Lecture Notes in Computer Science 15054

The series Lecture Notes in Computer Science (LNCS), including its subseries Lecture Notes in Artificial Intelligence (LNAI) and Lecture Notes in Bioinformatics (LNBI), has established itself as a medium for the publication of new developments in computer science and information technology research, teaching, and education.

LNCS enjoys close cooperation with the computer science R & D community, the series counts many renowned academics among its volume editors and paper authors, and collaborates with prestigious societies. Its mission is to serve this international community by providing an invaluable service, mainly focused on the publication of conference and workshop proceedings and postproceedings. LNCS commenced publication in 1973.

S. Akshay · Aina Niemetz ·
Sriram Sankaranarayanan
Editors

Automated Technology for Verification and Analysis

22nd International Symposium, ATVA 2024
Kyoto, Japan, October 21–25, 2024
Proceedings, Part I

Springer

Editors
S. Akshay
Indian Institute of Technology Bombay
Mumbai, Maharashtra, India

Aina Niemetz
Stanford University
Stanford, CA, USA

Sriram Sankaranarayanan
University of Colorado
Boulder, CO, USA

ISSN 0302-9743 ISSN 1611-3349 (electronic)
Lecture Notes in Computer Science
ISBN 978-3-031-78708-9 ISBN 978-3-031-78709-6 (eBook)
https://doi.org/10.1007/978-3-031-78709-6

This Springer imprint is published by the registered company Springer Nature Switzerland AG
The registered company address is: Gewerbestrasse 11, 6330 Cham, Switzerland

Preface

We are pleased to present the volume of regular and tool papers that appeared at the 22nd International Symposium on Automated Technology for Verification and Analysis (ATVA 2024). ATVA 2024 was held in Kyoto, Japan from the 21st to the 25th of October, 2024. ATVA is a forum for research in theoretical and practical aspects of automated analysis, verification and synthesis. It seeks to connect research communities from various parts of Asia with international research communities and industry.

ATVA 2024 received 73 submissions (77 original submissions with 4 withdrawals), of which 20 were accepted as regular papers and 4 as tool papers, while 49 were rejected. All submitted papers went through a rigorous review process with at least 3 double-blind reviews per paper, followed by an online discussion among PC members overseen by the PC chairs. The quality of the accepted papers, as perceived by the expert reviewers, was quite high: all accepted papers had a champion and overall positive scores from the reviewers.

This edition of ATVA featured three prestigious keynote speakers, who were invited to deliver one-hour-long keynote talks covering "hot" research topics and discussing new and interesting research directions:

- Orna Kupferman from Hebrew University, Jersusalem, Israel, delivered a keynote talk titled "Playing Games with Automata".
- Anne-Kathrin Schmuck from Max-Planck Institute for Software Systems, Kaiserslautern, Germany, delivered a keynote talk titled "Strategy Templates – Robust Certified Interfaces for Interactive Systems".
- Naoki Kobayashi from the University of Tokyo, Japan, delivered a keynote talk titled "Higher-Order Fixpoint Logic for Automated Program Verification".

The conference was preceded by half-day tutorials on two important tools that are widely used in formal verification.

- A tutorial on CVC5 by Haniel Barbosa from Universidade Federal de Minas Gerais, Belo Horizonte, Brazil, discussed the design, usage and application of the state-of-the-art SMT solver CVC5.
- A tutorial on the software verification tool suite VeriAbs by Priyanka Darke and R. Venkatesh from TCS Research, Pune, India, discussed the design, usage and application of VeriAbs.

In addition to the tutorials, a full day mentoring workshop was organized by Anna Lukina, TU Delft, The Netherlands; Andrew (Haoze) Wu, Amherst College, USA; and Zhenya Zhang, Kyushu University, Japan. The mentoring workshop featured speakers and panelists at various stages in their careers and provided a forum for junior researchers to consider various career options and avenues for research in the broad area of formal methods. We thank the mentoring workshop organizers for their hard work and dedication to the community.

We thank the technical program committee and external reviewers for their hard work in reviewing the papers submitted to ATVA 2024 and helping us put together a technical program consisting of high-quality papers. The program committee was made up of 62 members who represent the leading researchers in the core areas of ATVA including formal methods, hardware and software verification, automated reasoning, programming languages, logic, cyber-physical systems and theoretical computer science. Each paper was anonymized to ensure a "double-blind" review process. Each paper received three reviews, resulting in 219 reviews in total. ATVA 2024 featured a rebuttal process, wherein authors were provided an opportunity to respond to a draft of the review that the PC members took into account during the online discussions. The online discussion period lasted nearly two weeks. During this process, PC members were asked to "champion" papers that they felt should be included in the ATVA 2024 conference program. Every accepted paper had a "champion" who argued for the inclusion of the paper in the ATVA 2024 program, and overall positive review scores from all the reviewers. Also, the author responses were taken into account during the discussion. Many of the reviewers revised their review and scores based on the author responses. A meta-review written by one of the reviewers or a PC chair summarized the discussions surrounding a paper, where appropriate. We acknowledge the EasyChair conference management system for ensuring that the submission and review processes could be coordinated in a smooth and easy manner.

ATVA 2024 featured an artifact evaluation process spearheaded by our artifact evaluation chairs: Martin Jonáš from Masaryk University, Czech Republic, Mathias Preiner from Stanford University, USA, and Yoni Zohar from Bar-Ilan University, Israel. They put together an artifact evaluation committee consisting of researchers in the field with a particular interest in implementation and application of formal verification and analysis tools. Authors were encouraged to submit artifacts in addition to their submitted papers. Artifact submission was mandatory for tool papers and voluntary for regular research papers. The purpose of submitting artifacts is to support the claims made in the paper and to allow other researchers to check the data sets, obtain the results, check their validity and potentially also reuse the benchmarks and the implemented tools in their own research. For tool papers, it serves the additional purpose of providing a working version of the tool that can be used during the review process.

The artifact evaluation was held in two separate rounds: the first round of artifact evaluations was held concurrently with the peer review process for all papers. Submission of artifacts during this round was compulsory for all tool papers. After the acceptance notifications for the papers were sent out, a second round of artifact evaluation was conducted. This was optional and open to all accepted (regular research) papers.

The reviewing process for both artifact evaluation rounds was performed in two stages: Each artifact was first "smoke tested" to give the authors an opportunity to resolve minor technical issues with the artifact. Subsequently, each artifact was reviewed based on our evaluation criteria for functionality, availability and reusability by at least three members of the artifact evaluation committee. For tool papers, the artifact evaluation committee assessment was considered during the discussions by the technical program committee. The artifact evaluation results played a critical role in these discussions. A total of 17 artifacts were submitted: 10 artifacts for the tool papers and 7 artifacts for the regular research papers. Overall 14 of these artifacts were accepted by the committee. We thank the artifact evaluation committee for their hard work in ensuring fair and timely artifact reviews. We hope that the artifact evaluation process will remain a fixture for future versions of ATVA.

We thank the organizing committee headed by the ATVA 2024 General Chair Ichiro Hasuo from the National Institute of Informatics, Tokyo, Japan, for hosting the conference, organizing the venue, finances, registration and webpages and generally supporting the program committee in every step of the process. Special thanks go to Takashi Suwa for designing the logo and artifact evaluation badges. We thank our industry sponsors: DENSO and Mitsubishi Electric; Organizational sponsors: The Kyoto University Foundation and the JST ERATO HASUO Metamathematics for Systems Design Project. Last but not least, we thank our award sponsor and proceedings publisher: Springer.

October 2024

S. Akshay
Aina Niemetz
Sriram Sankaranarayanan
Martin Jonáš
Mathias Preiner
Yoni Zohar

Organization

General Chair

Ichiro Hasuo	National Institute of Informatics, Japan

Program Committee Chairs

S. Akshay	Indian Institute of Technology Bombay, India
Aina Niemetz	Stanford University, USA
Sriram Sankaranarayanan	University of Colorado Boulder, USA

Local Organization Chair

Masaki Waga	Kyoto University, Japan

Artifact Evaluation Committee Chairs

Martin Jonáš	Masaryk University, Czech Republic
Mathias Preiner	Stanford University, USA
Yoni Zohar	Bar-Ilan University, Israel

Publicity Chair

Jie An	National Institute of Informatics, Japan

Sponsorship Chair

Masaaki Konishi	National Institute of Informatics, Japan

Poster Chairs

Koko Muroya	Kyoto University, Japan
Yudai Tanabe	Tokyo Institute of Technology, Japan

Program Committee

Erika Ábrahám	RWTH Aachen University, Germany
Kyungmin Bae	Pohang University, Republic of Korea
Christel Baier	TU Dresden, Germany
Gogul Balakrishnan	Google, USA
Saddek Bensalem	VERIMAG, France
Dirk Beyer	LMU Munich, Germany
Armin Biere	University of Freiburg, Germany
Michael Blondin	Université de Sherbrooke, Canada
Sourav Chakraborty	Indian Statistical Institute, India
Xin Chen	University of New Mexico, USA
Yu-Fang Chen	Academia Sinica, Taiwan
Yunja Choi	Kyungpook National Univ., Republic of Korea
Thao Dang	CNRS/VERIMAG, France
Pallab Dasgupta	Synopsys, USA
Rayna Dimitrova	CISPA Helmholtz Center for Information Security, Germany
Susanna Donatelli	Universitá di Torino, Italy
Alexandre Duret-Lutz	EPITA Research Lab (LRDE), France
Souradeep Dutta	University of Pennsylvania, USA
Pascal Fontaine	Université de Liège, Belgium
Amir K. Goharshady	Hong Kong Univ. of Science and Technology, China
Blaise Genest	CNRS, France
Stéphane Graham-Lengrand	SRI International, USA
Ashutosh Gupta	IIT Bombay, India
Liana Hadarean	Amazon Web Services, USA
Ichiro Hasuo	National Institute of Informatics, Japan
Chih-Duo Hong	National Chengchi University, Taiwan
Matti Järvisalo	University of Helsinki, Finland
Jie-Hong Roland Jiang	National Taiwan University, Taiwan
Sebastian Junges	Radboud University, The Netherlands
Gowtham Kaki	University of Colorado Boulder, USA
Daniela Kaufmann	TU Wien, Austria
Sandra Kiefer	University of Oxford, UK

Katherine Kosaian	Iowa State University, USA
Orna Kupferman	Hebrew University, Israel
Yong Li	Chinese Academy of Sciences, China
Jianwen Li	East China Normal University, China
Shang-Wei Lin	Nanyang Technological University, Singapore
Kumar Madhukar	IIT Delhi, India
Tobias Meggendorfer	Lancaster University Leipzig, Germany
Benjamin Monmege	Aix-Marseille Université, France
Doron Peled	Bar-Ilan University, Israel
Sophie Pinchinat	IRISA Rennes, France
Jakob Piribauer	TU Dresden, Germany
Pavithra Prabhakar	Kansas State University, USA
Andrew Reynolds	University of Iowa, USA
Cesar Sanchez	IMDEA Software Institute, Spain
Ocan Sankur	University of Rennes & CNRS, France
Mate Soos	National University of Singapore, Singapore
B. Srivathsan	Chennai Mathematical Institute, India
Marielle Stoelinga	University of Twente, The Netherlands
Kohei Suenaga	Kyoto University, Japan
Tachio Terauchi	Waseda University, Japan
Ashish Tiwari	Microsoft, USA
Hazem Torfah	Chalmers University of Technology, Sweden
Hiroshi Unno	University of Tsukuba, Japan
Chao Wang	University of Southern California, USA
Bai Xue	Chinese Academy of Sciences, China
Akihisa Yamada	National Institute of Advanced Industrial Science and Technology, Japan
Đore Žikelić	Singapore Management University, Singapore

Artifact Evaluation Committee

Guy Amir	Hebrew University, Israel
Jie An	National Institute of Informatics, Japan
Lelio Brun	National Institute of Informatics, Japan
Marek Chalupa	IST Austria, Austria
Po-Chun Chien	LMU Munich, Germany
Solimul Chowdhury	University of Alberta, Canada
Greta Dolcetti	Ca' Foscari University of Venice, Italy
Burak Ekici	University of Oxford, UK
Katalin Fazekas	TU Wien, Austria
Hadar Frenkel	CISPA, Germany

Aman Goel	Amazon Web Services, USA
Petra Hozzová	TU Wien, Austria
Marek Jankola	LMU Munich, Germany
Mayuko Kori	SOKENDAI, Japan
Hanna Lachnitt	Stanford University, USA
Henrich Lauko	Trail of Bits, USA
Juneyoung Lee	Amazon, USA
Nian-Ze Lee	LMU Munich, Germany
Lorenz Leutgeb	Max Planck Institute for Informatics, Germany
Enrico Magnago	Amazon Web Services, USA
Vincent Mihalkovič	Masaryk University, Czech Republic
Samuel Pastva	IST Austria, Austria
Sophie Rain	TU Wien, Austria
Frédéric Recoules	CEA LIST, France
Gianluca Redondi	FBK, Italy
Kartik Sabharwal	University of Iowa, USA
Sota Sato	National Institute of Informatics, Japan
Hans-Jörg Schurr	University of Iowa, USA
Simon Schwarz	Max Planck Institute for Informatics, Germany
Joseph Scott	University of Waterloo, Canada
Masaki Waga	Kyoto University, Japan
Kazuki Watanabe	National Institute of Informatics, Japan
Andrew (Haoze) Wu	Amherst College, USA
Emily Yu	IST Austria, Austria
Zhenya Zhang	Kyushu University, Japan

Steering Committee

Yu-Fang Chen	Academia Sinica, Taiwan
Yunja Choi	Kyungpook National Univ., Republic of Korea
Ichiro Hasuo	National Institute of Informatics, Japan
Jie-Hong Roland Jiang	National Taiwan University, Taiwan
Doron A. Peled	Bar-Ilan University, Israel

Advisory Committee

E. Allen Emerson	University of Texas, Austin, USA
Teruo Higashino	Osaka University, Japan
Oscar H. Ibarra	University of California, Santa Barbara, USA
Insup Lee	University of Pennsylvania, USA

Farn Wang	National Taiwan University, Taiwan
Hsu-Chun Yen	National Taiwan University, Taiwan

Additional Reviewers

An, Jie
Bellier, Dylan
Chang, Tung-Che
Chatterjee, Abhranil
Chen, Tian-Fu
Cheng, Che
Fleury, Mathias
Fung, Long-Hin
Guttenberg, Roland
Hazra, Aritra
Hazra, Somnath
Ho, Kuo-Wei
Hozzová, Petra
Jabs, Christoph
Jankola, Marek
Joshi, Aniruddha
Kirst, Dominik
Klüppelholz, Sascha
Kruger, Loes
Liao, Yuke
Luque Cerpa, Alejandro
Marchand, Hervé
Rensink, Arend
Sen, Sayantan
Turrini, Andrea
van der Vegt, Marck
Vos, Daniël
Völker, Marcus
Wachowitz, Henrik
Waga, Masaki
Waldburger, Nicolas
Wienhöft, Patrick
Zhang, Guanqin

Higher-Order Fixpoint Logic for Automated Program Verification (Abstract of Invited Talk)

Naoki Kobayashi

University of Tokyo, Japan

Abstract. We present an overview of our recent project on automated program verification based on higher-order fixpoint logic HFL(Z), a higher-order logic equipped with fixpoint operators and integer arithmetic. Various problems for higher-order program verification can naturally be reduced to the validity checking problem for HFL(Z) formulas. Thus, an HFL(Z) validity checker can serve as a common backend for automated verification tools for higher-order programs. We explain why the HFL(Z) approach is preferable to other representative approaches to automated higher-order program verification, such as the one based on the model checking of higher-order recursion schemes. We also outline how an automated HFL(Z) validity checker can be constructed, and discuss the remaining challenges and future directions.

Contents – Part I

Learning for Verification and Synthesis

Contents – Part II

Invited Keynote and Tutorial Papers

Playing Games on Automata

Orna Kupferman(✉)

School of Engineering and Computer Science, Hebrew University, Jerusalem, Israel
orna@cs.huji.ac.il

Abstract. The interaction between a system and its environment corresponds to a game in which the system and the environment generate a word over the alphabet of assignments to the input and output signals. The system player wins if the generated word satisfies a desired specification. A correct reactive system has to satisfy its specification in all environments, and thus corresponds to a winning strategy for the system player in the above game. This view is the key to the game-based approach for reactive synthesis. It reduces synthesis to the problem of generating winning strategies in two-player games whose winning conditions are on-going behaviors, which can be specified by automata on infinite words. The paper presents the game-based approach, focusing on ways to cope with the fact that the game cannot be played over nondeterministic automata.

1 Introduction

Synthesis is the automated construction of systems from their specifications [8, 19]. Synthesis enables designers to focus on *what* the system should do rather on *how* it should do it. A reactive system interacts with its environment and should *realize* the specification, namely satisfy it against all possible environments. More formally, the specification is a language L of infinite words over the alphabet $2^{I \cup O}$, where I and O are sets of input and output signals, respectively, and the goal is to construct a reactive system that outputs assignments to the signals in O upon receiving assignments to the signals in I, such that the generated sequence of assignments, which can be viewed as an infinite computation in $(2^{I \cup O})^\omega$, is in L [19].

The common approach for solving the synthesis problem is to define a two-player game on top of a deterministic automaton $\mathcal{D}$ for L. The positions of the game are the states of $\mathcal{D}$. In each round of the game, one player (the environment) provides an assignment in 2^I to the input signals, the second player (the system) responds with an assignment in 2^O to the output signals, and the game proceeds to the corresponding successor state. More formally, when the game is in a position that corresponds to a state q of $\mathcal{D}$, the environment provides $i \in 2^I$, the system responds with $o \in 2^O$, and the game moves to the position associated with the single $(i \cup o)$-successor of q. The goal of the system is to respond in a way so that the sequence of visited positions satisfies the acceptance condition of $\mathcal{D}$, indicating that the generated computation is in L. The system has a

S. Akshay et al. (Eds.): ATVA 2024, LNCS 15054, pp. 3–21, 2025.
https://doi.org/10.1007/978-3-031-78709-6_1

winning strategy in the game iff the language L is realizable [11]. Moreover, an *(I/O)-transducer* that models a system that realizes the specification can be constructed from the winning strategy.

Now, if one replaces $\mathcal{D}$ by a nondeterministic automaton $\mathcal{A}$ for L, the response of the system to an assignment $i \in 2^I$ should include, in addition to an assignment $o \in 2^O$, also an $(i \cup o)$-successor of the current position. Letting the system resolve the nondeterminism makes sense, in particular that $\mathcal{A}$ has an accepting run on all computations in L. Letting the system resolve the nondeterminism is, however, problematic. The problem is that the choice of an $(i \cup o)$-successor should accommodate all possible future choices of the environment. In particular, if different future choices of the environment induce computations that are all in the language of $\mathcal{A}$ yet require different nondeterministic choices, the system cannot win. Thus, it might be that L is realizable and still the system has no winning strategy in the game played on $\mathcal{A}$.

The need to play the synthesis game on a deterministic automaton is a real barrier in practice. First, determinization constructions are very complicated and their implementation is very difficult. Second, they require the use of winning conditions that are more complex. In this paper we explain further the difficulty that nondeterminism imposes on games and survey two approaches that have been suggested to cope with it.

The first approach, introduced on [15], is based on *determinancy of games*, and the fact that the use of nondeterministic automata involves a *one-sided error*. To see the idea, consider a specification L, and recall that playing a game on a nondeterministic automaton for L may result in the system player losing even when L is realizable. Determinancy of games implies that whenever L is not realizable by the system, its complement is realizable by the environment. Thus, realizability of L can be checked also by playing the synthesis game on an automaton for its complement. In Sect. 4 we explain how the one-sided errors in the two checks can be combined in an algorithm that is played on automata for both L and its complement, and describe two interesting heuristics for reducing the one-sided error and coping with. The first heuristic refines the game by checking the *universal satisfiability* of the specification and its complement, and the second heuristic performs a subset-construction (rather than full determinization) on the underlying automata.

The second approach is based on playing the game on nondeterministic automata that can resolve their nondeterministic choices in a way that only depends on the past. The study of such automata started in [16], by means of tree automata for derived languages. It then continued by means of *good for games* word automata [12]. The idea is also used in [9] in the framework of cost functions, and we adopt the term *history determinism* that is used there.

Formally, a nondeterministic automaton $\mathcal{A}$ over an alphabet Σ and with state space Q is history deterministic (HD, for short) if there is a *strategy* $g : \Sigma^* \to Q$, such that for every word $w = \sigma_1 \cdot \sigma_2 \cdots \in \Sigma^\omega$, the sequence $g(w) = g(\epsilon)$, $g(\sigma_1)$, $g(\sigma_1 \cdot \sigma_2), \ldots$ is a run of $\mathcal{A}$ on w, and whenever w is accepted by $\mathcal{A}$, the run $g(w)$

is accepting. Thus, the strategy g maps each word $x \in \Sigma^*$ to the state that is visited after x is read.

In Sect. 5 we discuss HD automata, explain their application in the solution for the synthesis problem, and survey main results about them. We focus on the difference between HD automata and deterministic ones, and show that not only HD automata cannot always be pruned to deterministic ones [5], HD co-Büchi automata may in fact be exponentially more succinct than deterministic ones [13]. We also discuss the fact that for synthesis of (I, O)-transducers, one can work with *(I/O)-aware HD automata*, whose history-determinism can be defined with respect to the partition of the involved signals to inputs and outputs [10].

2 Preliminaries

2.1 Automata

A *nondeterministic word automaton* over a finite alphabet Σ is a tuple $\mathcal{A} = \langle \Sigma, Q, q_0, \delta, \alpha \rangle$, where Q is a set of states, $q_0 \in Q$ is an initial state, $\delta : Q \times \Sigma \to 2^Q \setminus \{\emptyset\}$ is a total transition function, and α is an acceptance condition. We say that $\mathcal{A}$ is *deterministic* if for every $q \in Q$ and $\sigma \in \Sigma$, we have that $|\delta(q, \sigma)| = 1$. For a state $q \in Q$, we use $\mathcal{A}^q$ to denote the automaton $\mathcal{A}$ with initial state q. That is, $\mathcal{A}^q = \langle \Sigma, Q, q_0, \delta, \alpha \rangle$. We sometimes refer to the transition function δ as a transition relation $\Delta \subseteq Q \times \Sigma \times Q$, where for every two states $q, s \in Q$ and letter $\sigma \in \Sigma$, we have that $\langle q, \sigma, s \rangle \in \Delta$ iff $s \in \delta(q, \sigma)$.

A *run* of $\mathcal{A}$ on $w = \sigma_1 \cdot \sigma_2 \cdots \in \Sigma^\omega$ is an infinite sequence of transitions $r = \langle r_0, \sigma_1, r_1 \rangle, \langle r_1, \sigma_2, r_2 \rangle, \langle r_2, \sigma_3, r_3 \rangle, \ldots \in \Delta^\omega$, such that $r_0 = q_0$, and for all $i \geq 0$, we have that $r_{i+1} \in \delta(r_i, \sigma_{i+1})$. The acceptance condition α determines which runs are "good". We consider here the *Büchi* and *co-Büchi* transition-based acceptance conditions, where $\alpha \subseteq \Delta$ is a subset of transitions. For a run r, let $\mathit{inf}(r) \subseteq \Delta$ be the set of transitions that r traverses infinitely often. Thus, $\mathit{inf}(r) = \{t \in \Delta : t = \langle r_i, \sigma_{i+1}, r_{i+1} \rangle$ for infinitely many i's$\}$. A run r of a Büchi automaton is *accepting* iff it traverses transitions in α infinitely often, thus $\mathit{inf}(r) \cap \alpha \neq \emptyset$. Dually, a run r of a co-Büchi automaton is accepting iff it traverses transitions in α only finitely often, thus $\mathit{inf}(r) \cap \alpha = \emptyset$. A run that is not accepting is *rejecting*. Note that as $\mathcal{A}$ is nondeterministic, it may have several runs on a word w. A word w is accepted by $\mathcal{A}$ if there is an accepting run of $\mathcal{A}$ on w. The language of $\mathcal{A}$, denoted $L(\mathcal{A})$, is the set of words that $\mathcal{A}$ accepts. Two automata are *equivalent* if their languages are equivalent.

We use three letter acronyms in {D,N} × {B,C} × {W} to denote classes of word automata. The first letter indicates whether this is a deterministic or nondeterministic automaton, and the second indicates the acceptance condition. For example, NBW is a nondeterministic Büchi automaton.

We say that a nondeterministic automaton is *history deterministic* (HD, for short) if its nondeterminism can be resolved based on the past [12]. Formally, a nondeterministic automaton $\mathcal{A} = \langle \Sigma, Q, q_0, \delta, \alpha \rangle$ is HD if there exists a function $g : \Sigma^* \to Q$ such that the following hold.

- The strategy g is compatible with q_0 and δ. That is, $g(\epsilon) = q_0$, and for every $w \in \Sigma^*$ and $\sigma \in \Sigma$, we have that $\langle g(w), \sigma, g(w \cdot \sigma)\rangle \in \Delta$.
- The strategy g "covers" all words in $L(\mathcal{A})$. That is, for every word $w = \sigma_1 \cdot \sigma_2 \cdots \in L(\mathcal{A})$, the run that g induces on w, namely $\langle g(\epsilon), \sigma_1, g(\sigma_1)\rangle$, $\langle g(\sigma_1), \sigma_2, g(\sigma_1 \cdot \sigma_2)\rangle, \ldots$, is accepting.

We then say that g *witnesses* the HDness of $\mathcal{A}$. Note that a state q of $\mathcal{A}$ may be reachable via different words, and g may suggest different transitions from q after different words are read. Thus, g need not induce a pruning of $\mathcal{A}$ to a deterministic automaton. Still, g itself is a deterministic strategy that resolves the nondeterminism in $\mathcal{A}$ in a way that only depends only on the past, namely on the word read so far.

2.2 Games

We consider *two-player turn-based* games played on graphs. The vertices of the game graph are partitioned between the players. Starting from an initial vertex, the players jointly move a token along the graph, with each player deciding the successor vertex whenever the token reaches a vertex he owns. Formally, a *game* is a tuple $G = \langle V_{\text{AND}}, V_{\text{OR}}, E, \alpha\rangle$, where V_{AND} and V_{OR} are disjoint sets of positions, owned by Player AND and Player OR, respectively. Let $V = V_{\text{AND}} \cup V_{\text{OR}}$. Then, $E \subseteq V \times V$ is an edge relation, and α is a winning condition, defining a subset of V^ω. A *play* is an infinite sequence of positions $v_0, v_1, \dots \in V^\omega$, such that for every index $i \geq 0$, we have that $\langle v_i, v_{i+1}\rangle \in E$. A play $\pi \in V^\omega$ is *winning* for Player OR if π satisfies α, and is winning for Player AND otherwise. We focus here on *Büchi* games, where $\alpha \subseteq V$ and π satisfies α if it visits the positions in α infinitely often. Note that since a play is winning for Player AND iff it is not winning for Player OR, the game is a co-Büchi game from the point of view of Player AND.

Recall that starting from some position $v_0 \in V$, the players generate a play in G by letting the player that owns the current position to choose a successor. Formally, in every round of the game, if the current position is $v \in V_j$, for $j \in \{\text{AND}, \text{OR}\}$, then Player j chooses a successor v' of v, and the play proceeds to position v'. A *strategy* for a player $j \in \{\text{AND}, \text{OR}\}$ is a function $f_j : V^* \times V_j \to V$ such that for every $u \in V^*$ and $v \in V_j$, we have that $\langle v, f_j(u, v)\rangle \in E$. Thus, a strategy for Player j maps the history of the game so far, when it ends in a position v owned by Player j, to a successor of v. A strategy f_j is *memoryless* if for every $u_1, u_2 \in V^*$ and $v \in V_j$, we have that $f_j(u_1 \cdot v) = f_j(u_2 \cdot v)$. Intuitively, a memoryless strategy for player j maps all the histories of the game that end in a position v, owned by player j, to the same successor of v. Note that we can describe a memoryless strategy for Player j by $f_j : V_j \to V$.

Two strategies $f_{\text{AND}}, f_{\text{OR}}$, and an initial position v_0 induce a play $\pi = v_0$, v_1, $v_2 \cdots \in V^\omega$, where for every $i \geq 0$, if $v_i \in V_j$, for $j \in \{\text{AND}, \text{OR}\}$, then $v_{i+1} = f_j((v_0, \ldots, v_{i-1}), v_i)$. We say that π is the *outcome* of f_{OR} and f_{AND} from v_0, and denote $\pi = \mathit{outcome}(v_0, f_{\text{OR}}, f_{\text{AND}})$.

We say that a position $v \in V$ is winning for Player OR if there exists a strategy f_{OR} such that for every strategy f_{AND}, we have that $outcome(v, f_{\text{OR}}, f_{\text{AND}})$ is winning for Player OR. We then say that f_{OR} is a *winning strategy* of Player OR from v. We define similarly winning positions and strategies for Player AND.

It is known that Büchi games are *determined*. That is, every position in a Büchi game is winning for exactly one of the players. Solving a game amounts to deciding which vertices are winning for Player OR. Since Büchi games are determined, the other vertices are winning for Player AND. Büchi games can be solved in quadratic time [23]. Moreover, a player wins in a Büchi game iff he has a memoryless winning strategy [22].

2.3 Synthesis

Consider two finite sets I and O of input and output signals, respectively. For two words $w_I = i_0 \cdot i_1 \cdot i_2 \cdots \in (2^I)^\omega$ and $w_O = o_0 \cdot o_1 \cdot o_2 \cdots \in (2^O)^\omega$, we define $w_I \oplus w_O$ as the word in $(2^{I \cup O})^\omega$ obtained by merging w_I and w_O. Thus, $w_I \oplus w_O = (i_0 \cup o_0) \cdot (i_1 \cup o_1) \cdot (i_2 \cup o_2) \cdots$.

An (I/O)*-transducer* models a finite-state system that generates assignments to the output signals while interacting with an environment that generates assignments to the input signals. Formally, an (I/O)-transducer is $\mathcal{T} = \langle I, O, S, s_0, \rho, \tau \rangle$, where S is a set of states, $s_0 \in S$ is an initial state, $\rho : S \times 2^I \to S$ is a transition function, and $\tau : S \times 2^I \to 2^O$ is labelling function.

The transducer $\mathcal{T}$ models an interaction between an environment that generates at each moment in time a letter in 2^I and a system that responds with letters in 2^O. Consider an input word $w_I = i_0 \cdot i_1 \cdots \in (2^I)^\omega$. The *run* of $\mathcal{T}$ on w_I is the sequence $s_0, s_1, s_2 \ldots$ such that for all $j \geq 0$, we have that $s_{j+1} = \rho(s_j, i_j)$. The *output* of $\mathcal{T}$ on w_I is then $w_O = o_1 \cdot o_2 \cdots \in (2^O)^\omega$, where $o_j = \tau(s_j, i_j)$ for all $j \geq 1$. Note that the environment initiates the interaction, with input i_0, to which the system responds with $\tau(s_0, i_0)$. The *computation of* $\mathcal{T}$ *on* w_I, denoted $\mathcal{T}(w_I)$, is then $w_I \oplus w_O$. Thus, $\mathcal{T}(w_I) = i_0 \cup o_1, i_1 \cup o_2, \ldots \in (2^{I \cup O})^\omega$.

Consider a specification $L \subseteq (2^{I \cup O})^\omega$. We say that an (I/O)-transducer $\mathcal{T}$ (I/O)*-realizes* L if for every input word $w_I \in (2^I)^\omega$, the computation of $\mathcal{T}$ on w_I is in L. In the *synthesis* problem, we are given a specification $L \subseteq (2^{I \cup O})^\omega$ and we have to decide whether L is (I/O)-realizable. In case the answer is positive, we also need to return an (I/O)-transducer that (I/O)-realizes L. The language L is typically given by a formula ψ in *linear temporal logic* (LTL, for short) [18]. Formulas of LTL are constructed from the set $I \cup O$ of signals using the usual Boolean operators and the temporal operators G ("always") and F ("eventually"), X ("next time") and U ("until"). The language induced by ψ is then $L_\psi = \{w : w \models \psi\}$.

3 From Synthesis to Games on Automata

In this section we describe the game-based approach to synthesis and explain why it is traditionally applied with deterministic automata. The game-based approach first translates the specification to an automaton:

Theorem 1. [24] For every LTL formula ψ, there is an NBW $\mathcal{A}_\psi$ with $2^{O(|\psi|)}$ states such that $L(\mathcal{A}_\psi) = \{w : w \models \psi\}$.

The input to the synthesis problems consists of the specification ψ, which we translate to an NBW, and a partition of the signals in ψ to I and O. Given an NBW $\mathcal{A} = \langle 2^{I \cup O}, Q, q_0, \delta, \alpha \rangle$ for the specification we wish to synthesize, we define the *synthesis game* $G_{\text{SYN}}(\mathcal{A}, I, O)$ as follows. The game proceeds in rounds. Let q be the position of the game at the beginning of some round. The round proceeds as follows. First, Player AND (the environment) chooses a letter $i \in 2^I$. Then, Player OR (the system) chooses a letter $o \in 2^O$ and a state $q' \in \delta(q, i \cup o)$, and the game proceeds to the position q'. Formally, we define $G_{\text{SYN}}(\mathcal{A}, I, O) = \langle V_{\text{AND}}, V_{\text{OR}}, E, \alpha \rangle$, where

- $V_{\text{AND}} = Q$,
- $V_{\text{OR}} = Q \times 2^I$, and
- $E = \{\langle q, \langle q, i \rangle \rangle : q \in V_{\text{AND}}$ and $i \in 2^I\} \cup \{\langle \langle q, i \rangle, q' \rangle :$ there is $o \in 2^O$ such that $q' \in \delta(q, i \cup o)\}$.

Intuitively, Player AND provides a sequence of assignments to the input signals, and Player OR responds with a sequence of assignments to the output signals and a run of $\mathcal{A}$ on the generated computation, aiming for a response that is an accepting run. We say that an automaton $\mathcal{A}$ over alphabet $2^{I \cup O}$ is *sound for* (I/O)*-realizability* if q_0 being a winning state for Player OR in $G_{\text{SYN}}(\mathcal{A}, I, O)$ implies that $\mathcal{A}$ is (I/O)-realizable. Then, $\mathcal{A}$ is *complete for* (I/O)*-realizability* if (I/O)-realizability of $\mathcal{A}$ implies that q_0 is a winning state for Player OR in $G_{\text{SYN}}(\mathcal{A}, I, O)$.

Example 1. Let $I = \{i\}$, $O = \{o\}$, and consider the specification $\psi = (i \leftrightarrow o) \wedge Xo$. Clearly, ψ is (I/O)-realizable, for example by a transducer that copies to o the value of i in the first cycle of the interaction and assigns true to o in the second cycle. In Fig. 1, we describe the DBW $\mathcal{D}_\psi$, which accepts exactly all the computations that satisfy ψ, and the game $G_{\text{SYN}}(\mathcal{D}_\psi, I, O)$. We label the transitions of $\mathcal{D}_\psi$ by strings in $\{00, 01, 10, 11\}$, indicating the assignment to i (the first bit) and o (the second bit). We label the edges of $G_{\text{SYN}}(\mathcal{D}_\psi, I, O)$ by 0 or 1, indicating the assignment to i (in edges that leave vertices owned by Player AND – the environment) and o (in edges that leave vertices owned by Player OR – the system). Since the only cycles in $\mathcal{D}_\psi$ are the accepting and rejecting sinks, we view $G_{\text{SYN}}(\mathcal{D}_\psi, I, O)$ as a reachability game with an objective q_{acc}.

It is easy to see that Player OR wins, with a strategy that moves the token to q_{acc}, namely one that copies to o the value of i in the first round and assigns true to o in the second round. □

We prove that all deterministic automata are sound and complete for (I/O)-realizability, all nondeterministic ones are sound, yet nondeterministic automata may not be complete.

Theorem 2. *Nondeterministic automata are sound for* (I/O)*-realizability.*

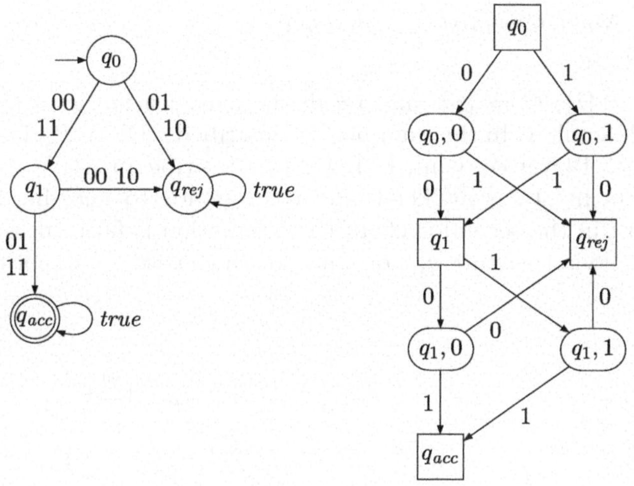

Fig. 1. The DBW $\mathcal{D}_\psi$ (left) and the game $G_{\text{SYN}}(\mathcal{D}_\psi, I, O)$ (right).

Proof. Consider a nondeterministic automaton $\mathcal{A} = \langle 2^{I \cup O}, Q, q_0, \delta, \alpha \rangle$. We show that if q_0 is winning for Player OR in $G_{\text{SYN}}(\mathcal{A}, I, O)$, then $\mathcal{A}$ is (I/O)-realizable.

Recall that the winner in a Büchi game has a memoryless winning strategy. Assume that q_0 is winning for Player OR in $G_{\text{SYN}}(\mathcal{A}, I, O)$, and let $f_{\text{OR}} : Q \times 2^I \to Q$ be a memoryless winning strategy for him. Recall that $f_{\text{OR}}(\langle q, i \rangle) = q'$ implies that there is $o \in 2^O$ such that $q' \in \delta(q, i \cup o)$. Thus, we can view the strategy of Player OR as a function $f_{\text{OR}} : Q \times 2^I \to Q \times 2^O$, which also specifies the assignment to the output signals according to which the successor state is chosen. Then, the strategy f_{OR} induces the (I/O)-transducer $\mathcal{T} = \langle I, O, Q \times 2^O, \langle q_0, \emptyset \rangle, \rho, \tau \rangle$, where ρ and τ are induced from f_{OR} in the expected way, thus for all states $q \in Q$ and inputs $i \in 2^I$, we have that $\langle \rho(q, i), \tau(q, i) \rangle = f_{\text{OR}}(q, i)$. □

Theorem 3. *Deterministic automata are complete for (I/O)-realizability.*

Proof. Consider a deterministic automaton $\mathcal{A} = \langle 2^{I \cup O}, Q, q_0, \delta, \alpha \rangle$. We show that if $\mathcal{A}$ is (I/O)-realizable, then q_0 is winning for Player OR in $G_{\text{SYN}}(\mathcal{A}, I, O)$.

Assume that $\mathcal{A}$ is (I/O)-realizable. Let $\mathcal{T} = \langle I, O, S, s_0, \rho, \tau \rangle$ be an (I/O)-transducer that (I/O)-realizes $\mathcal{A}$, and let $G_{\text{SYN}}(\mathcal{A}, I, O) = \langle Q, Q \times 2^I, E, \alpha \rangle$. We describe a (not necessarily memoryless) winning strategy f_{OR} for Player OR in $G_{\text{SYN}}(\mathcal{A}, I, O)$. For every prefix of a play $\pi = q_0, \langle q_0, i_0 \rangle, q_1, \langle q_1, i_1 \rangle, \ldots, q_k, \langle q_k, i_k \rangle$, we define $f_{\text{OR}}(\pi) = \delta(q_k, i_k \cup \tau(\rho(s_0, i_0 \cdot i_1 \cdots i_{k-1}), i_k)$. That is, f_{OR} follows the run of $\mathcal{T}$ on the generated computation, and when $\mathcal{T}$ is in state s and Player AND provides an assignment $i \in 2^I$, it extends the computation according to $\tau(s, i)$ and extends the run by moving to $\rho(s, i)$.

By the definition of $G_{\text{SYN}}(\mathcal{A}, I, O)$, all the outcomes of the game when Player OR uses f_{OR} are computations of $\mathcal{T}$. Since $\mathcal{T}$ (I/O)-realizes $\mathcal{A}$, the run of $\mathcal{A}$ on them is accepting, and so f_{OR} is indeed winning for Player OR. □

Theorem 4. *Nondeterministic automata are not complete for (I/O)-realizability.*

Proof. Let $I = \{i\}$, $O = \{o\}$, and recall the specification $\psi = (i \leftrightarrow o) \wedge Xo$ discussed in Example 1. In the example, we described a DBW $\mathcal{D}_\psi$ for ψ, inducing a game in which Player OR wins. In Fig. 2, we describe an NBW $\mathcal{A}_\psi$ for ψ. The nondeterminism in $\mathcal{A}_\psi$ is artificial, and corresponds to guessing whether the assignment to i in the second cycle of the interaction is false (in which case an accepting run is via the state q_1), or true (in which case an accepting run is via the state q_2).

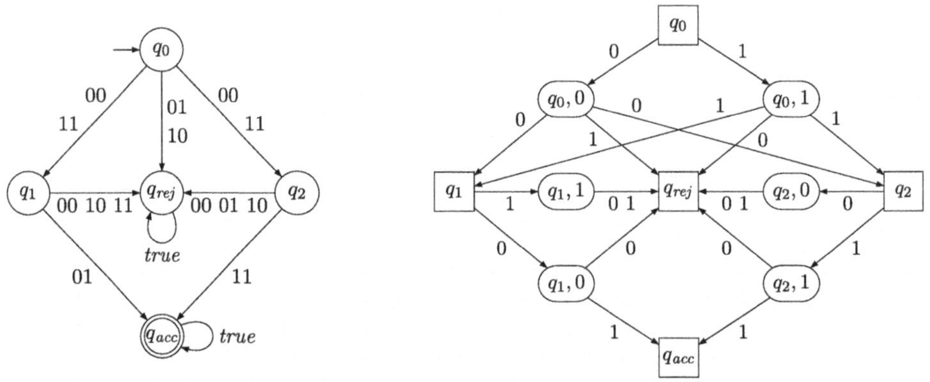

Fig. 2. The NBW $\mathcal{A}_\psi$ (left) and the game $G_{\text{SYN}}(\mathcal{A}_\psi, I, O)$ (right).

The game $G_{\text{SYN}}(\mathcal{A}_\psi, I, O)$ appears on the right. Note that if Player OR moves the token to q_1, Player AND responds with 0 (that is, $\neg i$), and if Player OR moves the token to q_2, Player AND responds with 1 (that is, i). In both cases, regardless of the response of Player OR in the next round, the token reaches q_{rej}. Thus, while $\mathcal{A}_\psi$ is (I/O)-realizable, Player OR does not have a winning strategy from q_0 in $G_{\text{SYN}}(\mathcal{A}_\psi, I, O)$. □

Beyond getting convinced about the specific example in the proof of Theorem 4, it is important to understand the conceptual difficulty that nondeterminism imposes on games. Whenever a nondeterministic automaton takes a nondeterministic transition, it makes a guess about the future. For example, when the NBW $\mathcal{A}_\psi$ from the proof branches from q_0 to q_1, it guesses that the next assignment to i is false, and when it branches to q_2, it guesses that the next assignment to i is true. While $\mathcal{A}_\psi$ has an accepting run on all the words in $L(\mathcal{A}_\psi)$, forcing Player OR to choose a successor state forces $\mathcal{A}_\psi$ to accept all the words that share the prefix generated so far with that same nondeterministic choice. In the example, when Player OR moves the token from $\langle q_0, 0\rangle$ or $\langle q_0, 1\rangle$ to the vertex q_1 in $G_{\text{SYN}}(\mathcal{A}_\psi, I, O)$, it restricts the runs of $\mathcal{A}_\psi$ on the generated words to ones that move from q_0 to q_1, namely to ones that guess that the next assignment to i is false, implying that Player AND wins by assigning true to i.

4 Using Determinancy of Games

The roles of the system and the environment in the synthesis setting may be switched, and we can talk about a formula ψ being (O/I)-realizable by the environment, meaning that there is an (O/I)-transducer $\mathcal{T}$ such that for every output sequence $w_O = o_0, o_1, o_2, \ldots \in (2^O)^\omega$, the computation of $\mathcal{T}$ on w_O satisfies ψ. Note that in order for switched settings to complement each other, we let the environment move first in both types of realizability. Thus, the settings are not completely dual. From determinancy of games, we know that for every specification ψ, either ψ is (I/O)-realizable by the system or $\neg\psi$ is (O/I)-realizable by the environment.

The soundness of nondeterministic automata for realizability suggests the following simple heuristic: Given an LTL formula ψ over $I \cup O$, let $\mathcal{A}_\psi$ and $\mathcal{A}_{\neg\psi}$ be NBWs for ψ and $\neg\psi$, respectively. We proceed as follows.

(1) Solve the game $G_{\text{SYN}}(\mathcal{A}_\psi, I, O)$.
(1.1) If the system wins, we are done: ψ is (I/O)-realizable and the winning strategy for the system induces a transducer that (I/O)-realizes ψ.
(1.2) If the environment wins, proceed to (2).
(2) Solve the game $G_{\text{SYN}}(\mathcal{A}_{\neg\psi}, O, I)$.
(2.1) If environment wins, we are done. Indeed, if $\neg\psi$ is (O/I)-realizable, then ψ is not (I/O)-realizable.
(2.2) If the system wins, proceed to (3).
(3) Continue to read this section.

Since $\mathcal{A}_\psi$ and $\mathcal{A}_{\neg\psi}$ are sound but not complete, we may reach Step 3 in the algorithm. Below we discuss a heuristic for coping with this situation.

Consider an LTL formula ψ over $I \cup O$. We say that ψ is *universally (I/O)-satisfiable* if for every input sequence $w_I \in (2^I)^\omega$, there is an output sequence $w_O \in (2^O)^\omega$ such that $w_I \oplus w_O$ satisfies ψ. It is not hard to see that (I/O)-realizability implies universal (I/O)-satisfiability, but not the other way around. For example, letting $I = \{i\}$ and $O = \{o\}$, the formula $\psi = G(Xi \leftrightarrow o)$ is universally (I/O)-satisfiable but not (I/O)-realizable. Indeed, once a transducer $\mathcal{T}$ sets the value of the signal o in the first round, the environment can assign $\neg o$ to i in the next round, causing the generated computation to violate $Xi \leftrightarrow o$ and hence also violate ψ.

As is the case with realizability, the roles of the system and the environment may be switched also in the context of universal satisfiability, and we can talk about a formula ψ being universally (O/I)-satisfiable, meaning that for every output sequence $w_O \in (2^O)^\omega$, there is an input sequence $w_I \in (2^I)^\omega$ such that $w_I \oplus w_O$ satisfies ψ. Note that for universal satisfiability, the identity of the player that moves first is irrelevant, and the definitions of universal (I/O)-satisfiability and universal (O/I)-satisfiability are completely dual.

Checking universal satisfaction is much simpler than checking realizability, not just from a theoretical point of view (the problem is EXPSPACE-complete [21]), but also in practice – universal satisfaction amounts to checking universality of an NBW, which can be done without determinization [17].

Below we describe the methodology for using universal satisfiability in the process of checking realizability.

Given an LTL formula ψ over I and O, we proceed as follows.

(1) Check universal (I/O)-satisfiability of ψ.
- **(1.1)** If the answer is negative, we are done. Indeed, if ψ is not universally (I/O)-satisfiable, then ψ is also not (I/O)-realizable.
- **(1.2)** If the answer is positive, proceed to (2).

(2) Check universal (O/I)-satisfiability of $\neg\psi$.
- **(2.1)** If the answer is negative, we are done. Indeed, if $\neg\psi$ is not universally (O/I)-satisfiable, then $\neg\psi$ is not (O/I)-realizable by the environment, implying that ψ is (I/O)-realizable by the system. Moreover, a transducer for ψ can simply generate the output sequence $w_O \in (2^O)^\omega$ for which for all $w_I \in (2^I)^\omega$ we have that $w_I \oplus w_O \models \psi$. The existence of such a sequence follows from $\neg\psi$ not being universally (O/I)-satisfiable, and the algorithm for checking universal (O/I)-satisfiability returns it.
- **(2.2)** If the answer is positive, proceed to (3).

(3) This is the interesting case: both ψ is universally (I/O)-satisfiable and $\neg\psi$ is universally (O/I)-satisfiable. Note that while it cannot be that both ψ and $\neg\psi$ are realizable, they can both be universally satisfiable. When this happens, we know that one of the players, the system or the environment, cannot arrange the responses that work for the universal satisfiability in the form of the strategy that is needed for realizability. In this case, continue to read this section.

As an example to an LTL formula that reaches Step (3) consider $\psi = G(Xi \leftrightarrow o)$. As discussed above, the formula ψ is universally (I/O)-satisfiable but not (I/O)-realizable. Note that $\neg\psi = F\neg(Xi \leftrightarrow o)$, which is universally (O/I)-satisfiable, and would thus reach Step (3). In fact, all LTL formulas ψ that are universally (I/O)-satisfiable but not (I/O)-realizable are such that $\neg\psi$ is (O/I)-realizable, and hence $\neg\psi$ is universally (O/I)-satisfiable, and so the application of the algorithm on them reaches Step (3).

Below we describe a heuristic for handling specifications that reach Step (3). The idea is to apply the subset construction on $\mathcal{A}_\psi$ and $\mathcal{A}_{\neg\psi}$, aiming to refine the universal satisfiability checks by taking into account the history of the game. In more detail, rather than checking the universal satisfiability of ψ and $\neg\psi$ once, here we check the specifications induced by ψ and $\neg\psi$ after each finite history of the interaction between the system and the environment. This is done by performing a subset construction on $\mathcal{A}_\psi$ and $\mathcal{A}_{\neg\psi}$. While the latter involves an exponential blow up in the state spaces of $\mathcal{A}_\psi$ and $\mathcal{A}_{\neg\psi}$, it is independent of the acceptance condition, and can be implemented symbolically.

Let $\mathcal{A}_\psi = \langle 2^{I \cup O}, S, S_0, \rho, \alpha\rangle$ and $\mathcal{A}_{\neg\psi} = \langle 2^{I\cup O}, S', S'_0, \rho', \alpha'\rangle$ be NBWs for ψ and $\neg\psi$, respectively. Let $\mathcal{U}_\psi$ be the pre-automaton (that is, and automaton without an acceptance condition) obtained by applying the subset construction to $\mathcal{A}_\psi$ and $\mathcal{A}_{\neg\psi}$. Thus, $\mathcal{U}_\psi = \langle 2^{I\cup O}, 2^S \times 2^{S'}, \langle S_0, S'_0\rangle, \delta\rangle$, where for all $\langle P, P'\rangle \in 2^S \times 2^{S'}$ and $\sigma \in 2^{I\cup O}$, we have that $\delta(\langle P, P'\rangle, \sigma) = \langle \rho(P, \sigma), \rho'(P', \sigma)\rangle$. For a state $\langle P, P' \rangle$ of $\mathcal{U}_\psi$, let $L(\mathcal{A}_\psi^P)$ and $L(\mathcal{A}_{\neg\psi}^P)$ be the languages of $\mathcal{A}_\psi$ and $\mathcal{A}_{\neg\psi}$ with initial sets P and P', respectively. We say that a set $P \in 2^S$ is *system hopeful* if for all $w_I \in (2^I)^\omega$, there is $w_O \in (2^O)^\omega$ such that $w_I \oplus w_O \in L(\mathcal{A}_\psi^P)$. We say that a set $P' \in 2^{S'}$ is *environment hopeful* if for all $w_O \in (2^O)^\omega$, there is $w_I \in (2^I)^\omega$ such that $w_I \oplus w_O \in L(\mathcal{A}_{\neg\psi}^{P'})$. Thus, system hopefulness coincides with universal (I/O)-satisfaction, except that instead of talking about satisfaction of an LTL formula we talk about the membership in the language of $\mathcal{A}_\psi^P$. Dually, environment hopefulness refers to membership in $\mathcal{A}_{\neg\psi}^{P'}$.

Consider a state $\langle P, P' \rangle \in 2^S \times 2^{S'}$ of $\mathcal{U}_\psi$. It is possible to decide in space exponential in the length of ψ whether P is system hopeful and whether P' is environment hopeful. Indeed, the check is similar to the check for universal satisfaction. For the case of system hopefulness, we project $\mathcal{A}_\psi^P$ on 2^I and check that the obtained NBW is universal. For environment hopefulness we do the same, with $\mathcal{A}_{\neg\psi}^{P'}$ and a projection on 2^O.

We can now describe the heuristic that can be applied in Step (3).

(3) Consider the game $G_{\text{SYN}}(\mathcal{U}_\psi, I, O)$.

(3.1) If the system has a strategy to reach a state $\langle P, P' \rangle$ such that P is system-hopeful and P' is not environment-hopeful, then we are done. Indeed, ψ is realizable, and we can also have a transducer for it.

(3.2) If the environment has a strategy to reach a state $\langle P, P' \rangle$ such that P' is environment-hopeful and P is not system-hopeful, then we are done. Indeed, in a manner dual to the one above, $\neg\psi$ is realizable by the environment.

(3.3) If we get here, both the system and the environment have strategies to stay forever in the region of states that are both system-hopeful and environment-hopeful. At this point we give up and turn to solve the realizability problem using one of the traditional algorithms (or continue and read Sect. 5). The information gathered during our algorithm is still useful and enables us to restrict the realizability game to states in the region of hopeful states (all the other states are replaced by two states – one is winning for the system and one is winning for the environment).

5 Using History-Deterministic Automata

Recall that an HD automaton can resolve its nondeterministic choices in a way that only depends on the past. Obviously, there exist HD automata: deterministic ones, or nondeterministic ones that are *determinizable by pruning* (DBP); that is, ones that just add transitions on top of a deterministic automaton. In fact, the HD automata constructed in [12] are DBP.[1] Before we describe some theoretical properties of HD automata, let us first show that the ability to resolve

[1] As explained in [12], the fact that the HD automata constructed there are DBP does not contradict their usefulness in practice, as their transition relation is simpler than the one of the embodied deterministic automaton and it can be defined symbolically.

nondeterministic choices in a way that depends on the past makes HD automata sound and complete for synthesis.

Theorem 5. *History deterministic automata are sound and complete for (I/O)-realizability.*

Proof. Since all nondeterministic automata are sound for (I/O)-realizability, we only have to prove completeness. Consider an HD automaton $\mathcal{A} = \langle 2^{I \cup O}, Q, q_0, \delta, \alpha \rangle$. Let $g : (2^{I \cup O})^* \rightarrow Q$ be a strategy that witnesses the HDness of $\mathcal{A}$. We show that if $\mathcal{A}$ is (I/O)-realizable, then q_0 is winning for Player OR in $G_{\text{SYN}}(\mathcal{A}, I, O)$.

Assume that $\mathcal{A}$ is (I/O)-realizable. Let $\mathcal{T} = \langle I, O, S, s_0, \rho, \tau \rangle$ be an (I/O)-transducer that (I/O)-realizes $\mathcal{A}$, and let $G_{\text{SYN}}(\mathcal{A}, I, O) = \langle Q, Q \times 2^I, E, \alpha \rangle$. We describe a winning strategy f_{OR} for Player OR in $G_{\text{SYN}}(\mathcal{A}, I, O)$. For every prefix of a play $\pi = q_0, \langle q_0, i_0 \rangle, q_1, \langle q_1, i_1 \rangle, \ldots, q_k, \langle q_k, i_k \rangle$, let $s_0, s_1, \ldots, s_k$ be the run of $\mathcal{T}$ on $i_0, i_1, \ldots, i_k$, and let $o_0, o_1, \ldots, o_k$ be the sequence of outputs generated by $\mathcal{T}$. Thus, for all $j \geq 0$, we have that $o_j = \tau(s_j, i_j)$. We define $f_{\text{OR}}(\pi) = g(i_0 \cup o_o \cdot i_1 \cup o_1 \cdots i_k \cup o_k)$. Since g is an HD strategy for $\mathcal{A}$, the strategy f_{OR} is well defined, in the sense that it returns a state $q_{k+1} \in \delta(q_k, i_k \cup o_k)$. By the definition of $G_{\text{SYN}}(\mathcal{A}, I, O)$, all the outcomes of the game when Player OR uses f_{OR} are computations of $\mathcal{T}$. Since $\mathcal{T}$ (I/O)-realizes $\mathcal{A}$, these computations are in the language of $\mathcal{A}$, and as g is an HD-strategy for $\mathcal{A}$, the run that g induces on them is accepting. Hence, f_{OR} is winning for Player OR, and we are done. □

Remark 1 [**(I/O)-aware HD automata**]. The definition of HD automata involves strategies that resolve nondeterminism by mapping each prefix in $(2^{I \cup O})^*$ to the transition that should be taken after reading the prefix. In the context of synthesis, it is useful to distinguish between nondeterminism due to I and O. In order for an automaton to be complete for (I/O)-realizability, both types on nondeterminism should be resolved in a way that depends only on the past; but while nondeterminism in I is hostile, and all I-futures should be accepted, nondeterminism in O is cooperative, and a single O-future may be accepted.

In [10], we introduced and studied (I/O)-*aware HD automata*, which make use of this distinction. More formally, an automaton $\mathcal{A}$ over $2^{I \cup O}$ is (I/O)-aware HD if for every word $w_I \in (2^I)^\omega$, if w_I is *hopeful*, namely it can be paired with a word $w_O \in (2^O)^\omega$ to a computation accepted by $\mathcal{A}$, then the pairing as well as the accepting run of $\mathcal{A}$ can be produced in an on-line manner, thus in a way that only depends on the past. It is shown in [10] that (I/O)-aware HD automata are sound and complete for (I/O)-realizability, and are unboundedly more succinct than deterministic and even HD automata. □

It is not hard to see that in the context of automata on finite words, every HD automaton is DBP. For automata on infinite words, the situation is much more involved and many questions concerning HD automata are still open. We describe here two key results that highlight the difference between deterministic and HD automata on infinite words. We show that not only HD automata need not be DBP, they may be exponentially more succinct than deterministic ones. We start with HD-NBWs, and show that a strategy that witnesses HDness may need to resolve the nondeterminism in a different manner in different visits to the same state of the NBW.

Theorem 6. *[5] There are HD-NBWs that are not determinizable by pruning.*

Proof. Consider the NBW $\mathcal{A}$ appearing in Fig. 3. We prove that $\mathcal{A}$ is HD and is not DBP. Note that $\mathcal{A}$ gets stuck (and rejects) when it reads words that are not in $(a0+a1)^\omega$. We claim that $L(\mathcal{A}) = L$, for

$$L = \{w \in (a0+a1)^\omega : w \text{ has infinitely many infixes of the form } a0a0 \text{ or } a1a1\}.$$

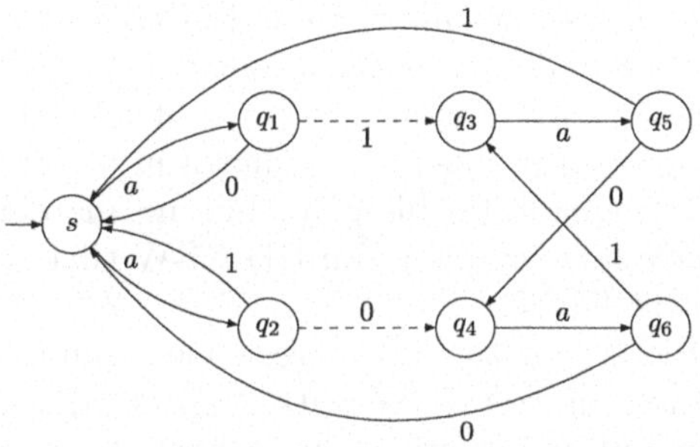

Fig. 3. A HD-NBW that is not DBP. Dashed transitions are in α.

In order to see that $L(\mathcal{A}) \subseteq L$, note that if a word in $(a0+a1)^\omega$ is not in L, and thus it has only finitely many infixes of the form $a0a0$ or $a1a1$, then it has a suffix $(a0a1)^\omega$. Also, when a run of $\mathcal{A}$ traverses an α-transition when reading such a suffix, then after taking the α-transition, it keeps looping at the q_3, q_5, q_4, q_6 cycle and never traverses an α-transition again. In order to see that $L \subseteq L(\mathcal{A})$, note that after reading a prefix in $(a0+a1)^*$, a run of $\mathcal{A}$ is in state s, q_3, or q_4. If the run is in state s or q_4 and reads $a0a0$, then it can traverse an α-transition and return to s, and if it is in state q_3 and reads $a0a0$, then it reaches the state s. Also, reading $a1$ from s, a run can return to s. Thus, reading $a0a0$ infinitely often enables a run to traverse α-transitions infinitely often, and similarly for $a1a1$.

We continue and prove that $\mathcal{A}$ is HD. We do so by describing a strategy f that witnesses its HDness. Note that there is one nondeterministic transition in $\mathcal{A}$: reading a in state s, a run can proceed to q_1 or q_2. We define f so that whenever $\mathcal{A}$ is in state s and reads a, it directs the run to proceed as follows. If the run has just started or s was reached from q_6 or q_2, then the run continues to q_1; if s was reached from q_5 or q_1, then the run continues to q_2. First, note that the above strategy can be described by means of a function with domain $\{a, 0, 1\}^*$. For example, $f(a) = q_1$, $f(a0a) = q_2$, and $f(a1a1a) = q_2$. In addition, the strategy guarantees that all words in the language are accepted. Indeed, reading $a0a0$ either leads to a traversal of an α-transition or leads to s, where the next $a0a0$ or $a1a1$ leads to a traversal of an α-transition, and similarly for $a1a1$.

It is left to prove that $\mathcal{A}$ is not DBP. Recall that there are two ways to make $\mathcal{A}$ deterministic by pruning: either prune the a transition from s to q_1 or the a-transition from s to q_2. We show that both ways result in a DBW whose language is strictly contained in that of $\mathcal{A}$. First, if we prune the transition from s to q_1, then the obtained tDBW rejects the word $(a1)^\omega$, which is in $L(\mathcal{A})$. Indeed, the singe run on it is $(s, q_2)^\omega$, which is rejecting. Dually, if we prune the transition from s to q_2, then the single run of the obtained DBW on the word $(a0)^\omega$, which is in $L(\mathcal{A})$, is $(s, q_1)^\omega$, which is rejecting. Thus, $\mathcal{A}$ is an HD-NBW that is not DBP. □

Note that Theorem 6 does not imply that HD-NBWs are more succinct than DBWs. In fact, the HD-NBW $\mathcal{A}$ in the proof can be easily determinized by merging the states q_1 and q_2. The succinctness of HD-NBWs with respect to DBWs is an intriguing open problem. It is shown in [3,13] that HD-NBWs can be determinized with a quadratic blow-up, but no matching lower bounds is known. In fact, we have no example to an HD-NBW that is smaller in even one state from an equivalent DBW.

For HD-NCWs, the succinctness picture is clear, and includes a surprising exponential succinctness of HD-NCW with respect to DCWs. The beautiful proof, by Kuperberg and Skrzypczak, shows how the past can direct a nondeterministic automaton how to resolve its nondeterministic choices, and to do it in a way that significantly reduces the state space of the automaton. Below we present the key ideas of the proof.

Theorem 7. [13] There is an infinite family of languages $L_1, L_2, L_3, \ldots$ such that for every $n \geq 1$, the following holds.

1. There is an HD-NCW with $2n$ states that recognizes L_n.
2. Every DCW that recognizes L_n needs at least $\frac{2^n}{2n}$ states.

Proof. For $n \geq 1$, let $[n] = \{0, 1, \ldots, 2n-1\}$. We define the language L_n over the alphabet $\Sigma = \{I, Z, X, H\}$. Each letter in Σ is a (possibly partial) function $\sigma : [n] \to [n]$, as described in Fig. 4.

The functions I, X, and Z are one-one and onto: for every $x \in [n]$, we have that $I(x) = x$, $Z(x) = (x+1) \bmod 2n-1$, and X agrees with I, except for $x \in \{0, 1\}$, where $X(0) = 1$ and $X(1) = 0$. The function H is partial; it agrees with I, except for $x = 0$, where $H(0)$ is undefined. Thus, the letters induce permutations on $[n]$, with H inducing a permutation only on $[n] \setminus \{0\}$.

We view a finite word w as the partial function $w : [n] \to [n]$ obtained by composing its letters. Thus, if $w = \sigma_1 \cdot \sigma_2 \cdots \sigma_l$, then for all $i \in [n]$, we have that $w(i) = \sigma_l(\cdots \sigma_2(\sigma_1(i)))$. It is convenient to associate with each word $w \in \Sigma^*$ a grid of dimensions $(|w| + 1) \times 2n$, and lines that start in "floors" in $[n]$ and traverse the floors along the grid according to the permutations induced by the

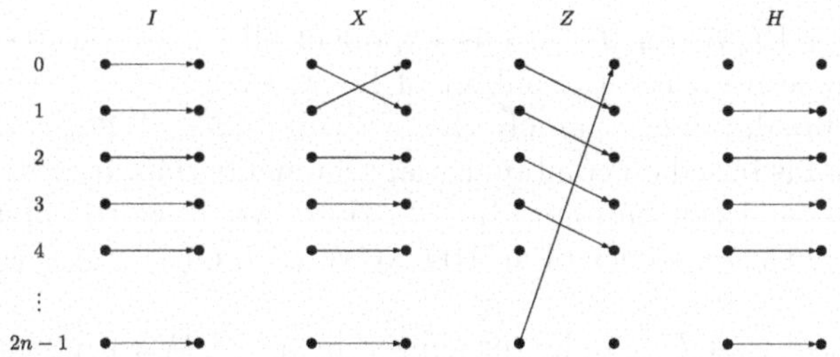

Fig. 4. The permutations induced by the letters I, X, Z, and H.

letters in w. As $H(0)$ is undefined, a line that reaches floor 0 before H is read has a "hole" in the corresponding position in the grid. Figure 5 describes the grid associated with the word $IXHZZXHZ$ when $n = 2$ and $n = 3$.

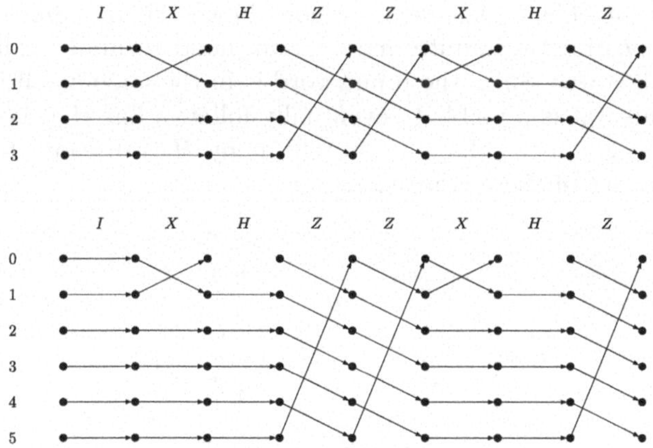

Fig. 5. The grid induced by the word $IXHZZXHZ$ when $n = 2$ (top) and $n = 3$ (bottom).

An infinite word $u \in \Sigma^\omega$ corresponds to an infinite sequence of compositions of its letters, and thus the horizontal dimension of the grid associated with it is infinite. We define L_n as the set of words in Σ^ω whose grid contains an infinite line; that is, a line that has only finitely many holes. For example, back to Fig. 5, it is not hard to see that the infinite word $u = w^\omega$, for $w = IXHZZXHZ$ is in L_2. Indeed, when $n = 2$, we have that $w(0) = 0$ and $w(2) = 2$, and so the lines starting at floors 0 and 2 are never cut. On the other hand, $u \notin L_3$. Indeed, when $n = 3$, we have that $w(0) = 4$, $w(2) = 5$, $w(3) = 0$, $w(4) = 2$, whereas $w(1)$ and $w(5)$ are undefined. Accordingly, $w^5(i)$ is undefined for all $i \in [3]$, implying that lines from all floors are cut whenever w^5 is read. Therefore, the grid of u contains no infinite line, and so $u \notin L_3$.

Intuitively, a DCW for L_n needs exponentially many states as it has to remember in its state space the subset of floors whose lines have not been cut since the last "break point", namely the last time since all floors have been cut. The formal proof is based on combinatorial arguments that are less related to the issue of HDness, and can be found in [13]. Here, we prove the first claim in the theorem, namely the existence of an HD-NCW with $O(n)$ states that recognizes L_n.

It is easy to see that L_n can be recognized by an NCW with $2n$ states. Indeed, an NCW can simply guesses a line to follow, and to initiate its guess whenever the line it follows is cut. Specifically (see $\mathcal{A}_2$ in Fig. 6), the NCW $\mathcal{A}_n$ has state space $\{q_0, \ldots, q_{2n-1}\}$ and for all $i \in [n]$, it visits q_i when the line it follows is in floor i. The initial state of $\mathcal{A}_n$ is arbitrarily set to q_0, and the transition function updates the floor according to the letter it reads. For example, when $\mathcal{A}_n$ is in state q_i and reads I, it stays in q_i, when it reads X, if stays in q_i for $i \in \{2, \ldots, 2n-1\}$, moves to q_1 from q_0, and moves to q_0 from q_1. Nondeterminism is required when $\mathcal{A}_n$ reads the letter H in state q_0, thus when it follows a line that is in floor 0 and the line is cut. Then, $\mathcal{A}_n$ guesses a new floor to follow. Since all floors are candidates for hosting an infinite line, $\mathcal{A}_n$ can nondeterministically move from q_0 with H to all states. Since the input word is in the language if it contains an infinite line, thus if it is possible to eventually follow a line that is never cut, we want an accepting run to take only finitely many H-transitions from the state q_0, thus α is the set of these transitions.

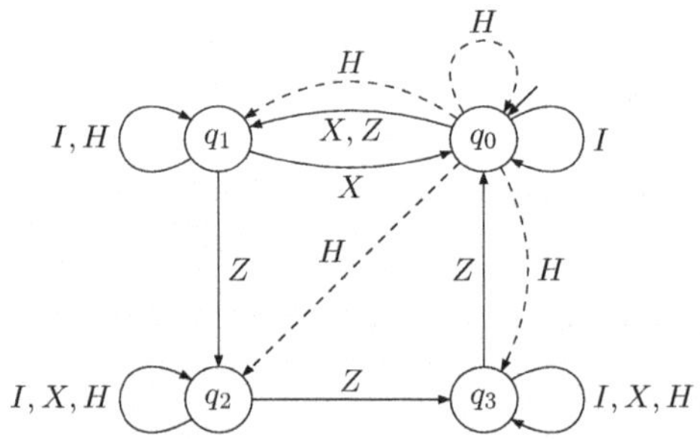

Fig. 6. The HD-NCW $\mathcal{A}_2$ that recognizes L_2.

It is less easy to see that the NCW $\mathcal{A}_n$ is in fact HD. In order to see this, consider the following HD strategy $g : \Sigma^* \to Q$. First, $g(\epsilon) = q_0$, thus all runs start in state q_0, which is the only initial state of $\mathcal{A}_n$. Whenever a run is in state q_0 after reading a prefix u and it reads H, it proceeds to the state q_i such that the line that is now in floor i is the longest among all lines in the graph. Formally, for all words $u \in \Sigma^*$ and floors $i \in [n]$, let *seniority*(u, i) be the length of the longest suffix u' of u such that there is $j \in [n]$ with $u'(j) = i$. Then, if $u \in \Sigma^*$ is such that $g(u) = q_0$, then $g(u \cdot H) = q_i$, for the minimal $i \in [n]$ that maximizes *seniority*(u, i). Note that the choice of the minimal i is arbitrary, and it is required in order to decide between lines with the same seniority. Note also that it is possible to implement the HD strategy g by maintaining the order of seniority among the different floors during the run, thus it indeed depends only on the history of the run. Finally, as an infinite line would eventually obtain the maximal seniority, it is guaranteed that following the strategy g leads to accepting all words in the language: in all of then, the run that follows g eventually follows an infinite line. □

The two results we described here about the succinctness of HD-automata with respect to deterministic ones are just two examples to the interesting and extensive research that has been done in the last years about HD automata. Research includes richer types of HD automata, both in terms of the acceptance condition, and in settings like alternating, weighted, or pushdown automata [6,7], the problem of deciding HDness [4], the relation of HDness to other restrictions on nondeterminism [2], minimization and canonization of HD automata [1,20], and many more [14].

6 Discussion

We presented two approaches for coping with the fact that playing the synthesis game on top of a nondeterministic automaton is incomplete. Essentially, the problem with using a nondeterministic automaton follows from the fact that the system generates its responses in an on-line manner. Consequently, as long as computations agree on their prefix, the system generates the same run on them. This limits the way in which the system may use different nondeterministic choices on different computations.

The two approaches we suggested are different, yet they both address the need of the system to respond with an accepting run in an on-line manner. In the case of HD automata, this is done directly, as HD automata are capable of resolving their nondeterministic choices in an on-line manner. In the approach that is based on determinancy of games and universal satisfiability, this hides in the difference between realizability and universal satisfiability. To see this, recall that in universal satisfiability, each input sequence should be matched with an output sequence. This matching can be done in an off-line manner. In realizability, on the other hand, this matching should be done in an on-line manner. Moving from checking realizability to checking universal satisfiability thus examines the realizability problem in the case the system could respond, with both an output assignment and a run of the automaton, in an off-line manner.

References

1. Abu Radi, B., Kupferman, O.: Minimization and canonization of GFG transition-based automata. Log. Meth. Comput. Sci. **18**(3) (2022)

2. Abu Radi, B., Kupferman, O., Leshkowitz, O.: A hierarchy of nondeterminism. In: 46th International Symposium on Mathematical Foundations of Computer Science. LIPIcs, vol. 202, pp. 85:1–85:21 (2021)
3. Abu Radi, B., Kupferman, O., Leshkowitz, O.: Easy complementation of history-deterministic büchi automata. In: 22nd International Symposium on Automated Technology for Verification and Analysis. LNCS. Springer (2024)
4. Bagnol, M., Kuperberg, D.: Büchi good-for-games automata are efficiently recognizable. In: Proceedings of the 38th Conference on Foundations of Software Technology and Theoretical Computer Science. LIPIcs, vol. 122, pp. 16:1–16:14. Schloss Dagstuhl - Leibniz-Zentrum fuer Informatik (2018)
5. Boker, U., Kuperberg, D., Kupferman, O., Skrzypczak, M.: Nondeterminism in the presence of a diverse or unknown future. In: Fomin, F.V., Freivalds, R., Kwiatkowska, M., Peleg, D. (eds.) ICALP 2013. LNCS, vol. 7966, pp. 89–100. Springer, Heidelberg (2013). https://doi.org/10.1007/978-3-642-39212-2_11
6. Boker, U., Kuperberg, D., Lehtinen, K., Skrzypczak, M.: On the succinctness of alternating parity good-for-games automata. In: Proceedings of the 40th Conference on Foundations of Software Technology and Theoretical Computer Science. LIPIcs, vol. 182, pp. 41:1–41:13. Schloss Dagstuhl - Leibniz-Zentrum für Informatik (2020)
7. Boker, U., Lehtinen, K.: When a little nondeterminism goes a long way: an introduction to history-determinism. ACM SIGLOG News **10**(1), 177–196 (2023)
8. Church, A.: Logic, arithmetics, and automata. In: 1962 Proceedings of the International Congress of Mathematicians, pp. 23–35. Institut Mittag-Leffler (1963)
9. Colcombet, T.: The theory of stabilisation monoids and regular cost functions. In: Albers, S., Marchetti-Spaccamela, A., Matias, Y., Nikoletseas, S., Thomas, W. (eds.) ICALP 2009. LNCS, vol. 5556, pp. 139–150. Springer, Heidelberg (2009). https://doi.org/10.1007/978-3-642-02930-1_12
10. Faran, R., Kupferman, O.: On (I/O)-aware good-for-games automata. In: 18th International Symposium on Automated Technology for Verification and Analysis. LNCS, vol. 12302, pp. 161–178. Springer, Heidelberg (2020)
11. Mazala, R.: Infinite games. In: Grädel, E., Thomas, W., Wilke, T. (eds.) Automata Logics, and Infinite Games. LNCS, vol. 2500, pp. 23–38. Springer, Heidelberg (2002). https://doi.org/10.1007/3-540-36387-4_2
12. Henzinger, T.A., Piterman, N.: Solving games without determinization. In: Ésik, Z. (ed.) CSL 2006. LNCS, vol. 4207, pp. 395–410. Springer, Heidelberg (2006). https://doi.org/10.1007/11874683_26
13. Kuperberg, D., Skrzypczak, M.: On determinisation of good-for-games automata. In: Proceedings of the 42nd International Colloquium on Automata, Languages, and Programming, pp. 299–310 (2015)
14. Kupferman, O.: Using the past for resolving the future. Front. Comput. Sci. **4**, 1114625 (2022)
15. Kupferman, O., Sadigh, D., Seshia, S.A.: Synthesis with clairvoyance. In: 7th International Haifa Verification Conference. LNCS, vol. 7261, pp. 5–19. Springer, Heidelberg (2011)
16. Kupferman, O., Safra, S., Vardi, M.Y.: Relating word and tree automata. Ann. Pure Appl. Logic **138**(1–3), 126–146 (2006)
17. Kupferman, O., Vardi, M.Y.: Weak alternating automata are not that weak. ACM Trans. Comput. Log. **2**(2), 408–429 (2001)
18. Pnueli, A.: The temporal semantics of concurrent programs. Theoret. Comput. Sci. **13**, 45–60 (1981)

19. Pnueli, A., Rosner, R.: On the synthesis of a reactive module. In: Proceedings of the 16th ACM Symposium on Principles of Programming Languages, pp. 179–190 (1989)
20. Schewe, S.: Minimising good-for-games automata is NP-complete. In: Proceedings of the 40th Conference on Foundations of Software Technology and Theoretical Computer Science. LIPIcs, vol. 182, pp. 56:1–56:13. Schloss Dagstuhl - Leibniz-Zentrum für Informatik (2020)
21. Sistla, A.P., Vardi, M.Y., Wolper, P.: The complementation problem for Büchi automata with applications to temporal logic. Theoret. Comput. Sci. **49**, 217–237 (1987)
22. Thomas, W.: On the synthesis of strategies in infinite games. In: Mayr, E.W., Puech, C. (eds.) STACS 1995. LNCS, vol. 900, pp. 1–13. Springer, Heidelberg (1995). https://doi.org/10.1007/3-540-59042-0_57
23. Vardi, M.Y., Wolper, P.: Automata-theoretic techniques for modal logics of programs. J. Comput. Syst. Sci. **32**(2), 182–221 (1986)
24. Vardi, M.Y., Wolper, P.: Reasoning about infinite computations. Inf. Comput. **115**(1), 1–37 (1994)

Strategy Templates
– Robust Certified Interfaces for Interacting Systems

Ashwani Anand, Satya Prakash Nayak(✉), and Anne-Kathrin Schmuck

Max Planck Institute for Software Systems (MPI-SWS), Kaiserslautern, Germany
{ashwani,sanayak,akschmuck}@mpi-sws.org

Abstract. This invited paper unifies our recent work on the automated synthesis of strategy templates as robust certified interfaces for interacting autonomous systems. Strategy templates are similar to classical strategies typically computed by reactive software synthesis but contain a huge set of relevant strategies in a succinct and simple data structure. This *permissiveness* allows efficient adaptations to new specifications as well as robustness to unexpected actuation failures during runtime. In addition to these favorable engineering properties of strategy templates for cyber-physical systems (CPS), their permissiveness, efficient computability, and adaptability enables their use for the automated synthesis of *certified interfaces* among different interacting CPS. This paper discusses the foundations and applications of this novel *control-inspired distributed reactive synthesis framework* for different cooperation and partial-observation settings common for interacting CPS.

Keywords: Rational Synthesis · Cooperative Synthesis · Strategy Templates · Negotiation · Graph Games · Robustness

1 Introduction

The holy grail of autonomy and artificial intelligence are technological systems that deploy a *reliable seamless and strategic interaction* with each other, which requires the design of *robust certified interfaces* for their interaction. In recent years, this problem has been addressed by a combination of *formal methods* (rooted in theoretical computer science) and *control theory* (rooted in engineering) [5,11–13,15], due to two main observations: first, and more obviously, the trustworthiness of software is the main object of study within the formal methods community, naturally leading to an intersection of concerns for embedded software within cyber-physical systems (CPS). The second, usually non-obvious reason, is that strategic decisions in higher control layers of autonomous CPS are largely event-based, naturally leading to discrete, transition-based models,

Authors are ordered randomly, denoted by (,) and the publicly verifiable record of the randomization is available at www.aeaweb.org/journals/policies/random-author-order/search?. The authors are supported by the DFG projects SCHM 3541/1-1 and 389792660 TRR 248-CPEC.

S. Akshay et al. (Eds.): ATVA 2024, LNCS 15054, pp. 22–41, 2025.
https://doi.org/10.1007/978-3-031-78709-6_2

such as automata, formal languages or logic. In both cases, so called *reactive* (software) systems are particularly related to feedback control. Here, the computations of a software component are influenced by inputs from the outside which might, in turn, be effected by their outputs, which forms a *logical feedback loop* between the (software) system and its (software) environment.

This connection between reactive software and feedback control is well known and existing work bridges both fields by either (i) enhancing classical feedback control with formal methods, or (ii) enhancing reactive synthesis with physical dynamics.However, methods that efficiently *integrate both* to address the challenges of *seamless strategic feedback* among autonomous CPS are still in their infancy. This invited paper outlines how our recent research addresses this gap by *rethinking distributed reactive synthesis* from a control perspective for *robust certified interface design* in higher layers of the CPS control software stack.

Distributed Reactive Synthesis is concerned with the automated computation of implementations of interacting reactive software components, given specifications for each component in linear temporal logic (LTL). While this classical synthesis problem is known to be undecidable, we consider a common variant where the strategic interaction capabilities of the components are known and modelled as a P-player game graph G. However, in contrast to most previous work, we assume that players only know their own objective Φ_p along with G and compute their own strategy π_p independently under this knowledge. In addition, during runtime, each player only observes the current moves of other players, but does not know their strategy, and hence, cannot use this knowledge to condition its strategy on. Given such an instance, this paper presents our novel techniques to *synthesize robust certified interfaces* for fully cooperating [3] and rationally interacting [10] players, which allows them to adapt their local strategies efficiently both during (offline) synthesis and during (online) deployment.

The main ingredient of our framework is the realization of these interfaces by *strategy templates.* We first introduced strategy templates as *novel robust and adaptable logical controllers* for single systems [2]. Strategy templates are similar to classical strategies typically computed by reactive synthesis but contain a huge set of relevant strategies in a succinct and simple data structure. This *permissiveness* allows efficient adaptations to new specifications as well as robustness to unexpected actuation failures during runtime. In addition, strategy template synthesis only requires mild modifications of the classical reactive synthesis algorithms and therefore enjoys identical computational complexities.

In addition to the favorable engineering properties of strategy templates for CPS control, their permissiveness, efficient computability, and adaptability enables their use for the synthesis of *certified interfaces* among different interacting CPS. Here the fundamental idea is to iteratively *co-synthesize* templates both as *assumptions* and as *guarantees* by individual players which are iteratively refined into certified interfaces. While assume-guarantee reasoning has proven useful in verification, where all component implementations are known, assume-guarantee *synthesis* usually encounters a chicken-and-egg problem – without component implementations, no contracts can be obtained and without contracts, no respecting implementations can be synthesized. Our work fills this gap by locally computing *permissive templates* which retain as many feasible ways of cooperation as possible to allow for a distributed implementation to be eventually discovered by their iterative and distributed refinement. In particular, our frameworks does not only address safety – which naturally allows for maximal permissiveness – but to also enable *certified interactive progress*, which is known to be very challenging already for verification.

In Summary, our *iterative synthesis frameworks* are

- *expressive* – we consider parity specifications to model system objectives;
- *privacy concerned* – specifications and strategy choices of systems are not directly shared or handled centrally;
- *computationally tractable* – the efficient computability and adaptability properties of strategy templates allow for reasonable synthesis times; and
- *ensured to terminate* – due to careful under-approximations of templates which prevent game graph modifications in between iterations.

Further, the resulting *strategy templates* form a robust certified interface for interacting CPS due to their

- *full decentralization of strategy choices* – during runtime, the correct interaction of components is achieved by any locally chosen strategy, as long as each one satisfies the (previously iteratively synthesized) local template;
- *their robustness* – the full decentralization of strategy choices retains the local robustness and adaptability of strategy templates during deployment.

In addition, we have recently shown the applicability of strategy templates beyond distributed reactive synthesis. In particular, we have

- introduced a *hierarchical control framework* which combines low-level (fast) physical feedback control with high-level (slow) logical feedback control in a novel seamless manner [9] powered by the use of strategy templates as *vertical interfaces* between both control layers, and
- used strategy templates to build a *progress guided refinement framework* for the synthesis of embedded software via *infinite-state reactive program games* [14], which can efficiently handle synthesis problem which are non-tractable by any existing partial solvers for this (undecidable) synthesis problem.

Outline. This invited paper is based on our recent work [1–3, 10], to which we refer for an in-depth discussion of related work, the proposed synthesis algorithms, their correctness proofs and their experimental evaluations along with many illustrative examples. In contrast, this invited paper illustrates the underlying similarities and differences of these algorithms. After recalling preliminaries in Sect. 2 and the general notion of strategy templates in Sect. 3, the discussion of the iterative synthesis frameworks in Sect. 4 provides a novel joint view on the negotiation frameworks for cooperative [3] and rational [10] players. This allows us to extend our cooperative framework from 2 to P players, which gives additional insights about the permissiveness and termination nature of our synthesis frameworks, not contained in our previous work. In addition, Sect. 5 provides a new, unpublished algorithm for strategy template based control *under partial observation*, typically present in autonomous CPS applications.

2 Preliminaries

This section introduces notation and preliminaries used throughout the paper.

Notation. We use $\mathbb{N}$ to denote the set of natural numbers including zero. Given two natural numbers $a, b \in \mathbb{N}$ with $a \leq b$, we use $[a; b]$ to denote the set $\{n \in \mathbb{N} \mid a \leq n \leq b\}$. The notations Σ^* and Σ^ω, respectively, denote the set of finite and infinite words over the finite alphabet Σ. Given two words $u \in \Sigma^*$ and $v \in \Sigma^* \cup \Sigma^\omega$, the concatenation of u and v is written as the word uv.

2.1 Infinite Games over Finite Graphs

We use games over finite graphs as an abstract model for the interaction dynamics within in a distributed CPS. This section introduces notation and preliminaries on this modeling formalism.

Game Graphs. A *P-player (turn-based) game graph* is a tuple $G = (V, E, v_0)$ where (V, E, v_0) is a finite, directed graph with *vertices* V and *edges* E, and $v_0 \in V$ is an initial vertex. For such a game graph, let $\mathtt{P} = [1; P]$ be the set of players such that $V = \bigcup_{p \in \mathtt{P}} V_i$ is partitioned into vertices of P players in $\mathtt{P}$. We write E_p, $p \in \mathtt{P}$, to denote the edges from Player p's vertices, i.e., $E_p = E \cap (V_p \times V)$. Further, we write $V_{\neg p}$ and $E_{\neg p}$ to denote the set $\bigcup_{q \neq p} V_p$ and $\bigcup_{q \neq p} E_q$, respectively. A *play* from a vertex u_0 is a finite or infinite sequence of vertices $\rho = u_0 u_1 \ldots$ with $(u_j, u_{j+1}) \in E$ for all $j \geq 0$.

Winning Conditions. Given a game graph G, a *winning condition* (or *objective*) is a set of plays specified using a formula Φ in *linear temporal logic* (LTL) over the vertex set V, i.e., LTL formulas whose atomic propositions are sets of vertices from V. We write $\mathcal{L}(\Phi) \subseteq V^\omega$ to denote the set of plays that satisfy Φ. The standard definitions of ω-regular languages and LTL are omitted for brevity and can be found in standard textbooks [4]. In particular, we consider *parity objectives* given by the LTL formula

$$Parity(\mathbb{C}) := \bigwedge_{i \in_{\text{odd}} [0;d]} \left(\Box\Diamond C^i \implies \bigvee_{j \in_{\text{even}} [i+1;d]} \Box\Diamond C^j \right), \tag{1}$$

with *color set* $C^j = \{v : \mathbb{C}(v) = j\}$ for $0 \leq j \leq d$ of vertices for some *coloring function* $\mathbb{C} : V \to [0; d]$ that assigns each vertex a *color* (a.k.a. priority). Hence, $\mathcal{L}(Parity(\mathbb{C}))$ contains all plays ρ for which the highest color appearing infinitely often is even. We note that every game with an arbitrary ω-regular winning condition can be reduced to a parity game (possibly with a larger vertex set) [4].

Games. A *P-player (single-objective) game* is a tuple $\mathcal{G} = (G, \Phi)$, where G is a game graph, and Φ is the *winning condition* over G. A *P-player multi-objective game* is a pair $\mathcal{G} = (G, (\Phi_p)_{p\in\mathsf{P}})$ where G is a P-player game graph and each Φ_p is an *objective* for Player p over G. We call a $\mathcal{G}$ a parity game if all involved winning conditions are parity objectives.

Strategies. A strategy of Player p, $p \in \mathsf{P}$, is a function $\pi_p\colon V^*V_p \to V$ such that for every $\rho v \in V^*V_p$, it holds that $(v, \pi_p(\rho v)) \in E$. A strategy profile for a set of players $\mathsf{P}' \subseteq \mathsf{P}$ is a tuple $(\pi_p)_{p\in\mathsf{P}'}$ of strategies, one for each player in P'. To simplify notation, we write $\mathsf{P}_{\neg p}$ and $\pi_{\neg p}$ to denote the set $\mathsf{P} \setminus \{p\}$ and their strategy profile $(\pi_q)_{q\in\mathsf{P}\setminus\{p\}}$, respectively. Given a strategy profile $(\pi_p)_{p\in\mathsf{P}'}$, we say that a play $\rho = u_0u_1\dots$ is a $(\pi_p)_{p\in\mathsf{P}'}$*-play* if for every $p \in \mathsf{P}'$ and for all $\ell \geq 1$, it holds that $u_{\ell-1} \in V_p$ implies $u_\ell = \pi_p(u_0 \dots u_{\ell-1})$.

Winning. Given a game graph G, a play ρ in G is *winning* for objective Φ if it satisfies Φ, i.e., $\rho \in \mathcal{L}(\Phi)$. A strategy profile $(\pi_p)_{p\in\mathsf{P}'}$ for $\mathsf{P}' \subseteq \mathsf{P}$ is winning for objective Φ from a vertex v, denoted by $(\pi_p)_{p\in\mathsf{P}'} \models_v \Phi$, if every $(\pi_p)_{p\in\mathsf{P}'}$-play from v satisfies Φ. We write $(\pi_p)_{p\in\mathsf{P}'} \models \Phi$ if v is the initial vertex. We collect all vertices from which there exists a strategy profile for players in P' that satisfies Φ in the winning region[1] $\langle\!\langle \mathsf{P}' \rangle\!\rangle \Phi$.

We note two special cases. First, if $\mathsf{P}' = \{p\}$, $\pi_p \models_v \Phi$ requires that Player p wins from v against all strategies of players in $\mathsf{P}_{\neg p}$. If $|\mathsf{P}| = 2$, this corresponds to the classical notion of *adversarial winning* in zero-sum games. Second, given a multi-objective game $(G, (\Phi_p)_{p\in\mathsf{P}})$ and the full set of players $\mathsf{P}' = \mathsf{P}$, $(\pi_p)_{p\in\mathsf{P}} \models \bigwedge_{p\in\mathsf{P}} \Phi_p$ denotes a *cooperatively winning* strategy profile.

Rational Winning. To formalize a third type of winning that sits between adversarial and cooperative winning, we use the concept of *winning secure equilibria (WSE)* [7] to introduce *rationality* among players. A WSE is a Nash equilibrium where every player's main goal is to satisfy their own objective Φ_p, and, as a secondary goal, falsify the objectives of the other players. Given a P-player multi-objective game $(G, (\Phi_p)_{p\in\mathsf{P}})$, a *WSE* is a strategy profile $(\pi_p)_{p\in\mathsf{P}'}$ for $\mathsf{P}' \subseteq \mathsf{P}$ such that (i)$(\pi_p)_{p\in\mathsf{P}'} \models \bigwedge_{p\in\mathsf{P}'} \Phi_p$; and (ii)for every strategy π'_p of Player $p \in \mathsf{P}'$ with $\mathsf{P}'' = \mathsf{P}' \setminus \{p\}$, it holds that $(\pi'_p, (\pi_q)_{q\in\mathsf{P}''}) \not\models \bigwedge_{q\in\mathsf{P}''} \Phi_q \Rightarrow (\pi'_p, (\pi_q)_{q\in\mathsf{P}''}) \not\models \Phi_p$. Intuitively, item (i) ensures that the strategy profile satisfies all player's objective, whereas item (ii) ensures that no player can improve, i.e., falsify another player's objective without falsifying their own objective, by deviating from the prescribed strategy.

We call a strategy profile $(\pi_p)_{p\in\mathsf{P}}$ *rationally winning* if it is a WSE over $(G, (\Phi_p)_{p\in\mathsf{P}})$ for the full set of players P, i.e. $\mathsf{P}' = \mathsf{P}$.

---

[1] Slightly abusing notation, we write $\langle\!\langle p \rangle\!\rangle \Phi$ for singleton sets of players $\mathsf{P}' = \{p\}$.

2.2 Permissive Templates

In principle, a template is simply an LTL formula Λ over a game graph G. We will, however, restrict attention to four distinct types of such formulas, and interpret them as a succinct way to represent a set of strategies for each player, in particular all strategies that *follow* Λ. Formally, a Player p strategy π_p *follows* Λ if every π_p-play belongs to $\mathcal{L}(\Lambda)$, i.e., $\pi_p \models_v \Lambda$ for all $v \in V$. The exposition in this section follows the presentation in [1] where more illustrative examples and intuitive explanations can be found.

Safety Templates. Given a set $S \subseteq E$ of *unsafe edges*, the safety template is defined as $\Lambda_{\text{UNSAFE}}(S) := \square \wedge_{e \in S} \neg e$, where an edge $e = (u, v)$ is equivalent to the LTL formula $u \wedge \bigcirc v$. A safety template requires that an edge to S should never be taken.

Live-Group Templates. A *live-group* $H = \{e_j\}_{j \geq 0}$ is a set of edges $e_j = (s_j, t_j)$ with source vertices $src(H) := \{s_j\}_{j \geq 0}$. Given a set of live-groups $H_\ell = \{H_i\}_{i \geq 0}$ we define a live-group template as $\Lambda_{\text{LIVE}}(H_\ell) := \bigwedge_{i \geq 0} \square \lozenge src(H_i) \Rightarrow \square \lozenge H_i$. A live-group template requires that if some vertex from the source of a live-group is visited infinitely often, then some edge from this group should be taken infinitely often by the following strategy.

Conditional Live-Group Templates. A *conditional live-group* over G is a pair (R, H_ℓ), where $R \subseteq V$ and H_ℓ is a set of live groups. Given a set of conditional live groups $\mathcal{H}$ we define a *conditional live-group template* as $\Lambda_{\text{COND}}(\mathcal{H}) := \bigwedge_{(R, H_\ell) \in \mathcal{H}} (\square \lozenge R \Rightarrow \Lambda_{\text{LIVE}}(H_\ell))$. A conditional live-group template requires that for every pair (R, H_ℓ), if some vertex from the set R is visited infinitely often, then a following strategy must follow the live-group template $\Lambda_{\text{LIVE}}(H_\ell)$. We write $(\cdot, H_\ell)$ if there exists $R \subseteq V$, such that (R, H_ℓ) is a conditional live group.

Co-liveness Templates. Given a set of *co-live* edges D, a co-live template is defined as $\Lambda_{\text{COLIVE}}(D) := \bigwedge_{e \in D} \lozenge \square \neg e$. A co-liveness template requires that edges in D are only taken finitely often.

Composed Templates. A template $\Lambda := \Lambda_{\text{UNSAFE}}(S) \wedge \Lambda_{\text{COLIVE}}(D) \wedge \Lambda_{\text{COND}}(\mathcal{H})$ will be associated with the tuple $(S, D, \mathcal{H})$, denoted by $\Lambda \lhd (S, D, \mathcal{H})$, in the rest of the paper. Similarly, $\Lambda \lhd (S, D, H_\ell)$ denotes the template $\Lambda := \Lambda_{\text{UNSAFE}}(S) \wedge \Lambda_{\text{COLIVE}}(D) \wedge \Lambda_{\text{LIVE}}(H_\ell)$. We further note that the conjunction of two templates $\Lambda \lhd (S, D, \mathcal{H})$ and $\Lambda' \lhd (S', D', \mathcal{H}')$ is equivalent to the template $(\Lambda \wedge \Lambda') \lhd (S \cup S', D \cup D', \mathcal{H} \cup \mathcal{H}')$ by the definition of conjunction of LTL formulas.

Player Specific Templates. It will be customary to separate templates to restrict single players. Hence, a template $\Lambda \lhd (S, D, \mathcal{H})$ over G is called a *p-template* for some $p \in \mathsf{P}$ if all edges used in the template are Player p's edges, i.e., $S \cup D \cup \overline{H} \subseteq E_p$, where $\overline{H} := \bigcup \{H \in H_\ell \mid (\cdot, H_\ell) \in \mathcal{H}\}$. Furthermore, given any template $\Lambda \lhd (S, D, H_\ell)$, one can extract a p-template $\Lambda|_{E_p}$ by restricting the edges used to E_p, i.e., $\Lambda|_{E_p} \lhd (S \cap E_p, D \cap E_p, H_\ell|_{E_p})$ with $H_\ell|_{E_p} = \{H \cap E_p \mid H \in H_\ell\}$. Similarly, for $\Lambda \lhd (S, D, \mathcal{H})$, we define $\Lambda|_{E_p} \lhd (S \cap E_p, D \cap E_p, \mathcal{H}|_{E_p})$ with $\mathcal{H}|_{E_p} = \{(R, H_\ell|_{E_p}) \mid (R, H_\ell) \in \mathcal{H}\}$.

3 Strategy Templates for Adversarial Winning

This section introduces the concept of strategy templates as a generalization of strategies in zero-sum games over finite graphs, i.e., in games where it is only one player's goal to satisfy the given objective Φ, while all other players try to achieve its negation (see Fig. 1 (top, right) for an illustration of this scenario). This setting reduces to a zero-sum *two-player game* between the protagonist, who must satisfy Φ and the antagonist (i.e., the collection of all other players) who try to satisfy $\neg\Phi$. The content in this section is taken from [2] and included in this paper for completeness.

*Example 1 (**Illustrative Example**).* To appreciate the simplicity and easy adaptability of our strategy templates, consider the game graph in Fig. 1 (left). The first winning condition $\Phi^0 = \Box\neg e$ requires vertex e to never be seen along a play. This can be enforced by Player 0 from vertices $\mathcal{W}_0 = \{a, b, c, d, f\}$ called the *winning region*. The safety template $\Pi_0^0 = \Lambda_{\text{UNSAFE}}(e_{ce})$ ensures that the game always stays in $\mathcal{W}_0$ by forcing the edge e_{ce} to never be taken. It is easy to see that every Player 0 strategy that follows this rule results in plays which are winning if they start in $\mathcal{W}_0$. Now consider the second winning condition $\Phi^1 = \Box\Diamond\{c, f, g\}$ which requires vertex c, f, or g to be seen infinitely often. This induces the template $\Pi_0^1 = \Lambda_{\text{LIVE}}(\{e_{bc}\}) \wedge \Lambda_{\text{LIVE}}(\{e_{ab}\})$ with two live groups which requires that whenever vertex b (resp. vertex a) is seen infinitely often, edge e_{bc}

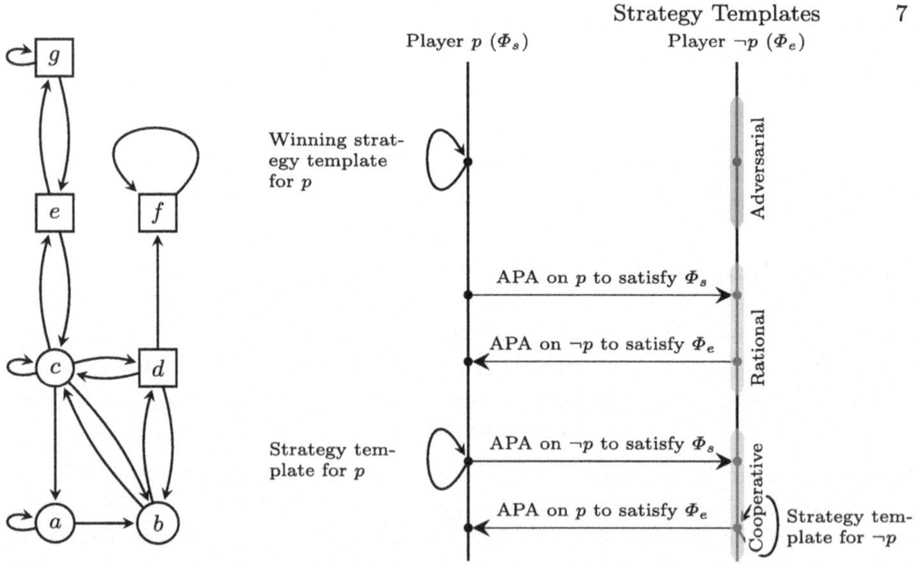

Fig. 1. (Left) A 2-player game graph with Player 0 (circle) and Player 1 (square) vertices. (Right) A graph showing the communication between Player p and Player $\neg p$ for different behaviors of Player $\neg p$. Self loop denotes the information that is computed for self and is not shared with others.

(resp. edge e_{ab}) needs to be taken infinitely often. It is easy to see that any strategy that complies with this edge-condition is winning for Player 0 from any vertex and there are infinitely many such compliant winning strategies. Finally, we consider condition $\Phi^2 = \Diamond\Box\neg b$ requiring vertex b to be seen only finitely often. This induces the co-liveness template $\Pi_0^2 = \Lambda_{\text{COLIVE}}(e_{cb}, e_{cd}, e_{ab})$ requiring that all edges from Player 0 vertices which unavoidably might lead to vertex b, i.e., e_{cb}, e_{cd}, e_{ab}, are taken only finitely often.

Winning Strategy Templates. Intuitively, a strategy template is a p-template Π_p which is used by Player p to extract a strategy for themself. We say a strategy template Π_p is *winning from a vertex* v for a game (G, Φ) if every Player p strategy following the template Π_p is winning from v. Moreover, we say a strategy template Π_p is *winning* if it is winning from every vertex in $\langle\langle p\rangle\rangle\Phi$.

The algorithm to compute a winning strategy template in a parity game lies in same time complexity class as the standard algorithm, i.e., Zielonka's algorithm [16], for solving parity games. This leads to the following result:

Proposition 1 ([2], **Thm. 4**). *Given a parity game with game graph G and coloring function $\mathbb{C}\colon V \to [0, d]$, a winning strategy template can be computed in $\mathcal{O}\left(|V|^{d+\mathcal{O}(1)}\right)$ time.*

Remark 1. While objectives like safety ($\Box\neg V'$), Büchi ($\Box\Diamond V'$), and co-Büchi ($\Diamond\Box V'$) are weaker than parity objectives and are subsumed by the latter, the winning strategy templates for these objectives can be computed in the matching time of their respective standard algorithms, i.e., $\mathcal{O}(m), \mathcal{O}(nm)$, and $\mathcal{O}(nm)$, respectively [2, Theorem 1–3], where $n = |V|, m = |E|$. Moreover, for safety objectives we can compute maximally permissive strategy templates (see below).

Permissiveness of Winning Strategy Templates. We call Π_p *maximally permissive* for $\mathcal{G}$, if every Player p strategy π which is winning in $\mathcal{G}$ also follows Π_p. It is easy to see that safety templates are naturally maximally permissive. However, while live-group templates capture infinitely many winning strategies in Büchi games, they *may not be* maximally permissive (see Ex. 2). As shown in the example, the strategy templates may fail to capture strategies with memory that can react to environment strategies and put less restriction on the system if the environment unexpectedly starts helping the system.

Example 2. Consider the game as in Ex. 1 with objective $\Phi^1 = \Box\Diamond\{c, f, g\}$. Our algorithm outputs the Player 0 strategy template $\Pi_0^1 = \Lambda_{\text{LIVE}}(\{e_{bc}\}) \wedge \Lambda_{\text{LIVE}}(\{e_{ab}\})$ as in Ex. 1. Now consider the winning strategy π_0 of Player 0 with memory that takes edge e_{ab} from a, takes e_{cb} from c, and takes e_{bc} for play suffix db and e_{bd} for every other play ending in b. This strategy does not follow the template—the play $(cbd)^\omega$ is in $\mathcal{L}(\pi_0)$ but not in $\mathcal{L}(\Pi_0)$.

Adaptability through Strategy Templates. Since the strategy templates provide structured guidelines for the systems to satisfy their tasks, we can now combine templates for individual objectives to obtain new templates to satisfy dynamic objectives. More formally, for instance, given two objectives Φ and Φ', we can obtain a strategy template by combining her templates Π_0 and Π_0' for the individual objectives, and one may observe that all strategies compliant with $\Pi_0 \wedge \Pi_0'$ are winning for $\Phi \wedge \Phi'$. This observation allows for more efficient recomputation of strategies when objectives for the system arrives one after another—compute the strategy template for the newest parity objective and conjunct it with the existing strategy template [2, Sec. 5.1, Alg. 4]. Consider the game as in Ex. 1 with objective $\Phi^1 = \Box\Diamond\{c, f, g\}$. The strategy template for Player 0 is Π_0^1 as in Ex. 1. Now, if another objective $\Phi^0 = \Box\neg e$ is added, for which the strategy template is $\Pi_0^0 = \Lambda_{\text{UNSAFE}}(e_{ce})$, then the template $\Pi_0^1 \wedge \Pi_0^0$—making e_{ce} unsafe—is a winning strategy template for $\Phi^1 \wedge \Phi^0$.

In addition to their compositionality, strategy templates also allow for local strategy adaptations in case of edge unavailability faults. Consider again the game in Ex. 1 with objective $\Phi^2 = \Diamond\Box\neg b$, for which the strategy template is $\Pi_0^2 = \Lambda_{\text{COLIVE}}(e_{cb}, e_{cd}, e_{ab})$. Suppose that Player 0 follows the strategy π: $c \mapsto a$, $a \mapsto b$, $b \mapsto c$, which is compliant with Π_0^2. If the edge e_{ca} becomes unavailable, we would need to re-solve the game for the modified game graph $G' = (V, E' = E \setminus \{e_{ca}\})$. However, we see that the strategy π': $c \mapsto c$, $a \mapsto b$ and $b \mapsto c$ is actually compliant with Π_0^2 over G'. This allows us to obtain a new strategy in linear time without re-solving the game if edges become temporary unavailable during deployment.

While these examples demonstrate the potential of templates for strategy adaptation (both during synthesis and during deployment), there exist scenarios where conflicts arise from these adaptations, as illustrated next.

Example 3. Consider the game in Ex. 1 with objectives Φ^1, for which the strategy template is Π_0^1. If Player 0 is now required to satisfy an additional objective $\Phi^2 = \Diamond\Box\neg b$, for which the strategy template is Π_0^2, then the composition of the templates $\Pi_0^1 \wedge \Pi_0^2$ marks the edge e_{ab} as live and co-live simultaneously. This causes a conflict at a—if the play arrives infinitely often at a, there is no edge that can be taken to follow the templates. Hence, to remove the conflicts, we must ensure that a is not visited infinitely often. So, we re-solve the game with an additional objective $\Diamond\Box\neg a$.

Conflict-Free Templates and Strategy Extraction. The previous examples demonstrated that a winning strategy can be efficiently computed from a template, if it is *conflict-free*. Formally, a template $\Lambda \lhd (S, D, \mathcal{H})$ over game graph $G = (V, E)$ is *conflict-free* if (i) every vertex v has an outgoing edge that is neither co-live nor unsafe, i.e., $E \cap (v \times V) \not\subseteq S \cup D$, and (ii) in every live-group $H \in H_\ell$ s.t. $(\cdot, H_\ell) \in \mathcal{H}$, every source vertex v has an outgoing edge in H that is neither co-live nor unsafe, i.e., $H \cap (v \times V) \not\subseteq S \cup D$.

Note that checking (i)-(ii) can be done independently for every vertex, and hence, checking whether a template is conflict-free can be done in linear time. In addition, whenever the existentially quantified edge in (i) and (ii) exists, a strategy that alternates between all these edges follows the given template. This results in a linear time extraction of a strategy from a conflict-free template as restated below.

Theorem 1 (**[3], Prop. 21**). *Given a template Λ over a game graph (V, E, v_0), checking whether Λ is conflict-free can be done in $\mathcal{O}(|E|)$ time. Moreover, if Λ is conflict-free, a strategy following Λ can also be extracted in $\mathcal{O}(|E|)$ time.*

We further showed in [2, Sec.4] that strategy templates directly computed for a parity objective are always conflict free. Conflicts only arise from the above-mentioned adaptations due to changes in the specification or the game graph.

Practical Evaluation. Using our prototype tool PeSTel[2], we evaluated the synthesis and adaptability of strategy templates on over 200 examples of parity games adapted from the SYNTCOMP benchmark suite [8]. Our analysis shows that the cheap local adaptation of templates usually does not create conflicts, effectively avoiding the computational overhead of re-computation. In addition, our experiments show that the observed non-permissiveness of strategy templates for specifications beyond safety never yielded a reduced winning region compared to its exact computation for all 200 considered benchmark instances (see [2, Sec.6] for more details). This suggests that our technique can synthesize and adapt strategy templates for large problem class efficiently in practice.

4 Contract-Based Distributed Reactive Synthesis

While the previous section has introduced strategy templates for zero-sum games, we now consider the more common instance where every player, i.e., every component, has their own objective, leading us to *multi-objective* P-player games. For this setting, we first consider *rational players*, i.e., players whose goal is to satisfy their own objective, and only if their objective is not at risk, are adversarial to others. Thereby, rational players might still 'accidentally' help others while perusing their own objective (see Fig. 1 (middle, right) for an illustration of this scenario), and hence, do not need to be treated fully adversarially. While rational players allow for a very robust notion of interaction, the assumption of systems always ultimately being adversarial, might not always be realistic. In particular, if interacting CPS are co-synthesized the design of one component could take the needs of other components into account if these needs are known, resulting in a *cooperative* negotiation framework (see Fig. 1 (bottom, right)).

Within this section, we present the outlined synthesis frameworks of fully cooperating [3] and rationally interacting [10] players jointly. In order to do so, we first give a unified view of the underlying synthesis principles in Sect. 4.1 and then elaborate on the different algorithms for their realization in Sect. 4.2 and Sect. 4.3, respectively. In particular, this novel joint presentation extents our work on cooperative strategies from two players (as presented in [3]) to P-players – becoming en-par with our work on rationally interacting players [10]. In addition, the joint presentation of both frameworks reveals their fundamental similarities and differences, which have not been presented in this form before.

[2] Repository URL: https://github.com/satya2009rta/pestel.

4.1 Contracted Specifications

Both negotiation frameworks for multi-objective games rely on the iterative computation of a new set of objectives, one for each player, such that each player can independently realize these new objectives (e.g., by a local (zero-sum) strategy template). The main intuition behind the design of this – to be computed – new specification profile, is that it should (i) ensure that any such local realization results in a global strategy profile that is winning, w.r.t. the given cooperation mode (soundness), while (ii) enable each player to realize this specification fully locally (decentralization), and (iii) not loosing any winning strategy profile on the way (maximal). This is formalized via contracted specifications next.

Definition 1 (Contracted Specifications). *Given a game* $(G, \{\Phi_p\}_{p\in \mathsf{P}})$, *a specification profile* $\{\varphi\}_{p\in \mathsf{P}}$ *is said to be a* cooperatively contracted specification CCS *(resp. a* rationally contracted specification RCS*) if it is both*

(i) sound*: any* $(\pi_p)_{p\in \mathsf{P}}$ *with* $\pi_p \models \varphi_p$ *is cooperatively (resp. rationally) winning;*
(ii) decentralized*: it holds that* $v_0 \in \langle\langle p\rangle\rangle\varphi_p$ *for all* $p \in \mathsf{P}$.

In addition, CCSs and RCSs are called maximal *if* $\mathcal{L}(\bigwedge_{p\in \mathsf{P}} \varphi_p) = \mathcal{L}(\bigwedge_{p\in \mathsf{P}} \Phi_p)$.

With this, the decentralized synthesis problem reduces to the computation of such contracted specifications. In both frameworks, this computation relies on the ability to iteratively refine an over-approximation of possible strategies a component might use in a (globally) winning strategy profile. The main insight that enables this efficiently, is that templates can be used for this purpose. Now, however, not strategy, but *assumption templates* $\Psi_{\mathsf{P}'}$ on players in $\mathsf{P}' \subseteq \mathsf{P}$ are used by the other players to over-approximate strategies of players P'. In order to realize the outlined strategy over-approximation and enable an iterative framework which results in contracted specifications, *adequately permissive assumptions* are needed.

Definition 2 (APA; adapted from [1]). Given a P-player game graph $G = (V, E, v_0)$ and a specification Φ, we say that an assumption template $\Psi_{\mathsf{P}'}$ is an *adequately permissive assumption (APA)* on players $\mathsf{P}' \subseteq \mathsf{P}$ for Φ if it is

(i) *sufficient*: there exists a strategy profile $(\pi_p)_{p\notin \mathsf{P}'}$ such that for every strategy profile $(\pi_p)_{p\in \mathsf{P}'}$ of players in P' with $(\pi_p)_{p\in \mathsf{P}'} \models \Psi_{\mathsf{P}'}$, we have $(\pi_p)_{p\in \mathsf{P}} \models \Phi$;
(ii) *implementable*: $\langle\langle \mathsf{P}'\rangle\rangle\Psi_{\mathsf{P}'} = V$; and
(iii) *permissive*: $\mathcal{L}(\Psi_{\mathsf{P}'}) \supseteq \mathcal{L}(\Phi)$.

Intuitively, sufficiency ensures that Ψ provides a sufficient restriction on player P' strategies under which the others can ensure Φ. Further, implementability ensures that Ψ can be ensured by the players in P' without any help from the other players. Finally, permissiveness ensures that the assumption does not prevent any winning strategy profile from being realized.

Note that computing APAs on players P' can be reduced to computing APAs on one player in a 2-player game by considering the players in P' as one player and all other players as another player. We can therefore use our algorithm from [1] to compute APAs for two-player parity games in polynomial time.

Algorithm 1. ComputeRCS($\mathcal{G}$); adapted from [10, Alg.1]

Input: A P-player multi-objective parity game $\mathcal{G} = (G = (V, E, v_0), (\Phi_p)_{p \in \mathsf{P}})$.
Output: A rationally contracted specification $(\varphi_p)_{p \in \mathsf{P}}$.
1: $\Psi_p \leftarrow \mathsf{True}\ \forall p \in \mathsf{P}$
2: **return** RecursiveRCS($\mathcal{G}, (\Psi_p)_{p \in \mathsf{P}}$)

3: **procedure** RecursiveRCS($\mathcal{G}, (\Psi_p)_{p \in \mathsf{P}}$)
4: $\quad \Psi_{\neg p} \leftarrow \bigwedge_{q \neq p} \Psi_q\ \forall p \in \mathsf{P}$
5: $\quad \varphi_p \leftarrow \Psi_p \wedge (\Psi_{\neg p} \Rightarrow \Phi_p)\ \forall p \in \mathsf{P}$
6: $\quad$ **if** $v_0 \in \bigcap_{p \in \mathsf{P}} \langle\langle p \rangle\rangle \varphi_p$ **then**
7: $\quad\quad$ **return** $(\varphi_p)_{p \in \mathsf{P}}$
8: $\quad \Psi'_p \leftarrow \Psi_p \wedge$ ComputeAPA($G, \Psi_{\neg p} \wedge \Phi_p, p$) $\forall p \in \mathsf{P}$
9: $\quad$ **return** RecursiveRCS($\mathcal{G}, (\Psi'_p)_{p \in \mathsf{P}}$)

Lemma 1 ([1, Thm. 4]). *Given a P-player game graph $G = (V, E, v_0)$ and a parity specification $\Phi = Parity(\mathbb{C})$, an APA on a set of players $\mathsf{P}' \subseteq \mathsf{P}$ for Φ can be computed, if one exists, in time $\mathcal{O}(|V|^4)$. We write* [3] ComputeAPA(G, Φ, P') *to denote the procedure that returns this APA if it exists; and* False, *otherwise.*

It remains to show how contracted specifications are computed via the iterative refinement of APAs for rationally [10] and cooperatively [3] interacting players, which will be presented in Sect. 4.2 and Sect. 4.3, respectively.

4.2 Rationally Contracted Specifications

Intuitively, rationally interacting agents are intrinsically selfish. They are primed on achieving their own objective. However, through this selfishness they *might* – accidentally – help others. Towards computing a contracted specification over rational agents, we first over-approximate the way in which players (accidentally) help each other by letting each Player p compute an APA Ψ_p *on themself* by executing the procedure ComputeAPA(G, Φ_p, p). Intuitively, Ψ_p collects all restrictions on Player p strategies (i.e., moves they *choose themself*) s.t. the resulting play *can* be winning for Φ_p if others cooperate (somehow). It therefore *over-approximates* the set of all Player p strategies which could possibly form a rationally winning strategy profile with the other players. As a consequence, the intersection $\Psi_{\neg p} = \bigwedge_{q \neq p} \Psi_q$ *under-approximates* the way in which other players (accidentally) help Player p.

Computation. The main idea of algorithm 1, called ComputeRCS($\mathcal{G}$), is therefore to iteratively refine the assumptions $(\Psi_p)_{p \in \mathsf{P}}$ on every player – via RecursiveRCS – until $(\varphi_p)_{p \in \mathsf{P}}$ with $\varphi_p := \Psi_p \wedge (\Psi_{\neg p} \Rightarrow \Phi_p)$ (computed in line 5) is a RCS. By Def. 1 this requires that Player p is able to choose a Player p

[3] With slight abuse of notation, we also call the algorithm ComputeAPA(G, Φ, P') if Φ is an arbitrary ω-regular specification. Then the game is converted into a parity game first (with a possibly exponentially larger state space) by standard methods [4].

strategy π_p s.t. $\pi_p \models \varphi_p$ i.e., π_p must (a) satisfy Ψ_p against all strategies of other players (which follows from Def. 2 as Ψ_p is an APA on Player p) and (b) satisfy its specification Φ_p against all other players strategies which satisfy $\Psi_{\neg p} = \bigwedge_{q \neq p} \Psi_q$. Whether (b) holds[4] is tested by intersecting all winning regions $\langle\langle p \rangle\rangle \varphi_p$ (line 6) to obtain the winning region that is achievable by any strategy profile $(\pi_p)_{p \in \mathsf{P}}$ with $\pi_p \models \varphi_p$. If this check fails, the assumptions $(\Psi_p)_{p \in \mathsf{P}}$ are strengthened by re-calling RECURSIVERCS (line 8).

As $\Psi_p = \mathsf{True}$ for each $p \in \mathsf{P}$ in the first iteration (line 1), we see that the first time COMPUTEAPA is called in line 8 we have $\Psi'_p = \text{COMPUTEAPA}(G, \Phi_p, p)$. In all further iterations COMPUTEAPA is called with the restricted specifications $\Phi'_p := \Psi_{\neg p} \wedge \Phi_p$ for all players (line 8). This tightens the objective for Player p by incorporating the knowledge on how other players are *surely* cooperating, as $\Psi_{\neg p}$ is an *under-approximation* of their (accidental) help. As a result, the new assumptions are stricter than earlier ones, i.e., $\mathcal{L}(\Psi'_p) \subseteq \mathcal{L}(\Psi_p)$, and hence, more informative for the computation of rationally contracted strategies.

Upon termination of COMPUTERCS($\mathcal{G}$), the resulting specification profile is indeed a *maximal RCS*, as formalized next.

Theorem 2 ([10, Thm. 1]). *Given a P-player game $\mathcal{G}$ with game graph $G = (V, E, v_0)$ and parity specifications $(\Phi_p)_{p \in \mathsf{P}}$, if the algorithm* COMPUTERCS($\mathcal{G}$) *terminates, then it outputs a* maximal RCS $(\varphi_p)_{p \in \mathsf{P}}$.

Example 4. Consider the game graph in Fig. 1 restricted to set of vertices $\{c, d, e, f, g\}$, with specification $\Phi_0 = \Diamond\Box\{e, f, g\}$ for Player 0 and $\Phi_1 = \Diamond\Box\{e, g\}$ for Player 1, and initial vertex c. Then first we observe that neither player can satisfy their specification by themselves. Then the APA computed by Player 0 is $\Psi_0 = \Lambda_{\text{COLIVE}}(e_{cc})$, and that computed by Player 1 is $\Psi_1 = \Lambda_{\text{UNSAFE}}(e_{df}) \wedge \Lambda_{\text{COLIVE}}(e_{ec})$. Intuitively, Ψ_0 ensures that the play does not get stuck in vertex c, and progress is made towards Player 0's goal set. Similarly, Ψ_1 ensures that the play does not reach a region from which satisfying Φ_0 becomes infeasible, and ensures progress towards vertex g happens. We note that Player 0 accidentally ends up helping Player 1, by trying to leave c. Hence, in the next iteration, Player p actually can realize their contract $\varphi_p = \Psi_p \wedge (\Psi_{\neg p} \Rightarrow \Phi_p)$, which gives us a maximal RCS.

Approximation and Termination. While COMPUTERCS outputs a maximal RCS *when it terminates*, it is unfortunately not guaranteed to terminate. This is due to the fact that the procedure COMPUTEAPA needs a parity game as an input. While $(\Phi_p)_{p \in \mathsf{P}}$ are assumed to be parity objectives, this is general not true for $\Psi_{\neg p} \wedge \Phi_p$ in later calls to RECURSIVERCS. Therefore, COMPUTEAPA might need to change the game graph in each iteration to reduce it to a parity game. While the *language* of the computed APA is guarantee to shrink in every iteration (due to line 8), this does not guarantee termination of Alg. 1 as such a language still contains an infinite number of words. Due to the possibly repeated

[4] Note that $\langle\langle p \rangle\rangle \Psi_p = V$ from Def. 2(ii).

changes in the game graph for APA computation, the finiteness of the underlying model can also not be used as a termination argument.

To address this problem, we provide a modified version of ComputeRCS [10, Sec.5] where the APAs computed by ComputeAPA in line 8 are over-approximated by assumptions which are only implementable and permissive, but not necessarily sufficient. This is done by restricting each assumption template to its safety and co-live part which allows to encode the resulting additional restrictions for players directly as parity specifications over the *original game graph* and thereby ensuring termination. Luckily, as assumptions are only computed on each protagonist themselves, the resulting algorithm is still sound. Moreover, this variant terminates in same time as that for solving parity games (i.e., quasi-polynomial time) and still computes maximal RSCs [10]. However, due to the over-approximation, this variant of ComputeRCS might fail to compute an RCS in every case where ComputeRCS would have succeeded.

4.3 Cooperatively Contracted Specifications

Similar to the rationally contracted specifications, we can also compute *cooperatively* contracted specifications by utilizing APAs. Here, a player can *rely* on other players to help. However, in order to give every player as much freedom as possible in (locally) choosing their strategy, we want to reduce this help to the necessary minimum. In the iterative algorithm for computing cooperatively contracted specifications every player therefore computes how *other* players *must help* her to make her own objective Φ_p realizable. Such an assumption $\Psi_{\neg p}$ on all other players $\mathtt{P}_{\neg p}$ can be computed by the procedure ComputeAPA$(G, \Phi_p, \mathtt{P}_{\neg p})$. In order to isolate the required help for each player, one needs to separate the resulting templates into Player q-templates $\Psi_{\neg p}|_{E_q}$ for each player $q \neq p$. With this, every Player p now gets new objectives from every other player in $\mathtt{P}_{\neg p}$, that specifies the help player p needs to provide for others. Hence, $\Psi'_p \leftarrow \bigwedge_{q \neq p} \Psi_{\neg q}|_{E_p}$ is an additional objective for Player p, strengthening its objective to $\varphi_p \leftarrow \Psi_p \wedge (\Psi_{\neg p} \Rightarrow \Phi_p)$.

This, maybe surprisingly, shows that the computation of contracted strategies for cooperating players is actually identical to their computation for rational players (see line 5 in Alg. 1). The difference however, lies in the use of ComputeAPA to compute Ψ'_p. More importantly, also the interpretation of $(\varphi_p)_{p \in \mathtt{P}}$ being a contracted specification changes for cooperating players. Here, (b), i.e., satisfying $\Psi_{\neg p} \Rightarrow \Phi_p$ is now the easy part, as this follows directly from $\Psi_{\neg p}$ being an APA on $\mathtt{P}_{\neg p}$ for Φ_p. However, (a), i.e., ensuring to provide all requested help to others, contained in Ψ_p, might result in unrealizability of Φ_p. Then Player p must ask for more help from others, and hence, strengthen her assumption on them. The resulting refinement of assumptions requires $\Psi_{\neg p}$ to be strengthened to ComputeAPA$(G, \varphi_p, \mathtt{P}_{\neg p})$ in future iterations.

Computation. Given the above intuition, we introduce the procedure ComputeCCS(G) – which computes CCSs – by modifying the assumption computation in line 8 of Alg. 1 to $\Psi'_p \leftarrow \bigwedge_{q \neq p}$ ComputeAPA$(G, \varphi_p, \mathtt{P}_{\neg q})|_{E_p}$ for all

Algorithm 2. NEGOTIATE($\mathcal{G}$); adapted from [3, Alg.1]

Input: A P-player game $\mathcal{G}$ with game graph $G = (V, E, v_0)$ and parity specifications $(\Phi_p)_{p\in\mathsf{P}}$.
Output: A cooperatively contracted specification $(\varphi_p)_{p\in\mathsf{P}}$ and templates $(\Lambda_p)_{p\in\mathsf{P}}$.

```
𝒲ᵢ, 𝒞ₚ, Πₚ, Ψ¬ₚ ← COMPUTETEMP(G, Φₚ, p), ∀p ∈ P
if ∧_{p∈P}(Πₚ ∧ Ψ¬ₚ) is conflict-free then
    Ψₚ ← ⋀_{q≠p} Ψ¬q|_{Eₚ} ∀p ∈ P
    φₚ ← Ψₚ ∧ (Ψ¬ₚ ⇒ Φₚ) ∀p ∈ P
    return (φₚ)_{p∈P}, (Ψₚ ∧ Πₚ)_{p∈P}
else
    Φₚ ← Φₚ ∧ □(⋂_{p∈P} 𝒲ᵢ) ∧ ◇□¬(⋃_{p∈P} 𝒞ₚ) , ∀ p ∈ P
    return NEGOTIATE(G, Φ'₀, Φ'₁)
```

$p \in \mathsf{P}$. While it can be proven that, whenever COMPUTECCS terminates, the resulting specification profile $(\varphi_p)_{p\in\mathsf{P}}$ is indeed a CCS, it is in general *not maximal.* This is due to the fact that the separation of APAs into Player p templates might make them lose their permissiveness, resulting in potentially non-maximal CCSs. This phenomenon of lacking permissiveness is similar to the observation discussed in Ex. 2, i.e. that winning strategy templates are not maximally permissive in zero-sum games. There we have seen that strategy templates exclude strategies the protagonist can only use if the antagonist (unexpectedly) helps. The same phenomenon occurs when splitting APAs: it is not always needed that all players actually help – if one player decides to help, some obligations can be lifted from other players, leading to cooperative strategies not contained in the resulting CCS.

Interestingly, this over-approximation of assumptions by their restriction to players is already enough to obtain a terminating version of COMPUTECCS. In contrast to the terminating version of COMPUTERCS, we do not need to further restrict templates only to their safety and co-live parts. Due to the now cooperative nature of the game, also live-group templates can be directly encoded as new parity objectives over the same game graph. In particular, this implies that for two-player games (addressed in [3]) which do not require the restriction of APAs (as $|\mathsf{P}_{\neg p}| = 1$ for all $p \in \mathsf{P} = \{1, 2\}$), this terminating version of COMPUTERCS (which is called NEGOTIATE in [3, Alg.1]) indeed computes *maximal CCSs.*

The NEGOTIATE **Algorithm for** P**-Player Games.** In order to complete the picture, Alg. 2 presents the formal extension of NEGOTIATE [3, Alg.1] to P-player games, following the structure of COMPUTERCS for an easier exposition in the scope of this paper. Here, the re-encoding of contracted strategies into parity games is realized by an updated version of the procedure COMPUTEAPA($G, \Phi, \mathsf{P}_{\neg q}$), called COMPUTETEMP($G, \Phi, q$), which computes the winning region $\langle\langle \mathsf{P} \rangle\rangle \Phi$, the conflict region $\mathcal{C}$ that needs to be avoided eventually, and a strategy template Π_q for Player q, along with the APA on players $\mathsf{P}_{\neg q}$. With this, the realizability check of the specification profiles $(\Phi'_p)_{p\in\mathsf{P}}$ reduces to checking if all assumption and strategy templates are conflict-free. If this is not the case, the new parity objective is obtained by adding the requirements to (i) always stay in the winning region and (ii) eventually avoid the conflict region.

Due to the cooperative nature of the game, the algorithm terminates in polynomial time. Furthermore, the use of localness of templates ensures that the algorithm does not depend on the initial vertex, and hence, for every vertex v for which there exists a cooperatively winning strategy profile, i.e., for every $v \in \langle\langle \mathsf{P} \rangle\rangle \bigwedge_{p \in \mathsf{P}} \Phi_p$ the algorithm outputs a CCS even for the modified game graph (V, E, v). This follows directly from the results in [3], and is formalized below.

Theorem 3. *Given a P-player game $\mathcal{G}$ with game graph $G = (V, E, v_0)$ and parity specifications $(\Phi_p)_{p \in \mathsf{P}}$, the algorithm* Negotiate($\mathcal{G}$) *terminates in $\mathcal{O}(P\,|V|^6)$ time and outputs a profile $(\varphi_p)_{p \in \mathsf{P}}$ that is CCS w.r.t. every game graph (V, E, v) with $v \in \langle\langle \mathsf{P} \rangle\rangle \bigwedge_{p \in \mathsf{P}} \Phi_p$. If $|\mathsf{P}| = 2$, $(\varphi_p)_{p \in \mathsf{P}}$ is also maximal.*

Example 5. Consider the game graph in Fig. 1 restricted to set of vertices $\{c, d, e, f, g\}$, with specification $\Phi_0 = \square\lozenge\{e\}$ for Player 0 and $\Phi_1 = \lozenge\square\{e, g\}$ for Player 1, and initial vertex c. Again, neither player can satisfy the specifications on their own. Then in Alg. 1 (to compute RCS), the APA computed by Player 0 is $\Psi_0 = \Lambda_{\text{LIVE}}(\{e_{cc}\})$, and that computed by Player 1 is $\Psi_1 = \Lambda_{\text{UNSAFE}}(e_{df}) \wedge \Lambda_{\text{COLIVE}}(e_{ec})$. In the next iteration, Player 1 can satisfy her specification $\varphi_1 := \Psi_1 \wedge (\Psi_0 \Rightarrow \Phi_1)$ by herself, but Player 0 can not satisfy $\varphi_0 := \Psi_0 \wedge (\Psi_1 \Rightarrow \Phi_0)$. Moreover, the new APAs and specifications will remain same in the next iterations, and hence, the algorithm will not terminate with a CCS. In fact, for the rational setting, no CSS exists for this game.

However, in the cooperative setting, Player 0 computes the assumption $\Psi_1 = \Lambda_{\text{UNSAFE}}(e_{df}) \wedge \Lambda_{\text{LIVE}}(\{e_{ge}\})$ on Player 1, and strategy template $\Pi_0 = \Lambda_{\text{LIVE}}(\{e_{ce}\})$. Similarly, Player 1 computes $\Psi_0 = \Lambda_{\text{COLIVE}}(e_{cc}, e_{cd})$ on Player 0, and $\Pi_1 = \Lambda_{\text{UNSAFE}}(e_{df}) \wedge \Lambda_{\text{COLIVE}}(e_{ec})$. Then since $\Psi_0 \wedge \Pi_0$ and $\Psi_1 \wedge \Pi_1$ are conflict free, the negotiation terminates with these templates for Player 0 and Player 1 respectively. Intuitively, Player 0 brings the token to e from c, and Player 1 ensures that the token does not leave $\{e, g\}$ infinitely often. Then due to Ψ_1, Player 1 also brings the token to e infinitely often. Hence, on cooperating, both agents can satisfy their respective specification.

Remark 2. In principle, conflict free strategy templates Π_p can be extracted for all players from a computed RCS or CCS $(\varphi_p)_{p \in \mathsf{P}}$ by using Prop. 1 on each φ_p. However, as already hinted at by the previous example, we show that Negotiate($\mathcal{G}$) can directly output conflict-free strategy templates without additional computational overhead [3]. As contracted specifications $(\varphi_p)_{p \in \mathsf{P}}$ fully decentralize a given multi-objective game $\mathcal{G} = (G, (\Phi_p)_{p \in \mathsf{P}})$ into locally realizable specifications φ_p, their respective winning strategy template Π_p ensures that any strategy π_p following Π_p will result in a winning strategy profile $(\Phi_p)_{p \in \mathsf{P}}$ for $\mathcal{G}$.

5 Utilizing Templates Under Partial Observation

This section will *not* discuss the *synthesis* of strategy templates under partial observation. Instead, we assume that the interaction between players is known during synthesis, but players have to actually *play* under partial observation which requires the extraction of a *partial observation strategy* from (full-observation) strategy templates Π_p.[5]. For simplicity, we use a partial observation setting where players cannot distinguish all vertices in the graph but still take turns when playing. We use the well known knowledge-based abstraction of games under partial observation (see e.g. [6]) to build an abstraction over so-called *knowledge states* for each player, which collects all vertices of the game that a player can currently not distinguish (given the past history of the play). We then intersect all templates of vertices combined in these knowledge states. If the resulting (knowledge-based) template is non-conflicting, a strategy can be extracted in analogy to Theorem. 1.

The extraction of partial observation strategies from templates formalized in this section has not been presented before. Its soundness, however, follows directly from the known properties of knowledge-based abstractions and conflict free templates and is therefore not explicitly proven.

5.1 Preliminaries

As every player might have different partial observation settings, the knowledge abstraction is different for every player. Further, in order to build these abstractions in a sound manner, we need to make Player p choices along their moves explicit by adding a label to Player p transitions in a game graph[6].

p-Labelled Game Graphs. Let $G = (V, E, v_0)$ be a P-player game graph. Then a corresponding p-labled game graph is a tuple ${}^pG = (V, v_0\, {}^p\Sigma, {}^p\Delta)$ s.t.

- ${}^p\Sigma$ is a finite alphabet with $\bot \in {}^p\Sigma$
- $(u, \bot, v) \in {}^p\Delta$ iff $(u, v) \in E_{\neg p}$, and
- $(u, v) \in E_p$ iff there exists a *unique* $\bot \neq \sigma \in {}^p\Sigma$ s.t. $(u, \sigma, v) \in {}^p\Delta$.

Sightly abusing notation, we write ${}^p\Delta(U, \sigma)$ for some $\emptyset \neq U \subseteq V$ and $\sigma \in \Sigma$ to denote all states $v \in V$ s.t. $(u, \sigma, v) \in {}^p\Delta$ for some $u \in U$.

Vertex Covers and Partitions. Vertex subsets $\Gamma \subseteq 2^V \setminus \emptyset$ form a *cover* of V. If for all $\gamma, \gamma' \in \Gamma$ with $\gamma \neq \gamma'$ holds that $\gamma \cap \gamma' = \emptyset$, a cover is called a *partition.* Covers induce a mapping $\Gamma^{\Uparrow} : V \to 2^\Gamma$ s.t. $\gamma \in \Gamma^{\Uparrow}(v)$ iff $v \in \gamma$. If Γ is a partition, its holds that $|\Gamma^{\Uparrow}(v)| = 1$. Then we slightly abuse notation to write $\Gamma^{\Uparrow}(v) = \gamma$. We call covers and partitions *player-respecting* if for all $\gamma \in \Gamma$, $u, v \in \gamma$ and $q \in \mathsf{P}$ holds $u \in V_q$ iff $v \in V_q$.

Knowledge-Based Abstractions. Let ${}^pG$ be a p-labelled game graph and ${}^p\Gamma$ a player-respecting[7] *partial observation partition* which groups all states that

[5] This complies with the concept of *output-feedback control* from engineering, where control strategies are synthesized offline under full state information, but need to operate based on measurements containing only partial state information.

[6] Note that such labels are not needed in full observation settings, as discussed in previous sections, as moves are then uniquely determined by the edge successors.

[7] By assuming ${}^p\Gamma$ to be player-respecting, we assume that each player sees who is playing. This retains the turn-based nature in the abstract game. Otherwise, concurrent abstract games are obtained which are out of the scope of this paper.

are indistinguishable for Player p. Then we define a *knowledge-based abstraction* ${}^{p}\widehat{G}$ of ${}^{p}G$ under ${}^{p}\Gamma$ in the usual way, by using the interaction structure between players captured in ${}^{p}G$.

Definition 3. *A* knowledge-based abstraction $\mathtt{abstract}({}^{p}G, {}^{p}\Gamma, p)$ *of a p-labelled game graph* ${}^{p}G = (V, v_0\, {}^{p}\Sigma, {}^{p}\Delta)$ *under the player-preserving partial observation partition* ${}^{p}\Gamma \subseteq 2^V \setminus \emptyset$ *is a tuple* ${}^{p}\widehat{G} = ({}^{p}\widehat{\Gamma}, {}^{p}\widehat{\gamma}_0, {}^{p}\Sigma, {}^{p}\widehat{\Delta})$ *s.t.*

- ${}^{p}\widehat{\Gamma} \subseteq 2^V$ *and for all* $\widehat{\gamma} \in {}^{p}\widehat{\Gamma}$ *and* $u, v \in \widehat{\gamma}$ *holds that* ${}^{p}\Gamma^{\Uparrow}(v) = {}^{p}\Gamma^{\Uparrow}(u)$*;*
- ${}^{p}\widehat{\gamma}_0 := {}^{p}\Gamma^{\Uparrow}(v_0)$*;*
- $(\widehat{v}, \sigma, \widehat{u}) \in {}^{p}\widehat{\Delta}$ *iff there exists* $\gamma \in {}^{p}\Gamma$ *s.t.* $\widehat{u} = {}^{p}\Delta(\widehat{v}, \sigma) \cap \gamma \neq \emptyset$.

We observe that the state space ${}^{p}\widehat{\Gamma}$ of ${}^{p}\widehat{G}$ is a player- and observation-preserving cover of V with its induced abstraction map ${}^{p}\widehat{\Gamma}^{\Uparrow}$. With this, we denote by ${}^{p}\widehat{\Gamma}_q$ the set of knowledge-states $\widehat{\gamma}$ of Player p which are owned by player q, i.e., $\widehat{\gamma} \subseteq V_q$.

5.2 Extracting Partial Observation Strategies

In this section, we show how a Player p strategy template in a p-labelled game graph ${}^{p}G$ can be abstracted into a Player p strategy template in Player p's knowledge abstraction ${}^{p}\widehat{G}$. In order to formalize this abstraction, we need to first extend strategy templates to labelled games.

Labelled Strategy Templates. Let ${}^{p}G$ be a p-labelled game graph. Then the *enabled state-action pairs* for Player p in ${}^{p}G$ are collected in the set ${}^{p}A := \{(v, \sigma) \in V_p \times {}^{p}\Sigma \mid \exists v' \in V.\, (v, \sigma, v') \in {}^{p}\Delta\}$. Then a p-labelled strategy template is a tuple ${}^{p}\Pi \lhd ({}^{p}S, {}^{p}D, {}^{p}\mathcal{H})$ with ${}^{p}S \subseteq {}^{p}A$, ${}^{p}D \subseteq {}^{p}A$, and ${}^{p}\mathcal{H}$ containing pairs of form $(R, {}^{p}H_\ell)$ for $R \subseteq V$ and ${}^{p}H_\ell \subseteq {}^{p}A$. We note that, due to the deterministic definition of transition labels in ${}^{p}G$ for Player p edges E_p in G, every Player p strategy template over G corresponds to a unique p-labelled strategy template in ${}^{p}G$.

Knowledge-Based Strategy Templates. Given a p-labelled game graph ${}^{p}G$ and a corresponding knowledge-based abstraction ${}^{p}\widehat{G}$ with state space ${}^{p}\widehat{\Gamma}$ and enabled state-action pairs ${}^{p}\widehat{A}$, we extend the partition mapping ${}^{p}\widehat{\Gamma}^{\Uparrow}$ induced by ${}^{p}\widehat{\Gamma}$ to sets of state-action pairs $\alpha \subseteq {}^{p}A$ in the obvious way, i.e., ${}^{p}\widehat{\Gamma}^{\Uparrow}(\alpha) := \{(\widehat{v}, \sigma) \in {}^{p}\widehat{A} \mid (v, \sigma) \in \alpha, \widehat{v} \in {}^{p}\widehat{\Gamma}^{\Uparrow}(v)\}$.

With this, a p-labled strategy template ${}^{p}\Pi$ in ${}^{p}G$ naturally corresponds to an abstract strategy template ${}^{p}\widehat{\Pi}$ in ${}^{p}\widehat{G}$

Definition 4. *Given a p-labelled game graph* ${}^{p}G$*, a corresponding knowledge-based abstraction* ${}^{p}\widehat{G}$ *with state space* ${}^{p}\widehat{\Gamma}$ *and a p-labelled strategy template* ${}^{p}\Pi \lhd ({}^{p}S, {}^{p}D, {}^{p}\mathcal{H})$ *over* ${}^{p}G$*, its corresponding knowledge-based strategy template* ${}^{p}\widehat{\Pi} \lhd ({}^{p}\widehat{S}, {}^{p}\widehat{D}, {}^{p}\widehat{\mathcal{H}})$ *is defined by* ${}^{p}\widehat{S} := {}^{p}\widehat{\Gamma}^{\Uparrow}({}^{p}S)$, ${}^{p}\widehat{D} := {}^{p}\widehat{\Gamma}^{\Uparrow}({}^{p}D)$*, and* ${}^{p}\widehat{\mathcal{H}} := \{(\widehat{R}, {}^{p}\widehat{H_\ell}) \mid (R, {}^{p}H_\ell) \in {}^{p}\mathcal{H}\}$ *with* $\widehat{R} = \{\widehat{\gamma} \in {}^{p}\widehat{\Gamma} \mid \widehat{\gamma} \cap R \neq \emptyset\}$ *and* ${}^{p}\widehat{H_\ell} = \{{}^{p}\widehat{\Gamma}^{\Uparrow}({}^{p}H) \mid {}^{p}H \in {}^{p}H_\ell\}$.

Given the above construction, one can use a computed strategy template Π_p in the original game graph to compute a p-labelled knowledge-based template ${}^p\widehat{\Pi}$ which can be used to extract a Player p strategy ${}^p\widehat{\pi}_p$ following ${}^p\widehat{\Pi}$ in ${}^p\widehat{G}$ via Thm. 1, if ${}^p\widehat{\Pi}$ is *conflict-free* in ${}^p\widehat{G}$. As knowledge-based abstractions ensure that every history of a play corresponds to a unique Player p state, ${}^p\widehat{\pi}_p$ is a well-defined observation-preserving strategy in ${}^pG$.

If ${}^p\widehat{\Pi}$ is not *conflict-free* in ${}^p\widehat{G}$, on can add these conflicts to the original synthesis problem by updating the parity specifications in the iterative algorithms of Sect. 4 and resolve them by another iteration of the respective synthesis algorithms before attempting a strategy extraction again. As this does not require a change in the game graph, the resulting extension of the iterative synthesis algorithms always terminates. It is however not complete, as synthesizing an observation-based winning strategy profile might require to encode the knowledge-based state structure into the negotiation algorithms.

References

1. Anand, A., Mallik, K., Nayak, S.P., Schmuck, A.K.: Computing adequately permissive assumptions for synthesis. In: Sankaranarayanan, S., Sharygina, N. (eds.) Tools and Algorithms for the Construction and Analysis of Systems, pp. 211–228. Springer, Cham (2023)
2. Anand, A., Nayak, S.P., Schmuck, A.: Synthesizing permissive winning strategy templates for parity games. In: Enea, C., Lal, A. (eds.) Computer Aided Verification - 35th International Conference, CAV 2023, Paris, France, July 17-22, 2023, Proceedings, Part I. Lecture Notes in Computer Science, vol. 13964, pp. 436–458. Springer (2023). https://doi.org/10.1007/978-3-031-37706-8_22
3. Anand, A., Schmuck, A., Nayak, S.P.: Contract-based distributed logical controller synthesis. In: Ábrahám, E., Jr., M.M. (eds.) Proceedings of the 27th ACM International Conference on Hybrid Systems: Computation and Control, HSCC 2024, Hong Kong SAR, China, May 14-16, 2024, pp. 11:1–11:11. ACM (2024). https://doi.org/10.1145/3641513.3650123
4. Baier, C., Katoen, J.P.: Principles of Model Checking. MIT Press (2008)
5. Belta, C., Yordanov, B., Gol, E.: Formal Methods for Discrete-Time Dynamical Systems, Studies in Systems, Decision and Control, vol. 15. Springer (2017)
6. Chatterjee, K., Doyen, L., Henzinger, T.A., Raskin, J.F.: Algorithms for omega-regular games with imperfect information. Logical Methods Comput. Sci. **3** (2007)
7. Chatterjee, K., Henzinger, T.A., Jurdziński, M.: Games with secure equilibria. Theoret. Comput. Sci. **365**(1–2), 67–82 (2006)
8. Jacobs, S., et al.: The reactive synthesis competition (SYNTCOMP): 2018–2021. arXiv preprint arXiv:2206.00251 (2022)
9. Nayak, S.P., Egidio, L.N., Della Rossa, M., Schmuck, A.K., Jungers, R.M.: Context-triggered abstraction-based control design. IEEE Open J. Control Syst. **2**, 277–296 (2023). https://doi.org/10.1109/OJCSYS.2023.3305835

10. Nayak, S.P., Schmuck, A.: Most general winning secure equilibria synthesis in graph games. In: Finkbeiner, B., Kovács, L. (eds.) Tools and Algorithms for the Construction and Analysis of Systems - 30th International Conference, TACAS 2024, Held as Part of the European Joint Conferences on Theory and Practice of Software, ETAPS 2024, Luxembourg City, Luxembourg, April 6-11, 2024, Proceedings, Part III. LNCS, vol. 14572, pp. 173–193. Springer (2024). https://doi.org/10.1007/978-3-031-57256-2_9
11. Reissig, G., Weber, A., Rungger, M.: Feedback refinement relations for the synthesis of symbolic controllers. TAC **62**(4), 1781–1796 (2017)
12. Saha, S., Julius, A.A.: An MILP approach for real-time optimal controller synthesis with metric temporal logic specifications. In: 2016 American Control Conference (ACC), pp. 1105–1110 (2016). https://doi.org/10.1109/ACC.2016.7525063
13. Sanfelice, R.G.: Hybrid Feedback Control. Princeton University Press (2020)
14. Schmuck, A.K., Heim, P., Dimitrova, R., Nayak, S.P.: Localized attractor computations for infinite-state games. In: Gurfinkel, A., Ganesh, V. (eds.) Computer Aided Verification. CAV 2024. LNCS, vol. 14683, pp. 135–158. Springer, Cham (2024). https://doi.org/10.1007/978-3-031-65633-0_7
15. Tabuada, P.: Verification and Control of Hybrid Systems - A Symbolic Approach. Springer (2009). http://www.springer.com/mathematics/applications/book/978-1-4419-0223-8
16. Zielonka, W.: Infinite games on finitely coloured graphs with applications to automata on infinite trees. Theoret. Comput. Sci. **200**(1), 135–183 (1998)

The VeriAbs Tool Suite for Code Verification

Priyanka Darke[1], Bharti Chimdyalwar[1](✉), R. Venkatesh[1], and Supratik Chakraborty[2]

[1] TCS Research, Pune, India
bharti.c@tcs.com
[2] Indian Institute of Technology, Bombay, India

Abstract. In large real life programs, loops and arrays are the main challenges to scaling up verification. Overcoming this challenge requires a portfolio of specialised techniques. Accordingly, we at TCS Research have developed a portfolio of loop and array abstraction techniques to scale up verification in practice. Naturally, a collection of such techniques can verify programs from a wider variety of classes than each individual technique. This collection of techniques in addition to well known verification techniques like bounded model checking form the portfolio used in the VeriAbs framework. In order to improve the likelihood that a suitable technique from the portfolio is applied to the input program, the techniques are often prioritized into a sequence, also called a verification *strategy*, to verify each input program. VeriAbs uses four such strategies, each defined manually using domain expertise and experimentation. One of the suitable strategies is selected for verification based on the class of the input program. This approach to program verification has shown success and won several gold medals in the Competition on Software Verification (SV-COMP) 2019–23.

In practice, defining verification strategies manually is time consuming and not extensible. Towards this, machine learning methods have been proposed recently to predict strategies automatically for each input program. It is a challenge to define useful program features that can describe a program well enough to the learner to predict a useful strategy from the given portfolio of techniques. We present a novel approach to alleviate this challenge as implemented in VeriAbsL, a tool that uses machine learning methods to predict strategies for an input program using VeriAbs's portfolio. VeriAbsL was developed in 2023, and since then has won a silver and a gold medal at SV-COMP 2023–24. To summarise, in this paper we present (1) a few proprietary loops and array abstraction techniques in VeriAbs's portfolio, (2) the manually defined method of strategy selection as implemented in VeriAbs, (3) the machine learning method of strategy prediction as implemented in VeriAbsL, (4) a comparison of VeriAbs's portfolio with another state-of-art portfolio-based verifier, and (5) a comparison of strategy selection implemented in VeriAbs with a novel strategy prediction implemented in VeriAbsL.

S. Akshay et al. (Eds.): ATVA 2024, LNCS 15054, pp. 42–64, 2025.
https://doi.org/10.1007/978-3-031-78709-6_3

1 Introduction

It is well known that a diverse set of programs cannot be verified using a single technique, necessitating the adoption of specialized techniques to effectively verify different classes of programs. This led to the development of portfolio-based verification in which verifiers act as an abstraction of a set of verification techniques. Such verifiers incorporate a portfolio of verification techniques that complement each others strengths and weaknesses while empowering the portfolio-based verifier. Typically their portfolio constitutes of diverse model checking and abstract interpretation techniques. State of the art verifiers like VeriAbs [4], CPAchecker [8] and Ultimate Automizer [32] have been developed based on this principle. To maximize the benefits of the portfolio, several techniques from the portfolio with similar strengths and applicability to the input program are often invoked in a sequence by the portfolio-based verifier until it either successfully verifies the program using one of the techniques or runs out of resources. Such a sequence of techniques is called a *strategy* and strategy selection for an input program is an active field of research. On the other hand, predicate discovery using interpolation, lazy predicate abstraction, and counter-example guided abstraction refinement (CEGAR) are advanced methods commonly utilized to scale verification. Consequently, these methods are central to the portfolios of most well known portfolio-based verifiers such as CPAchecker [8] and Ultimate Automizer [32]. But popular implementations of predicate abstraction and interpolation are unable to precisely reason about quantified invariants [33]. Due to this they cannot precisely reason about loops modifying inductive data structures like arrays. Further, several of these implementations are unable to reason precisely about mathematical operations (which are commonly performed in loops) [33]. Consequently, the presence of loops often causes techniques of these portfolios to get stuck in CEGAR loops. Finally, the biggest limitation of most portfolio-based verifiers is that in pursuit of soundness they do not exploit the advantages of bounded model checking (BMC) in the presence of loops [5].

Bounded model checking (BMC) is another model checking technique complementary to abstraction-driven model checking. It allows for a precise representation of a program as a logical formula by unwinding loops and the usage of advanced SAT/SMT solvers over this formula to produce error traces or safety proofs. It has shown great success in practice in terms of its ability to successfully find bugs in programs. Its main limitation is its inability to verify programs of unknown bounds. In other words, it cannot scale for safe programs or programs containing deep bugs due to loops with large, infinite or unknown bounds. This limitation of BMC particularly impacts its ability to verify industrial reactive systems which are implemented as infinite reactive loops and consequently have infinite bounds. Loops modifying large arrays that manipulate large amounts of data are also common in industrial programs. Large arrays commonly lead to a state space explosion limiting the scalability of BMC. As mentioned earlier, these are the main reasons why most portfolios do not use BMC for programs with unknown bounds [5]. Further, non-linear arithmetic operations when performed in loops can blow up the size of the SAT formula generated by a bounded model checker, limiting its scalability. Due to the above reasons we can conclude that model checking both precise and abstract program representations is either not scalable or lacks precision in the presence of loops performing array manipulations or mathematical operations.

To maximise scalability we present the VeriAbs tool suite that incorporates a portfolio in which a majority of the techniques perform an abstraction directed at eliminating loops which are the main bottleneck towards a scalable verification using BMC. The novel loop and array abstraction techniques in VeriAbs's portfolio primarily perform a syntax guided abstraction rather than the property directed ones popularly used by other portfolios. To perform these abstractions we analyze the body of each loop along with the syntax of its program statements. Accordingly we perform abstractions by accelerating variables assigned in loop bodies to eliminate loops. For this we non-deterministically count the number of times each condition in the loop body holds and accelerate the variables accordingly. The above produces an abstraction which is devoid of loops or contains loops of known small bounds. On such programs BMC can scale well. Here BMC is used as a black-box on the abstraction. By itself the bounded model checker can use property-directed analyses while generating the SAT/SMT formula for the solvers. Similarly, the SAT/SMT solvers can use advanced property directed methods to verify the input logical formula.

The usefulness of the novel loop and array directed abstractions (rather than the property-directed abstractions) are manifold and can be seen from our experiments on the well known error reachability benchmarks of the Competition on Software Verification (SV-COMP). We observed that close to 60% of the programs successfully verified by VeriAbs are verified using the various loop and array abstraction techniques in its portfolio. Also, close to 70% of the programs not verified by CPAchecker can be verified by the loop and array abstraction methods implemented in the VeriAbs tool suite. In this paper, we present the VeriAbs tool suite, which is composed of (1) a carefully selected portfolio of verification techniques that uses both property-directed and syntax-directed abstraction techniques but majorly syntax-directed abstractions, (2) the VeriAbs tool: which uses manually defined strategies to verify input programs, (3) the tool VeriAbsL: which implements strategies predicted by machine learning for verification abilities superior to VeriAbs, (4) a comparison of VeriAbs's portfolio with that of CPAchecker's.

To summarise, VeriAbs's portfolio of verification techniques stands out from other well known portfolios because (1) it mainly incorporates verification techniques that enhance the scalability of BMC by performing loops and arrays-driven abstractions. (2) It abstracts once at a certain level and then does not refine the loops and arrays-driven abstractions at all. While other portfolios over-approximate and then always try to refine [9]. (3) It applies BMC to explore the state space of the original program such that it finds sufficient bounds to produce valid counter-example traces or sound safety proofs. On the other hand, like other portfolios, it uses explicit state model checking, abstract interpretation, predicate abstraction, and interpolation whenever it cannot abstract loops and arrays. Overall, in this paper we present:

- Two of our most useful proprietary loops and array abstraction techniques in Sect. 2.
- The VeriAbs tool, its portfolio, and its strategy selection approach in Sects. 3.
- The VeriAbsL tool and its portfolio driven machine learning approach for strategy prediction in Sects. 4, 5 and 6.
- An extensive evaluation of the VeriAbs tool suite on 11222 SV-COMP 2024 ReachSafety benchmarks in Sect. 7 showing the advantages of (a) using loops and arrays-driven abstractions over CPAChecker in Sect. 7.1, a well known portfolio-based verifier, and (b) our training methodology over manually crafted strategies in VeriAbs in Sect. 7.2.

Next we describe the portfolio of the VeriAbs tool suite.

2 A Portfolio of Abstractions for a Scalable Verification

As mentioned earlier, loops and arrays in programs are the main bottleneck towards scaling model checking techniques in practice. In this paper, we describe two of the most successful proprietary loop and array abstraction techniques invented at TCS Research to scale up formal verification using BMC on industrial code. We first present a loop abstraction technique.

2.1 Loop Abstraction Followed by BMC (LABMC)

Bounded Model Checking (BMC) can effectively detect property violations in an input program up to a bounded execution length [3]. However, it cannot validate properties encoded in the programs containing loops of unknown or large bounds. To use bounded model checking for proving program properties even in the presence of such loops, VeriAbs uses a technique called Loop Abstraction followed by BMC or LABMC [25]. This technique abstracts the given program by over-approximating variables modified within each loop and replacing each original loop with a new loop having a smaller fixed bound. The new program with abstracted loops is then passed to an off-the-shelf bounded model checker to verify the given assertions. VeriAbs uses C Bounded Model Checker (CBMC) [22] to verify the program with abstracted loops. As all abstracted loops have fixed (small) bounds, CBMC does not get stuck in unwinding the loops before moving to verify the given property. The abstractions presented by LABMC are sound abstractions of the original loop. Hence, when BMC proves safety of a property on an abstract program, it is *safe* on the original program too. We refer the interested reader to [25] for the technical details and the soundness proof.

For a given loop in the input program, we refer to the variables modified by the loop as *output variables*. These are further classified as *input-output* variables, which are read as well as modified in the loop body, and *pure output* variables,

```
1 x=0; M=*;
2 while (x < M)
3 {
4     x += 2;
5 }
6 assert(!(x % 2));
```

(a) C Program 1

```
for(i=0; i!=M; i++)
{
   assert(i <= M);
}
```

(b) C Program 2

```
1  //Initial value
2  x0 = x;
3
4  //Abstract loop
5  for(j=0; j<1 && x<M; j++)
6  {
7   k = *;
8   x = x0 + 2 * k;
9   assume(x < M);
10  //Original loop body
11  x += 2;
12 }
13
14 //!(loop-condition)
15 assume(!(x < M));
16
17 assert(!(x % 2));
```

(c) Abstract Program 1

```
i0 = i; //Initial value
//Base case :
if(i != M) {
   assert(i <= M);
   i++;
}
//Hypothesis:kth iteratn.
for(j=0; j<1 && i!=M; j++) {
   k = *;
   i = i0 + i * k;
   assume (i!=M && i<=M);
   i++;
}
//Check:(k+1)th iteratn.
if(i != M) {
  assert(i <= M);
  i++;
}
//!(loop condition)
assume(!(i != M));
```

(d) Abstract Program 2

Fig. 1. Motivating Example: Loop Abstraction using LABMC

which are only modified in the loop body. LABMC over-approximates all *output* variables of every loop. We explain this with the help of a C program in Fig. 1a, selected from the Loops sub-category of SV-COMP 2024 benchmarks [1]. This is a safe program with respect to the safety property encoded as assertion outside the loop, at line number 6. Due to the unknown bound of the loop, state-of-the-art bounded model checkers cannot prove the validity of this assertion [1]. The portfolios of verifiers CPAchecker and Pesco [42,43] get stuck in refinement loops and consequently cannot verify this program either. Figure 1c shows the abstraction of the program as generated by LABMC. The abstract loop contains acceleration assignments [25] to *input-output* variables to capture the effect of multiple loop iterations on them and hence on the behavior of the loop. Line 8 in Fig. 1c shows the acceleration assignment corresponding to the *input-output* variable x. Here, x_0 is the value of x before the loop, incremented k times in the loop by a constant value 2. Here k is an abstraction of the number of times x gets modified in the actual loop as the value of k is chosen non-deterministically (line 7). This makes the assignment to x an over-approximation. In the abstraction, acceleration assignments are followed by the original loop body (line 11) under the assumption of the loop-condition at line 9. This loop body also over-approximates the *pure output variables* as all variables read in the loop body thus impacting the values of *pure output variables* are over-approximated using acceleration. The new abstract loop iteration count (line 5) is number of *output variables* present in original loop as that will be the maximum number of iterations needed in the abstraction if at least one distinct variable was modified in each iteration of the abstract loop [25]. In this way, all *output* variables of the loop are over-approximated and an abstract loop with fixed (small) bound is generated. After the abstract loop, the loop condition is assumed to not hold (ensured by an assume statement at line 15). CBMC proves the safety of the input property in the abstraction as shown in Fig. 1c, which it was unable to on the original program. Acceleration techniques for different types of *input-output* variables which are modified (un)conditionally in the loop body are presented in [25].

When the property to be verified is within the loop, LABMC further improves the precision of its analysis using *induction*. Consider the safe program with respect to encoded property as assertion on line 3 of Fig. 1b and its abstraction in Fig. 1d. LABMC first generates a base case (lines 3–6) with the first iteration of the original loop that asserts the input property (line 4 of Listing 1d). Subsequently, the induction hypothesis, i.e. the property holds for an arbitrary k iterations of the loop, is generated as *for* loop as shown on line 8. This *for* loop is an abstraction of the original loop and represents k iterations of the original loop. It is generated as described previously. But it additionally contains an assumption as shown on line 11 in Fig. 1d. This means that until the end of the kth iteration only those executions in which the property holds will be considered by the model checker. Next, in the induction step, the $(k+1)^{th}$ iteration of the loop is generated (lines 15–18) and the property is asserted (line 16). CBMC proves the safety of asserted properties (line 4 and 16) in the abstraction shown in Fig. 1d, which it was unable to on the original program.

Over-approximating loops this way allows bounded model checking to prove properties of programs containing loops of large or unknown bounds. It also allows the avoidance of CEGAR loops which in such cases could hinder successful verification. Abstracting loops in general also helps to scale up program analyses and prove properties of industry strength programs. This is shown by applying LABMC to detect static analysis false warnings [21,28] in industrial practice. LABMC could detect upto 70% of warnings reported by state-of-the-art static analyzers [21] as false warnings on different industrial embedded applications.

To summarise, LABMC is useful for programs with loops in which variables are modified through linear arithmetic operations. *Abstract acceleration* [25] is used to capture the cumulative effect of several loop iterations on these variables. In cases where the modification of variables within loops cannot be precisely accelerated, they are simply assigned non-deterministic values [26]. While the above abstraction is useful in practice, it cannot be used to precisely abstract different elements of arrays when quantified invariants are required. This gives rise to the need for a more refined loop abstraction in the presence of arrays modified in loops. Next we present one such array abstraction technique invented at TCS Research.

2.2 Array Pruning

Array abstraction techniques transform programs having large or even infinite state space into abstract programs with finite state space, which can be verified by any bounded model checker. Consider a program P with encoded property ϕ. Suppose that P, ϕ can be transformed into a finite state abstract program P' and property ϕ', such that if the property ϕ' holds in program P' then ϕ holds in P. Then it is sufficient to analyze P' for property ϕ' to show that ϕ holds in P. In the subsequent section, we describe *array pruning*, the most successful array abstraction technique devised by us as per its performance in the Array sub-category of SV-COMP 2024.

```
int N;
int max (int x[N]){
  int i,ret=0;
  for (i=0;i<N;i++)
    ret=ret<x[i]?x[i]:ret;
  return ret;
}
int main (){
  N = nondet();
  if (N > 1) {
    int x[N],temp,ret,ret2;

    ret = max(x);
    temp=x[0];
    for(int i=0;i<N-1;i++){
       x[i]=x[i+1];
    }
    x[N-1]=temp;
    ret2=max(x);
    if(ret != ret2)
          error();
  }
  return 1;
}
```

(a) Input Program

```
int N;
int max (int x[2]){
  int i,ret=0;
  for (i=0;i<2;i++)
    ret=ret<x[i]?x[i]:ret;
  return ret;
}
int main (){
  N = nondet();
  if (N > 1) {
    int x[2],temp,ret,ret2;
    x[0],x[1]=nondet();
    ret = max(x);
    temp=x[0];
    for(int i=0;i<1;i++){
       x[i]=x[i+1];
    }
    x[1]=temp;
    ret2=max(x);
    if(ret != ret2)
          error();
  }
  return 1;
}
```

(b) Abstraction

Fig. 2. Motivating Example: Loop Pruning

In this technique [36], we make use of the fact that there are programs where proving properties or finding errors for the initial segment of an array is sufficient to prove the property or find an error for the entire array. Consider the program shown in Fig. 2a. Function *main* computes maximum value in the array x, before and after rotating the array elements. Later, it checks whether the two maximum values computed are equal. Since the maximum element of the array remains the same before and after rotating the array, so, the program is safe. This program cannot be verified by the techniques in other well known portfolios.

The technique ensures that for each run in the input program there exists an equivalent run in the abstract program, which infers that if a run violates the property in the input program then some run will also violate the property in the abstract program. Consider a run of the program in which in first call to *max* the variable *ret* is updated by the iterations $t_1, t_2, t_3, .., $ and t_n. Since *ret* is being updated under the condition $ret < x[i]$, the inequality $0 < x[t_1] < x[t_2] < ... < x[t_n]$ holds. Transitively, the inequality $0 < x[t_n]$ holds. So, if we execute this loop only once but with value of $x[0]$ as value of $x[t_n]$ in the original run, value of ret will be same as in the original run.

The array of size one and a single iteration is sufficient in the abstract program to construct the equivalent run. However, another iteration of the loop is included to account for the effect of the rotation. The challenge is in identifying the kind of loops for which this observation holds and if so then what is the number of iterations required for the loops. The constraints under which the technique works are defined in [36], and if a program satisfies these constraints then the technique computes the bound of the loops which are sufficient to prove the property. For the example case, the resulting abstract program is shown in Fig. 2b.

2.3 A Novel Portfolio of Abstraction Techniques

A few more abstraction techniques were found at TCS Research to scale formal verification in practice. These include array abstraction techniques such as *loop shrinking* [39], *tiling* [16], *full program induction* [17], and *difference invariants* [18]. Further, we implemented three *loop invariant generation* techniques. The first one uses fuzz testing and program syntax analysis to guess and check candidate loop invariants [41]. The second and third techniques uses a backward analysis [27] that eliminates paths leading to the error in the loop's abstraction and *k-induction* [20] to find loop invariants, respectively. We also implemented an *abstract interpretation* technique called *k-path interval analysis* [38] to analyze the input program. This technique is an extension of the standard interval domain. The above techniques when applied intelligently in a sequence enable the verification of a broader variety of programs than when each technique is applied individually. In the next section, we present VeriAbs that implements four such sequences using the proprietary abstraction techniques mentioned above along with a few well known formal verification techniques.

3 VeriAbs: Verification by Abstraction

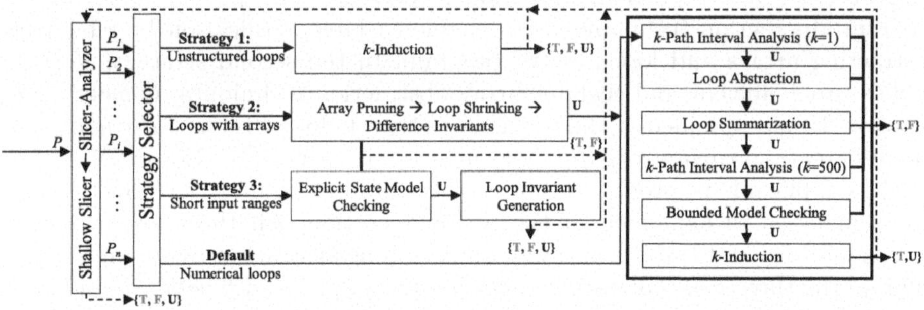

Fig. 3. VeriAbs's Architecture (T: True, F: False, **U**: Unknown)

VeriAbs is a strategy selection based reachability verifier that can verify properties encoded as assertions in C programs [23]. As shown in Fig. 3, to verify a program P, first P is sliced into n slices using a sequence of two slicers [23] [24] which do not use a property directed analysis. For each slice P_i, $1 \leq i \leq n$, a strategy selector identifies the structural and behavioral features of the slice using a light-weight static analysis, to select a predefined sequence of techniques, called a *strategy*, from a set of predefined strategies [4,23]. The program P is safe if each slice P_i is safe, and P is unsafe if any slice P_i is unsafe. If program P cannot be sliced, then the strategy is selected for P itself.

The strategies are assigned priorities based on their order of presentation and are selected in a sequential manner, with each strategy designed for a specific type of programs. The *first strategy* is meant for programs with unstructured control-flow, the *second strategy* for programs that process arrays in loops, and the *third strategy* for programs with inputs having short ranges. If a program does not fall into any of these categories, the *default* strategy is selected. The chosen strategy consists of a sequence of techniques that are applied to verify the program [4,23]. Each technique in each strategy is invoked with a predefined time limit. If the technique succeeds in proving the validity of the input assertion(s) within the predefined time-limit, it returns the verification result as T (True - program safe). If the technique finds a counterexample that violates any assertion, it returns the verification result as F (False - program failed). In case a technique is unable to verify the program or runs out of resources, the next technique in the sequence is invoked. If all techniques within a strategy are unable to verify the program or run out of resources, the overall result is reported as U (unknown). The details of these predefined strategies of VeriAbs are presented in [4,23]. We next present a short summary of each technique in VeriAbs's portfolio.

3.1 VeriAbs's Portfolio

As can be seen in Fig. 3, VeriAbs incorporates a diverse range of eleven verification techniques that use formal verification methods such as program abstraction, abstract interpretation, and model checking. The primary goal of the program abstraction techniques is to enable scalable verification by effectively abstracting arrays and loops in the program. In the second strategy, VeriAbs applies three efficient and scalable array abstraction techniques, namely, *array pruning* [37] as explained in the previous section, followed by *loop shrinking* [39] and *difference invariants (Diffy)* [18] mentioned earlier. It also uses LABMC which is applicable to programs that modify variables in linear arithmetic operations in loops as explained in the previous section. All the above are over-approximations and BMC scales well on programs abstracted by them. VeriAbs employs the three *loop invariant generation* techniques and *k-path interval analysis* [38] explained in Sect. 2.3 to analyze loops. In VeriAbs, the latter is performed twice, with $k = 1$ and $k = 500$, aiming at high scalability and accuracy, respectively.

Model checking is applied in two forms - *bounded model checking* and *explicit state model checking* (ESMC). VeriAbs uses the C Bounded Model Checker or CBMC [22] for BMC. To ensure soundness it performs a series of calls to CBMC in order to assert if all loops in the original program have been unwound sufficiently to verify the input property. ESMC is applied when dealing with programs containing loops where variables have small finite domains or discrete sets of values. ESMC is suitable for exploring small state spaces comprehensively. The portfolio also contains k-induction as implemented by CPAchecker [6]. This technique uses property-directed k-induction with invariants continuously refined using a configurable program analysis. It is useful for loops where loop abstraction using LABMC is a challenge. Next, we describe VeriAbsL, another tool in the VeriAbs tool suite, that uses machine learning for strategy prediction.

4 VeriAbsL: Verification by Learning Strategies from a Portfolio

As mentioned earlier, a verification strategy is a prioritized sequence of techniques, custom selected for a given problem, from a portfolio of verification techniques. They have been defined manually in tools like VeriAbs and CPAchecker using domain expertise and extensive experimentation. Such pre-defined strategies although useful are not flexible because whenever a new class of programs is encountered, a new set of strategies and a corresponding new strategy selection algorithm have to be defined. In other words, manually defined strategies and strategy selection verifiers are not scalable. For instance, in VeriAbs, the second strategy contains 9 techniques in which several calls to BMC are made until sufficient unwinding bounds are obtained. This makes this strategy expensive and often on large programs VeriAbs runs out of resources before the last technique in the strategy is tried. To overcome this limitation, a recent trend has been to use machine learning (ML) to train strategy predictors for programs (see e.g. [29,40,42,43]). Next we the following definitions used in the subsequent paper.

Definition 1 (Feature Vector). *A feature or a program feature is a quantifiable attribute used to capture and abstract specific syntactic and/or semantic attributes of an input program. A vector of such features is called a feature vector.*

For instance, if we use features like `hasloops` to denote presence of loops and `has-known-loop-bound` to represent presence of known bounded loops for a given program, then the feature vector `(hasloops, has-known-loop-bound)` evaluating to boolean `(1, 1)` can summarize the presence of loops in the program and their characteristics.

Definition 2 (Portfolio-Driven Feature). *A program feature is considered to be portfolio-driven if it represents a strength or a weakness of some techniques, but not all, in the portfolio.*

When a program feature is a strength or a weakness of all techniques in the portfolio, then all techniques will either be able to verify the program or not. Thus their order in the strategy will not matter. Hence, such features are not portfolio driven. For instance, '`has-known-loop-bound`' feature indicates a strength of BMC, like it can verify the program in Fig. 4, while k-induction [6] need not, making it a portfolio-driven feature.

4.1 Portfolio-Driven Boolean Features for Feature Relevance

The right set of features representing the input program can lead to better learning models. This in turn can predict a strategy closer to the optimal for a given program with a property specification, and consequently impact the effectiveness of the portfolio either positively or negatively. Consider strategies in VeriAbs. They are selected using boolean representations of the strengths of the techniques in its portfolio, and the order in which they are selected is based on the strengths and weaknesses of the techniques. This method of strategy selection used in VeriAbs was a huge success with its rich portfolio and boolean feature representation for strategy selection. This hints at using carefully chosen features tailored to the verification techniques in the portfolio to improve strategy prediction. Since VeriAbs implements only four manually defined strategies, it relies on three boolean features to select among them. The fourth strategy is used if none of the first three are selected. But learning strategies allows us to use many more features that express all techniques in the portfolio. Thus, in continuation to VeriAbs's method of strategy selection, we propose features to be the representations of the strengths and weaknesses of various techniques in VeriAbs's portfolio. In general, for any given portfolio, we propose the usage of a boolean set of features that represent the strengths and weaknesses of the various techniques in that portfolio for ML-driven strategy prediction. We term such features as *Portfolio Driven Boolean Features* (PDBF).

```
int i;
for (i = 0; i < 1000000; i += 2) ;
assert(i == 1000000);
```

Fig. 4. A sample program [2]

Table 1 presents the set of PDBF we implement in VeriAbsL and are the strengths and weaknesses of some but not all techniques in VeriAbs's portfolio. As discussed earlier, since a majority techniques in VeriAbs's portfolio are designed to handle different classes of loops in the programs, over 70% of the features are related to variables modified in loops. The first four features in Table 1 correspond to the first three strategies present in VeriAbs. On the other hand, the last strategy in VeriAbs, referred to as the *default* strategy, is a useful generic strategy that incorporates a large number of techniques. Thus, as mentioned earlier, VeriAbs can run out of time in this strategy before trying all its techniques or before reaching a useful technique. Therefore, the remaining PDBF in the table represent strengths and weaknesses of techniques within the *default* strategy to guide the learner to predict the most useful technique early in the strategy. Experimental results showcase that portfolio-driven boolean features have helped improve overall verification abilities of VeriAbs's portfolio on a large set of diverse SV-COMP benchmarks. In the next section we present the ML approach used in VeriAbsL.

5 Strategy Prediction in VeriAbsL

In this section, we first present the notation and terminology used in the subsequent discussion. Let,

P be the input program encoded with the property assertion ϕ
T the portfolio of techniques
N the number of techniques in the portfolio, $|T| = N$
T_i a technique in the portfolio, $T_i \in T$, $1 \leq i \leq N$
S a strategy or a permutation of techniques in portfolio T, $S = (T_{i_1}, T_{i_2}, \ldots, T_{i_N})$

R_i the result True (T), False (F) or Unknown (U) when technique T_i verifies program P, $R_i \in \{\text{T}, \text{F}, \text{U}\}$

Table 1. Portfolio-driven boolean features

Loop Patterns
Goto-labels in loop
Forward backward goto-edges forming loops
Array element modified in loop
Loops of short input ranges
Constant assignments in loop
Linearly accelerated variables in loop
Linear operations in loop
All variables in a loop are self recurrent
Variables in loop are mutually dependent
Non-linear operations in loop
Statically loop bound is known
Loop has infinite bound
Control Flow Patterns
No loops in program
Program has more than one loop
Program has nested loop
Recursive program

We use a neural network (NN) with multi-class classification and categorical cross-entropy as a loss function for learning [45]. The output of the NN is a vector of normalized weights $W = \langle w_1, \ldots, w_N \rangle, \Sigma_{i=1}^{N} w_i = 1$. Each weight w_i, is a measure of the predicted effectiveness of each corresponding technique $T_i \in T$ on the input program P. In VeriAbsL, strategy prediction is modelled as a ranking function $G : \{0,1\}^n \rightarrow T^N$, where n is the number of program features, and N is the number of techniques in the portfolio. The domain of the ranking function is the set of all possible feature vectors, and the range is the set of all possible verification strategies for the given portfolio.

A strategy, S, is an ordered set of techniques, where more effective techniques are ranked higher (that is before others with lower effectiveness). A technique T_i is more effective than another technique T_j if it can verify a program P successfully while T_j cannot, or if T_i needs lesser time than T_j to verify P. Techniques that cannot verify a program P, or can verify with the same computational time are considered to be equally effective. The order of equally effective techniques within a strategy is decided arbitrarily. It is important to note that the relative effectiveness of techniques must always be interpreted in the context of specific parameters, such as computing platform, available memory, and timeout. The ordering is obtained by controlled measurements during training for a specific parameter set, and a trained model can be used to predict the order for an unseen program only when the same parameters are used for verification. Our approach is however parameter-agnostic and can be used for any parameter combination. Nevertheless, its prediction is meaningful only when the same parameter combination is used during training and evaluation.

In reality, the NN predicts a real-valued weight for each technique, and techniques with higher predicted weights are ranked higher. Thus strategy prediction is modelled as a function which accepts a feature vector X, and implements an NN to predict weights W indicating the effectiveness of the respective techniques $T_i \in T$, to generate a strategy of techniques S satisfying the following constraint:

$$\forall T_i, T_j \in S, \forall w_i, w_j \in W, w_i > w_j \implies T_i \prec T_j$$

Here $T_i \prec T_j$ indicates that the NN predicted that T_i is at least as effective as T_j, thus technique T_i precedes technique T_j in the predicted strategy S. Note that $T_i \prec T_j$ does not necessarily mean T_i is at least as effective as T_j, instead it is just such a prediction by the NN.

Next we present a learning model implemented in VeriAbsL for strategy prediction.

5.1 Learning Model

VeriAbsL learns a model $M_1 : \{0,1\}^n \rightarrow 1\text{-}hot(N)$, where n is the number of program features, and N is the number of techniques in the portfolio. The domain of this model is the set of all possible boolean feature vectors representing all possible programs. The range of output *label* of model M_1 is the set of all possible boolean vectors of size N that are one-hot encoded [30]. Each output label vector represents the most effective technique in the portfolio T for the program represented by the given feature vector X. The output label is one-hot encoded to represent the technique $T_i, 1 \leq i \leq N$, from portfolio T that verified the program in the *least* amount of time. Thus for a program P represented by feature vector X, the model M_1 learns B given by,

$$M_1(X) = B \in 1\text{-}hot(N)$$

where $b_i \in B$ is set to one when technique $T_i \in T$ solves the program P represented by X in the least amount of time. Let technique T_i verify program P in time t_i to produce result R_i, then

$$b_i = \begin{cases} 1, & \text{if } R_i \neq \mathsf{U} \wedge \forall T_k \in T, i \neq k \Rightarrow (R_k = \mathsf{U} \vee t_i \leq t_k) \\ 0, & \text{otherwise} \end{cases}$$

If multiple techniques are found to verify program P in the same shortest amount of time during the training phase, one of those techniques is arbitrarily selected and its corresponding variable b_i is set to 1 for output labelling during training.

It is significant that although we train the model using data in which the output for every input is one-hot encoded, when actually using the trained model for an input program, we use the weights assigned by the learned model to each technique in the portfolio and use these to obtain a strategy which is an ordered sequence of techniques. Thus, although we train the model using one-hot output labels, we use it to generate a ranked sequence of techniques.

Illustrative Example. We explain strategy prediction using an illustrative example. Consider a feature vector, $X = (g, c, l, p, b)$. Here let, g be TRUE iff the input program P has global variables, c be TRUE iff P has control-flow statements, l stand for the presence of loops, p for presence of pointers, and b for the presence of loops of known bounds. The valuation of this feature vector for the program shown in Fig. 4 will be $X = (11101)$. Let there be three techniques in the portfolio, BMC denoted by B, interval-analysis denoted by I_a [38], and symbolic execution denoted by S_e [19]. A sample training data label for X can be given by $Y = \langle(B,1),(I_a,0),(S_e,1)\rangle$, or $Y = (101)$ for convenience, when the techniques corresponding to the components of Y are understood. The bits corresponding to BMC and symbolic execution are set to TRUE since they can verify program P, while interval analysis cannot. Accordingly one way to label the input with the corresponding output for training can be as follows: $\{(11101, 101)\}$.

But as mentioned earlier, the labelling is one-hot encoded based on the time taken by each technique to verify the program. Let BMC take 0.5 s, and symbolic execution 0.4 s to verify the program. Consequently the training data for this program will be given by $\{(11101, 001)\}$. Since symbolic execution is the fastest technique, only the bit corresponding to it is set to TRUE. Let the prediction by model M_1 for the same program be as follows: $Y' = \langle(B,0.3),(I_a,0.2),(S_e,0.5)\rangle$. Then the predicted strategy will be (S_e, B, I_a) as per the predicted weights.

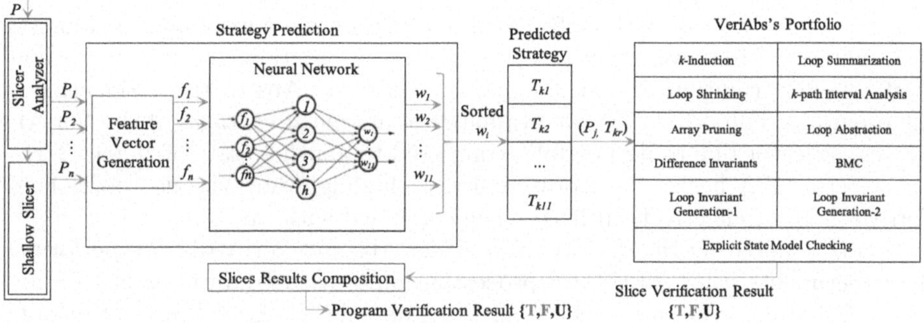

Fig. 5. VeriAbsL Architecture (**T**: True, **F**: Fail, **U**: Unknown)

6 VeriAbsL Architecture

The architecture of VeriAbsL is depicted in Fig. 5. In this architecture, P represents the input program encoded with property assertions. Like VeriAbs, first the input program P is sliced using a sequence of slicers. Then for each slice, P_j, $1 \le j \le n$, verification starts by passing it to the feature vector generation module to generate the feature vector $f_1, \ldots, f_n$ using known static analysis tools and techniques. This feature vector is then passed to trained Neural Network(NN). This trained NN has four layers: an input layer with neurons equal to the number of features, two hidden layers with half the neurons of the previous layer, and an output layer with 11 neurons representing verification techniques in the VeriAbs portolio. The total number of neurons in the hidden layers is less than the total number of neurons in the input and output layers to prevent underfitting and overfitting. Here, the loss function is categorical cross-entropy, and the output layer uses the softmax activation function for multi-class classification. This neural network design is characterized by its compact size and is trained on a limited dataset, which enables exceptionally fast training. The NN translates the feature vector $f_1, \ldots, f_n$ into a vector of measures of effectiveness $(w_1, \ldots, w_N)$ of the corresponding verification techniques $T_1, \ldots, T_N$ in the portfolio. Each output node of the NN corresponds to a specific verification technique T_i, and the value w_i generated by the network at that node represents a measure of effectiveness of the corresponding technique T_i for the slice P_j. The values w_i at all output nodes of the neural network are sorted in decreasing order and mapped to the techniques, and the resulting ordered techniques constitute the predicted strategy $(T_{k1}, \ldots, T_{kr})$. It verifies the slice using this predicted strategy and lastly, similar to VeriAbs, composes the result of verifying each slice. In the next section we present our experiments performed using VeriAbs, VeriAbsL and CPAchecker.

7 Experimentation

In this section, we assess the effectiveness of VeriAbs's portfolio by conducting two analyses. First, we carry out a program-by-program analysis to demonstrate the contribution of each technique within VeriAbs to the verification of the programs. Following that, we evaluate the unique advantages of the VeriAbs strategy selector due to its portfolio compared to another state-of-the-art strategy selector CPAchecker [5]. Additionally, we highlight how the rich portfolio of VeriAbs is most effectively utilized when combined with ML-based strategy prediction by comparing the performance of VeriAbs and VeriAbsL. We performed the experiments using 20 central processing units with Ubuntu 20.04 LTS and 64 GB RAM, allowing up to 900 s per program (matching SV-COMP's timeout).

ReachSafety Benchmarks. In our experimentation, we used the ReachSafety benchmarks from SV-COMP 2024 [1] meant to check for error reachability. They constitute a diverse set of 11222 C programs, each encoded with verification properties. Out of these, 8323 programs satisfy the encoded properties and 2899 violate one or more encoded properties. These benchmarks are distributed into categories based on program functionality and features listed as follows: Arrays, BitVectors, Combinations, ControlFlow, ECA, Floats, Heap, Loops, ProductLines, Recursive, Sequentialized, XCSP, Hardware, Hardness, and Fuzzle [1]. These benchmarks have been contributed and categorised by researchers and practitioners globally.

7.1 Effectiveness of VeriAbs's Portfolio

Technique-wise Contribution. Overall VeriAbs successfully verified 68.5% of the total programs in ReachSafety category. The percentage programs solved by each technique is presented in Fig. 6. *Array Abstraction* includes three techniques - array pruning, loop shrinking and difference invariants or Diffy [18]. We make the following observations from the data presented in Fig. 6:

- TCS's proprietary techniques for array abstraction, loop abstraction, and invariant generation account for 61% of the programs successfully verified.

– The next significant contributors are BMC and ESMC, collectively accounting for 35% of the total programs successfully verified. ESMC's success is primarily due to an efficient proprietary implementation which can explore the entire state space without running out of memory and time for programs with small input ranges. BMC is effective due to the statically computed bounds provided by VeriAbs to the off-the-shelf bounded model checker and because we use BMC incrementally to compute sufficient program bounds.

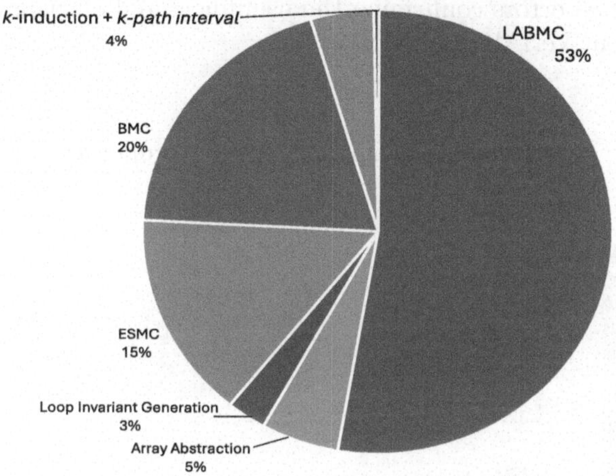

Fig. 6. Technique-wise distribution in VeriAbs

VeriAbs Unique Contribution. To assess the unique contribution of VeriAbs, we compared the programs it verified with those verified by the well-known state-of-the-art strategy selector CPAchecker [5]. VeriAbs successfully verified 1,729 programs (22%) of the total programs that CPAchecker could not verify. The technique-wise distribution of these 1,729 programs is illustrated in Fig. 7. Below are some key observations derived from this data.

– VeriAbs successfully verified 830 of the above 1729 programs (48%) by using LABMC (Sect. 2.1 and invariant generation techniques presented in Sect. 2.3. As metioned earlier, these techniques create an abstract program that is devoid of loops or contains loops of known small bounds on which BMC is applied. On these programs, CPAchecker applied either the *single-loop* or *other* strategy [5], but it timed out. Within the *single-loop* or *other* strategy in CPAchecker invokes Symbolic Execution [14] followed by Value Analysis [15], Predicate Abstraction [12], CPA-DF [7], and interpolation-based model checking [13].
– The array abstraction techniques array pruning, loop shrinking and difference invariants cumulatively verified 350 (20%) programs. CPAchecker does not have specialized techniques for verifying array programs in its portfolio.

- BMC and ESMC verified 518 (30%) programs and primarily identified bugs. CPAChecker incorporates both techniques in its portfolio. However, it applies BMC only to loop-free programs unlike VeriAbs which computes bounds using BMC incrementally or using interval analysis to enable BMC in finding bugs. Finding program bounds has also helped in proving program safety because approximately 44% programs verified by BMC were safe. Additionally, VeriAbs applies ESMC to programs with short input ranges, allowing for complete exploration of the state space. In comparison, CPAChecker uses a single-loop strategy for such programs, which mostly resulted in timeouts. All these programs contained errors confirming the usefulness and efficiency of the ESMC implemented in VeriAbs's portfolio.

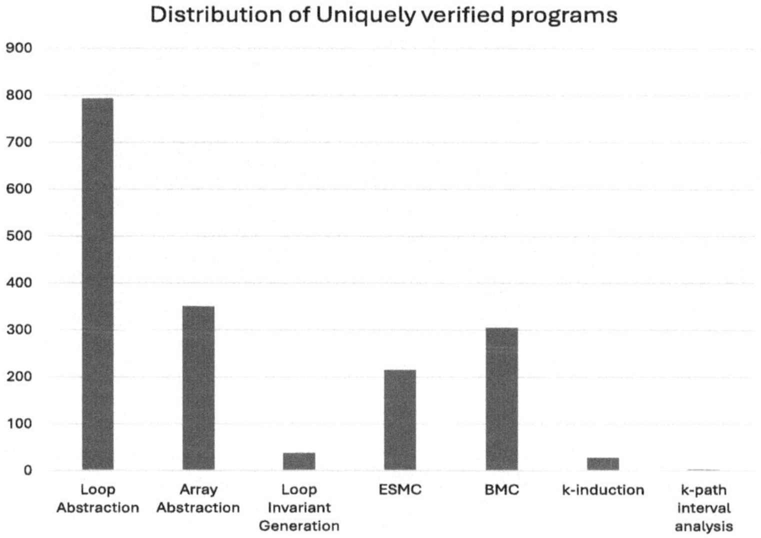

Fig. 7. VeriAbs's unique technique-wise contribution in comparison with CPAchecker

Conclusion. Both evaluations emphasize that VeriAbs has a rich portfolio of techniques distinguishing it as a best-in-class verification tool. Its unique loop and array abstraction techniques play a key role in its success.

7.2 Comparison of VeriAbs and VeriAbsL

Table 2. Comparison on SV-COMP 2024 ReachSafety benchmarks

Test Data	VeriAbs	VeriAbsL
11222	7690	**8234**
Total % verified	68.5	**73.4**

We compare the performance of VeriAbs and VeriAbsL with respect to number of programs verified by both these tools on SV-COMP 2024 ReachSafety benchmarks. We begin by describing the training and test data used by VeriAbsL.

Training and Test Data for VeriAbsL. With the aim of using a small set of training data, we randomly selected 12% (648) of the SV-COMP 2022 ReachSafety programs out of total 5400. SV-COMP'22 ReachSafety programs are distributed into 12 categories, and a 12% random selection allows for a training data that is equally distributed over all classes of programs represented by each of the 12 categories in SV-COMP 2022. To perform data labelling, we executed each verification technique for upto 900 s on each program in the training data. As discussed earlier, output label for each program is the successful technique that took least execution time. The training process is fully automated, employing a utility that randomly picks programs from the input set, creates feature vectors, and generates output labels for each program. On the other hand, the SV-COMP 2024 ReachSafety category benchmarks serve as the test data. Each year structurally and functionally distinct benchmarks have been added to the SV-COMP benchmarks repository. We thus used latest benchmarks to evaluate VeriAbsL using portfolio-driven boolean features.

Evaluation. Table 2 shows the programs successfully verified by VeriAbs and VeriAbsL. VeriAbsL verified approximately 5% more programs than VeriAbs. Unlike VeriAbs, VeriAbsL learns from a larger strategy space, accommodating up to $N!$ strategies, where N is number of techniques in the portfolio. Moreover, it can classify programs using an extensive set of features, encompassing up to 2^n categories of programs, where n is the number of features. This enables VeriAbsL to verify more programs successfully. Some key observations while comparing the performance of VeriAbs and VeriAbsL are as follows:

- On the programs verified successfully by VeriAbs, it tried 62% more techniques compared to VeriAbsL. This is because 66% of the programs verified by VeriAbsL use one of the first three techniques in the predicted strategies, whereas in VeriAbs, only 8% programs were verified by one of first three techniques in the manually defined strategies.
- VeriAbsL verified 544 more programs than VeriAbs as explained below:
  - VeriAbsL verified 720 programs for which VeriAbs ran out of time due to the selection of ineffective manually defined strategies.
  - VeriAbs verified 176 programs that VeriAbsL could not. These programs required techniques that were not present as output labels in the randomly selected training data, causing VeriAbsL to never predict them early in a strategy. Consequently, less effective techniques were prioritized, resulting in timeouts.

Conclusion. The rich portfolio of VeriAbs is most effectively utilized when combined with ML-based strategy prediction, even when trained on a limited dataset.

8 Related Work

We categorize the related work into three areas - portfolio, strategy selection and ML-based strategy prediction.

Portfolio. For scalable verification, different abstraction based techniques such as predicate discovery using interpolation [34], lazy predicate abstraction [35], and counter-example guided abstraction refinement (CEGAR) [15] being utilized. But popular implementations of predicate abstraction and interpolation are unable to precisely reason about quantified loop invariants [33]. Consequently, the presence of loops often causes techniques to get stuck in CEGAR loops. In contrast, abstraction techniques present in VeriAbs portfolio aim towards eliminating loops or make them small bounded loops and apply BMC over abstracted programs. Experimental result shows the unique effectiveness of these techniques.

Strategy Selection. CPAChecker [5] and UAutomiser [31] are popular strategy selectors with wide variety of techniques in their portfolio. Another approach is cooperative verification [10], where a portfolio of techniques collaboratively exchange verification summaries, harnessing the strengths of multiple tools for better results. Past efforts have introduced platforms and languages to facilitate this cooperative verification [11]. Experimental results indicate that VeriAbs's strategy selection approach, which leverages program features and constructs while considering the strengths and weaknesses of techniques in the portfolio, effectively maximizes the capabilities of well-known techniques such as BMC and ESMC.

ML-based Strategy Prediction. To enhance the overall accuracy of verification, machine learning techniques have been employed in algorithm selection. MUX [44] and Verifolio [29], which are ML-based algorithm selectors that uses manual feature engineering approach for learning. VERIABSL employs similar idea but they diverge in several key aspects. Table 3 presents the comparative study.

Table 3. Comparative study of Manual Feature Engineering approaches

Aspect	Verifolio	MUX	VeriAbsL
Feature Selection	Based on tool compatibility and constructs	Structural features over the program-property pairs	Systematic approach using domain expertise
Feature Representation	Integer or rational number representing counts or frequencies of program constructs	Integer counts of program constructs	Boolean variable to capture attributes of syntax, or semantics of a program
Static Analysis for feature computation	Yes	Yes	Yes
Training Methodology	Support vector Machine	Support vector Machine	Neural Network

Our experiments indicate that a portfolio-driven boolean representation of features helped improve verification accuracy of best-in-class verifier. Other ML-based strategy selectors, such as PeSCo [42], Graves and CST [43], rely on automatic feature engineering using program graphs. The main focus of these graph-based approaches is to generate features based on program structure rather than emphasizing semantic information related to verification techniques. In contrast, VeriAbsL uses lightweight static analysis to extract program features, making it efficient in obtaining essential semantic information.

9 Conclusion

Loops and arrays in programs pose significant challenges for scalable software verification. TCS Research has developed innovative loop and array abstraction techniques to enhance verification scalability. These techniques, combined with well-known model checking and abstract interpretation techniques, form the portfolio of the VeriAbs tool suite for reachability verification of C programs. This comprehensive suite of techniques and strategy-selection made the VeriAbs tool a best-in-class tool as shown by the results of the international competition on software verification (SV-COMP). Experimental results demonstrate that on the SV-COMP 2024 benchmarks, TCS's proprietary abstraction techniques accounted for 61% of the total programs verified by VeriAbs. Moreover, 22% of these verified programs were uniquely verified by VeriAbs when compared to CPAchecker, outperforming the well-known strategy selector CPAchecker. This unique contribution is primarily attributed to TCS's novel techniques. Furthermore, by leveraging machine learning, the strategy predictor VeriAbsL effectively utilizes VeriAbs's portfolio, verifying 73.3% of the programs, which is 5% more than VeriAbs. Overall, these results underscore the significant impact of VeriAbs's portfolio on scalable software verification.

References

1. SV-COMP 2024 Benchmarks. http://sv-comp.sosy-lab.org/2024/benchmarks.php
2. SV-COMP Benchmarks Repository. https://gitlab.com/sosy-lab/benchmarking/sv-benchmarks/tree/svcomp22
3. Schuele, T., Schneider, K.: Bounded model checking of infinite state systems: exploiting the automata hierarchy. In: MEMOCODE '04, pp. 17–26, Washington, DC, USA. IEEE Computer Society (2004)
4. Afzal, M., et al.: VeriAbs: verification by abstraction and test generation. In: ASE, pp. 1138–1141 (2019)
5. Baier, D., et al.: CPAchecker 2.3 with strategy selection. In: Finkbeiner, B., Kovács, L., (eds.) Tools and Algorithms for the Construction and Analysis of Systems. Springer, Cham (2024)
6. Beyer, D., Dangl, M., Wendler, P.: Boosting k-induction with continuously-refined invariants. In: CAV, pp. 622–640 (2015)
7. Beyer, D., Chien, P.C., Lee, N.Z.: CPA-DF: a tool for configurable interval analysis to boost program verification. In: 38th IEEE/ACM International Conference on Automated Software Engineering, ASE 2023, Luxembourg, September 11-15, 2023, pp. 2050–2053. IEEE (2023)

8. Beyer, D., Dangl, M.: Strategy selection for software verification based on Boolean features - a simple but effective approach. In: ISoLA (2). LNCS, vol. 11245, pages 144–159. Springer (2018)
9. Beyer, D., Henzinger, T.A., Théoduloz, G.: Program analysis with dynamic precision adjustment. In: 23rd IEEE/ACM International Conference on Automated Software Engineering (ASE 2008), 15-19 September 2008, L'Aquila, Italy, pp. 29–38. IEEE Computer Society (2008)
10. Beyer, D., Kanav, S.: CoVeriTeam: on-demand composition of cooperative verification systems. In: Fisman, D., Rosu, G. (eds.) TACAS 2022, Munich, Germany, April 2-7, 2022, Proceedings, Part I. LNCS, vol. 13243, pp. 561–579. Springer (2022)
11. Beyer, D., Kanav, S., Richter, C.: Construction of verifier combinations based on off-the-shelf verifiers. In: Johnsen, E.B., Wimmer, M. (eds) FASE 2022, Munich, Germany, April 2-7, 2022, Proceedings. LNCS, vol. 13241, pp. 49–70. Springer (2022)
12. Beyer, D., Erkan Keremoglu, M., Wendler, P.: Predicate abstraction with adjustable-block encoding. In: Bloem, R., Sharygina, N. (eds.) Proceedings of 10th International Conference on Formal Methods in Computer-Aided Design, FMCAD 2010, Lugano, Switzerland, October 20-23, pp. 189–197. IEEE (2010)
13. Beyer, D., Lee, N.Z., Wendler, P.: Interpolation and sat-based model checking revisited: adoption to software verification. arXiv preprint arXiv:2208.05046 (2022)
14. Beyer, D., Lemberger, T.: CPA-SymExec: efficient symbolic execution in CPAchecker. In: Huchard, M., Kästner, C., Fraser, G. (eds.) Proceedings of the 33rd ACM/IEEE International Conference on Automated Software Engineering, ASE 2018, Montpellier, France, September 3-7, 2018, pp. 900–903. ACM (2018)
15. Beyer, D., Löwe, S.: Explicit-state software model checking based on CEGAR and interpolation. In: Cortellessa, V., Varró, D. (eds.) Fundamental Approaches to Software Engineering - 16th International Conference, FASE 2013, Held as Part of the European Joint Conferences on Theory and Practice of Software, ETAPS 2013, Rome, Italy, March 16-24, 2013. Proceedings. LNCS, vol. 7793, pp. 146–162. Springer (2013)
16. Chakraborty, S., Gupta, A., Unadkat, D.: Verifying array manipulating programs by tiling. In: International Static Analysis Symposium, pp. 428–449. Springer (2017)
17. Chakraborty, S., Gupta, A., Unadkat, D.: Verifying array manipulating programs with full-program induction. In: International Conference on Tools and Algorithms for the Construction and Analysis of Systems (TACAS), pp. 22–39. Springer (2020)
18. Chakraborty, S., Gupta, A., Unadkat, D.: Diffy: inductive reasoning of array programs using difference invariants. In: Computer Aided Verification (CAV), pp. 911–935. Springer (2021)
19. Chalupa, M., Mihalkovic, V., Rechtácková, A., Zaoral, L., Strejcek, J.: Symbiotic 9: string analysis and backward symbolic execution with loop folding - (competition contribution). In: Fisman, D., Rosu, G. (eds.) 28th TACAS. LNCS, vol. 13244, pp. 462–467. Springer (2022)
20. Chimdyalwar, B., Darke, P., Chauhan, A., Shah, P., Kumar, S., Venkatesh, R.: VeriAbs: verification by abstraction (competition contribution). In: TACAS (2017)
21. Chimdyalwar, B., Darke, P., Chavda, A., Vaghani, S., Chauhan, A.: Eliminating static analysis false positives using loop abstraction and bounded model checking. In: FM, pp. 573–576 (2015)
22. Clarke, E. Kroening, D., Lerda, F.: A tool for checking ANSI-C programs. In: TACAS, pp. 168–176 (2004)

23. Darke, P., Agrawal, S., Venkatesh, R.:VERIABS: a tool for scalable verification by abstraction (competition contribution). In: Proceedings TACAS (2). LNCS, vol. 12652. Springer (2021)
24. Darke, P., Chimdyalwar, B., Agrawal, S., Kumar, S., Venkatesh, R., Chakraborty, S. VeriAbsL: scalable verification by abstraction and strategy prediction (competition contribution). In: Sankaranarayanan, S., Sharygina, N. (eds.) 29th TACAS 2023 Paris, France, April 22-27, 2023, Proceedings, Part II. LNCS, pp. 588–593. Springer (2023)
25. Darke, P., Chimdyalwar, B., Venkatesh, R., Shrotri, U., Metta, R.: Over-approximating loops to prove properties using bounded model checking. In: DATE, pp. 1407–1412 (2015)
26. Darke, P., Khanzode, M., Nair, A., Shrotri, U., Venkatesh, R.: Precise analysis of large industry code. In: APSEC (2012)
27. Darke, P., Shah, T., Venkatesh, R.: A refinement to loop abstraction for bounded model checking. In: TCS Internal Technical Report (2018)
28. Darke, P., Chimdyalwar, B., Chauhan, A., Venkatesh, R.: Efficient safety proofs for industry-scale code using abstractions and bounded model checking. In: ICST (2017)
29. Demyanova, Y., Pani, T., Veith, H., Zuleger, F.: Empirical software metrics for benchmarking of verification tools. In: Knoop, J., Zdun, U. (eds.) Software Engineering 2016, pp. 67–68, Bonn. Gesellschaft für Informatik e.V (2016)
30. Hancock, J.T., Khoshgoftaar, T.M.: Survey on categorical data for neural networks. J. Big Data **7**(1), 1–41 (2020). https://doi.org/10.1186/s40537-020-00305-w
31. Heizmann, M., et al.: Ultimate automizer and the search for perfect interpolants - (competition contribution). In: TACAS, vol. 2, pp. 447–451 (2018)
32. Heizmann, M., et al.: Ultimate automizer and the search for perfect interpolants, pp. 447–451 (2018)
33. Henzinger, T.A., Jhala, R., Majumdar, R., McMillan, K.L.: Abstractions from proofs. ACM SIGPLAN Notices **49**(4S), 79–91 (2014)
34. Hojjat, H., Iosif, R., Konečný, F., Kuncak, V., Rümmer, P.: Accelerating interpolants. In: Chakraborty, S., Mukund, M. (eds.) ATVA, pp. 187–202. Berlin, Heidelberg (2012)
35. Kroening, D., Lewis, M., Weissenbacher, G.: Under-approximating loops in C programs for fast counterexample detection. In: Computer Aided Verification (CAV). LNCS, vol. 8044. Springer (2013)
36. Kumar, S.: Scaling up property checking (2019). https://www.cse.iitb.ac.in/~as/thesis_soft.pdf
37. Kumar, S., Afzal, M., Venkatesh, R.: Property checking array programs using array pruning. In: TCS Internal Technical Report (2018)
38. Kumar, S., Chimdyalwar, B., Shrotri, U.: Precise range analysis on large industry code. In: ESEC/FSE, pp. 675–678 (2013)
39. Kumar, S., Sanyal, A., Venkatesh, R., Shah, P.: Property checking array programs using loop shrinking. In: TACAS (2018)
40. Leeson, W., Dwyer, W.B.: Graves-CPA: a graph-attention verifier selector (competition contribution). In: Fisman, D., Rosu, G. (eds.) TACAS, pp. 440–445. Springer, Cham (2022)
41. Prabhu, S., Madhukar, K., Venkatesh, R.: Efficiently learning safety proofs from appearance as well as behaviours. In: SAS (2018)
42. Richter, C., Hüllermeier, E., Jakobs, M.-C., Wehrheim, H.: Algorithm selection for software validation based on graph kernels. Autom. Softw. Eng. **27**, 153–186 (2020). https://doi.org/10.1007/s10515-020-00270-x

43. Richter, C., Wehrheim, H.: Attend and represent: a novel view on algorithm selection for software verification. In: ASE, pp. 1016–1028 (2020)
44. Tulsian, V., Kanade, V., Kumar, R., Lal, A., Nori, A.V.: MUX: algorithm selection for software model checkers. In: Devanbu, P., Kim, S., Pinzger, M. (eds.) 11th MSR 2014, Proceedings, May 31 - June 1, 2014, Hyderabad, India, pp. 132–141. ACM (2014)
45. Zhang, A., Lipton, Z.C., Li, M., Smola, A.J.: Dive into Deep Learning. Cambridge University Press (2023). https://D2L.ai

Automata and Games

Easy Complementation of History-Deterministic Büchi Automata

Bader Abu Radi(✉), Orna Kupferman(✉), and Ofer Leshkowitz(✉)

School of Engineering and Computer Science, Hebrew University, Jerusalem, Israel
bader.aburadi@gmail.com, orna@cs.huji.ac.il, oleshkowitz@gmail.com

Abstract. A *history deterministic* (HD) automaton can successfully resolve its nondeterministic choices in a way that only depends on the past. Formally, an HD automaton has a strategy that maps each finite word to the transition to be taken after the word is read, and following this strategy results in accepting all the words in the language of the automaton. HD automata can replace deterministic automata in several applications, most notably reactive synthesis, and they attract a lot of interest in the research community.

In 2015, Kuperberg and Skrzypczak proved that an HD Büchi automaton $\mathcal{A}$ can be determinized with a quadratic blow-up in the state space. The suggested construction also implicitly induces an HD co-Büchi automaton of linear size that complements $\mathcal{A}$. The construction is based on a series of transformations on an HD strategy for $\mathcal{A}$, which has two drawbacks. First, the construction is conceptually hard to understand. Second, since the state space of the HD strategy is exponential, so is the runtime of a procedure implementing the construction.

In this paper, we describe a direct complementation procedure for HD Büchi automata. Our procedure is based on removal of transitions from $\mathcal{A}$ itself, which can be done in polynomial time. It results in an HD Büchi automaton equivalent to $\mathcal{A}$ on top of which we define a complementing HD co-Büchi automaton of linear size. A deterministic equivalent automaton of size quadratic in $\mathcal{A}$ can then be defined in polynomial time too. We also prove a quadratic lower bound on the size of an HD strategy for HD Büchi automata.

1 Introduction

Nondeterminism allows a computing machine to examine several possible actions simultaneously [19]. In the setting of automata on finite words, nondeterminism does not add to the expressive power of deterministic automata, yet enables the definition of exponentially more succinct automata. In the setting of *automata on infinite words* [6], nondeterminism is more involved. Acceptance in such automata is determined according to the set of transitions that are traversed infinitely often along the run. For example, in *Büchi* automata (tNBW and tDBW, for nondeterministic and deterministic Büchi word automata, respectively), the acceptance condition is a subset α of transitions, and a run is

S. Akshay et al. (Eds.): ATVA 2024, LNCS 15054, pp. 67–88, 2025.
https://doi.org/10.1007/978-3-031-78709-6_4

accepting iff it visits α infinitely often.[1] Consequently, the *subset construction*, which is useful for determinization of automata on finite words, does not work for automata on infinite words, as it does not maintain information on the history of runs beyond the state they have reached. In fact, NBWs are strictly more expressive than DBWs [17].

Automata on infinite objects are used in *specifications*, *verification*, and *synthesis* of reactive systems [13,21]. In some applications, such as verification, algorithms can be based on nondeterministic automata, whereas in other applications, such as synthesis and control, algorithms are based on deterministic automata, and thus involve a complicated determinization construction [20] or acrobatics for circumventing determinization [8,16]. Essentially, the problem with nondeterminism is that it amounts to guessing the future, and in many applications, the use of nondetermnistic automata means that the same guess is applied to all futures, which is too restrictive.

In [9], Henzinger and Piterman introduced *history deterministic* (HD) automata, which capture this difficulty in a very clean way. A nondeterministic automaton is HD if it can to resolve its nondeterministic choices in a way that only depends on the past.[2] Formally, a nondeterministic automaton $\mathcal{A}$ over an alphabet Σ is HD if there is a strategy g that maps each finite word $u \in \Sigma^*$ to the transition to be taken after u is read; and following g results in accepting all the words in the language of $\mathcal{A}$. Note that a state q of $\mathcal{A}$ may be reachable via different words, and g may suggest different transitions from q after different words are read.

The simplest class of HD automata are deterministic ones. Another simple class consists of nondeterministic automata that are *determinizable by pruning* (DBP); that is, ones that just add transitions on top of a deterministic automaton. Clearly, DBP automata are HD, as witnessed by a strategy that follows the embodied deterministic automaton. In fact, it is not hard to see that HD nondeterministic automata on finite words are always DBP. Moving to automata on infinite words, the picture is different. On the one hand, in terms of expressive power, HD automata are not more expressive than deterministic ones [15,18]. On the other hand, HD automata need not be DBP [3], and they constitute an interesting and intriguing class of automata, many of whose properties are still unknown [5,14].

In [12], Kuperberg and Skrzypczak study determinization of HD automata. They focus on Büchi auotmata and their dual *co-Büchi* automata (denoted tDCW and tNCW, for the deterministic and nondeterministic classes). For HD-

[1] Traditionally, the study of automata on infinite words assume *state-based* acceptance conditions, which specify the set of states that should be visited infinitely or finitely often. Here, we assume *transitions-based* acceptance, which turns out to be cleaner in our study.

[2] The notion used in [9] is *good for games* (GFG) automata, as they address the difficulty described above in the context of games played on top of a nondeterministic automaton. As it turns out, the property of being good for games varies in different settings, and history determinism is useful for applications beyond games [7,15], and so we opt for using the term HD.

tNCWs, the picture is well understood: Every HD-tNCW can be determinized with an exponential blow-up, and this bound is tight [12]. For Büchi automata, Kuperberg and Skrzypczak proved that an HD-tNBW $\mathcal{A}$ can be determinized with a quadratic blow-up in the state space, and no lower bound is known. The suggested determinization construction also implicitly induces an HD-tNCW of linear size that complements $\mathcal{A}$.

Essentially, the construction in [12] starts with computing an HD strategy g for $\mathcal{A}$ that is based on the subset-construction, and is therefore exponential. It then considers a *parity game* defined on top of the product of $\mathcal{A}$ and g. Using ranks that are defined on top of the game, the construction identifies properties of $\mathcal{A}$ and g that are used in order to modify them while preserving $\mathcal{A}$'s language and HDness.

While the construction cleverly solves the open problem of polynomial determinization of HD-tNBWs, it has two drawbacks. First, its implementation is complex: it is based on a product with an exponential HD strategy and thus requires exponential time, and it involves optimal strategies in parity games. Second, the construction involves ranks obtained by analyzing a game played on top of both $\mathcal{A}$ and g. This makes the construction very hard to understand. In addition, it is difficult to gain a conceptual understanding of HDness from it.

In this paper we suggest an alternative complementation construction for HD-tNBWs, which addresses the above two drawbacks. Our construction is direct, and can be implemented in time polynomial in $\mathcal{A}$. We show that a complementing automaton can be defined on top of the state space of $\mathcal{A}$, after removing from it transitions that are not essential for its language or its HDness. We prove the correctness of our construction by analyzing the structure of a witness HD strategy. Thus, as in [12], we analyze HD strategies, yet we are able to avoid ranks and games, and the analysis is used only for proving correctness – the construction itself is independent of such a strategy. This makes the proof cleaner, shorter, and easier to understand.

Our complementation construction also yields a new determinization construction: once we complement $\mathcal{A}$ to an HD-tNCW, a tDBW equivalent to $\mathcal{A}$ can be defined on top of the product of $\mathcal{A}$ and its complement [3]. Thus, in polynomial time we also determinize $\mathcal{A}$ with a quadratic blow-up. Our construction also implies a quadratic upper bound for the size of HD strategies. We show that the bound is tight. That is, we show that for every $n \geq 1$, there is an HD-tNBW $\mathcal{A}_n$ (in fact, even one that is *deterministic in the limit*) such that $\mathcal{A}_n$ has $O(n)$ states and every HD strategy for $\mathcal{A}_n$ needs at least n^2 states. Note that this does not imply a quadratic lower bound for determinization of HD-tNBWs. Indeed, it only implies that determinization constructions that are based on pruning strategies are at least quadratic, suggesting that a linear determinization construction, if exists, must involve redirectioning of transitions.

We believe that our results contribute not only to efficient complementation and determinization constructions for HD Büchi automata, but also to better understanding of history determinism.

2 Preliminaries

For a finite nonempty alphabet Σ, an infinite *word* $w = \sigma_1 \cdot \sigma_2 \cdots \in \Sigma^\omega$ is an infinite sequence of letters from Σ. For positions $1 \leq i \leq j$, we use $w[i,j]$ to denote the finite infix $\sigma_i \cdot \sigma_{i+1} \cdots \sigma_j$ of w, and use $w[i,\infty]$ to denote the infinite suffix $\sigma_i \cdot \sigma_{i+1} \cdots$. A *language* $L \subseteq \Sigma^\omega$ is a set of infinite words. We use $\overline{L}$ to denote the complement of L, thus $\overline{L} = \Sigma^\omega \setminus L$. We sometimes refer also to finite words, namely elements in Σ^*, and denote the empty word by ϵ.

A *nondeterministic automaton* on infinite words is $\mathcal{A} = \langle \Sigma, Q, q_0, \delta, \alpha \rangle$, where Σ is an alphabet, Q is a finite set of *states*, $q_0 \in Q$ is an *initial state*, $\delta : Q \times \Sigma \to 2^Q \setminus \emptyset$ is a *transition function*, and α is an *acceptance condition*, to be defined below. We extend δ to sets of states and finite words in the expected way. Thus, $\delta(S, u)$ is the set of states that $\mathcal{A}$ may reach when it reads the word $u \in \Sigma^*$ from some state in $S \in 2^Q$. Formally, $\delta : 2^Q \times \Sigma^* \to 2^Q$ is such that for every $S \in 2^Q$, finite word $u \in \Sigma^*$, and letter $\sigma \in \Sigma$, we have that $\delta(S, \epsilon) = S$, $\delta(S, \sigma) = \bigcup_{s \in S} \delta(s, \sigma)$, and $\delta(S, u \cdot \sigma) = \delta(\delta(S, u), \sigma)$. Note that δ is *full*, thus $|\delta(q, \sigma)| \geq 1$ for every state $q \in Q$ and letter $\sigma \in \Sigma$. If $|\delta(q, \sigma)| = 1$ for every state $q \in Q$ and letter $\sigma \in \Sigma$, then $\mathcal{A}$ is *deterministic*. In a deterministic automaton $\mathcal{A}$, we view δ and its extension to words as a function $\delta : Q \times \Sigma^* \to Q$. We sometimes refer to the transition function δ as a transition relation $\Delta \subseteq Q \times \Sigma \times Q$, where for every two states $q, s \in Q$ and letter $\sigma \in \Sigma$, we have that $\langle q, \sigma, s \rangle \in \Delta$ iff $s \in \delta(q, \sigma)$.

An *run* of $\mathcal{A}$ on an infinite word $w = \sigma_1 \cdot \sigma_2 \cdots \in \Sigma^\omega$, is an infinite sequence $r \in \Delta^\omega$ of successive transitions that are traversed while reading w. Thus, $r = \langle r_0, \sigma_1, r_1 \rangle, \langle r_1, \sigma_2, r_2 \rangle, \langle r_2, \sigma_3, r_3 \rangle, \ldots$ is such that $r_0 = q_0$, and for all $i \geq 0$, we have that $r_{i+1} \in \delta(r_i, \sigma_{i+1})$. We sometimes also consider runs of $\mathcal{A}$ on a finite words $w = \sigma_1 \cdot \sigma_2 \cdots \sigma_k \in \Sigma^*$, where $r = \langle r_0, \sigma_1, r_1 \rangle, \langle r_1, \sigma_2, r_2 \rangle, \ldots, \langle r_{k-1}, \sigma_k, r_k \rangle$, and then similarly $r_0 = q_0$, and for all $0 \leq i \leq k-1$, we have that $r_{i+1} \in \delta(r_i, \sigma_{i+1})$. The acceptance condition α determines which runs are "good". We consider here the *Büchi* and *co-Büchi* transition-based acceptance conditions, where $\alpha \subseteq \Delta$ is a subset of transitions. For an infinite run r, let $\mathit{inf}(r) \subseteq \Delta$ be the set of transitions that r traverses infinitely often. Thus, $\mathit{inf}(r) = \{t \in \Delta : t = \langle r_i, \sigma_{i+1}, r_{i+1} \rangle$ for infinitely many i's$\}$. A run r of a Büchi automaton is *accepting* iff it traverses transitions in α infinitely often, thus $\mathit{inf}(r) \cap \alpha \neq \emptyset$. Dually, a run r of a co-Büchi automaton is accepting iff it traverses transitions in α only finitely often, thus $\mathit{inf}(r) \cap \alpha = \emptyset$. A run that is not accepting is *rejecting*. For finite words the acceptance condition α is a subset of *accepting states*. Thus, $\alpha \subseteq Q$ and a run r is *accepting* if the last state in r belongs to α. Note that as $\mathcal{A}$ is nondeterministic, it may have several runs on a word w. The word w is accepted by $\mathcal{A}$ if there is an accepting run of $\mathcal{A}$ on w. The language of $\mathcal{A}$, denoted $L(\mathcal{A})$, is the set of words that $\mathcal{A}$ accepts.

Two automata are *equivalent* if their languages are equivalent. For a state $q \in Q$, we define $\mathcal{A}^q = \langle \Sigma, Q, q, \delta, \alpha \rangle$. Thus, $\mathcal{A}^q$ is obtained from $\mathcal{A}$ by setting the initial state to q. Then, two states $q, s \in Q$ are *equivalent*, denoted $q \sim_\mathcal{A} s$, if $L(\mathcal{A}^q) = L(\mathcal{A}^s)$. When $\mathcal{A}$ is clear from the context, we omit it and write $L(q) = L(s)$, $q \sim s$, etc.

We use tDBW, tDCW, tNBW and tNCW to denote deterministic Büchi, deterministic co-Büchi, nondeterministic Büchi and nondeterministic co-Büchi word automata with a transition-based acceptance condition.

A nondeterministic automaton $\mathcal{A}$ is *semantically deterministic* (*SD*, for short) if different nondeterministic choices lead to equivalent states. Thus, for all states $q \in Q$, and transitions $\langle q, \sigma, s_1 \rangle, \langle q, \sigma, s_2 \rangle \in \Delta$, it holds that $s_1 \sim s_2$. Consider two states q and s in an SD automaton $\mathcal{A}$. It is easy to see that if $q \sim_{\mathcal{A}} s$, then for every $\sigma \in \Sigma$, $q' \in \delta(q, \sigma)$, and $s' \in \delta(s, \sigma)$, we have that $q' \sim_{\mathcal{A}} s'$. An iterative application of the above property, termed the *SDness property*, implies also that for every word $x \in \Sigma^*$, if $q' \in \delta(q, x)$, and $s' \in \delta(s, x)$, we have that $q' \sim_{\mathcal{A}} s'$. In particular, for all finite words x, all the states in $\delta(q_0, x)$ are equivalent. Intuitively, it means that a run of an SD automaton is allowed to take finitely many 'bad' nondeterministic choices; when reading a word in the language there is always a chance to generate an accepting run.

An automaton $\mathcal{A}$ is *history deterministic* (*HD*, for short) if its nondeterminism can be resolved based on the past, thus on the prefix of the input word read so far. Formally, $\mathcal{A}$ is *HD* if there is a *strategy* $g : \Sigma^* \to Q$ such that the following hold:

1. The strategy g is consistent with the transition function. That is, $g(\epsilon) = q_0$, and for every finite word $u \in \Sigma^*$ and letter $\sigma \in \Sigma$, we have that $\langle g(u), \sigma, g(u \cdot \sigma) \rangle \in \Delta$.
2. Following g causes $\mathcal{A}$ to accept all the words in $L(\mathcal{A})$. That is, for every infinite word $w = \sigma_1 \cdot \sigma_2 \cdots \in \Sigma^\omega$, if $w \in L(\mathcal{A})$, then the run $\langle g(\epsilon), \sigma_1, g(w[1,1]) \rangle$, $\langle g(w[1,1]), \sigma_2, g(w[1,2]) \rangle, \langle g(w[1,2]), \sigma_2, g(w[1,3]) \rangle, \ldots$, which we denote by $g(w)$, is an accepting run of $\mathcal{A}$ on w.

We say that the strategy g is an *HD strategy* for $\mathcal{A}$, and that g *witnesses* $\mathcal{A}$'s HDness. We say that a transition $\langle q, \sigma, s \rangle \in \Delta$ is *used by* g if there is $u \in \Sigma^*$ such that $g(u) = q$ and $g(u \cdot \sigma) = s$. Note that every deterministic automaton is HD.

For an automaton $\mathcal{A}$, we say that a state q of $\mathcal{A}$ is *HD* if $\mathcal{A}^q$ is HD. We use HD-tNBW and HD-tNCW to denote history deterministic tNBWs and tNCWs, respectively.

Consider a directed graph $G = \langle V, E \rangle$. A *strongly connected set* in G (SCS, for short) is a set $C \subseteq V$ such that for every two vertices $v, v' \in C$, there is a (possibly empty) path from v to v'. A SCS is *maximal* if it is maximal with respect to containment, that is, for every non-empty set $C' \subseteq V \setminus C$, it holds that $C \cup C'$ is not a SCS. The *maximal strongly connected sets* are also termed *strongly connected components* (SCCs, for short).

Consider a tNBW $\mathcal{A} = \langle \Sigma, Q, q_0, \delta, \alpha \rangle$. Let $G_{\mathcal{A}}^{black} = \langle Q, E_{\mathcal{A}}^{black} \rangle$ be the directed graph with $\langle q, q' \rangle \in E_{\mathcal{A}}^{black}$ iff there is a letter $\sigma \in \Sigma$ such that $\langle q, \sigma, q' \rangle \in \Delta \setminus \alpha$. Thus, $E_{\mathcal{A}}^{black}$ is induced by transitions of $\mathcal{A}$ that are not in α. The *black components* of $\mathcal{A}$, denoted by $\mathcal{B}(\mathcal{A})$, are the SCCs of $G_{\mathcal{A}}^{black}$. For a state $q \in Q$, we denote the black component containing q by $black(q)$.

We say that a tNBW $\mathcal{A}$ is *normal* if transitions between different black components are α transitions. Since a run of $\mathcal{A}$ that traverses infinitely many transitions between black components does not get stuck in a black component, and is thus accepting, every tNBW can be made normal by adding to α transitions between black components. Note that normalization can be done in linear time and does not change the set of runs nor their classification to accepting and rejecting runs. In particular, normalization maintains HDness. We thus assume that all tNBWs are normal.

We refer to transitions in $\Delta \setminus \alpha$ as *black transitions* and to transitions in α as *green transitions*. Note that in a normal tNBWs, all transitions between black components are green.[3] For a finite or infinite run $r = \langle r_0, \sigma_1, r_1 \rangle, \langle r_1, \sigma_2, r_2 \rangle, \ldots$, we say that r is black if r is empty or consists of only black transitions. Otherwise, we say that r is green. Thus, r is green if there is $j \geq 0$ such that $\langle r_j, \sigma_j, r_{j+1} \rangle \in \alpha$. Note that $\mathcal{A}$ is normal iff for all states $q \in Q$, black runs from q do not leave $black(q)$. We define the *black language* of q, denoted $L_{black}(\mathcal{A}^q)$, as the set of infinite words w such that there is a black run of $\mathcal{A}^q$ on w.

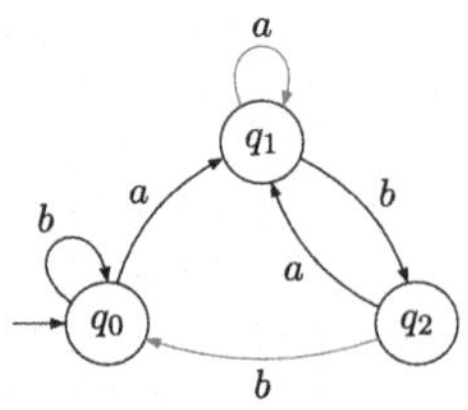

Example 1. The tDBW $\mathcal{A}$ on the right is not normal. Indeed, $\mathcal{B}(\mathcal{A}) = \{\{q_0\}, \{q_1, q_2\}\}$, and the transition $\langle q_0, a, q_1 \rangle$, which connects two black components, is black. Note that the run of $\mathcal{A}$ on the word $w = (ab)^\omega$ does not traverse α, and so $w \in L_{black}(\mathcal{A}^{q_0})$. Normalizing $\mathcal{A}$, the transition $\langle q_0, a, q_1 \rangle$ becomes green. Then, the word w is no longer in $L_{black}(\mathcal{A}^{q_0})$, yet the run on it traverses only one green transition, and is thus rejecting.

3 Observations on HD Strategies

Recall that each HD automaton has an HD strategy that witnesses its HDness. By [4], each HD automaton has a *finite-state* HD strategy, namely one generated by a *finite-state transducer*. In this section we define *super-tight* HD-tNBWs, which are HD-tNBWs whose HDness is witnessed by a strategy with some helpful properties. We then use this strategy in order to complement HD-tNBWs.

3.1 Tight HD Automata

Consider an HD-tNBW $\mathcal{A} = \langle \Sigma, Q, q_0, \delta, \alpha \rangle$. We view an HD strategy for $\mathcal{A}$ as a *(Σ/Q)-transducer*, namely a finite-state machine that given inputs in Σ, generates outputs in Q. Formally, the HD strategy is given by $g = \langle \Sigma, Q, M, m_{init}, \rho, \tau \rangle$, where M is a finite set of states, $m_{init} \in M$ is an initial state, $\rho : M \times \Sigma \to M$ is a transition function that is guarded by the inputs in Σ, and $\tau : M \to Q$ labels each state by a state in Q. We extend ρ to finite words by $\rho(m, \epsilon) = m$ and $\rho(m, u \cdot a) = \rho(\rho(m, u), a)$, for all $u \in \Sigma^*$ and

[3] Note also that there can be green transitions among states that belong to the same black component, for example the transition $\langle q_1, a, q_1 \rangle$ in Example 1 is a green transition inside $black(q_1)$.

$a \in \Sigma$. Then, for $u \in \Sigma^*$, we let $g(u) \in Q$ be the state suggested by g on u. I.e., $g(u) = \tau(\rho(m_{init}, u))$. We refer to the states of g as *memories*, and say that $m \in M$ is a memory of a state $q \in Q$ if $\tau(m) = q$. We assume that all memories in HD strategies are reachable. Recall that g is an HD strategy for $\mathcal{A}$, and so in particular induce legal runs of $\mathcal{A}$. I.e., for all $m, m' \in M$ and $\sigma \in \Sigma$ such that $m' = \rho(m, \sigma)$, we have that $\langle \tau(m), \sigma, \tau(m') \rangle$ is a transition of $\mathcal{A}$.

Recall that the labeling function $\tau : M \to Q$ of g maps each memory in g to its state in $\mathcal{A}$. We extend τ to sets of memories in the expected way. Thus, for $C \subseteq M$, we have that $\tau(C) = \{\tau(m) : m \in C\}$.

Let $\mathcal{A}_g$ be the tDBW obtained by letting $\mathcal{A}$ follow g. Formally, $\mathcal{A}_g = \langle \Sigma, M, m_{init}, \rho, \alpha_g \rangle$, where $\alpha_g = \{\langle m, \sigma, m' \rangle \in M \times \Sigma \times M : m' = \rho(m, \sigma)$ and $\langle \tau(m), \sigma, \tau(m') \rangle \in \alpha\}$. The following observations follow easily from the definitions and the fact we assume that all memories are reachable.

Lemma 1. *[4] Consider an HD-tNBW* $\mathcal{A} = \langle \Sigma, Q, q_0, \delta, \alpha \rangle$ *and let* $g = \langle \Sigma, Q, M, m_{init}, \rho, \tau \rangle$ *be a strategy witnessing its HDness.*

1. *For every memory* $m \in M$ *in* $\mathcal{A}_g$*, we have that* $L(\mathcal{A}_g^m) = L(\mathcal{A}^{\tau(m)})$.
2. *For every two memories* $m, m' \in M$ *in* $\mathcal{A}_g$ *with* $\tau(m) = \tau(m')$*, we have that* $L(\mathcal{A}_g^m) = L(\mathcal{A}_g^{m'})$.

The notion of *tightness* for HD automata and strategies is introduced in [4] for Rabin automata with state-based acceptance. Here, we focus on the special case of Büchi automata and a setting with transition-based acceptance. An HD-tNBW $\mathcal{A}$ is *tight* with respect to an HD strategy g if all the transitions of $\mathcal{A}$ are used by g, and for all memories m and m' with $\tau(m) = \tau(m')$, if $m \neq m'$, then there is a black path from m to m' in $\mathcal{A}_g$. Equivalently, if all memories of a state $q \in Q$ belong to the same black component of $\mathcal{A}_g$. We say that $\mathcal{A}$ is *tight* if it is tight with respect to some HD strategy.

Tightness is achieved by starting with some witness strategy g, and then repeatedly (1) removing from $\mathcal{A}$ transitions that are not used by g and (2) merging memories m and m' of the same state such that there is no black path from m' to m. Intuitively, by removing m and redirecting transitions that go to m into m', we save one memory of $\tau(m)$ and we continue to accept all words in $L(\mathcal{A})$, as between successive traversals of transitions that have been redirected, there is at least one traversal of a transition between different black components. As $\mathcal{A}$ is normal, the latter are green. Formally, we have the following.

Lemma 2. *[4] Every HD-tNBW* $\mathcal{A}$ *can be made tight.*

Proof. Let $g = \langle \Sigma, Q, M, m_{init}, \rho, \tau \rangle$ be a strategy witnessing $\mathcal{A}$'s HDness. To make $\mathcal{A}$ tight with respect to g, we repeatedly apply the following modifications to $\mathcal{A}$ and g:

1. Remove all transitions of $\mathcal{A}$ that are not used by g.
2. If there are memories $m \neq m'$ with $\tau(m) = \tau(m')$ such that m is unreachable from m' in $\mathcal{A}_g$ or m is reachable from m' only via paths that visit α_g, then modify g by removing the memory m and redirecting transitions to m to m' (in particular, if m is the initial memory of g, then we make m' initial).

Before we prove that the modifications result in an equivalent and tight HD-tNBW, we note that they only involve removal of transitions in $\mathcal{A}$. Indeed, the first step clearly only removes transitions, and the second only redirects transitions in the strategy g. In more details, the redirection in the second step is of transitions of the form $\langle m'', \sigma, m\rangle$ to $\langle m'', \sigma, m'\rangle$ for memories m and m' with $\tau(m) = \tau(m') = s$. Accordingly, both transitions follow the transition $\langle \tau(m''), \sigma, s\rangle$ in $\mathcal{A}$, and so the redirection in g follows transitions in $\mathcal{A}$.

We prove that in each iteration, if we start with an HD-NBW $\mathcal{A}$ and a strategy g that witnesses its HDness, the modification results in an HD-tNBW $\mathcal{A}'$ and function g' such that $L(\mathcal{A}') = L(\mathcal{A})$ and g' witnesses the HDness of $\mathcal{A}'$. Then, since the modification of $\mathcal{A}$ into $\mathcal{A}'$ at most removes transitions from $\mathcal{A}$, it follows that $\mathcal{A}'$ is an equivalent HD-tNBW that is embodied in $\mathcal{A}'$.

It is easy to see that the above holds for modifications in the first step. Indeed, since removal of transitions that are not used by g does not restrict the language of $\mathcal{A}$, we have that $L(\mathcal{A}') = L(\mathcal{A})$, and g stays an HD strategy for $\mathcal{A}'$.

We proceed to the modifications in the second step, thus the replacement of g by g'. There, we prove that $L(\mathcal{A}'_{g'}) \subseteq L(\mathcal{A}_g)$, implying that $L(\mathcal{A}') = L(\mathcal{A})$ with g' being an HD strategy for $\mathcal{A}'$.

Let m and m' be memories in $\mathcal{A}_g$ such that g' is obtained from g by removing the memory m and redirecting to m' the transitions to m. Consider an accepting run r_g of $\mathcal{A}_g$ of g on some word $w \in L(\mathcal{A}_g)$. Let $r_{g'} = \langle m'_0, \sigma_1, m'_1\rangle, \langle m'_1, \sigma_2, m'_2\rangle, \ldots$ be the run of $\mathcal{A}_{g'}$ on w. We prove that $r_{g'}$ is accepting.

Let $k \geq 0$ be the number of times that $r_{g'}$ takes redirected transitions to m'. Formally, $k = |\{i \geq 0 : \rho(m'_i, \sigma_{i+1}) = m\}|$. Note that if m is not reachable from m', then once $r_{g'}$ visits m', it never reaches m, and so it never takes a redirected transition. Hence, if $k = \infty$, the reason for the modification in the second step is that m is reachable from m' only via green runs. Therefore, $r_{g'}$ traverses at least one green transition between each pair of successive redirected transitions. It follows that when $k = \infty$, we have that $r_{g'}$ is accepting.

We continue to the case $1 \leq k < \infty$. Let $i \geq 0$ be the last index in $r_{g'}$ in which a redirected transition is taken. Thus, $i \geq 0$ is such that $m'_i = m'$ and for all $j > i$, the j-th transition in $r_{g'}$ is an original transition of g. That is, $\rho(m'_{j-1}, \sigma_j) = m'_j$, for all $j > i$. Accordingly, the suffix of $r_{g'}$ from the i-th position coincides with the run of $\mathcal{A}_g^{m'}$ on the suffix $w[i+1, \infty]$. This, it is left to show that $\mathcal{A}_g^{m'}$ accepts $w[i+1, \infty]$. The strategy g' witnesses that $\tau(m') \in \delta(q_0, w[1, i])$. Since $w \in L(\mathcal{A})$, it follows by the SDness of $\mathcal{A}$ that $w[i+1, \infty] \in L(\mathcal{A}^{\tau(m')})$. Then, since all memories are reachable, Lemma 1 implies that $w[i+1, \infty] \in L(\mathcal{A}_g^{m'})$. Therefore, $\mathcal{A}_g^{m'}$ accepts $w[i+1, \infty]$, and we are done. □

Tight HD-tNBWs have some nice properties. For example, tight HD-tNBWs are SD. To see why, observe that if $\mathcal{A}$ has two transitions $\langle q, \sigma, s_1\rangle, \langle q, \sigma, s_2\rangle \in \Delta$ with $s_1 \not\sim s_2$, then no strategy that witnesses the HDness of $\mathcal{A}$ can use both transitions [12]. Indeed, if $\langle q, \sigma, s_1\rangle$ is used by an HD strategy, then $L(s_2) \subseteq L(s_1)$.

Another advantage of a tight strategy g is that the partition into black components in $\mathcal{A}$ induces a partition to black components in $\mathcal{A}_g$. Formally, we have the following.

Lemma 3. *If $\mathcal{A}$ is tight with respect to g, then for all memories $m, m' \in M$, it holds that $\tau(m') \in black(\tau(m))$ iff $m' \in black(m)$.*

Proof. Consider an HD-tNBW $\mathcal{A} = \langle \Sigma, Q, q_0, \delta, \alpha \rangle$ that is tight with respect to $g = \langle \Sigma, Q, M, m_{init}, \rho, \tau \rangle$. We prove that for all memories $m, m' \in M$, it holds that $\tau(m')$ is reachable via a black run of $\mathcal{A}^{\tau(m)}$ iff m' is reachable via a black run of $\mathcal{A}_g^m$. By the symmetry between m and m' and the definition of black components, it follows that $\tau(m') \in black(\tau(m))$ iff $m' \in black(m)$.

Assume first that m' is reachable via a black run of $\mathcal{A}_g^m$. Consider a black run $r = \langle m_0, \sigma_1, m_1 \rangle, \langle m_2, \sigma, m_3 \rangle, \ldots, \langle m_{k-1}, \sigma_k, m_k \rangle$ of $\mathcal{A}_g^m$ to m', thus $m_0 = m$ and $m_k = m'$. By definition of α_g, we have that $\langle \tau(m_i), \sigma_{i+1}, \tau(m_{i+1}) \rangle \notin \alpha$ for all $0 \leq i \leq k-1$. Hence, the corresponding run mapped by τ is a black run of $\mathcal{A}^{\tau(m)}$ to $\tau(m')$, as required.

Assume now that $\tau(m')$ is reachable via a black run of $\mathcal{A}^{\tau(m)}$. If $\tau(m) = \tau(m')$, then m and m' are both memories of the same state and since g is tight it follows that $m' \in black(m)$. In particular, m' is reachable via a black run in $\mathcal{A}_g^m$ as required. Otherwise, the black run from $\tau(m)$ to $\tau(m')$ is a non empty run. That is, there exists a black run $r = \langle p_0, \sigma_1, p_1 \rangle, \langle p_2, \sigma, p_3 \rangle, \ldots, \langle p_{k-1}, \sigma_k, p_k \rangle$ of $\mathcal{A}^{\tau(m)}$ to $\tau(m')$, thus $p_0 = \tau(m)$ and $p_k = \tau(m')$. Since g is tight, all transitions are used by g, and hence there are memories $m'_0, m_1, m'_1, m_2, m'_2, \ldots m'_{k-1}, m_k \in M$, such that $\langle m'_{i-1}, \sigma_i, m_i \rangle$ is a black transition of $\mathcal{A}_g$ and $\langle \tau(m'_{i-1}), \sigma_i, \tau(m_i) \rangle = \langle p_{i-1}, \sigma_i, p_i \rangle$ for all $1 \leq i \leq k$. Let $m_0 = m$ and $m'_k = m'$. Since for all $0 \leq i \leq k$ the memories m_i and m'_i are both memories of the same state, it follows by tightness that there are words $w_0, w_1, w_2, \ldots, w_k \in \Sigma^*$ such that the run of $\mathcal{A}_g^{m_i}$ over w_i is black and reaches m'_i. It then follows that the run of $\mathcal{A}_g^{m_0}$ on the word $w_0 \cdot \sigma_1 \cdot w_1 \cdot \sigma_2 \cdots \sigma_k \cdot w_k$ is black and reaches m'_k. That is, $m' = m'_k$ is reachable via a black run in $\mathcal{A}_g^m = \mathcal{A}_g^{m_0}$ and we are done. □

An immediate consequence of Lemma 3 is that if $\mathcal{A}$ is normal and tight with respect to g, then $\mathcal{A}_g$ is normal as well. Indeed, if $\langle m, \sigma, m' \rangle$ is black, then $\langle \tau(m), \sigma, \tau(m') \rangle$ is black, and so since $\mathcal{A}$ is normal we have that $\tau(m') \in black(\tau(m))$. Then, by Lemma 3 it follows that $m' \in black(m)$.

3.2 Fast Memories

Consider a normal HD-tNBW $\mathcal{A} = \langle \Sigma, Q, q_0, \delta, \alpha \rangle$ that is tight with respect to a strategy $g = \langle \Sigma, Q, M, m_{init}, \rho, \tau \rangle$. Let $\mathcal{A}_g = \langle \Sigma, M, m_{init}, \rho, \alpha_g \rangle$.

For a memory $m \in M$ and a state $q \in Q$, we say that m *covers* q if for every word $w \in \Sigma^+$, and run r from q on w, if r is green, then so is the run of $\mathcal{A}_g$ from m on w. Thus, m covers q if for every word $w \in \Sigma^+$, runs of $\mathcal{A}^q$ on w cannot traverse an α transition before the run of $\mathcal{A}_g^m$ on w traverses an α_g transition. Intuitively, if m covers q, and $\tau(m)$ is a state equivalent to q, then following the strategy g from m is better than following any other run from $\mathcal{A}^q$, in the sense that the former traverses an α transition faster.

It is not difficult to see that the cover relation is transitive in the sense that if m covers $\tau(m')$ and m' covers q, then m covers q. Formally we have the following.

Lemma 4. *Consider states $q, p \in Q$ and memories $m, m_q \in M$, such that m_q is a memory of q. If m covers q and m_q covers p, then m covers p.*

Proof. Consider a word $w \in \Sigma^+$ for which there exists a green run of $\mathcal{A}$ from p. We need to show that the run of $\mathcal{A}_g$ on w from m is green as well. Since m_q covers p it follows that the run of $\mathcal{A}_g$ on w from m_q is green. So m_q witnesses that there exists a green run of $\mathcal{A}$ on w from q. Then similarly, as m covers q it follows that the run of $\mathcal{A}_g$ on w from m is green and we are done. □

In contrast to the transitivity in Lemma 4, the covering relation needs not be reflexive. Thus, there may be a memory m, a word $w \in \Sigma^+$, and a run of $\mathcal{A}^{\tau(m)}$ on w that traverses a green transition while the run of $\mathcal{A}^m$ on w is black. We say that a memory m is *fast* if m covers $\tau(m)$. We then say that a state $q \in Q$ is *fast* if there exists a fast memory of q. It is not hard to see that the property of being fast is preserved along black paths. Formally, we have the following.

Lemma 5. *For all states $q \in Q$, if q is fast, then all states in black(q) are fast.*

Proof. Consider a fast memory m_q of q. We prove that all the memories in *black*(m_q) are fast. Since, by Lemma 3, each state $q' \in$ *black*(q) has a memory $m_{q'} \in$ *black*(m_q) with $\tau(m_{q'}) = q'$, the claim follows.

Consider a memory $m \in$ *black*(m_q). Let $m_0, \ldots, m_l$ be a path from m_q to m in *black*(m_q), thus $m_0 = m_q$ and $m_l = m$. We prove that m is fast. The proof proceeds by an induction on l. First, if $l = 0$, then $m = m_q$, and we are done. For $l > 0$, consider the black transition $\langle m_{l-1}, \sigma, m_l \rangle$. Let $p_{l-1} = \tau(m_{l-1})$ and $p_l = \tau(m_l)$. By the induction hypothesis, the memory m_{l-1} is fast, and so m_{l-1} covers p_{l-1}. Hence, as $\langle m_{l-1}, \sigma, m_l \rangle$ is black, the transition $\langle p_{l-1}, \sigma, p_l \rangle$ cannot be green, and so it is black.

Assume towards contradiction that m_l is not fast. That is, m_l does not cover p_l. Then, there exists a word $w \in \Sigma^+$ on which there exists a green run r_l from p_l, while the run of $\mathcal{A}_g^{m_l}$ on w is black. Consider the word $\sigma \cdot w$. The sequence $r = \langle p_{l-1}, \sigma, p_l \rangle \cdot r_l$ is a green run of $\mathcal{A}^{p_{l-1}}$ on $\sigma \cdot w$. On the other hand, since $\langle m_{l-1}, \sigma, m_l \rangle$ is black, the run of $\mathcal{A}_g^{m_{l-1}}$ on $\sigma \cdot w$ is black. Thus, the word $\sigma \cdot w$ witnesses that m_{l-1} does not cover p_{l-1}, and we have reached a contradiction to m_{l-1} being fast. □

We now argue that each memory covers an equivalent fast state. We first need the following lemma.

Lemma 6. *Consider a state $q \in Q$. For every memory m_q of q, there is a state s equivalent to q such that m_q covers s.*

Proof. Let $\mathcal{A}_g = \langle \Sigma, M, m_{init}, \rho, \alpha_g \rangle$. Consider a memory m_q of q. Assume towards contradiction that for all states s equivalent to q it holds that m_q does not cover s. We prove that for all $s_0 \sim_{\mathcal{A}} q$ we can define a word $x_1 \in \Sigma^+$ and a state $s_1 \in Q$ equivalent to q, such that the following holds:

1. The run of $\mathcal{A}_g$ on x_1 from m_q is a black cycle. I.e., the run of $\mathcal{A}_g$ on x_1 from m_q does not traverse α_g transitions and is such that $\rho(m_q, x_1) = m_q$.
2. There is a green run r_1 on x_1 from s_0 to some state s_1 equivalent to q.

Note that then, as $q \sim_{\mathcal{A}} s_1$, and by assumption m_q does not cover s_1, we can use the same argument to also define $x_2 \in \Sigma^+$, and $s_2 \in Q$ with similar properties. I.e., the run of $\mathcal{A}_g$ on x_2 from m_q is a black cycle, whereas there is a green run r_2 on x_2 from s_1 that reaches a state s_2 equivalent to q. Repeating this argument inductively, we end up with an infinite word $w = x_1 \cdot x_2 \cdot x_3 \cdots$ such that, on the one hand, the run of $\mathcal{A}_g$ from m_q on w does not traverse α_g, and so $w \notin L(\mathcal{A}_g^{m_q}) = L(\mathcal{A}^q)$, and on the other hand, the concatenation of the runs $r_1, r_2, \ldots$ on the subwords $x_1, x_2, \ldots$, is a run r of $\mathcal{A}^{s_0}$ on w that traverses infinitely many green transitions. Recall that a run is rejecting iff it is eventually black, and so the induced run r is accepting, and we reached a contradicting to the fact that $q \sim_{\mathcal{A}} s_0$. Taking $s_0 = q$ completes the proof.

We define x_1 as follows. As m_q does not cover s_0, there is a word $y_1 \in \Sigma^+$ such that the run of $\mathcal{A}_g$ from m_q on y_1 is black, yet there is a green run of $\mathcal{A}$ from s_0 on y_1 that reaches some state s'_1. Let $m_1 = \rho(m_q, y_1)$. Recall that $\mathcal{A}_g$ is normal, and so $m_1 \in black(m_q)$. Hence, there is a word $z_1 \in \Sigma^*$ such that the run of $\mathcal{A}_g$ from m_1 on z_1 is black and reaches m_q. We define $x_1 = y_1 \cdot z_1$, and $s_1 \in Q$ to be some state reachable from s'_1 with a run on z_1. By the above, the run of $\mathcal{A}_g$ on x_1 from m_q is a black cycle, and there is a green run of $\mathcal{A}$ on x_1 from s_0 to s_1. As $q \sim s_0$, and $q \in \delta(q, x_1)$ and $s_1 \in \delta(s_0, x_1)$, the SDness property implies that s_1 is equivalent to q. □

Since M is finite, the transitivity of the "covers" relation (Lemma 4), together with Lemma 6, imply the following.

Lemma 7. *For every memory m, there is a fast state p_m such that p_m is equivalent to $\tau(m)$ and m covers p_m. In particular, every state in Q has an equivalent fast state in Q.*

Intuitively, Lemma 7 implies that the set of fast states of $\mathcal{A}$ can represent the languages of all the states of $\mathcal{A}$. In Lemma 8 below we show that this representation can be carried on to a small set of fast memories – one for each fast state.

Lemma 8. *Consider an HD strategy g. For every state $q \in Q$, if q is fast, then we can modify g so that it has only a single memory of q.*

Proof. Let $g = \langle \Sigma, Q, M, m_{init}, \rho, \tau \rangle$. Consider a fast state $q \in Q$, and let m_q be a fast memory of q. We define a strategy g' in which m_q is the only memory of q. Essentially, all the transitions of g that lead to other memories of q are directed in g' to m_q. Formally, $g' = \langle \Sigma, Q, M', m'_{init}, \rho', \tau \rangle$, where M' is obtained by removing from M all the memories of q but m_q, the initial state m'_{init} stays m_{init}, unless it is a memory of q that is no longer in M', in which case $m'_{init} = m_q$, and ρ' is such that for all $m \in M$ and $\sigma \in \Sigma$, if $\tau(\rho(m, \sigma)) = q$, then $\rho'(m, \sigma) = m_q$, and otherwise $\rho'(m, \sigma) = \rho(m, \sigma)$.

We prove that $L(\mathcal{A}_g) = L(\mathcal{A}_{g'})$. For that, we first prove that m_q is fast also with respect to g'. That is, for all words $w \in \Sigma^+$, if there is a green run of $\mathcal{A}^q$ on w, then the run of $\mathcal{A}_{g'}^{m_q}$ on w is green. Assume by way of contradiction that m_q is not fast with respect to g' and let $w = \sigma_1 \cdot \sigma_2 \cdots \sigma_k \in \Sigma^+$ be a minimal witness for that. That is, there is a green run of $\mathcal{A}^q$ on w, the run r' of $\mathcal{A}_{g'}^{m_q}$ on w is black, and there is no word shorter than w for which the above hold.

As m_q is fast with respect to g, the run $r = \langle r_0, \sigma_1, r_1 \rangle, \ldots, \langle r_{k-1}, \sigma_k, r_k \rangle$ of $\mathcal{A}_g^{m_q}$ on w is green. Consider the black run $r' = \langle r'_0, \sigma_1, r'_1 \rangle, \ldots, \langle r'_{k-1}, \sigma_k, r'_k \rangle$ of $\mathcal{A}_{g'}^{m_q}$ on w, and consider the minimal index $1 \leq i \leq k$ in which r and r' differ. Thus, for all $1 \leq j < i$, we have that $r_j = r'_j$, $r'_i = m_q$, and $r_i = m'_q$ for some memory m'_q of q with $m'_q \neq m_q$. Note that such an index i must exist. In fact, $i < k$, as otherwise the runs of $\mathcal{A}^q$ on w generated by r and r' are identical, contradicting the fact that the former run is green whereas the latter is black.

We claim that the suffix $w' = \sigma_{i+1} \cdot \sigma_{i+2} \cdots \sigma_k$ of w also witnesses that m_q is not fast with respect to g', contradicting the minimality of w. Since i is minimal and the run r' is black, the fact that the run r is green implies that r traverses a green transition only after its first i transitions, thus when it reads w' from m'_q. Hence, there is a green run of $\mathcal{A}^q$ on w'. On the other hand, the run of $\mathcal{A}_{g'}^{m_q}$ on w' is a suffix of the run r', and is black. If follows that w' is a shorter witness to m_q not being fast, and we have reached a contradiction.

We can now prove that $L(\mathcal{A}_{g'}) = L(\mathcal{A}_g)$. Since $L(\mathcal{A}_{g'}) \subseteq L(\mathcal{A}) = L(\mathcal{A}_g)$, it is enough to prove that $L(\mathcal{A}_g) \subseteq L(\mathcal{A}_{g'})$. Consider a word $w \in L(\mathcal{A}_g)$, and let $r = \langle m_0, \sigma_1, r_m \rangle, \langle m_1, \sigma_2, m_2 \rangle, \ldots$ be the accepting run of $\mathcal{A}_g$ on w. We show that the run $r' = \langle m'_0, \sigma_1, m'_1 \rangle, \langle m'_1, \sigma_2, m'_2 \rangle, \ldots$ of $\mathcal{A}_{g'}$ on w is accepting to. To begin with, as memories of the same state are equivalent in $\mathcal{A}_g$, the SDness property implies that for all $i \geq 0$, we have that $L(\mathcal{A}_g^{m_i}) = L(\mathcal{A}_g^{m'_i})$. We say that an index $i \geq 0$ is a *jumping index* if r' uses the memory m_q at m'_i instead of some other memory of q. Thus, $m'_i = m_q$ whereas $m_i \neq m_q$.

For $i \geq 0$ let $r[i, \infty]$ be the suffix of r from the i-th tranistion. Thus, $r[i, \infty]$ is the run of $\mathcal{A}_g^{m_i}$ on $w[i+1, \infty]$. The run $r'[i, \infty]$ is defined similarly with respect to r'. Assume first that r' has finitely many jumping indices, and let $j \geq 0$ be the last such index. Then, the run $r'[j, \infty]$ coincides with the run of $\mathcal{A}_g^{m'_j}$ on the suffix $w[j+1, \infty]$. By the SDness property, we have that $\mathcal{A}_g^{m_j} \sim \mathcal{A}_g^{m'_j}$. Since $r[j, \infty]$ is an accepting run of $\mathcal{A}_g^{m_j}$ on $w[j+1, \infty]$, we conclude that $w[j+1, \infty] \in \mathcal{A}_g^{m'_j}$, and thus r' is an accepting run on w.

Now, if the run r' has infinitely many jumping indices, we claim that r' traverses infinitely many green transitions, and is thus accepting. Assume towards contradiction that r' traverses only finitely many green transitions. Thus, there is a jumping index $i \geq 0$ such that $r'[i, \infty]$ is a black run on the suffix $w[i+1, \infty]$.

As $L(\mathcal{A}_g^{m_i}) = L(\mathcal{A}_g^{m'_i})$ and $w[i+1,\infty] \in L(\mathcal{A}_g^{m_i})$, there is a green run of $\mathcal{A}_g^{m'_i}$ on $w[i+1,j]$, for some $j \geq i+1$. Then, since i is a jumping index, we have that $m'_i = m_q$. Since m_q is fast with respect to g', then $r'[i,\infty]$ traverses a green transition upon reading $w[i+1,j]$, contradicting the fact that $r'[i,\infty]$ is black. □

4 An Efficient Complementation Construction

In this section, we present our efficient complementation construction. As in [12], our starting point is an HD-tNBW[4] $\mathcal{A}$ and a finite-state HD strategy for $\mathcal{A}$. In [12], the strategy is manipulated until every state of $\mathcal{A}$ has only linearly many "copies" in the obtained HD strategy, implying that the strategy can be viewed as an equivalent deterministic automaton of quadratic size. Here, the "copies" are induced by the fast states $\mathcal{A}$, which, as we argue below, can be identified efficiently. Also, while [12] uses the manipulated strategy only for determinization, we observe that it induces also an HD-tNCW of linear size that complements $\mathcal{A}$, and so we gain both a linear complementation and a quadratic determinization constructions.

Consider an HD-tNBW $\mathcal{A}$. We construct an HD-tNCW that complements $\mathcal{A}$ in two steps: (1) Trimming redundant transitions from $\mathcal{A}$, and (2) Defining a co-Büchi acceptance condition on top of the state space of the trimmed HD-tNBW.

The correctness of the construction follows from the analysis in Sect. 3. Essentially, we show that trimming of redundant transitions makes the identification of fast memories easy, and that the complementing HD-tNCW can be defined on top of the state space of fast states.

Consider an HD-tNBW $\mathcal{A} = \langle \Sigma, Q, q_0, \delta, \alpha \rangle$. We say that $\mathcal{A}$ is *maximally-trimmed* if we cannot remove transitions from $\mathcal{A}$ and obtain an equivalent HD-tNBW. Note that the latter condition means that for every $t \in \Delta$, the automaton obtained from $\mathcal{A}$ by removing t from Δ either rejects some words that $\mathcal{A}$ accepts, or has the same language as $\mathcal{A}$, but is no longer HD. Intuitively, transitions in maximally-trimmed HD-tNBWs are used by every HD strategy.

Theorem 1. *Every HD-tNBW can be made maximally-trimmed in polynomial time.*

Proof. Consider an HD-tNBW $\mathcal{A} = \langle \Sigma, Q, q_0, \delta, \alpha \rangle$. We repeatedly remove transitions from Δ while maintaining $\mathcal{A}$'s language and HDness. Formally, let $t_1, \ldots, t_m$ be an order on the transitions in Δ. Starting with $i = 1$, we check whether the tNBW obtained from $\mathcal{A}$ by removing t_i is an equivalent HD-tNBW. If so, we remove t_i. In any case, we increase i by 1. Since removal of a transition cannot make another transition redundant, the order in which the transitions are

[4] The construction in [12] starts with an HD-NBW, thus one with *state-based* acceptance. Since every HD-NBW can be translated to an equivalent HD-tNBW on the same structure, our setting is more general.

checked is not important.[5] Hence, by definition, once $i = m + 1$, the procedure terminates and we end up with a maximally-trimmed HD-tNBW.

Since checking HDness and language equivalence for HD-tNBWs can be done in polynomial time [2], and since the number of times each transition in Δ is examined is linear in $|\Delta|$, the whole procedure is polynomial in $\mathcal{A}$. Note that normalizing a maximally-trimmed HD-NBW leaves it maximally-trimmed. Indeed, normalization does not change the classification of runs to accepting or rejecting, and so a transition t can be removed after normalization iff there is an HD strategy that does not use t also before normalization. □

Consider an HD-tNBW $\mathcal{A} = \langle \Sigma, Q, q_0, \delta, \alpha \rangle$. We say that a state $q \in Q$ is *deterministic* if for all letters $\sigma \in \Sigma$, it holds that $|\delta(q, \sigma)| = 1$. A set $B \in \mathcal{B}(\mathcal{A})$ is a *black deterministic component* if all states $q \in B$ are deterministic.

Lemma 9. *Consider a maximally trimmed HD-tNBW $\mathcal{A}$. For every state q of $\mathcal{A}$, we have that q is fast iff $black(q)$ is a deterministic black component.*

Proof. First, as detailed in the proof of Lemma 2, making an HD-tNBW tight involves removal of transitions as long as some condition, which is stronger than the one used in maximal trimming, is valid. Hence, all maximally trimmed HD-tNBW are tight, and so the analysis in Sect. 3 applies to them. Let g be the HD-strategy of $\mathcal{A}$.

We first prove that if $black(q)$ is deterministic, then q is fast. Let m be a memory of q. Assume that a word $w \in \Sigma^+$ is such that the run of $\mathcal{A}_g^m$ on w is black. Then, as transitions in $\mathcal{A}_g$ are induced by transitions in $\mathcal{A}$, there exists a black run of $\mathcal{A}^q$ on w. Since $black(q)$ is deterministic, there is a unique run of $\mathcal{A}^q$ on w, and so all runs of $\mathcal{A}^q$ are black. It follows that if $\mathcal{A}^q$ has a green run on $w \in \Sigma^+$, then the run of $\mathcal{A}_g^m$ on w is green. That is, m covers q and since $\tau(m) = q$ we have that q is fast.

We continue to the second direction and prove that if q is fast, then $black(q)$ is deterministic. Consider a fast state q, and assume by way of contradiction that $black(q)$ is not deterministic. There is a state p in $black(q)$ and a letter $\sigma \in \Sigma$ such that $\delta(p, \sigma)$ is not a singleton. By Lemma 5, the state p is fast too. Also, by Lemma 8, we can obtain from g an HD strategy g' in which p has a unique memory m. We claim that the strategy g' witnesses that a maximal-trimming of $\mathcal{A}$ should have made p deterministic. Formally, consider the HD-tNBW $\mathcal{A}'$ obtained from $\mathcal{A}$ by trimming from $\mathcal{A}$ all the σ-successors of p but the one used by m. The strategy g' witnesses that $\mathcal{A}'$ is an HD-tNBW equivalent to $\mathcal{A}$. Thus, $\mathcal{A}$ is not maximally trimmed, and we reached a contradiction. □

We can now describe the complementation construction.

Theorem 2. *Let $\mathcal{A}$ be a maximally-trimmed HD-tNBW. We can construct in polynomial time an HD-tNCW $\mathcal{C}$ such that $L(\mathcal{C}) = \overline{L(\mathcal{A})}$, and the state space of $\mathcal{C}$ is contained in the state space of $\mathcal{A}$.*

[5] Note that different orders may lead to different HD-tNBWs, but they are all maximally trimmed.

Proof. Let $\mathcal{A} = \langle \Sigma, Q, q_0, \delta, \alpha \rangle$. Recall that $\mathcal{A}$ is normal, implying that black transitions from black components stay in the same black component. We define the HD-tNCW $\mathcal{C} = \langle \Sigma, Q', q'_0, \delta', \beta \rangle$ as follows.

- $Q' = \{q \in Q : q$ belongs to a deterministic black component of $\mathcal{A}\}$.
- The state $q'_0 \in Q'$ is chosen such that $q_0 \sim_{\mathcal{A}} q'_0$.
- Since Q' contains only deterministic states of $\mathcal{A}$, we know that for all $q \in Q'$ and $\sigma \in \Sigma$, we have that $\delta(q, \sigma) = \{s\}$, for some state $s \in Q$. The transition function $\delta'(q, \sigma)$ then depends on whether s belongs to Q', and is defined as follows.
  - (original transitions) If $s \in Q'$, then $\delta'(q, \sigma) = \{s\}$. In this case, we have that $\langle q, \sigma, s \rangle \in \beta$ iff $\langle q, \sigma, s \rangle \in \alpha$.
  - (new transitions) If $s \notin Q'$, then $\delta'(q, \sigma) = \{p \in Q' : p \sim_{\mathcal{A}} s\}$. In this case, $\langle q, \sigma, p \rangle \in \beta$ for all $p \in \delta'(q, \sigma)$.

  Thus, if s is in Q', then it is the only σ-successor of q, and the transition to it is in β iff the corresponding transition of $\mathcal{A}$ is in α. If s is not in Q', then the σ-successors of q in $\mathcal{C}$ are all the states in Q' that are $\sim_{\mathcal{A}}$-equivalent to s, and the transition to them is in β.

Since checking language equivalence for HD-tNBWs can be done in polynomial time, so are the checks required for the definition of the new transitions.

We first prove that $\mathcal{C}$ is well defined. By Lemma 9, the set Q' is the set of fast states/ By Lemma 7, for every $q \in Q$ there exists a states $s \in Q'$ equivalent to q. Hence, the initial state q'_0 is well defined, and $\delta'(q, \sigma)$ is non-empty for all $q \in Q'$ and $\sigma \in \Sigma$. Moreover, a transition $\langle p, \sigma, p' \rangle$ of $\mathcal{C}$ belongs to β iff the unique σ transition from p in $\mathcal{A}$ is green and hence belongs to α.

We prove that $\mathcal{C}$ is an HD-tNCW with $L(\mathcal{C}) = \overline{L(\mathcal{A})}$. Note that by the SDness of $\mathcal{A}$, the definition of δ', and the choice of q'_0 to be one that is equivalent to q_0, we have that that for all $u \in \Sigma^*$, all states in $\delta'(q'_0, u)$ are $\sim_{\mathcal{A}}$-equivalent to all states in $\delta(q_0, u)$ (the proof is by an easy induction on $|u|$). In particular, the state $g(u) \in \delta(q_0, u)$, reached by g on u, is equivalent to all states in $\delta(q_0, u) \cup \delta'(q'_0, u)$. So overall, for all $q \in \delta(q_0, u)$ and for all $p \in \delta'(q'_0, u)$ it holds that $q \sim_{\mathcal{A}} g(u) \sim_{\mathcal{A}} p$. We refer to this as the "equivalence property".

We first prove that $L(\mathcal{C}) \subseteq \overline{L(\mathcal{A})}$. Let $r = \langle q'_0, \sigma, q'_1 \rangle, \langle q'_1, \sigma_2, q'_2 \rangle, \ldots$ be an accepting run of $\mathcal{C}$ on some word $w = \sigma_1 \cdot \sigma_2 \cdot \sigma_3 \cdots \in \Sigma^\omega$. Let $i \geq 0$ be such that r does not traverse β after time i. I.e., $\langle q'_j, \sigma_{j+1}, q'_{j+1} \rangle \notin \beta$ for all $j \geq i$. By definition of β this means that all transitions after time i are original black transitions of $\mathcal{A}$, and so the suffix of r from the i-th position is a rejecting run of $\mathcal{A}^{q'_i}$ on the suffix $w[i+1, \infty]$. Let $q = g(w[1, i])$. Then, by the equivalence property, we have $q'_i \sim_{\mathcal{A}} q$ and so $w[i+1, \infty] \notin L(\mathcal{A}^q) = L(\mathcal{A}^{q'_i})$. Thus, by the SDness of $\mathcal{A}$ the latter implies that $w \notin L(\mathcal{A})$ and we are done with the first direction.

We continue and prove that $\mathcal{C}$ is HD and $\overline{L(\mathcal{A}_g)} \subseteq L(\mathcal{C})$. Since $L(\mathcal{A}_g) = L(\mathcal{A})$ this will complete the second direction. We do so by defining a strategy $f : \Sigma^* \to Q'$ such that for all $w \notin L(\mathcal{A}_g)$, we have that $f(w)$ is an accepting run of $\mathcal{C}$ on w. We define f to be such that we always take original transitions of $\mathcal{A}$ as long as possible, and whenever all σ-transitions from $f(u)$ are new transitions, we pick one that is to a fast state covered by $g(u \cdot \sigma)$. Such a state exists by Lemma 7. Formally, for a memory $m \in M$, let p_m be some fast state equivalent to $\tau(m)$ such that m covers p_m. Let $f(\epsilon) = q'_0$, and for all $u \in \Sigma^*$ and $\sigma \in \Sigma$, let $s \in Q$ and $m \in M$ be such that $\delta(f(u), \sigma) = \{s\}$ and $m = \rho(m_{init}, u \cdot \sigma)$, and define $f(u \cdot \sigma)$ as follows:

$$f(u \cdot \sigma) = \begin{cases} s & \text{if } s \in Q' \\ p_m & \text{otherwise} \end{cases}$$

Note that in the case that $s \notin Q'$ then $\delta'(q, \sigma) = \{p \in Q' : p \sim_{\mathcal{A}} s\}$ and $p_m \sim_{\mathcal{A}} \tau(m) = g(u \cdot \sigma)$, and by the equivalence property $g(u \cdot \sigma) \sim_{\mathcal{A}} p$ for all $p \in \delta'(q, \sigma)$. Thus, the fast state p_m indeed belongs to $\delta'(q, \sigma)$, and f is well defined.

Consider a word $w \notin L(\mathcal{A}_g)$ and let r_g be the run of $\mathcal{A}_g$ on w. For $j \geq 0$, let $m_j = \rho(m_{init}, w[1, j])$ be the j-th memory reached by r_g on w. Similarly, let r_f be the run of $\mathcal{C}$ generated by f on w, and, for $j \geq 0$, let $q'_j = f(w[1, j])$ be the j-th fast state reached by r_f. By the equivalence property, it holds that $\tau(m_j) \sim_{\mathcal{A}} q'_j$, for all $j \geq 0$. In particular, $w[j+1, \infty] \notin L(\mathcal{A}_g^{m_j}) = L(\mathcal{A}^{q'_j})$.

Moreover, since $w \notin \mathcal{A}_g$, it holds that r_g is eventually black. That is, there exists an index $i_0 \geq 0$, such that after position i_0, the run r_g traverses no more green transitions. Note that if r_f takes finitely many new transitions, then there exists $j \geq 0$ such that the j-th suffix of r_f coincides with the run of $\mathcal{A}^{q'_j}$ on $w[j+1, \infty]$. Since $w[j+1, \infty] \notin L(\mathcal{A}^{q'_i})$, it follows that r_f also takes finitely many original α transitions. Thus, if r_f takes finitely many new transitions, then r_f is co-Büchi accepting with respect to β, which is the union of new transitions and original α transitions. We conclude the proof by proving that r_f takes at most one new transition after position i_0.

Assume that f takes at least one new transition after position i_0. Let $i_1 > i_0$ be the first position it does so. By the definition of f, we have that $m_{i_1} = \rho(m_{init}, w[1, i_1])$ covers q'_{i_1}. Now, as $i_1 > i_0$, the run of $\mathcal{A}_g^{m_{i_1}}$ on $w[i_1+1, \infty]$ is black, and since m_{i_1} covers q'_{i_1}, all the runs of $\mathcal{A}^{q'_{i_1}}$ on $w[i_1+1, \infty]$ are black too. In fact, since q'_{i_1} belongs to a deterministic black component, it follows that $\mathcal{A}^{q'_{i_1}}$ has a unique run on $w[i_1+1, \infty]$. Since f follows the unique original transitions as long this is possible, the i_1-th suffix of r_f coincides with the run of $\mathcal{A}^{q'_{i_1}}$ on $w[i_1+1, \infty]$, and is hence an original run with no new transitions. □

We conclude this section by a determinization construction that makes use of the complementation construction. The construction is based on a construction from [3,14], which generates a deterministic automaton for a language L from HD automata for L and $\overline{L}$. Here, we use a slight variant, where the automata for both L and $\overline{L}$ use transition-based acceptance conditions.

Theorem 3. *Let $\mathcal{A}$ be an HD-tNBW with n states, and $\mathcal{C}$ be an HD-tNCW for $\overline{L(\mathcal{A})}$ with m states. We can determinize $\mathcal{A}$ in polynomial time, obtaining a tDBW with at most $n \cdot m$ states.*

Proof. Let $\mathcal{A} = \langle \Sigma, Q, q_0, \delta, \alpha \rangle$, and $\mathcal{C} = \langle \Sigma, Q', q'_0, \delta', \beta \rangle$. Consider the tNBW $\mathcal{P}$ obtained by taking the product of $\mathcal{A}$ with $\mathcal{C}$ and requiring runs to satisfy the acceptance condition of $\mathcal{A}$. Thus, $\mathcal{P} = \langle \Sigma, Q \times Q', \langle q_0, q'_0 \rangle, \eta, \alpha \times \Delta' \rangle$, where for every state $\langle q, q' \rangle \in Q \times Q'$ and letter $\sigma \in \Sigma$, we have that $\eta(\langle q, q' \rangle, \sigma) = \delta(q, \sigma) \times \delta'(q', \sigma)$, and a transition $\langle \langle q, q' \rangle, \sigma, \langle p, p' \rangle \rangle$ is accepting iff the corresponding transition $\langle q, \sigma, q' \rangle$ of $\mathcal{A}$ is accepting. Since the transition functions of $\mathcal{A}$ and $\mathcal{C}$ are full, the product of $\mathcal{A}$ with $\mathcal{C}$ is also full and so $L(\mathcal{P}) = L(\mathcal{A})$. We prove that $\mathcal{P}$ can be pruned to an equivalent tDBW.

Consider the following game between Player $\exists$ and Player $\forall$. The game is played on $\mathcal{P}$ and starts from position $\langle q_0, q'_0 \rangle$. When the game is in position $\langle q, q' \rangle \in Q \times Q'$, Player $\forall$ chooses a letter $\sigma \in \Sigma$, and Player $\exists$ chooses a successor position $\langle s, s' \rangle \in \eta(\langle q, q' \rangle, \sigma)$. The outcome ρ of an interaction between the players is an infinite sequence of Σ-labeled transitions of $\mathcal{P}$. That is, $\rho = (\langle q_0, q'_0 \rangle, \sigma_1, \langle q_1, q'_1 \rangle), (\langle q_1, q'_1 \rangle, \sigma_2, \langle q_2, q'_2 \rangle), (\langle q_2, q'_2 \rangle, \sigma_3, \langle q_3, q'_3 \rangle \ldots$. Note that ρ combines a run $r = \langle q_0, \sigma_1, q_1 \rangle, \langle q_1, \sigma_2, q_2 \rangle, \ldots$ of $\mathcal{A}$ with a run $r' = \langle q'_0, \sigma_1, q'_1 \rangle, \langle q'_1, \sigma_2, q'_2 \rangle, \ldots$ of $\mathcal{C}$, both on the word $w = \sigma_1 \cdot \sigma_2 \cdot \sigma_3 \cdots$ obtained by concatenating the letters chosen by Player $\forall$.

The winning condition for Player $\exists$ is that either r satisfies α or r' satisfies β. This winning condition can be specified by a transition-based parity condition with three colors. Thus, $\gamma : (Q \times Q') \times \Sigma \times (Q \times Q') \to \{0, 1, 2\}$ and an outcome ρ is winning for Player $\exists$ if $\max \gamma(\inf(\rho))$ is even.

For all $q, p \in Q$, $q', p' \in Q'$, and $\sigma \in \Sigma$ we define $\gamma(\langle q, q' \rangle, \sigma, \langle p, p' \rangle)$ as follows.

$$\gamma(\langle q, q' \rangle, \sigma, \langle p, p' \rangle) = \begin{cases} 0 \text{ if } \langle q, \sigma, p \rangle \notin \alpha \text{ and } \langle q', \sigma, p' \rangle \notin \beta \\ 1 \text{ if } \langle q, \sigma, p \rangle \notin \alpha \text{ and } \langle q', \sigma, p' \rangle \in \beta \\ 2 \text{ if } \langle q, \sigma, p \rangle \in \alpha \end{cases}$$

Outcomes ρ with $\max \gamma(\inf(\rho)) = 0$ are outcomes in which r' satisfies β, outcomes ρ with $\max \gamma(\inf(\rho)) = 2$ are outcomes in which r that satisfies α, and outcomes ρ with $\max \gamma(\inf(\rho)) = 1$ are such that r' does not satisfy β and r does not satisfy α. Note that r and r' are both runs above the same word in automata that complement each other, and so at most one of them is accepting. Since an outcome ρ is winning for Player $\exists$ if $\max \gamma(\inf(\rho)) \in \{0, 2\}$, the function γ specifies outcomes in which at least one of the runs are accepting.

It is easy to see that following the HD strategies of $\mathcal{A}$ and $\mathcal{C}$ is a winning strategy for Player $\exists$. Indeed, this strategy guarantees that if the word w is in $L(\mathcal{A})$, the run r is accepting in $\mathcal{A}$ and thus satisfies the Büchi condition α, namely infinitely many moves of priority 2 are played. Conversely, if $w \in \overline{L(\mathcal{A})}$, then while the run r is clearly rejecting, the run r' is accepting in $\mathcal{C}$ and thus eventually only moves of priority 0 are taken. Since every word is either in $L(\mathcal{A})$ or in $\overline{L(\mathcal{A})}$, the winning condition for Player $\exists$ is always satisfied.

It is known that parity games admit memoryless strategies and that a memoryless strategy can be computed in polynomial time for parity games with a fixed number of colors [10,11]. Hence, we can compute in polynomial time a memoryless winning strategy for Player $\exists$. Such a strategy maps each position $\langle q, q' \rangle \in Q \times Q'$ and letter $\sigma \in \Sigma$ to a position $\langle s, s' \rangle$, and induces the required pruning of $\mathcal{P}$ into a deterministic automaton. □

Combining Theorems 2 and 3, we have the following.

Corollary 1. *Let $\mathcal{A}$ be an HD-tNBW with n states. There is a tDBW equivalent to $\mathcal{A}$ with at most n^2 states. Moreover, the determinization can be done in polynomial time.*

5 On the Size of HD Strategies

The quadratic determinization construction for HD-tNBWs described in Theorem 1 implies a quadratic upper bound for the size of HD strategies. Indeed, given an HD-tNBW $\mathcal{A}$ with state space Q, the equivalent tDBW has state space $Q \times Q$, where a state $\langle q, q' \rangle$ can be viewed as a memory of the state q. In this section we show that the bound is tight – thus there are HD-tNBWs whose HD strategy must be quadratic.

Theorem 4. *For every $n \geq 1$, there is an HD-tNBW $\mathcal{A}_n$ such that $\mathcal{A}_n$ has $O(n)$ states and every HD strategy for $\mathcal{A}_n$ needs at least n^2 states.*

Proof. Consider $n \geq 3$. Let $[n] = \{1, 2, \ldots, n\}$. We define $\mathcal{A}_n = \langle [n] \cup \{\#\}, Q_n, a_1, \Delta_n, \alpha_n \rangle$ as follows (See $\mathcal{A}_3$ in Fig. 1. For clarity, #-transitions are dashed in the figure and their # label is omitted).

- The state space $Q_n = \{a_i, b_i, c_i, d_i : i \in [n]\}$ is partitioned into four levels, each of size n. We refer to the states $a_1, \ldots, a_n$ as "the a-states" of $\mathcal{A}_n$, they constitute the first level of states, and similarly for b-, c-, and d-states, and the second, third, and fourth level, respectively.
- Transitions are only between adjacent levels, and Δ_n is the union of the following sets of transitions.
  - #-transitions from the first and third levels: $\{\langle a_i, \#, b_j \rangle : j \neq i \in [n]\} \cup \{\langle c_i, \#, d_i \rangle : i \in [n]\}$,
  - transitions from the second level: $\{\langle b_j, i, a_j \rangle : j \neq i \in [n]\} \cup \{\langle b_j, j, c_j \rangle : j \in [n]\}$, and
  - transitions from the fourth level: $\{\langle d_i, j, c_j \rangle : i, j \in [n]\}$.
- The set of accepting transitions (colored green in the figure) is $\alpha_n = \{\langle b_j, j, c_j \rangle : j \in [n]\} \cup \{\langle d_i, i, c_i \rangle : i \in [n]\}$. Thus, transitions from the second to the third level are accepting (note that these transitions are traversed at most once in each run, and so their membership in α is arbitrary), and reading i in state d_i, we go to c_i via an accepting transition.

Let L_n be the set of words w of the form $(\# \cdot [n])^\omega$ such that there is $i \in [n]$ such that the subword $\#i\#i$ appears infinitely often in w. We prove that $L(\mathcal{A}_n) = L_n$.

It is easy to see that $\mathcal{A}_n$ accepts only words of the form $(\# \cdot [n])^\omega$. It is less easy to see that it accepts a word $w \in (\# \cdot [n])^\omega$ iff there is $i \in [n]$ such that the subword $\#i\#i$ appears infinitely often in w. To see this, note that the only nondeterminizm in $\mathcal{A}_n$ is in the #-transitions from the first level. Once a run of $\mathcal{A}_n$ reaches the component that consists of the third and fourth levels, it stays there forever, it is deterministic, and it accepts only words in L_n. Thus, if a word is accepted, it is in L_n.

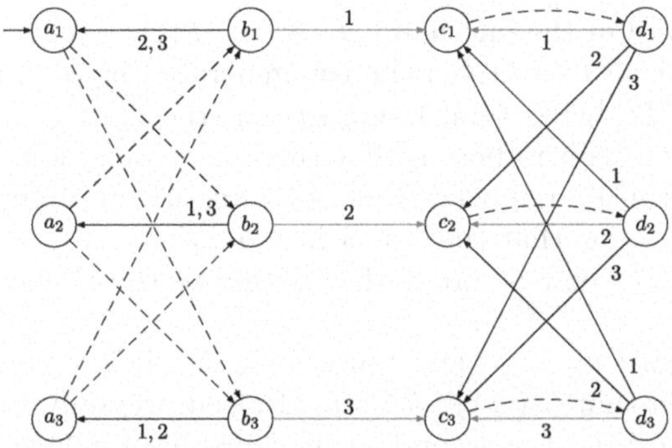

Fig. 1. The HD-tNBW $\mathcal{A}_3$.

For the other direction, consider a word $w \in L_n$. Recall that the tNBW is deterministic in the limit, and its deterministic component recognizes L_n. So it will be enough to show that there is a run on w that enters the deterministic levels. In fact, we will prove that there is a strategy to generates a run that enters the deterministic levels for all $w \in L_n$. Assume by induction that we have generated on a prefix $u \in (\# \cdot [n])^*$ that ends with $i \in [k]$, a run that reached some a-state a_j. Thus by the time we finished reading u we have yet fulfilled our goal to reach a deterministic c-state. By definition of δ, if we go back from the b level to the a level with an i-transition, then it is to an a-state different from a_i. Thus $i \neq j$. Now if we move from a_j upon reading $\#$ to b_i, then in the next step we'll succeed and move to the third level iff the next letter will be i. Notice that if in the limit we always fail, then it means that we have never seen even a single good pattern in $\{\#k\#k : k \in [n]\}$. Since $w \in L_n$, it follows that at least one such pattern exists, and so after a finite amount of time the strategy enters the deterministic levels and from there the only deterministic run must be accepting.

The strategy described above requires each a-state to have $n-1$ memories – one for each letter with which the state was reached. Accordingly, as every a-state can be reached with $(n-1)$ letters, a finite-state transducer that models this strategy needs at least $n(n-1)$ memories for the first level, and then at least one memory for each of the other $3n$ states, so overall at least n^2+2n memories. We now prove that this is optimal. That is, that a minimal HD strategy for $\mathcal{A}_n$ needs at least n^2+2n memories. Note that this does not imply that every tDBW for L_n needs $\Omega(n^2)$ states. In particular, the deterministic component that consists of the third and fourth levels of $\mathcal{A}_n$ can serve as a linear tDBW for L_n.

Consider a minimal HD strategy $g = \langle [n] \cup \{\#\}, M, m_{init}, \rho, \tau \rangle$ for $\mathcal{A}_n$. We prove that each a-state a_i has at least $n-1$ memories in M, and hence by the same analysis as above g has at least n^2+2n memories. Observe that if g has less than $n-1$ memories of some a-state a_i, then at least one of the non-deterministic $\#$-transitions from a_i are not used, and hence $\mathcal{A}_n$ is not maximally trimmed. Indeed, Let $\mathcal{A}'_n$ be a tNBW obtained from $\mathcal{A}_n$ by trimming out transitions unused by g. On the one hand, $L(\mathcal{A}'_n) \subseteq L(\mathcal{A}_n)$, and on the other hand g witnesses that for all $w \in L(\mathcal{A}_n)$ the run generated by g on w is an accepting run also in $\mathcal{A}'_n$. So $L(\mathcal{A}_n) \subseteq L(\mathcal{A}'_n)$ and g is an HD strategy for $\mathcal{A}'_n$ as well.

Assume by way of contradiction that there is a transition #-transition from some a-state that can be removed from $\mathcal{A}_n$ while maintaining its language and HDness. W.l.o.g. assume that the transition $\langle a_1, \#, b_2 \rangle$ can be removed, and let $h : ([n] \cup \{\#\})^* \to Q_n$ be a strategy that witnesses the HDness of the obtained tNBW.

Consider the word $w_1 = (\#1)^\omega$. Since $w_1 \in L_n$, it is accepted, and so there must be $i_1 \geq 0$ such that $h((\#1)^{i_1}\#) = b_1$. Indeed, the only way for a run to be accepted is to move from the second to the third level, which can be done only by reading the letter 1 from the state b_1. Let $x_1 = (\#1)^{i_1}\#2\#2$ and consider now the word $w_2 = x_1 \cdot (\#1)^\omega$. When a run of $\mathcal{A}_n$ on w_2 follows h, it reads the first occurrence of the letter 2 from state b_1. Hence, the run continues to the state a_1, and after reading the next #, it continues to a state b_j for some $j \neq 2$. Indeed, the transition $\langle a_1, \#, b_2 \rangle$ does not exist. Hence, upon reading the next 2, it moves to the state a_j. As $w_2 \in L_n$, continuing to follow h eventually leads the run again to b_1. That is, there is $i_2 \geq 0$ such that $h(x_1 \cdot (\#1)^{i_2}\#) = b_1$. We let $x_2 = x_1 \cdot (\#1)^{i_2}\#2\#2$ and note again that when h reads x_2, it reaches a state b_j for some $j \neq 2$. We can now continue and define an infinite sequence of words $x_1, x_2, x_3, \ldots$, where each x_i is a proper prefix of x_{i+1} and contains at least i occurrences of the subword #2#2. In addition, for all $i \geq 1$ the run of $\mathcal{A}_n$ on x_i, when following h, never leaves the first and second levels. Thus, in the limit, we get a word with infinitely many occurrences of #2#2 for which the run of $\mathcal{A}_n$ generated by h is rejecting, and we reach a contradiction. □

Note that the automaton $\mathcal{A}_n$ used in the proof of Theorem 4 is *deterministic in the limit*: all accepting runs eventually reach a deterministic component. On the one hand, this makes the lower bound stronger, as it shows that the quadratic lower bound applies even for HD-tNBWs of a restricted class. In particular, note that the quadratic strategy is needed in order to make a single successful guess, which has the flavor of weak HD-tNBWs, which are known to be DBP [4]. On the other hand, it makes the result weaker, as by making one of the c-states initial, we get an equivalent tDBW. The latter concern can be easily addressed, by making the automaton $\mathcal{A}_n$ a bit more complicated by directing the accepting transitions from the fourth level back to the first level, namely defining $\delta(d_i, i) = a_i$ rather than $\delta(d_i, i) = c_i$. It is not hard to see that all the considerations made above for $\mathcal{A}_n$ apply also for this variant (which is the extension to n letters of the HD-NBW used in [3] in order to show than HD-NBWs need not be DBP).

References

1. Aminof, B., Kupferman, O., Lampert, R.: Reasoning about online algorithms with weighted automata. In: Proceedings 20th ACM-SIAM Symposium on Discrete Algorithms, pp. 835–844 (2010)

2. Bagnol, M., Kuperberg, D.: Büchi good-for-games automata are efficiently recognizable. In: Proceedings 38th Conference on Foundations of Software Technology and Theoretical Computer Science. LIPIcs, vol. 122, pp. 16:1–16:14. Schloss Dagstuhl - Leibniz-Zentrum fuer Informatik (2018)
3. Boker, U., Kuperberg, D., Kupferman, O., Skrzypczak, M.: Nondeterminism in the presence of a diverse or unknown future. In: Fomin, F.V., Freivalds, R., Kwiatkowska, M., Peleg, D. (eds.) ICALP 2013. LNCS, vol. 7966, pp. 89–100. Springer, Heidelberg (2013). https://doi.org/10.1007/978-3-642-39212-2_11
4. Boker, U., Kupferman, O., Skrzypczak, M.: How deterministic are Good-For-Games automata? In: Proceedings 37th Conference on Foundations of Software Technology and Theoretical Computer Science, vol. 93, pp. 18:1–18:14. Leibniz International Proceedings in Informatics (LIPIcs) (2017)
5. Boker, U., Lehtinen, K.: When a little nondeterminism goes a long way: an introduction to history-determinism. ACM SIGLOG News **10**(1), 177–196 (2023)
6. Büchi, J.R.: On a decision method in restricted second order arithmetic. In: Proceedings International Congress on Logic, Method, and Philosophy of Science, 1960, pp. 1–12. Stanford University Press (1962)
7. Colcombet, T.: The theory of stabilisation monoids and regular cost functions. In: Albers, S., Marchetti-Spaccamela, A., Matias, Y., Nikoletseas, S., Thomas, W. (eds.) ICALP 2009. LNCS, vol. 5556, pp. 139–150. Springer, Heidelberg (2009). https://doi.org/10.1007/978-3-642-02930-1_12
8. Esparza, J., Kretínský, J., Sickert, S.: One theorem to rule them all: a unified translation of LTL into ω-automata. In: Proceedings 33rd IEEE Symposium on Logic in Computer Science, pp. 384–393 (2018)
9. Henzinger, T.A., Piterman, N.: Solving games without determinization. In: Ésik, Z. (ed.) CSL 2006. LNCS, vol. 4207, pp. 395–410. Springer, Heidelberg (2006). https://doi.org/10.1007/11874683_26
10. Jutla, C.S.: Determinization and memoryless winning strategies. Inf. Comput. **133**(2), 117–134 (1997)
11. Klarlund, N.: Progress measures, immediate determinacy, and a subset construction for tree automata. In: Proceedings 7th IEEE Symposium on Logic in Computer Science, pp. 382–393. IEEE Computer Society (1992)
12. Kuperberg, D., Skrzypczak, M.: On determinisation of good-for-games automata. In: Proceedings 42nd International Colloquium on Automata, Languages, and Programming, pp. 299–310 (2015)
13. Kupferman, O.: Automata theory and model checking. In: Handbook of Model Checking, pp. 107–151. Springer (2018)
14. Kupferman, O.: Using the past for resolving the future. Front. Comput. Sci. **4** (2022)
15. Kupferman, O., Safra, S., Vardi, M.Y.: Relating word and tree automata. Ann. Pure Appl. Logic **138**(1–3), 126–146 (2006)
16. Kupferman, O., Vardi, M.Y.: Safraless decision procedures. In: Proceedings 46th IEEE Symposium on Foundations of Computer Science, pp. 531–540 (2005)
17. Landweber, L.H.: Decision problems for ω-automata. Math. Syst. Theory **3**, 376–384 (1969)
18. Niwinski, D., Walukiewicz, I.: Relating hierarchies of word and tree automata. In: Proceedings 15th Symposium on Theoretical Aspects of Computer Science. LNCS, vol. 1373. Springer (1998)
19. Rabin, M.O., Scott, D.: Finite automata and their decision problems. IBM J. Res. Dev. **3**, 115–125 (1959)

20. Safra, S.: On the complexity of ω-automata. In: Proceedings 29th IEEE Symposium on Foundations of Computer Science, pp. 319–327 (1988)
21. Vardi, M.Y., Wolper, P.: Reasoning about infinite computations. Inf. Comput. **115**(1), 1–37 (1994)

A Decremental Algorithm for Fair Büchi Games

Irmak Sağlam(✉), Anne-Kathrin Schmuck, and Munko Tsyrempilon

Max Planck Institute for Software Systems (MPI-SWS), Kaiserslautern, Germany
{isaglam,akschmuck}@mpi-sws.org

Abstract. This paper provides the first decremental algorithm for fair Büchi games. It efficiently recalculates the winning region under the deletion of *live* edges in the underlying game graph.

Our algorithm addresses the unique challenges posed by fair Büchi games such as exponential-memory strategies and the non-monotonicity of the winning region under edge deletion. This prevents a straight forward extension of dynamic algorithms from (normal) Büchi games, in particular Jurdziński's small progress measures, on which these algorithms rely.

The main contribution of this paper is the definition of a specialized (one-digit) progress measure for fair Büchi games and its correctness proof. We further derive a decremental algorithm for fair Büchi games using a fixed-point calculation entailed by this progress measure. We show that the (non-optimized) prototype implementation of our decremental algorithm outperforms an (optimized) fair Büchi game solver on a large class of benchmarks. By this, our work not only expands the scope of dynamic algorithms but also underscores the benefit of tailored solutions for specific game structures such as fair Büchi games.

Keywords: games on graphs · fairness · two-player games · Büchi games · decremental algorithms · dynamic algorithms

1 Introduction

Büchi games are extensively used as modeling abstractions in the context of correct-by-construction synthesis of reactive software or hardware. In particular, two player games on graphs have been extensively used in the context of cyber-physical system design [4,26]. Within this context, the class of *strong* ***transition*** *fairness constrains* [2,12,22] has recently gained some interest due to their computational tractability. While *strong fairness* encoded by a Streett condition necessarily incurs a high additional cost in synthesis [11], strong transition fairness can be handled almost "for free" [3,13,24]. Intuitively, strong transition fairness constrains limit strong fairness to individual transitions, allowing them

I. Sağlam and A.-K. Schmuck—Supported by the DFG project SCHM 3541/1-1.

S. Akshay et al. (Eds.): ATVA 2024, LNCS 15054, pp. 89–109, 2025.
https://doi.org/10.1007/978-3-031-78709-6_5

to be handled mostly locally during synthesis. Büchi games enriched with strong transition fairness constrains are called *fair Büchi games*.

Despite their limited expressive power, transition fairness constrains naturally arise in resource management [5], in abstractions of continuous-time physical processes for planning [1,7–9,21,23] and controller synthesis [17,20,28], which makes them interesting to study. However, in many such scenarios, it is realistic to assume that the underlying game graph is subject to addition and deletion of edges (e.g. due to an agent discovering its environment or enriching/restricting its own actuation capabilities). Having posed an initial question on the graph such as reachability, or Büchi; ideally we want to recover the answer to the same question on the altered graph efficiently, without solving the new game from scratch. Algorithms that achieve this are called *dynamic*. A dynamic algorithm is called *decremental* if the altered graph is obtained from the original graph by ommiting edges; it is called *incremental* if it is obtained by adding edges.

In this work, we give the first *decremental algorithm* for *fair Büchi games*. In particular, we restrict our attention to the special scenario where fair environment edges – edges which are (i) owned by the (adversarial) environment player, and (ii) are equipped with strong transition fairness constrains – are removed from the graph. This scenario is relevant in the context of logical controller synthesis for non-linear stochastic dynamical systems. This insight goes back to a chain of work by Mallik and others [3,16–18], who show that such dynamical systems can be abstracted into two-player games with fairness constrains only acting on the environment player. Here, the game graph of an abstract two-player game (between *system* and *environment*) is obtained from a discretization of the underlying dynamics. *Environment* owns fair outgoing edges, which model the non-determinism and uncertainty introduced by the (conservative) abstraction process. The number of fair edges is determined by the support of the noise acting on the dynamics. This uncertainty is typically reduced when the system operates, as more detailed information about the system dynamics can be captured, directly leading to the removal of fair environment transitions in the graph. A decremental algorithm for *fair games* would allow to efficiently update the logical controller during exploration.

Motivated by this application, we introduce a decremental algorithm for *fair Büchi games*. Decremental algorithms go back to the graph-theoretic work by Even and Shiloach in 1981 [25] where the reachability problem on undirected graphs under one-by-one deletion of edges is studied. More recently, Chatterjee and Henzinger gave dynamic algorithms for Büchi games [6]. Their work generalizes the Even-Shiloach algorithm to infinite games while giving (dual) fixed-point based proofs using Jurdziński's small progress measures [15].

While our decremental algorithm for *fair* Büchi games is based on the same insight, the progress measure for *fair* Büchi games does not follow directly from [15] as the environment-player strategies are not memoryless in such games.

The main contribution of this paper is the definition of a (one-digit) progress measure for fair Büchi games and its correctness proof. This enables a decremental algorithm for fair Büchi games using a fixed-point calculation entailed by this progress measure. This algorithm is more involved than the one for (normal) Büchi games in [6] as we cannot rely on an intrinsic monotonicity of the problem w.r.t. the deletion of edges. We show on a set of practically motivated benchmarks, in 80% of all instances the (non-optimized) prototype implementation of our decremental algorithm outperforms the optimized BDD-based symbolic algorithm FairSyn [16] which solves the changed game from scratch.

Conceptually, this paper shows that small progress measure based dynamic algorithms can be derived for synthesis problems where strategies are *not memoryless* and whose dynamic recomputation cannot rely on an *intrinsic monotonicity* of the problem. We believe that this paves the way to a larger class of efficient dynamic algorithms for challenging synthesis problems.

2 A Decremental Algorithm for Büchi Games

This section recalls all necessary notation from (normal) Büchi games in Subsect. 2.1 and describes their decremental algorithm [6] in Subsect. 2.3 which is based on Jurdziński's small progress measures for Parity games [15], specialized to Büchi games in Subsect. 2.2.

2.1 Preliminaries

We use $\mathbb{N}$ to denote the set of natural numbers including zero. Let Σ be a finite set. Then Σ^* and Σ^ω denote the sets of finite and infinite words over Σ.

Game Graphs. A *game graph* is a tuple $G = (V, V_0, V_1, E)$ where (V, E) is a finite directed graph with *edges* E and *vertices* V partitioned into Player 0 and Player 1 vertices, V_0 and V_1, respectively. For $v \in V$, $E(v)$ denotes its successor set $\{w \mid (v, w) \in E\}$. Without loss of generality, we can assume that all vertices in V have at least one outgoing edge. A *play* originating at a vertex v_0 is an infinite sequence of vertices $\pi = v_0v_1 \ldots \in V^\omega$ with $v_{i+1} \in E(v_i)$ for all $i \in \mathbb{N}$. We denote the restriction of a game graph G to a subset $V' \subseteq V$ as $G|_{V'} = (V \cap V', V_0 \cap V', V_1 \cap V', E \cap V' \times V')$.

LTL Winning Conditions. Given a game graph G, we consider winning conditions specified using a formula Φ in *linear temporal logic* (LTL) over the vertex set V, that is, we consider LTL formulas whose atomic propositions are sets of vertices. In this case the set of desired infinite plays is given by the semantics of Φ which is an ω-regular language $\mathcal{L}(\Phi) \subseteq V^\omega$. The standard definitions of ω-regular languages and LTL are omitted for brevity and can be found in standard textbooks [2]. A game $\mathcal{G} = \langle G, \Phi \rangle$ is a game graph G under the winning condition Φ. A play π is winning for Player 0 in $\langle G, \Phi \rangle$ if $\pi \in \mathcal{L}(\Phi)$, i.e. $\pi \models \Phi$. We denote the restriction of a game $\mathcal{G}$ to a subset $V' \subseteq V$ as $\mathcal{G}|_{V'} = \langle G|_{V'}, \Phi \rangle$.

Strategies. A *strategy* for Player j over the game graph G is a function $\mu^j : V^* \cdot V_j \to V$ with the constraint that for all $u \cdot v \in V^* \cdot V_j$ it holds that $\mu^j(u \cdot v) \in E(v)$. A play $\pi = v_0v_1 \ldots \in V^\omega$ is compliant with μ^j if for all $i \in \mathbb{N}$ holds that $v_i \in V_j$ implies $v_{i+1} = \mu^j(v_0 \ldots v_i)$. A strategy μ^j is winning for

Player j from a subset V' of vertices of the game $\langle G, \Phi \rangle$ if all plays π in G that start at a vertex in V' and are compliant with μ^j are winning for the player w.r.t. Φ. The winning region of Player j is the maximal set $V' \subseteq V$ that is winning for Player j, which is denoted by $\mathsf{Win}_j(G)$, or simply Win_j whenever G is clear from the context. By Borel determinacy theorem [19], any game defined by LTL winning conditions is determined. That is, V is a disjoint union of the winning regions, $V = \mathsf{Win}_0 \uplus \mathsf{Win}_1$. A strategy μ is called *positional* iff for all $w_1, w_2 \in V^*$, $\mu(w_1 \cdot v) = \mu(w_2 \cdot v)$. In this case we denote the unique outgoing edge μ assigns a vertex v as $\mu(v)$.

Büchi Games. Büchi games are particular games over a game graph G where the winning condition is given by a subset of vertices called *Büchi vertices.* Formally, a Büchi game is a tuple $\mathcal{G} = \langle V, V_0, V_1, E, \chi \rangle$, where (V, V_0, V_1, E) is a game graph and $\chi \subseteq V$ are Büchi vertices. A play $\pi = v_0 v_1 \ldots$ is winning for Player 0 iff $\chi \cap \inf(\pi) \neq \emptyset$, where $\inf(\pi)$ is the set of vertices visited infinitely often in π. Otherwise the play is winning for Player 1.

Winning Strategies in Büchi Games. Büchi games are determined, as their winning conditions can easily be expressed as LTL conditions. Moreover, it is well-known that Büchi games are positionally determined, meaning both players have positional winning strategies from their respective winning regions [10].

2.2 Valid-for-Büchi Progress Measures

Small progress measures have been introduced by Jurdziński in [15] as a space-efficient fixed-point based solution algorithm for parity games. Here we give its restriction to Büchi games and briefly explain its function.

Progress Measures. Given a Büchi game $\mathcal{G} = \langle V, V_0, V_1, E, \chi \rangle$, with $|V| = n$, a *progress measure* is a function $\rho : V \to [1, n-1] \cup \{\top\}$ with the convention that $\top > i$ for all $i \in [1, n-1]$, $\top \geq n$, $\top + 1 = \top$ and $\top \geq \top$. Intuitively, progress measures are used to compute the winning region of a Büchi game by locally updating the measure of each vertex using a *lifting function* until the least fixed-point is reached. The least fixed-point progress measure assigns each vertex in V an integer if it is in the winning region of Player 0 and $\top$ if it is in the winning region of Player 1. Formally, a progress measure ρ is called a *valid-for-Büchi progress measure* if for all $v \in V$, the following holds

$$\rho(v) \begin{cases} \geq \min_{(v,w) \in E} \rho(w) + 1, & v \in V_0 \setminus \chi; \\ \geq \max_{(v,w) \in E} \rho(w) + 1, & v \in V_1 \setminus \chi; \\ = \top, & v \in V_0 \cap \chi,\ \forall (v,w) \in E\,.\, \rho(w) = \top; \\ = 0, & v \in V_0 \cap \chi,\ \exists (v,w) \in E \text{s.t.} \rho(w) \neq \top; \\ = \top, & v \in V_1 \cap \chi,\ \exists (v,w) \in E \text{ s.t. } \rho(w) = \top; \\ = 0, & v \in V_1 \cap \chi,\ \forall (v,w) \in E\,.\, \rho(w) \neq \top. \end{cases}$$

The operators $\geq$ and $\leq$ are defined on a progress measure ρ with respect to point-wise comparison. That is, for $\bowtie \in \{\leq, \geq\}$; $\rho \bowtie \rho'$ iff for all $v \in V$, $\rho(v) \bowtie \rho'(v)$.

Lifting Function. With this, we can define the *lifting function* on $\mathcal{G}$, which incrementally updates the progress measure ρ for individual vertices $v \in V$. Intuitively, each update minimally increases the value of v to ensure ρs validity on v. Formally, the lifting function $\mathsf{Lift}^{\mathcal{G}}$ receives a progress measure ρ and a vertex v, and outputs a new progress measure $\rho' := \mathsf{Lift}^{\mathcal{G}}(\rho, v)$ that agrees with ρ on all vertices except v. For $\rho'(v)$, one of the following holds:

- $v \in V_0 \setminus \chi$: $\rho'(v) := \min_{(v,w)\in E} \rho(w) + 1$ if $\rho'(v) < n$, and $\rho'(v) := \top$ otherwise;
- $v \in V_1 \setminus \chi$: $\rho'(v) := \max_{(v,w)\in E} \rho(w) + 1$ if $\rho'(v) < n$, and $\rho'(v) := \top$ otherwise;
- $v \in V_0 \cap \chi$: $\rho'(v) := \top$ if $\forall (v,w) \in E \,.\, \rho(w) = \top$, and $\rho'(v) := 0$ otherwise;
- $v \in V_1 \cap \chi$: $\rho'(v) := \top$ if $\exists (v,w) \in E \,.\, \rho(w) = \top$, and $\rho'(v) = 0$ otherwise.

In order to comprehend why the lifting function can be effectively utilized in a fixed-point procedure that terminates with desired properties, we must first recognize that the progress measures on a finite set V with the least element $\rho_0 : V \to \{0\}$ and the greatest element $\rho_\top : V \to \{\top\}$ constitute a complete (finite) lattice under the pointwise comparison relation $\bowtie$. Then the Knaster-Tarski theorem [27] confirms that any monotonic function operating on this complete lattice possesses a least fixed-point. Moreover, if the lattice is finite, this least fixed-point can be obtained by iterative application of a monotonic function, starting from the lattice's least element (ρ_0), until the fixed-point is reached in a finite number of steps. With this understanding, the effective properties of the lifting function are derived from its monotonicity, formalized next.

Lemma 1 ([15]). *Let $\mathcal{G}$ be a Büchi game. Then the function $\mathsf{Lift}^{\mathcal{G}}$ is monotonic, i.e., $\mathsf{Lift}^{\mathcal{G}}(\rho, v) \leq \mathsf{Lift}^{\mathcal{G}}(\rho', v)$ for all $v \in V$ whenever $\rho \leq \rho'$.*

We call the algorithm which takes a lifting function $\mathsf{Lift}^{\mathcal{G}}$ and a progress measure ρ (s.t. $\rho_0 \leq \rho \leq \rho^*$) as input, and returns the least fixed-point ρ^* of $\mathsf{Lift}^{\mathcal{G}}$ by $\textsc{IterativeLift}(\mathsf{Lift}^{\mathcal{G}}, \rho)$. If $\mathsf{Lift}^{\mathcal{G}}$ is monotonic, it indeed does not matter in which order vertices are lifted by $\mathsf{Lift}^{\mathcal{G}}$ (one-at-a-time) as long as every vertex is eventually lifted until its progress measure value does not change anymore. The fact that Büchi games can be solved by $\textsc{IterativeLift}$ is established next.

Theorem 1 ([15]). *Let $\mathcal{G}$ be a Büchi game and ρ^* be the least fixed-point of the function $\mathsf{Lift}^{\mathcal{G}}$. Then ρ^* is a valid-for-Büchi progress measure and a vertex v is in Win_0 if and only if $\rho^*(v) \in [1, n-1]$.*

The proof of Theorem 1 in [15] (when restricted to the Büchi case) essentially shows that on the vertex subset $V_{\mathbb{N}} = \{v \in V \mid \rho^*(v) \neq \top\} \subseteq V$, there exists a positional Player 0 strategy σ such that all loops in plays compliant with σ contain a Büchi vertex. This implies that starting from any vertex in $V_{\mathbb{N}}$, Player 0 can win the game $\mathcal{G}$ by following the strategy σ.

We will see that this argument does not to work for proving a similar result on fair Büchi games (Theorem 2) as winning Player 0 strategy may contain cycles *without* Büchi vertices in *fair* Büchi games, as discussed in Sect. 4.

Algorithm 1. DecrementalBuechi

Require: $\mathcal{G} = \langle V, V_0, V_1, E, \chi \rangle$ a Büchi game, $(u, u') \in E_0$, ρ^* least fixed-point of $\mathsf{Lift}^{\mathcal{G}}$

function DecrementalBuechi($\mathcal{G}, \rho^*, (u, u')$)

  $\mathcal{G}' \leftarrow \langle V, V_0, V_1, E \setminus \{(u, u')\}, \chi \rangle$

  $\rho'^* \leftarrow$IterativeLift($\mathsf{Lift}^{\mathcal{G}'}, \rho^*$)

  return ρ'^*

Ensure: ρ'^* is the least fixed-point of $\mathsf{Lift}^{\mathcal{G}'}$.

2.3 Decremental Solution Algorithms

A *decremental (solution) algorithm* for Büchi games allows for efficient "updating" of the winning regions after they have been computed, should the underlying game graph be altered by removal of edges. Progress measures are particularly well-suited for dynamic adaptation, as the nature of their update rules, encoded into the lifting function, are inherently local. In addition, Theorem 1 implies that least fixed-point ρ^* of the lifting function $\mathsf{Lift}^{\mathcal{G}}$ allows to directly extract the winning regions $\mathsf{Win}_0 = V|_{\mathbb{N}} = \{v \in V \mid \rho^*(v) \neq \top\}$ and $\mathsf{Win}_1 = V|_{\top} = \{v \in V \mid \rho^*(v) = \top\}$. Therefore, the decremental algorithm DecrementalBuechi taken from [6] and given as pseudo-code in Algorithm 1, reduces to "updating" the least fixed-point ρ^* after edge removal.

In order to ensure that $\rho'^* :=$ DecrementalBuechi($\mathcal{G}, \rho^*, (u, u')$) is indeed the least fixed-point of $\mathsf{Lift}^{\mathcal{G}'}$, it needs to hold that $\rho^* \leq \rho'^*$. Only then, the warm-starting of the function IterativeLift with ρ^* instead of ρ_0 indeed results in the least fixed-point of $\mathsf{Lift}^{\mathcal{G}'}$. This is achieved by restricting edge removals to Player 0 edges, i.e. requiring $(u, u') \in E_0$. This restriction intuitively grants Player 0 less flexibility in choosing its next move in $\mathcal{G}'$ compared to $\mathcal{G}$. Consequently, any vertex that belongs to the winning region of Player 0 in $\mathcal{G}'$ also belongs to the winning region in $\mathcal{G}$. This reflects the principle that vertex values can only move upward (closer to $\top$, and thus to Win_1) when transitioning from ρ^* to ρ'^*.

We will see that the condition $\rho^* \leq \rho'^*$ does not hold in *fair* Büchi games, leading to a modified algorithm DecrementalFairBuechi (Algorithm 2).

3 Fair Büchi Games

Before introducing progress measures for fair Büchi games in Sect. 4 and a decremental algorithm in Sect. 5, this section formalizes *fair Büchi games* along with all necessary notation. This section is based on [3,24] where odd-fair parity games are studied. Fair Büchi games are odd-fair parity games over two colors.

Fair Büchi Games. A *fair Büchi game* $\mathcal{F}$ is a tuple $(\mathcal{G}, E^{\ell})$, where $\mathcal{G} = \langle V, V_0, V_1, E, \chi \rangle$ is a Büchi game, $E^{\ell} \subseteq E \cap (V_1 \times V)$ is a subset of edges, called *live edges* which originate from Player 1 vertices and $V^{\ell} \subseteq V_1$, the domain of the relation E^{ℓ}, is called *live vertices*. The live edges induce a *strong transition fairness constraint* – whenever a live vertex v is visited infinitely often, every outgoing live edge $(v, w) \in E^\ell$ needs to be taken infinitely often. Formally, a play π in $\mathcal{G}$ is called *fair* if the LTL formula[1]

$$\alpha := \bigwedge_{(v,w)\in E^\ell}(\Box\Diamond v \implies \Box\Diamond(v \wedge \bigcirc w)) \tag{1}$$

holds along π, i.e. $\pi \models \alpha$. A play π is winning for Player 0 in $\mathcal{F}$ iff $\pi \not\models \alpha$ or $\chi \cap \mathrm{inf}(\pi) \neq \emptyset$. Dually, π is winning for Player 1 iff $\pi \models \alpha$ and $\chi \cap \mathrm{inf}(\pi) = \emptyset$. A Player 1 strategy τ is called *fair* if all plays compliant with ρ are fair. A strategy μ is winning for Player j in $\mathcal{F}$ if all plays compliant with μ are winning for Player j in $\mathcal{F}$. This entails that any winning Player 1 strategy τ is necessarily fair.

Winning Strategies in Fair Büchi Games. It is known that in odd-fair parity games Player 0 has positional winning strategies and Player 1 has exponential memory winning strategies and that the exponential memory requirement for Player 1 is tight [13,24]. These memory requirements extend to fair Büchi games: the positionality of Player 0 strategies directly follow since fair Büchi games are fair parity games over two colours; the exponential memory requirement for Player 1 already holds for two colours [13, Lemma 1].

Strategy Subgraphs. For a fair Büchi game $\mathcal{F} = (\langle V, V_0, V_1, E, \chi\rangle, E^\ell)$, we can represent Player 0 and Player 1 winning strategies with subgraphs on their respective winning regions.

A *Player 0 strategy subgraph* $\mathcal{S}$ on $V' \subseteq V$ is given by a fair Büchi game $\mathcal{S} = (\mathcal{G}', E^\ell \cap E')$ where $\mathcal{G} = \langle V', V_0 \cap V', V_1 \cap V', E', \chi \cap V'\rangle$ where for each $v \in V_1 \cap V'$, $E'(v) = E(v)$. Note that since $\mathcal{S}$ is a game, E' is deadend-free and is a subset of $V' \times V'$. $\mathcal{S}$ is called *winning (for Player 0)* iff all fair plays in $\mathcal{S}$ are winning for Player 0. For a Player 0 positional strategy σ on $V' \subseteq V$, the strategy subgraph of σ is defined similarly where for each $v \in V_0 \cap V'$, $E'(v) = \{\sigma(v)\}$, and is denoted by $\mathcal{F}^\sigma|_{V'}$. It is easy to see that σ is winning iff $\mathcal{F}^\sigma|_{V'}$ is.

A *Player 1 strategy subgraph* on $V' \subseteq V$ is defined similarly where this time for each $v \in V_0 \cap V'$, $E'(v) = E(v)$ and for each $v \in V_1 \cap V'$, $(*)$ if v lies on a cycle in the subgraph (indicating v may be taken infinitely often), then $E^\ell(v) \subseteq E'(v)$. $\mathcal{S}$ is called *winning (for Player 1)* iff all plays in $\mathcal{S}$ are winning for Player 1. Due to $(*)$, there always exists a fair Player 1 strategy on V' that takes only the edges in $\mathcal{S}$. If $\mathcal{S}$ is winning, clearly this strategy is also winning.

4 Solving Fair Büchi Games via Progress Measures

This section presents the main contribution of this paper, which is the construction of *valid-for-fair-Büchi* progress measures, and the pairing lifting function which can be used to compute the winning regions in a fair Büchi game. In essence, this section mimics the results from Sect. 2.2 for *fair* Büchi games.

[1] Here, $\Box$, $\Diamond$ and $\bigcirc$ stand for the LTL operators 'always', 'eventually' and 'next'.

4.1 Valid-for-Fair-Büchi Progress Measures

Given a fair Büchi game $\mathcal{F}$ with vertex set V, progress measures $\rho : V \to [1, n-1] \cup \{\top\}$ are defined analogously to the Büchi case. The main difference lies in the definition of a *valid* progress measure for fair Büchi games. This time we need to distinguish between (i) live vertices - all of which belong to Player 1 (ii) not live Player 1 vertices and (iii) Player 0 vertices.

Definition 1. *Given a fair Büchi game* $\mathcal{F} = (\langle V, V_0, V_1, E, \chi\rangle, E^\ell)$*, a progress measure* $\rho : V \to [1, n-1] \cup \{\top\}$ *is called a* valid-for-fair-Büchi progress measure *if for all* $v \in V$ *holds that*

$$\rho(v) \begin{cases} \geq \min_{(v,w)\in E^\ell} \rho(w) + 1, & v \in V^\ell \setminus \chi,\ \forall (v,w) \in E \,.\, \rho(w) \neq \top; \\ \geq \min_{(v,w)\in E} \rho(w) + 1, & v \in V_0 \setminus \chi; \\ \geq \max_{(v,w)\in E} \rho(w) + 1, & v \in (V_1 \setminus V^\ell) \setminus \chi; \\ = \top, & v \in V_0 \cap \chi,\ \forall (v,w) \in E \,.\, \rho(w) = \top; \\ = 0, & v \in V_0 \cap \chi,\ \exists (v,w) \in E \ s.t.\ \rho(w) \neq \top; \\ = \top, & v \in V_1,\ \exists (v,w) \in E \ s.t.\ \rho(w) = \top; \\ = 0, & v \in V_1 \cap \chi,\ \forall (v,w) \in E \,.\, \rho(w) \neq \top; \end{cases}$$

For the rest of the paper, whenever clear from the context, we will call *valid-for-fair-Büchi* progress measures, simply *valid* progress measures.

4.2 Lifting Valid Progress Measures

As before, the lifting function on $\mathcal{F}$ updates a progress measure ρ by minimally increasing the value of each vertex v to ensure the validity of ρ w.r.t. v.

Definition 2. *Given a fair Büchi game* $\mathcal{F} = (\langle V, V_0, V_1, E, \chi\rangle, E^\ell)$*, a progress measure* ρ *over* V *and a vertex* $v \in V$*, the* lifting function $\mathsf{FairLift}^{\mathcal{F}}$ *returns a progress measure* $\rho' = \mathsf{FairLift}^{\mathcal{F}}(\rho, v)$ *s.t.* $\rho(w) = \rho'(w)$ *for* $w \neq v$ *and* $\rho'(v)$ *s.t.*

- $v \in V^\ell \setminus \chi$: $\rho'(v) = \min_{(v,w)\in E^\ell} \rho(w) + 1$ *if* $\forall (v,w) \in E \,.\, \rho(w) \neq \top$ *and* $\rho'(v) < \top$*; else* $\rho'(v) = \top$;
- $v \in V_0 \setminus \chi$: $\rho'(v) = \min_{(v,w)\in E} \rho(w) + 1$ *if* $\rho'(v) < n$*; else* $\rho'(v) := \top$;
- $v \in (V_1 \setminus V^\ell) \setminus \chi$: $\rho'(v) = \max_{(v,w)\in E} \rho(w) + 1$ *if* $\rho'(v) < n$*; else* $\rho'(v) := \top$;
- $v \in V_0 \cap \chi$: $\rho'(v) = \top$*, if* $\forall (v,w) \in E \,.\, \rho(w) = \top$*; else* $\rho'(v) = 0$;
- $v \in V_1 \cap \chi$: $\rho'(v) = \top$*, if* $\exists (v,w) \in E \,.\, \rho(w) = \top$*; else* $\rho'(v) = 0$.

We have seen in Sect. 2.2, that in order to use $\mathsf{FairLift}^{\mathcal{F}}$ in a fixed-point type fashion to solve $\mathcal{F}$, it needs to be monotonic over the complete (finite) lattice formed by progress measures on V, analogous to Lemma 1, which is proven next.

Lemma 2. *Let* $\mathcal{F} = (\langle V, V_0, V_1, E, \chi\rangle, E^\ell)$ *be a fair Büchi game. Then the function* $\mathsf{FairLift}^{\mathcal{F}}$ *is monotonic, i.e.,* $\mathsf{FairLift}^{\mathcal{F}}(\rho, v) \leq \mathsf{FairLift}^{\mathcal{F}}(\rho', v)$ *for all* $v \in V$ *whenever* $\rho \leq \rho'$.

Proof. Consider two progress measures $\rho_1 \leq \rho_2$ over V and a vertex $v \in V$. Let $\rho'_i = \mathsf{FairLift}^{\mathcal{F}}(\rho_i, v)$ for $i \in \{1, 2\}$. We show that $\rho'_1 \leq \rho'_2$. Note that for all $w \neq v$, $\rho'_i(w) = \rho_i(w)$, so it is sufficient to show $\rho'_1(v) \leq \rho'_2(v)$. To see the statement holds, it is sufficient to go over the cases given above under the observation that min and max operations are monotonic.

As in Subsect. 2.2, it follows from the Knaster-Tarski theorem and Lemma 2, that for any fair Büchi game $\mathcal{F}$, the least fixed-point ρ^* of $\mathsf{FairLift}^{\mathcal{F}}$ exists. Moreover, ρ^* can be achieved by repeatedly applying $\mathsf{FairLift}^{\mathcal{F}}$ to the initial progress measure $\rho_0 : V \to \{0\}$ a finite number of times. We call the algorithm which takes a lifting function $\mathsf{FairLift}^{\mathcal{F}}$ and a progress measure ρ (s.t. $\rho_0 \leq \rho \leq \rho^*$) as input, and returns least fixed-point ρ^* of $\mathsf{FairLift}^{\mathcal{F}}$ by $\textsc{IterativeLift}(\mathsf{FairLift}^{\mathcal{F}}, \rho)$. Due to the monotonicity of $\mathsf{FairLift}^{\mathcal{F}}$ it indeed does not matter in which order vertices are lifted (one-at-a-time) as long as every vertex is lifted until its progress measure value does not change again.

It remains to be shown that the least fixed-point ρ^* is indeed *valid* and allows the extraction of the winning regions, analogously to Theorem 1.

Theorem 2. *Let $\mathcal{F}$ be a fair Büchi game and ρ^* be the least fixed-point of the function $\mathsf{FairLift}^{\mathcal{F}}$. Then ρ^* is a valid-for-fair-Büchi progress measure and $v \in \mathsf{Win}_0$ if and only if $\rho^*(v) \in [1, n-1]$.*

Unfortunately, generalizing the proof of Theorem 1 to Theorem 2 proves challenging. This is because for a Player 0 strategy σ to be winning, it is no longer required for all cycles in its strategy subgraph $\mathcal{F}^{\sigma}|_{V'}$ to contain Büchi vertices. As discussed in the last paragraph of Subsect. 2.2, this formed the bases of the proof for Theorem 1. We illustrate the existence of Büchi-free cycles in winning Player 0 strategy subgraphs on fair Büchi games in Fig. 1.

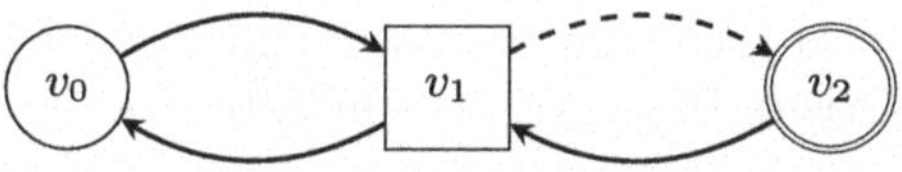

Fig. 1. A fair Büchi game $\mathcal{F}$, which is itself a winning Player 0 strategy subgraph. The circle and square nodes indicate Player 0 and 1 nodes, respectively. Live edges are dashed and Büchi nodes are encircled twice. The game is winning for Player 0 as all fair plays see the Büchi node v_2. However, there exists a cycle $v_0 - v_1$ without Büchi nodes in the subgraph.

Due to the existence of non-winning cycles in winning strategy subgraphs of Player 0 in fair Büchi games, the proof of Theorem 2 becomes substantially more involved than the proof of Theorem 1. It reduces to showing that:

(i) ρ^* is a valid-for-fair-Büchi progress measure,
(ii) all vertices v with $\rho^*(v) \in [1, n-1]$ are winning for Player 0, i.e. $V_{\mathbb{N}} \subseteq \mathsf{Win}_0$ where $V_{\mathbb{N}} := \{v \in V \mid \rho^*(v) \neq \top\} \subseteq V$, and

(iii) all vertices v with $\rho^*(v) = \top$ are winning for Player 1, i.e., $V_\top \subseteq \mathsf{Win}_1$ where $V_\top := \{v \in V \mid \rho^*(v) = \top\} \subseteq V$

While (i), i.e., the validity of ρ^*, can be readily deduced from its definition, parts (ii) and (iii) are proven separately in the following subsections.

4.3 Vertices in $V_\mathbb{N}$ Are Winning for Player 0

Given the premises of Theorem 2 this section proves $V_\mathbb{N} \subseteq \mathsf{Win}_0$. I.e., we show that for any $v \in V$, the fact that $\rho^*(v) \in [1, n-1]$ implies that $v \in \mathsf{Win}_0$. Towards this goal, we construct a positional Player 0 strategy σ on $\mathcal{F}|_{V_\mathbb{N}}$ and show that σ is indeed winning for Player 0 on $V_\mathbb{N}$, which shows that $v \in \mathsf{Win}_0$ for all $v \in V_\mathbb{N}$.

Formally, we define σ to be a positional Player 0 strategy s.t. $\sigma(v) = w$ for some fixed $w \in E(v)$ s.t. $\rho^*(w) = \min_{(v,v')\in E} \rho^*(v')$, i.e., σ always chooses a successor with the minimal value. Now we show that all fair plays π that start in $V_\mathbb{N}$ and are compliant with σ (i) do not leave $V_\mathbb{N}$ and (ii) visit a Büchi vertex infinitely often, i.e., are indeed winning for Player 0.

Proof of (i). Due to the validity of ρ^*, for any Player 0 vertex v in $V_\mathbb{N}$ it has a successor w with $\rho^*(w) \neq \top$; and therefore $\sigma(v) \neq \top$. For any Player 1 vertex v in $V_\mathbb{N}$, all its successors w has $\rho^*(w) \neq \top$. Thus we conclude that π never reaches a vertex w with $\rho^*(w) = \top$; i.e. it doesn't leave $V_\mathbb{N}$.

Proof of (ii). We will show that all fair plays π in the strategy subgraph $\mathcal{F}^\sigma|_{V_\mathbb{N}}$ visit a Büchi vertex infinitely often.

Claim (1). Let v be the first vertex of π and $\rho^*(v) = k \neq 0$. Then π visits a vertex w with $\rho^*(w) \leq k - 1$.

The correctness of (ii) follows from Claim 1. Given that (i) confirms that π stays in $V_\mathbb{N}$; and the only vertices w in π with $\rho^*(w) = 0$ are the Büchi vertices, we can inductively infer from the claim that each suffix of π will eventually reach a Büchi vertex. Thus, π visits Büchi vertices infinitely often.

Proof (Claim 1). Let $\pi = w_0 w_1 \ldots$. We proceed by induction on $\rho^*(w_0)$.

Base case: Let $\rho^*(w_0) = m$ where $m = \max\{\rho^*(v) \mid v \in V_\mathbb{N}\}$. Either for all $i \in \mathbb{N}$, $\rho^*(w_i) = m$, or there exists an i s.t. $\rho^*(w_i) \leq m-1$. In the latter, the base case is satisfied. We show that the former cannot hold. By pigeonhole principle, π needs to visit a specific vertex w with $\rho^*(w) = m$ infinitely often. Unless $w \in V^\ell$, by the validity of ρ^*, for all edges $(w, u) \in E$, we have that $\rho^*(u) \leq m-1$, which reveals a contradiction. On the other hand, if $w \in V^\ell$, there can exist an edge (w, u) in the strategy subgraph where $\rho^*(u) = m$, and π can take this edge. However, there also exists a live outgoing edge (w, u') with $\rho^*(u') = m - 1$; and as w is seen infinitely often, (w, u') is in the strategy sugraph, and is eventually taken in π. This reveals another contradiction and establishes the base case.

Inductive Hypothesis: We assume the claim holds for $\rho^*(w_0) > k$.

Inductive Step: We show that the claim holds for $\rho^*(w_0) = k$. The proof is similar to the base case. First assume there are only finitely many $i \in \mathbb{N}$ with

$\rho^*(w_i) = k$. Then there either exists an i with $\rho^*(w_i) < k$ (in which case we are done), or for all i, $\rho^*(w_i) \geq k$. In the latter, there exist infinitely many i with $\rho^*(w_i) > k$, and the claim of the inductive step follows from the I.H.

Now assume there are infinitely many $i \in \mathbb{N}$ with $\rho^*(w_i) = k$. By pigeonhole principle, there exists a specific w with $\rho^*(w) = k$ visited infinitely often in π. Analogously to the base case, if $w \notin V^\ell$, its successor u in π has $\rho^*(u) \leq k-1$, and we are done. On the other hand if $w \in V^\ell$, there exists a live edge (w, u) in the strategy subgraph with $\rho^*(u) = k-1$, that is eventually visited in π. This finishes the proof of the inductive step, and therefore that of the claim. □

4.4 Vertices in $V_\top$ Are Winning for Player 1

Given the premises of Theorem 2 this section proves that $V_\top \subseteq \mathsf{Win}_1$, i.e., for any $v \in V$ holds that $\rho^*(v) = \top$ implies $v \in \mathsf{Win}_1$. Towards this goal, we will show that there always exists a winning Player 1 strategy τ on $\mathcal{F}|_{V_\top}$ which shows that $V_\top \subseteq \mathsf{Win}_1$. We first introduce new concepts before attempting the proof.

Lifting Histories. The first observation we use is the fact that the least fixed-point ρ^* is independent of the order of lifting over V. That is, regardless of how one chooses the next $v \in V$ when applying $\mathsf{FairLift}^{\mathcal{F}}$ starting from ρ_0, we will reach a unique least fixed-point ρ^* after finitely many steps. To remember in which order the vertices got lifted to reach a progress measure ρ s.t. $\rho_0 \leq \rho \leq \rho^*$ we keep a history of lifted vertices.

Definition 3. *A* lifting history[2] *of a progress measure ρ that is obtained by a finite application of* $\mathsf{FairLift}^{\mathcal{F}}$ *to ρ_0 is the sequence of vertices* $\texttt{hist} = v^1, v^2, \ldots, v^m$ *corresponding to a sequence of progress measures $\rho^0, \rho^1, \ldots, \rho^m$ such that $\rho^0 = \rho_0$, $\rho^m = \rho$ and for all $i \in [1, n-1]$, $\rho^i = \mathsf{FairLift}^{\mathcal{F}}(\rho_{i-1}, v^i)$. In addition, we call the smallest integer k satisfying $\rho^k(v) = \rho(v)$, the* last lifter *of v.*

Intuitively, v^i are the vertices that are lifted in order and ρ^i are the progress measures after lifting vertex v^i. Further, if k is the last lifter of v, v is lifted to its current value in ρ during the lifting of v^k in ρ^{k-1}, and achieved its current value in ρ^k. We know $\rho^k(v)$ cannot be modified in the following lifts since the sequence $\rho^0, \rho^1, \ldots, \rho^m$ is monotonically increasing. Furthermore, $v = v^k$ since $\rho^{k-1}(w) = \rho^k(w)$ for all $w \neq v^k$. Note that the lifting history of a progress measure need not be unique.

Dependency Functions. The next ingredient is a partial function $\texttt{dep}_{\rho,\texttt{hist}} : V \to 2^V$, called *dependency function*, that assigns a vertex a set of its successors based on a progress measure ρ and a lifting history $\texttt{hist}$ of ρ. Intuitively, for a v, we define $\texttt{dep}_{\rho,\texttt{hist}}(v)$ to be the set of its successors responsible for lifting v to its current value, from Player 1's perspective. When v is lifted due to the minimum value among a subset of its successors, we assign $\texttt{dep}_{\rho,\texttt{hist}}(v)$ to this whole responsible set. This assignment reflects that Player 1 must win from all

[2] Whenever we talk about the lifting history of a progress measure ρ, we will consider it implicitly given that $\rho_0 \leq \rho \leq \rho^*$ holds.

its successors in this set. If $v \in V_0$, this is clear since Player 0 gets to choose the successor within this set. If $v \in V^\ell$ the correspondance holds because Player 1 may need to visit off successors in this set, $E^\ell(v)$. Conversely, if v's value results from the maximum value among its successors, $\mathtt{dep}_{\rho,\mathtt{hist}}(v)$ is assigned to this specific successor. When $v \in V_1 \setminus V^\ell$. This is evidents since Player 1 gets to choose its successor. For $v \in V^\ell$ and $\rho(v') = \top$ for a $v' \in E$, the correspondance still holds since $\rho(v') = \top$ indicates that v has an *escape strategy* from v', that never visits v again.

The next definition formalizes this intuition.

Definition 4. *A* dependency function *is a partial function* $\mathtt{dep}_{\rho,\mathtt{hist}} : V \to 2^V$ *where* ρ *is a progress measure and* $\mathtt{hist}$ *is a lifting history of* ρ. $\mathtt{dep}_{\rho,\mathtt{hist}}$ *is not* defined *on* $v \in V$ *iff (a)* v *was never lifted, i.e.* $v \notin \mathtt{hist}$, *or (b)* $v \in \chi$ *and* $\rho(v) = 0$. *Let* $v \in V$ *s.t.* $\mathtt{dep}_{\rho,\mathtt{hist}}(v)$ *is defined and* k *is the last lifter of* v. *Then*

- *if* $v \in V_0$: $\mathtt{dep}_{\rho,\mathtt{hist}}(v) := E(v)$;
- *if* $v \in V_1$, $\rho(v) = \top$ *and* $\exists w \in E(v)$. $\rho_{k-1}(w) = \top$: $\mathtt{dep}_{\rho,\mathtt{hist}}(v) := \{w'\}$ *s.t.* $\rho(w') = \top$;
- *else if* $v \in V^\ell$: $\mathtt{dep}_{\rho,\mathtt{hist}}(v) = E^\ell(v)$;
- *else if* $v \in V_1 \setminus V^\ell$: $\mathtt{dep}_{\rho,\mathtt{hist}}(v) = \{w\} \subseteq E(v)$ *s.t.* $\rho_k(w) = \max_{w' \in E(v)} \rho_{k-1}(w')$.

Further, given a vertex $v \in V$, *the transitive closure of* $\mathtt{dep}_{\rho,\mathtt{hist}}(v)$ *is the set* $\mathtt{depset}^*_{\rho,\mathtt{hist}}(v)$, *which is defined as the least fixed-point of* $\mathtt{depset}^i_{\rho,\mathtt{hist}}(v)$ *s.t.* $\mathtt{depset}^0_{\rho,\mathtt{hist}}(v) = \{v\}$ *and*

$$\mathtt{depset}^i_{\rho,\mathtt{hist}}(v) = \mathtt{depset}^{i-1}_{\rho,\mathtt{hist}}(v) \cup \mathtt{dep}_{\rho,\mathtt{hist}}(\mathtt{depset}^{i-1}_{\rho,\mathtt{hist}}(v)), \tag{2}$$

where, for a set $V' \subseteq V$, $\mathtt{dep}_{\rho,\mathtt{hist}}(V')$ *denotes* $\bigcup_{v \in V'} \mathtt{dep}_{\rho,\mathtt{hist}}(v)$.

Whenever $\mathtt{hist}$ is clear from the context, we simply write $\mathtt{dep}_\rho$ or $\mathtt{depset}_\rho$.

We observe that the assignments of $\mathtt{dep}_{\rho,\mathtt{hist}}(v)$, where Player 0 vertices v have $\mathtt{dep}_{\rho,\mathtt{hist}}(v) = E(v)$ and for Player 1 vertices v, where $\mathtt{dep}_{\rho,\mathtt{hist}}(v)$ is either one successor of v, or is $E^\ell(v)$; reminds Player 1 strategy subgraphs from Sect. 3. In fact, if $\rho = \rho^*$ and $v \in V_\top$, the dependency function induces a Player 1 strategy subgraph on $V_\top$, as formalized next.

Proposition 1. *Let* $\mathcal{F}$ *a fair Büchi game,* ρ^* *the least fixed-point of* $\mathsf{FairLift}^{\mathcal{F}}$ *and* $\mathtt{hist}$ *a lifting history of* ρ^*. *Further, define a graph* $\mathcal{S}$ *induced by* $\mathtt{dep}_{\rho^*,\mathtt{hist}}$ *as a fair Büchi game* $(\mathcal{G}', E^\ell \cap E')$ *where* $\mathcal{G}' = \langle V_\top, V_0 \cap V_\top, V_1 \cap V_\top, E', \chi \cap V_\top \rangle$ *and for all* $v \in V_\top$, $E'(v) = \mathtt{dep}_{\rho^*,\mathtt{hist}}(v)$. *Then* $\mathcal{S}$ *is a Player 1 strategy subgraph.*

The proof of Proposition 1 relies on the observation that whenever $v \in V_1$ lies on a cycle in E', $\mathtt{dep}_{\rho^*,\mathtt{hist}}$ contains all its live successors. As we do not use Proposition 1 in the final proof, we omit the formal argumentation.

We now note that if every strategy subgraph induced by ρ^* would be winning for Player 1 we would now be able to prove the overall claim. Unfortunately, whether such a subgraph is winning depends on the particular lifting history used, as illustrated in the next example.

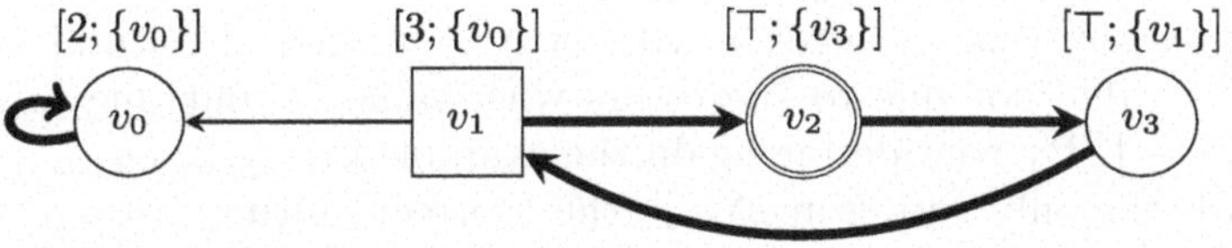

Fig. 2. A fair Büchi game $\mathcal{F}$; each vertex is annotated with $[\rho_5(v);\ \mathtt{dep}_{\rho,\mathtt{hist}}(v)]$. The Player 1 strategy induced by $\mathtt{dep}_{\rho,\mathtt{hist}}$ is indicated by thick arrows.

Example 1. Consider a game graph as in Fig. 2. Whole graph is winning for Player 1 with the positional Player 1 strategy τ that assigns $\tau(v_1) = v_0$. So, for all v_i, $\rho^*(v_i) = \top$. Now consider the lifting history $\mathtt{hist}^* = v_0, v_0, v_1, v_3, v_2, v_1, v_0, v_0$ of ρ^*. The last lifter of v_1 is 6; meaning v_1 was lifted for the last time at ρ_5, to its current value $\top$. Next to each vertex, their values in ρ_5 is depicted; together with $\mathtt{dep}_{\rho_5,\mathtt{hist}_5}$ where $\mathtt{hist}_5 = v_0, v_0, v_1, v_3, v_2$. When v_1 is lifted for the last time in ρ_5, it gets $\rho_6(v_1) = \top$ due to its successor v_2; and obtains $\mathtt{dep}_{\rho_5,\mathtt{hist}_5 \cdot v_1}(v_1) = \mathtt{dep}_{\rho^*,\mathtt{hist}^*}(v_1) = \{v_2\}$. If we look at the strategy subgraph induced by $\mathtt{dep}_{\rho^*,\mathtt{hist}^*}$, it prescribes the successor v_2 to v_1; which is making the subgraph losing by forming a cycle with a Büchi vertex, $v_1 - v_2 - v_3$. Therefore, it is not a winning strategy subgraph. However, if we consider the lifting history $\mathtt{hist}' = v_0, v_0, v_0, v_0, v_1, v_3, v_2$ of ρ^*, we can see that the graph induced by $\mathtt{dep}_{\rho^*,\mathtt{hist}'}$ is a winning Player 1 strategy subgraph; consistent with τ.

Proof Outline. Example 1 shows that $\mathtt{dep}_{\rho^*,\mathtt{hist}^*}$ is susceptible to different lifting orders and might not lead to a winning Player 1 strategy subgraph. The remainder of this section provides a proof (based on the concepts introduced before) on the existence of a winning Player 1 strategy subgraph on $V_\top$. Specifically, we will show that there exist a sequence of vertex subsets $\emptyset = Q_0 \subset Q_1 \subset \cdots \subset Q_m = V_\top$ and winning Player 1 strategy subgraphs $\mathcal{S}_0, \mathcal{S}_1, \ldots, \mathcal{S}_m$ on the respective vertex sets. As $Q_m = V_\top$ the fact that $\mathcal{S}_m$ is a winning Player 1 strategy subgraph then will conclude that $V_\top \subseteq \mathsf{Win}_1$.

We first observe that the base case of the outlined induction is trivial, as $Q_0 = \emptyset$. This implies that $\mathcal{F}|_{Q_0}$ has an empty vertex set. By choosing $\mathcal{S}_0 := \mathcal{F}|_{Q_0}$ we see that this is a trivially winning Player 1 strategy subgraph and $Q_0 \subseteq \mathsf{Win}_1$. In order to formalize the induction step, we need two more concepts.

Definition 5. *Let ρ be a progress measure with $\rho_0 \leq \rho \leq \rho^*$ and* $\mathtt{hist} = v_1, \ldots, v_m$ *be a lifting history of ρ. We say that the vertex $v = v_i$ in* $\mathtt{hist}$ died of natural causes, *denoted by $v \in \mathsf{D}_{\mathtt{hist}}$, if $\rho(v) = \top$, k is the last lifter of v and*

- $v \in V_0$ *and* $\min_{(v,w)\in E} \rho_{k-1}(w) = n - 1$,
- $v \in V_1 \setminus V^\ell$ *and* $\max_{(v,w)\in E} \rho_{k-1}(w) = n - 1$,
- $v \in V^\ell$ *and* $\min_{(v,w)\in E^\ell} \rho_{k-1}(w) = n - 1$ *and* $\nexists w \in E(v)\ .\ \rho_{k-1}(w) = \top$.

We will denote $\mathsf{D}_{\mathtt{hist}}$ *with* D *whenever* $\mathtt{hist}$ *is clear from the context.*

Intuitively, we say that a vertex v with $\rho(v) = \top$ died of natural causes if it received this value not due to successors with value $\top$, but due to successors with value $n-1$. By considering again the example in Fig. 2, $D_{\texttt{hist}^*} = \{v_0, v_3\}$; whereas v_0 is the only vertex in $D_{\texttt{hist}'}$, the "correct" lifting history.

Definition 6. *For a vertex subset $Q \subseteq V$, we call ρ_Q a* transitional progress measure *if ρ_Q is obtained by applying $\mathsf{FairLift}^{\mathcal{F}}$ repeatedly on ρ_0 and*

$$\rho_Q(v) = \begin{cases} 0, & \textit{if } v \notin Q; \\ \top, & \textit{if } v \in Q. \end{cases} \tag{3}$$

We have the following crucial observation.

Lemma 3. *Let $\mathcal{S}$ be a winning Player 1 strategy subgraph of $\mathcal{F}$ on the vertex subset Q. Then there exists a transitional progress measure ρ_Q and $Q \subseteq V_\top$.*

Proof. As $\mathcal{S}$ is a separate fair Büchi game that is winning for Player 1, the vertices of $\mathcal{S}$ can be lifted independently from the rest of the vertices in $\mathcal{F}$. Further, we know from Subsect. 4.3 that $\mathsf{Win}_1 \subseteq V_\top$. As $\mathcal{S}$ is winning, all nodes $v \in Q$ have $\rho^*(v) = \top$. This gives us the existence of ρ_Q that only lifts the nodes in Q, and lifts them until they all reach $\rho^*(v)$.

The Induction Step. Assume that for $i-1$, $Q_{i-1} \subseteq V_\top$ and $\mathcal{S}_{i-1}$ is a winning Player 1 strategy subgraph on Q_{i-1} with transitional progress measure $\rho_{Q_{i-1}}$ (due to Lemma 3). Further, we assume $Q_{i-1} \subsetneq V_\top$, as otherwise $Q_m = Q_{i-1}$ and we are done. We will show that there exists Q_i s.t. $Q_{i-1} \subsetneq Q_i \subseteq V_\top$ and a winning Player 1 strategy subgraph $\mathcal{S}_i$ over Q_i.

Since $Q_{i-1} \subsetneq V_\top$ we have $\rho_{Q_{i-1}} < \rho^*$. Now assume that we apply $\mathsf{FairLift}^{\mathcal{F}}$ to $\rho_{Q_{i-1}}$. It follows from the monotonicity of $\mathsf{FairLift}^{\mathcal{F}}$ that after a finite number of lifts (leading to the progress measure ρ) there exists a first vertex $w \in V_\top \setminus Q_{i-1}$ s.t. $\rho(w) = \top$. We use this w to construct Q_i by adding $\texttt{depset}^*_\rho(w)$ to Q_{i-1}. It remains to show the existence of a winning Player 1 strategy subgraph $\mathcal{S}_i$ on Q_i.

Claim (2). There exists a winning Player 1 strategy subgraph $\mathcal{S}_i$ on the vertex set $Q_i = Q_{i-1} \cup \texttt{depset}^*_\rho(w)$ that agrees with $\mathcal{S}_{i-1}$ on Q_{i-1}.

Proof (Claim 2). Let $E_{Q_{i-1}}$ be the edge set of $\mathcal{S}_{i-1}$. Observe that either $w \in \mathsf{D}$, or (i) $w \in V_1$ and there exists a $u \in E(w)$ s.t. $u \in Q_{i-1}$ and $\texttt{dep}_\rho(w) = \{u\}$, or (ii) $w \in V_0$ and $\texttt{dep}_\rho(w) = E(w) \subseteq Q_{i-1}$. If (i) or (ii) holds, $\mathcal{S}_i$ on the vertex set $Q_i = Q_{i-1} \cup \{w\}$ and edge set $E' = E_{Q_{i-1}} \cup \texttt{dep}_\rho(w)$ is a winning Player 1 strategy subgraph. It is winning since every play starting at w, moves to Q_{i-1} in the next step and stays there (since the edges $E_{Q_{i-1}}$ stay in Q_{i-1}). The fact that there are no cycles on w in E' justifies the lack of live edges of w in E' and shows that $\mathcal{S}_i$ is indeed a Player 1 strategy subgraph. Therefore, for the case $w \notin \mathsf{D}$; we obtain the desired winning Player 1 strategy subgraph $\mathcal{S}_i$.

Now let $w \in \mathsf{D}$. We define $\mathcal{S}_i$ on the vertex set $Q_i = Q_{i-1} \cup \texttt{depset}^*_\rho(w)$ with the edge set $E' = E_{Q_{i-1}} \cup \{(u, u') \mid u \in \texttt{depset}^*_\rho(w) \text{ and } u' \in \texttt{dep}_\rho(u)\}$. We will first show that $\mathcal{S}_i$ is a strategy subgraph. For this, it is enough to show that for all $u \in (\mathtt{depset}^*_\rho(w) \cap V^\ell) \setminus Q_{i-1}$, it holds that $E^\ell(u) \subseteq E'$. This follows from the construction of dependency sets: Whenever a vertex $u \in V^\ell$ did not obtain its value in its last lifter, due to a successor with value $\top$; $\mathtt{dep}_\rho(u)$ contains $E^\ell(u)$. Since w is the only vertex in $\mathtt{depset}^*_\rho(w) \setminus Q_{i-1}$ with value $\top$, and it has died of natural causes; the condition holds for all $u \in (\mathtt{depset}^*_\rho(w) \cap V^\ell) \setminus Q_{i-1}$.

Now let's show that $\mathcal{S}_i$ is winning. For this, it is enough to show that any play π starting at $Q_i \setminus Q_{i-1}$, either visits a vertex from Q_i or never sees a Büchi vertex. In the former, π is winning for Player 1 since eventually π stays in $\mathcal{S}_{i-1}$. We will show an equivalent statement; that is $Q_i \setminus Q_{i-1}$ contains no Büchi vertices.

Before we start, we define the length of a finite path by the number of transitions in it, and denote it with $\mathtt{len}$. E.g. $\mathtt{len}(u) = 0$ and $\mathtt{len}(u_0 \to u_1 \to u_2) = 2$.

Claim (3). Let $v, u \in \mathtt{depset}^*_\rho(w) \setminus Q_{i-1}$ where v is a Büchi vertex and there is a path from u to v in E'. Further, let r be the length of a minimal length path from v to u in E'. Then $\rho(u) \leq r$.

Proof (Claim 3). We will proceed by induction. Since all vertices in $\mathtt{depset}^*_\rho(w)$ either have a natural number ρ-value, or (in the case of w) are in D; all Büchi vertices in the set have $\rho(v) = 0$. This concludes the base case. Now assume the claim holds for all u with a minimal path of length $r - 1$ to v. We will show that the claim holds for a u with minimal path of length r to v. Let k be the last lifter of u. Then either $u \in V_1 \setminus V^\ell$ and $\mathtt{dep}_{\rho^k}(u) = \mathtt{dep}_\rho(u) = \{u'\}$; or $u \in V_0 \cup V^\ell$ and $\mathtt{dep}_{\rho^k}(u) = \mathtt{dep}_\rho(u)$ is a subset $S \subseteq E(u)$. In the first case, u' has a $(r-1)$–length minimal path to v; and by inductive hypothesis and the monotonicity of $\mathsf{FairLift}$ we get $\rho^k(u) \leq \rho(u) \leq r - 1$; which gives us $\rho(u) = \rho^k(u') + 1 \leq r$. In the second case, there exists a successor $u' \in S$ that has a $(r-1)$–length minimal path to v. Therefore, $\rho^k(u') \leq \rho(u) \leq r - 1$. By construction, $\rho^k(u) = \min\{u' \mid u' \in S\} + 1$. Therefore, $\rho(u) = \rho^k(u) \leq \rho(u') + 1 = r$. □

Now observe that for every $v \in \mathtt{depset}^*_\rho(w) \setminus Q_{i-1}$, there exists a minimal length path from w to v in E'. Minimal length paths do not contain cycles and therefore have length at most $n - 2$. Therefore, if there exists a $v \in \chi$ in this set, there exists an at most $(n-2)$–length minimal length path from w to v. The by claim, $\rho(w) \leq n - 2$, which leads to a contradiction.

We therefore establish that $\mathtt{depset}^*_\rho(w) \setminus Q_{i-1}$ contains no Büchi vertices, and finish the proof of Claim 2. □

This concludes the proof of the inductive step; establishing $V_\top \subseteq \mathsf{Win}_1$. □

5 Decremental Algorithm for Fair Büchi Games

This section presents a decremental algorithm for fair Büchi games. Due to Theorem 2, we can again utilize the idea behind the decremental algorithm for (normal) Büchi games (see Sect. 2.3) and only "update" the least fixed-point ρ^* after the fair edge $(u, u') \in E^\ell$ got removed from the fair Büchi Game $\mathcal{F} =$

Algorithm 2. DECREMENTALFAIRBUECHI

Require: $\mathcal{F} = (\langle V, V_0, V_1, E, \chi\rangle, E^\ell)$ a fair Büchi game, $(u, u') \in E^\ell$, ρ^* the least fixed-point of $\mathsf{FairLift}^{\mathcal{F}}$

1: **function** DECREMENTALFAIRBUECHI($\mathcal{F}, \rho^*, (u, u')$)
2: $\quad \mathcal{F}' \leftarrow (\langle V, V_0, V_1, E \setminus \{(u, u')\}, \chi\rangle, E^\ell \setminus \{(u, u')\})$
3: $\quad \rho^{\mathsf{reset}} \leftarrow$RESETPM($\mathcal{F}', \rho^*, u$)
4: $\quad \rho'^* \leftarrow$ITERATIVEFAIRLIFT($\mathsf{FairLift}^{\mathcal{F}'}, \rho^{\mathsf{reset}}$)
5: $\quad$ **return** ρ'^*

Ensure: ρ'^* is the least fixed-point of $\mathsf{FairLift}^{\mathcal{F}'}$.

$(\langle V, V_0, V_1, E, \chi\rangle, E^\ell)$. This results in the algorithm DECREMENTALFAIRBUECHI, given as pseudo-code in Algorithm 2.

Compared to Algorithm 1, Algorithm 2 additionally includes line 3 where the progress measure of vertices whose values in $\rho^*_{\mathcal{F}'}$ might decrease compared to their values in ρ^* is reset to 0. This was not required in Algorithm 1 as we could ensure that $\rho^* \leq \rho'^*$ for the considered edge removals. The function RESETPM is given as pseudocode[3] in Algorithm 3 and ensures in turn that $\rho^{\mathsf{reset}} \leq \rho'^*$. With this, it follows again from the monotonicity of $\mathsf{FairLift}^{\mathcal{F}'}$ that the computation of its least fixed-point ρ'^*can be warm-started with ρ^{reset} in line 4 in Algorithm 2, instead of initializing this iteration with ρ_0.

Intuitively, ρ^{reset} is computed by setting $\rho^{\mathsf{reset}} = \rho^*$ if the value of u cannot decrease after the edge removal. Otherwise, $\rho^{\mathsf{reset}}(v) = 0$ for all vertices v that can reach u by a play over $\mathcal{F}'$ (including u), collected in the set $Pre^*(\mathcal{F}', u)$, and $\rho^{\mathsf{reset}}(v) = \rho^*(v)$ for all other vertices.

Algorithm 3. RESETPM

Require: $\mathcal{F}' = (\langle V, V_0, V_1, E, \chi\rangle, E^\ell)$ a fair Büchi game, $u \in V^\ell$, ρ a progress measure

function RESETPM($\mathcal{F}', \rho, u$)
$\quad \rho^{\mathsf{reset}} \leftarrow \rho$
$\quad$ **if** $\rho(u) = \top$ **then**
$\quad\quad Succ^\top \leftarrow \{w \mid (u, w) \in E \text{ and } \rho(w) = \top\}$
$\quad\quad$ **if** $Succ^\top \subseteq Pre^*(\mathcal{F}', u)$ **then**
$\quad\quad\quad$ **for** $w \in Pre^*(\mathcal{F}', u)$ **do** $\rho^{\mathsf{reset}}(w) \leftarrow 0$
$\quad$ **else**
$\quad\quad$ **if** $\mathsf{FairLift}^{\mathcal{F}'}(\rho, u)(u) < \rho(u)$ **then**
$\quad\quad\quad$ **for** $w \in Pre^*(\mathcal{F}', u)$ **do** $\rho^{\mathsf{reset}}(w) \leftarrow 0$
$\quad$ **return** ρ^{reset}

Ensure: $\rho^{\mathsf{reset}} \leq \rho'^*$ where ρ'^* is the least fixed-point of $\mathsf{FairLift}^{\mathcal{F}'}$.

It remains to show that Algorithm 2 and Algorithm 3 are sound, i.e., indeed ensure their claim.

[3] Here, $Pre^*(\mathcal{F}', u)$ is the set of vertices v that have a path to u in $\mathcal{F}'$, including u. I.e., there exists a play $\pi = w_0 w_1 \ldots$ over $\mathcal{F}'$ s.t. $w_0 = v$ and $w_i = u$ for some $i \in \mathbb{N}$.

Theorem 3. *Given a fair Büchi game* $\mathcal{F} = (\langle V, V_0, V_1, E, \chi\rangle, E^\ell)$*, an edge* $(u, u') \in E^\ell$ *and the least fixed-point* ρ^* *of* $\mathsf{FairLift}^{\mathcal{F}}$*, let* $\mathcal{F}'$ *be as in line 2 of Algorithm 2 and* $\rho^*_{\mathcal{F}'}$ *the least fixed-point of* $\mathsf{FairLift}^{\mathcal{F}'}$*. Then it holds that*

- $\rho^{\mathtt{reset}} \leq \rho^*_{\mathcal{F}'}$ *for* $\rho^{\mathtt{reset}} := \text{ResetPM}(\mathcal{F}', \rho^*, u)$*, and*
- $\rho'^* = \rho^*_{\mathcal{F}'}$ *for* $\rho'^* := \text{DecrementalFairBuechi}(\mathcal{F}, \rho^*, (u, u'))$*.*

Proof. We first observe that Theorem 3(ii) directly follows from Theorem 3(i) due to the fact that according to Theorem 2, repetitive application of $\mathsf{FairLift}^{\mathcal{F}'}$ on any ρ s.t. $\rho_0 \leq \rho \leq \rho^*_{\mathcal{F}'}$ guarantees that $\rho^*_{\mathcal{F}'} = \text{IterativeFairLift}(\mathsf{FairLift}^{\mathcal{F}'}, \rho)$. It therefore remains to show that Theorem 3(i) indeed holds.

Firstly, observe that the maximal set of vertices whose values may *change* due to the removal of the edge, is $Pre^*(\mathcal{F}, u)$ (which is equivalent to $Pre^*(\mathcal{F}', u)$ since u is trivially in this set.). This is simply because disconnected vertices do not influence each other's values during the lifting operation. Now assume that $\rho^*_{\mathcal{F}'}(u) \geq \rho^*(u)$. Then the monotonicity of $\mathsf{FairLift}$ implies that the values of u's predecessors cannot decrease. Thus, for correctness, it suffices to detect when u satisfies $\rho^*_{\mathcal{F}'}(u) < \rho^*(u)$ and reset $Pre^*(u)$.

We will discuss that if u does satisfy this condition, it will be detected by one of the if conditions in line 5 or 8 of Algorithm 3, resulting $Pre^*(\mathcal{F}', u)$ to be reset. Assume $\rho^*(u) = \top$ and $\rho^*_{\mathcal{F}'}(u) \neq \top$. We know for sure that u will preserve its value $\top$, if it has a successor w in $\mathcal{F}'$ with $\rho^*(w) = \top$, and in addition, there exists no path from w to u in $\mathcal{F}$, and equivalently in $\mathcal{F}'$. Then we can ensure that $\rho^*_{\mathcal{F}'}(w) = \top$, and therefore $\rho^*_{\mathcal{F}'}(u)$ remains $\top$ as well. In such cases $S_\top \not\subseteq Pre^*(\mathcal{F}', u)$, and the if-clause in line 5 is avoided. Otherwise, the algorithm enters the if-clause.

Now assume $\rho^*(u) \neq \top$ and $\rho^*_{\mathcal{F}'}(u) < \rho^*(u)$. By construction of $\mathsf{FairLift}$, this scenario is possible only if u' is the sole live successor of u, and $\max\{\rho(w) \mid (u, w) \in E \setminus E^\ell\} < \rho^*(u')$. Let w be the successor holding this value. Even if $w \in Pre^*(\mathcal{F}', u)$, that fact that $\rho^*(w) < \rho^*(u)$ ensures that a possible increase in the value of u, cannot increase the value of w in $\rho^*_{\mathcal{F}'}$. Therefore, we know that $\rho^*_{\mathcal{F}'}(u) < \rho^*(u)$. We can detect this case simply by lifting u once in ρ^* and checking if the value of u decreases (line 8). If this is not the case, we can guarantee that $\rho^*(u) \leq \rho^*_{\mathcal{F}'}$.

Remark 1. We note that one can refine the set $Pre^*(\mathcal{F}', u)$ for resetting ρ^* by utilizing the backward-dependency sets of each vertex instead of the entire backward-reachability set.

Remark 2. Our approach assumes the removed edge (u, u') is not the sole outgoing edge of u in $\mathcal{F}$, as winning conditions for finite plays are not specified in this framework. Depending on the definitions of winning conditions for finite plays, Algorithm 3 can be modified to reset potentially decreasing vertices correctly.

Remark 3. We remark that Algorithm 2 can easily be generalized to the setting where multiple edges are removed by considering a set $R \subseteq E^\ell$ of removed edges and repeating the operations outlined in Algorithm 3 for each edge in R within a loop. Again, this algorithm can be optimized by carefully optimizing the order of computations for $Pre^*(\mathcal{F}', u)$ with $u \in R$.

6 Experimental Evaluation

This section provides experimental results generated with a prototype implementation of the DecrementalFairBuechi algorithm (Algorithm 2) as a proof-of-concept without additional heuristics to optimize its performance. In a nutshell we explore whether, given a fair Büchi game $\mathcal{F}$, its winning regions Win_0 & Win_1 and a removed edge (u, u'), our decremental algorithm computes new winning regions Win'_0 & Win'_1 for the new game $\mathcal{F}'$ significantly faster than an algorithm which recomputes Win'_0 & Win'_1 for $\mathcal{F}'$ from scratch.

Experimental Setup. We let our (non-optimized) decremental algorithm compete against an efficient BBD-based implementation of a symbolic algorithm for fair Büchi games from [3] implemented in the tool FairSyn [16]. We also extract the progress measure ρ^* for $\mathcal{F}$ (used as the input for Algorithm 2) from the last iteration of the fixed-point computation via FairSyn which computes Win_0 for $\mathcal{F}$. Intuitively, $\rho^*(v) := \top$ for all $v \notin \mathsf{Win}_0$ and $\rho^*(v) := \mathsf{rank}(v)$ for all $v \in \mathsf{Win}_0$, where rank denotes the iteration where v was first added to Win_0 in the last global iteration of FairSyn (see [3] for details).

Regarding the implementation of IterativeFairLift (line 4 in Algorithm 2) we could use any heuristic to pick vertices to be lifted until a new fixed-point is reached. We employ the *predecessor lifting with maximum measure propagation* from [29]. This algorithm lifts a progress measure ρ by prioritising the lifting of a vertex v if the increase of v's value after lifting will be the greatest amongst all vertices. This algorithm is shown to be more efficient than a naive version, as well as other heuristics implemented in [29].

Benchmark Generation. We generated fair Büchi game instances manipulating 54 benchmark instances of the PGAME_Synth_2021 dataset of the SYNT-COMP benchmark suite [14], with the number of vertices ranging from 100 to 44k. The dataset contains examples of parity games. We construct fair Büchi game instances $\mathcal{F}$ by collecting all vertices with even priorities in the Büchi set and turning 30% of all Player 1 vertices to live vertices. For each live vertex, we make 50% of all its outgoing edges live. To construct $\mathcal{F}'$ from $\mathcal{F}$, we randomly select the live edge to be removed. The experiments were performed on a machine equipped with Intel(R) Core(TM) i5-6600 CPU and 8 GB RAM. We implement all our algorithms in C++. We set a standard timeout of one hour.

Experimental Results. On 2 of the considered 54 examples both the recomputation and the decremental algorithm time out. The computation times for the remaining 52 instances are detailed in Appendix A and summarized in Fig. 3. We see that DecrementalFairBuechi outperforms FairSyn in 80% of the considered instances. Group 1 mostly contains instances where ResetPM concluded that no reset was needed. In this case, running the decremental algorithm

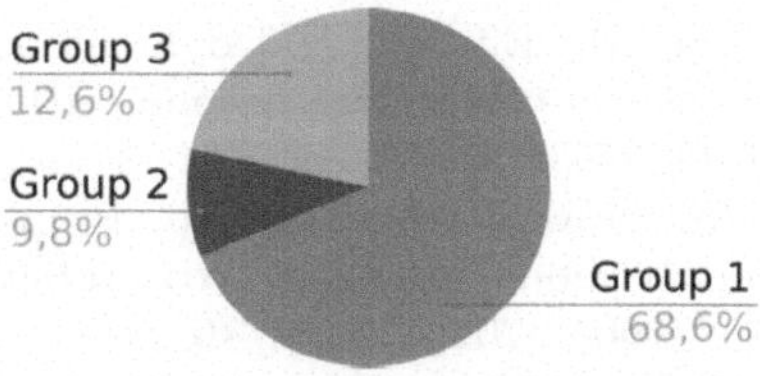

Fig. 3. Comparison between the recomputation of Win_0' & Win_1' with FairSyn [16] and their dynamic adaptation using DecrementalFairBuechi. Group 1: DecrementalFairBuechi is significantly faster; Group 2: DecrementalFairBuechi is proportionally faster; Group 3: FairSyn is faster.

is substantially more efficient than recalculating the winning regions; especially if we are dealing with bigger game graphs. The second group mostly contains instances where some vertices are reset; but the predecessor set $Pre^*(\mathcal{F}', u)$ is not very big. Since lifting is a time-consuming algorithm, this groups computation time for DecrementalFairBuechi is significantly larger than for Group 1; but still polynomially better than recomputation via FairSyn. For this group, a better performance of DecrementalFairBuechi can be achieved by optimizing the computation of the reset-set (see Remark 1). Finally, the third group mainly contains instances where u's value decreases due to the edge deletion; and $Pre^*(\mathcal{F}', u)$ is quite large.

In order to benefit from both algorithms, one could combine them based on the relative size of the reset-set $Pre^*(\mathcal{F}', u)$ w.r.t. to the size of V. Given a treshold r we can use DecrementalFairBuechi if the relative reset set is small, and FairSyn otherwise.

References

1. Aminof, B., Giacomo, G.D., Rubin, S.: Stochastic fairness and language-theoretic fairness in planning in nondeterministic domains. In: Beck, J.C., Buffet, O., Hoffmann, J., Karpas, E., Sohrabi, S. (eds.) Proceedings of the Thirtieth International Conference on Automated Planning and Scheduling, Nancy, France, 26–30 October 2020, pp. 20–28. AAAI Press (2020). https://ojs.aaai.org/index.php/ICAPS/article/view/6641
2. Baier, C., Katoen, J.: Principles of Model Checking. MIT Press (2008)
3. Banerjee, T., Majumdar, R., Mallik, K., Schmuck, A., Soudjani, S.: Fast symbolic algorithms for omega-regular games under strong transition fairness. TheoretiCS **2** (2023). https://doi.org/10.46298/theoretics.23.4
4. Belta, C., Yordanov, B., Gol, E.A.: Formal Methods for Discrete-Time Dynamical Systems, vol. 15. Springer, Cham (2017). https://doi.org/10.1007/978-3-319-50763-7
5. Chatterjee, K., de Alfaro, L., Faella, M., Majumdar, R., Raman, V.: Code aware resource management. Formal Methods Syst. Des. **42**(2), 146–174 (2013). https://doi.org/10.1007/s10703-012-0170-4

6. Chatterjee, K., Henzinger, M.: Efficient and dynamic algorithms for alternating büchi games and maximal end-component decomposition. J. ACM **61**(3) (2014). https://doi.org/10.1145/2597631
7. Cimatti, A., Pistore, M., Roveri, M., Traverso, P.: Weak, strong, and strong cyclic planning via symbolic model checking. Artif. Intell. **147**(1–2), 35–84 (2003). https://doi.org/10.1016/S0004-3702(02)00374-0
8. Daniele, M., Traverso, P., Vardi, M.Y.: Strong cyclic planning revisited. In: Biundo, S., Fox, M. (eds.) ECP 1999. LNCS (LNAI), vol. 1809, pp. 35–48. Springer, Heidelberg (2000). https://doi.org/10.1007/10720246_3
9. D'Ippolito, N., Rodríguez, N., Sardiña, S.: Fully observable non-deterministic planning as assumption-based reactive synthesis. J. Artif. Intell. Res. **61**, 593–621 (2018). https://doi.org/10.1613/jair.5562
10. Emerson, E.A., Jutla, C.S.: On simultaneously determinizing and complementing omega-automata. In: Proceedings of the Fourth Annual Symposium on Logic in Computer Science LICS 1989, Pacific Grove, California, USA, 5–8 June 1989, pp. 333–342. IEEE Computer Society (1989)
11. Emerson, E.A., Jutla, C.S.: The complexity of tree automata and logics of programs **29**, 132–158 (1999). https://doi.org/10.1137/S0097539793304741
12. Francez, N.: Fairness. Springer, Heidelberg (1986)
13. Hausmann, D., Piterman, N., Sağlam, I., Schmuck, A.: Fair omega-regular games. In: Kobayashi, N., Worrell, J. (eds.) Foundations of Software Science and Computation Structures - 27th International Conference, FoSSaCS 2024, Held as Part of the European Joint Conferences on Theory and Practice of Software, ETAPS 2024, Luxembourg City, Luxembourg, 6–11 April 2024, Proceedings, Part I. LNCS, vol. 14574, pp. 13–33. Springer, Cham (2024). https://doi.org/10.1007/978-3-031-57228-9_2
14. Jacobs, S., et al.: The reactive synthesis competition (SYNTCOMP): 2018–2021. CoRR abs/2206.00251 (2022). https://doi.org/10.48550/arXiv.2206.00251
15. Jurdziński, M.: Small progress measures for solving parity games. In: Reichel, H., Tison, S. (eds.) STACS 2000. LNCS, vol. 1770, pp. 290–301. Springer, Heidelberg (2000). https://doi.org/10.1007/3-540-46541-3_24
16. Majumdar, R., Mallik, K., Rychlicki, M., Schmuck, A., Soudjani, S.: A flexible toolchain for symbolic Rabin games under fair and stochastic uncertainties. In: Enea, C., Lal, A. (eds.) Computer Aided Verification - 35th International Conference, CAV 2023, Paris, France, 17–22 July 2023, Proceedings, Part III. LNCS, vol. 13966, pp. 3–15. Springer, Cham (2023). https://doi.org/10.1007/978-3-031-37709-9_1
17. Majumdar, R., Mallik, K., Schmuck, A.K., Soudjani, S.: Symbolic control for stochastic systems via finite parity games. Nonlinear Anal. Hybrid Syst. **51**, 101430 (2024). https://doi.org/10.1016/j.nahs.2023.101430
18. Majumdar, R., Mallik, K., Soudjani, S.: Symbolic controller synthesis for büchi specifications on stochastic systems. In: Ames, A.D., Seshia, S.A., Deshmukh, J. (eds.) HSCC 2020: 23rd ACM International Conference on Hybrid Systems: Computation and Control, Sydney, New South Wales, Australia, 21–24 April 2020, pp. 14:1–14:11. ACM (2020). https://doi.org/10.1145/3365365.3382214
19. Martin, D.A.: Borel determinacy. Ann. Math. **102**(2), 363–371 (1975)
20. Nilsson, P., Ozay, N., Liu, J.: Augmented finite transition systems as abstractions for control synthesis. Discrete Event Dyn. Syst. **27**(2), 301–340 (2017). https://doi.org/10.1007/s10626-017-0243-z

21. Pistore, M., Traverso, P.: Planning as model checking for extended goals in non-deterministic domains. In: International Joint Conference on Artificial Intelligence (2001). https://api.semanticscholar.org/CorpusID:18603460
22. Queille, J., Sifakis, J.: Fairness and related properties in transition systems - a temporal logic to deal with fairness. Acta Informatica **19**, 195–220 (1983). https://doi.org/10.1007/BF00265555
23. Ramírez, M., Sardiña, S.: Directed fixed-point regression-based planning for non-deterministic domains. In: Chien, S.A., Do, M.B., Fern, A., Ruml, W. (eds.) Proceedings of the Twenty-Fourth International Conference on Automated Planning and Scheduling, ICAPS 2014, Portsmouth, New Hampshire, USA, June 21–26 2014. AAAI (2014). https://doi.org/10.1609/icaps.v24i1.13629
24. Sağlam, I., Schmuck, A.: Solving odd-fair parity games. In: Bouyer, P., Srinivasan, S. (eds.) 43rd IARCS Annual Conference on Foundations of Software Technology and Theoretical Computer Science, FSTTCS 2023, 18–20 December 2023, IIIT Hyderabad, Telangana, India. LIPIcs, vol. 284, pp. 34:1–34:24. Schloss Dagstuhl - Leibniz-Zentrum für Informatik (2023). https://doi.org/10.4230/LIPICS.FSTTCS.2023.34
25. Shiloach, Y., Even, S.: An on-line edge-deletion problem. J. ACM **28**(1), 1–4 (1981). https://doi.org/10.1145/322234.322235
26. Tabuada, P.: Verification and Control of Hybrid Systems - A Symbolic Approach. Springer, New York (2009). https://doi.org/10.1007/978-1-4419-0224-5
27. Tarski, A.: A lattice-theoretical fixpoint theorem and its applications. Pac. J. Math. **5**, 285–309 (1955). https://api.semanticscholar.org/CorpusID:13651629
28. Thistle, J.G., Malhamé, R.: Control of ω-automata under state fairness assumptions. Syst. Control Lett. **33**(4), 265–274 (1998)
29. Verver, M.: Practical improvements to parity game solving (2013). https://api.semanticscholar.org/CorpusID:44613658

Games with Weighted Multiple Objectives

Orna Kupferman(✉) and Noam Shenwald

School of Computer Science and Engineering,
The Hebrew University, Jerusalem, Israel
orna@cs.huji.ac.il, noam.shenwald@mail.huji.ac.il

Abstract. Games with multiple objectives arise naturally in synthesis of reactive systems. We study *games with weighted multiple objectives*. The winning objective in such games consists of a set α of underlying objectives, and a weight function $w : 2^{\alpha} \to \mathbb{N}$ that maps each subset S of α to a reward earned when exactly all the objectives in S are satisfied. The goal of a player may be to maximize or minimize the reward. As a special case, we obtain games where the goal is to maximize or minimize the number of satisfied objectives, and in particular satisfy them all (a.k.a. generalized conditions). A weight function allows for a much richer reference to the underlying objectives: prioritizing them, referring to desired and less desired combinations, and addressing settings where we cannot expect all sub-specifications to be satisfied together.

We focus on settings where the underlying objectives are all *Büchi*, *co-Büchi*, *reachability*, or *avoid* objectives, and the weight function is non-decreasing (a.k.a. *free disposal*). For each of the induced classes (that is, type of underlying condition, type of optimization, and type of weight function), we solve the problem of deciding the game and analyze its tight complexity. We also study the tight memory requirements for each of the players. Finally, we consider general weight functions, which make the setting similar to the one of Boolean Muller objectives.

Keywords: Two-player zero-sum games · ω-regular objectives · Weighted games · Strategies and memory

1 Introduction

Synthesis is the automated construction of a system from its specification [37]. A *reactive* system interacts with its environment and has to satisfy its specification in all environments [23]. A useful way to approach synthesis of reactive systems is to consider the situation as a *game* between the system and its environment. In the *turn-based* setting, the game is played on a graph whose vertices are partitioned between the system and the environment: starting from an initial vertex, the players jointly generate a *play*, namely a path in the graph, with each player deciding the successor vertex when the play reaches a vertex she owns. The objectives of the players refer to the infinite play that they generate. Each objective α defines a subset of V^{ω} [33], where V is the set of vertices of the

S. Akshay et al. (Eds.): ATVA 2024, LNCS 15054, pp. 110–132, 2025.
https://doi.org/10.1007/978-3-031-78709-6_6

game graph. In some settings, the specification of α is *behavioral*: the vertices in V are labeled by assignments to a set AP of atomic propositions – these with respect to which the system is defined, and α is a language of infinite words in $(2^{AP})^\omega$. In other settings (and in the process of reasoning about behavioral specifications), the specification of α is *structural*: it is specified as an ω-regular objective on V [5].

The most basic ω-regular objectives are *reachability* [27] and *Büchi* [10], and their respective dual *avoid* (also known as *safety*) and *co-Büchi* objectives. Both are given by a set of vertices $\alpha \subseteq V$. A play satisfies a reachability objective α if it visits a vertex in α at least once, and it satisfies a Büchi objective α if it visits some vertex in α infinitely often.

Traditional synthesis is Boolean: a computation satisfies a specification or it does not. In many applications, the setting is not Boolean. Quantitative aspects may arise from the setting itself, for example when actions involve costs or rewards (cf., energy games [12]) or when the assignments to the atomic propositions are multi-valued [22]. A key challenge in these settings is an evaluation of an infinite sequence of values using measures like its mean-payoff, discounted sum, etc. [1,6,7,24]. Quantitative aspects may also arise from the specification, which may refer to the *quality* in which the specification is satisfied [2]. In particular, in *Objective LTL* [29], a specification consists of a set of LTL formulas, along with a function mapping each subset of them to a reward earned when exactly all the formulas in the subset are satisfied.

The quantitative setting enables the designer to combine many aspects of the synthesized system, for example when studying trade-offs between the satisfaction value of a multi-valued specification and the budget used for activating sensors [3,18], gaining control [4,31], paying tolls [32], or consuming energy [11]. The richness of the setting, as well as the fact that synthesis typically handles a conjunction of requirements, makes games with *multiple objectives* of special interest. In these games, the objectives of the players are specified by a collection of ω-regular objectives. In the Boolean setting, this includes games with *generalized Büchi* [14], *generalized co-Büchi* [30], *generalized parity* [15], *generalized reachability* [21], and *generalized reactivity* (GR(1)) [14,36] objectives. In addition to the deterministic turn-based setting, these games have been studied in various richer settings, like concurrent, stochastic, and energy games [8,13,17,41].

In this work we add a quantitative aspect to multiple objectives by weighing them. We introduce and study *games with weighted multiple objectives*. Consider a game graph with vertices in V. An objective in our game is a tuple $\langle \alpha, w, t \rangle$ where $\alpha \subseteq 2^V$, is a set of objectives that are all Büchi (B), co-Büchi (C), reachability (R), or avoid (A) objectives, $w : 2^\alpha \rightarrow \mathbb{N}$ is a weight function that maps each subset S of α to a reward earned when exactly all the objectives in S are satisfied, and $t \geq 0$ is a threshold. Consider a play ρ, and let $S \subseteq \alpha$ be the set of objectives in α that ρ satisfies. For example, if α consists of Büchi objectives, then exactly all the sets in S are visited infinitely often in ρ, and if α consists of avoid objectives, then exactly all the sets in S are never visited along ρ. Then, the satisfaction value of the play ρ in the game is $w(S)$. An objective can be viewed as a *maximization* objective, in which case the goal is to maximize its satisfaction value (and t serves as a lower bound) or a *minimization* objective, in which case the goal is to minimize its satisfaction value (and t serves as an upper bound).[1]

Weighted objectives enable the user to prioritize different scenarios. The different objectives in α may correspond, for example, to different types of grants given by a server or different storage options in the cloud. Using the weight function w, the user can then express the utility of different combinations of grants, storage options, locations, and more. As a concrete example, consider a warehouse robot assigned to navigate and fulfill item-retrieval requests from shelves. The environment issues the requests, and the system directs the robot. The setting can be modeled by a game-graph whose vertices correspond to locations in the warehouse. The robot's objective encompasses both the retrieval of items from appropriate shelves and logistical tasks such as visiting charging stations or navigating areas covered by security cameras. Different sets of locations within the warehouse are associated with varying rewards, reflecting diverse priorities related to requested items, specific shelves for retrieval, and the logistical considerations.

Studying games with weighted multiple objectives, we focus on *non-decreasing* weight functions (a.k.a. functions that respect *free disposal* [35]): for every two sets $S, S' \subseteq \alpha$, if $S \subseteq S'$, then $w(S) \leq w(S')$. We use the acronym MaxWB in order to denote a weighted maximization objective game with underlying Büchi objectives, and similarly for minimization objectives and the other classes of underlying objectives. For example, in MinWR games, the system aims to minimize the weight of reachability objectives. We also consider the special case where w counts the number of objectives satisfied, thus $w(S) = |S|$, and so the goal is to maximize (Max) or minimize (Min) the number of objectives satisfied. Note that the generalized conditions mentioned above are a special case of the latter, with $t = |\alpha|$. Here, we call them *All* objectives, and refer also to their dual *Exists* objectives. For example, AllB is a generalized Büchi game.

For all classes of games with weighted multiple objectives, we study the problem of *deciding the winner* in the game: the system wins a MaxW (MinW) game with objective $\langle \alpha, w, t \rangle$ if it has a strategy ensuring a satisfaction value at least (at most, respectively) t in all plays. Note that while the winning criterion is Boolean, by searching for the largest or smallest t with which the system wins, we can solve also the *optimization* (rather than *decision*) variants of the problem.

In order to satisfy an objective, a player may need to choose different successors of a vertex in different visits to the vertex. Indeed, a-priori, choices may depend not only on the current vertex but also on the history of the play so far. The number of histories is unbounded, and extensive research has concerned the

[1] As we elaborate in Remark 1, our setting can easily capture also a semantics in which the satisfaction value of the play ρ is $w(S) - w(\alpha \setminus S)$; thus when players are punished (in the maximization variant, or rewarded, in the minimization variant) for objectives that are not satisfied.

memory requirements for players in games with ω-regular objectives, namely the minimal number of equivalence classes to which the histories can be partitioned [9,19,39]. In particular, *memoryless* strategies depend only on the current vertex in the game, thus all histories are in one equivalence class. We study the memory requirements in games with weighted multiple objectives.

Our results about the complexity of deciding a game and the memory requirements are summarized in Table 1 below.[2] Hardness results hold already for the cases of Max and Min objectives, thus when w is uniform. It is not hard to see that games with weighted multiple objectives can be dualized in two manners: a MaxWB objective can be dualized to either a MinWB objective or a MaxWC objective. Consequently, when we study both MaxWB and MinWB games, we also cover MaxWC and MinWC games, and similarly for reachability and avoid games. Thus, with an appropriate dualization of the weight function and the threshold (see Proposition 1), the table includes the results also for co-Büchi and avoid objectives.

Table 1. Complexity and memory requirements for objectives $\langle \alpha, w, t \rangle$. The definitions of the measures $\mathsf{width}(\alpha, w, t)$, $\mathsf{equiv}(\alpha, w, t)$, and $\mathsf{sepwidth}(\alpha, w, t)$ can be found in Sects. 3 and 4.

	deciding the winner	memory requirements
AllB	PTIME [14]	$\|\alpha\|$ [19]
ExistsC		1 [20]
MaxWB	co-NP-complete (Theorem 5)	$\mathsf{width}(\alpha, w, t)$ (Theorem 4)
MinWB	NP-complete (Theorem 5)	1 (Theorem 2)
AllR	PSPACE-complete [21]	$2^{\|\alpha\|} - 1$ [21]
ExistsA		$\binom{\|\alpha\|}{\|\alpha\|/2}$ [21]
MaxWR	PSPACE-complete (Theorem 12)	$\mathsf{equiv}(\alpha, w, t)$ (Theorem 8)
MinWR		$\mathsf{sepwidth}(\alpha, w, t)$ (Theorem 11)

Below we highlight the main conclusions from our complexity results. Recall that single-objective reachability and Büchi games can be solved in PTIME, and both players have memoryless strategies [27,40]. Interestingly, while reachability

[2] While the problem of deciding games has several parameters (the game, the number of objectives, the weight function, and the threshold), a parameterized analysis is not of much interest, as fixing the game also fixes the number of objectives, and, as we shall show, once the number of objectives is fixed, all the decision problems can be solved in polynomial time.

objectives are typically easier than Büchi (in particular, the PTIME above is linear for reachability and quadratic for Büchi), the fact Büchi refers to limit behaviors makes it easier when we move to multiple objectives. Indeed, moving to AllB and AllR objectives, the complexity stays in PTIME for Büchi and jumps to PSPACE for reachability [14,21]. Also, the system player now needs memory, polynomial in the case of Büchi and exponential in the case of reachability [19,21]. Intuitively, this follows from the fact that detecting satisfaction of Büchi objectives, one may ignore visits to the objectives along the play, whereas detecting satisfaction of reachability objectives, one must keep track of all visits. In particular, in AllB objectives, one can detect the underlying objectives in a round-robin fashion, which is impossible in AllR. How does this difference affect weighted multiple objectives? Our results show that the jump to PSPACE in AllR games is sufficiently high to solve also MaxWR games, and the memory requirements are bounded by these in AllR games. That is, as detailed in Sect. 4, the measures $\mathsf{equiv}(\alpha, w, t)$ and $\mathsf{sepwidth}(\alpha, w, t)$ are bounded by $2^{|\alpha|} - 1$ and $\binom{|\alpha|}{|\alpha|/2}$, respectively. For Büchi objectives, MaxWB games are still easier than MaxWR games, yet are much harder than AllB games, and the memory requirements are higher. In particular, as detailed in Sect. 3, the measure $\mathsf{width}(\alpha, w, t)$ may be exponential in $|\alpha|$.

From a technical point of view, while both MaxWB and MaxWR objectives can be translated to equivalent AllB and AllR objectives, such a translation lead to optimal upper bounds only in the case of Büchi. Also, our lower bounds involve games and reductions that capture the difference between generalized and weighted objectives.

Finally, we show that games with weighted Büchi and reachability objectives with general (that is, not necessarily non-decreasing) weight functions correspond to games with Boolean *Muller* objectives, which describe the exact sets of vertices that should be visited infinitely often (termed B-Muller), or reached (termed R-Muller, a.k.a. *weak-Muller* or *Staiger-Wagner*). The correspondence enables us to lift known results about games with Muller objectives. In particular, deciding Muller games of both types is PSPACE-complete [26,34], implying membership in PSPACE for MaxWB and MaxWR games with general weight function. Thus, restricting attention to non-decreasing function makes a difference in the complexity only when the underlying objectives are Büchi. As for the memory requirements, for B-Muller, it can be analyzed using *Zielonka trees* [19], and for R-Muller it was studied in [25]. In fact, results relating the structure of Zielonka trees and the memory requirements for the corresponding objective [9] suggest an alternative proof also for the analysis of the memory requirements for non-decreasing weight functions, which we describe in the full version.

In Sect. 6, we discuss further extensions of the setting, in particular the connection between changes in the type of the underlying objectives (for example, to parity) and changes to the class of weight functions.

Due to the lack of space, examples and some proofs are omitted or given partially, and can be found in the full version.

2 Preliminaries

2.1 Two-Player Games

A *two-player game graph* is a tuple $G = \langle V_1, V_2, v_0, E\rangle$, where V_1, V_2 are disjoint sets of vertices, controlled by Player 1 and Player 2, respectively, and we let $V = V_1 \cup V_2$. Then, $v_0 \in V$ is an initial vertex, and $E \subseteq V \times V$ is a total edge relation, thus for every $v \in V$, there is $u \in V$ such that $(v, u) \in E$. The size of G, denoted $|G|$, is $|E|$, namely the number of edges in it.

In the beginning of a play in the game, a token is placed on v_0. Then, in each turn, the player that owns the vertex that hosts the token chooses a successor vertex and moves the token to it. Together, the players generate a *play* $\rho = v_0, v_1, \ldots$ in G, namely an infinite path that starts in v_0 and respects E: for all $i \geq 0$, we have that $(v_i, v_{i+1}) \in E$.

For $i \in \{1, 2\}$, a *strategy* for Player i is a function $f_i : V^* \cdot V_i \to V$ that maps prefixes of plays that end in a vertex that belongs to Player i to possible extensions in a way that respects E. That is, for every $\rho \in V^*$ and $v \in v_i$, we have that $(v, f_i(\rho \cdot v)) \in E$. Intuitively, a strategy for Player i directs her how to move the token, and the direction may depend on the history of the game so far.

A strategy is *finite-memory* if it is possible to replace the unbounded histories in $V^* \cdot V_i$ by finite memories. Formally, a *memory structure* for a game graph $G = \langle V_1, V_2, v_0, E\rangle$ is $\mathcal{M} = \langle M, \mu_0, \delta\rangle$, consisting of a finite set M of memory states, an initial memory state $\mu_0 \in M$, and an update function $\delta : M \times E \to M$. A memory structure is similar to an automaton with alphabet E, which is executed in parallel to the game: it starts from μ_0 and reads the edges traversed by the token. Formally, a strategy for Player i that relies on $\mathcal{M}$ replaces the dependency on the history of the play by dependency on the current vertex of the game and the current memory state of $\mathcal{M}$. Thus, the strategy is given by a function $f_i : M \times V_i \to V$, such that for all $\mu \in M$ and $v \in V_i$, we have that $(v, f_i(\mu, v)) \in E$. When the current memory state is μ and the token is in vertex $v \in V_i$, Player i moves the token to $f_i(\mu, v)$ and $\mathcal{M}$ moves to state $\delta(\mu, (v, f_i(\mu, v)))$. The strategy f_i is *memoryless* if it relies on a memory structure with a single memory state. It is thus given by a function $f_i : V_i \to V$.

A *profile* is a tuple $\pi = \langle f_1, f_2\rangle$ of strategies, one for each player. The *outcome* of a profile $\pi = \langle f_1, f_2\rangle$ is the play obtained when the players follow their strategies in π. Formally, $\mathsf{Outcome}(\pi) = v_0, v_1, \ldots \in V^\omega$ is such that for all $j \geq 0$, we have that $v_{j+1} = f_i(v_0, v_1, \ldots, v_j)$, where $i \in \{1, 2\}$ is such that $v_j \in V_i$. For finite-memory strategies, the definition is similar, with f_i being defined over memory states.

A *two-player game* is a pair $\mathcal{G} = \langle G, \psi\rangle$, where $G = \langle V_1, V_2, v_0, E\rangle$ is a two-player game graph, and ψ is a winning condition for Player 1, specifying a subset of V^ω, namely the set of plays in which Player 1 wins. The game is zero-sum, thus Player 2 wins when the play does not satisfy ψ. A strategy f_1 is a *winning strategy* for Player 1 if for every strategy f_2 for Player 2, we have that Player 1 wins in $\langle f_1, f_2\rangle$, thus $\mathsf{Outcome}(\langle f_1, f_2\rangle)$ satisfies ψ. Dually, a strategy

f_2 for Player 2 is a winning strategy for Player 2 if for every strategy f_1 for Player 1, we have that Player 2 wins in $\langle f_1, f_2 \rangle$. We say that Player i *wins* in $\mathcal{G}$ if she has a winning strategy. A game is *determined* if Player 1 or Player 2 wins it. For $m \geq 1$, we say that Player i wins in $\mathcal{G}$ with memory m if she has a winning strategy that relies on a memory structure of size m.

2.2 Weighted Multiple Objectives

For a play $\rho = v_0, v_1, \ldots$, we denote by *reach*(ρ) the set of vertices that are visited at least once along ρ, and we denote by *inf*(ρ) the set of vertices that are visited infinitely often along ρ. That is, $reach(\rho) = \{v \in V :$ there exists $i \geq 0$ such that $v_i = v\}$, and $inf(\rho) = \{v \in V :$ there are infinitely many $i \geq 0$ such that $v_i = v\}$. For a set of vertices $\alpha \subseteq V$, a play ρ satisfies the *reachability* objective α iff $reach(\rho) \cap \alpha \neq \emptyset$, and satisfies the *Büchi* objective α iff $inf(\rho) \cap \alpha \neq \emptyset$. The objectives dual to reachability and Büchi are *avoid* and *co-Büchi*, respectively. Formally, a play ρ satisfies an avoid objective α iff $reach(\rho) \cap \alpha = \emptyset$, and satisfies a co-Büchi objective α iff $inf(\rho) \cap \alpha = \emptyset$.

A *weighted objective* is a pair $\langle \alpha, w \rangle$, where $\alpha = \{\alpha_1, \ldots, \alpha_m\}$ is a set of m objectives, all of the same type, and $w : 2^\alpha \to \mathbb{N}$ is a weight function that maps subsets of objectives in α to natural numbers. [3] For $m \geq 1$, let $[m] = \{1, \ldots, m\}$. We assume that w is *non-decreasing*: for every sets $S, S' \subseteq \alpha$, if $S \subseteq S'$, then $w(S) \leq w(S')$. In the context of game theory, non-decreasing functions are very useful, as they correspond to settings with *free disposal*, namely when satisfaction of additional objectives does not decrease the utility [35]. We also assume that $w(\emptyset) = 0$. Note that we can set $w(\emptyset)$ to 0 preserving the non-decrease of w. A non-decreasing weight function is *additive* if for every set $S \subseteq \alpha$, the weight of S equals to the sum of weights of the singleton subsets that constitute S. That is, $w(S) = \sum_{\alpha_i \in S} w(\{\alpha_i\})$. An additive weight function is thus given by $w : \alpha \to \mathbb{N}$, and is extended to sets of objectives in the expected way, thus $w(S) = \sum_{\alpha_i \in S} w(\alpha_i)$, for every $S \subseteq \alpha$. Finally, an additive weight function is *uniform* if $w(\alpha_i) = 1$ for all $\alpha_i \in \alpha$. Thus, for all $S \subseteq \alpha$, we have that $w(S) = |S|$.

For a play ρ, let $\mathsf{sat}(\rho, \alpha) \subseteq \alpha$ be the set of objectives in α that are satisfied in ρ. The *satisfaction value* of $\langle \alpha, w \rangle$ in ρ, denoted $\mathsf{val}(\rho, \alpha, w)$, is then the weight of the set of objectives in α that are satisfied in ρ. That is, $\mathsf{val}(\rho, \alpha, w) = w(\mathsf{sat}(\rho, \alpha))$.

For every vertex $v \in V$, we denote by $\mathsf{obj}(v)$ the set of objectives that contain v, thus $\mathsf{obj}(v) = \{\alpha_i \in \alpha : v \in \alpha_i\}$. We extend the function obj to sets of vertices in the expected way; thus, for $U \subseteq V$, we have that $\mathsf{obj}(U) = \bigcup_{v \in U} \mathsf{obj}(v) = \{\alpha_i \in \alpha : \alpha_i \cap U \neq \emptyset\}$.

[3] One could also define multiple weighted objectives with mixed types of objectives. Essentially, combining objectives of the same polarity (that is, Buchi and reachability, or co-Buchi and avoid), we expect the properties of the game to be dominated by the complexity of the harder objective. Then, combining objectives with different polarities (for example, Buchi and co-Buchi), things become more complicated, as the combined objectives have the flavor of Rabin or Streett objectives.

Weighted objectives can be viewed as either maximization or minimization objectives. That is, in general non-decreasing weighted functions, the goal is to maximize or minimize the weight of the set of objectives satisfied, and in uniform additive weight functions, the goal is to maximize or minimize their number. A special case of the latter, known in the literature as *generalized* conditions, is when we aim to satisfy all or at least one objective. We denote different classes of weighted objectives by acronyms in {MaxW, MinW, Max, Min, All, Exists} × {R, A, B, C}, where the first letter describes the way we refer to the satisfaction value, and the second letter describes the objectives type (reachability, avoid, Büchi, or co-Büchi).

Formally, for a play $\rho \in V^\omega$, an objective type $\gamma \in \{\text{R, A, B, C}\}$, an objective $\alpha \subseteq 2^V$, a weight function $w : 2^\alpha \to \mathbb{N}$, and a threshold $t \in \mathbb{N}$, we have the following winning conditions.

- ρ satisfies a MaxW-γ objective $\langle \alpha, w, t\rangle$ if $\mathsf{val}(\rho, \alpha, w) \geq t$.
- ρ satisfies a MinW-γ objective $\langle \alpha, w, t\rangle$ if $\mathsf{val}(\rho, \alpha, w) \leq t$.
- ρ satisfies a Max-γ objective $\langle \alpha, t\rangle$ if $|\mathsf{sat}(\rho, \alpha)| \geq t$.
- ρ satisfies a Min-γ objective $\langle \alpha, t\rangle$ if $|\mathsf{sat}(\rho, \alpha)| \leq t$.
- ρ satisfies an All-γ objective α if $|\mathsf{sat}(\rho, \alpha)| = |\alpha|$.
- ρ satisfies an Exists-γ objective α if $|\mathsf{sat}(\rho, \alpha)| \geq 1$.

We also consider *strict satisfaction*, where the bound set by the threshold is strict. For example, ρ strictly satisfies a MinW-γ objective $\langle \alpha, w, t\rangle$ if $\mathsf{val}(\rho, \alpha, w) < t$. Note that as a consequence of Martin's determinacy theorem [33], games with multiple weighted objectives are determined.

Weighted objectives may be dualized in two ways, by complementing either the type of the objective or the way we refer to the satisfaction value. For an objective type $\gamma \in \{\text{R, A, B, C}\}$, let $\tilde{\gamma}$ be the dual objective, thus $\tilde{R} = A$ and $\tilde{B} = C$. Consider an objective $\psi = \langle \alpha, w, t\rangle$. The dual weight function of w, denoted $\tilde{w}$, is defined, for every $S \subseteq \alpha$, by $\tilde{w}(S) = w(\alpha) - w(\alpha \setminus S)$. The dual threshold of t, denoted $\tilde{t}$, is defined as $w(\alpha) - t$. Then, the *dual objective of* ψ, denoted $\tilde{\psi}$, is $\langle \alpha, \tilde{w}, \tilde{t}\rangle$. Note that for an additive weight function, we have that $\tilde{w} = w$. The following lemma follows directly from the definitions.

Lemma 1. *For every objective* ψ*, we have that* $\tilde{\tilde{\psi}} = \psi$*. Also, if* ψ *is non-decreasing, then* $\tilde{\psi}$ *is non-decreasing.*

Proof. For the first claim, recall that $w(\emptyset) = 0$ and note that $\tilde{\tilde{t}} = \tilde{w}(\alpha) - \tilde{t} = (w(\alpha) - w(\emptyset)) - (w(\alpha) - t) = t$, and for every $S \subseteq \alpha$, we have that $\tilde{\tilde{w}}(S) = \tilde{w}(\alpha) - \tilde{w}(\alpha \setminus S) = (w(\alpha) - w(\emptyset)) - (w(\alpha) - w(\alpha \setminus (\alpha \setminus S))) = w(S)$.

For the second claim, assume that w is non-decreasing, and consider two sets $S, S' \subseteq \alpha$. If $S \subseteq S'$, then $(\alpha \setminus S') \subseteq (\alpha \setminus S)$. Since w is non-decreasing, this implies that $w(\alpha \setminus S') \leq w(\alpha \setminus S)$, and so $\tilde{w}(S) = w(\alpha) - w(\alpha \setminus S) \leq w(\alpha) - w(\alpha \setminus S') = \tilde{w}(S')$, as required. □

Proposition 1 below formalizes the different types of dualities.

Proposition 1. *Consider a play ρ, and an objective $\psi = \langle \alpha, w, t \rangle$ with objectives of type γ. The following are equivalent.*

1. *The play ρ satisfies the MaxW-γ objective ψ.*
2. *The play ρ does not strictly satisfy the MinW-γ objective ψ.*
3. *The play ρ does not strictly satisfy the MaxW-$\tilde{\gamma}$ objective $\tilde{\psi}$.*
4. *The play ρ satisfies the MinW-$\tilde{\gamma}$ objective $\tilde{\psi}$.*

Proof. The equivalence between 1 and 2, as well as between 3 and 4, follow immediately from the definitions. We prove the equivalence between 1 and 4, which completes the proof. Let S be the set of γ-objectives in α that ρ satisfies. The set of $\tilde{\gamma}$-objectives in α that ρ satisfies is then $\alpha \setminus S$. Clearly, $w(S) \geq t$ iff $w(\alpha) - w(S) \leq w(\alpha) - t$. Thus, by the definition of $\tilde{w}$ and $\tilde{t}$, we have that $w(S) \geq t$ iff $\tilde{w}(\alpha \setminus S) \leq \tilde{t}$. Hence, ρ satisfies the MaxW-γ objective $\langle \alpha, w, t \rangle$ iff ρ satisfies the MinW-$\tilde{\gamma}$ objective $\langle \alpha, \tilde{w}, \tilde{t} \rangle$, and we are done. □

A special case of Proposition 1 is that ρ satisfies an All-γ condition, which is a special case of Max-γ with $t = m$, iff it does not satisfy the Exists-$\tilde{\gamma}$ condition. Finally, note that for $\gamma \in \{R, B\}$, we have that ρ satisfies an Exists-γ objective α iff ρ satisfies the Exists-γ singleton objective $\{\cup \alpha\}$. Dually, for $\gamma \in \{A, C\}$, we have that ρ satisfies an All-γ objective α iff ρ satisfies the All-γ singleton objective $\{\cup \alpha\}$.

Recall that in zero-sum games, the objectives of the players complement each other. Thus, by Proposition 1, for every objective type γ, when Player 1 has a MaxW-γ or, equivalently, a MinW-$\tilde{\gamma}$ objective, Player 2 has a MinW-γ or, equivalently, a MaxW-$\tilde{\gamma}$ objective. In addition, our definition below of the size of an objective ψ is such that $|\psi| = |\tilde{\psi}|$. Consequently, Proposition 1 enables us to lift results on B and R objectives to C and A objectives, respectively.

We define the *size* of a game G as the size of its edge relation, and define the size of an objective $\psi = \langle \alpha, w, t \rangle$ with a non-decreasing weight function as the size of w, defined as follows. First, we define the *length* of a weight function w, denoted $|w|$, as $\sum_{S \subseteq \alpha} w(S)$. Then, we define the *size* of w as $\min\{|w|, |\tilde{w}|\}$. Thus, the size of w as the length of the shorter function among w and $\tilde{w}$. Note that w can indeed be encoded in $|w|$ bits (in fact, for our upper bounds, one can also replace $w(S)$, which corresponds to an encoding of the weights in unary, by $\log w(S)$, which corresponds to a binary encoding), and our upper bounds are such that one can work with an encoding of either w or $\tilde{w}$. Moreover, when w is additive, our bounds hold also when we define its length by $\sum_{\alpha_i \in \alpha} w(\alpha_i)$.

Remark 1. **[Games with penalties]** In *games with penalties*, the satisfaction value of an objective $\psi = \langle \alpha, w, t \rangle$ in a play ρ, denoted $\mathsf{valp}(\rho, \alpha, w)$, is $w(\mathsf{sat}(\rho, \alpha)) - w(\alpha \setminus \mathsf{sat}(\rho, \alpha))$. Thus, objectives that are not satisfied reduce the satisfaction value. Note that the satisfaction value of a play may be negative. For example, if $\mathsf{sat}(\rho, \alpha) = \emptyset$, then $\mathsf{valp}(\rho, \alpha, w) = w(\emptyset) - w(\alpha) = -w(\alpha)$.

Our setting can easily capture games with penalties. Formally, as we show below, for every objective $\psi = \langle \alpha, w, t \rangle$, we can define, in linear time, an objective $\psi' = \langle \alpha, w', t' \rangle$, such that for every play ρ, we have that $\mathsf{valp}(\rho, \alpha, w) \geq t$ iff

$\mathsf{val}(\rho, \alpha, w') \geq t'$. Accordingly, a game with penalties with objective ψ is equivalent to a game in our setting and objective ψ'.

Given ψ, we define $w'(S) = \frac{1}{2}(w(\alpha) + w(S) - w(\alpha \setminus S))$, for all $S \subseteq \alpha$, and define $t' = \frac{1}{2}(w(\alpha) + t)$. Note that indeed, for every $S \subseteq \alpha$, we have that $\mathsf{val}(\rho, \alpha, w) \geq t$ iff $w(S) - w(\alpha \setminus S) \geq t$ iff $\frac{1}{2}(w(\alpha) + w(S) - w(\alpha \setminus S)) \geq \frac{1}{2}(w(\alpha) + t)$ iff $\mathsf{valp}(\rho, \alpha, w') \geq t'$.

For example, if w is additive and uniform, then the satisfaction value of a play ρ with $\mathsf{sat}(\rho, \alpha) = S$ in a setting with penalties is $|S| - |\alpha \setminus S| = 2 \cdot |S| - |\alpha|$. Accordingly, $\mathsf{valp}(\rho, \alpha, w) \geq t$ iff $2|S| - |\alpha| \geq t$. Note that then, $w'(S) = \frac{1}{2}(|\alpha| + |S| - |\alpha \setminus S|) = |S|$ and $t' = \frac{1}{2}(|\alpha| + t)$. Thus, $\mathsf{val}(\rho, \alpha, w) \geq t$ iff $2|S| - |\alpha| \geq t$ iff $|S| \geq \frac{1}{2}(|\alpha| + t)$ iff $\mathsf{valp}(\rho, \alpha, w') \geq t'$, as required. □

3 Weighted Büchi and co-Büchi Games

In this section we study weighted Büchi and co-Büchi games: the problem of deciding the winner, and the memory requirements for winning strategies for both players. We first show that every MaxWB objective has an equivalent AllB objective of exponential size. This enables us to use known results about AllB games, yet involves an exponential increase in the complexity. We show that MaxWB objectives (in fact, already MaxB objectives) are indeed exponentially more complex than AllB objectives.

Consider a MaxWB game $\langle G, \langle \alpha, w, t \rangle \rangle$, with $\alpha = \{\alpha_1, \ldots, \alpha_m\}$. We say that a set $S \subseteq \alpha$ is *t-short* if $w(S) < t$, and is *max-t-short* if S is t-short and maximal, in the sense that $w(S') \geq t$ for all $S' \subseteq \alpha$ such that $S \subsetneq S'$. A set $S \subseteq \alpha$ is *t-essential* if $\alpha \setminus S$ is max-t-short. Thus, S is t-essential iff $w(\alpha \setminus S) < t$ and S is minimal. We define the *width* of $\langle \alpha, w, t \rangle$, denoted $\mathsf{width}(\alpha, w, t)$, as the number of max-$t$-short (or, equivalently, t-essential) subsets of α.

Remark 2. **[On the size of** $\mathsf{width}(\alpha, w, t)$**]** It is not hard to see that $\mathsf{width}(\alpha, w, t)$ need not be polynomial in $|\alpha|$ or t. In particular, for MaxB games with m objectives and threshold t, namely when $w(\alpha_i) = 1$ for all $\alpha_i \in \alpha$, we have that $\mathsf{width}(\alpha, w, t) = \binom{m}{t-1}$. That is, the number of different subsets of α of size $t - 1$. In the general case, the calculation of $\mathsf{width}(\alpha, w, t)$ coincides with calculating the number of 0/1 Knapsack solutions for a knapsack of size t and items with weights w. The problem is #P-complete, with some known polynomial-time approximation schemes [38]. □

Theorem 1. *Every MaxWB objective $\langle \alpha, w, t \rangle$ has an equivalent AllB objective of size $\mathsf{width}(\alpha, w, t)$. That is, for every MaxWB game $\langle G, \langle \alpha, w, t \rangle \rangle$, there is an AllB objective α' such that the winning vertices for Player 1 in $\langle G, \langle \alpha, w, t \rangle \rangle$ coincide with these in $\langle G, \alpha' \rangle$, and $|\alpha'| = \mathsf{width}(\alpha, w, t)$.*

Proof. Let $\psi = \langle \alpha, w, t \rangle$, with $\alpha = \{\alpha_1, \ldots, \alpha_m\}$. We define α' as the AllB objective that contains every set $\cup S$ for sets $S \subseteq \alpha$ that are t-essential. Recall that $\cup S \subseteq V$. We prove that the MaxWB condition ψ is equivalent to the AllB condition α'. Consider a play ρ in G, and let $S = \mathsf{sat}(\rho, \alpha)$. We show that

$w(S) \geq t$ iff $S \cap S' \neq \emptyset$ for every t-essential set S'. We then conclude that ρ satisfies ψ iff ρ satisfies the Büchi objective $\cup S'$ for every t-essential set S', thus satisfies α'.

Assume first that $w(S) \geq t$. For every t-essential set S' we have that $w(\alpha \setminus S') < t$. Since w is non-decreasing and $w(S) \geq t$, it follows that $S \nsubseteq \alpha \setminus S'$, therefore $S \cap S' \neq \emptyset$. Assume now that $w(S) < t$, and let S' be a max-t-short set S' such that $S \subseteq S'$. Hence, for the t-essential set $\alpha \setminus S'$ it holds that $S \cap (\alpha \setminus S') = \emptyset$. □

3.1 Memory Requirements

In this section we study the memory requirements of strategies in MaxWB games. We show that while Player 2 can use memoryless strategies, Player 1 needs memory of exponential size, thus exponentially more than the one required in AllB games.

We start with Player 2, where things are easy.

Theorem 2. *Player 2 wins a MaxWB game iff she has a memoryless winning strategy.*

Proof. By Theorem 1, for every MaxWB game $\langle G, \psi \rangle$, there exists an AllB objective α' such that Player 2 wins in $\langle G, \psi \rangle$ iff Player 2 wins in $\langle G, \alpha' \rangle$. Player 2 in AllB games has an ExistsC objective. The latter is a special case of a Rabin objective, and hence, by [20], Player 2 wins $\langle G, \psi \rangle$ iff she has a memoryless winning strategy. □

For Player 1, the construction in the proof of Theorem 1 also gives an upper bound on the memory requirements. Indeed, since a winning strategy of Player 1 in an AllB game with m sets needs memory of size at most m [19], the construction implies a $\mathsf{width}(\alpha, w, t)$ upper bound on the size of the memory required for Player 1 in MaxWB games. Below we prove a matching lower bound. In the full version, we provide an alternative analysis of the memory requirements in MaxWB games, based on an analysis of the Zielonka trees they induce.

Theorem 3. *For every $m, t \in \mathbb{N}$ and a non-decreasing function $f : 2^{[m]} \rightarrow \mathbb{N}$, we can construct a MaxWB game $\mathcal{G}_{m,f,t} = \langle G_{m,f,t}, \langle \alpha, w, t \rangle \rangle$, such that all the following hold.*

1. *$|\alpha| = m$.*
2. *$w(\{\alpha_i : i \in S\}) = f(S)$ for every $S \subseteq [m]$.*
3. *Player 1 wins $\mathcal{G}_{m,w,t}$, yet every winning strategy for Player 1 requires memory $\mathsf{width}(\alpha, w, t)$.*

Proof. Consider $m, t \in \mathbb{N}$, and a non-decreasing function $f : 2^{[m]} \rightarrow \mathbb{N}$. We say that a set $S \subseteq [m]$ is *t-good* if $f(S) \geq t$, and is *min-t-good* if S is t-good and minimal, in the sense that $f(S') < t$ for all $S' \subset S$. If for every $i \in [m]$, there exists a min-t-good set S such that $i \in S$, then we define $\mathcal{X}$ as the set of min-t-good subsets of $[m]$. Otherwise, we define $\mathcal{X}$ as the set of t-good subsets of $[m]$. Note that for every $i \in [m]$, there exists $S \in \mathcal{X}$ such that $i \in S$.[4]

The MaxWB game $\mathcal{G}_{m,f,t}$ proceeds as follows (see formal definition and example in the full version). From the initial vertex v_0, Player 2 chooses a set $S \in \mathcal{X}$, Player 1 chooses an objective vertex $i \in S$, and the game returns to the initial vertex, where again Player 2 chooses a set, and so on. The objective of Player 1 is to visit infinitely often a set S of objectives vertices such that $f(S) \geq t$.

Since Player 2 can only choose among t-good sets, it is easy to see that Player 1 has a winning strategy in $\mathcal{G}_{m,f,t}$. We prove that every winning strategy f_1 for Player 1 needs at least $\mathsf{width}([m], f, t)$ different memory states. Since $w(\{\alpha_i : i \in S\}) = f(S)$ for every $S \subseteq [m]$, we conclude that every winning strategy f_1 for Player 1 needs at least $\mathsf{width}(\alpha, w, t)$ different memory states. We do this by presenting a strategy for Player 2 that forces every winning strategy f_1 to visit the initial vertex v_0 with $\mathsf{width}([m], f, t)$ different memory states.

Consider $i \in [m]$ and a memory state μ of f_1. We say that i is *avoided* in μ if for every play that starts in v_0 while in μ, the next objective vertex that f_1 chooses is not i. That is, i is avoided in μ if no matter which set vertex S Player 2 chooses from v_0, the strategy f_1 chooses from S an objective vertex that is not i. For every memory state μ, we denote by $avoid(\mu)$ the set of $i \in [m]$ that are avoided in μ.

Consider a max-t-short set $S \subseteq [m]$. We show that Player 2 has a strategy that leads the play to v_0 with a memory state μ_S of f_1 such that $S \subseteq avoid(\mu_S)$. This is done by describing a strategy f_S for Player 2 such that if not all $i \in S$ are avoided in the current memory state μ of f_1, the play returns to v_0 while visiting only objective vertices $i \in S$. Since $f(S) < t$, f is non-decreasing, and f_1 is a winning strategy, the above cannot continue forever, and so f_1 eventually reaches a memory state in which all $i \in S$ are avoided. The strategy f_S is defined as follows. Recall that not all $i \in S$ are avoided in μ. Thus, by definition, and since for every $i \in [m]$ there exists $S' \in \mathcal{X}$ such that $i \in S'$, there exists $i \in S$ and a set S' such that when Player 2 goes to the set vertex S', the strategy f_1 proceeds from S' to i. The strategy f_S then proceeds to S'. As required, the play then returns to v_0 while visiting only objectives vertices $i \in S$.

To complete the proof, we show that Player 2 can lead the play to a memory state μ with $avoid(\mu) = S$, for every max-t-short set S of $[m]$. We then proceed to describe a strategy for Player 2 that forces the play to visit as many memory states of f_1 as there are max-t-short sets, which implies the claim.

Consider a max-t-short set S of $[m]$, and let μ_S be such that $S \subseteq avoid(\mu_S)$. Since max-t-short sets are maximal, we have that $f(S \cup \{i\}) \geq t$ for all $i \in [m]$ such that $i \notin S$. Therefore, $S \cup \{i\} \nsubseteq avoid(\mu_S)$. Indeed, when Player 2 proceeds from v_0 to a vertex set S' such that S' is a min-t-good set and $S' \subseteq S \cup \{i\}$, Player 1 must proceed to an objective in S', which thus cannot be avoided. Hence, $S = avoid(\mu_S)$.

[4] The proof is valid also when $\mathcal{X}$ is defined as the set of t-good sets. Our definition, however, emphasizes the intuition behind the memory requirements for Player 1, which is the fact that every $i \in [m]$ is included in some of the t-good sets.

By the above, for every max-t-short set S of $[m]$, Player 2 has a strategy f_S that leads the play to v_0 with a memory state μ_S of f_1 such that $avoid(\mu_S) = S$. Consider a strategy of Player 2 that follows some order $S_1, S_2, \ldots, S_{\mathsf{width}([m],f,t)}$ on the max-t-short subsets of $[m]$, starts with $i = 1$, applies the strategy f_{S_i} until the play reaches v_0 with a memory state μ_{S_i} such that $avoid(\mu_{S_i}) = S_i$, and then switches to $f_{S_{i+1}}$, and so on until all max-t-short subsets are covered. Then, $\mathsf{Outcome}(\langle f_1, f_2\rangle)$ visits v_0 with $\mathsf{width}([m], f, t) = \mathsf{width}(\alpha, w, t)$ different memory states of f_1, and we are done. □

We can now conclude with a tight bound for the memory required to Player 1.

Theorem 4. *A winning strategy for Player 1 in a MaxWB game* $\mathcal{G} = \langle G, \langle \alpha, w, t\rangle\rangle$ *requires memory* $\mathsf{width}(\alpha, w, t)$.

3.2 Decidability

In this section we study the decidability of MaxWB games, and show that they (in fact, already their MaxB special cases) are exponentially harder than AllB games.

Theorem 5. *Deciding MinWB (MaxWB) games is NP-complete (co-NP-complete, respectively). Hardness in NP (co-NP) applies already for MinB (MaxB, respectively) games. Fixing the number of underlying objectives, the problem is in PTIME.*

Proof. We prove the results for MinWB. The ones for MaxWB follow from determinacy of MinWB games.

We start with the upper bound. By Theorem 2, Player 1 wins a MinWB game iff she has a memoryless winning strategy. As we argue below, checking whether a given memoryless strategy for Player 1 is winning can be done in polynomial time, implying membership in NP.

Consider a MinWB game $\langle G, \langle \alpha, w, t\rangle\rangle$, with $\alpha = \{\alpha_1, \ldots, \alpha_m\}$. Let $G = \langle V_1, V_2, v_0, E\rangle$. For a memoryless strategy $f_1 : V_1 \to V$ for Player 1, let $G_{f_1} = \langle V, E_{f_1}\rangle$ be the sub-graph of G obtained by removing all edges not taken by f_1. Thus $\langle v, u\rangle \in E_{f_1}$ iff $f_1(v) = u$. Clearly, f_1 is winning iff all the paths from v_0 in G_{f_1} satisfy $\langle G, \langle \alpha, w, t\rangle\rangle$.

Note that there exists a path ρ in G_{f_1} such that $\mathsf{sat}(\rho, \alpha, w) \geq t$ iff there exists a non-trivial strongly connected component (SCC) C in G_{f_1} such that $w(\mathsf{obj}(C)) \geq t$. Accordingly, f_1 is a winning strategy for Player 1 iff $w(\mathsf{obj}(C)) < t$ for every non-trivial SCC C reachable from the initial vertex in G_{f_1}. Since the latter can be checked in polynomial time, we are done. Note that the check is polynomial also when the weight function is dualized, thus when $\tilde{w}$ is given. Indeed, we need to calculate $w(\mathsf{obj}(C))$ only for linearly many SCCs.

When the number of underlying objectives is fixed, we have that the corresponding AllB game from the proof of Theorem 1 is of polynomial size. Thus, a

MaxWB game can be decided in polynomial time by solving the corresponding AllB game.

For the lower bound, we describe a reduction from SAT to MinB That is, as detailed in the full version, given a propositional formula φ in CNF, we construct a MinB game $\mathcal{G}_\varphi$ such that φ is satisfiable iff Player 1 wins $\mathcal{G}_\varphi$. Intuitively, we define $\mathcal{G}_\varphi$ so that Player 2 can require Player 1 to prove that every clause of φ is evaluated to **true** by asking Player 1 to choose a literal in the clause that is assigned **true**. Choosing a literal l involves a visit in a vertex associated with l. Accordingly, there exists a satisfying assignment to φ iff Player 1 can choose her responses so that at most n literals are visited infinitely often. □

4 Weighted Reachability and Avoid Games

In this section we study weighted reachability and avoid games: the problem of deciding the winner, and the memory requirements for both players.

First, it is not hard to see that the construction in Theorem 1 applies also to reachability objectives, thus every MaxWR objective has an equivalent AllR objective of exponential size.

Theorem 6. *Every MaxWR objective $\langle \alpha, w, t \rangle$ has an equivalent AllR objective of size* $\mathsf{width}(\alpha, w, t)$.

Known results about AllR games then imply upper bounds on the complexity of MaxWR games. Specifically, deciding AllR games is PSPACE-complete and the memory requirement for the players in AllR games are exponential in the number of reachability objectives. Combining this with the construction in Theorem 6, suggests a solution for MaxWR games. Since, however, $\mathsf{width}(\alpha, w, t)$ need not be polynomial in α, this is not optimal, and below we describe an algorithm that works on the MaxWR objective without translating it to an AllR objective, and is optimal.

Consider a MaxWR game $\mathcal{G} = \langle G, \langle \alpha, w, t \rangle \rangle$, with $G = \langle V_1, V_2, v_0, E \rangle$ and $\alpha = \{\alpha_1, \ldots, \alpha_m\}$. Recall that a set $S \subseteq \alpha$ is t-short if $w(S) < t$. We denote by $\mathfrak{S}$ the set of all t-short subsets of α, and we define the *volume* of $\langle \alpha, w, t \rangle$, denoted $\mathsf{volume}(\alpha, w, t)$, as the number of t-short subsets of α. Recall that $\mathsf{width}(\alpha, w, t)$ is the number of max-t-short subsets of α, thus the measure volume is much bigger than the measure width. Below we describe a reachability game $\mathcal{G}'$ of size $|G| \cdot \mathsf{volume}(\alpha, w, t)$, such that Player 1 wins $\mathcal{G}$ iff Player 1 wins $\mathcal{G}'$. Intuitively, $\mathcal{G}'$ follows the play in G while remembering the set of reachability objectives satisfied so far. Player 1 wins in a play in G' when the corresponding play in G satisfies $\langle \alpha, w, t \rangle$. We use the construction of $\mathcal{G}'$ in order to prove that Player 1 wins $\mathcal{G}$ iff she can force the satisfaction of $\langle \alpha, w, t \rangle$ within $|V| \cdot |\alpha|$ steps (see full proof in the full version), which we then use to prove various results for MaxWR games. Note that the reduction also implies that tools for solving reachability games can be used for solving MaxWR games.

Theorem 7. *For every MaxWR game $\mathcal{G} = \langle G, \langle \alpha, w, t\rangle\rangle$, there exists a reachability game $\mathcal{G}' = \langle G', \alpha'\rangle$ such that $|G'| = |G| \cdot \mathsf{volume}(\alpha, w, t)$ and the following are equivalent.*

1. *Player 1 wins in $\mathcal{G}$.*
2. *Player 1 wins in $\mathcal{G}'$.*
3. *Player 1 has a winning strategy in $\mathcal{G}'$ that satisfies α' within $|V| \cdot |\alpha|$ steps.*
4. *Player 1 has a winning strategy in $\mathcal{G}$ that satisfies $\langle \alpha, w, t\rangle$ within $|V| \cdot |\alpha|$ steps.*

4.1 Memory Requirements

In this section we study the memory requirements of winning strategies for both players in MaxWR games.

Memory Requirements for Player 1. We start with studying the memory requirement for Player 1 in a MaxWR game $\mathcal{G} = \langle G, \langle \alpha, w, t\rangle\rangle$. For a pair of t-short sets $S, S' \in \mathfrak{S}$, we say that S and S' are *equivalent* if for every t-short set $Q \in \mathfrak{S}$, we have that $w(S \cup Q) \geq t$ iff $w(S' \cup Q) \geq t$. Then, for every t-short set $S \in \mathfrak{S}$, the *equivalence class* of S, denoted $[S]$ is the set of t-short sets $S' \in \mathfrak{S}$ such that S and S' are equivalent. We denote by $\mathfrak{E}$ the set of different equivalence class of $\mathfrak{S}$. Below we show that the memory requirement for Player 1 is the number of equivalence classes of the MaxWR objective, denoted $\mathsf{equiv}(\alpha, w, t)$.

Note that for every MaxWR objective $\langle \alpha, w, t\rangle$ in which every t-short set is equivalent only to itself, for example, every MaxR objective, we have that $\mathsf{equiv}(\alpha, w, t) = \mathsf{volume}(\alpha, w, t)$. Also note that for an AllR objective α, we have that $\mathsf{equiv}(\alpha) = \mathsf{volume}(\alpha) = 2^{|\alpha|} - 1$, which coincides with the known memory requirement for Player 1 in AllR games [21].

Theorem 8. *A winning strategy for Player 1 in a MaxWR game with objective $\langle \alpha, w, t\rangle$ requires memory $\mathsf{equiv}(\alpha, w, t)$.*

Proof. The upper bound follows from the proof of Theorem 7. Indeed, it can be shown that Player 1 wins $\mathcal{G}$ iff she has a winning strategy that relies on a memory structure with memory states in $\mathfrak{S}$, and it is easy to see that we can replace them with memory states in $\mathfrak{E}$ in the expected way, and $|\mathfrak{E}| = \mathsf{equiv}(\alpha, w, t)$.

For the lower bound, for every $m, t \in \mathbb{N}$ and a non-decreasing function $f : 2^{[m]} \to \mathbb{N}$, we construct a MaxWR game that proceeds as follows (see formal definition and example in the full version). From the initial vertex v_0, Player 2 chooses an *init-set vertex* S, for some $S \in \mathfrak{S}$. From S, the game proceeds to a vertex v_1, from which Player 1 chooses an *equivalence-class vertex* $[S]$, for some $[S] \in \mathfrak{E}$. From $[S]$, Player 2 chooses a *final-set vertex* S', for some $S' \in \mathfrak{S}$ such that $f(S \cup S') \geq t$, or chooses an *inter-set vertex* S', for some $S' \in \mathfrak{S}$ such that $f(S \cup S') < t$, and $[S] \neq [S \cup S']$. Every final-set vertex is self-looped with no other outgoing edges, and from every inter-set vertex the game proceeds back to v_1. The objective of Player 1 is to reach set vertices that together form a set $S \subseteq [m]$ such that $f(S) \geq t$.

It is easy to see that Player 1 has a winning strategy in $\mathcal{G}_{m,f,t}$, as f is non-decreasing, and from every equivalence-class vertex $[S]$ Player 2 chooses a final-set vertex that corresponds to $S' \in \mathfrak{S}$ such that $f(S \cup S') \geq t$, or an inter-set vertex that corresponds to $S' \in \mathfrak{S}$ such that $[S] \neq [S \cup S']$. We prove that every winning strategy f_1 for Player 1 has at least $|\mathfrak{E}| = \mathsf{equiv}(\alpha, w, t)$ different memory states.

We show that for every $[S] \in \mathfrak{E}$, Player 2 has a strategy $f_{[S]}$ that causes f_1 to eventually proceed from v_1 to the equivalence-class vertex $[S]$. Since there are $\mathsf{equiv}(\alpha, w, t)$ equivalence class vertices, that are all reached via the same vertex for Player 1, we conclude that f_1 has at least $\mathsf{equiv}(\alpha, w, t)$ different memory states.

Consider $[S] \in \mathfrak{E}$. The strategy $f_{[S]}$ for Player 2 proceeds as follows. From the initial vertex v_0, the strategy $f_{[S]}$ chooses the init-set vertex S. Then, while Player 1 chooses from v_1 an equivalence-class vertex $[S']$ such that $[S'] \neq [S]$: if there exists $Q \in \mathfrak{S}$ such that $f(S' \cup Q) \geq t$ and $f(S \cup Q) < t$, the strategy $f_{[S]}$ proceeds from $[S']$ to the final-set vertex Q, thus the game ends while satisfying the set of reachability objectives $\{\alpha_i \in \alpha : i \in S \cup Q\}$; otherwise, the strategy $f_{[S]}$ proceeds from $[S']$ to the inter-set vertex S, thus the set of reachability objectives satisfied is still $\{\alpha_i \in \alpha : i \in S\}$. Below we show that indeed Player 2 can choose the inter-set vertex S from the equivalnce-class vertex $[S']$. Then, since f_1 is a winning strategy and $f(S) < t$, we have that eventually the play $\mathsf{Outcome}(\langle f_1, f_{[S]}\rangle)$ reaches the equivalence-class vertex $[S]$.

It is thus left to show that for every $[S'] \in \mathfrak{E}$ such that there does not exist $Q \in \mathfrak{S}$ for which $f(S' \cup Q) \geq t$ and $f(S \cup Q) < t$, we have that Player 2 can proceed from the equivalence-class vertex $[S']$ to the inter-set vertex S. Since $[S] \neq [S']$ and $f(S \cup Q) \geq t$ for every $Q \in \mathfrak{S}$ such that $f(S' \cup Q) \geq t$, we have that $f(S' \cup S) < t$. We also have that there exists $Q \in \mathfrak{S}$ such that $f(S \cup Q) \geq t$ and $f(S' \cup Q) < t$; thus, $f(S' \cup S \cup Q) \geq t$, and so $[S'] \neq [S' \cup S]$. Since $f(S' \cup S) < t$ and $[S'] \neq [S' \cup S]$, we have that there exists an edge between $[S']$ and the inter-set vertex S by the definition of $G_{m,f,t}$. □

Memory Requirements for Player 2. We continue to Player 2, and study her memory requirement in a MaxWR game $\mathcal{G} = \langle G, \langle \alpha, w, t\rangle\rangle$. For this, we introduce the *separated-width* measure of $\langle \alpha, w, t\rangle$, and show that the memory requirement for Player 2 coincides with it.

Consider a MaxWR objective $\langle \alpha, w, t\rangle$, with $\alpha = \{\alpha_1, \ldots, \alpha_m\}$. For two t-short sets S, S' of α, we say that S and S' are *separated* iff there exist max-t-short sets $Q \subseteq \alpha$ and $Q' \subseteq \alpha$ such that $S \subseteq Q$ and $S' \nsubseteq Q$, and $S' \subseteq Q'$ and $S \nsubseteq Q'$. We say that a set $\mathfrak{P} \subseteq \mathfrak{S}$ of t-short sets is *pairwise separated* iff for every two sets $S, S' \in \mathfrak{P}$, we have that S and S' are separated. Then, the *separated-width* of $\langle \alpha, w, t\rangle$, denoted $\mathsf{sepwidth}(\alpha, w, t)$, is the maximal size of a pairwise separated set of t-short sets of α. That is, $\mathsf{sepwidth}(\alpha, w, t) = \max\{|\mathfrak{P}| : \mathfrak{P} \subseteq \mathfrak{S} \text{ and } \mathfrak{P} \text{ is pairwise separated}\}$.

Note that for the special case of AllR objectives, two sets $S, S' \in \mathfrak{S}$ are separated iff $S \not\subset S'$ and $S' \not\subset S$: First, it is easy to see that if $S \subset S'$ (similarly, if $S' \subset S$), then S and S' are not separated, since for every max-m-short set Q such that $S' \subseteq Q$, we also have that $S \subseteq Q$. For the second direction, if $S \not\subset S'$ and $S' \not\subset S$, then for every $\alpha_i \in S' \setminus S$, we have that $Q = \alpha \setminus \{\alpha_i\}$ is a max-m-short set such that $S \subseteq Q$ and $S' \nsubseteq Q$, and for every $\alpha_i \in S \setminus S'$, we have that $Q' = \alpha \setminus \{\alpha_i\}$ is a max-m-short set such that $S' \subseteq Q'$ and $S' \nsubseteq Q'$, thus S and S' are separated. Hence, $\mathsf{sepwidth}(\alpha)$ is the maximal size of a set $\mathfrak{P} \subseteq \mathfrak{S}$ such that $S \not\subset S'$, for every $S, S' \in \mathfrak{P}$. In particular, $\mathsf{sepwidth}(\alpha) = \binom{m}{m/2}$, which coincides with the known memory requirement for Player 2 in AllR games.

We return to the case of non-decreasing weight functions and start with the upper bound. Consider a vertex $v \in V$ and a t-short set S of α. We say that Player 2 *S-wins from v* if Player 2 has a strategy to win from v, given that the objectives in S have already been satisfied. Such a strategy is called an *S-winning strategy*. Note that since w is non-decreasing, then if Player 2 S-wins from v, then Player 2 also S'-wins from v, for every $S' \subseteq S$. We denote by $\mathsf{good}(v)$ the set of sets $S \subseteq \alpha$ such that Player 2 S-wins from v and S is maximal, in the sense that Player 2 does not S'-win from v, for all $S' \subseteq \alpha$ such that $S \subset S'$. First, we state that the set $\mathsf{good}(v)$ is pairwise separated (see full proof in the full version).

Lemma 2. *For every vertex $v \in V$ and two sets $S, S' \in \mathsf{good}(v)$, we have that S and S' are separated.*

We conclude that $|\mathsf{good}(v)| \leq \mathsf{sepwidth}(\alpha, w, t)$ for every vertex $v \in V$. We use this bound in order to prove an upper bound on the memory requirement for Player 2, which we prove to be tight.

Theorem 9. *Player 2 wins a MaxWR game $\mathcal{G} = \langle G, \langle \alpha, w, t \rangle \rangle$ iff she has a winning strategy that uses at most $\mathsf{sepwidth}(\alpha, w, t)$ different memory states.*

Proof. Consider a MaxWR game $\mathcal{G} = \langle G, \langle \alpha, w, t \rangle \rangle$, and assume Player 2 wins $\mathcal{G}$. Recall the reachability game $\mathcal{G}' = \langle G', \alpha' \rangle$ constructed from $\mathcal{G}$ in the proof of Theorem 7. Also recall that Player 2 wins $\mathcal{G}$ iff Player 2 wins $\mathcal{G}'$. Since $\mathcal{G}'$ is a reachability game, Player 2 has a memoryless winning strategy, which we use to construct a winning strategy for Player 2 in $\mathcal{G}$ with $\mathsf{sepwidth}(\alpha, w, t)$ memory states.

For every vertex $v \in V$, let $\pi_v : [|\mathsf{good}(v)|] \to \mathsf{good}(v)$ be an arbitrary function that induces an order on the sets in $\mathsf{good}(v)$. By Lemma 2, we have that $|\mathsf{good}(v)| \leq \mathsf{sepwidth}(\alpha, w, t)$. Indeed, $\mathsf{good}(v)$ is pairwise separated, thus its size is bounded by the maximal size of a pairwise separated subset of $\mathfrak{S}$, which is $\mathsf{sepwidth}(\alpha, w, t)$. Below we describe a winning strategy for Player 2 in $\mathcal{G}$ with memory states in $[\mathsf{sepwidth}(\alpha, w, t)]$. Intuitively, when the play is in a vertex v and a memory state $1 \leq i \leq \mathsf{sepwidth}(\alpha, w, t)$, the set of reachability objectives satisfied so far is some $S \subseteq \pi_v(i)$.

Recall that a play in G' follows the play in G while remembering the set S of reachability objectives satisfied so far. Thus, Player 2 wins from a vertex $\langle v, S \rangle$ in G' iff Player 2 S-wins from v in G. Consider a memoryless winning strategy f_2 for Player 2 in $\mathcal{G}'$. We use f_2 to define the following strategy f'_2 for Player 2 in $\mathcal{G}$. The strategy f'_2 relies on the memory structure $\mathcal{M} = \{\{1, \ldots, \mathsf{sepwidth}(\alpha, w, t)\}, i_0, \delta\}$, where the initial memory state is $i_0 = \min\{i \in [|\mathsf{good}(v_0)|] : \mathsf{obj}(v_0) \subseteq \pi_{v_0}(i)\}$, and $\delta(i, \langle v, u\rangle) = \min\{j \in [|\mathsf{good}(u)|] : \pi_v(i) \cup \mathsf{obj}(u) \subseteq \pi_u(j)\}$, for every $1 \leq i \leq \mathsf{sepwidth}(\alpha, w, t)$ and $\langle v, u\rangle \in E$. Then, for every $v \in V_2$ and $1 \leq i \leq |\mathsf{good}(v)|$, we define $f'_2(v, i) = f_2(\langle v, \pi_v(i)\rangle)$.

We show that f'_2 is a winning strategy for Player 2 in $\mathcal{G}$. The strategy f_2 is winning from every vertex $\langle v, S\rangle$ in G' such that $S \in \mathsf{good}(v)$, thus f'_2 is an $\pi_v(i)$-winning strategy from v while in a memory state $1 \leq i \leq |\mathsf{good}(v)|$. Since the play induced by f'_2 is in a vertex v and a memory state i when the set S of reachability objectives satisfied so far is such that $S \subseteq \pi_v(i)$, and every $\pi_v(i)$-winning strategy is also an S-winning strategy for Player 2 from v, we conclude that f'_2 is a winning strategy for Player 2 in $\mathcal{G}$. □

We continue to the lower bound.

Theorem 10. *For every $m, t \in \mathbb{N}$ and a non-decreasing function $f : 2^{[m]} \to \mathbb{N}$, we can construct a MaxWR game $\mathcal{G}_{m,f,t} = \langle G_{m,f,t}, \langle \alpha, w, t\rangle\rangle$ such that all the following hold.*

1. *$|\alpha| = m$.*
2. *$w(\{\alpha_i : i \in S\}) = f(S)$, for every $S \subseteq [m]$.*
3. *Player 2 wins $\mathcal{G}_{m,f,t}$, yet every winning strategy for Player 2 requires memory* $\mathsf{sepwidth}(\alpha, w, t)$.

Proof. For every $m, t \in \mathbb{N}$ and a non-decreasing function $f : 2^{[m]} \to \mathbb{N}$, let $\mathfrak{P}$ be a pairwise separated subset of $\mathfrak{S}$ of maximal size. The MaxWR game $\mathcal{G}_{m,f,t}$ proceeds as follows (see formal definition in the full version): First, Player 1 chooses a set $S \in \mathfrak{P}$, then Player 2 chooses a set $S' \in \mathfrak{P}$, from which Player 1 can choose any max-t-short set Q such that $f(S' \cup Q) < t$. Then, the objective of Player 1 is to reach set vertices that form a set $S \subseteq [m]$ with $f(S) \geq t$.

As we formally prove in the full version, every winning strategy for Player 2 matches the choice of set in $\mathfrak{P}$ Player 1 makes from v_1, thus every winning strategy for Player 2 requires $|\mathfrak{P}|$ different memory states.

Consider a strategy f_2 for Player 2 in $\mathcal{G}_{m,f,t}$ such that there exist two different sets $S, S' \in \mathfrak{P}$ such that when Player 1 chooses S, Player 2 chooses S'. Recall that there exists a maximal set $Q \in \mathfrak{S}$ such that $S' \subseteq Q$ and $S \not\subseteq Q$. It is easy to see that in this case f_2 is not a winning strategy for Player 2. Indeed, when Player 1 chooses S and Q as described above, we have that the satisfaction value is $f(S \cup Q)$. Since $S \not\subseteq Q$ and Q is maximal, we have that $f(S \cup Q) \geq t$. □

We can now conclude with a tight bound for the memory required to Player 2.

Theorem 11. *A winning strategy for Player 2 in a MaxWR game with objective $\langle \alpha, w, t\rangle$ requires memory* $\mathsf{sepwidth}(\alpha, w, t)$.

4.2 Decidability

We continue to the complexity of deciding whether Player 1 wins a MaxWR game.

Theorem 12. *Deciding the winner in a MaxWR game is PSPACE-complete. Fixing the number of underlying objectives, the problem is in PTIME.*

Proof. For the upper bound, we describe an alternating Turing machine (ATM) T that runs in polynomial time, such that T accepts a MaxWR game $\mathcal{G}$ iff Player 1 wins in $\mathcal{G}$. The idea (see details in the full version) is similar to the upper-bound proof for deciding AllR games [21]. The ATM simulates the given MaxWR game $\mathcal{G} = \langle G, \langle \alpha, w, t \rangle \rangle$ for $|V| \cdot |\alpha|$ steps, and writes on the tape the set S of reachability objectives from α that are satisfied. After $|V| \cdot |\alpha|$ steps are completed, the ATM T calculates $w(S)$, proceeds to an accepting state if $w(S) \geq t$, and proceeds to a rejecting state otherwise.

When the number of underlying objectives is fixed, we have that the corresponding reachability game from the proof of Theorem 7 is of polynomial size. Thus, a MaxWR game can be decided in polynomial time by solving the corresponding reachability game.

The lower bound follows from the PSPACE-hardness of deciding whether Player 1 wins in AllR games [21]. □

5 General Weight Functions

In this section we show that weighted multiple objectives with general (that is, not necessarily non-decreasing) weight functions are equivalent to *Muller* objectives, and we lift results known for Muller games to games with weighted multiple objectives.

Consider a game $G = \langle V_1, V_2, v_0, E \rangle$, and a finite set C of colors. A *Muller objective* is a pair $\langle \mathcal{F}, \chi \rangle$, where $\mathcal{F} \subseteq 2^C$ is a set of subsets of C, and $\chi : V \to 2^C$ is a coloring function that maps vertices to colors in C. We extend χ to sets of vertices in the expected way, thus $\chi(U) = \bigcup\{\chi(v) : v \in U\}$. We define the *size* of a Muller objective $\langle \mathcal{F}, \chi \rangle$ as $|\mathcal{F}|$, namely the number of sets in $\mathcal{F}$. Then, the size of a general weight function $w : 2^\alpha \to \mathbb{N}$ is $\sum_{S \in 2^\alpha} w(S)$.

Muller objectives have been studied mainly with a semantics that refers to the set of states visited in a play infinitely often. Here, we denote them as B-Muller. A play ρ satisfies the B-Muller objective $\langle \mathcal{F}, \chi \rangle$ iff $\chi(\mathit{inf}(\rho)) \in \mathcal{F}$. That is, if the set of colors of the vertices that appear infinitely often in ρ is a member of $\mathcal{F}$. For a semantics that refers to the set of states that the play reaches (a.k.a. weak-Muller games or Staiger-Wagner games [25,34]), we have that ρ satisfies $\langle \mathcal{F}, \chi \rangle$ iff $\chi(\mathit{reach}(\rho)) \in \mathcal{F}$. We refer to this semantics as R-Muller objectives.

A *two-player B-Muller (or R-Muller) game* is a tuple $\mathcal{G} = \langle G, \psi \rangle$, where G is a two-player game graph, and $\psi = \langle \mathcal{F}, \chi \rangle$ is a B-Muller (or R-Muller) objective for Player 1.

Theorem 13 below shows that Muller games are reducible to weighted multiple objective games with general weight functions, and vice versa.

Theorem 13. *1. Every MaxWB (and MaxWR) objective $\psi = \langle \alpha, w, t \rangle$ with a general weight function has an equivalent B-Muller (R-Muller, respectively) objective of size $|\{S \subseteq \alpha : w(S) \geq t\}|$.*
2. Every B-Muller (and R-Muller) objective $\psi = \langle \mathcal{F}, \chi \rangle$ with a set of colors C has an equivalent MaxWB (MaxWR, respectively) objective with a general weight function of size $|\psi|$.

Proof. We start with the first claim. Let $\psi = \langle \alpha, w, t \rangle$. We define $\psi' = \langle \mathcal{F}, \chi \rangle$ with the set of colors α, where the Muller set $\mathcal{F} \subseteq 2^\alpha$ is such that $\mathcal{F} = \{S \subseteq \alpha : w(S) \geq t\}$, and the coloring function $\chi : V \to 2^\alpha$ is such that $\chi(v) = \mathsf{obj}(v)$ for every $v \in V$. It is easy to see that for every play ρ, we have that ρ satisfies ψ iff ρ satisfies ψ', and $|\psi'| = |\{S \subseteq \alpha : w(S) \geq t\}|$.

For the second claim, consider a set of colors C, and let $\psi = \langle \mathcal{F}, \chi \rangle$, with $\mathcal{F} \subseteq 2^C$. We define $\psi' = \langle \alpha, w, 1 \rangle$, where $\alpha = \{\alpha_i\}_{i \in C}$, with $\alpha_i = \chi^{-1}(i)$, for every $i \in C$. Then, for every $S \in 2^\alpha$, we have that $w(S) = 1$ for every $S \in \mathcal{F}$, and $w(S) = 0$ for every $S \notin \mathcal{F}$. It is easy to see that for every play ρ, we have that ρ satisfies ψ iff ρ satisfies ψ', and since $|w| = |\{S \subseteq \alpha : w(S) = 1\}|$, we have that $|w| = |\psi|$. □

Since the problems of deciding B-Muller and R-Muller games are PAPCE-complete [19,26,34], we can conclude with the following.

Theorem 14. *Deciding the winner in MaxWB and MaxWR games with general weight functions is PSPACE-complete.*

As for the memory requirements for winning strategies, by Theorem 13, given a MaxWB or MaxWR objective ψ with a general weight function, the memory requirement for a winning strategy for Player 1 in a game with objective ψ coincides with the memory requirement for a winning strategy for Player 1 in the Muller game with an objective $\langle \mathcal{F}, \chi \rangle$ equivalent to ψ. For B-Muller games, the picture is well understood – the memory requirements are these required for the Zielonka tree $\mathcal{Z}_\mathcal{F}$. For R-Muller games, the memory requirements are exponential, and heuristics for their minimization have been studied in [25].

6 Discussion

We studied many aspects of weighted multi-objectives games. In the area of ω-regular games, researchers have extensively studied the expressive power and complexity of different types of Boolean objectives [28]. In the context of weighted multiple objectives, there are two parameters to the type of an objective: the class of the underlying objectives and the class of the weight function.

We focused on non-decreasing weight functions and showed that moving to general weight functions leads to the expressive power (and computational price) of Boolean Muller games. In the context of *bidding* in game theory, researchers have studied additional interesting classes of weight functions [35] (Chap. 11). We find it interesting to study restrictions on weight functions as a mean for defining objectives that are simpler than Muller, and are different from the simplification studied so far in the Boolean setting.

One can also study weighted multiple objective games in which the underlying objectives are stronger than Büchi and reachability, in particular games with underlying *parity* objectives. By [16], generalized parity games have the flavor of Streett games (in particular, their decidability is co-NP-complete). Also, it is not hard to see that Muller objectives can be translated to weighted multiple parity objectives with a non-decreasing weight function (as opposed to general weight functions, required in the translation of Muller to weighted multiple Büchi objectives). Thus, while weighted multiple parity objectives are of interest, the inherited complexity of parity dominates the complexity that has to do with the weights. Consequently, we find their study less interesting than that of multiple Büchi or reachability objectives.

Acknowledgments. This research was supported by the Israel Science Foundation, Grant 2357/19, and European Research Council, Advanced Grant ADVANSYNT.

References

1. de Alfaro, L., Henzinger, T., Majumdar, R.: Discounting the future in systems theory. In: Proc. 30th Int. Colloq. on Automata, Languages, and Programming. Lecture Notes in Computer Science, vol. 2719, pp. 1022–1037 (2003)
2. Almagor, S., Boker, U., Kupferman, O.: Formalizing and reasoning about quality. J. ACM **63**(3), 24:1–24:56 (2016)
3. Almagor, S., Kuperberg, D., Kupferman, O.: Sensing as a complexity measure. Int. J. Found. Comput. Sci. **30**(6–7), 831–873 (2019)
4. Avni, G., Henzinger, T., Chonev, V.: Infinite-duration bidding games. J. ACM **66**(4), 31:1–31:29 (2019)
5. Bloem, R., Chatterjee, K., Jobstmann, B.: Graph games and reactive synthesis. In: Handbook of Model Checking., pp. 921–962. Springer (2018)
6. Bohy, A., Bruyère, V., Filiot, E., Raskin, J.-F.: Synthesis from LTL specifications with mean-payoff objectives. In: Piterman, N., Smolka, S.A. (eds.) TACAS 2013. LNCS, vol. 7795, pp. 169–184. Springer, Heidelberg (2013). https://doi.org/10.1007/978-3-642-36742-7_12
7. Boker, U., Chatterjee, K., Henzinger, T., Kupferman, O.: Temporal specifications with accumulative values. In: Proceedings of the 26th IEEE Symposium on Logic in Computer Science, pp. 43–52 (2011)
8. Bouyer, P., Brenguier, R., Markey, N., Ummels, M.: Concurrent games with ordered objectives. In: Birkedal, L. (ed.) FoSSaCS 2012. LNCS, vol. 7213, pp. 301–315. Springer, Heidelberg (2012). https://doi.org/10.1007/978-3-642-28729-9_20
9. Bouyer, P., N, F., Randour, M., Vandenhove, P.: How to play optimally for regular objectives? (2023)
10. Büchi, J.: On a decision method in restricted second order arithmetic. In: Proceedings of the International Congress on Logic, Method, and Philosophy of Science. 1960, pp. 1–12. Stanford University Press (1962)
11. Chatterjee, K., Doyen, L.: Energy and mean-payoff parity markov decision processes. In: 36th International Symposium on Mathematical Foundations of Computer Science, pp. 206–218 (2011)

12. Chatterjee, K., Doyen, L.: Energy parity games. Theoret. Comput. Sci. **458**, 49–60 (2012)
13. Chatterjee, K., Doyen, L., Henzinger, T., Raskin, J.F.: Generalized mean-payoff and energy games. In: Proc. 30th Conf. on Foundations of Software Technology and Theoretical Computer Science. LIPIcs, vol. 8, pp. 505–516. Schloss Dagstuhl - Leibniz-Zentrum für Informatik (2010)
14. Chatterjee, K., Dvorak, W., Henzinger, M., Loitzenbauer, V.: Conditionally optimal algorithms for generalized büchi games. In: 41st Int. Symp. on Mathematical Foundations of Computer Science. LIPIcs, vol. 58, pp. 25:1–25:15. Schloss Dagstuhl – Leibniz-Zentrum für Informatik (2016)
15. Chatterjee, K., Henzinger, T.A., Piterman, N.: Generalized parity games. In: Seidl, H. (ed.) FoSSaCS 2007. LNCS, vol. 4423, pp. 153–167. Springer, Heidelberg (2007). https://doi.org/10.1007/978-3-540-71389-0_12
16. Chatterjee, K., Henzinger, T.A., Piterman, N.: Strategy logic. In: Proceedings of the 18th International Conference on Concurrency Theory, pp. 59–73 (2007)
17. Chatterjee, K., Komárková, Z., Kretínský, J.: Unifying two views on multiple mean-payoff objectives in markov decision processes. In: Proceedings of the 30th IEEE Symposium on Logic in Computer Science, pp. 244–256 (2015)
18. Chatterjee, K., Majumdar, R., Henzinger, T.A.: Controller synthesis with budget constraints. In: Egerstedt, M., Mishra, B. (eds.) HSCC 2008. LNCS, vol. 4981, pp. 72–86. Springer, Heidelberg (2008). https://doi.org/10.1007/978-3-540-78929-1_6
19. Dziembowski, S., Jurdzinski, M., Walukiewicz, I.: How much memory is needed to win infinite games. In: Proceedings of the 12th IEEE Symposium on Logic in Computer Science, pp. 99–110 (1997)
20. Emerson, E., Jutla, C.: The complexity of tree automata and logics of programs. In: Proceedings of the 29th IEEE Symposium on Foundations of Computer Science, pp. 328–337 (1988)
21. Fijalkow, N., Horn, F.: The surprizing complexity of reachability games. CoRR **abs/1010.2420** (2010)
22. Gurfinkel, A., Chechik, M.: Multi-valued model-checking via classical model-checking. In: Proceedings of the 14th International Conference on Concurrency Theory, pp. 263–277. Springer-Verlag (2003)
23. Harel, D., Pnueli, A.: On the development of reactive systems. In: Apt, K. (ed.) Logics and Models of Concurrent Systems, NATO Advanced Summer Institutes, vol. F-13, pp. 477–498. Springer (1985)
24. Henzinger, T.: From Boolean to quantitative notions of correctness. In: Proceedings of the 37th ACM Symposium on Principles of Programming Languages, pp. 157–158 (2010)
25. Holtmann, M.: Memory and delay in regular infinite games. Ph.D. thesis, RWTH Aachen University (2011)
26. Hunter, P., Dawar, A.: Complexity Bounds for Regular Games. MFCS 2005. LNCS, vol. 3618, pp. 495–506. Springer, Heidelberg (2005). https://doi.org/10.1007/11549345_43
27. Immerman, N.: Number of quantifiers is better than number of tape cells. J. Comput. Syst. Sci. **22**(3), 384–406 (1981)
28. Kupferman, O.: Automata theory and model checking. In: Handbook of Model Checking, pp. 107–151. Springer (2018)
29. Kupferman, O., Perelli, G., Vardi, M.Y.: Synthesis with rational environments. Ann. Math. Artif. Intell. **78**(1), 3–20 (2016). https://doi.org/10.1007/s10472-016-9508-8

30. Kupferman, O., Piterman, N., Vardi, M.Y.: Safraless Compositional Synthesis. In: Ball, T., Jones, R.B. (eds.) CAV 2006. LNCS, vol. 4144, pp. 31–44. Springer, Heidelberg (2006). https://doi.org/10.1007/11817963_6
31. Kupferman, O., Shenwald, N.: Games with trading of control. In: Proceedings of the 34th Internatinoal Conference on Concurrency Theory. Leibniz International Proceedings in Informatics (LIPIcs), vol. 279, pp. 19:1–19:17. Schloss Dagstuhl – Leibniz-Zentrum für Informatik (2023)
32. Kupferman, O., Tamir, T.: Alternating reachability games with behavioral and revenue objectives. In: Proceeedings of the 22nd Interenational Conferene on Logic for Programming Artificial Intelligence and Reasoning (2018)
33. Martin, D.: Borel determinacy. Ann. Math. **65**, 363–371 (1975)
34. Neumann, J., Szepietowski, A., Walukiewicz, I.: Complexity of weak acceptance conditions in tree automata. Inf. Process. Lett. **84**(4), 181–187 (2002)
35. Nisan, N., Roughgarden, T., Tardos, E., Vazirani, V.: Algorithmic Game Theory. Cambridge University Press (2007)
36. Piterman, N., Pnueli, A., Saar, Y.: Synthesis of reactive(1) designs. In: Proceedings of the 7th International Conference on Verification, Model Checking, and Abstract Interpretation. LNCS, vol. 3855, pp. 364–380. Springer (2006)
37. Pnueli, A., Rosner, R.: On the synthesis of a reactive module. In: Proceedings of the 16th ACM Symposium on Principles of Programming Languages, pp. 179–190 (1989)
38. Rizzi, R., Tomescu, A.: Faster fptases for counting and random generation of knapsack solutions. Inf. Comput. **267**, 135–144 (2019)
39. Thomas, W.: On the synthesis of strategies in infinite games. In: Mayr, E.W., Puech, C. (eds.) STACS 1995. LNCS, vol. 900, pp. 1–13. Springer, Heidelberg (1995). https://doi.org/10.1007/3-540-59042-0_57
40. Vardi, M., Wolper, P.: Automata-theoretic techniques for modal logics of programs. J. Comput. Syst. Sci. **32**(2), 182–221 (1986)
41. Velner, Y., Chatterjee, K., Doyen, L., Henzinger, T., Rabinovich, A., Raskin, J.F.: The complexity of multi-mean-payoff and multi-energy games. Inf. Comput. **241**, 177–196 (2015)

Concurrent and Distributed Systems

Proving Cutoff Bounds for Safety Properties in First-Order Logic

Raz Lotan(✉), Eden Frenkel, and Sharon Shoham

Tel Aviv University, Tel Aviv, Israel
lotanraz@tauex.tau.ac.il

Abstract. First-order logic has been established as an important tool for modeling and verifying intricate systems such as distributed protocols and concurrent systems. These systems are parametric in the number of nodes in the network or the number of threads, which is finite in any system instance, but unbounded. One disadvantage of first-order logic is that it cannot distinguish between finite and infinite structures, leading to spurious counterexamples. To mitigate this, we offer a verification approach that captures only finite system instances. Our approach is an adaptation of the cutoff method to systems modeled in first-order logic. The idea is to show that any safety violation in a system instance of size larger than some bound can be simulated by a safety violation in a system of a smaller size. The simulation provides an inductive argument for correctness in finite instances, reducing the problem to showing safety of instances with bounded size. To this end, we develop a framework to (i) encode such simulation relations in first-order logic and to (ii) validate the simulation relation by a set of verification conditions given to an SMT solver. We apply our approach to verify safety of a set of examples, some of which cannot be proven by a first-order inductive invariant.

1 Introduction

Many recent works [2,4,5,15,24,25,34,35,44,45] have used first-order logic for deductive or automatic verification of distributed protocols, concurrent programs, and other systems that operate over unbounded domains. Most of these works are based on the notion of an *inductive invariant* as a way of verifying safety properties—properties of all reachable states of a system. An inductive invariant is a property that holds in the initial states of the system and is preserved by the steps of the system. The system, its properties and its inductive invariants are all specified using first-order formulas, which allows to build on the success of first-order provers and SMT solvers, with or without theories, for automatically discharging the verification conditions that establish correctness of the system.

Using first-order logic for modeling and verifying systems and their inductive invariants has significant benefits. First, first-order logic provides a natural and expressive specification language that, thanks to uninterpreted relation and function symbols as well as quantifiers, is able to model unbounded domains,

S. Akshay et al. (Eds.): ATVA 2024, LNCS 15054, pp. 135–159, 2025.
https://doi.org/10.1007/978-3-031-78709-6_7

such as network topologies, sets of messages, quorums of processes, and so on. In fact, first-order logic is Turing-complete as a specification language for systems [34]. Second, first-order logic benefits from a plethora of automatic solvers that already exhibit impressive performance and continue to improve rapidly.

Unfortunately, using first-order logic for encoding and verifying systems and their inductive invariants also has several crucial downsides. One obstacle is that it is not always possible to express a suitable inductive invariant in first-order logic. Another problem arises from the inability of first-order logic to distinguish between finite and infinite structures. This may lead to spurious infinite counterexamples to induction [9], or even to spurious violations of the property, in cases where all finite instances of the system satisfy a desired property, but some infinite instances do not (see Example 1). Because we are usually only interested in finite, albeit unbounded, instances (e.g., a finite number of processes), violations caused by infinite instances are spurious.

In this work, we mitigate the aforementioned obstacles by (i) considering a *finite-domain* semantics for first-order transition systems that only includes the finite instances of the system (of any size), and (ii) devising a deductive approach for establishing a *cutoff* for a first-order transition system and a safety property under the finite-domain semantics via a *size-reducing simulation* between instances of the system. The simulation relation is encoded and validated using first-order logic. This allows us to take the finite-domain semantics into account in the verification process, while still using first-order solvers to discharge the resulting verification conditions.

Cutoffs are widely used in the context of parameterized systems. A parameterized system is a family of transition systems $T = \{T_n\}_n$, one for each natural number $n \in \mathbb{N}$. The parameter n can represent the number of nodes in a distributed network, the number of threads running a concurrent program, the length of an array or a linked list, etc. The parameterized system T satisfies a property P if T_n satisfies P for all n. A number k is a cutoff for the system T and the property P if, to verify that T satisfies P, it suffices to verify that T_n satisfies P for all $n \leq k$. Cutoffs therefore allow to reduce the verification of the unbounded system T to verification of a system where n is bounded by k. The cutoff method, introduced by [11], proposes to establish that k is a cutoff for T by proving that for every $n > k$, T_n is simulated by $T_{n'}$ for some $n' < n$.

Much like a parameterized system, a first-order specification of a transition system induces a family of transition systems, except that instead of a numeric parameter, the instances are defined by the domain of their states. We can therefore adapt the cutoff method to verify all the finite instances of a first-order transition system (i.e., instances obtained by fixing a finite domain): instead of a simulation between any T_n for $n > k$ and some $T_{n'}$ with $n' < n$, we need to show a simulation between any instance with a finite domain of size $> k$ and some instance with a strictly smaller domain.

The key technical contribution of our work is a realization of the cutoff method for first-order transition systems using a size-reducing simulation relation between finite instances of the system. A size-reducing simulation relation can be understood as proving the induction step in a proof by induction on the size of the domain. It therefore lifts correctness of instances of size at most k to all finite instances, but *not* to infinite instances. As a result, it may succeed to verify first-order specifications that only satisfy their property w.r.t. the finite-domain semantics and not w.r.t. the first-order semantics. Moreover, as already demonstrated in previous work [19], verification by simulation (akin to induction on domain size) may sometimes be easier than verification based on inductive invariants (akin to induction on time), and can succeed in cases where an inductive invariant cannot be expressed in first-order logic.

We propose a first-order encoding of a size-reducing simulation relation for a first-order transition system. We further show how to verify the correctness of such a (user-provided) encoding by a set of verification conditions that are encoded as first-order formulas and discharged by an automatic solver.

Our first challenge is to ensure that the simulation relation is size-reducing in finite domains. While first-order logic can express the property that the size of a set is exactly k, at most k or at least k, for any specific number k, it cannot directly compare the sizes of sets of arbitrary sizes. Our solution is to guarantee size reduction by defining the smaller domain as a subset of the larger domain obtained by deleting one element. The element to be deleted is specified by a (user-provided) formula. For finite instances, this ensures that the size of the domain decreases.

The next challenge arises from the definition of a simulation relation, which involves quantification over states: *every* successor state of the larger state must be simulated by *some* successor state of the smaller state. When states are modeled using uninterpreted functions and relations, this leads to higher-order quantification. To facilitate a first-order encoding of the verification conditions, we strengthen the definition of the simulation relation. Namely, we replace the existential quantification over a simulating successor state of the smaller state by universal quantification, stating that *every* state that simulates the larger successor state is a successor of the smaller state. To ensure that the universal quantification is not satisfied vacuously, we require the (inductive) totality of the simulation relation.

Contributions. The main contributions of this paper are:

- We define the finite-domain semantics of first-order specifications of transition systems, formulate the notion of cutoffs, and define size-reducing simulations as a way of proving cutoffs for finite-domain first-order transition systems (Sect. 3).
- We develop an approach for defining and validating size-reducing simulation relations in first-order logic (Sect. 4).
- We implement a tool that receives as input a first-order specification of a transition system and a safety property, as well as a first-order encoding of a size-reducing simulation relation, and validates the simulation relation using the Z3 [29] SMT solver (Sect. 5).

– We demonstrate the applicability of the approach by verifying a set of examples of distributed protocols and concurrent systems, including some that cannot be verified by classical techniques based on inductive invariants (Sect. 5).

The rest of the paper is organized as follows: Sect. 2 provides the necessary background on transition systems in first-order logic, Sects. 3 to 5 present the above contributions, Sect. 6 discusses related work and Sect. 7 concludes the paper. Due to space considerations we defer all proofs to the full version of this paper [27].

2 Preliminaries

This section provides a brief background on transition systems, first-order logic and first-order specifications of transition systems and properties.

Transition Systems. a transition system T is given by $T = (S, I, R)$, where S is the set of states, $I \subseteq S$ is the set of initial states, and $R \subseteq S \times S$ is the transition relation. A trace of T is a sequence of states $(s_i)_{i=0}^{t}$ such that $s_0 \in I$ and for every $0 \leq i < t$ we have $(s_i, s_{i+1}) \in R$. We denote by $R^\star$ the reflexive transitive closure of R. A state s is reachable if there exists a trace $(s_i)_{i=0}^{t}$ such that $s_t = s$. A safety property is given by a set of states $P \subseteq S$. We say that T satisfies P, denoted $T \models P$, if every reachable state of T is in P. A set of states $J \subseteq S$ is an inductive invariant of T if for any state $s \in I$ we have $s \in J$ and for any two states $(s, s') \in R$ such that $s \in J$ we have $s' \in J$. Note that if J is an inductive invariant and $J \subseteq P$ then $T \models P$.

First-Order Logic. We consider first-order logic with equality. For simplicity of the presentation, we consider the single-sorted, uninterpreted version of first-order logic, i.e., without background theories. However, in practice, we use many-sorted first-order logic and allow some sorts and symbols to be interpreted by arbitrary background theories. See Sect. 4.5 for more details.

A first-order vocabulary Σ consists of relation and function symbols, where function symbols with arity zero are also called constant symbols. Terms t over Σ are either variables x or function applications $f(t_1, \ldots, t_m)$. Formulas are defined recursively, where atomic formulas are either $t_1 = t_2$ or $r(t_1, \ldots, t_m)$ where r is a relation symbol. Non-atomic formulas are built using connectives $\neg, \wedge, \vee, \rightarrow$ and quantifiers $\forall, \exists$. We denote by $\mathit{Vars}(\alpha)$ the variables of a formula α, by $\mathit{FV}(\alpha)$ the free variables of α, and write $\alpha(x_1, \ldots, x_m)$ when $\mathit{FV}(\alpha) \subseteq \{x_1, \ldots, x_m\}$. We denote a sequence $x_1, \ldots, x_m$ by $\boldsymbol{x}$ when m is clear from context.

A structure for Σ is a pair $s = (\mathcal{D}, \mathcal{I})$ where $\mathcal{D}$ is a domain (a nonempty set of elements), denoted $\mathrm{dom}(s)$, and $\mathcal{I}$ is an interpretation that maps each relation and function symbol to an appropriate construct over the domain. We denote by $\mathrm{struct}(\Sigma)$ the set[1] of all structures for Σ. We define the cardinality (size) of s,

[1] Technically, $\mathrm{struct}(\Sigma)$ is not a well-defined set in the sense of set theory (since we allow the domain of a structure to be an arbitrary set). However, for the sake of this paper we can restrict the domains to be subsets of $\mathbb{N}$ without loss of generality.

denoted $|s|$, to be $|\mathrm{dom}(s)|$. For two structures $s = (\mathcal{D}, \mathcal{I})$ and $s_\times = (\mathcal{D}_\times, \mathcal{I}_\times)$, we say that $s_\times$ is a substructure of s if $\mathcal{D}_\times \subseteq \mathcal{D}$, for every relation $r \in \Sigma$ with arity m we have $\mathcal{I}_\times(r) = \mathcal{I}(r) \cap \mathcal{D}_\times^m$ and for every function $f \in \Sigma$ with arity m we have $\mathcal{I}_\times(f) = \mathcal{I}(f)|_{\mathcal{D}_\times^m}$. For a formula α with free variables $FV(\alpha)$, a structure $s = (\mathcal{D}, \mathcal{I})$ and an assignment $v : FV(\alpha) \to \mathcal{D}$ mapping each free variable in α to an element from the domain, we write $s, v \models \alpha$ to denote that the pair (s, v) satisfies α, defined as usual. For a variable x and a domain element d, we write $[x \to d]$ for the assignment $v : \{x\} \to \mathcal{D}$ with $v(x) = d$. For two formulas α, β (not necessarily closed), we write $\alpha \implies \beta$ to denote the validity of $\alpha \to \beta$.

For a vocabulary Σ and an identifier o, we denote by Σ^o the vocabulary $\{a^o \mid a \in \Sigma\}$. We assume that $\Sigma \cap \Sigma^o = \emptyset$. For a formula (or term) α over Σ we denote by α^o the formula (respectively, term) over Σ^o obtained by substituting each symbol $a \in \Sigma$ by $a^o \in \Sigma^o$. With abuse of notation, we sometimes consider an interpretation $\mathcal{I}$ for Σ as an interpretation for Σ^o where $\mathcal{I}(a^o) = \mathcal{I}(a)$, or, similarly, an interpretation $\mathcal{I}^o$ of Σ^o as an interpretation for Σ.

First-Order Specifications of Transition Systems. We consider transition systems given by a first-order logic specification $\mathcal{T} = (\Sigma, \Gamma, \iota, \tau)$ where Σ is a vocabulary, Γ is a closed formula over Σ that acts as a finitely-axiomatizable background theory, ι is a closed formula over Σ that specifies initial states, and τ is a closed formula defined over vocabulary $\Sigma \uplus \Sigma'$ that specifies the transition relation. Intuitively, the unprimed copy of Σ specifies the pre-state of a transition, while the primed copy specifies the post-state. Some symbols in Σ may be declared immutable, in which case τ preserves their interpretation.

Any domain $\mathcal{D}$ defines a transition system $T_\mathcal{D} = (S_\mathcal{D}, I_\mathcal{D}, R_\mathcal{D})$ where $S_\mathcal{D}$ is the set of structures $s \in \mathrm{struct}(\Sigma)$ with $\mathrm{dom}(s) = \mathcal{D}$ that satisfy the axioms, i.e., $s \models \Gamma$; $I_\mathcal{D}$ is the set of states $s \in S_\mathcal{D}$ that satisfy ι; and the transition relation $R_\mathcal{D}$ is the set of all pairs of states $((\mathcal{D}, \mathcal{I}), (\mathcal{D}, \mathcal{I}'))$ where, when we identify $\mathcal{I}$ as an interpretation of Σ and $\mathcal{I}'$ as an interpretation of Σ' we have $(\mathcal{D}, \mathcal{I} \uplus \mathcal{I}') \models \tau$.

The standard first-order semantics of $\mathcal{T}$ is then given by the transition system $T_{\mathrm{fol}} = (S_{\mathrm{fol}}, I_{\mathrm{fol}}, R_{\mathrm{fol}})$ where $S_{\mathrm{fol}}, I_{\mathrm{fol}}, R_{\mathrm{fol}}$ are the (disjoint) union of their counterparts in $T_\mathcal{D}$ over all domains $\mathcal{D}$ (see footnote 1 for well-definedness of the union). Note that every trace of T_{fol} is a trace of $T_\mathcal{D}$ for some domain $\mathcal{D}$. This is because $(s, s') \in R_{\mathrm{fol}}$ implies $\mathrm{dom}(s) = \mathrm{dom}(s')$. We refer to $T_\mathcal{D}$ as a system instance of T_{fol}.

Safety properties and inductive invariants are also specified by closed first-order formulas over Σ. A safety specification φ induces a safety property $P = \{s \in S_{\mathrm{fol}} \mid s \models \varphi\}$ for T_{fol}. With abuse of notation we will also consider P as a safety property of $T_\mathcal{D}$ for any domain $\mathcal{D}$ instead of writing $P \cap S_\mathcal{D}$.

3 The Cutoff Method for First-Order Transition Systems

The standard first-order semantics T_{fol} of a transition system specification $\mathcal{T}$ is often an abstraction of the intended semantics in the sense that it considers as a state *any* first-order structure (that satisfies Γ), whereas in many cases the intended semantics only considers finite structures. In this section we define a finite-domain semantics $\mathcal{T}_{\text{fin}}$ for $\mathcal{T}$, where the size of states (structures) is finite but unbounded. The finite-domain semantics induces a parameterized system, where the parameter is the size of the (finite) domain. We then formulate the cutoff method, based on the notion of a size-reducing simulation, in the context of first-order transition systems, as a way of reducing safety verification of $\mathcal{T}_{\text{fin}}$ to safety verification of a *bounded* transition system, whose states are of size at most k.

3.1 Finite-Domain Semantics of a First-Order Transition System

The finite-domain semantics of a first-order specification of a transition system $\mathcal{T}$ is given by the transition system $\mathcal{T}_{\text{fin}} = (S_{\text{fin}}, I_{\text{fin}}, R_{\text{fin}})$ where $S_{\text{fin}}, I_{\text{fin}}, R_{\text{fin}}$ are defined similarly to the corresponding definitions in $\mathcal{T}_{\text{fol}}$, except that only *finite* domains are included. Note that a semantics that *bounds* the domain size by some $k \in \mathbb{N}$ can be captured with the standard first-order semantics by adding to Γ the formula $\text{size}_{\leq k} := \exists x_1, \ldots, x_k . \forall x. \bigvee_i (x = x_i)$ as an axiom. However, the same cannot be done to capture the finite-domain semantics since finiteness of the domain is not definable in first-order logic.

Every trace of $\mathcal{T}_{\text{fin}}$ is also a trace of $\mathcal{T}_{\text{fol}}$. Hence, every safety property that is satisfied by $\mathcal{T}_{\text{fol}}$ is also satisfied by $\mathcal{T}_{\text{fin}}$, but the converse need not hold, as demonstrated by the following example.

Example 1 (TreeTermination). Consider a simple termination detection protocol for nodes arranged in a rooted tree (which captures the second phase of a simple broadcast protocol [38]). Upon receiving an ack from all its children, a node terminates and sends an ack to its parent, except for the root, which does not have a parent. The protocol satisfies the safety property that if the root has declared termination then all nodes have terminated as well.

A first-order specification of this protocol is given in Fig. 1. The tree structure is modeled as proposed in [32], by a relation leq, axiomatized to induce a tree, with the intention that leq(X, Y) indicates that Y is a descendant of X in the tree. The axioms in Example 1 ensure that leq is a partial order with the root as its minimum and Example 1 guarantees the tree structure. The formula child(Y, X) indicates that Y is a child of X by asserting that X is a predecessor of Y in the order.

For finite instances, the specification satisifies safety: any node X in the tree is connected to the root by a finite sequence of predecessor steps. It follows by induction on the length of this sequence that if the root terminated, so did X. The induction step follows from the precondition of terminate, which ensures that a node terminates only after its children sent it acks, and so already terminated.

While this proof is correct, it uses induction on the length of tree paths, and as a consequence, relies on the finiteness of the tree. In fact, if we allow infinite structures, the safety property may be violated. A counterexample trace for an infinite instance of the protocol is given in Fig. 2. In the example, the partial order is in fact a total order that consists of infinitely many nodes, all

```
sort node
immutable constant root : node
immutable relation leq(node,node)
axiom ∀X. leq(root,X) ∧ leq(X,X)
axiom ∀X,Y. leq(X,Y) ∧ leq(Y,X) → X=Y
axiom ∀X,Y,Z. leq(X,Y) ∧ leq(Y,Z)
           → leq(X,Z)
axiom ∀X,Y,Z. leq(Y,X) ∧ leq(Z,X)
           → leq(Y,Z) ∨ leq(Z,Y)
def child(Y,X) := leq(X,Y) ∧ X≠Y ∧
           ∀Z.leq(Z,Y) ∧ Z≠Y →leq(Z,X)
relation termd(node)
relation ack(node,node)
init ¬termd(X)
init ¬ack(X,Y)

transition terminate(n: node)
  assume ∀X. child(X,n) → ack(X,n)
  ∀X. termd'(X) = termd(X) ∨ (X = n)
  ∀X,Y. ack'(X,Y) = ack(X,Y) ∨ child(n,Y)

safety termd(root) → ∀X. termd(X)
```

Fig. 1. First-order specification of the TreeTermination protocol.

of which are larger than the root, but for none the root is a predecessor. The counterexample consists of a single step, where the root, which has no children and therefore satisfies the pre-condition of the termination transition vacuously, terminates, even though all the other nodes did not terminate.

In the sequel, we develop an approach that mimics induction over the state size and is able to verify the protocol for all finite instances by showing that every instance with more than 2 nodes is simulated by an instance where some node other than the root is deleted.

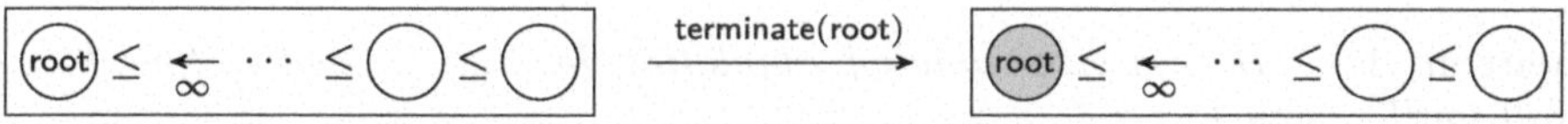

Fig. 2. A counterexample to safety of TreeTermination over infinite structures, depicted as a trace of two states related by the transition relation: the first is an initial state, and the second violates safety. The order of nodes in each state is depicted by $\leq$ and terminated nodes are depicted by shading.

3.2 Establishing Cutoffs by Size-Reducing Simulations

To verify first-order transition systems under the finite-domain semantics, we adapt the cutoff method to fit the first-order setting. Fix a first order specification $\mathcal{T}$, its corresponding transition systems $\{T_{\mathcal{D}}\}_{\mathcal{D}}$, its finite-domain semantics T_{fin}, a safety specification φ, and the induced safety property P. We define the notion of a cutoff for T_{fin} and P as an adaptation of the standard definition [31].

Definition 1. *A natural number k is a* cutoff *for T_{fin} and P if*

$$T_{\text{fin}} \models P \qquad \Longleftrightarrow \qquad T_{\mathcal{D}} \models P \text{ for all } \mathcal{D} \text{ with } |\mathcal{D}| \leq k.$$

Generally speaking, cutoffs allow to reduce verification of parameterized systems to verification of bounded systems: if k is a cutoff, then it suffices to verify $T_{\mathcal{D}}$ for domains $\mathcal{D}$ with $|\mathcal{D}| \leq k$ in order to deduce that $T_{\text{fin}} \models P$. Traditionally (e.g., in [11]), cutoffs are investigated for *classes* of transition systems and properties. Since Definition 1 considers cutoffs for a specific specification of a transition system and a specific safety property, a cutoff always exists: if $T_{\text{fin}} \models P$, then $T_{\mathcal{D}} \models P$ for any finite $\mathcal{D}$, making any k a cutoff. Similarly, if $T_{\text{fin}} \not\models P$, then there exists a violating trace with some finite domain $\mathcal{D}$, making $k = |\mathcal{D}|$ a cutoff. The challenge our work addresses, and what makes cutoffs useful for verification, is to establish a cutoff without checking whether $T_{\text{fin}} \models P$. To do so, we use the notion of a size-reducing simulation.

Definition 2. *A* size-reducing simulation *for T_{fin}, P and a bound k is a relation $H \subseteq S_{\text{fin}} \times S_{\text{fin}}$ such that:*

1. *Size Reduction: For every pair $(s^h, s^\ell) \in H$ we have $|s^\ell| < |s^h|$.*
2. *Initiation: For every state $s^h \in I_{\text{fin}}$ with $|s^h| > k$ there exists $s^\ell \in I_{\text{fin}}$ such that $(s^h, s^\ell) \in H$.*
3. *Simulation: For every pair $(s^h, s^\ell) \in H$ and $s^{h\prime} \in S_{\text{fin}}$ such that $(s^h, s^{h\prime}) \in R_{\text{fin}}$ there exists $s^{\ell\prime} \in S_{\text{fin}}$ such that $(s^{h\prime}, s^{\ell\prime}) \in H$ and $(s^\ell, s^{\ell\prime}) \in R^\star_{\text{fin}}$.*
4. *Fault Preservation: For every pair $(s^h, s^\ell) \in H$, if $s^h \notin P$ then $s^\ell \notin P$.*

Usually (e.g., in [11,31]) simulation relations for showing cutoffs are defined between different instances of the parameterized system. Instead, a size-reducing simulation is a self-simulation of T_{fin}, which is more natural in this context.

Theorem 1. *If H is a size-reducing simulation for T_{fin}, P and k, then k is a cutoff for T_{fin} and P.*

Intuitively, the theorem holds because we can use H to translate a trace violating P in system instances of (finite) size larger than k to a (perhaps shorter/longer) trace violating P in a system instance with a smaller domain. Then, continuing by induction, we get a violating trace of size smaller than k. Thus if no counterexample to safety exists for system instances whose domain size is at most k, no counterexample exists for T_{fin}, making k a cutoff.

Our goal is to encode size-reducing simulations in first-order logic. As written, items 2 and 3 involve alternation between universal and existential quantification over states. Since states are first-order structures, explicitly quantifying over them requires higher-order quantification. Note, however, that if a claim only involves universal quantification over states, the quantification can remain implicit by checking (first-order) validity. We use this observation to strengthen Definition 2 to a *strong* size-reducing simulation, by over-approximating the existential quantification using universal quantification together with a totality requirement that guarantees the universal quantification is not vacuous.

Namely, the existential quantification specifies the existence of a state $s^{\ell\prime}$ that simulates $s^{h\prime}$ and is a successor of s^ℓ. When turning it into universal quantification, we can either quantify over all successor states and require that they are all simulating, or vice versa. We choose the latter option. We also strengthen the requirement $(s^\ell, s^{\ell\prime}) \in R^\star_{\text{fin}}$ to $(s^\ell, s^{\ell\prime}) \in R_{\text{fin}}$ or $s^\ell = s^{\ell\prime}$, hence removing the existential quantification on intermediate states. This is illustrated in Fig. 3. The totality check then requires that a simulating state exists initially and that it continues to hold inductively. These still involve existential quantification over states, and we will see in the next section how to reduce them to first-order quantification for the specific class of size-reducing relations that we use.

Definition 3. *A* strong size-reducing simulation *for T_{fin}, P and k is a relation $H \subseteq S_{\text{fin}} \times S_{\text{fin}}$ such that:*

1. *Size Reduction: For every pair $(s^h, s^\ell) \in H$ we have $|s^\ell| < |s^h|$.*
2. *Strong Initiation: For every pair $(s^h, s^\ell) \in H$, if $s^h \in I_{\text{fin}}$ then $s^\ell \in I_{\text{fin}}$.*
3. *Strong Simulation: For all pairs $(s^h, s^\ell) \in H$ and $(s^{h\prime}, s^{\ell\prime}) \in H$, if $(s^h, s^{h\prime}) \in R_{\text{fin}}$ and $\text{dom}(s^\ell) = \text{dom}(s^{\ell\prime})$ then $(s^\ell, s^{\ell\prime}) \in R_{\text{fin}}$ or $s^\ell = s^{\ell\prime}$.*
4. *Fault Preservation: For every pair $(s^h, s^\ell) \in H$, if $s^h \notin P$ then $s^\ell \notin P$.*
5. *Inductive Totality:*
   - *For every $s^h \in I_{\text{fin}}$ with $|s^h| > k$ there exists $s^\ell \in S_{\text{fin}}$ s.t. $(s^h, s^\ell) \in H$.*
   - *For every pair $(s^h, s^{h\prime}) \in R_{\text{fin}}$, if there exists s^ℓ s.t. $(s^h, s^\ell) \in H$ then there exists $s^{\ell\prime} \in S_{\text{fin}}$ s.t. $(s^{h\prime}, s^{\ell\prime}) \in H$ and $\text{dom}(s^\ell) = \text{dom}(s^{\ell\prime})$.*

Note that in the strong simulation requirement we do not consider all states $s^{\ell\prime}$ that simulate s^ℓ but only those that have $\text{dom}(s^\ell) = \text{dom}(s^{\ell\prime})$, since each trace is confined to one system instance. As a result, we also need to require the domain equality in the totality of item 5.

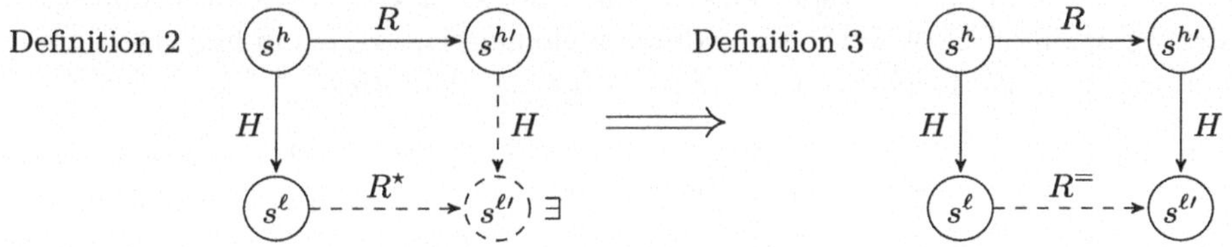

Fig. 3. Strengthening of simulation to strong simulation: solid nodes are universally quantified while the dashed node is existentially quantified; solid edges represent assumptions and dashed edges represent conclusions. $R^=$ is a shorthand for $R \cup \text{id}_S$.

Lemma 1. *A strong size-reducing simulation is a size-reducing simulation.*

The converse of Lemma 1 does not hold. In fact, a transition system may have a size-reducing simulation but no strong size-reducing simulation. Moreover, while size-reducing simulations are as powerful as inductive invariants as a proof rule [31], the proof does not carry over to strong size-reducing simulations.

4 First-Order Encoding of Size-Reducing Simulations

In this section we show how to encode and validate a strong size-reducing simulation in first-order logic. To circumvent the need to express and verify size reduction in first-order logic, we consider a certain class of strong size-reducing simulations, where the pairs (s^h, s^ℓ) in the relation are such that s^ℓ is obtained from s^h by deleting an element in its domain and updating the interpretation of all symbols. We propose a first-order encoding of such relations and show how to validate that the relation defined by this encoding is a strong size-reducing simulation using a set of verification conditions expressible in first-order logic.

For the remainder of the section, fix a first-order specification $\mathcal{T} = (\Sigma, \Gamma, \iota, \tau)$, a safety specification φ and a natural number k. Let T_{fin} be the finite-domain semantics associated with $\mathcal{T}$ and P the safety property associated with φ.

4.1 Encoding Size-Reducing Relations Using Substructures

A strong size-reducing simulation is a relation between states that satisfies certain requirements. To specify a relation between states (structures) we rely on the standard approach of using a formula over a double vocabulary $\Sigma^h \uplus \Sigma^\ell$, where the interpretation of Σ^h represents the "high" state s^h, and the interpretation of Σ^ℓ represents the "low" state s^ℓ. However, since a model of a formula (even when it is a two-vocabulary formula) has a single domain, such an encoding does not account for size reduction of the domain. Our observation is that we can enforce size reduction by deleting an element from the domain. Thus, we use a formula $\eta(z)$ over $\Sigma^h \uplus \Sigma^\ell$ to specify a size-reducing relation, where the deleted element is specified using the free variable z. In a model of $\eta(z)$, the interpretation of Σ^h represents s^h and the state s^ℓ is a substructure of the interpretation of Σ^ℓ with the same domain elements as s^h, excluding the element assigned to z. We formalize this by the following definition.

Definition 4. *Let $\eta(z)$ be a formula over $\Sigma^h \uplus \Sigma^\ell$, $(\mathcal{D}, \mathcal{I}^h \uplus \mathcal{I}^\ell)$ a structure over $\Sigma^h \uplus \Sigma^\ell$ and $d_0 \in \mathcal{D}$ such that $(\mathcal{D}, \mathcal{I}^h \uplus \mathcal{I}^\ell), [z \mapsto d_0] \models \eta(z)$. Then for $\mathcal{D}_\times = \mathcal{D} \setminus \{d_0\}$, if there exists an interpretation $\mathcal{I}^\ell_\times$ such that $(\mathcal{D}_\times, \mathcal{I}^\ell_\times)$ is a substructure of $(\mathcal{D}, \mathcal{I}^\ell)$, we say that $s^\ell = (\mathcal{D}_\times, \mathcal{I}^\ell_\times)$ is an* η-substructure *of $s^h = (\mathcal{D}, \mathcal{I}^h)$. The* size-reducing relation *of η is the relation*

$$H_\eta = \left\{(s^h, s^\ell) \in \text{struct}(\Sigma) \times \text{struct}(\Sigma) \mid s^\ell \textit{ is an } \eta\textit{-substructure of } s^h\right\}.$$

An example of a pair $(s^h, s^\ell) \in H_\eta$ is depicted in Fig. 4 along with the structure $(\mathcal{D}, \mathcal{I}^h \uplus \mathcal{I}^\ell)$ and the element $d_0 \in \mathcal{D}$ that induces them, assuming that $(\mathcal{D}, \mathcal{I}^h \uplus \mathcal{I}^\ell), [z \mapsto d_0] \models \eta(z)$. In the example: $\mathcal{D} = \{1, 2, 3, 4\}$, $d_0 = 3$, $\mathcal{I}^h = \{\mathsf{leq} : \{(1,2), (1,3), (3,4), (1,4)\}, \mathsf{root} : 1, \mathsf{ack} : \{(4,3)\}, \mathsf{termd} : \{4\}\}$ and $\mathcal{I}^\ell = \{\mathsf{leq} : \{(1,2), (1,3), (3,4), (1,4)\}, \mathsf{root} : 1, \mathsf{ack} : \{(4,1)\}, \mathsf{termd} : \{4\}\}$. This induces the pair $(s^h, s^\ell) \in H_\eta$ where $s^h = (\mathcal{D}, \mathcal{I}^h)$, $s^\ell = (\mathcal{D}_\times, \mathcal{I}^\ell_\times)$, $\mathcal{D}_\times = \{1, 2, 4\}$ and $\mathcal{I}^\ell_\times = \{\mathsf{leq} : \{(1,2), (1,4)\}, \mathsf{root} : 1, \mathsf{ack} : \{(4,1)\}, \mathsf{termd} : \{4\}\}$. The choice $d_0 = 4$ would give a different pair in H_η.

Lemma 2. *For a formula $\eta(z)$ over $\Sigma^h \uplus \Sigma^\ell$, and a pair $(s^h, s^\ell) \in H_\eta$ such that s^h is finite, we have $|s^\ell| < |s^h|$.*

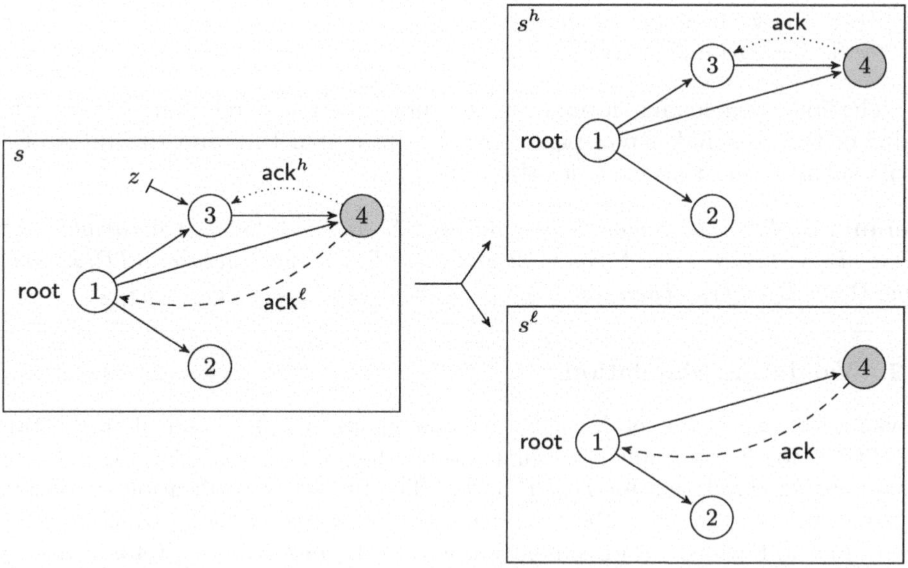

Fig. 4. Left: a structure $s = (\mathcal{D}, \mathcal{I}^h \uplus \mathcal{I}^\ell)$ and an assignment $[z \mapsto d_0]$ that satisfy $\eta(z)$. The h and ℓ copies of root, leq and termd are interpreted in the same way, so these interpretations are depicted jointly. leq$(\cdot,\cdot)$ is depicted by solid arrows and termd$(\cdot)$ is depicted by shading. The interpretation of the two copies of ack$(\cdot,\cdot)$ are depicted by dashed and dotted arrows. Right: the derived high and low structures: $s^h = (\mathcal{D}, \mathcal{I}^h)$ and $s^\ell = (\mathcal{D}_\times, \mathcal{I}^\ell_\times)$, with the relations and constants depicted in the same way.

Lemma 2 states that, when restricting to finite structures, H_η is size-reducing. This holds by construction. In the sequel, we define a set of verification conditions that guarantee the rest of the required properties of Definition 3.

In order to encode the verification conditions, we need to be able to reason about the states $(s^h, s^\ell) \in H_\eta$. The state s^h is captured by $\eta(z)$ directly. However, s^ℓ is defined by a substructure that excludes the element assigned to z from the domain of $\eta(z)$. As a result, we need to exclude z when reasoning about s^ℓ. For this purpose, we define, for a formula α and a variable $z \notin \mathit{Vars}(\alpha)$, the z-excluded representation, denoted $[\alpha]_{\setminus z}$. The z-excluded representation is the formula obtained from α by adding to each quantifier a guard that excludes z. This ensures that the evaluation of $[\alpha]_{\setminus z}$ on a structure with domain $\mathcal{D}$ with z assigned to $d_0 \in \mathcal{D}$ is the same as the evaluation of α on a substructure with domain $\mathcal{D} \setminus \{d_0\}$ (if such a substructure exists, see Sect. 4.3).

Definition 5. *For a formula α and a variable $z \notin \mathit{Vars}(\alpha)$, the z-excluded representation of α, denoted $[\alpha]_{\setminus z}$, is a formula defined inductively as follows:*

- $[\alpha]_{\setminus z} = \alpha$ *if* $\alpha = r(t_1, \ldots, t_m)$ *or* $\alpha = (t_1 = t_2)$
- $[\neg\beta]_{\setminus z} = \neg[\beta]_{\setminus z}$
- $[\beta_1 \bowtie \beta_2]_{\setminus z} = [\beta_1]_{\setminus z} \bowtie [\beta_2]_{\setminus z}$ *for* $\bowtie \in \{\wedge, \vee, \rightarrow\}$

- $[\forall x.\beta]_{\setminus z} = \forall x.(x \neq z) \rightarrow [\beta]_{\setminus z}$
- $[\exists x.\beta]_{\setminus z} = \exists x.(x \neq z) \wedge [\beta]_{\setminus z}$

The following lemma formalizes the aforementioned relation between the value of the z-excluded representation of α in a structure and the value of α in its substructure that excludes the value of z.

Lemma 3. *Let α be a closed formula over Σ and $z \notin Vars(\alpha)$ a variable. Let $(\mathcal{D}, \mathcal{I})$ be a structure for Σ, $d_0 \in \mathcal{D}$ and $(\mathcal{D}_\times, \mathcal{I}_\times)$ a substructure of $(\mathcal{D}, \mathcal{I})$ such that $\mathcal{D}_\times = \mathcal{D} \setminus \{d_0\}$. Then $(\mathcal{D}_\times, \mathcal{I}_\times) \models \alpha \iff (\mathcal{D}, \mathcal{I}), [z \mapsto d_0] \models [\alpha]_{\setminus z}$.*

4.2 Validating Simulation

Given a formula $\eta(z)$ over $\Sigma^h \uplus \Sigma^\ell$, we now go on to define a set of verification conditions for $\mathcal{T}$, φ, k and $\eta(z)$ that ensure that $H_\eta \cap (S_{\text{fin}} \times S_{\text{fin}})$ is a strong size-reducing simulation for T_{fin}, P and k. The full set of verification conditions is listed in Fig. 5. In this subsection we introduce three of them, which guarantee strong initiation, strong simulation and fault preservation (items 2 to 4 of Definition 3). Having already ensured size reduction (item 1) in Lemma 2, the next subsection addresses the final requirement: inductive totality (item 5).

In all verification conditions, we use the appropriate copies of the vocabulary to refer to high states (Σ^h) and low states (Σ^ℓ) and to pre-states (unprimed) and post-states (primed). We use $\eta(z)$ to encode pairs of states related by simulation and the z-excluded representation to encode properties of the low state in a pair. For this purpose, we assume w.l.o.g. that the variable z does not appear in the system and safety specification $\Gamma, \iota, \tau, \varphi$ (this can be achieved by renaming).

Verification conditions (1) and (3) are straight forward encodings of strong initiation and fault preservation, respectively.

Verification condition (2) establishes strong simulation. It requires that any transition between high-states is reflected by a transition between their simulating low states or by a stutter, provided that the low states have the same domain. The assumption that the high and low states are related by the simulation relation is encoded by asserting $\eta(z)$ (for the pre-states) and $\eta'(z)$ (for the post-states). Crucially, we use the same variable z to ensure that we refer to low states with the same domain. We encode a stutter by the formula id_Σ given by $\text{id}_\Sigma := \bigwedge_{r \in \Sigma} (\forall \boldsymbol{x}.\ r'(\boldsymbol{x}) \leftrightarrow r(\boldsymbol{x})) \wedge \bigwedge_{f \in \Sigma} (\forall \boldsymbol{x}.\ f'(\boldsymbol{x}) = f(\boldsymbol{x}))$.

Lemma 4. *Let $\eta(z)$ be a formula over $\Sigma^h \uplus \Sigma^\ell$. If verification conditions (1)–(3) of Fig. 5 are valid then $H_\eta \cap (S_{\text{fin}} \times S_{\text{fin}})$ satisfies items 2 to 4 of Definition 3.*

4.3 Guaranteeing and Validating Totality

So far, we have considered an arbitrary formula $\eta(z)$. We now define a syntactic restriction on $\eta(z)$, that, along with four verification conditions, guarantees that

(1)	$\Gamma^h \wedge \iota^h \wedge \eta(z) \implies [\iota]^\ell_{\setminus z}$	[ι-preservation]
(2)	$\Gamma^h \wedge \Gamma^{h\prime} \wedge \eta(z) \wedge \eta'(z) \wedge \tau^h \implies [\tau \vee \mathrm{id}_\Sigma]^\ell_{\setminus z}$	[τ-preservation]
(3)	$\Gamma^h \wedge \neg\varphi^h \wedge \eta(z) \implies [\neg\varphi]^\ell_{\setminus z}$	[$\neg\varphi$-preservation]
(4)	$\Gamma^h \wedge \eta(z) \implies \mathsf{closure}_\Sigma(z)^\ell$	[projectability]
(5)	$\Gamma^h \wedge \eta(z) \implies [\Gamma]^\ell_{\setminus z}$	[Γ-preservation]
(6)	$\Gamma^h \wedge \iota^h \wedge \mathsf{size}_{>k} \implies \exists z.\theta(z)$	[θ-initation]
(7)	$\Gamma^h \wedge \Gamma^{h\prime} \wedge \theta(z) \wedge \tau^h \implies \theta'(z)$	[θ-consecution]

Fig. 5. Verification conditions establishing strong size-reducing simulation for a high-low update $\eta(z)$ with precondition $\theta(z)$, $\mathcal{T} = (\Sigma, \Gamma, \iota, \tau)$, φ and k.

the induced size-reducing relation $H_\eta \cap (S_{\mathrm{fin}} \times S_{\mathrm{fin}})$ is inductively total (item 5 of Definition 3). Namely, we consider formulas $\eta(z)$ that consist of a precondition $\theta(z)$ and update formulas for all the symbols in the vocabulary. For such formulas, called high-low updates, we show how to encode the remaining existential quantification over states in the definition of inductive totality by first-order quantification.

Definition 6. *A formula $\eta(z)$ over the vocabulary $\Sigma^h \uplus \Sigma^\ell$ is a* high-low update *if it has the form:*

$$\eta(z) = \theta(z) \wedge \bigwedge_{r \in \Sigma} (\forall \boldsymbol{x}.\ r^\ell(\boldsymbol{x}) \leftrightarrow \alpha_r(\boldsymbol{x}, z)) \wedge \bigwedge_{f \in \Sigma} (\forall \boldsymbol{x}.\ f^\ell(\boldsymbol{x}) = t_f(\boldsymbol{x}, z))$$

where $\theta(z)$ is a formula over Σ^h, for every relation symbol $r \in \Sigma$ of arity m, α_r is a formula over Σ^h with $m+1$ free variables, and for every function symbol $f \in \Sigma$ with arity m, t_f is a term over Σ^h with $m+1$ free variables. We call θ the precondition *for η, each α_r the* update formula *for r and each t_f the* update term *for f.*

Intuitively, for a high-low update $\eta(z)$ with precondition $\theta(z)$, to any high state and assignment to z that satisfies the precondition $\theta(z)$, $\eta(z)$ defines the low state as a deterministic update from the high state, according to the formulas α_r and terms t_f. For example, we can use $\theta(z)$ to specify that the deleted element must be different from all constants, and we can update all relation and function symbols to their values in the high state (we refer to this as a trivial update). However, since the low state is obtained by deleting an element, we still need to make sure that, after the deletion, the updates result in a well-defined substructure, and, furthermore, that the structure is in fact a state (satisfies Γ). This is done by additional verification conditions. First, we formalize the precise guarantee of a high-low update:

Lemma 5. *Let $\eta(z)$ be a high-low update with precondition $\theta(z)$ and $(\mathcal{D}, \mathcal{I}^h)$ a structure with $d_0 \in \mathcal{D}$ such that $(\mathcal{D}, \mathcal{I}^h), [z \mapsto d_0] \models \theta(z)$. Then there exists an interpretation $\mathcal{I}^\ell$ such that $(\mathcal{D}, \mathcal{I}^h \uplus \mathcal{I}^\ell), [z \mapsto d_0] \models \eta(z)$.*

The lemma states that whenever the high-state satisfies $\theta(z)$ for some value of z, there exists $\mathcal{I}^\ell$ such that $\eta(z)$ holds. By Definition 4, to obtain the simulating state of the high-state, we then take a substructure which excludes the assigned value of z. To ensure that a substructure can be obtained in this way, we must verify that for any function symbol f, its interpretation remains a total function when we restrict its domain and range by discarding the assigned value of z. To ensure that a state is obtained, we further need to verify that the resulting substructure satisfies the axioms. These properties are guaranteed by verification conditions (4) and (5), where $\text{closure}_\Sigma(z) := \bigwedge_{f\in\Sigma} \text{closed}_f(z)$ and $\text{closed}_f(z) := \forall \boldsymbol{x}.\ (\wedge_{i=1}^{m} x_i \neq z) \rightarrow f(\boldsymbol{x}) \neq z$.

If the aforementioned verification conditions hold, we know that any high state that satisfies $\theta(z)$ has a corresponding low state in $H_\eta \cap (S_{\text{fin}} \times S_{\text{fin}})$. To guarantee inductively totality it remains to ensure that the precondition $\theta(z)$ holds over appropriate high states. Verification condition (6) requires that for all initial high states with size larger than k there exists z such that $\theta(z)$ holds (note the existential quantification). The size constraint is encoded by $\text{size}_{>k} := \exists x_1, \dots, x_{k+1}.\ \wedge_{i,j}\ x_i \neq x_j$. Verification condition (7) ensures that totality is maintained over transitions between high states by requiring that $\theta(z)$ is maintained, i.e., if $\theta(z)$ holds, then so does $\theta'(z)$. To ensure that the low states corresponding to the high pre-state and the high post-state have the same domain, we use the same variable z in $\theta(z)$ and $\theta'(z)$. This ensures that we can delete the same element that is deleted in the pre-state in the post state, leading to the same domain.

Lemma 6. *Let $\eta(z)$ be a high-low update with precondition $\theta(z)$, if verification conditions (4)–(7) of Fig. 5 are valid, then $H_\eta \cap (S_{\text{fin}} \times S_{\text{fin}})$ satisfies item 5 of Definition 3.*

Remark 1. The main role of $\theta(z)$ is to specify the deleted element in a high state in a simulation pair. However, it can also be used to restrict the high states, which may be necessary to make verification conditions (2)–(5) valid. This can be done by conjoining to the deletion condition in $\theta(z)$ a closed formula over Σ^h that serves as an invariant. In this case, the inductive totality checks verify that the invariant is inductive, ensuring soundness of the restriction.

4.4 Putting It All Together

The following theorem summarizes the soundness of the first-order encoding of a strong size-reducing simulation by a high-low update.

Theorem 2. *If all the verification conditions for a high-low update $\eta(z)$, $\mathcal{T}$, φ and k (Fig. 5) are valid, then $H_\eta \cap (S_{\text{fin}} \times S_{\text{fin}})$ is a strong size-reducing simulation for T_{fin}, P and k. Consequently, k is a cutoff for T_{fin} and P.*

Back to Example 1. Figure 6 encodes a high-low update that induces a size-reducing simulation for establishing a cutoff of 2 for the TreeTermination protocol (Example 1). In this example, violation of safety is witnessed by a node that did not terminate even though the root terminated. To allow the high-low update to refer to the node inspected by the property, we first Skolemize the negated safety property into $\mathsf{termd}(\mathsf{root}) \land \neg\mathsf{termd}(\mathsf{n_{sk}})$, where $\mathsf{n_{sk}}$ is a fresh immutable constant that is added to the first-order specification of the transition system. The original transition system violates the universally quantified safety property if and only if the transition system augmented with $\mathsf{n_{sk}}$ violates the Skolemized property. (A similar Skolemization is performed in all of our examples.) The precondition of the high-low update is then: $\theta(z) = (z \neq \mathsf{n_{sk}}^h \land z \neq \mathsf{root}^h)$, i.e., the deleted element z is required to be different than both the root and the violating node $\mathsf{n_{sk}}$, which ensures fault preservation. The update of the ack relation is specified by the formula α_{ack}, which says that messages bypass the deleted node. The other updates are trivial and thus not specified in Fig. 6. α_{ack} and the resulting high-low update are given below.

$$\alpha_{\mathsf{ack}}(x, y, z) = (\mathsf{ack}^h(x, y) \land x \neq z \land y \neq z)$$
$$\lor\ (\mathsf{ack}^h(x, z) \land \mathsf{child}^h(z, y)) \lor (\mathsf{child}^h(x, z) \land \mathsf{ack}^h(z, y))$$
$$\eta(z) = \theta(z) \land (\forall x, y.\ \mathsf{leq}^\ell(x, y) \leftrightarrow \mathsf{leq}^h(x, y)) \land (\forall x.\ \mathsf{termd}^\ell(x) \leftrightarrow \mathsf{termd}^h(x))$$
$$\land\ (\forall x, y.\ \mathsf{ack}^\ell(x, y) \leftrightarrow \alpha_{\mathsf{ack}}(x, y, z)) \land (\mathsf{root}^\ell = \mathsf{root}^h) \land (\mathsf{n_{sk}}^\ell = \mathsf{n_{sk}}^h)$$

The structure in the left of Fig. 4 is an example of a model for $\eta(z)$ (the Skolem constant, which is omitted from Fig. 4, can be interpreted to any node other than node 3). With this definition of a high-low update, all the verification conditions are valid. To see that τ-preservation holds, consider a transition $\mathsf{terminate}(n)$ in the high state. If n is equal to the deleted node z, all changes made by the transition are lost in the projection, so the transition is simulated by a stutter in the low state. If $n \neq z$, the transition is simulated by $\mathsf{terminate}(n)$ in the low states: if z is a child of n, then the updates to ack guarantee that the precondition for the transition still holds in the low state; if z is the parent of n, the updates to ack guarantee that the updated post-state is indeed the post-state of the transition; finally, if z is not a child nor a parent of n, the simulation is clear. We emphasize that when using our approach, validating the verification conditions for the given high-low update is delegated to an SMT solver (see Sect. 5.1 for explanation of the hint in Fig. 6).

```
bound node 2        # default value
condition(z: node) =  z ≠ n_sk ∧ z ≠ root        # default formula
update ack(x: node, y: node, z: node) =
    (ack(x,y) ∧ x ≠ z ∧ y ≠ z) ∨ (ack(x,z) ∧ child(z,y)) ∨ (child(x,z) ∧ ack(z,y))
hint terminate(n_h: node, n_ℓ: node, z: node) = (n_ℓ = n_h)
```

Fig. 6. Encoding of a high-low update for Example 1.

4.5 Extension to a Many-Sorted Vocabulary

We considered a single sort in the vocabulary used to specify $\mathcal{T}$, which the finite-domain semantics treats as finite but unbounded. Our approach generalizes to transition systems specified using many-sorted first-order logic, including interpreted sorts and symbols. In this case, the finite-domain semantics affects only the sorts that are designated as finite. The finite sorts and corresponding symbols are required to be uninterpreted, which means that they may only be restricted by a finitely-axiomatizable background theory (e.g., the theory of rooted trees as in Example 1). Other sorts and symbols may be interpreted, i.e., defined by arbitrary background theories, including ones that are not finitely-axiomatizable (e.g., linear integer arithmetic).

To handle multiple finite sorts, we apply our approach iteratively, each time establishing a cutoff for a single finite sort s by finding a size-reducing simulation for that sort. When proving a cutoff for s, we define the cardinality of a structure as the cardinality of $\mathcal{D}(\mathsf{s})$, and replace $\mathcal{D}$ with $\mathcal{D}(\mathsf{s})$ in the definition of a cutoff and size-reducing simulation. The variable z used as a free variable in a high-low update is of sort s, and in the definition of H_η we define $\mathcal{D}_\times(\mathsf{s}) = \mathcal{D}(\mathsf{s}) \setminus \{d_0\}$. Finally, in the definition of a z-excluded representation and $\text{closed}_f(z)$ we add the guard $x \neq z$ only for variables x of the sort s. Then, when moving on to establish a cutoff for the next sort we restrict the cardinality of s to the established cutoff bound using the axiom $\text{size}_{\leq k}$. In some cases, the order in which we apply our method matters. Specifically, when we have a function f from finite sort s_1 to finite sort s_2, it is natural to first show a cutoff for s_1.

5 Implementation and Evaluation

5.1 Implementation

The implementation of our method, which is available at [26], is built on top of the open-source verification tool `mypyvy` [43]. `mypyvy` allows a user to provide a first-order specification of a transition system $\mathcal{T}$ and a safety property φ. To run our tool, the user additionally provides a cutoff bound for one of the system's sorts, as well as a high-low update specified as a deletion condition for $\theta(z)$ along with update formulas and terms for relation and function symbols (Definition 6). When omitted, the deletion condition is assigned the default formula $\bigwedge_c z \neq c$ where c ranges over the immutable constants, including Skolem constants, and the cutoff bound is assigned the number of immutable constants. Similarly, for an update term the default is $\alpha_r(\boldsymbol{x}_h, z) = r^h(\boldsymbol{x}_h)$ and for an update formula the default is $t_f(\boldsymbol{x}_h, z) = f^h(\boldsymbol{x}_h)$. Invariants of the system can also be provided, and are conjoined to $\theta(z)$ as described in Remark 1. For instance, the user input for Example 1 is given in Fig. 6. Our tool generates the verification conditions described in Fig. 5 and validates them using the SMT solver Z3 [29]. If Z3 establishes that some verification condition is invalid, it generates a counterexample, which is a model of the negated verification condition. In such cases, the counterexample can point the user towards finding an appropriate fix for the high-low update.

Optimizations. Of the verification conditions in Fig. 5, item (2) is the most challenging for the solver. This is because τ often has an $\exists^*$ prefix (quantifying over transition arguments) followed by nested quantifiers, as can be seen in Example 1. Since τ appears on both sides of the implication in verification condition (2), quantifier alternations are introduced, which are difficult for SMT solvers to handle. To expedite this check, we split it into a separate check for each transition (disjunct) of τ, strengthening the simulation requirement. Furthermore, we let the user provide hints for the existential quantifiers (arguments) on the right-hand side of the implication, as described next. Generally speaking, the queries of verification condition (2) have the form $(\exists \boldsymbol{x}_h.\alpha(\boldsymbol{x}_h, z)) \implies (\exists \boldsymbol{x}_\ell.\beta(\boldsymbol{x}_\ell, z))$, where α and β are potentially complicated formulas with nested quantifiers. We propose verifying the above using a user-provided *hint* $\gamma(\boldsymbol{x}_h, \boldsymbol{x}_\ell, z)$ that satisifies

- *totality:* $\alpha(\boldsymbol{x}_h, z) \implies \exists \boldsymbol{x}_\ell.\gamma(\boldsymbol{x}_h, \boldsymbol{x}_\ell, z)$,
- *sufficiency:* $\alpha(\boldsymbol{x}_h, z) \wedge \gamma(\boldsymbol{x}_h, \boldsymbol{x}_\ell, z) \implies \beta(\boldsymbol{x}_\ell, z)$.

In this way we break the query into two, eliminating the existential quantification over $\beta(\boldsymbol{x}_\ell, z)$, and introducing one over $\gamma(\boldsymbol{x}_h, \boldsymbol{x}_\ell, z)$. The idea is for $\gamma(\boldsymbol{x}_h, \boldsymbol{x}_\ell, z)$ to be much simpler than $\beta(\boldsymbol{x}_h, z)$, which reduces the number of quantifier alternations and significantly improves performance. In some cases we use hints of the form $\gamma(\boldsymbol{x}_h, \boldsymbol{x}_\ell, z) = (\boldsymbol{x}_\ell = \boldsymbol{t}(\boldsymbol{x}_h, z))$, where $\boldsymbol{t}(\boldsymbol{x}_h, z)$ are terms. In such cases, totality is trivial and we have completely eliminated the existential quantification. In the TreeTermination example we give a hint of this form for the transition terminate, see Fig. 6. The hint says that the transition terminate in high states with argument $\mathsf{n_h}$ is simulated in low states by the same argument, $\mathsf{n}_\ell = \mathsf{n_h}$ (or by a stutter).

5.2 Results

We evaluate our approach on examples from various previous works, listed in Table 1. We use mypyvy with Z3 version 4.12.2.0, run on a laptop running Windows, with a Core-i7 2.8 GHz CPU. All run-times are under 10 s.

Table 1 summarizes our results. Each row describes one example. As described in Sect. 4.5, for transition systems with multiple finite sorts we apply our approach iteratively, in which case each iteration is described using a separate row in the order of application. For each example, the columns list its sorts and their semantics, the sort for which we show a cutoff together with the cutoff bound, how many relation and function symbols are given update terms and formulas (instead of using default values), whether an invariant is given, and how many transitions are given hints. For all examples the default formula for the deletion condition is used. In the sorts column, "s : fin" indicates that s is an uninterpreted sort with the finite-domain semantics, "s : k" indicates that s is an uninterpreted sort with the bounded semantics with bound k (this is encoded by the axiom $\text{size}_{\leq k}$), and "int" stands for the interpreted integer sort.

Next, we briefly describe each of the examples.

TreeTermination. Our motivating example from Example 1, originally from [38]. Crucially, this example cannot be proved by means of an inductive invariant as it is only safe under the finite-domain semantics.

Table 1. Summary of Results.

Example	Sorts & Semantics	Cutoff	Updates	Inv	Hints
TreeTermination	node: fin	node: 2	1/3	✓	1/1
EchoMachine	round: fin, value: fin	round: 3	0/3	✓	0/2
	round: 3, value: fin	value: 2	0/3	×	0/2
ToyConsensus	value: fin, quorum: fin, node: fin	value: 2	1/3	✓	0/2
	value: 2, quorum: fin, node: fin	quorum: 2	0/3	×	0/2
	value: 2, quorum: 2, node: fin	node: 4	0/3	×	1/2
LockServer	node: fin	node: 2	1/5	✓	0/5
ListToken	node: fin	node: 3	2/7	✓	1/3
PlusMinus	thread: fin, int	thread: 1	1/3	✓	0/2
EqualSum	thread: fin, index: fin, int	thread: 2	0/8	×	0/1
	thread: 2, index: fin, int	index: 2	3/8	✓	0/1
EqualSumOrders	thread: fin, index: fin, int	thread: 2	0/8	×	0/1
	thread: 2, index: fin, int	index: 4	3/8	✓	0/1

EchoMachine. Taken from [9]. A simple distributed protocol where values are echoed in rounds which are linearly ordered. A value may be echoed in some round if there exists some previous round that echoed it. The safety property is that the value echoed in all rounds is unique. [9] shows a simple inductive invariant that implies safety over finite structures but not in the first-order semantics; we use the same invariant in a high-low update to establish safety.

ToyConsensus. Taken from [40]. A simple consensus protocol with three finite sorts, including sort quorum, which is axiomatized to ensure a nonempty intersection for any two quorums. We highlight this example as an example where the order of application on sorts matters. Specifically, after we show a cutoff of 2 for the sort quorum, we can instantiate the quorum intersection axiom and Skolemize the node in the intersection of any pair of quorums, giving 4 Skolem constants. We can then freely delete any other node.

LockServer. Taken from [34]. A simple mutual exclusion protocol. In this example, our approach does not simplify the proof since to prove simulation the high-low update must include an invariant that suffices to prove safety directly.

ListToken. A custom example where a token travels along a linked list, modeled with a next relation. An invariant that proves safety would require talking about the transitive closure of next, which cannot be done in FOL. Instead, our approach based on simulation avoids the need to reason about the transitive closure. The high-low update changes the next relation to skip over the deleted node, and moves the token accordingly.

PlusMinus. Taken from [18]. A simple concurrent program where any number of threads each move between two program locations, incrementing and then decrementing a shared counter, which must always remain non-negative. In [18], it is shown that no Ashcroft invariant proves its safety. Intuitively, an inductive invariant would need to count the number of threads in some program location, which is problematic in FOL. Instead, the high-low update undoes increments to the counter by the deleted thread.

EqualSum. Taken from [14]. A simple concurrent program where threads sum over elements of an array. The safety property is that any two threads that terminate hold the same sum. An inductive invariant would need to record sums of array segments of unbounded length, which is not clear how to express in FOL. Our approach easily establishes a cutoff of 2 for sort thread. Then, to establish a cutoff for sort index, the high-low update deletes an array element and subtracts it from the sum of any thread pointing to a higher index.

EqualSumOrders. A variant of EqualSum where every thread holds a different order on the indices of the array. Unlike EqualSum, in this variant the order of application of our method on the sorts matters. To prove the cutoff for sort index we use a similar Skolemization to the one used in ToyConsensus.

Limitations. While our approach is applicable to some examples that cannot be verified by previous approaches, it has limitations. The definition of a high-low update does not specify how the state should be updated to obtain a simulation relation. In our examples, we used the high-low update to undo all changes that involved the deleted element z in all transitions so far. In this way, transitions that are completely undone are simulated by stutters. For some examples, it is hard to keep track of the changes that need to be undone, and it requires some instrumentation. For example, in the ToyConsensus example, when a value is chosen by some quorum we change the model to keep track of the quorum that chose it, and not only the fact that it was chosen. In some cases, undoing the changes that involved z causes transitions of other elements to be impossible to simulate, for example, if the transition has a guard on some global variable, affected by z.

6 Related Work

Parameterized verification of safety properties is a widely-researched problem. Many works [12,16–18,25,36,44] have developed techniques to infer inductive invariants for parameterized systems in first-order logic. Such techniques are bound to fail if no satisfactory invariant exists in the language considered, or if the system is only safe in the finite instances. Our approach is deductive and based on the notion of cutoffs [1,3,10,11,21–23,28,31,41,42]. Most cutoff results guarantee that a cutoff always exists for a class of systems and properties. In turn, the system specification is much more limited. Our work proposes a framework for establishing cutoffs for a specific first-order transition system and property. Next we focus on the works closest to ours.

Cutoffs by Simulation Relations. In [5], the cutoff method is utilized for safety verification of distributed protocols specified in FOL. They automatically generate and check a simulation relation between an arbitrary system instance and a cutoff instance.We, on the other hand, encode a simulation relation between system instances that differ in size by 1, and not directly to the cutoff instance. In this way, our work captures an inductive argument over the state size, which lets it capture the finite-domain semantics. In contrast, [5] cannot verify examples such as Example 1 that are only correct in finite instances. Additionally, the simulation relation in [5] is defined by mapping all elements in any instance to the elements of the cutoff instance such that transitions are preserved, while we use a partial mapping of elements with updates that allow to undo transitions. Relying on a fixed total mapping of elements is bound to fail in examples such as PlusMinus, where threads move between program locations. In [8], a cutoff result is given for a parameterized mutual-exclusion protocol by giving a simulation relation between system instances that differ in size by 1. Their proof of simulation is manual, and uses an unbounded number of steps, which cannot be automated by an SMT solver. [19] formulates the notion of a simulation-inducing squeezer for safety properties, which is essentially a *deterministic* size-reducing simulation with a slightly weaker notion of stuttering. This work is evaluated only on deterministic sequential array programs and cannot capture transition systems defined in FOL. Other works [6,7] automatically generate proofs for program assertions by induction on some size parameter. These methods are currently limited to programs manipulating arrays.

Mitigating Limitations of FOL. [4,20,32,33,39,40] use the Effectively Propositional (EPR) [37] decidable logic of FOL to model and verify transition systems. EPR has the finite-model property: any satisfiable formula has a finite model. In the case of safety verification, this has the effect of capturing the finite-domain semantics. However, it is not always clear how to ensure that the verification conditions are in EPR. When the verification conditions are outside of EPR, as in Example 1, infinite models may arise. [9] finds such models and shows that they can sometimes be eliminated by induction axioms. [30] develops an approach for automatically generating induction axioms for systems modeled using algebraic data-types. [2] takes an alternative approach to modeling systems in FOL, separating the specification of topology from the specification of the protocol.

Mitigating Limitations of Inductive Invariants. In [14], programs whose inductive invariants are not expressible in FOL (or are too complex) are verified by finding an inductive invariant for a reduction of the program obtained by reordering execution steps, relying on commutativity. Counting Proofs [13] create proofs that keep track of the number of threads that satisfy some properties, akin to examples like PlusMinus.

7 Conclusion

We have presented a framework for specifying and validating size-reducing simulations in first-order logic as a way to establish cutoffs for the finite-domain semantics of first-order transition systems. Size-reducing simulations mimic induction over the domain size, which is sometimes simpler than induction over time, and, notably, leverages the finite-domain semantics.

As our evaluation shows, our framework manages to verify some examples that cannot be verified by previous approaches. We leave automating the search for a high-low update to future work. In this context we note that without hints our verification conditions are not in EPR, and therefore SMT solvers sometimes struggle to find models when a query is not valid, which might be an obstacle for automation.

It is possible to extend our approach to a larger class of size-reducing simulations, e.g., by allowing to delete more than one domain element, or relaxing the deterministic updates to other syntactic restrictions that still guarantee Lemma 5. We did not find such extensions necessary in the examples we considered. Another interesting direction for future research is to consider a wider range of properties, including liveness properties. While the definition of a size-reducing simulation can be extended naturally, the more intricate structure of traces that satisfy liveness properties seems to be a challenge.

Acknowledgement. We thank Neta Elad, Shachar Itzhaky and Orna Grumberg for helpful advice. The research leading to these results has received funding from the European Research Council under the European Union's Horizon 2020 research and innovation programme (grant agreement No [759102-SVIS]). This research was partially supported by the Israeli Science Foundation (ISF) grant No. 2117/23.

References

1. Abdulla, P., Haziza, F., Holík, L.: Parameterized verification through view abstraction. Int. J. Softw. Tools Technol. Transfer **18**(5), 495–516 (2015). https://doi.org/10.1007/s10009-015-0406-x
2. Ashmore, R., Gurfinkel, A., Trefler, R.J.: Local reasoning for parameterized first order protocols. In: NASA Formal Methods - 11th International Symposium, NFM 2019, Houston, TX, USA, May 7-9, 2019, Proceedings. Lecture Notes in Computer Science, vol. 11460, pp. 36–53. Springer (2019). https://doi.org/10.1007/978-3-030-20652-9_3
3. Außerlechner, S., Jacobs, S., Khalimov, A.: Tight cutoffs for guarded protocols with fairness. In: Jobstmann, B., Leino, K.R.M. (eds.) VMCAI 2016. LNCS, vol. 9583, pp. 476–494. Springer, Heidelberg (2016). https://doi.org/10.1007/978-3-662-49122-5_23
4. Ball, T., Bjørner, N., Gember, A., Itzhaky, S., Karbyshev, A., Sagiv, M., Schapira, M., Valadarsky, A.: Vericon: towards verifying controller programs in software-defined networks. SIGPLAN Not. **49**(6), 282–293 (jun 2014). https://doi.org/10.1145/2666356.2594317

5. Bhat, S.G., Nagar, K.: Automating cutoff-based verification of distributed protocols. In: 2023 Formal Methods in Computer-Aided Design (FMCAD), pp. 75–85 (2023). https://doi.org/10.34727/2023/isbn.978-3-85448-060-0_15
6. Chakraborty, S., Gupta, A., Unadkat, D.: DIFFY: inductive reasoning of array programs using difference invariants. In: Silva, A., Leino, K.R.M. (eds.) CAV 2021. LNCS, vol. 12760, pp. 911–935. Springer, Cham (2021). https://doi.org/10.1007/978-3-030-81688-9_42
7. Chakraborty, S., Gupta, A., Unadkat, D.: Full-program induction: verifying array programs sans loop invariants. Int. J. Softw. Tools Technol. Transf. **24**(5), 843–888 (2022). https://doi.org/10.1007/S10009-022-00676-W
8. Clarke, E.M., Grumberg, O., Browne, M.C.: Reasoning about networks with many identical finite-state- processes. In: Proceedings of the Fifth Annual ACM Symposium on Principles of Distributed Computing, pp. 240-248. PODC '86, Association for Computing Machinery, New York, NY, USA (1986). https://doi.org/10.1145/10590.10611
9. Elad, N., Padon, O., Shoham, S.: An infinite needle in a finite haystack: Finding infinite counter-models in deductive verification. Proc. ACM Program. Lang. **8**(POPL) (jan 2024). https://doi.org/10.1145/3632875
10. Emerson, E.A., Kahlon, V.: Reducing model checking of the many to the few. In: Automated Deduction - CADE-17, 17th International Conference on Automated Deduction, Pittsburgh, PA, USA, June 17-20, 2000, Proceedings. Lecture Notes in Computer Science, vol. 1831, pp. 236–254. Springer (2000). https://doi.org/10.1007/10721959_19
11. Emerson, E.A., Namjoshi, K.S.: Reasoning about rings. In: Proceedings of the 22nd ACM SIGPLAN-SIGACT Symposium on Principles of Programming Languages, pp. 85–94. POPL '95, Association for Computing Machinery, New York, NY, USA (1995). https://doi.org/10.1145/199448.199468
12. Fang, Y., McMillan, K.L., Pnueli, A., Zuck, L.D.: Liveness by Invisible Invariants. In: Najm, E., Pradat-Peyre, J.-F., Donzeau-Gouge, V.V. (eds.) FORTE 2006. LNCS, vol. 4229, pp. 356–371. Springer, Heidelberg (2006). https://doi.org/10.1007/11888116_26
13. Farzan, A., Kincaid, Z., Podelski, A.: Proofs that count. SIGPLAN Not. **49**(1), 151–164 (jan 2014). https://doi.org/10.1145/2578855.2535885
14. Farzan, A., Klumpp, D., Podelski, A.: Commutativity simplifies proofs of parameterized programs. Proc. ACM Program. Lang. **8**(POPL) (jan 2024). https://doi.org/10.1145/3632925
15. Feldman, Y.M.Y., Wilcox, J.R., Shoham, S., Sagiv, M.: Inferring inductive invariants from phase structures. In: Dillig, I., Tasiran, S. (eds.) Computer Aided Verification. pp. 405–425. Springer International Publishing, Cham (2019). https://doi.org/10.1007/978-3-030-25543-5_23
16. Gurfinkel, A., Shoham, S., Meshman, Y.: SMT-based verification of parameterized systems. In: Proceedings of the 2016 24th ACM SIGSOFT International Symposium on Foundations of Software Engineering, pp. 338–348. FSE 2016, Association for Computing Machinery, New York, NY, USA (2016). https://doi.org/10.1145/2950290.2950330
17. Hance, T., Heule, M., Martins, R., Parno, B.: Finding invariants of distributed systems: It's a small (enough) world after all. In: 18th USENIX Symposium on Networked Systems Design and Implementation (NSDI 21), pp. 115–131. USENIX Association (Apr 2021). https://www.usenix.org/conference/nsdi21/presentation/hance

18. Hoenicke, J., Majumdar, R., Podelski, A.: Thread modularity at many levels: a pearl in compositional verification. In: Proceedings of the 44th ACM SIGPLAN Symposium on Principles of Programming Languages, pp. 473–485. POPL '17, Association for Computing Machinery, New York, NY, USA (2017). https://doi.org/10.1145/3009837.3009893
19. Ish-Shalom, O., Itzhaky, S., Rinetzky, N., Shoham, S.: Putting the squeeze on array programs: Loop verification via inductive rank reduction. In: Verification, Model Checking, and Abstract Interpretation, pp. 112–135. Springer International Publishing, Cham (2020). https://doi.org/10.1007/978-3-030-39322-_6
20. Itzhaky, S., Banerjee, A., Immerman, N., Lahav, O., Nanevski, A., Sagiv, M.: Modular reasoning about heap paths via effectively propositional formulas. In: The 41st Annual ACM SIGPLAN-SIGACT Symposium on Principles of Programming Languages, POPL '14, San Diego, CA, USA, January 20-21, 2014, pp. 385–396. ACM (2014). https://doi.org/10.1145/2535838.2535854
21. Jaber, N., Wagner, C., Jacobs, S., Kulkarni, M., Samanta, R.: Quicksilver: modeling and parameterized verification for distributed agreement-based systems. Proc. ACM Program. Lang. **5**(OOPSLA) (oct 2021). https://doi.org/10.1145/3485534
22. Jacobs, S., Sakr, M.: Analyzing guarded protocols: Better cutoffs, more systems, more expressivity. In: Verification, Model Checking, and Abstract Interpretation - 19th International Conference, VMCAI 2018, Los Angeles, CA, USA, January 7-9, 2018, Proceedings. Lecture Notes in Computer Science, vol. 10747, pp. 247–268. Springer (2018). https://doi.org/10.1007/978-3-319-73721-8_12
23. Kaiser, A., Kroening, D., Wahl, T.: Dynamic cutoff detection in parameterized concurrent programs. In: Computer Aided Verification, 22nd International Conference, CAV 2010, Edinburgh, UK, July 15-19, 2010. Proceedings. Lecture Notes in Computer Science, vol. 6174, pp. 645–659. Springer (2010). https://doi.org/10.1007/978-3-642-14295-6_55
24. Karbyshev, A., Bjørner, N., Itzhaky, S., Rinetzky, N., Shoham, S.: Property-directed inference of universal invariants or proving their absence. J. ACM **64**(1) (mar 2017). https://doi.org/10.1145/3022187
25. Koenig, J.R., Padon, O., Shoham, S., Aiken, A.: Inferring invariants with quantifier alternations: Taming the search space explosion. In: Tools and Algorithms for the Construction and Analysis of Systems - 28th International Conference, TACAS 2022, Munich, Germany, April 2-7, 2022, Proceedings, Part I. Lecture Notes in Computer Science, vol. 13243, pp. 338–356. Springer (2022). https://doi.org/10.1007/978-3-030-99524-9_18
26. Lotan, R., Frenkel, E., Shoham, S.: Proving cutoff bounds for safety-properties in first-order logic (artifact). Zenodo (2024). https://doi.org/10.5281/zenodo.12664114
27. Lotan, R., Frenkel, E., Shoham, S.: Proving cutoff bounds for safety properties in first-order logic (full version) (2024). https://arxiv.org/abs/2408.10685
28. Maric, O., Sprenger, C., Basin, D.A.: Cutoff bounds for consensus algorithms. In: Computer Aided Verification - 29th International Conference, CAV 2017, Heidelberg, Germany, July 24-28, 2017, Proceedings, Part II. Lecture Notes in Computer Science, vol. 10427, pp. 217–237. Springer (2017).https://doi.org/10.1007/978-3-319-63390-9_12

29. de Moura, L., Bjørner, N.: Z3: an efficient SMT solver. In: Ramakrishnan, C.R., Rehof, J. (eds.) TACAS 2008. LNCS, vol. 4963, pp. 337–340. Springer, Heidelberg (2008). https://doi.org/10.1007/978-3-540-78800-3_24
30. Murali, A., Peña, L., Blanchard, E., Löding, C., Madhusudan, P.: Model-guided synthesis of inductive lemmas for FOL with least fixpoints. Proc. ACM Program. Lang. **6**(OOPSLA2), 1873–1902 (2022). https://doi.org/10.1145/3563354
31. Namjoshi, K.S.: Symmetry and completeness in the analysis of parameterized systems. In: Cook, B., Podelski, A. (eds.) VMCAI 2007. LNCS, vol. 4349, pp. 299–313. Springer, Heidelberg (2007). https://doi.org/10.1007/978-3-540-69738-1_22
32. Padon, O.: Deductive Verification of Distributed Protocols in First-Order Logic. Ph.D. thesis, Tel Aviv University, Israel (2018). https://tau.primo.exlibrisgroup.com/permalink/972TAU_INST/bai57q/alma9932991300004146
33. Padon, O., Losa, G., Sagiv, M., Shoham, S.: Paxos made epr: decidable reasoning about distributed protocols. Proc. ACM Program. Lang. **1**(OOPSLA) (oct 2017). https://doi.org/10.1145/3140568
34. Padon, O., McMillan, K.L., Panda, A., Sagiv, M., Shoham, S.: Ivy: Safety verification by interactive generalization. In: PLDI '16: Proceedings of the 37th ACM SIGPLAN Conference on Programming Language Design and Implementation, pp. 614–630 (Jun 2016). https://doi.org/10.1145/2908080.2908118
35. Padon, O., Wilcox, J.R., Koenig, J.R., McMillan, K.L., Aiken, A.: Induction duality: primal-dual search for invariants. Proc. ACM Program. Lang. **6**(POPL) (jan 2022). https://doi.org/10.1145/3498712
36. Pani, T., Weissenbacher, G., Zuleger, F.: Thread-modular counter abstraction: automated safety and termination proofs of parameterized software by reduction to sequential program verification. Formal Methods in System Design, pp. 1–38 (10 2023). https://doi.org/10.1007/s10703-023-00439-6
37. Ramsey, F.P.: On a Problem of Formal Logic, pp. 1–24. Birkhäuser Boston, Boston, MA (1987). https://doi.org/10.1007/978-0-8176-4842-8_1
38. Segall, A.: Distributed network protocols. IEEE Transactions on Information Theory **29**(1), 23–35 (1983). https://doi.org/10.1109/TIT.1983.1056620
39. Tamir, O., Taube, M., McMillan, K.L., Shoham, S., Howell, J., Gueta, G., Sagiv, M.: Counterexample driven quantifier instantiations with applications to distributed protocols. Proc. ACM Program. Lang. **7**(OOPSLA2) (oct 2023). https://doi.org/10.1145/3622864
40. Taube, M., et al.: Modularity for decidability of deductive verification with applications to distributed systems. SIGPLAN Not. **53**(4), 662–677 (jun 2018). https://doi.org/10.1145/3296979.3192414
41. Tran, T., Konnov, I., Widder, J.: Cutoffs for symmetric point-to-point distributed algorithms. In: Networked Systems - 8th International Conference, NETYS 2020, Marrakech, Morocco, June 3-5, 2020, Proceedings. Lecture Notes in Computer Science, vol. 12129, pp. 329–346. Springer (2020). https://doi.org/10.1007/978-3-030-67087-0_21
42. Wagner, C., Jaber, N., Samanta, R.: Enabling bounded verification of doubly-unbounded distributed agreement-based systems via bounded regions. Proc. ACM Program. Lang. **7**(OOPSLA1) (2023). https://doi.org/10.1145/3586033
43. Wilcox, J.R., Feldman, Y.M.Y., Padon, O., Shoham, S.: mypyvy: A research platform for verification of transition systems in first-order logic. In: Computer Aided Verification, pp. 71–85. Springer Nature Switzerland, Cham (2024). https://doi.org/10.1007/978-3-031-65630-9_4

44. Yao, J., Tao, R., Gu, R., Nieh, J.: DuoAI: Fast, automated inference of inductive invariants for verifying distributed protocols. In: 16th USENIX Symposium on Operating Systems Design and Implementation (OSDI 22), pp. 485–501. USENIX Association, Carlsbad, CA (Jul 2022). https://www.usenix.org/conference/osdi22/presentation/yao
45. Yao, J., Tao, R., Gu, R., Nieh, J., Jana, S., Ryan, G.: DistAI: data-driven automated invariant learning for distributed protocols. In: 15th USENIX Symposium on Operating Systems Design and Implementation (OSDI 21), pp. 405–421. USENIX Association (Jul 2021). https://www.usenix.org/conference/osdi21/presentation/yao

Distribution of Reconfiguration Languages Maintaining Tree-Like Communication Topology

Daniel Hausmann, Mathieu Lehaut(✉), and Nir Piterman

University of Gothenburg and Chalmers University of Technology, Gothenburg, Sweden

lehaut@chalmers.se

Abstract. We study how to distribute trace languages in a setting where processes communicate via reconfigurable communication channels. That is, the different processes can connect and disconnect from channels at run time. We restrict attention to communication via tree-like communication architectures. These allow channels to connect more than two processes in a way that maintains an underlying spanning tree and keeps communication continuous on the tree. We make the reconfiguration explicit in the language allowing both a centralized automaton as well as the distributed processes to share relevant information about the current communication configuration. We show that Zielonka's seminal result regarding distribution of regular languages for asynchronous automata can be generalized in this setting, incorporating both reconfiguration and more than binary tree architectures.

1 Introduction

Over the past years, computing devices have proliferated to the point where they are ubiquitous. These devices are not only lightweight and affordable but also highly prevalent and mobile. They are used, for example, in sensor networks or multi-agent or multi-robot systems. In such applications, communication requires mobility and ad-hoc connectivity depending on need and availability. Indeed, participants in communications frequently leave or join specific tasks or groups and change who they communicate with based on, e.g., requirements or location. This prompts us to explore how communication dynamics evolve when dealing with numerous mobile participants that have to collaborate effectively.

We consider an extension of Zielonka's asynchronous automata – a canonical formalism for distributed systems with a fixed communication architecture [13]. A system consists of multiple finite-state automata called processes. Processes communicate by synchronizing on channels. While in asynchronous automata processes share their full state information in every communication, here, we replace this with information sharing through data exchange. The data exchange

Supported by the ERC Consolidator grant D-SynMA (No. 772459).

S. Akshay et al. (Eds.): ATVA 2024, LNCS 15054, pp. 160–180, 2025.
https://doi.org/10.1007/978-3-031-78709-6_8

allows to define how processes update their local states without knowing the number of participants in a communication or their identity. A communication happens only if all involved participants are ready for it. Thus, a single process can block communications they are not ready to accept. The considered extended asynchronous automata allow processes to decide in every state to which channels they wish to be connected to. Thus, their connectivity may change from transition to transition at run time. They can easily establish groups and change the set of processes they communicate with. This extension is called *reconfigurable asynchronous automata* (RAA), and was first defined in [11]. RAA are inspired by the attribute-based communication calculus [1,3] and by channeled transition systems (CTS) [4], but are simplified to include only one form of communication (CTS include both broadcast and multicast channels, the latter corresponding to the type of communication allowed here).

Asynchronous automata are notable due to Zielonka's seminal result on *distributivity* of regular languages [13]. Namely, for every regular language that respects the independence of communications in a given fixed communication architecture, it is possible to define a team of processes who distribute the original language. That is, their distributed interaction reproduces the regular language. In other words, one can build a *distributed* implementation from a *centralized* specification. Zielonka's result is quite involved and is source for much ongoing research work on establishing a better understanding of the result [2,6–8,12]. Here we concentrate on the restriction of this result to the case where processes communicate via an acyclic binary communication architecture [10]. That is, every channel is binary (between two processes) and the graph of channels forms a tree. Distribution in this restricted setting is much better understood: the tree enables a distribution construction where the state space of every process is only quadratic in the state space of the original deterministic automaton that (centrally) recognizes the language. In comparison, in the general case, the distribution construction incurs exponential blow-up (with a non-linear exponent).

As mentioned, in asynchronous automata every channel has a fixed set of processes connected to it, while our framework allows processes to connect and disconnect to/from channels. We call this process *reconfiguration*, as processes reconfigure their communication interfaces, and we call the way they are connected at a certain point in time the *communication architecture*. In order to extend Zielonka's distribution results to our automata we make reconfiguration explicit in the communication. This allows both the centralized and the distributed systems to follow how the communication architecture changes. We do that by including, with every communication, instructions regarding how the communication architecture is changed and do not allow other (invisible) changes to the architecture. Based on this information, the centralized automaton can keep track of the communication architecture. We make this notion explicit by considering deterministic automata that keep track of both the current run of the automaton, as well as the changing communication architecture. The instructions that we include allow changes in the structure of a tree by reversing the order between parent and child vertices and by transferring a child vertex to its parent or to another child. In addition, we allow joining or leaving channels in restricted ways that preserve the connectivity as *tree-like*. A communication architecture is tree-like if it has an underlying spanning tree and allows communication that is local with respect to this tree. That is, all communication is continuous on the tree. We show that the allowed reconfigurations enable transfer between any two tree-like communication architectures (in multiple steps).

Based on these definitions of reconfigurations and reconfiguration languages, we show that regular languages of reconfigurations can be distributed if they satisfy a reasonable structure constraint corresponding to the independence of communications. That is, they can be recognized by reconfigurable asynchronous automata that connect to channels according to the instructions given to them and are only aware of communications they participate in. To this end, we generalize the construction of Krishna and Muscholl [10] by adding to it a part that follows distributively the communication architecture. We show that these additional parts allow to keep track of how to update the local view of the global state. They allow to do so also in the context of communication that is not necessarily binary (as mentioned, we support tree-like communication architectures in which channels may subsume more than two participants provided they are continuous on the spanning tree). This, as far as we know, has not been recognized even for fixed communication structures. The distribution constructs processes whose number of states is polynomial in the number of states of a centralized automaton but also keeps track of potentially exponentially many options for the way the communication architecture is arranged around a process.

The paper is organized as follows. In Sect. 2 we define automata, asynchronous automata, and reconfigurable asynchronous automata. In Sect. 3 we define tree-like communication architectures and how they change. Section 4 shows how reconfiguration is exposed through the communication itself, and defines requirements on languages that enable distribution. We show in Sect. 5 the distribution construction and its correctness and conclude in Sect. 6. Omitted proofs and full details of the distribution construction can be found in the full version of this paper [9].

2 Automata and Reconfigurable Asynchronous Automata

Deterministic Finite Automata. Given a set of letters Σ, a deterministic finite automaton is $\mathcal{D} = (S, s^0, \Delta, F)$, where S is a finite set of states, $s^0 \in S$ is an initial state, $\Delta : S \times \Sigma \to S$ is a partial transition function, and $F \subseteq S$ is a set of accepting states. Given a word $w = a_0 \cdots a_{n-1}$, a run of A on w is $r = s_0, \ldots, s_n$ such that $s_0 = s^0$ and for every $0 \leq i < n$ we have $s_{i+1} = \Delta(s_i, a_i)$. A run is accepting if $s_n \in F$ and then w is accepted by $\mathcal{D}$. The language of $\mathcal{D}$, denoted by $\mathcal{L}(\mathcal{D})$, is the set of words accepted by $\mathcal{D}$.

An *independence relation* is a symmetric relation $I \subseteq \Sigma \times \Sigma$. Two words $u = u_1 \cdots u_n$ and $v = v_1 \cdots v_n$ are said to be I-indistinguishable, denoted by $u \sim_I v$, if one can start from u, repeatedly switch two consecutive independent letters, and end up with v. That is, for all $(a, b) \in I$ and all $u, v \in \Sigma^*$, we have

$uabv \sim_I ubav$. We denote by $[u]_I$ the I-equivalence class of a word $u \in \Sigma^*$. Let $\mathcal{A} = (S, s_0, \Delta, F)$ be a deterministic automaton over Σ. We say that $\mathcal{A}$ is I-diamond if for all pairs of independent letters $(a, b) \in I$ and all states $s \in S$, we have $\Delta(s, ab) = \Delta(s, ba)$. If $\mathcal{A}$ has this property, then a word u is accepted by $\mathcal{A}$ if and only if all words in $[u]$ are accepted.

Asynchronous Automata. Let $\mathbb{P}$ be a finite set of *processes*. A *communication architecture* is $\mathbb{C} : \Sigma \to 2^{\mathbb{P}}$, associating with each letter the subset of processes reading it. We put $\mathbb{C}^{-1}(p) = \{a \in \Sigma \mid p \in \mathbb{C}(a)\}$. A distributed alphabet is $(\Sigma, \mathbb{C})$, where $\mathbb{C}$ is a communication architecture. It induces an independence relation $I(\mathbb{C}) \subseteq \Sigma \times \Sigma$ by $(a, b) \in I(\mathbb{C})$ iff $\mathbb{C}(a) \cap \mathbb{C}(b) = \emptyset$. We say that $\mathbb{C}$ is binary if for each $a \in \Sigma$ we have $|\mathbb{C}(a)| = 2$. A binary $\mathbb{C}$ induces a tree if the graph $(\mathbb{P}, E)$, where $(p, q) \in E$ iff $\mathbb{C}(a) = \{p, q\}$ for some $a \in \Sigma$, is a tree.

An *asynchronous automaton* (in short: AA) [13] over distributed alphabet $(\Sigma, \mathbb{C})$ and processes $\mathbb{P}$ is $\mathcal{B} = ((S_p)_{p\in\mathbb{P}}, (s_p^0)_{p\in\mathbb{P}}, (\delta_a)_{a\in\Sigma}, Acc)$ such that:

- S_p is the finite set of states for process p, and $s_p^0 \in S_p$ is its initial state,
- $\delta_a : \prod_{p\in\mathbb{C}(a)} S_p \to \prod_{p\in\mathbb{C}(a)} S_p$ is a partial transition function for letter a that only depends on the states of processes in $\mathbb{C}(a)$ and changes them,
- $Acc \subseteq \prod_{p\in\mathbb{P}} S_p$ is a set of accepting states.

A global state of $\mathcal{B}$ is $\mathbf{s} = (s_p)_{p\in\mathbb{P}}$, giving the state of each process. For global state $\mathbf{s}$ and subset $P \subseteq \mathbb{P}$, we denote by $\mathbf{s}{\downarrow}_P = (s_p)_{p\in P}$ the subset of $\mathbf{s}$ of states from processes in P. A run of $\mathcal{B}$ on a word $a_1a_2\ldots a_n$ is a sequence $\mathbf{s}_0a_1\mathbf{s}_1a_2\ldots\mathbf{s}_n$ such that for all $0 < i \leq n$, $\mathbf{s}_i \in \prod_{p\in\mathbb{P}} S_p$, $a_i \in \Sigma$, satisfying $\mathbf{s}_0 = (s_p^0)_{p\in\mathbb{P}}$ and the following relation: $\mathbf{s}_i{\downarrow}_{\mathbb{C}(a_i)} = \delta_{a_i}(\mathbf{s}_{i-1}{\downarrow}_{\mathbb{C}(a_i)})$ and $\mathbf{s}_i{\downarrow}_{\mathbb{P}\setminus\mathbb{C}(a_i)} = \mathbf{s}_{i-1}{\downarrow}_{\mathbb{P}\setminus\mathbb{C}(a_i)}$. A run is accepting if $\mathbf{s}_n$ belongs to Acc. The word $a_1a_2\ldots$ is accepted by $\mathcal{B}$ if such an accepting run exists (note that automata are deterministic but runs on certain words may not exist). The language of $\mathcal{B}$, denoted by $\mathcal{L}(\mathcal{B})$, is the set of words accepted by $\mathcal{B}$.

We say that a language $\mathcal{L}$ over $(\Sigma, \mathbb{C})$ is *distributively recognized* if there exists an asynchronous automaton $\mathcal{B}$ such that $\mathcal{L}(\mathcal{B}) = \mathcal{L}$.

Theorem 1 ([10,13]). *Given an $I(\mathbb{C})$-diamond deterministic automaton $\mathcal{D}$, there exists an AA that distributively recognizes this language. In general if $\mathcal{D}$ has n states then every process in the AA has $2^{O(n^2)}$ states. If $\mathbb{C}$ induces a tree, then every process in the AA has $O(n^2)$ states.*

Reconfigurable Asynchronous Automata. We present Asynchronous Automata with reconfiguration. Here the communication architecture is modified dynamically during a run. We fix a finite set $\mathbb{P}$ of processes and a finite set CH of channels (intuitively corresponding to the alphabet).

Let $\mathbb{D}$ be a finite set of synchronization data contents. A *reconfigurable asynchronous automaton* (RAA) over alphabet CH and processes $\mathbb{P}$ is $\mathcal{A} = ((S_p)_{p\in\mathbb{P}}, (s_p^0)_{p\in\mathbb{P}}, (\delta_p)_{p\in\mathbb{P}}, (L_p)_{p\in\mathbb{P}}, (F_p)_{p\in\mathbb{P}})$, where

- S_p and s_p^0 are as before,
- $\delta_p : S_p \times (\mathbb{D} \times \mathrm{CH}) \rightharpoonup S_p$ is the partial transition function, where $\delta_p(s, (d, c)) = s'$ means going from state s to s', reading a data on channel c with content d. We write $(s, (d, c), s') \in \delta$ for $\delta(s, (d, c)) = s'$,
- $L_p : S_p \to 2^{\mathrm{CH}}$ is a listening function such that $c \in L_p(s)$ if there is a transition of the form $(s, (d, c), s') \in \delta_p$, i.e. state s must be listening to channel c if there is some transition from s involving a data on c.
- $F_p : S_p \times \mathbb{D} \to \{\bot, \top\}$ is an acceptance function.

Global states of $\mathcal{A}$ are as before. A run of $\mathcal{A}$ is $\mathbf{s}_0 m_1 \mathbf{s}_1 m_2 \ldots \mathbf{s}_n$, where for all $0 < i \leq n$, $\mathbf{s}_i = (s_p^i)_{p \in \mathbb{P}}$ is a global state, $m_i = (d_i, c_i) \in \mathbb{D} \times \mathrm{CH}$, satisfying $\mathbf{s}_0 = (s_p^0)_{p \in \mathbb{P}}$ and all the following:

1. $\exists p$ s.t. $c_i \in L_p(s_p^{i-1})$,
2. $\forall p$ s.t. $c_i \in L_p(s_p^{i-1}), (s_p^{i-1}, (d_i, c_i), s_p^i) \in \delta_p$, and
3. $\forall p$ s.t. $c_i \notin L_p(s_p^{i-1}), s_p^i = s_p^{i-1}$.

In plain words, there is a transition upon reading channel name c if all processes listening to c have an according transition, with at least one process listening to c, whereas those processes that do not listen to c are left unchanged. Note that if some process listens to c but does not implement the transition, then that transition is blocked. A run is accepting if for some $d \in \mathbb{D}$ and for all $p \in \mathbb{P}$ we have $F_p(s_n^p, d) = \top$. That is, acceptance happens only if all processes can agree on a data value d that is accepted by all. The language of $\mathcal{A}$, denoted by $\mathcal{L}(\mathcal{A})$, is the set of words over CH of the form $c_0 c_1 \ldots$ such that there exists an accepting run of the form $\mathbf{s}_0(d_0, c_0)\mathbf{s}_1(d_1, c_1)\ldots$, i.e. we focus only on the sequence of channels where data is sent, and drop the states and data contents.

Example 2. Figure 1 shows an example RAA over channels $\mathrm{CH} = \{a, b, c\}$ and three processes $\mathbb{P} = \{p, q, r\}$, with the listening function given by the labels to the right of the individual states. Here we take a singleton set $\mathbb{D} = \{d\}$ as the set of data contents, so for readability purposes it is omitted from the transitions. Note that when process p is in state s_2, it is listening to channel c but no c-transition is implemented, therefore a communication on c is impossible (similarly for q and t_2). So the only way a communication can happen on c is when p and q are in s_1 and t_1 respectively, which means only process r listens to c. We then set $F_p(x, d) = \top$ for all $p \in \mathbb{P}$ and $x \in S_p$. The language accepted by this RAA is the set of all sequences such that in any prefix ending with a communication on c, we have an even number of a and b:

$$\mathcal{L}(\mathcal{A}) = \left\{ v_0 \ldots v_n \in \{a, b, c\}^* \;\middle|\; \begin{array}{r} \forall i \,.\, v_i = c \text{ implies } a_\sharp(v_0 \ldots v_i) =_{mod2} 0 \\ \text{and } b_\sharp(v_0 \ldots v_i) =_{mod2} 0 \end{array} \right\},$$

where $\sigma_\sharp(w)$ is the number of occurrences of letter σ in word w.

We say that an RAA over CH and $\mathbb{P}$ has a fixed communication architecture if for all $p \in \mathbb{P}$ and all $s, s' \in S_p$ we have $L_p(s) = L_p(s')$. That is, the listening

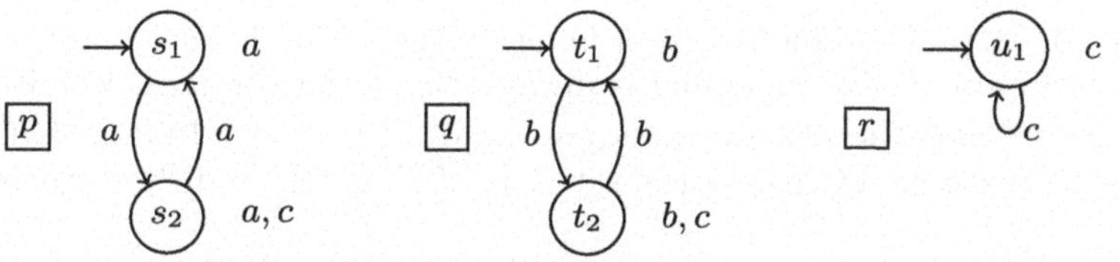

Fig. 1. An RAA $\mathcal{A}$ over three processes.

function of each process never changes. In that case, there is an obvious definition of a communication architecture $\mathbb{C}$.

Lehaut and Piterman showed that RAA with fixed architecture and asynchronous automata are different notations for the same object.

Lemma 3 ([11]). *There is an isomorphism between RAA with fixed communication architecture and asynchronous automata.*

3 Tree-Like Communication Architecture with Reconfiguration

We have defined what it means for a communication architecture to be a tree. Now we extend this in two orthogonal directions. First, we are interested in a more general communication architecture that is *tree-like* rather than a tree. Second, we consider the fact that for RAA (unlike AA) the communication architecture can change over time. This is made formal below.

3.1 Tree-Like Communication Architecture

As before, let $\mathbb{P}$ be a set of processes and CH a set of channels, both finite. A communication architecture is tree-like if there is a tree that spans channels that connect more than two processes. Formally, we have the following.

Let $|\mathbb{P}| = n$ and let us denote by $[n]$ the set $\{0, ..., n-1\}$, and put $[n]^+ = [n] \setminus \{0\}$. A *tree* over $\mathbb{P}$ is a tree $T = (\mathbb{P}, r, E, \ell)$ where $\mathbb{P}$ is the set of nodes, of which $r \in \mathbb{P}$ is the *root*, $E \subseteq \mathbb{P}^2$ is the set of *edges* (so that $|E| = n - 1$) that is cycle free, and $\ell :\ \mathrm{E} \to [n]^+$ is a *labeling bijection* that maps each edge to a strictly positive integer.

Definition 4. *We say that* $\mathfrak{A} = (\mathbb{C}, T)$*, where* $\mathbb{C}$ *is a communication architecture and* T *is a tree, is a* tree-like communication architecture *(short: TCA) if:*

1. $|\mathbb{C}(c)| \geq 2$ *for all channels* $c \in \mathrm{CH}$,
2. *for all channels* $c \in \mathrm{CH}$*, the set* $\mathbb{C}(c)$ *is connected in* T*, i.e. if* $p, q \in \mathbb{C}(c)$*, then all processes along the path from* p *to* q *in* T *are also in* $\mathbb{C}(c)$*, and*
3. *if* $(p, q) \in E$*, then there is a channel* $c \in \mathrm{CH}$ *such that* $p, q \in \mathbb{C}(c)$.

Condition 1 prevents a channel from being trivial.[1] Condition 2 ensures that a communication on a given channel is always "local" in the tree. Finally, condition 3 ensures that the tree does not consist of disconnected parts. Let $\mathcal{T}_{\mathrm{CH}}^{\mathbb{P}}$ be the set of all possible TCA over the sets CH of channels and $\mathbb{P}$ of processes.

Example 5. Fix sets $\mathbb{P} = \{p_1, \ldots, p_5\}$ of processes and $\mathrm{CH} = \{c_1, c_2, c_3\}$ of communication channels. Then $\mathfrak{A} = ((\mathbb{C}(c_1), \mathbb{C}(c_2), \mathbb{C}(c_3)), T)$ as given in Fig. 2 is a tree-like communication architecture rooted in p_1:

1. All channels have at least 2 members,
2. Every channel is connected in T,
3. All edges in T are covered by at least one channel.

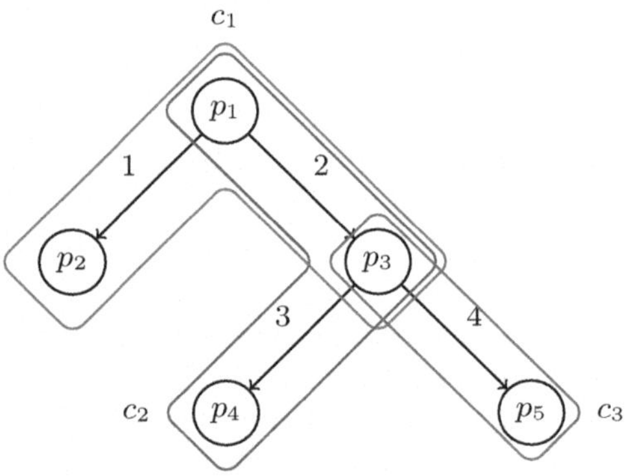

Fig. 2. A tree-like communication architecture: the spanning tree is given by the black edges, while the communication architecture is drawn with one color group for each channel. Edges labels are drawn next to each edge with a matching color.

We fix notation regarding the spanning tree $T = (\mathbb{P}, r, E, \ell)$ of a TCA that will be useful later on. For $p \neq r$, we let $e^{\uparrow}(p) \in E$ denote the parent edge of p; it is the only edge (p, q) (or (q, p)) that leads from p toward the root r. We also refer to q as the parent of p. We then let $E^{\downarrow}(p) \subseteq E$ denote the set of children edges of p, which are all edges that p is part of, except for $e^{\uparrow}(p)$. Similarly, processes that can be found by following edges from $E^{\downarrow}(p)$ are the children of p. Finally, put $E^{\updownarrow}(p) = \{e^{\uparrow}(p)\} \uplus E^{\downarrow}(p)$ for any $p \neq r$ and $E^{\updownarrow}(r) = E^{\downarrow}(r)$. A neighbor of p is either p's parent or one of its children. T' being a subtree of T, denoted by $T' \leq T$, is defined as usual.

A tree $T = (\mathbb{P}, r, E, \ell)$ can be observed locally by the processes. Formally, the *neighborhood* of a process $p \in \mathbb{P}$ is a tuple $N_p = (e_p^{\updownarrow}, E_p^{\downarrow}) \in [n] \times 2^{[n]^+}$, with the intuition that when T is known then $e_p^{\updownarrow} = \ell(e^{\uparrow}(p))$ and $E_p^{\downarrow} = \ell(E^{\downarrow}(p))$. Given

[1] We could allow channels with only 1 participant with few modifications. A channel with 0 participants will stay at 0 forever, thus being useless to the computation.

a family $N = (N_p)_{p \in \mathbb{P}}$ of neighborhoods, we say that the family is consistent if there exists exactly one $r \in \mathbb{P}$ such that $e_r^\uparrow = 0$ and $e_r^\uparrow \notin E_q^\downarrow$ for all $q \in \mathbb{P}$, and for all $p \neq r$ there exists exactly one $q \in \mathbb{P}$ such that $e_p^\uparrow \in E_q^\downarrow$. In that case, we define $\mathbb{T}(N) = (\mathbb{P}, r, E, \ell)$ where r is the unique process as defined in the previous condition, $E = \{(p,q) \mid e_p^\uparrow \in E_q^\downarrow\}$, and $\ell(p,q) = e_p^\uparrow$. One can easily check that if N is consistent, then $\mathbb{T}(N)$ is a well-defined tree over $\mathbb{P}$. Finally, we extend these notions to subsets $P \subseteq \mathbb{P}$, where a consistent family $N = (N_p)_{p \in P}$ (with the $e_r^\uparrow = 0$ condition dropped) induces a tree $\mathbb{T}(N)$ (that is a subtree of the entire spanning tree).

3.2 Reconfiguration Operations

We want to support reconfiguration operations to change from one TCA to another. Fix $\mathfrak{A} = (\mathbb{C}, T)$ with the same notation as before. There will be two kinds of operations: those affecting only the spanning tree, and those affecting only the channel memberships. Those operations are only valid when specific conditions (that depend on which operation is involved) on the TCA are satisfied; if a condition is not satisfied then the result of that operation is undefined.

As the TCA will change due to those operations, it is more convenient to specify edges and processes in terms of integers from $[n]$, with each integer being associated to the process for which the label of the parent edge is that integer, with integer 0 being associated to the root r of the tree. Abusing notations, we use e to denote actual edges in a tree as well as integers in $[n]$, with the understanding that one goes from one to the other using the labelling bijection ℓ. With that idea in mind, we define for any tree T the function $\pi : [n] \to \mathbb{P}$ where $\pi(0) = r$ and $\pi(e) = p$ such that p is the unique process with $\ell(e^\uparrow(p)) = e$ for any $e \neq 0$.

As operations for changing the spanning tree, we define a *swap* operation and a *move* operation. All operations involve a communication on some channel, say $c \in \mathrm{CH}$. See Fig. 3 for an illustration.

- A swap along an edge $e = (p, q)$ between a process p and its parent q, both of which must be listening to c, switches their positions and makes p the parent of q in the new architecture. To ensure condition 2 of Definition 4 is maintained, this operation can only be done if p is listening to all channels that both q and the parent of q are listening to.[2]
  Formally, we want to define the operation $\mathrm{SWAP}^c(e)(\mathfrak{A})$ where $\mathfrak{A}$ is a TCA and $e \in [n]^+$. Let $p = \pi(e)$ and q be the parent of p in T. For this operation to be defined, we must have $p, q \in \mathbb{C}(c)$; moreover if q is not the root and q' is the parent of q then we must have $p \in \mathbb{C}(c')$ for every $c' \in \mathrm{CH}$ such that $q, q' \in \mathbb{C}(c')$.
  If those conditions are satisfied, then we define $\mathrm{SWAP}^c(e)(\mathfrak{A}) = (\mathbb{C}, T')$ with $T' = (\mathbb{P}, r', E', \ell')$ as follows. If $q = r$ then $r' = p$ and both E' and ℓ' are unchanged. Otherwise $r' = r$, $E' = E \setminus \{(q, q')\} \uplus \{(p, q')\}$, and $\ell'(p, q') = \ell(q, q')$, $\ell'(e) = \ell(e)$ for all other edges e.

[2] Alternatively, we could make p connect to those channels as a result of the operation.

- A move of p to q changes the position of a non-root p in the tree so that the new parent of p after the operation is q. For this operation to be legal there are three conditions required. Let q' be the parent of p before the operation. First, q must be a neighbor of q', i.e. p can only be moved to either the parent of its parent or to one of its siblings. Second, q and q' must both be part of the communication on c (but p need not be part of it). Finally, moving p to q must not disconnect any channel that was shared by p and q'.
  Formally, the operation $\text{MOVE}^c(e, e')(\mathfrak{A})$ with $e \in [n]^+$ and $e' \in [n]$ is defined for $e \neq e'$ when, with $p = \pi(e)$, $q = \pi(e')$, and q' being the parent of p in T: 1) q' is a neighbor of q, 2) $q, q' \in \mathbb{C}(c)$, and 3) $q \in \mathbb{C}(c')$ for all c' such that $p, q' \in \mathbb{C}(c')$. Then we define $\text{MOVE}^c(e, e')(\mathfrak{A}) = (\mathbb{C}, T')$ where $T' = (\mathbb{P}, r, E \setminus \{(p, q')\} \uplus \{(p, q)\}, \ell')$ such that $\ell'(p, q) = \ell(p, q')$ and the rest is unchanged.

Consider the tree-like communication architecture in Fig. 2. Under this architecture, $\text{SWAP}^{c_1}(1)$ is possible as both p_1 and p_2 are connected to c_1 and p_1 is the root. The only swap not possible in this architecture is $\text{SWAP}^{c_3}(4)$. Indeed, this operation would leave c_2 and c_1 disconnected. The operation $\text{MOVE}^{c_1}(3, 2)$ is possible as it leaves p_4 connected to c_2. On the other hand, operation $\text{MOVE}^{c_3}(3, 4)$ is not possible since it would result in c_2 being disconnected around p_5.

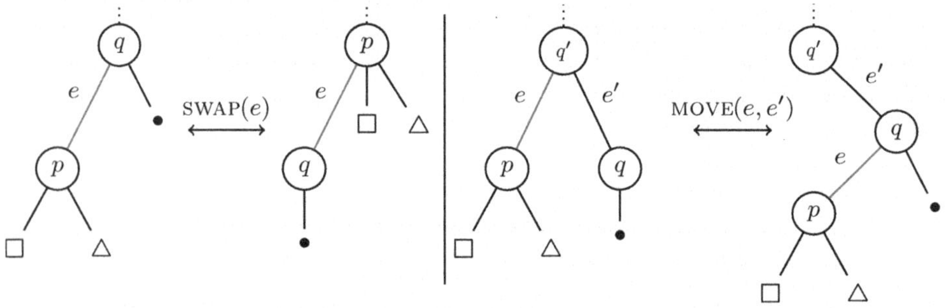

Fig. 3. Illustration of SWAP and MOVE operations.

There are also two operations that change channel membership but leave the underlying spanning tree unchanged.

- The *connect* operation allows a process $p \in \mathbb{C}(c)$ to join some specified channel c'. This can happen provided that there is a process adjacent to p that is contained in both $\mathbb{C}(c)$ and $\mathbb{C}(c')$. Intuitively this corresponds to that process "inviting" p to join channel c' via a communication on c.
  Operation $\text{CONN}^c(e, c')(\mathfrak{A})$ is defined for $e \in [n]$ if, with $p = \pi(e)$, $p \notin \mathbb{C}(c')$ and there exists q a neighbor of p such that $p, q \in \mathbb{C}(c)$ and $q \in \mathbb{C}(c')$. Then we define $\text{CONN}^c(e, c')(\mathfrak{A}) = (\mathbb{C}', T)$ with $\mathbb{C}'(c') = \mathbb{C}(c) \uplus \{p\}$ and $\mathbb{C}'(x) = \mathbb{C}(x)$ for all $x \neq c'$.

– Conversely, the *disconnect* operation allows $p \in \mathbb{P}_c$ to stop listening to c, as long as it does not result in breaking the conditions of Definition 4.
  Formally, $\mathbb{C}(c)$ must have size at least 3. Furthermore, p must be at the boundary of c, i.e. there is exactly one neighbor q that is also in $\mathbb{C}(c)$. Finally, there must be a different channel $c' \neq c$ such that both p and q are in $\mathbb{C}(c')$. If all of these conditions are satisfied, then for $e \in [n]$ and $p = \pi(e)$ we define $\textsc{disc}^c(e)(\mathfrak{A}) = (\mathbb{C}', T)$ with $\mathbb{C}'(c) = \mathbb{C}(c) \setminus \{p\}$ and $\mathbb{C}'(x) = \mathbb{C}(x)$ for all $x \neq c$.

Consider the tree-like communication architecture in Fig. 2. Under this architecture, it is possible to connect p_2 to c_2 by the communication $\textsc{conn}^{c_1}(1, c_2)$. It is, however, impossible to connect p_2 to c_3 as no neighbor of p_2 is connected to it. Disconnect operations are only possible for c_1 and c_2 as they have more than 2 processes listening to them. However, $\textsc{disc}^{c_2}(3)$ is not possible as it leaves p_4 disconnected. On the other hand, $\textsc{disc}^{c_2}(0)$ is possible. Similarly, the only disconnect possible from c_1 is p_3: $\textsc{disc}^{c_1}(2)$. See Fig. 4 for an illustration.

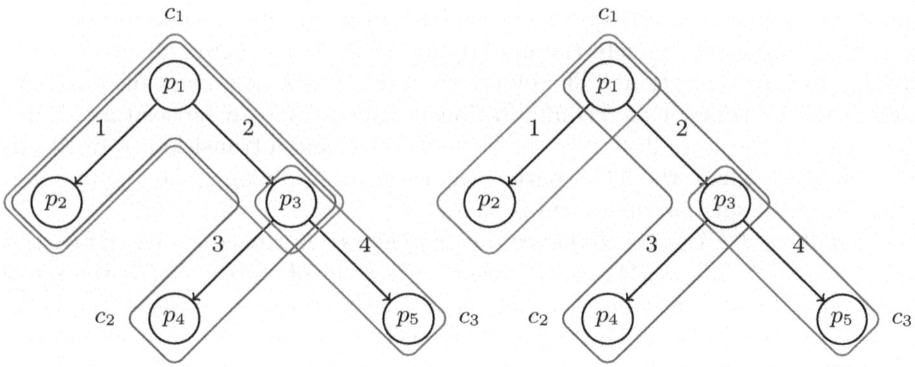

Fig. 4. The results of applying $\textsc{conn}^{c_1}(1, c_2)$ and $\textsc{disc}^{c_1}(2)$, respectively, to the tree-like communication architecture in Fig. 2.

For any of the four introduced operations, we write op($\mathfrak{A}$) to denote that op is valid from $\mathfrak{A}$ and results in op($\mathfrak{A}$). We show that all those operations preserve the properties of a TCA.

Lemma 6. *If* $\mathfrak{A}$ *is a TCA then* op($\mathfrak{A}$) *is also a TCA.*

We also show that those operations are universal, meaning that one can go to any TCA using a sequence with only those four operations.

Lemma 7. *If* $\mathfrak{A}$ *and* $\mathfrak{A}'$ *are in* $\mathcal{T}_{\mathrm{CH}}^{\mathbb{P}}$, *then there is a sequence of reconfiguration operations leading from* $\mathfrak{A}$ *to* $\mathfrak{A}'$.

4 Reconfiguration Languages

4.1 Automata over Reconfiguration Languages

We define *reconfiguration languages*, which are basically languages that also include information about reconfiguration of a TCA. Formally, we fix $\mathbb{P}$ and CH, as well as the set $[n]$ as defined before. Then we define the set of operations $Op = \{\text{NOP}, \text{SWAP}(e), \text{MOVE}(e, e'), \text{CONN}(e', c), \text{DISC}(e')\}$ with $e \in [n]^+$, $e' \in [n]$ and $c \in \text{CH}$; NOP denotes the empty operation that does not change the TCA and is always valid (i.e. no conditions are needed for this operation). All other operations mirror those defined previously. Then we let $\Sigma = \text{CH} \times Op$ be the *reconfiguration alphabet.* A reconfiguration language is a language over this alphabet. We note that operations as applied to TCAs include the channel name on which they were sent in them. We write op^c of the operation on TCA that arises from sending op on channel c. For example, if $\text{op} = \text{MOVE}(e, e')$ then $\text{op}^c = \text{MOVE}^c(e, e')$.

Now we want to define what it means for an automaton to recognize a reconfiguration language. Intuitively, a generic DFA over this alphabet would be missing some component, namely the underlying TCA that is being affected by the reconfigurations operations. Therefore, we introduce a new class of automata tailored to the concept of reconfiguration languages. It can be seen as a DFA where part of the state describes the current TCA, and a transition (c, op) leads to a new state where the TCA part is the result of applying op to the previous TCA, provided such an operation is valid.

Formally a *DFA for reconfiguration languages*, shortened to RL-DFA, is a tuple $\mathcal{A} = (\Sigma, S, \mathcal{T}^{\mathbb{P}}_{\text{CH}}, s_0, \mathfrak{A}_0, \Delta, F)$, where S is a set of states, $\mathcal{T}^{\mathbb{P}}_{\text{CH}}$ is the set of TCA over CH and $\mathbb{P}$ as defined earlier, $s_0 \in S$ is the initial state, $\mathfrak{A}_0 \in \mathcal{T}^{\mathbb{P}}_{\text{CH}}$ is the initial TCA, $\Delta : S \times \Sigma \rightharpoonup S$ is the partial transition function, and $F \subseteq S$ is the set of accepting states. As hinted, a *configuration* of $\mathcal{A}$ is a pair $(s, \mathfrak{A}) \in S \times \mathcal{T}^{\mathbb{P}}_{\text{CH}}$ indicating the current state and current TCA of $\mathcal{A}$. In runs, we require that all transitions in Δ are valid with respect to the current TCA, i.e. if the current TCA is $\mathfrak{A}$ then $\Delta(s, (c, \text{op}))$ can be taken only if $\text{op}^c(\mathfrak{A})$ is defined. A *run* of $\mathcal{A}$ over word $w = (c_1, \text{op}_1), \ldots, (c_k, \text{op}_k) \in \Sigma^*$ is the sequence

$$(s_0, \mathfrak{A}_0) \xrightarrow{(c_1, \text{op}_1)} (s_1, \mathfrak{A}_1) \xrightarrow{(c_2, \text{op}_2)} \ldots \xrightarrow{(c_k, \text{op}_k)} (s_k, \mathfrak{A}_k)$$

where for all $1 \le i \le k$, $s_i = \Delta(s_{i-1}, (c_i, \text{op}_i))$ and $\mathfrak{A}_i = \text{op}_i^{c_i}(\mathfrak{A}_{i-1})$. Notice, that, as $\text{op}_i(\mathfrak{A}_{i-1})$ is undefined if op_i is not possible in $\mathfrak{A}_{i-1}$, this means that all operations in a run are possible. So, for some word the associated run does not exist if at some point the necessary transition does not exist in the automaton or because from the reached architecture the next operation would not be valid. We say that configuration $(s, \mathfrak{A})$ is reachable, if there is a run visiting it. Word $w \in \Sigma^*$ is accepted if the run over w ends in a state $s_k \in F$, and the language accepted by $\mathcal{A}$, $\mathcal{L}(\mathcal{A})$, is the set of words accepted by $\mathcal{A}$.

4.2 Distributivity of a Language

We start from a centralized language given by an RL-DFA $\mathcal{A}$. The goal is to build a distributed system able to recognize the same language using only the communication architecture given by following the language. This distributed system should be in the form of an RAA $\mathcal{A}$, as defined in Sect. 2.

Let us define our notion of distribution. Intuitively, an RAA distributes an RL-DFA if both automata recognize the same language, and if they agree, on all runs, on the sequences of communication architectures that they construct. In runs of the centralized RL-DFA, the communication architecture occurs explicitly in each configuration; in runs of the distributed RAA, the communication architecture features only implicitly, but to be able to define our notion of distribution, we assume that the neighborhood of a process can be extracted from its local states, using a family of functions $(N_p)_{p\in\mathbb{P}}$. Finally, one should be able to deduce the state of the centralized automaton by looking at the product of the local states in the RAA, using a function D.

Formally, let $\mathcal{A} = (\Sigma, S, \mathcal{T}_{\mathrm{CH}}^{\mathbb{P}}, s_0, \mathfrak{A}_0, \Delta, F)$ be a RL-DFA and let $\mathcal{A}_{\|} = ((S_p)_{p\in\mathbb{P}}, (s_p^0)_{p\in\mathbb{P}}, (\delta_p)_{p\in\mathbb{P}}, (L_p)_{p\in\mathbb{P}}, (F_p)_{p\in\mathbb{P}})$ be an RAA over Σ (slightly adapting the definition to accept this extended alphabet). We say that $\mathcal{A}_{\|}$ *distributes* $\mathcal{A}$ if there is a family $(N_p : S_p \to [n] \times 2^{[n]^+})_{p\in\mathbb{P}}$ of functions and a function $D : \prod_{p\in\mathbb{P}} S_p \to S$ such that for all words $w = (c_1, \mathrm{op}_1), \ldots, (c_k, \mathrm{op}_k) \in \Sigma^*$ with

$$\rho = (s_0, \mathfrak{A}_0) \xrightarrow{(c_1,\mathrm{op}_1)} (s_1, \mathfrak{A}_1) \xrightarrow{(c_2,\mathrm{op}_2)} \ldots \xrightarrow{(c_k,\mathrm{op}_k)} (s_k, \mathfrak{A}_k)$$

being the run of $\mathcal{A}$ on w, we have that the run of $\mathcal{A}_{\|}$ on w is of shape

$$\rho_{\|} = (s_p^0) \xrightarrow{(d_1,(c_1,\mathrm{op}_1))} (s_p^1) \xrightarrow{(d_2,(c_2,\mathrm{op}_2))} \ldots \xrightarrow{(d_k,(c_k,\mathrm{op}_k))} (s_p^k),$$

where for all $0 \le i \le k$, we have

1. $\mathfrak{A}_i = \left((\mathbb{C} : c \mapsto \{p \in \mathbb{P} \mid c \in L_p(s_p^i)\}\right), \mathbb{T}((N_p(s_p^i))_{p\in\mathbb{P}}))$, that is, $\mathfrak{A}_i$ is the architecture arising from collecting the listening functions of all processes and building the tree from their local knowledge,
2. $s_i = D((s_p^i)_{p\in\mathbb{P}})$, and
3. $s_k \in F$ if and only if $\exists d \in \mathbb{D}.\forall p \in \mathbb{P}.F_p((s_p^k), d) = \top$.

Recall that $d_1 d_2 \ldots d_k \in \mathbb{D}^*$ is the data used for coordination when communicating while reading w. Finally, if the run of $\mathcal{A}$ on w is undefined, then so is the run of $\mathcal{A}_{\|}$. Note that by definition $L(\mathcal{A}) = L(\mathcal{A}_{\|})$ whenever $\mathcal{A}_{\|}$ distributes $\mathcal{A}$.

4.3 Diamond Closed RL-DFA

In general, it is not the case that any RL-DFA can be distributed. For instance, one can create a language which only accepts the word $(c_1, \mathrm{NOP}), (c_2, \mathrm{NOP})$ for two channels c_1 and c_2 that do not share a common process; such a pattern can not be accepted in a distributed way as processes in c_2 have no way to "wait" until the communication in c_1 happens. A distributed language would thus have to accept also the communication $(c_2, \text{NOP}), (c_1, \text{NOP})$. Intuitively, for a centralized language to be distributable, the existence and result of $\Delta(s,(c,\text{op}))$ should only depend on the history of processes participating in the communication on c. In other words, if no process can distinguish between two different communications, then those two communications should end in the same configuration. In the non-reconfiguration case, i.e. for DFA where the communication architecture is fixed, this property can be ensured by checking syntactically that the DFA has the I-diamond property: for any two *independent* channels a and b, meaning that there is no process listening to both a and b, we have that $\Delta(s, ab) = \Delta(s, ba)$ for all states s. Obviously this does not work in the case of RL-DFA, as two channels can be independent in one TCA but not in another; thus we need to redefine what it means to be independent.

Given a TCA $\mathfrak{A} = (\mathbb{C}, T)$, we say that two actions (c_1, op_1) and (c_2, op_2) are $\mathfrak{A}$-dependent if there exists $p \in \mathbb{P}$ such that p listens to c_1 in either $\mathfrak{A}$ or $\text{op}_1^{c_1}(\mathfrak{A})$ *and* process p listens to c_2 in either $\mathfrak{A}$ or $\text{op}_2^{c_2}(\mathfrak{A})$. Otherwise, we say that (c_1, op_1) and (c_2, op_2) are $\mathfrak{A}$-independent. In other words, (c_1, op_1) and (c_2, op_2) are $\mathfrak{A}$-dependent iff there is some process p that can distinguish between the two communications $(c_1, \text{op}_1), (c_2, \text{op}_2)$ and $(c_2, \text{op}_2), (c_1, \text{op}_1)$ starting from $\mathfrak{A}$. Alternatively, using the properties of TCAs, (c_1, op_1) and (c_2, op_2) are $\mathfrak{A}$-independent iff there exists an edge e in T that if removed splits T in two smaller TCA $\mathfrak{A}_1 = (\mathbb{C}_1, T_1)$ and $\mathfrak{A}_2 = (\mathbb{C}_2, T_2)$ and such that (c_i, op_i) is valid in the restricted TCA $\mathfrak{A}_i$ for $i \in \{1, 2\}$. In simpler terms, those two actions are independent because they operate in disjoint parts of the tree. It is possible to see that the two definitions are equivalent by considering the set of processes participating in each, observing that they are disjoint, and choosing an edge that disconnects them.

From now on, we assume that the centralized RL-DFA $\mathcal{A}$ is diamond closed:

Definition 8 (Diamond closed RL-DFA). *An RL-DFA $\mathcal{A}$ is said to be* diamond closed *when for all reachable configurations $(s, \mathfrak{A}) \in S \times \mathcal{T}_{\text{CH}}^{\mathbb{P}}$ and all $\mathfrak{A}$-independent actions (c_1, op_1) and (c_2, op_2),*

$$\Delta(s, (c_1, \text{op}_1)(c_2, \text{op}_2)) = \Delta(s, (c_2, \text{op}_2)(c_1, \text{op}_1)).$$

We extend the definition of independence to sequences, so that $w_1, w_2 \in \Sigma^*$ are independent if all possible interleavings are indistinguishable. Formally, we define the notion recursively. The empty sequence ε is $\mathfrak{A}$-independent with any word w for any TCA $\mathfrak{A}$, and $w_1 = (c_1, \text{op}_1) \cdot w_1'$ is $\mathfrak{A}$-independent with $w_2 = (c_2, \text{op}_2) \cdot w_2'$ if (c_1, op_1) and (c_2, op_2) are $\mathfrak{A}$-independent and w_1' and w_2 are $\text{op}_1^{c_1}(\mathfrak{A})$-independent and w_1 and w_2' are $\text{op}_2^{c_2}(\mathfrak{A})$-independent. If $\mathcal{A}$ is diamond closed with $(s, \mathfrak{A})$ being a reachable configuration, and w_1 and w_2 are two $\mathfrak{A}$-independent words, then we have that $\Delta(s, w_1 w_2) = \Delta(s, w_2 w_1) = \Delta(s, w)$ for any w that is an interleaving of w_1 and w_2.

We end on a property satisfied by diamond closed RL-DFA that will be used in the next section. Fix a reachable configuration $(s, \mathfrak{A})$ and let w_1 and w_2 be two $\mathfrak{A}$-independent words. Let $s_1 = \Delta(s, w_1)$, $s_2 = \Delta(s, w_2)$, and let C be the set of channels involved in w_2. We claim that one can compute the diamond closure $s' = \Delta(s, w_1 w_2)$ knowing only s, s_1, s_2, and C.

Lemma 9 ([5,10]). *Let $\mathcal{A}$ be a diamond closed RL-DFA. There is a function* $\mathrm{Diam} : S^3 \times 2^{\mathrm{CH}} \to S$ *such that if $(s, \mathfrak{A}), s, s_1, w_1, s_2, w_2, C, s'$ are all defined as described above, then* $\mathrm{Diam}(s, s_1, s_2, C) = s'$.

To understand the need for this function, let us give a quick intuition for the construction in the case of a fixed tree with binary channels given in [10]. There, the goal of the construction is to distribute a diamond closed DFA $\mathcal{A}$ into an asynchronous automaton. Each process will maintain a state of $\mathcal{A}$ that is the most recent state visited by $\mathcal{A}$ according to the knowledge of this process. This does not necessarily coincide with the actual state of $\mathcal{A}$, as some communication happening without this process involved can change the state of $\mathcal{A}$. Then when two processes communicate they will share their information in order to update their knowledge about the state of $\mathcal{A}$. To that end, both processes need to agree on what was the state the last time they communicated with each other and what each side has been doing independently since that time. With a tree structure, this is actually easy: each child also maintain the state of $\mathcal{A}$ during the last communication with their parent, and by the structure of the tree everything that happened with the child since then is independent from what happened with the parent. So on a communication between a parent and one of its children, let s be the state after their last communication, s_1 and s_2 be the most up-to-date states known by the parent and its child respectively, and C the set of channels belonging in the subtree rooted in the child. Then one can combine the information known by the parent and the child by computing $\mathrm{Diam}(s, s_1, s_2, C)$, without needing to know the full sequences w_1, w_2 that were done separately on each side since s.

In our setting, communications can include more than two participants. To that end, we naturally extend the Diam function to work on trees. Let T be a tree where each node is labeled by a pair (s^1, s^2) of states and a set C of channels, with the intuition that s^1 is the last state in common that the process at this node has with its parent, s^2 is the most recent state this process knows, and C is the set of channels that can be found in the subtree rooted in that node. Let p be the root of T, labeled by (s_r^1, s_r^2, C_r), and assume that p has k children labeled (s_i^1, s_i^2, C_i) and leading to tree T_i for $i \in \{1, \dots, k\}$. Then we define the function TDiam recursively in the following way:

$$\mathrm{TDiam}(T) = \begin{cases} s_r^2 & \text{if } k = 0, \\ \mathrm{Diam}(s_1^1, \mathrm{TDiam}(T \setminus T_1), \mathrm{TDiam}(T_1), C_1) & \text{otherwise.} \end{cases}$$

Basically we just iterate the Diam function on all children of a parent, then repeat in all levels of the tree until we get to the root. Note that the state(p) function from [10] is equivalent to $\mathrm{TDiam}(T_p)$ where T_p is the tree rooted in p.

We now have all the tools needed to state our construction.

5 Distribution of Diamond Closed RL-DFA

We show that the language of a diamond closed RL-DFA can be distributed to collaborating RAAs. The different processes of the RAA maintain their knowledge of the architecture as well as their knowledge regarding the states of the RL-DFA that the computation has reached. We then show that based on the communication that each process participates in, they can keep this information updated so that it is maintained correctly and corresponds to the respective configurations of the RL-DFA.

More formally we have the following. We fix the finite sets $\mathbb{P}$ and CH of processes and channels, respectively, and let $n = |\mathbb{P}|$. Given an RL-DFA $\mathcal{A} = (\Sigma, S, \mathcal{T}_{\mathrm{CH}}^{\mathbb{P}}, s_0, \mathfrak{A}_0, F, \Delta)$, the goal of this section is to show how to build an RAA $\mathcal{A}_{\|} = ((S_p)_{p\in\mathbb{P}}, (s_p^0)_{p\in\mathbb{P}}, (\delta_p)_{p\in\mathbb{P}}, (L_p)_{p\in\mathbb{P}}, (F_p)_{p\in\mathbb{P}})$ that distributes $\mathcal{A}$. Toward this goal, we describe the maintained information in the states of each process.

5.1 Local Information to Be Maintained

Each process p stores in its states S_p some local information about the communication architecture as well as some information about the state of the centralized automaton. Recall that we associate each edge in the tree with an integer in $[n]^+$. A state $s_p \in S_p$ then is a tuple of the form $\langle (s^1, s^2), L, (e^\uparrow, E^\downarrow), cc, dc\rangle$ where:

- $(s^1, s^2) \in S \times S$ is a pair of states of the centralized automaton, with s^1 being the state during the last communication involving both p and its parent, and s^2 the most up-to-date state known by p.
- $L \subseteq \mathrm{CH}$ is the set of channels that p listens to, i.e. $L_p(s_p) = L$. In the corresponding TCA, it means that $c \in L$ iff $p \in \mathbb{C}(c)$.
- $(e^\uparrow, E^\downarrow) \in [n] \times 2^{[n]^+}$ are the edge leading to the parent of p (or 0 for the root) and the set of edges leading to the children of p respectively. The edge $e^\uparrow$ serves as a proxy for the identity of p and its position in the tree. Let $E^\updownarrow$ denote the set $\{e^\uparrow\} \uplus E^\downarrow$.
- $cc : E^\updownarrow \to 2^L$ is the set of *connected channels* shared by p and each of its neighbors. For instance, $cc(e^\uparrow)$ is exactly the set of channels that both p and its parent listen to. As we want to maintain a TCA, these sets should never be empty by condition 3 of Definition 4.
- $dc : E^\updownarrow \to 2^{\mathrm{CH}\setminus L}$ indicates for each direction leading away from p which set of channels can be found in that direction that p does not listen to (dc stands for *disconnected channels*). Intuitively, we have $c \in dc(e)$ for some $e \in E^\updownarrow$ if all processes that listen to channel c can be found in the subtree obtained by following the edge whose label is e. By condition 2 of Definition 4, any channel $c \in \mathrm{CH} \setminus L$ can only be found in at most one direction, otherwise $\mathbb{C}(c)$ would be disconnected due to p not being contained in this set; and by condition 1, c can be found in at least one direction. Thus dc can also be seen as a partition of $\mathrm{CH} \setminus L$ over $E^\updownarrow$.

The first component, that is the pair of states of the centralized automaton, is identical to the construction in [10]. The rest of the components are used to represent a TCA in a distributed way and help maintain it under reconfiguration operations.

Recall that we fixed $\mathcal{A} = (\Sigma, S, s_0, F, \Delta)$ and an initial TCA $\mathfrak{A}_0 = (\mathbb{C}_0, T_0)$. Let $T_0 = (\mathbb{P}, r_0, E_0, \ell_0)$. By abuse of notation, we extend ℓ_0 to set of edges. The initial state of process $p \neq r_0$ is

$$s_p^0 = \langle (s_0, s_0), \mathbb{C}_0^{-1}(p), (\ell_0(e^{\uparrow}(p)), \ell_0(E^{\downarrow}(p))), cc_p^0, dc_p^0 \rangle$$

where cc_p^0 and dc_p^0 are defined as follows:

$$cc_p^0(e) = \{c \in \mathrm{CH} \mid p, q \in \mathbb{C}_0(c) \text{ where } q \text{ is the neighbor of } p \text{ along edge } \ell^{-1}(e)\}$$
$$dc_p^0(e) = \left\{ c \in \mathrm{CH} \,\middle|\, \begin{array}{l} p \notin \mathbb{C}_0(c) \wedge \text{ there is a path in } T_0 \text{ from } p \text{ starting} \\ \text{with edge } \ell^{-1}(e) \text{ reaching some } q \text{ with } q \in \mathbb{C}_0(c) \end{array} \right\}$$

For $p = r_0$, component $\ell_0(e^{\uparrow}(p))$ (which is undefined) is set to 0 instead; all other components are defined same as above with $cc_p(0) = dc_p(0) = \emptyset$.

We are now ready to start the description of the transition function Δ_p of each process p. Transitions will vary based on which reconfiguration operation occurs, and the data sent along the communication will reflect this. However, there is some basic common data that is needed for synchronization, even when no reconfiguration happens. We start by describing this data in the next section.

5.2 Common Synchronization Data

Under every communication, processes participating in the communication share as part of the data the information they have regarding the subtree of processes participating in the communication. Namely, on a communication in channel c only the processes in $\mathbb{C}(c)$ participate. The shared data will allow every process to independently build the subtree of c's participants, check that there is no inconsistency in the data sent, and then compute the newest state by taking the diamond closure over the states sent by all other processes in the correct order. Based on this computation, and potentially requiring additional data, each process updates their state.

Formally, the data sent is of the following form:

$$\begin{aligned} \mathit{SyncData} = \{&((s_1^1, s_1^2), e_1^{\uparrow}, E_1^{\downarrow}, C_1), \ldots, ((s_k^1, s_k^2), e_k^{\uparrow}, E_k^{\downarrow}, C_k) \mid \\ &2 \leq k \leq n \ \wedge \ \forall 1 \leq i \leq k.(s_i^1, s_i^2) \in S^2, e_i^{\uparrow} \in [n], E_i^{\downarrow} \subseteq [n]^+, C_i \subseteq \mathrm{CH}\} \end{aligned}$$

A process p agrees only to data of this form that is consistent both with p's local view and with itself; otherwise p will simply block this communication. Consider a data sync $= ((s_1^1, s_1^2), e_1^{\uparrow}, E_1^{\downarrow}, C_1), \ldots, ((s_k^1, s_k^2), e_k^{\uparrow}, E_k^{\downarrow}, C_k) \in \mathit{SyncData}$, we define $T_{\mathrm{sync}} = \mathbb{T}((e_i^{\uparrow}, E_i^{\downarrow})_{1 \leq i \leq k})$. Each node of T_{sync} is associated to one index i between 1 and k, and is labeled by (s_i^1, s_i^2, C_i). For all processes $p \in \mathbb{P}$, given p's a local state $s_p = \langle (s^1, s^2), L, (e^{\uparrow}, E^{\downarrow}), cc, dc \rangle$, we say that data

$$\mathrm{sync} = ((s_1^1, s_1^2), e_1^{\uparrow}, E_1^{\downarrow}, C_1), \ldots, ((s_k^1, s_k^2), e_k^{\uparrow}, E_k^{\downarrow}, C_k) \in \mathit{SyncData}$$

is *consistent* with s_p for channel c, if $c \in L$ and the following conditions hold:

- The subtree T_{sync} is defined.
- There are no two $i \neq j$ such that $e_i^{\uparrow} = e_j^{\uparrow}$.
- There is $i \leq k$ such that $(s_i^1, s_i^2) = (s^1, s^2)$, $e_i^{\uparrow} = e^{\uparrow}$, $E_i^{\downarrow} = \{e \in E^{\downarrow} \mid c \in cc(e)\}$, and for all $e \in E_i^{\downarrow}$, there exists $j \leq k$ such that $e_j^{\uparrow} = e$ and $C_j = dc(e)$.

We denote by $\sigma(\text{sync}) = \text{TDiam}(T_{\text{sync}})$ the newest up-to-date state of the centralized automaton $\mathcal{A}$ according to processes that listen to c agreeing on data sync. It follows that the information in the synchronization data is sufficient for computing the diamond closure for all the processes participating in the communication.

We describe the transition function for all possible reconfiguration operations.

5.3 Transition on Reconfiguration Operation

With no reconfiguration operation (NOP). Under a (c, NOP) communication, the TCA remains unchanged. In the distributed automaton, this is reflected in that only the first component of each local state needs to be updated. As the TCA is unchanged, no additional information is required in addition to the synchronization data.

Consider p's local state $s_p = \langle (s^1, s^2), L, (e^{\uparrow}, E^{\downarrow}), cc, dc \rangle$. Let $\sigma(\text{sync}) = \text{TDiam}(T_{\text{sync}})$. Then, $\delta_p(s_p, (\text{sync}, (c, \text{NOP})))$ is defined if and only if sync is consistent with s_p for c and $s' = \Delta(\sigma(\text{sync}), (c, \text{NOP}))$ is defined. We put

$$\delta_p(s_p, (\text{sync}, (c, \text{NOP}))) = \langle (\text{ID-IF-ROOT}_c^{s_p}(s'), s'), L, (e^{\uparrow}, E^{\downarrow}), cc, dc \rangle, \text{ where}$$
$$\text{ID-IF-ROOT}_c^{s_p}(s') = \begin{cases} s^1 & \text{if } p \text{ is the root of the subtree of } c \text{ (i.e. } c \notin cc(e^{\uparrow}) \text{)}, \\ s' & \text{otherwise.} \end{cases}$$

On SWAP(e). A communication $(c, \text{SWAP}(e))$ along an edge $e = (p, q)$ swaps the position of a non-root process p and its parent q in the TCA. Note that p is identified by being the unique process whose parent edge is e, and similarly q is the unique process for which e is a child edge. Recall that this operation is only possible if p listens to every channel that is shared by q and the parent of q, so as to not break connectivity after swapping. Thus the distributed automaton should also ensure that this condition is satisfied; this requires additional information sent in the data during communication. If this condition is satisfied, then p and q swap their upward edges and update their cc and dc components accordingly. We invite the reader to refer to the appendix for the full details of the construction, for this operation as well as the following ones.

On MOVE(e,e'). A $\text{MOVE}(e, e')$ changes the position of the process p whose parent edge is e to become one of q's children (where q is the process whose parent edge is e'), assuming that q was a neighbor of p's original parent, which we call q'. Another condition is that any channel shared by p and its original parent q' must also be shared by its new parent q; this set of channels needs to be sent as part of the data as in the previous operation. Notably, p itself does not need to be part of the communication, as nothing changes in the TCA from its point of view. As for process q, it needs to add e to the set of its children edges, and know what set of channels are found in p's subtree to update its state correctly; those will be provided in the communication by q'. Process q' itself removes e from its children edges, and changes its dc to reflect p's new position.

On CONN*(e,c')*. On a CONN(e, c') communication sent on channel c, and with p being the process whose parent edge is e, p starts listening to c'. This requires the existence of a process, say q, that is a neighbor of p and that listens to both c and c'. To check this, an additional edge will be sent as part of the data, with that edge representing process q (which will block the communication if it does not fit the required conditions). As a result of this, p and q will have to update their cc and dc components.

On DISC*(e)*. Finally, a DISC(e) operation on channel c makes the process p whose parent edge is e disconnect from c. Several conditions need to be satisfied for this to be possible. First, exactly one neighbor q of p must be in c, which can be checked from the tree T_c. There must be at least two processes other than p listening to c, which again can be seen in the size of T_c. Lastly, there must be at least one other channel c' shared by p and q; both of those can check this by looking at their cc component. If those are satisfied, then p disconnects fron c and p and q update their cc and dc.

5.4 Acceptance and Correctness

The last component that remains to be defined is the acceptance condition F_p. To that end, we define *global* synchronization data, which is basically some synchronization data sync that includes all processes instead of being restricted to only those participating in a communication. Formally, we say that

$$\text{sync} = ((s_1^1, s_1^2), e_1^\uparrow, E_1^\downarrow, C_1), \ldots, ((s_n^1, s_n^2), e_n^\uparrow, E_n^\downarrow, C_n) \in \mathit{SyncData}$$

is globally consistent with s_p if:

- T_{sync} is defined,
- $\forall i. e_i^\uparrow = i - 1$, i.e. each process is seen once in order of their parent edge,
- with $i = e_p^\uparrow + 1$, we have $s_i^1 = s_p^1, s_i^2 = s_p^2, e_i^\uparrow = e_p^\uparrow, E_i^\downarrow = E_p^\downarrow$,
- $\forall e \in E_p^\downarrow . C_{e+1} = dc_p(e)$.

We then put $F_p(s_p, \text{sync}) = \top$ if and only if sync is globally consistent with s_p and $\sigma(\text{sync}) \in F$.

Let $\mathcal{A}_p = (S_p, s_p^0, \delta_p, L_p, F_p)$ as defined throughout this section and let $\mathcal{A}_\parallel = ((S_p)_{p\in\mathbb{P}}, (s_p^0)_{p\in\mathbb{P}}, (\delta_p)_{p\in\mathbb{P}}, (L_p)_{p\in\mathbb{P}}, (F_p)_{p\in\mathbb{P}})$. We state our main result as follows.

Theorem 10. *If $\mathcal{A}$ is diamond closed, then $\mathcal{A}_\parallel$ distributes $\mathcal{A}$.*

5.5 Complexity and Non-reconfigurable Case

We analyze the complexity of the proposed construction. A state of a process p is of the form $s_p = \langle (s^1, s^2), L, (e^\uparrow, E^\downarrow), cc, dc \rangle$, and a global state $\mathbf{s} = (s_p)_{p \in \mathbb{P}}$ is a product of the states for each process. The first component is of the shape $(s^1, s^2) \in S^2$, so the number of states in the constructed automaton has quadratic dependency on the size of S. Next, L is a subset of CH, $e^\uparrow$ and $E^\downarrow$ combined are a subset of $[n]$ (recall that $n = |\mathbb{P}|$), and cc and dc are partitions of CH over $[n]$. Combining all those together, we get that S_p has size quadratic in S and exponential in both CH and $\mathbb{P}$. Since in our setting n is fixed, a global state $\mathbf{s}$ takes space logarithmic in S and polynomial in CH and $\mathbb{P}$. Notice that the set $\mathcal{T}_{\mathrm{CH}}^{\mathbb{P}}$ of all possible TCAs is also exponential in CH and $\mathbb{P}$, and as $\mathcal{A}$ is assumed to be diamond closed, its state set must relate to this set. Therefore, overall, we get the following result.

Theorem 11. *The size of $\mathcal{A}_{\parallel}$ is polynomial in the size of $\mathcal{A}$.*

Our construction is also a generalization of the construction of Krishna and Muscholl [10]. That is, assume no reconfiguration operation happens during a run over w (i.e. we only have NOP operations in w). In the run of the centralized automaton $\mathcal{A}$, this means that the TCA never changes, and remains $\mathfrak{A}_0$ throughout the run. Similarly in the run of $\mathcal{A}_{\parallel}$, only the first component (s^1, s^2) in each process state gets updated; the remaining components stay as they were initially. We can then build a simpler $\mathcal{A}_{\parallel}$ by removing those fixed parts and only keeping the pair of states, dropping the complexity down to simply polynomial in S. This new construction corresponds to the one from [10], but generalized to tree-like architectures instead of trees in which all channels are binary. If we further restrict channels to be binary in the now fixed architecture, we get back exactly the same construction. Indeed if $\mathbb{C}(c) = \{p, q\}$ with p being the parent of q then $\mathrm{TDiam}(T_c)$ reduces to $\mathrm{Diam}(s_q^1, s_p^2, s_q^2, C_q)$ which is the way updates are computed in Krishna and Muscholl's construction.

6 Conclusion

We define automata over reconfiguration languages, along with a notion of distribution by reconfigurable asynchronous automata, as well as a semantic (confluence) property that ensures distributability. Our construction imposes a tree-like communication architecture, but supports both communication channels with an arbitrary number of members, as well as reconfiguration of the communication architecture, and therefore significantly extends the construction from [10] that is restricted to fixed architectures with binary channels that are arranged in a tree. Our distribution method retains the quadratic dependency on the number of states of the central automaton from [10], but uses additional data for the distribution of the (changing) communication architecture.

Future works include generalizing this result to general communication topologies. There are several difficulties involved. First, devising the set of atomic reconfiguration operations that will allow to gradually transform an architecture into any possible other architecture. These operations need to be "locally safe", that is allow processes to update their view of the architecture so that the global architecture can still be captured and that enough information about independence is maintained locally. Second, the diamond property of the centralized automaton becomes more involved and requires careful analysis of how independence changes over time and operations. Finally, follow up on Zielonka's construction in its full complexity and extend it with reconfiguration. We need to both add and update the information that processes maintain about the architecture, as well as use this information in order to understand (and update others about) the progress of the global computation.

References

1. Abd Alrahman, Y., De Nicola, R., Loreti, M.: A calculus for collective-adaptive systems and its behavioural theory. Inf. Comput. **268**, 104457 (2019). https://doi.org/10.1016/J.IC.2019.104457
2. Adsul, B., Gastin, P., Kulkarni, S., Weil, P.: An expressively complete local past propositional dynamic logic over Mazurkiewicz traces and its applications. In: Logic in Computer Science, LICS 2024, pp. 1–13 (2024). https://doi.org/10.1145/3661814.3662110
3. Alrahman, Y.A., De Nicola, R., Loreti, M., Tiezzi, F., Vigo, R.: A calculus for attribute-based communication. In: Symposium on Applied Computing, SAC 2015, pp. 1840–1845 (2015). https://doi.org/10.1145/2695664.2695668
4. Abd Alrahman, Y., Piterman, N.: Modelling and verification of reconfigurable multi-agent systems. Auton. Agent. Multi-Agent Syst. **35**(2), 1–36 (2021). https://doi.org/10.1007/s10458-021-09521-x
5. Cori, R., Métivier, Y., Zielonka, W.: Asynchronous mappings and asynchronous cellular automata. Inf. Comput. **106**(2), 159–202 (1993). https://doi.org/10.1006/INCO.1993.1052
6. Genest, B., Gimbert, H., Muscholl, A., Walukiewicz, I.: Optimal Zielonka-type construction of deterministic asynchronous automata. In: Automata, Languages and Programming, ICALP 2010. LNCS, vol. 6199, pp. 52–63. Springer (2010).https://doi.org/10.1007/978-3-642-14162-1_5
7. Genest, B., Muscholl, A.: Constructing exponential-size deterministic zielonka automata. In: Bugliesi, M., Preneel, B., Sassone, V., Wegener, I. (eds.) ICALP 2006. LNCS, vol. 4052, pp. 565–576. Springer, Heidelberg (2006). https://doi.org/10.1007/11787006_48
8. Gimbert, H.: Distributed asynchronous games with causal memory are undecidable. Logical Methods Comput. Sci. **18** (2022). https://doi.org/10.46298/LMCS-18(3:30)2022
9. Hausmann, D., Lehaut, M., Piterman, N.: Distribution of reconfiguration languages maintaining tree-like communication topology. CoRR **abs/2408.10708** (2024). https://doi.org/10.48550/arXiv.2408.10708
10. Krishna, S., Muscholl, A.: A quadratic construction for Zielonka automata with acyclic communication structure. Theor. Comput. Sci. **503**, 109–114 (2013). https://doi.org/10.1016/j.tcs.2013.07.015

11. Lehaut, M., Piterman, N.: Adding reconfiguration to Zielonka's asynchronous automata. In: Games, Automata, Logics, and Formal Verification, GANDALF 2024. EPTCS (2024), to appear 2024
12. Mukund, M., Sohoni, M.A.: Keeping track of the latest gossip in a distributed system. Distributed Comput. **10**(3), 137–148 (1997). https://doi.org/10.1007/S004460050031
13. Zielonka, W.: Notes on finite asynchronous automata. RAIRO Theor. Inform. Appl. **21**(2), 99–135 (1987). https://doi.org/10.1051/ita/1987210200991

Dynamic Partial Order Reduction for Transactional Programs on Serializable Platforms

Parosh Aziz Abdulla[1], Ashutosh Gupta[2], Shankara Narayanan Krishna[2], and Omkar Tuppe[2](✉)

[1] Uppsala University, Uppsala, Sweden
parosh@it.uu.se
[2] IIT Bombay, Mumbai, India
{akg,krishnas,omkarvtuppe}@cse.iitb.ac.in

Abstract. In this paper, we present a stateless model checking algorithm for establishing the correctness of database backed applications modeled as transactional programs under the strongest isolation level, namely serializability. We show that our algorithm is sound, complete, optimal and runs with polynomial memory consumption. In contrast, existing DPOR algorithms for transactional programs work only with weak isolation levels exploring exponentially many more equivalence classes of executions than what serializability permits. We report an implementation of our algorithm by applying it to several thousands of litmus tests as well as challenging database backed applications from the literature.

1 Introduction

Concurrent systems are ubiquitous. At the lowest level of system design, concurrency manifests at the chip level as multi core architectures. At the highest level, we have distributed databases and geo-replicated systems such as Facebook, Insta and X. Applications such as e-commerce platforms and cloud based storage systems involve concurrently connected clients and use relational databases. An anamoly which is very common in these distributed concurrent systems is when different clients observe different versions of the underlying data. To circumvent this, databases often use strong isolation levels (also known as consistency models), which offer the same version of data to all clients at any point of time.

The strongest known isolation level is that of *Serializability* (SER) [33] which ensures the highest synchronization between all processes. This high level of synchronization, although easy for a user to understand and program with, makes it difficult to achieve good performance guarantees. As an alternative, many databases go with weaker isolation levels and consistency guarantees such as weak causal consistency (CC) [13,35], causal memory (CM) [6,35], causal convergence (CCv) [16], read atomicity (ReadAt)[12,18] as well as read committed (ReadCom) [11,12]. In all these weak isolation levels, the sets of updates visible

S. Akshay et al. (Eds.): ATVA 2024, LNCS 15054, pp. 181–202, 2025.
https://doi.org/10.1007/978-3-031-78709-6_9

to different processes may differ and read actions may return values that cannot be obtained with serializability. Thus, weaker consistency guarantees exhibit several extra behaviours than serializability. As a result, weaker models are harder to reason [15], the extra behaviours result in application bugs [37], and the underlying application is loaded with several behaviours which it may not be able to handle.

Model Checking Applications on Serializable Platforms. Model checking [20] is a technique which explores the state space of a program in a systematic manner covering all possible executions of the program. The problem with this approach is that the number of executions can grow exponentially large in the number of concurrent processes. Partial order reduction (POR) [21,25,34] is an approach which limits the number of explored executions without compromising on system coverage. In POR, the notion of "equivalent" executions is used, where two executions are equivalent if one can be obtained from the other by swapping independent execution steps which come one after the other. Thus, POR enables the partitioning of the entire state space into equivalence classes of executions, and at least one execution per equivalence class is explored. Dynamic partial order reduction (DPOR) [23] is a technique which explores the execution state space by tracking the equivalence classes on the fly. DPOR is usually coupled with Stateless model checking (SMC) [26] to do the exploration without storing the visited states (hence the name "stateless").

There are several works on DPOR algorithms for shared memory programs under weak memory such as TSO, PSO or release-acquire (RA) [2,4,27,32], [1,38]. DPOR algorithms have also been developed for weak consistency models such as CC, CCv and CM [5]. These DPOR algorithms are all sound, complete and optimal, although they incur an exponential memory. Recently, [28,29] proposed a DPOR algorithm which is applicable to a range of weak memory models incurring only polynomial space while being also sound, complete and optimal. All these papers work on shared memory programs and do not address the verification of transactional programs, which model database applications.

In this regard, [14] proposes a DPOR algorithm for transactional programs where all transactions operate under one of the weak isolation levels namely, causal convergence (CC), read atomicity (ReadAt) and read committed (ReadCom). Figure 1 illustrates a simple transactional program with two processes, each having $i+1$ transactions, $i \geq 1$. A transaction (enclosed in boxes in Fig. 1) is a sequence of instructions which are executed atomically, with no interleaving of any other instructions. Under serializability (SER), executions of this program fall into two equivalence classes for all $i \geq 1$, corresponding to the possible ways in which transactions making a write can be ordered with respect to the other transactions. These equivalence classes are called execution graphs. In this case, these two classes (Fig. 1 (a) and (b)) correspond to which among t_1, t_2 get executed first.

Nodes of the execution graphs are the transactions, while the edges come from relations between transactions. po is the "program order" which orders transactions in the order they appear in the same process. co_x is a "coherence order" between transactions writing to the variable x. All variables are initialized to value 0, and this is written by the initial transaction $\mathcal{T}_{init}$. In 1(a), t_1 writes 1 to x, and the co_x from $\mathcal{T}_{init}$ to t_1 represents the coherence order for x when the value of x is changed from 0 to 1. Likewise, the rf_y edge from $\mathcal{T}_{init}$ to t_1 represents reading the initial value 0 from y (rf stands for reads from). Since the value of y read is not 1, the next transaction in the first process can execute, and is connected by the po from t_1. It writes 1 to z_1, and there is a co_{z_1} edge from $\mathcal{T}_{init}$ to it. Whenever t_2 happens, it writes 1 to y (the co_y from $\mathcal{T}_{init}$ to t_2 depicts the coherence order for y) and reads the value 1 from x (t_1 rf_x t_2). The rest of the transactions in the second process do not get executed since t_2 aborts on reading 1 from x. In 1(b), t_2 goes first, writes 1 to y and reads the initial value 0 from x. The rest of the transactions in the second process can execute, and the variable z_1 has only one value to read from, namely the initial value 0 from $\mathcal{T}_{init}$. Note that t_1 aborts and exits reading 1 from y.

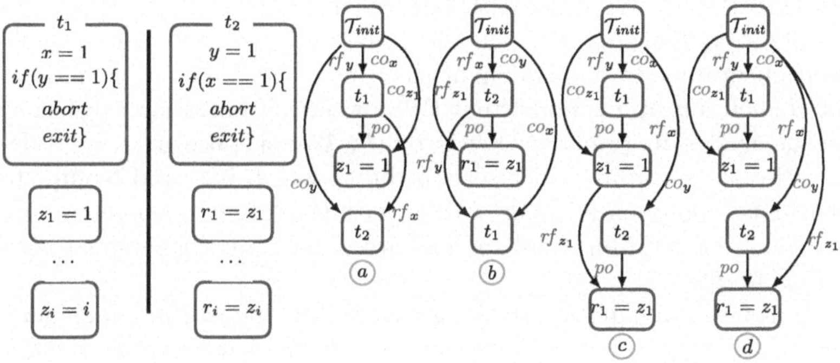

Fig. 1. A parameterized program on the left. Execution graphs for $i = 1$ on the right. Only (a) and (b) are consistent for SER, while all (a)-(d) are consistent for weak isolation levels. For $i \geq 1$, weak isolation levels have $2^i + 2$ consistent graphs, while SER has only 2 graphs. The lazy approach explores all 2^i+2 graphs. The eager approach explores only (a) and (b).

Under weak isolation levels, executions of this program (with $i = 1$) fall under 4 equivalence classes 1(a)-1(d). The main difference is that since t_2 is not "causally related" to t_1, it can read the initial value of x even after t_1 writes 1 to x; likewise t_1 can read both values for y. This is shown in 1(c), 1(d) respectively where both t_1, t_2 read the initial values as depicted by $\mathcal{T}_{init}$ rf_x t_2 and $\mathcal{T}_{init}$ rf_y t_1. This allows the second transactions of both processes to be executed; in particular, z_1 can read both values 0, 1 even after the value 1 is written to z_1. (c) depicts z_1 reading 1 while (d) depicts z_1 reading 0. Under weak isolation levels, each z_i has two possible values to read from, resulting in $2^i + 2$ execution graphs.

The algorithm proposed in [14] enumerates all po, rf execution graphs under weak isolation levels and outputs one representative from each equivalence class.

Their equivalence classes are defined by po-rf execution graphs; two graphs are equivalent if they have the same po, rf edges. The algorithm is sound, complete and optimal; further, it incurs only polynomial space like [28]. [14] handles serializability (SER) and snap shot isolation (SI) which are strong isolation levels by following the "lazy consistency" approach. In this approach, all po-rf execution graphs consistent with respect to weak isolation are generated first. Checking if a po-rf execution graph is consistent for weak isolation levels amounts to checking some acyclicity condition and is in polytime. From the generated execution graphs, [14] removes all those which are inconsistent with respect to SER. Checking if a given po-rf execution graph $\mathcal{G}$ is consistent under SER amounts to synthesizing a total co relation such that, in the extended graph, $(po \cup rf \cup co \cup ow)^+$ is acyclic where $ow = rf^{-1}; co$. This is known to be an NP-complete problem [24]. This makes the construction of efficient SMC algorithms significantly more challenging for serializability than for weak isolation levels. Now, we explain the key features and contributions of our work.

Our Contributions. We work with full execution graphs (on po, rf, co) where co is total. Our equivalence is the classical Mazurkiewicz equivalence [30], where two execution graphs are equivalent if they have the same po, rf and co edges. Checking if such a graph is consistent [19] for SER is polytime : just check that there are no cycles in $(po \cup rf \cup co \cup ow)^+$. We propose a DPOR algorithm for transactional programs under serializability which is sound, complete, optimal and also uses polynomial space. We go with the "eager consistency" approach where only those execution graphs which are consistent with respect to serializability are generated.

Our algorithm is a generic swapping based SMC algorithm which generalizes the approach of [28] to handle transactions. Each read event in a transaction produces many exploration branches, corresponding to each transaction which has been executed in the past containing a matching write event. In addition, write events in transactions to be executed, are also considered as potential sources to be read, for the read events in transactions which have been already visited, by swapping these transactions. Swapping is done in such a way that the new execution graph is feasible wrt serializability thereby ensuring soundness of our approach. Our algorithm is also complete and optimal : that is, no feasible execution graph is generated more than once, and no feasible graph is left out.

Key Challenges. The generalization of TruSt [28] to transactions is significantly more challenging and a straightforward adaptation does not work. The consistency checking procedures used in [28] and [14] cannot be adapted directly : the former does not handle transactions, while the latter work with weak isolation levels. This apart, one of the main challenges in the transactional case is in handling swaps. This happens when we have a transaction (say t_r) with read events on some variable x which can read from a transaction (say t_w) which writes to x, but appears later in the execution graph. The general idea behind the swap is to erase events which are "in between" t_r and t_w and schedule them later. Towards this, we implemented a procedure wherein, swapping t_r and t_w is allowed only when the transactions of the erased events respect a "co_x-maximality" condition with respect to the other transactions. The idea of *co*-maximality was also considered in [28]; however, their check was relatively straightforward since it only involved the events (and not transactions) appearing between the read r and the write w which were to be swapped. In our setting, there are many cases to be considered, depending on whether the erased event belongs to the transaction t_r or whether it belongs to a later transaction, and doing these maintaining optimality and not compromising on completeness is challenging.

We prove that following our notion of *co*-maximality, there is a unique way in which swaps can be done. This helps to achieve optimality and correctness. We designed data structures carefully so that we only store a single execution graph at any point of time, and all recursive calls update this graph when they are called, and they roll back on return. We have a fixed ordering on the processes (thereby transactions and events), and we only need a polynomial memory to roll back to the previous state. This recursive depth-first approach makes the explorations of branches disjoint from one another, and also to achieve polynomial space.

We evaluated our implementation TRANSER on (i) adaptations of thousands of litmus tests generated by the Herd tool [7] and verifying the correctness of our results, (ii) 5 sets of well known database-backed applications, as well as (iii) several parameterized versions of litmus tests and database applications. (iii) serves as a stress test for TRANSER. We compared the performance of TRANSER with Transactional-JPF, the implementation in [14] across all categories of benchmarks. In all cases, TRANSER significantly outperforms Transactional-JPF by several orders of magnitude.

Full details of all proofs and more details regarding the experiments can be found in an online full version of the paper. Here, we omit these for lack of space.

2 Transactional Programs

We consider transactional programs $\mathcal{P}$ consisting of a finite set of *threads* or *processes* $p \in \mathsf{Procs}$ that share a finite set $\mathbb{X}$ of shared variables ranging over a domain $\mathbb{V}$ of *values* that includes a special value 0. A process has a finite set of local registers that store values from $\mathbb{V}$. Each process is an ordered sequence of *transactions*. A transaction is an ordered sequence of *labeled instructions* built in a standard way from expressions and atomic commands, using standard control flow constructs (sequential composition, selection, and bounded loop constructs). Throughout the paper, we use x, y, z etc. for shared variables, $\mathtt{a}, \mathtt{b}, \mathtt{c}, \mathtt{d}, r$ for registers, and e for expressions. Expressions do not contain any shared variables.

Let $\mathcal{T}$ denote the set of all transactions in $\mathcal{P}$. Transactions are denoted by $t_1, t_2, t_3, \ldots$. A transaction $t \in \mathcal{T}$ in process p starts with a $\mathtt{begin}(p, t)$ instruction and ends with an $\mathtt{end}(p, t)$ instruction (in the figures, we simply enclose the code of a transaction in a box without explicit `begin` and `end` statements). The instructions in a transaction are write, read, assign and abort instructions apart from standard conditional flow constructs. A transaction is committed if it completes all its instructions ending with `end`. A transaction is aborted if it executes an abort instruction. Write instructions $x := e$ write to the shared variable x the value of expression e while read instructions $r := x$ read from the shared variable x into the local register r. Assignments have the form $r := e$ involving local registers and expressions. We assume that the control cannot pass from one transaction to another in a process without going through the `begin` and `end` instructions.

Each transaction in a process p has a transaction identifier $t.id$ (which is in $\mathbb{N}$). The transaction identifier id indicates that p has executed $id - 1$ transactions before t in the execution. If process p is the ordered sequence $t_1, t_2, \ldots, t_n$ of transactions, then, $t_i.id < t_j.id$ for $i < j$.

Events. An event corresponds to the effect of executing an instruction in $\mathcal{P}$. There are five types of events corresponding to the *beginning* of a transaction, *ending* of a transaction, *aborting* a transaction, *writing* a value to a shared variable and *reading* from a shared variable. A *write event* e in a transaction t is given by $(id, proc, t, \mathsf{wt}(x, v))$ where $id \in \mathbb{N}$ is the identifier of the event in transaction t, $proc$ is the process containing the event in transaction t, $x \in \mathbb{X}$ is a variable, and $v \in \mathbb{V}$ is a value. The event identifier id indicates that the transaction t has executed $id - 1$ events before e in the execution. When clear from the context, we simply write $\mathsf{wt}(x, v)$ for a write event. This corresponds to a write event happening in transaction t of process $proc$ writing the value v to variable x. Likewise, a *read event* e is given by $(id, proc, t, \mathsf{rd}(x))$ (or $\mathsf{rd}(x)$ when clear) where $x \in \mathbb{X}$. The read event e does not specify the particular value it reads; this value will be defined in an execution by specifying a write event from which e fetches its value. The beginning, end and the abort of a transaction t in process p are represented by events $(id, \mathsf{begin}(p, t))$, $(id, \mathsf{end}(p, t))$ and $(id, \mathsf{abort}(p, t))$ respectively (when clear from the context, we drop the id).

Let $\mathtt{E}$ denote the set of all events. For a write or read event e, we denote by $e.var$ the variable it writes to/reads from. For an event e, $e.tran$ denotes the transaction t containing e, $e.id$ denotes the id of e, and $e.type$ denotes the type (read/write/abort/begin/end) of e. For a begin event e in a transaction t, $e.id = 0$ since it is the first event in the transaction, likewise, the id of the end event in t is larger than the ids of all events in t. Since assignments do not change values of shared variables, they are not visible to other transactions. If a transaction t contains multiple write events $e_1, \ldots, e_j$ such that $e_i.var = e_k.var$ for all $1 \leq i, k \leq j$, then the write event e such that $e.id = max\{e_i.id \mid 1 \leq i \leq j\}$ is the only one which is visible to other transactions. If a transaction gets aborted due to an abort event, then the effect of the writes in it are not visible to other transactions.

For each variable $x \in \mathbb{X}$, we assume a special transaction called the *initializer* transaction t_{init_x}. Apart from the `begin`, `end` instructions, t_{init_x} contains only the write event $\mathsf{init}_x = \mathsf{wt}(x, 0)$ for x. This transaction is not part of any of the processes in the program and writes the value 0 to x before any process begins execution. We define $\mathcal{T}_{init} := \{t_{\mathsf{init}_x} \mid x \in \mathbb{X}\}$ as the set of initializer transactions. Let $\mathcal{T}^{\mathsf{wt},x}, \mathcal{T}^{\mathsf{rd},x}$ respectively denote the set of transactions having a write and read instruction on $x \in \mathbb{X}$.

Next, we define execution graphs which succinctly capture the set of executions of the program.

Execution Graphs and Axiomatic Framework for Serializability

An execution graph (`Egraph` for short) $\mathcal{G}$ is a tuple $\langle \mathcal{T}, po, rf, co, <_{\mathcal{G}} \rangle$, where $\mathcal{T}$ is the set of all *transactions* including the set $\mathcal{T}_{init}$ of initializer transactions. po (program order), rf (read-from), and co (coherence-order) are binary relations on $\mathcal{T}$ and $<_{\mathcal{G}}$ is a total order on the events $\mathtt{E}$ that satisfy:

- $t \; po \; t'$ if t, t' are transactions in the same process and $t.id < t'.id$. The relation po totally orders the transactions of each individual process. We assume that $t_{\mathsf{init}_x} \; po \; t$ for all transactions $t \in \mathcal{T}$ and for all variables x.
- For $x \in \mathbb{X}$, and transactions t, t', we have $t \; rf_x \; t'$ if the following are true. First, $t \in \mathcal{T}^{\mathsf{wt},x}$ and $t' \in \mathcal{T}^{\mathsf{rd},x}$; that is, t' reads the value written to x in t. If t has several write events on x, then the write event whose id is the largest in t is the one selected to read from. If $t' \in \mathcal{T}^{\mathsf{wt},x} \cap \mathcal{T}^{\mathsf{rd},x}$, and if the read event $e' = \mathsf{rd}(x)$ in t' is after some write event $e = \mathsf{wt}(x, v)$ in t' (that is, $e.id < e'.id$) then $t = t'$. That is, t' reads its own latest write if available. $rf = \bigcup_{x \in \mathbb{X}} rf_x$.
- For each $x \in \mathbb{X}$, co_x totally orders transactions in $\mathcal{T}^{\mathsf{wt},x}$. $co = \bigcup_{x \in \mathbb{X}} co_x$.
- $<_{\mathcal{G}}$ is a total order on the events which defines the order in which they are added to $\mathcal{G}$. This is also extended to say $t <_{\mathcal{G}} e$ (or $t <_{\mathcal{G}} t'$) for a transaction t and event e (or transactions t, t') if $e.tran$ (or t') was added to $\mathcal{G}$ after t.

We define over-writes(aka from-reads) as a derived relation $ow_x = rf_x^{-1}; co_x$ for any $x \in \mathbb{X}$, and $ow = \bigcup_{x \in \mathbb{X}} ow_x$. $\mathcal{G} = \langle \mathcal{T}, po, rf, co, <_{\mathcal{G}} \rangle$ can be viewed as a graph whose nodes are the transactions $\mathcal{T}$ and whose edges are defined by the relations po, rf, co and ow. The empty `Egraph` is defined as $\mathcal{G}_\emptyset := \langle \mathcal{T}_{init}, \emptyset, \emptyset, \emptyset, \emptyset \rangle$, containing only the initializer transactions, with all relations empty. An `Egraph` is consistent for serializability (SER) iff $(po \cup rf \cup co \cup ow)^+$ is acyclic. For example, the execution graphs in Fig. 1(a), (b) are consistent, while (c) and (d) are not. In both (c) and (d) we have an ow edge from t_1 to t_2 (wrt y) and from t_2 to t_1 (wrt x) resulting in a cycle.

3 DPOR Algorithm

We present our DPOR algorithm, which systematically generates, for any terminating program under SER, all consistent execution graphs $\mathcal{G}$. The main procedure is DPOR($\mathcal{P}$) which invokes the procedure Explore($\mathcal{P}, \mathcal{G}_\emptyset$), to explore all `Egraphs` of the input program $\mathcal{P}$ consistent under SER.

The Explore Procedure. Explore($\mathcal{P}, \mathcal{G}$) takes as input, a program $\mathcal{P}$ and a `Egraph` $\mathcal{G}$. The initial invocation is with the empty `Egraph` $\mathcal{G}_\emptyset$. If the current graph $\mathcal{G}$is not consistent, then (line 3) we return to the previous call and continue exploration. `NextEvent` (line 4) returns the next enabled event e following a

Algorithm 1: DPOR($\mathcal{P}$)

```
   Input: transactional program P
 1 Explore(P, G_∅)
 2 Procedure Explore(P, G)
 3     if ¬consistent(G) return
 4     switch e ← NextEvent (P, G) do
 5         case assertion violation do
 6             output "assertion violation in G"
 7         case ⊥ do                        // explored all events from P so no next event
 8             output "full egraph G"
 9         case e = begin(t) do                           // add transaction t to G
10             Explore(P, addTrans(G, t))
11         case e = (−, −, t, wt(x, v)) do                // add the write event to t
12             Explore(P, addWrite(G, t, e))
13         case e = (−, −, t, rd(x)) do
14             if isLocalRead(G, t, x) then               // e can read locally from t
15                 Explore(P, doLocalRead(G, t, e))
16             else
17                 set reversible(e) = true               // e cannot read locally
18                 for t_w ∈ T^{wt,x} do                  // add rf from t_w ∈ T^{wt,x} in G
19                     Explore(P, addRf(G, e, t_w, t))
20         case e = abort(t) do
21             Explore(P, aborted(G, t))
22         case e = end(t) do
23             for cos ∈ getAllCOs(P, G, t) do            // get all possible cos
24                 Explore(P, addCO(G, t, cos))
25             PostponedRfs(P, G, t)
```

fixed order $<_{\mathcal{G}}$. We explore processes from left to right : if processes are labeled $p_1, p_2, \cdots, p_n$, then transactions from p_i will be visited in the order they appear in p_i before transactions from p_{i+1}. On validating an assertion violation (line 6) in $\mathcal{G}$, the exploration stops.

- If the event e is $\mathsf{wt}(x, v)$, (line 11, Explore) then, first the value of x is updated in t : the last values written in t to each variable are maintained in the "local store" of t. We do not show this in the pseudo code of Explore. After this, we recursively call Explore.
- If the event e is $\mathsf{rd}(x)$, (line 13, Explore) then we first check (`isLocalRead`(), line 14) that is, whether e can read "locally". If t had a write to x, then the last value written to x will be available in the local store of t, and e can read locally, by reading from this value. The other possibility when e can read locally is if t has an earlier read r from x ($r.id < e.id$). In this case also, e reads locally : it reads the same value read in r and continues exploration (`doLocalRead`(), line 15). Otherwise, if e cannot read locally it proceeds to line 17. The flag `reversible`(e) (line 17, Explore) set to true denotes that the read event e needs to look outside its transaction to read. The default

initial value set to **reversible**(e) is false. For a transaction t with a read event $e = \mathsf{rd}(x)$ having **reversible**(e) as true, we explore in separate branches (line 19) all possible transactions $t_w \in \mathcal{T}^{\mathsf{wt},x}$ in $\mathcal{G}$ from which t can read. Note that if any of these lead to inconsistency, they will be removed in line 3. There may be transactions t' which will be added later to $\mathcal{G}$ during exploration, from which t can read. Such transactions t' are called *postponed* wrt t and the corresponding write in t' is a *postponed* write for e. When such a t' is added to $\mathcal{G}$ later, the algorithm will have a branch where t can read from t' (line 25, EXPLORE calls the procedure POSTPONEDRFS($\mathcal{P}, \mathcal{G}, t'$)).

- If e is $\mathsf{end}(t)$, then we recursively call on EXPLORE for all possible co options for each variable x s.t. $t \in \mathcal{T}^{\mathsf{wt},x}$ (line 24, EXPLORE). co edges are added to/from a transaction t when it is completed, that is, when $\mathsf{end}(t)$ is encountered. At the end of transaction t, corresponding to the last write per variable in t, we call POSTPONEDRFS (line 25). This call enables us to pair these writes in t as potential sources to be read from, for the reads in transactions which are dependent on postponed writes.

The POSTPONEDRFS($\mathcal{P}, \mathcal{G}, t_w$) Procedure. The inputs to this algorithm are the program $\mathcal{P}$, the current **Egraph** $\mathcal{G}$ and the transaction t_w having writes on some variable. For any transaction t, let $porf.t$ be all transactions which are po-rf-before t, that is, this is the set of all transactions t'' s.t. there is a path in $\mathcal{G}$ on po, rf edges from t'' to t. POSTPONEDRFS iterates through all read events r (line 3) for all $x \in \mathbb{X}$, for which t_w is postponed, satisfying the following conditions. Let $t_r = r.tran$ denote the transaction containing r.

[(i)] **reversible**(r) $= true$ (line 2). This condition is necessary for r to read from the writes of transactions other than the one it is in.
[(ii)] t_r must not be po-rf before t_w (line 3). If t_r is po-rf before t_w, adding the rf from t_w to t_r will create a cycle.
[(iii)] **isOptimal**($\mathcal{G}$, $Erased \cup \{r\}, t_w$) (line 5) must be true. **isOptimal** ($\mathcal{G}$, $Erased \cup \{r\}, t_w$) is a procedure that ensures optimality without compromising the completeness of the algorithm : namely, no execution graph is produced more than once, and each consistent execution graph is explored.

The set *Erased* (line 4) consists of events which are added after r (these are events e' such that $r <_{\mathcal{G}} e'$) in $\mathcal{G}$ such that (a) they are between r and the postponed write event w of r in the current transaction $t_w \in \mathcal{T}^{\mathsf{wt},-}$ (these are events e'' such that $r <_{\mathcal{G}} e'' <_{\mathcal{G}} w$) and (b) they are not from transactions $t'' \in porf.t_w$. The intuition is that events of *Erased* can be deleted from $\mathcal{G}$ after adding the rf edge from t_w to t_r.

For each read r fulfilling (i)-(iii) above, POSTPONEDRFS($\mathcal{P}, \mathcal{G}, t_w$) does the following. First, events $e \in Erased$ from $\mathcal{G}$ are removed (along with all co, rf edges associated to them). Then a new rf edge is added from t_w to t_r to obtain the new graph $\mathcal{G}'$ (line 6). In $\mathcal{G}'$, r is called reversed, we set **reversed**(r) $= true$. All feasible co options for t_w are considered in $\mathcal{G}'$ (**getAllCOs**) and each possible co extension recursively invokes EXPLORE (line 9). We set **reversible**(r) $= false$

(line 7) in $\mathcal{G}'$ for all reads $r' \in \mathbf{R}$ which are in transactions $t'' \in porf.t_w$. This is done for optimality : these reads have `reversible`$(r') = true$ in $\mathcal{G}$ and will be handled by the loop in line 3; we do not want to duplicate this in $\mathcal{G}'$.

Algorithm 2: PostponedRfs($\mathcal{P}, \mathcal{G}, t_w$)

1 **Procedure** PostponedRfs ($\mathcal{P}, \mathcal{G}, t_w$)
2   **let R** be set of `reversible` reads in $\mathcal{G}$
3   **for** $x \in \mathbb{X}, r = (-,-,t_r,\mathsf{rd}(x)) \in \boldsymbol{R}$ *s.t.* $t_r \notin porf.t_w$ *and* $t_w \in \mathcal{T}^{\mathsf{wt},x}$ **do**
4     $Erased \leftarrow \{e \in \mathcal{G}.\mathrm{E} \mid r <_{\mathcal{G}} e \wedge e.tran \notin porf.t_w\}$
    // $porf.t_w = \{t'' \mid$ there is a path in $\mathcal{G}$ on po, rf edges from t'' to $t_w\}$
5   **if** *isOptimal*($\mathcal{G}$, Erased $\cup \{r\}, t_w, r$) **then**
6       $\mathcal{G}' \leftarrow$ **addRf**($\mathcal{G}|_{E \setminus Erased}, r, t_w, t_r$), set **reversed(r)** = **True** in $\mathcal{G}'$
7   **for** each read $r \in \mathcal{G}' \cap \mathbf{R} \cap porf.t_w$ set **reversible**$(r) = False$
8   **for** $cos \in$ *getAllCOs*($\mathcal{P}, \mathcal{G}', t_w$) **do**
9   Explore($\mathcal{P}$, addCO($\mathcal{G}', t_w, cos$))
10 **Procedure isOptimal** ($\mathcal{G}, Erased, t_w, r$)
11   **for** *each event* $e \in Erased$ **do**
12   **if** $e = \mathsf{end}(r.tran)$ **then**
13   **for** $x \in \mathbb{X}, lw_x$: *lw_x is the last write on x in $r.tran$, $lw_x <_{\mathcal{G}} r$* **do**
14   **if** $\neg$(**isMax**($\mathcal{G}, lw_x, t_w, r$)) **then return** false
15   **if** $e = \mathsf{begin}(-) \vee e = \mathsf{end}(-) \vee$ *isLocalRead*(e) **then continue**
    // $RF(e)$ is the write from which e reads
16   **if** $e = \mathsf{rd}(x)$ **then if reversed(e)** $\wedge$ **RF(e)** $\in$ **Erased then return** false
17   **if** $\neg$(**isMax**($\mathcal{G}, e, t_w, r$)) **then return** false
18   **return** true
19 **Procedure isMax** ($\mathcal{G}, e, t_w, r$)
  //if e is a read, t_e is the transaction that $e.tran$ reads from
20   $t_e \leftarrow$ **if** $e = \mathsf{wt}(x, v)$ **then** $e.tran$ **else** $RF(e).tran$
  // collect the transactions $<_{\mathcal{G}}$ before e or $porf$ before t_w
21   **let Tset** = $\{t'' \mid t'' <_{\mathcal{G}} e.tran \vee t'' \in t_w.porf\}$
22   **if** $t_e \; co_{e.var} \; t''$ *for some* $t'' \in$ **Tset then**   // $e.var$ denotes the variable of e
23   **if** $e \notin r.tran$ **then return** false
24   **else**
25   **for** *each* $t'' \in$ **Tset** *s.t.* $(t_e, t'') \in co_x$ **do**
26   **if isGopt**($\mathcal{G}, r, t_w, t_e, t'', e$) **then continue else return** false
27   **return** true

Optimality with `isOptimal`$(\mathcal{G}, Erased, t_w, r)$. The inputs to `isOptimal` are the current execution graph $\mathcal{G}$, the transaction t_w containing the postponed write for the read event r, as well as the set *Erased* of events after r in $\mathcal{G}$ which can be deleted from $\mathcal{G}$. `isOptimal` iterates through events from *Erased*; let $e \in Erased$ be the current event explored in $\mathcal{G}$.

If the event e explored is a read (line 16, `isOptimal`) and has `reversed`$(e) = true$ then the postponed write w it has read from should not be from *Erased*. This is done to avoid redundancy. Note that line 9 of PostponedRfs explores

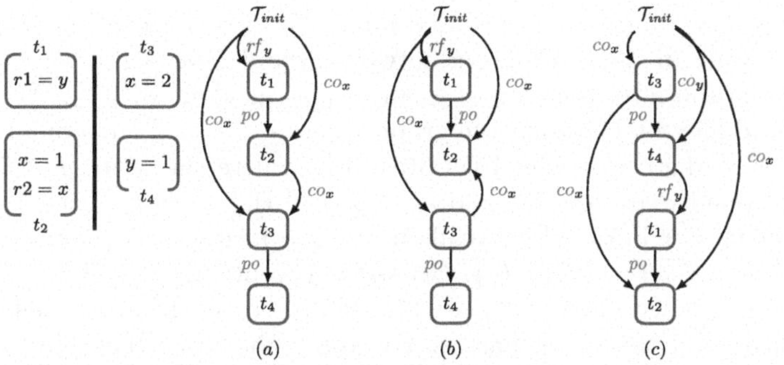

Fig. 2. Illustration for `isOptimal` when $e \notin r.tran$.

$\mathcal{G}'$ obtained by deleting events in *Erased* from $\mathcal{G}$, and this pairing of e with w will be covered in a later recursive call to EXPLORE when more events are added to $\mathcal{G}'$. To proceed, the read event e is such that `reversed`$(e) = false$, or it does not read from a write in *Erased* (these cases are checked in `isMax`, see below).

The `isMax` procedure to check co-maximality. Let t_e denote $e.tran$ if $e = \mathsf{wt}(x, v)$, and let it be the transaction that $e.tran$ reads from, if $e = \mathsf{rd}(x)$ (line 20, `isMax`). Let $Tset$ (line 21, `isMax`) denote all transactions t'' which were added to $\mathcal{G}$ before $e.tran$, as well as all those transactions which are in $porf.t_w$. To obtain optimality, `isMax` checks if t_e is "$co_{e.var}$-maximal" with respect to $Tset$.

$co_{e.var}$**-maximality of** t_e wrt $Tset$: t_e is $co_{e.var}$-maximal wrt $Tset$ if for all transactions $t'' \in Tset$, we have $t'' co_{e.var} t_e$.

(a) Assume that $e \notin r.tran$, and let the variable involved in e be x (either $e = \mathsf{wt}(x, v)$ or $e = \mathsf{rd}(x)$). We check if t_e violates co_x-maximality wrt $Tset$, that is, whether $t_e\ co_x\ t''$ for some $t'' \in Tset$ (line 22, `isMax`). If yes, then the optimality check fails : we will see the intuition below by separately considering the case when $e = \mathsf{wt}(x, v)$ and when $e = \mathsf{rd}(x)$.
   - Let $e = \mathsf{wt}(x, v)$. Skipping the test (is $t_e\ co_x\ t''$ for some $t'' \in Tset$) can result in redundancy, as illustrated in Figure 2. Both graphs 2(a) and 2(b) give rise to 2(c) if the test is skipped. Consider the execution graphs 2(a) and 2(b). In both of these, the write $y = 1$ in t_4 is a postponed write for the read $r1 = y$ (call this read r) in t_1. Consider the event e as the write $x = 1$ in transaction t_2 which is after r in both 2(a) and 2(b). Following the notation in POSTPONEDRFS, we have $t_e = e.tran = t_2$, $Erased = \{\text{events in } t_2\}$ and $Tset = \{\mathcal{T}_{init}, t_3\}$. Now, 2(a) has $t_2\ co_x\ t_3$ while 2(b) has $t_3\ co_x\ t_2$. Note that both 2(a) and 2(b) proceed in recursive calls of EXPLORE with the graph $\mathcal{G}'$ obtained from $\mathcal{G}$ by deleting t_2 and edges incident with t_2, then adding $t_4\ rf\ t_1$. To this graph $\mathcal{G}'$, events of t_2 are added later obtaining 2(c). The checks (line 22, line 23) in `isMax` ensures that only 2(b) proceeds, avoiding redundancy.

   To summarize, events of $t_e = e.tran$ are deleted (line 9) in the recursive

call to Explore, and scheduled later. Thus, two execution graphs which differ only in the co ordering between t_e and $Tset$ will both result in the same graph after deletion of t_e and edges incident with t_e. We avoid this redundancy by choosing the graph where t_e is $co_{e.var}$-maximal wrt $Tset$.

- Let $e = \mathsf{rd}(x)$. Consider Figs. 3(a), 3(b) where the write $y = 1$ in t_4 is a postponed write for the read $r1 = y$ (call this r) in t_1. Let e be the read event $r2 = x$ in t_2, which reads from $\mathcal{T}_{init}$ in Fig. 3(a). Then $t_e = \mathcal{T}_{init}$ in Fig. 3(a), $Tset = \{\mathcal{T}_{init}, t_3\}$, $Erased = \{\text{events in } t_2\}$ and $t_e\ co_x\ t_3$, hence the optimality check fails. In Fig. 3(b), e reads from t_3, hence $t_e = t_3$ in 3(b) and the check passes. We apply the same reasoning as above : $e.tran = t_2$ and its associated edges will be removed from the current execution graph $\mathcal{G}$ (from both (a),(b)) and will be scheduled later when exploring the new execution graph $\mathcal{G}'$, obtaining Fig. 3(c). We thus keep the graph where t_e is $co_{e.var}$-maximal with respect to the transactions in $Tset$ avoiding redundancy.

(b) Assume that $e \in r.tran$ and let the variable involved in e be x (either $e = \mathsf{wt}(x, v)$ or $e = \mathsf{rd}(x)$). Unlike (a), if t_e is not $co_{e.var}$-maximal wrt $Tset$, the optimality check does not fail immediately; in that case, we invoke `isGopt`$(\mathcal{G}, r, t_w, t_e, t'', e)$ (line 26 in `isMax`) which we describe through examples first.
Assume that $e = \mathsf{rd}(x)$. Then using the notation (line 20, `isMax`) we have $t_e\ rf\ e.tran$. Assuming t_e violates $co_{e.var}$-maximality wrt $Tset$, we have $t_e\ co_x\ t''$, for some $t'' \in Tset$. Then $e.tran$ is not reading the latest value written for x, visible to e. If we switch $t_e\ rf\ e.tran$ to $t''\ rf\ e.tran$, this may lead to inconsistency. This may be due to read events on other variables which are before (po-before) e in $e.tran$, and the switch to $t''\ rf\ e.tran$ may not be consistent with their rfs. If the switch leads to an inconsistent execution graph, then the optimality check succeeds, that is, the read must happen from t_e. However, if there is no inconsistency on switching to $t''\ rf\ e.tran$, then optimality fails.
Fig. 4 illustrates this when e is the read event $r2 = y$ in t_3. In Fig. 4(a), e reads from $t_e = \mathcal{T}_{init}$. The write $y = 4$ in t_4 is a postponed write for e. Further, $Erased = \emptyset$ and $Tset = \{t_1, t_2\}$. Now $t_e\ co_y\ t_2$. If we replace $t_e\ rf\ t_3$ with $t_2\ rf\ t_3$, then we obtain the inconsistent execution graph Figure 4(b). The inconsistency is due to the fact that the read $r1 = x$ in t_3 (po-before e) reads from t_1, and $t_2\ rf\ t_3$ induces $t_3\ ow_x\ t_2$ and a cycle. Thus, 4(a) passes the optimality check.
To illustrate an example when e is a write event in $r.tran$, consider the program in Fig. 5 and flip the order of the two events in t_1. The write $y = 1$ in t_4 is a postponed write for the read $r1 = y$ in t_1. Let e be the write $x = 1$ in t_1. Considering co, rf as in Fig. 5(a), $t_1\ co_x\ t_3$, and making $t_3\ co_x\ t_1$ will not give any inconsistency, and `isMax` fails the optimality check.

To summarize, let $\mathcal{G}$ be an execution graph such that $r = \mathsf{rd}(x)$ is a read which has a postponed write $w = \mathsf{wt}(x, v)$ in transaction t_w. Let $e \in Erased \cap r.tran$,

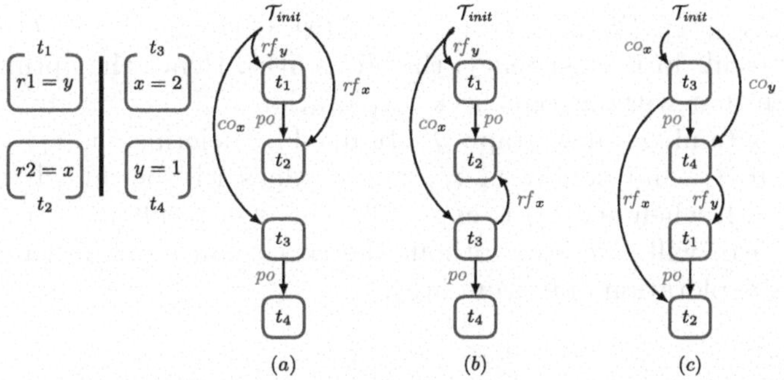

Fig. 3. Illustration of `isOptimal` when $e \notin r.tran$.

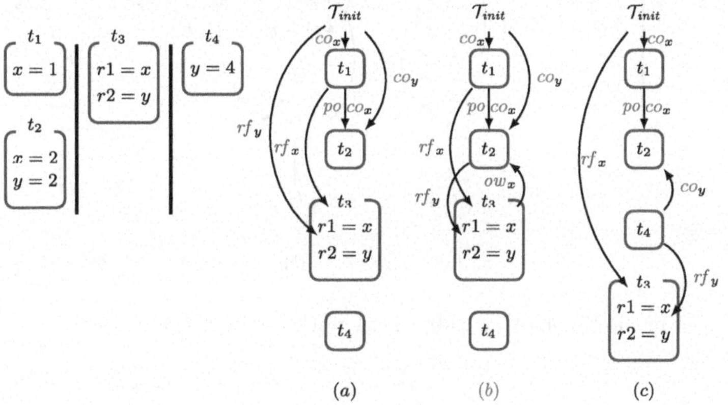

Fig. 4. Illustration of `isOptimal` when $e \in r.tran$.

and let t_e be as defined in line 20 of `isMax`. Further, let $t'' \in Tset$ be such that $e.tran\ co_x\ t''$. Then $\texttt{isGopt}(\mathcal{G}, r, t_w, t_e, t'', e)$ checks the following.

(1) Let e be a write. If switching $e.tran\ co_x\ t''$ to $t''\ co_x\ e.tran$ makes $\mathcal{G}$ inconsistent, then $\texttt{isGopt}(\mathcal{G}, r, t_w, t_e, t'', e)$ returns true; else it returns false.

(2) Let e be a read. If switching $t_e\ rf\ e.tran$ to $t''\ rf\ e.tran$ makes $\mathcal{G}$ inconsistent, then $\texttt{isGopt}(\mathcal{G}, r, t_w, t_e, t'', e)$ returns true; else it returns false.

(3) Let e be $\mathsf{end}(r.tran)$ in $\mathcal{G}$. Then $\mathsf{end}(r.tran) \in Erased$, and will be deleted in the next graph $\mathcal{G}'$, along with co edges incident on $r.tran$. For all $y \in \mathbb{X}$, let lw_y be the last write to y before r in $r.tran$. Then we make the same check as in (1) : given $\mathcal{G}$, first check if there exists some $t'' \in Tset$ such that $r.tran\ co_y\ t''$. If yes, check whether changing $r.tran\ co_y\ t''$ to $t''\ co_y\ r.tran$ makes $\mathcal{G}$ inconsistent. If yes, then $\texttt{isGopt}(\mathcal{G}, r, t_w, e.tran, t'', e)$ returns true, else it does not.

As an illustration, consider the execution graph $\mathcal{G}$ as Fig. 5(a). $y = 1$ in t_4 is a postponed write for the read r namely, $r1 = y$ in t_1, and let e be $\mathsf{end}(t_1)$. The write $x = 1$ is po-before r in t_1. Here, $t_e = r.tran = t_1$, $Erased = \{\mathsf{end}(t_1)\}$,

$Tset = \{T_{init}, t_3\}$. We have $t_1\ co_x\ t_3$ in 5(a). Changing $t_1\ co_x\ t_3$ to $t_3\ co_x\ t_1$ does not result in inconsistency; this gives 5(b). Hence the optimality check fails. Note that without the check, exploration will continue from both 5(a) and 5(b) obtaining a new graph $\mathcal{G}'$ obtained by deleting $\mathsf{end}(t_1)$, all co edges adjacent to t_1, and adding $t_4\ rf_y\ t_1$. co edges will be added to $\mathcal{G}'$ in the recursive call when $\mathsf{end}(t_1)$ is explored. This will result in 5(c). Thus, both 5(a) and 5(b) will give 5(c) without the check; our check discards 5(a) and continues exploration only from 5(b).

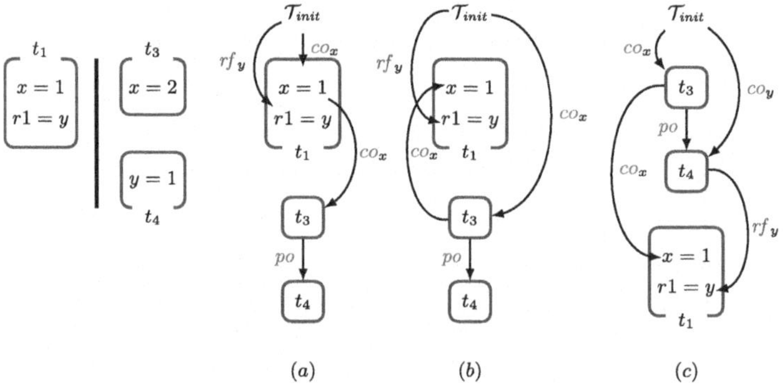

Fig. 5. Illustrating `isOptimal` with $e = \mathsf{end}(t_1) \in e.tran$.

Soundness, Completeness and Optimality of the DPOR Algorithm

Theorem 1. *Our DPOR algorithm for* SER *is sound, complete and optimal.*

Soundness. The DPOR algorithm is sound : this is easy to see, since the algorithm does not continue exploration from any SER-inconsistent execution graph. Line 3 of Algorithm 2 ensures this.

Completeness. The DPOR algorithm is complete in the sense that it does not miss any consistent and full execution graph. A full graph is one which is obtained when all processes have been executed to completion. The proof of completeness involves the following steps:

- We first show that starting from any execution graph $\mathcal{G}$, we can uniquely roll back to obtain the previous execution $\mathcal{G}_p$ (the full version describes an algorithm which computes $\mathcal{G}_p$ from $\mathcal{G}$). This is proved using the fact that we have a fixed order in exploring the processes, along with the conditions that allow a reversal to take place. To allow a reversal of a read r on some variable (say x), we check that transactions (other than $r.tran$) containing erased events respect "co_x-maximality". This is enforced by the `isOptimal` and `isMax` procedures and allows us to uniquely construct the previous execution graph $\mathcal{G}_p$.

- Second, we show that EXPLORE($\mathcal{P}, \mathcal{G}_p$) leads to the call of EXPLORE($\mathcal{P}, \mathcal{G}$). This shows that if $\mathcal{G}_p$ is reachable by the DPOR algorithm then $\mathcal{G}$ is also reachable.
- In the final step, we show that walking backward from $\mathcal{G}$ we have a unique sequence $\mathcal{G}_p, \mathcal{G}_{p-1}, \mathcal{G}_{p-2}, \ldots$, till we obtain $\mathcal{G}_\emptyset$. Thus, starting from EXPLORE($\mathcal{P}, \mathcal{G}_\emptyset$), we obtain $\mathcal{G}$.

Optimality. Optimality of the DPOR algorithm follows from the fact that each full, consistent execution graph $\mathcal{G}$ is output only once. Lines 19 and 24 of the EXPLORE procedure ensure that each recursive call to EXPLORE deals with an execution graph which has a different *rf* edge or a different *co* edge. Also, during the POSTPONEDRFS procedure, the reversal of a read r with the write from a transaction t_w is successful only when the "co_x-maximality" is respected by transactions containing erased events. As argued in completeness, for every (partial) execution graph $\mathcal{G}$, there exists a unique previous graph $\mathcal{G}_p$. If the DPOR algorithm explores $\mathcal{G}$ twice, it means that there are two different exploration sequences with respective previous execution graphs $\mathcal{G}_p$ and $\mathcal{G}_q$. This leads to a contradiction since we have a unique previous execution graph.

4 Experimental Evaluation

We have implemented our DPOR algorithm in a tool TRANSER and experimentally evaluated it against a wide variety of benchmarks. We also compare TRANSER with Transactional-JPF, the implementation of [14] which also handles SER by going through weak isolation levels. We show that TRANSER outperforms Transactional-JPF in all categories of benchmarks. For examples where the number of execution graphs under weak isolation levels are exponentially more than SER, this is expected; however, this is seen even in benchmarks where the number of consistent execution graphs are the same under SER and weak isolation levels.

TRANSER. TRANSER extends TruSt [28] and is capable of handling transactions. TRANSER takes C programs as input, and works at the LLVM IR level. It controls the exploration of the input program until it has explored all execution graphs using our DPOR algorithm, and detects user-provided assertion violations. We conduct all experiments on a Ubuntu 22.04.1 LTS with Intel Core i7-1165G7 and 16 GB RAM.

In the following sections, we describe the various categories of benchmarks we chose for evaluation, and also report on the performances of TRANSER and Transactional-JPF [14].

- Our first category of benchmarks is a set consisting of thousands of litmus tests. The main purpose of this set of experiments is to provide a sanity check for the correctness of TRANSER.
- The second category consists of a set of benchmarks inspired from real-world applications. This involves the following.

  - Shopping Cart [36]. This application allows users to add and remove items from their shopping cart and also to modify the quantities of the items in their cart.
  - Twitter [22]. This application allows users to follow other users, publish tweets, get new followers and also the tweets published by followers.
  - tpc-c [22]. This models an online shopping application with five kinds of transactions useful to read the stock of a product, creating a new order, getting the status, paying for an order and delivering the order.
  - Courseware [31]. This application manages the enrollment of students in various courses in an institute. It allows to create and delete courses, enrol students in courses if they have not reached the limit, remove the enrolment of a student from a course, and get the list of enrolled students.
  - Smallbank [17]. This application simulates a financial banking system. It allows customers to deposit a cheque, to check the savings amount and balance of customers, to send money from a customer account to others and to withdraw from the savings.
- The third category of benchmarks consists of paramaterized programs to study the scalability of TRANSER, when increasing the number of processes and transactions. For this scalability analysis, we consider parameterized versions of well known litmus tests as well as database-backed applications.

4.1 Litmus Tests

The first set of benchmarks includes litmus tests. These were created from the corresponding well known non-transactional litmus tests, which were generated using the Herd tool [7]. We generated 9815 litmus tests from Herd and instrumented them into transactional programs. These programs have assertions at the end which the test is known to satisfy or not. Each litmus test generated by Herd has a small number of instructions per process. In these litmus tests, the processes execute concurrently, and Herd checks whether an assertion is violated. We generated the expected results for these (non-transactional) litmus tests under sequential consistency and observed the behaviour of the transactional versions under SER. In all the transactional counterparts of these litmus tests, we observed the expected behaviour from both TRANSER as well as Transactional-JPF [14]. The time taken by TRANSER to evaluate all of the 9815 tests was at most 900 s. Transactional-JPF took 18,000 s on these.

4.2 Evaluation on Applications

We show the evaluation of 5 sets of applications in Table 1. We compare the performance of TRANSER against the implementation Transactional-JPF [8] of [14]. We considered multiple versions of these applications with increasing number of transactions and processes in the program. The number of transactions and then processes is enclosed in brackets as (transactions, processes). The first

Table 1. Evaluating behaviour of TRANSER on applications

Program	TRANSER		Transactional – JPF		
	Exec	Time	Exec(SER)	Exec(CC)	Time
courseware(9)(3)	48	1	48	81	7
courseware(10)(3)	54	3	54	2525	62
tpc-c(8)(3)	86	0.3	75	92	5
tpc-c(9)(4)	323	0.5	323	466	8
tpc-c(10)(4)	2086	6	1834	4955	63
twitter(9)(3)	19	0.1	19	34	2
twitter(10)(3)	62	0.5	62	229	6
twitter(14)(4)	858	1	286	1419	14
shoppingcart(9)(3)	10	0.1	10	16	1
shoppingcart(12)(4)	232	0.5	232	528	4
smallbank(10)(4)	157	0.6	157	356	10
smallbank(14)(5)	1216	2	1216	1344	54
tpc-c(14)(6)	19672	15	19672	69978	660
tpc-c(16)(6)	39344	68	(9215)*	(45174)*	1780

and second columns in Table 1 pertains to the number of execution graphs generated by TRANSER and the time taken. Transactional-JPF first generates execution graphs consistent under the weak isolation level causal consistency (CC) and then prunes away all those execution graphs which are not consistent under serializabilty. The second and third columns respectively show the number of execution graphs generated by Transactional-JPF [14] under CC and SER, and the fourth column shows the time taken by Transactional-JPF. Note that in all examples other than tpc-c(10)(4), the number of full execution graphs as well as *po*-*rf* execution graphs which are SER consistent are same. Only in the case of tpc-c(10)(4), there is a reduction in the number (1834) of *po*-*rf* graphs compared to the number of full execution graphs (2086). As can be seen from the table, Transactional-JPF generates several redundant execution graphs : courseware(10)(3) has only 54 consistent execution graphs under SER; Transactional-JPF generates 2525 execution graphs under CC and then prunes it away to 54. Likewise, tpc-c(10)(4) has 2086 SER consistent execution graphs and 4955 under CC. The time taken by TRANSER is also several magnitudes faster in comparison to Transactional-JPF.

Finally, the last row in Table 1 shows the number of executions explored by Transactional-JPF before it timeouts and crashes. tpc-c(16)(6) was obtained from tpc-c(14)(6) by adding two transactions t, t' such that t involves writes to two fresh variables while t' reads from them. The number of execution graphs is expected to double. However, Transactional-JPF outputs fewer execution graphs.

Table 2. Evaluating behaviour of TRANSER on parameterized benchmarks

Program	TRANSER		Transactional − JPF	
	Exec	Time	Exec(CC)	Time
LoadBuffer(6)(4)	29	0.4	50	0.4
LoadBuffer(9)(4)	494	1	2704	40
casrot(9)(9)	8597	2	8597	20
casrot(10)(10)	38486	8.8	38486	80
deliveryOrder(4)(2)	5	0.05	6	0.05
deliveryOrder(10)(2)	50	0.1	144	0.1
StoreBuffer(8)(6)	33	0.13	289	6
StoreBuffer(9)(7)	65	0.2	1089	24
StoreBuffer(10)(8)	129	0.35	4225	90
readers(12)(12)	2048	4	2048	13
readers(14)(14)	8192	18	8192	50
MP(4)(2)	4	0.06	4	0.1
MP(10)(4)	40	0.1	96	2
WriteSkew(2)(2)	2	0.04	2	1
WriteSkew(10)(2)	2	0.04	173	5
WriteSkew(12)(2)	2	0.04	1541	31

4.3 Evaluation on Parameterized Benchmarks and Applications

Table 2 and Fig. 6 show the evaluation of TRANSER and Transactional-JPF on parameterized benchmarks. The parameterization is done on the number of (transactions, processes). The first and second columns in Table 2 show the number of SER consistent execution graphs and the time taken by TRANSER; the third and fourth columns show the number of execution graphs (consistent under CC) and time taken by Transactional-JPF. It is worthy to note that all versions of programs "readers, casrot"[3] have the same number of consistent execution graphs under both SER and CC. For this program, Transactional-JPF has no redundant execution graphs computed. However, the time taken by Transactional-JPF is almost 10 times more than that taken by TRANSER. Next, consider programs "deliveryOrder"[10] and "MP[9]". For these, the difference in the number of execution graphs under SER and CC is moderate. However, Transactional-JPF takes almost 50 times more time than TRANSER in some of these. Finally, we have programs "WriteSkew"[9], "LoadBuffer, StoreBuffer" where the number of execution graphs under SER and CC vary drastically, the most pertinent example being WriteSkew. For these, TRANSER is faster (almost 800 times) than Transactional-JPF.

Figure 6 plots three graphs comparing the performance of TRANSER and Transactional-JPF on 16 parameterized applications (tpc-c(8)(6) to tpc-c(15)(6) as well as smallbank(8)(5) to smallbank(15)(5)). The first and second graph

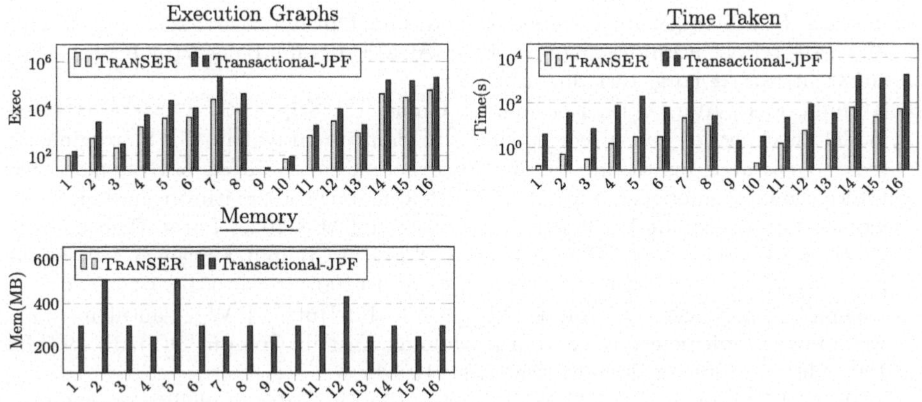

Fig. 6. Scalability analysis on a class of 16 applications.

compare the number of execution graphs explored and time taken respectively, the bar chart is plotted keeping these in logscale. The third graph shows the memory consumption; TRANSER consumes a maximum of 80–84 MB and hence does not show in the graph.

5 Conclusion

We have provided a DPOR algorithm for transactional programs under SER and also implemented the same as a tool TRANSER. Our experimental evaluation shows that TRANSER outperforms state of the art tools for transactional programs by several orders of magnitude. TRANSER can also be adapted to handle isolation levels such as snap shot isolation (SI) by appropriately modifying the consistency and optimality checks.

References

1. Abdulla, P.A., Aronis, S., Atig, M.F., Jonsson, B., Leonardsson, C., Sagonas, K.: Stateless model checking for tso and pso. In: Baier, C., Tinelli, C. (eds.) Tools and Algorithms for the Construction and Analysis of Systems, pp. 353–367. Springer, Berlin Heidelberg, Berlin, Heidelberg (2015)
2. Abdulla, P.A., Aronis, S., Jonsson, B., Sagonas, K.: Source sets: A foundation for optimal dynamic partial order reduction. J. ACM **64**(4), 25:1–25:49 (2017). https://doi.org/10.1145/3073408
3. Abdulla, P.A., Atig, M.F., Jonsson, B., Lång, M., Ngo, T.P., Sagonas, K.: Optimal stateless model checking for reads-from equivalence under sequential consistency. Proc. ACM Program. Lang. **3**(OOPSLA) (Oct 2019). https://doi.org/10.1145/3360576, https://doi.org/10.1145/3360576

4. Abdulla, P.A., Atig, M.F., Jonsson, B., Ngo, T.P.: Optimal stateless model checking under the release-acquire semantics. Proc. ACM Program. Lang. **2**(OOPSLA) (Oct 2018). https://doi.org/10.1145/3276505
5. Abdulla, P.A., Atig, M.F., Krishna, S., Gupta, A., Tuppe, O.: Optimal stateless model checking for causal consistency. In: Sankaranarayanan, S., Sharygina, N. (eds.) Tools and Algorithms for the Construction and Analysis of Systems - 29th International Conference, TACAS 2023, Held as Part of the European Joint Conferences on Theory and Practice of Software, ETAPS 2022, Paris, France, April 22-27, 2023, Proceedings, Part I. Lecture Notes in Computer Science, vol. 13993, pp. 105–125. Springer (2023). https://doi.org/10.1007/978-3-031-30823-9_6
6. Ahamad, M., Neiger, G., Burns, J.E., Kohli, P., Hutto, P.W.: Causal memory: Definitions, implementation, and programming. Distrib. Comput. **9**(1), 37–49 (Mar 1995). https://doi.org/10.1007/BF01784241
7. Alglave, J., Maranget, L., Tautschnig, M.: Herding cats: Modelling, simulation, testing, and data mining for weak memory. ACM Trans. Program. Lang. Syst. **36**(2) (jul 2014). https://doi.org/10.1145/2627752
8. anonymous: Transactional jpf (Apr 2023). https://doi.org/10.5281/zenodo.7824546
9. Beillahi, S.M., Bouajjani, A., Enea, C.: Checking robustness between weak transactional consistency models. In: Yoshida, N. (ed.) Programming Languages and Systems, pp. 87–117. Springer International Publishing, Cham (2021)
10. Beillahi, S.M., Bouajjani, A., Enea, C.: Robustness Against Transactional Causal Consistency. Logical Methods in Computer Science **Volume 17, Issue 1** (Feb 2021). https://doi.org/10.23638/LMCS-17(1:12)2021. https://lmcs.episciences.org/7149
11. Berenson, H., Bernstein, P., Gray, J., Melton, J., O'Neil, E., O'Neil, P.: A critique of ansi sql isolation levels. In: Proceedings of the 1995 ACM SIGMOD International Conference on Management of Data, pp. 1–10. SIGMOD '95, Association for Computing Machinery, New York, NY, USA (1995). https://doi.org/10.1145/223784.223785
12. Biswas, R., Enea, C.: On the complexity of checking transactional consistency. Proc. ACM Program. Lang. **3**(OOPSLA) (Oct 2019). https://doi.org/10.1145/3360591
13. Bouajjani, A., Enea, C., Guerraoui, R., Hamza, J.: On verifying causal consistency. SIGPLAN Not. **52**(1), 626–638 (Jan 2017). https://doi.org/10.1145/3093333.3009888
14. Bouajjani, A., Enea, C., Román-Calvo, E.: Dynamic partial order reduction for checking correctness against transaction isolation levels. Proc. ACM Program. Lang. **7**(PLDI), 565–590 (2023). https://doi.org/10.1145/3591243
15. Brutschy, L., Dimitrov, D.K., Müller, P., Vechev, M.T.: Serializability for eventual consistency: criterion, analysis, and applications. In: Castagna, G., Gordon, A.D. (eds.) Proceedings of the 44th ACM SIGPLAN Symposium on Principles of Programming Languages, POPL 2017, Paris, France, January 18-20, 2017, pp. 458–472. ACM (2017). https://doi.org/10.1145/3009837.3009895
16. Burckhardt, S.: Principles of eventual consistency. Found. Trends Program. Lang. **1**(1–2), 1–150 (2014). https://doi.org/10.1561/2500000011
17. Cahill, M.J., Röhm, U., Fekete, A.D.: Serializable isolation for snapshot databases. In: Wang, J.T. (ed.) Proceedings of the ACM SIGMOD International Conference on Management of Data, SIGMOD 2008, Vancouver, BC, Canada, June 10-12, 2008, pp. 729–738. ACM (2008). https://doi.org/10.1145/1376616.1376690

18. Cerone, A., Bernardi, G., Gotsman, A.: A framework for transactional consistency models with atomic visibility. In: Aceto, L., de Frutos-Escrig, D. (eds.) 26th International Conference on Concurrency Theory, CONCUR 2015, Madrid, Spain, September 1.4, 2015. LIPIcs, vol. 42, pp. 58–71. Schloss Dagstuhl - Leibniz-Zentrum für Informatik (2015). https://doi.org/10.4230/LIPICS.CONCUR.2015.58
19. Cerone, A., Gotsman, A.: Analysing snapshot isolation. J. ACM **65**(2), 11:1–11:41 (2018). https://doi.org/10.1145/3152396
20. Clarke, E.M., Emerson, E.A., Sistla, A.P.: Automatic verification of finite state concurrent systems using temporal logic specifications: A practical approach. In: Wright, J.R., Landweber, L., Demers, A.J., Teitelbaum, T. (eds.) Conference Record of the Tenth Annual ACM Symposium on Principles of Programming Languages, Austin, Texas, USA, January 1983, pp. 117–126. ACM Press (1983). https://doi.org/10.1145/567067.567080
21. Clarke, E.M., Grumberg, O., Minea, M., Peled, D.A.: State space reduction using partial order techniques. Int. J. Softw. Tools Technol. Transf. **2**(3), 279–287 (1999). https://doi.org/10.1007/s100090050035
22. Difallah, D., Pavlo, A., Curino, C., CudreMauroux, P.: Oltp-bench: An extensible testbed for benchmarking relational databases. Proc. VLDB Endowm. **7**, 277–288 (12 2013)
23. Flanagan, C., Godefroid, P.: Dynamic partial-order reduction for model checking software. In: Palsberg, J., Abadi, M. (eds.) Proceedings of the 32nd ACM SIGPLAN-SIGACT Symposium on Principles of Programming Languages, POPL 2005, Long Beach, California, USA, January 12-14, 2005, pp. 110–121. ACM (2005). https://doi.org/10.1145/1040305.1040315
24. Gibbons, P.B., Korach, E.: Testing shared memories. SIAM J. Comput. **26**(4), 1208–1244 (1997). https://doi.org/10.1137/S0097539794279614
25. Godefroid, P.: Partial-Order Methods for the Verification of Concurrent Systems - An Approach to the State-Explosion Problem, Lecture Notes in Computer Science, vol. 1032. Springer (1996). https://doi.org/10.1007/3-540-60761-7
26. Godefroid, P.: Model checking for programming languages using verisoft. In: Proceedings of the 24th ACM SIGPLAN-SIGACT Symposium on Principles of Programming Languages, pp. 174–186. POPL '97, Association for Computing Machinery, New York, NY, USA (1997). https://doi.org/10.1145/263699.263717
27. Kokologiannakis, M., Lahav, O., Sagonas, K., Vafeiadis, V.: Effective stateless model checking for C/C++ concurrency. Proc. ACM Program. Lang. **2**(POPL), 17:1–17:32 (2018). https://doi.org/10.1145/3158105
28. Kokologiannakis, M., Marmanis, I., Gladstein, V., Vafeiadis, V.: Truly stateless, optimal dynamic partial order reduction. Proc. ACM Program. Lang. **6**(POPL), 1–28 (2022). https://doi.org/10.1145/3498711
29. Kokologiannakis, M., Raad, A., Vafeiadis, V.: Model checking for weakly consistent libraries. In: McKinley, K.S., Fisher, K. (eds.) Proceedings of the 40th ACM SIGPLAN Conference on Programming Language Design and Implementation, PLDI 2019, Phoenix, AZ, USA, June 22-26, 2019, pp. 96–110. ACM (2019). https://doi.org/10.1145/3314221.3314609
30. Mazurkiewicz, A.: Trace theory. In: Advances in Petri Nets 1986. Part II on Petri Nets: Applications and Relationships to Other Models of Concurrency, pp. 279–324. Springer-Verlag, Berlin, Heidelberg (1987)
31. Nair, S.S., Petri, G., Shapiro, M.: Proving the safety of highly-available distributed objects. In: Müller, P. (ed.) Programming Languages and Systems, pp. 544–571. Springer International Publishing, Cham (2020)

32. Norris, B., Demsky, B.: A practical approach for model checking c/c++11 code. ACM Trans. Program. Lang. Syst. **38**(3) (May 2016). https://doi.org/10.1145/2806886
33. Papadimitriou, C.H.: The serializability of concurrent database updates. J. ACM **26**(4), 631–653 (1979). https://doi.org/10.1145/322154.322158
34. Peled, D.A.: All from one, one for all: on model checking using representatives. In: Courcoubetis, C. (ed.) Computer Aided Verification, 5th International Conference, CAV '93, Elounda, Greece, June 28 - July 1, 1993, Proceedings. Lecture Notes in Computer Science, vol. 697, pp. 409–423. Springer (1993). https://doi.org/10.1007/3-540-56922-7_34
35. Perrin, M., Mostefaoui, A., Jard, C.: Causal consistency: Beyond memory. SIGPLAN Not. **51**(8) (feb 2016). https://doi.org/10.1145/3016078.2851170
36. Sivaramakrishnan, K., Kaki, G., Jagannathan, S.: Declarative programming over eventually consistent data stores. SIGPLAN Not. **50**(6), 413–424 (jun 2015). https://doi.org/10.1145/2813885.2737981
37. Warszawski, T., Bailis, P.: Acidrain: Concurrency-related attacks on database-backed web applications. In: Salihoglu, S., Zhou, W., Chirkova, R., Yang, J., Suciu, D. (eds.) Proceedings of the 2017 ACM International Conference on Management of Data, SIGMOD Conference 2017, Chicago, IL, USA, May 14-19, 2017, pp. 5–20. ACM (2017). https://doi.org/10.1145/3035918.3064037
38. Zhang, N., Kusano, M., Wang, C.: Dynamic partial order reduction for relaxed memory models. In: Proceedings of the 36th ACM SIGPLAN Conference on Programming Language Design and Implementation, pp. 250–259. PLDI '15, Association for Computing Machinery, New York, NY, USA (2015). https://doi.org/10.1145/2737924.2737956

Learning for Verification and Synthesis

Deep-Reinforcement-Learning-Based Design Space Exploration for Time-Sensitive Networking

Yu-Cheng Wu, I-Ching Tseng, and Chung-Wei Lin(✉)

National Taiwan University, Taipei, Taiwan
b08901027@ntu.edu.tw, {d08922025,cwlin}@csie.ntu.edu.tw

Abstract. Time-Sensitive Networking (TSN) has emerged as a favorable option for real-time communication in Cyber-Physical Systems (CPSs), such as intelligent vehicles and industrial control systems, due to its capability of providing bounded end-to-end latencies. However, designing CPSs on a TSN network requires additional consideration of data flow schedulability and becomes an NP-hard combinatorial optimization problem. Therefore, a formal and efficient approach is desired to explore the design space with different combinations of data flow periods. Accordingly, we propose a novel design flow that preemptively generates a set of schedulable period lists, guaranteeing that all data flow deadlines can be met, to preclude the schedulability concern. We further employ Deep Reinforcement Learning (DRL) to optimize the searching process of these period lists. The experimental result demonstrates remarkable success where 97.02% solutions are found with 4.85× speed higher than a Satisfiability-Modulo-Theories-based method. The result of large-scale scenarios also reveals that our approach outperforms any other comparative method by at least 3.93× more schedulable period lists collected.

Keywords: Cyber-Physical Systems (CPSs) · Deep Reinforcement Learning (DRL) · Time-Sensitive Networking (TSN)

1 Introduction

The IEEE 802.1 Time-Sensitive Networking (TSN) task group has been developing the standards to define data transmission mechanisms over deterministic Ethernet networks [14], including time synchronization, traffic shaping, etc. Networks complying with these standards, namely TSN networks, facilitate real-time communication by introducing a globally synchronized clock with bounded precision, as defined in the IEEE 802.1AS standard [16]. Communication is performed via data flows consisting of frames with sizes equal to or less than the Ethernet Maximum Transmission Unit (MTU). Notably, data flows from the time-critical traffic class can be isolated and provided with bounded network latencies owing to the IEEE 802.1Qbv standard [12]. With time-aware shapers, network devices can control the transmission of data frames from each egress queue following a

S. Akshay et al. (Eds.): ATVA 2024, LNCS 15054, pp. 205–219, 2025.
https://doi.org/10.1007/978-3-031-78709-6_10

predetermined periodic schedule. Typically, the time slots assigned to the queues of the same egress port are mutually exclusive. This arrangement enables fully deterministic forwarding policies, which cannot be achieved with traditional non-scheduled networks.

To this point, TSN networks have become a promising solution to Cyber-Physical Systems (CPSs) requiring safety-critical and strict real-time communication, such as autonomous vehicles [2] and industrial control systems. However, scheduling the entire network is an NP-hard combinatorial problem. Furthermore, the generally considerable numbers of data frames and time slots lead to tremendous solution space. Although several algorithms have been proposed for TSN scheduling, *e.g.*, [6,11], the schedules are generated with all flow attributes predetermined and provided. This condition is overly strict for many modern CPSs requiring frequent updates and personalized supports, *e.g.*, over-the-air updates for intelligent vehicles, and personalization in Industry 4.0. Furthermore, designers cannot directly recognize whether data flows with particular attributes are schedulable when they plan all functional aspects of a TSN-based CPS. The testing process can be extremely time-consuming due to the high complexity of TSN scheduling, leading to inefficient design space exploration.

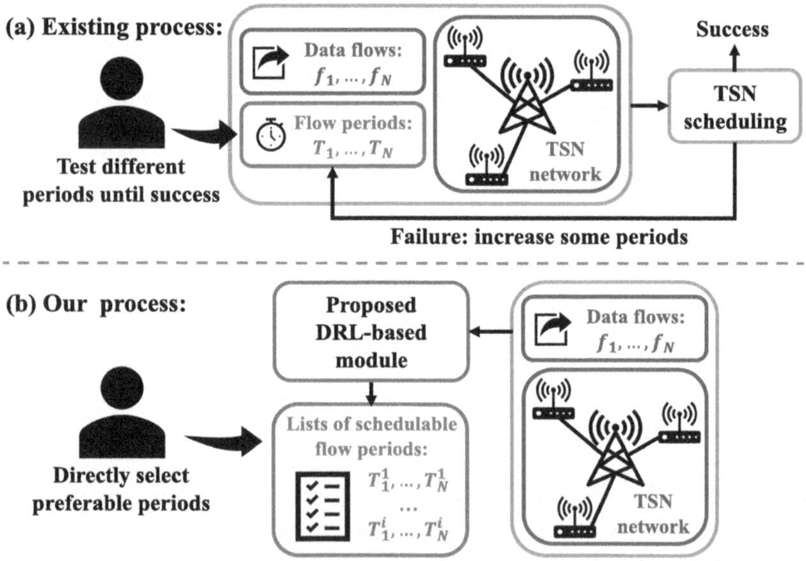

Fig. 1. Comparison between (a) the existing design process with TSN scheduling algorithms and (b) our direct design process, which precludes the schedulability concern in the system design phase and explores the design space with high quality and efficiency.

To address the problem, we propose an innovative design process that produces a set of period lists for data flows in advance, guaranteeing that the TSN network can be scheduled to meet all deadlines. Periods are one of the most critical flow attributes determining the schedulability of TSN networks. Moreover, compared with other attributes such as data flow sources and destinations, periods are much more flexible to different system needs and directly affect the system's performance. Here, take an autonomous vehicle, for instance. While the tank or battery can be monitored less frequently to reduce overhead, the data of the object detection sensors should be updated intensively. With our design flow, system designers only have to select a period list according to their needs without the concern for schedulability, as illustrated in Fig. 1.

Despite the significant advantages of our proposed design process, it may lead to sub-optimal system performance if the collected schedulable period lists are overly conservative. Accordingly, we present a methodology based on Deep Reinforcement Learning (DRL) [1]. DRL has already been applied to address several famous combinatorial optimization problems, including traveling salesman problem [4], maximum cut problem [3], bin packing problem [13], etc. A DRL framework typically comprises a deep neural network (DNN) agent and an environment, usually considered a black box. At each timestep, the agent takes a specific action according to the environment's state. The environment will then transition to the new state and return a reward to the agent. The agent's goal is to maximize the accumulated reward until the environment reaches the terminal state, and the series of interactions is defined as an episode. In this work, we modify DeepScheduler [11], a DRL-based TSN scheduler, to find schedulable period lists, which is much more complex than pure TSN scheduling.

To our best knowledge, no prior work has addressed the difficulties in considering schedulability during the system design phase of TSN-based CPSs. Our primary contributions can be summarized as follows:

1. **Improving the design flow for TSN-based CPSs**: Our proposed design procedure enables designers to focus on other system requirements without considering data flow schedulability on TSN networks.
2. **DRL-based technique for collecting schedulable period lists**: We design a DRL-based module to search for schedulable period lists for data flows on TSN networks efficiently and thoroughly.

To make this design flow even more useful to designers and closer to industrial applications, our ultimate goal is to enable the consideration of each solution's importance and prioritize the searching for more crucial ones. We believe that the DRL-based technique proposed in this work is a significant step toward this aim by first tackling the challenge of TSN schedulability concern.

Additionally, to evaluate the performance of our technique, we implement four other approaches for comparison in Sect. 5, including one based on Satisfiability Modulo Theories (SMT) [7], commonly used as the baseline in TSN scheduling, two trial-and-error methods with existing TSN scheduling algorithms, as depicted in Fig. 1(a), and one for ablation study. With no existing method capable of considering the priority of each solution, the number of solutions is a fair indicator of the Pareto front quality due to the scheduling inference property, which will be introduced in Sect. 4.2, and the degrees of flexibility for the following design. Therefore, all methodologies are evaluated with their run times and the numbers of the schedulable period lists found. An experimental result indicates that our approach finds 97.02% schedulable period lists with 4.85× speedup compared with an SMT-based method. Moreover, the results of large-scale cases suggest that our technique obtains at the minimum 3.93× more solutions than any other comparative method.

The rest of the paper is organized as follows. Section 2 summarizes the constraints and various algorithms for TSN scheduling. Section 3 elaborates on DeepScheduler [11], the basic framework of our module. Section 4 presents our DRL-based technique for finding schedulable period lists. Section 5 introduces comparative methods and experiments to evaluate the effectiveness of our design. Finally, Sect. 6 concludes this paper and provides future directions.

2 TSN Scheduling

A TSN scheduling algorithm aims to assign a time slot to each queued data frame for the transmission through a specific egress port connected to a physical link. All flow attributes should be provided during scheduling, including the size, the period, the path between the sender and receiver, etc. Several constraints should be satisfied to guarantee deterministic end-to-end latencies and are comprehensively discussed in [6]. Some of the most critical constraints include:

1. **Frame constraint**: The time slots assigned to each data flow should be within the respective period.
2. **Link constraint**: The time slots allocated to data frames transmitted through the same link should not overlap.
3. **Flow transmission constraint**: Transmission of a data frame through different links in its path should follow the sequential order in the time domain.
4. **End-to-end constraint**: For each data flow, the difference between the receiving time of the last frame and the sending time of the first data frame should not exceed the maximum end-to-end latency if specified.
5. **Frame isolation constraint**: Frames of different flows should not simultaneously be in the same queue.

Recently, several scheduling strategies have been proposed, and they can be divided into two categories, the SMT-based methodology [6] and other heuristic algorithms, *e.g.*, DeepScheduler [11], Tabu-search [8], Genetic algorithm [15], etc. The SMT-based method employs an SMT solver to search the entire solution space but with an exponentially growing run time. On the other hand, heuristic algorithms accelerate the scheduling process at the expense of scheduling ability. In other words, they may fail to schedule actually schedulable data flows but provide more reasonable run times.

3 DeepScheduler

DeepScheduler [11] applies DRL to strike an exceptional balance between run time and scheduling ability for TSN scheduling, outperforming SMT and other heuristic methods in most scenarios, especially those with large networks and numerous data flows. Owing to the advantage, we employ it as the fundamental design of our module. Here, we first give an overview of DeepScheduler [11] from the DRL perspective. In its framework, the state comprises the network topology, each device's time slot scheduling status, and the data flow attributes. The DNN agent determines the next data flow to be scheduled, which is the action, based on the current state. A heuristic algorithm subsequently schedules the selected flow, which can be viewed as the environment. The scheduling result will generate a reward and update the state for the next iteration. This repeated process terminates when a flow fails to be scheduled, or all scheduled successfully. Notably, the agent possesses encoders capable of handling different network topologies and data flows, introduced in Sect. 3.1 and Sect. 3.2, respectively. Section 3.3 further presents the scheduling procedure in detail.

3.1 Network Encoder

DeepScheduler [11] employs Graph Neural Network (GNN) to handle various network topologies. Typically, a network is transformed into a directed graph where each node represents a device, such as a switch, and each directed edge corresponds to a physical link. However, GNNs mostly perform tasks related to nodes' features, while TSN scheduling is mainly associated with links' conditions. Therefore, DeepScheduler [11] proposes an approach to reconstruct the graph where each node represents a link. If it is possible to transmit the same flow through two end-to-end connected links, edges with both directions are added between the nodes of the two links.

Moreover, to obtain the global information of the entire network, a super node S is inserted into the graph and connected to every other node by an edge pointing to S. Figure 2 provides an example of graph reconstruction. Each node in the graph contains a binary feature vector with a length equivalent to the number of time slots within the maximum available data flow period. The slot's size is precisely enough to transmit a frame with the MTU size. Except for node S, each entry indicates whether a slot has already been allocated to a data frame. As for node S, the feature is the element-wise average of all the others.

The type of GNN utilized is Message-Passing Neural Network (MPNN) [10]. MPNN includes an aggregation phase and an update phase at each time step. During the aggregation phase, each node produces a message from its hidden state by a function M and sends it to all the neighbors. Subsequently, every node aggregates the messages it receives by element-wise summation. Finally, each node updates its hidden state with the aggregated message by another function U during the update phase. DeepScheduler [11] implements M and U with Multi-Layer Perceptron (MLP). For the node of link l with its hidden state h_l and neighbors $\mathcal{N}(l)$, the forward passing process executed by a K-step MPNN

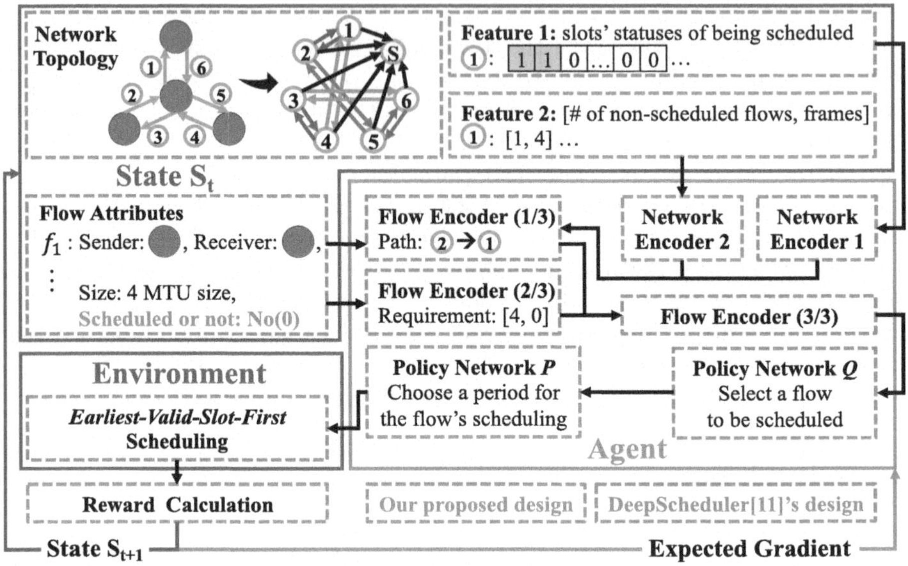

Fig. 2. Our DRL-based module for collecting schedulable period lists.

can be expressed as:

$$
\begin{aligned}
m_l^{t+1} &= \sum_{w \in \mathcal{N}(l)} M(h_l^t \parallel h_w^t), \\
h_l^{t+1} &= U(m_l^{t+1} \parallel h_l^t),
\end{aligned}
\qquad t = 0, 1, \ldots, (K-1), \tag{1}
$$

where $\parallel$ denotes vector concatenation. The binary feature of each link l is used as the initial hidden state h_l^0, and the final hidden state h_l^K is defined as the link embedding e_l.

3.2 Flow Encoder

The flow encoder proposed by DeepScheduler [11] comprises three components. The first component extracts the information on each data flow's path. Given a data flow routed through a sequence of links $[l_1, l_2, \ldots, l_N]$, link embeddings $[e_{l_1}, e_{l_2}, \ldots, e_{l_N}]$ are sequentially fed to a Gate Recurrent Unit (GRU) [5], which preserves the property of the order. For example, in Fig. 2, e_{l_2} and e_{l_1} are successively encoded for f_1. The path embedding p_i is defined as the final hidden state of the module. Second, an MLP generates the flow requirement embedding r_i from the attributes of each flow, including period and size. Finally, given a set of data flows $\mathcal{F}$, the embedding z_i of each flow $f_i \in \mathcal{F}$ is generated by:

$$
\begin{aligned}
h_i &= \mathrm{MLP}(e_S \parallel p_i \parallel r_i), \\
z_i &= \mathrm{MHA}(h_1, \ldots, h_i, \ldots, h_{|\mathcal{F}|})_i,
\end{aligned} \tag{2}
$$

where e_S is the super node's link embedding. The MHA is a Multi-Head Self-Attention [18] module that calculates each flow's final embedding z_i based on the relevance score of every (h_i, h_j) pair. To this end, all encoding is completed, and z_i will be utilized for scheduling.

3.3 Scheduling

Generally, large action space and long episodes lead to difficulties in convergence and low sample efficiency in DRL training. As the number of data frames is usually considerable, assigning time slots to each frame independently is impractical. Thus, DeepScheduler [11] simplified the task to a flow-level sequential decision process. In each iteration, a particular data flow is selected to be scheduled. An MLP policy network $Q : \mathbb{R}^{|z_i|} \rightarrow \mathbb{R}$ has been employed to generate a priority score for each flow f_i based on its final flow embedding z_i. With the Softmax function, the priority scores are transformed into the probability $\pi^s(f_i|s_t)$ of each flow f_i being selected, where s_t denotes the state that t flows have already been scheduled and should not be considered again. The selected flow is subsequently scheduled with the widely adopted Earliest-Valid-Slot-First algorithm (EVSF), *e.g.*, [8,15]. The algorithm traces the flow's path and allocates the first time slot satisfying all constraints introduced in Sect. 2 to the flow on each link. If the flow is successfully scheduled, the features of links in its path will be updated, and the entire process will repeat until all flows are scheduled, or a flow fails to be scheduled.

4 Methodology

Despite the exceptional capability of DeepScheduler [11] in TSN scheduling, it cannot be directly applied to our problem of finding schedulable period lists because the solution space expands drastically when we consider all data flow periods as variables instead of predetermined constants. Without a well-designed approach to explore different period combinations, the performance will be unsatisfactory even with DeepScheduler [11], which will be demonstrated in Sect. 5. Therefore, this section highlights our methodology incorporating DeepScheduler [11] with schedulable period list searching and achieving high efficiency. First, we introduce our modification on encoders obtaining information from the networks and data flows in Sect. 4.1. Second, Sect. 4.2 presents our approach for collecting schedulable period lists. Finally, Sect. 4.3 details our policy-based DRL training.

4.1 Encoders

As we must determine the periods of all flows by ourselves, unlike DeepScheduler [11], we need more information from network links other than the time slot statuses, especially the attributes of not yet scheduled data flows. Hence, we design another MPNN network encoder that processes the same graph but with a different initial hidden state. The new initial state contains two entries, including the number of flows routed through each link yet to be scheduled and the total number of frames of these flows. Taking Fig. 2 for instance, if f_1 is the only flow routed through link 1 and not scheduled, then the initial state is $[1, 4]$. We linearly project the new final hidden state and the original one into vectors with equal lengths and concatenate them as the new link embedding. The effectiveness of our additional network encoder is evaluated in Sect. 5. For the same reason, we remove the flow's period from the input of the flow attribute encoder because it is not provided in our design procedure and should be later determined by our module. Consequently, our version of the flow attribute vector only includes the flow's size and an additional boolean value indicating whether the flow has been scheduled, as the example of $[4, 0]$ for flow f_1 shown in Fig. 2.

4.2 Schedulable Period Lists

A set of schedulable period lists $\mathcal{P}$ needs to be produced in our proposed designing process for TSN-based CPSs, and the information needed for generating $\mathcal{P}$ is the same as that for the original TSN scheduling problem, including:

1. A network topology with a specified transmission rate.
2. A set of data flows $\mathcal{F} = \{f_1, f_2, \ldots, f_N\}$ with their sizes and paths between senders and receivers.
3. A set of available periods $\mathcal{T}$ provided by designers and supported by network devices.

In most prior works related to TSN scheduling, $\mathcal{T}$ satisfies a property as follows:

$$\bigwedge_{T^i, T^j \in \mathcal{T}} (T^i \mid T^j \vee T^j \mid T^i), \tag{3}$$

where $T^i \mid T^j$ denotes "T^j is divisible by T^i." The property can significantly reduce the complexity of schedulability analysis because any period list bounded below by a schedulable period list is also schedulable. The schedulability inference property can be expressed as:

$$[T_1, \ldots, T_N] \in \mathcal{P} \wedge \bigwedge_{i=1}^{N} (T_i' \in \mathcal{T} \wedge T_i' \geq T_i) \implies [T_1', \ldots, T_N'] \in \mathcal{P}. \tag{4}$$

To collect schedulable period lists, we insert another policy network $P : \mathbb{R}^{|z_i|} \to \mathbb{R}^{|\mathcal{T}|}$ after Q to produce the probabilities of all available periods being chosen. With the chosen period defined as T_i, the EVSF module will attempt to schedule the selected flow f_i with periods in $\{T_j \mid T_j \in \mathcal{T}, T_j \geq T_i\}$ following an ascending order. The process will repeat once a period is successfully scheduled or terminate when all attempts fail. For example, if $\mathcal{T} = \{1\,\text{ms}, 4\,\text{ms}, 16\,\text{ms}\}$ and $T_i = 4\,\text{ms}$, the module will scheduled f_i with the period of 4 ms and then 16 ms if the first attempt fails. Lines 3–15 in Algorithm 1 formally describe the procedure.

Algorithm 1: *Collecting Schedulable Period Lists*

Input : initial state s_0, maximum iterations I, number of flows N, available period set $\mathcal{T}$

Output: the set of schedulable period lists $\mathcal{P}$

1 $\mathcal{P} \leftarrow \varnothing$
2 **for** $i = 1$ *to* I **do**
3   **for** $t = 1$ *to* N **do**
4         $z_1, \ldots, z_N \leftarrow Encoders(s_{t-1})$
5         $f_j \leftarrow SampleFlow(PolicyQ(z_1, \ldots, z_N))$
6         $T_j \leftarrow SamplePeriod(PolicyP(z_j))$
7         $\mathcal{T}' \leftarrow \{T \mid T \in \mathcal{T} \wedge T \geq T_j\}$
8   **while** $\mathcal{T}'! = \varnothing$ **do**
9             $T_j \leftarrow min(\mathcal{T}')$
10   **if** $Schedule(s_{t-1}, f_j, T_j) = 1$ **then**
11                 $s_t \leftarrow UpdateState(s_{t-1}, f_j, T_j)$
12   *break*
13             $\mathcal{T}' \leftarrow \mathcal{T}' \setminus \{T_j\}$
14   **if** $\mathcal{T}' = \varnothing$ **then**
15   *break*
16   **if** $t = N$ **then**
17             $\mathcal{P}' \leftarrow \{[T'_1, \ldots, T'_N] \mid \bigwedge_{j=1}^{N}(T'_j \in \mathcal{T} \wedge T'_j \geq T_j)\}$
18             $\mathcal{P} \leftarrow \mathcal{P} \cup \mathcal{P}'$
19 **return** $\mathcal{P}$

4.3 DRL Training

During both training and testing, every set of data flows $\mathcal{F} = \{f_1, \ldots, f_N\}$ is scheduled with the actions, including flow and period selection, sampled based on the probabilities generated by the policy networks. If all flows are successfully scheduled with the period list $[T_1, \ldots, T_N]$, according to Eq. (4), all qualifying $[T'_1, \ldots, T'_N]$ will be added to the set of schedulable period lists $\mathcal{P}$, as Lines 16–18 in Algorithm 1. Each flow set is repetitively scheduled for I times, and I can be adjusted depending on how much time the user is willing to spend collecting schedulable period lists. As our goal is to produce $\mathcal{P}$ thoroughly and efficiently, we define the number of solutions, namely $|\mathcal{P}|$, as the reward for training.

Here, we exemplify an iteration with Fig. 2 and demonstrate its difference from that of DeepScheduler [11].

1. In the same way, the state includes data flow attributes, network topology, reconstructed into a new graph, and each device's time slot scheduling status. Additionally, we insert the information of each link's flows left to schedule. Take Link 1 for instance. The original Feature 1 suggests that only the first two time slots are already unavailable, and the added Feature 2 indicates that only one flow f_1, requiring 4 frames, is routed through the link and yet to be scheduled.

2. Our agent determines the minimum period for the scheduling attempts besides picking the specific flow, which expands the action space. For example, if $\mathcal{T} = \{1\,\text{ms}, 4\,\text{ms}, 16\,\text{ms}\}$, f_1 is selected, and the links that it passes have plenty more empty time slots than its frames, then the scheduling is very likely to start with the smallest period 1 ms; otherwise, it begins with 4 ms or 16 ms. The environment still operates with the EVSF algorithm but terminates only when all larger periods cannot be scheduled.
3. Each episode originally ends with a successful or failed scheduling with a 1 or 0 reward. However, as we define our reward as the number of solutions, the episode finishes after I runs of scheduling for all flows, with I's value assigned by users. For example, our module will receive a reward of 10 after finding 8, 0, and 2 more solutions in 3 independent runs.

With the additional policy network P iteratively making a policy π^p to determine the minimum available period for the flow selected based on Q's policy π^s, the policy π for finding schedulable period lists for a data flow set can be factorized as:

$$\pi(f_1, T_1, \ldots, f_N, T_N | s_0) = \prod_{t=1}^{N} \pi^s(f_t | s_{t-1}) \pi^p(T_t | f_t, s_{t-1}). \quad (5)$$

To maximize the expected reward $J = \mathbb{E}[R(a_\pi)]$, where a_π denotes the I times of actions sampled based on the policy π, we adopt policy gradient algorithm [17] for optimization, and the gradient is derived as:

$$\nabla_\theta J = \mathbb{E}[R(a_\pi) \sum_{i=1}^{I} \sum_{t=1}^{N} (\nabla_{\theta^s} log\pi^s(f_t^i | s_{t-1}^i) + \nabla_{\theta^p} log\pi^p(T_t^i | f_t^i, s_{t-1}^i))]. \quad (6)$$

θ, θ^s, and θ^p represent the parameters of the entire network, the policy network Q, and the policy network P, respectively. The policy gradient in Eq. (6) is estimated with Monte-Carlo sampling on batches of random data flow sets.

Generally, complex combinatorial problems lead to difficulty in convergence during DRL training. Furthermore, the estimation of the policy gradient in Eq. (6) is highly variant, which results in even more unstable optimization. Hence, we apply two skills to accelerate and stabilize the training process, including hard sample mining and incremental learning, as in [11]. The hard sample mining technique creates a fixed-size first-in-first-out buffer that keeps appending the data flow set with the lowest reward in the last batch. Accordingly, the training data is sampled from the union of the sets in the buffer and those in the current batch. On the other hand, incremental learning simply means gradually increasing the number of flows in a set during training.

5 Evaluation

5.1 Implementation

We apply two-step and three-step MPNNs for single-switch and multi-switch networks for all network encoders, respectively. The message and update function

M, Q are implemented with two-layer MLPs. We also employ two-layer MLPs for other components, including the encoder for flow requirements, the other encoder defined in Eq. (2), and the two policy networks Q, P. The MHA module for the final flow embedding has four heads, and the dimensions of all embeddings are 32 except that of flow requirement embedding r_i, which is 8. We train our DRL-based module for 400 epochs with 25 data flow sets per batch and a hard sample buffer with a size of 50 sets. As for the hardware environment, all experiments are conducted on a server with a 4-core Intel Core i7-6700 CPU, an NVIDIA GeForce RTX 3090 Ti GPU, and 64 GB memory.

5.2 Comparative Methods

SMT. An approach capable of finding all schedulable period lists is critical for evaluating the performance of other methods. In other words, it must be able to confirm whether a set of TSN data flows with specific periods are not schedulable. As mentioned in Sect. 2, only the SMT method has such capability. Consequently, we revise the approach in [6] by defining each flow's period, originally a constant, as a variable that can be any value in the set of available periods $\mathcal{T}$. Accordingly, the algorithm iteratively searches for a schedulable period list until no more lists can be found.

Ablated DRL. To evaluate the effectiveness of the additional network encoder introduced in Sect. 3.1, we apply the same DRL module in Fig. 2 but without our second network encoder for an ablation study.

Random EVSF. Random sampling is a straightforward and common approach for combinatorial problems. To better compare it with our methodology, we employ a similar process that utilizes EVSF to schedule each flow iteratively. Nonetheless, the scheduled flow and its period at each time step are randomly sampled.

Random DeepScheduler. This method represents the apparent trial-and-error approach system designers can use with DeepScheduler [11]. It repetitively and randomly samples a period list for data flows and determines the scheduling order with DeepScheduler [11]. Thus, it can also be viewed as the above random EVSF approach with a better scheduling algorithm.

5.3 Experimental Setup

Network Topologies. We experiment with three topology settings. The first two are static topologies consisting of 3 and 6 end systems connected to a single switch, respectively, where the former is illustrated in Fig. 2. The last one is much more complicated, with 6 switches randomly forming connected Erdős-Rényi Graphs, commonly used for network analysis [9], that link each pair of switches with a probability of 0.5, and every switch is also connected to 3 end systems. The link between any two devices is full-duplex and transmits a frame with the MTU size in 1/8 ms for single-switch topologies and 1/16 ms for the others.

Data Flows. During training and testing, the sender and receiver of each flow are randomly sampled among all end systems and cannot be the same. The path is randomly selected from all shortest paths for each flow, and the number of frames is uniformly distributed between 2 and 8. The set of available periods $\mathcal{T}$ includes 1, 4, and 16 ms. These settings have been used for simulations or even tested on real devices in several TSN scheduling works, such as [11]. We generate 8, 24, and 50 flows for three topology settings, respectively, and record the average number of schedulable period lists found over time in 40 repetitions for all three cases. The scenario with only 8 flows allows the SMT method to collect all schedulable period lists within a reasonable run time, enabling us to recognize the exact percentage of solutions found by the other methods. As for the other cases, we compare with the raw numbers of solutions.

5.4 Experimental Results

For the case with 8 flows, Fig. 3(a) indicates that while the SMT method collects 97.01% schedulable period lists in $1,000s$, our methodology reaches it in $206s$ (4.85× speedup) and eventually finds 97.83% solutions, nearly complete. Furthermore, the SMT method only finds 40.80% solutions in $206s$. Also, the random EVSF approach searches 11.40% and 3.52% fewer solutions than our technique in $206s$ and $1,000s$, respectively. However, the ablation study suggests nearly identical performance without our second network encoder. We attribute the result to the small number of flows and the relatively high ratio of schedulable period combinations.

Another observation in Fig. 3(a) is that the random DeepScheduler technique only finds 82.58% solutions in $1000s$, worse than the random EVSF approach. To verify DeepScheduler [11]'s advantage in scheduling ability, we randomly sample 1,000 period lists and schedule them with both DeepScheduler [11] and the random EVSF method. The result suggests that the latter finds 4.68% fewer solutions, but all period lists can be scheduled in 0.16× shorter time. Although the random DeepScheduler approach has a more extraordinary scheduling ability, the advantage is not significant because most period lists are either able or unable to be scheduled with both techniques. Instead, the high scheduling speed of the random EVSF method allows it to explore plenty more period lists and find more solutions.

Subsequently, we compare all methodologies in a larger scenario with 3 more end systems and 24 flows. Figure 3(b) showcases that our approach collects 10.6× and 86.2× more schedulable period lists than the random EVSF and the random DeepScheduler methods in 500 s, respectively. It also again validates the random DeepScheduler technique's disadvantage in exploring speed. Moreover, with more

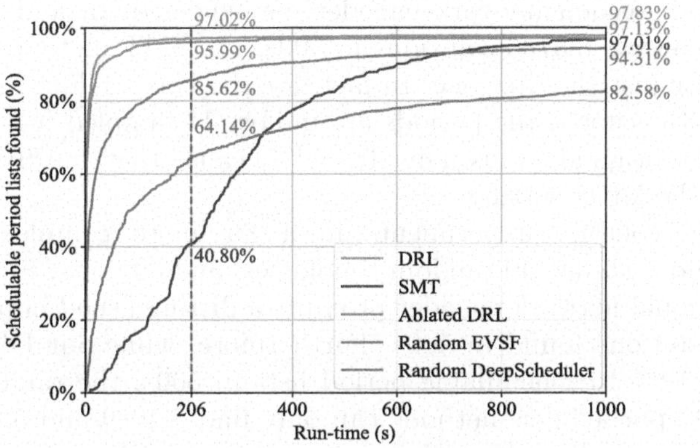

(a) 8 flows on a 4-device network.

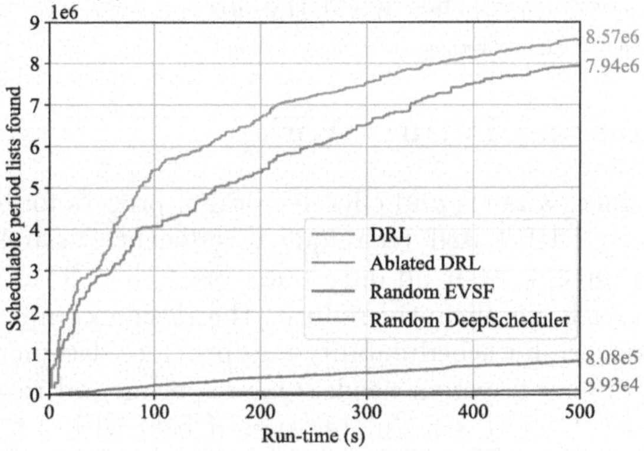

(b) 24 flows on a 7-device network.

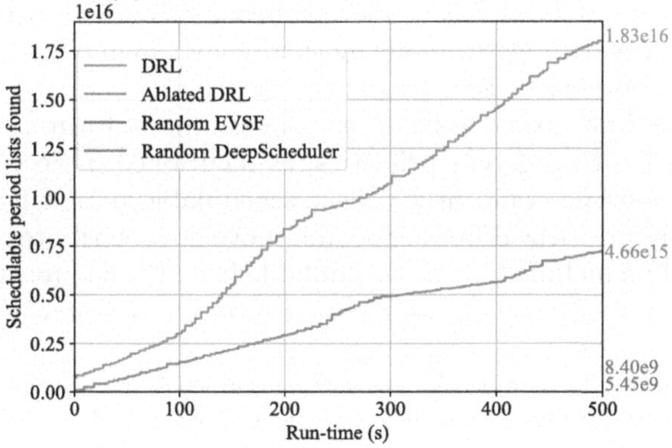

(c) 50 flows on 24-device random networks.

Fig. 3. Experimental results in scenarios with different scales. The percentages of schedulable period lists found are reported only in (a) because the SMT method cannot collect all solutions for (b) and (c) within reasonable run times.

transmitted data flows per link, the ablation study exhibits an improving 7.9% growth with our second network encoder, as expected. In addition, while our methodology collects $8.57e6$ solutions in $500s$, the SMT method spends $3,930s$ on searching for just the first one. In fact, for the two random methods, except for the case with 8 flows, the periods are uniformly sampled from $\{4\,\text{ms}, 16\,\text{ms}\}$ rather than the original $\{1\,\text{ms}, 4\,\text{ms}, 16\,\text{ms}\}$ because they hardly find even one solution with the latter setting.

Finally, we conduct experiments in a far more complex case with 6 switches, 18 end systems, 40 random topologies, and 50 flows. Figure 3(c) shows that our additional network encoder prompts a distinguished improvement with 3.93× more solutions found in $500s$. Furthermore, while our DRL-based technique collects $1.83e16$ schedulable period lists in $500s$, the random EVSF and the random DeepScheduler methods can only find $8.40e9$ and $5.45e9$ solutions, respectively. The results reflect that our methodology is increasingly advantageous over the other approaches when the size of network topologies and the number of data flows increase.

6 Conclusion and Future Work

This paper introduces a novel and effective design process for TSN-based CPSs. We also propose a DRL-based technique to efficiently search for schedulable period lists, guaranteeing that all data flows meet their deadlines on TSN networks. This approach significantly reduces the design complexity and cost by precluding the concern for schedulability and provides designers with great flexibility to satisfy different system needs. One experimental result indicates that our technique finds 97.02% schedulable period lists with 4.85× speedup compared with the baseline SMT method. The result of more extensive cases suggests our module collects at least 3.93× more solutions than any other comparative method. The results demonstrate our methodology's high efficiency and increasing advantage in large-scale scenarios.

Our work could be extended from two aspects in the future. First, data flows could be assigned with different priorities, as mentioned in Sect. 1. Accordingly, our DRL-based module could first collect schedulable period lists with smaller periods for highly prioritized flows. Second, more flow attributes, including sizes and paths, could be included in the schedulable lists. Both extensions will further expand our technique's scope of application in industrial practice.

Acknowledgments. This work is partially supported by Ministry of Education (MOE) in Taiwan under Grant Number NTU-113V2003-2, National Science and Technology Council (NSTC) in Taiwan under Grant Numbers NSTC-112-2636-E-002-010 and NSTC-112-2221-E-002-168-MY3, and ADLINK Technology Inc.

References

1. Arulkumaran, K., Deisenroth, M.P., Brundage, M., Bharath, A.A.: Deep reinforcement learning: a brief survey. IEEE Signal Process. Mag. **34**(6), 26–38 (2017)

2. Ashjaei, M., Bello, L.L., Daneshtalab, M., Patti, G., Saponara, S., Mubeen, S.: Time-Sensitive Networking in automotive embedded systems: state of the art and research opportunities. J. Syst. Architect. **117**, 102137 (2021)
3. Barrett, T., Clements, W., Foerster, J., Lvovsky, A.: Exploratory combinatorial optimization with reinforcement learning. In: AAAI Conference on Artificial Intelligence, vol. 34, pp. 3243–3250 (2020)
4. Bello, I., Pham, H., Le, Q.V., Norouzi, M., Bengio, S.: Neural combinatorial optimization with reinforcement learning. arXiv preprint arXiv:1611.09940 (2016)
5. Cho, K., Van Merriënboer, B., Bahdanau, D., Bengio, Y.: On the properties of neural machine translation: encoder-decoder approaches. arXiv preprint arXiv:1409.1259 (2014)
6. Craciunas, S.S., Oliver, R.S., Chmelík, M., Steiner, W.: Scheduling real-time communication in IEEE 802.1 Qbv Time Sensitive Networks. In: IEEE International Conference on Real-Time Networks and Systems, pp. 183–192 (2016)
7. De Moura, L., Bjørner, N.: Satisfiability modulo theories: introduction and applications. Commun. ACM **54**(9), 69–77 (2011)
8. Dürr, F., Nayak, N.G.: No-wait packet scheduling for IEEE Time-Sensitive Networks. In: IEEE International Conference on Real-Time Networks and Systems, pp. 203–212 (2016)
9. Fienberg, S.E.: A brief history of statistical models for network analysis and open challenges. J. Comput. Graph. Stat. **21**(4), 825–839 (2012)
10. Gilmer, J., Schoenholz, S.S., Riley, P.F., Vinyals, O., Dahl, G.E.: Neural message passing for quantum chemistry. In: International Conference on Machine Learning, pp. 1263–1272 (2017)
11. He, X., Zhuge, X., Dang, F., Xu, W., Yang, Z.: Deep-Scheduler: enabling flow-aware scheduling in Time-Sensitive Networking. In: IEEE International Conference on Computer Communications (2023)
12. ISO, IEC: 802.1 Qbv-2015 IEEE standard for local and metropolitan area networks-bridges and bridged networks-amendment 25: Enhancements for scheduled traffic (2016)
13. Laterre, A., et al.: Ranked reward: enabling self-play reinforcement learning for combinatorial optimization. arXiv preprint arXiv:1807.01672 (2018)
14. Messenger, J.L.: Time-sensitive networking: an introduction. IEEE Commun. Stand. Mag. **2**(2), 29–33 (2018)
15. Pahlevan, M., Obermaisser, R.: Genetic algorithm for scheduling time-triggered traffic in Time-Sensitive Networks. In: IEEE International Conference on Emerging Technologies and Factory Automation, pp. 337–344 (2018)
16. Rodrigues, S., Lv, J.: Synchronization in time-sensitive networking: an introduction to IEEE Std 802.1 AS. IEEE Commun. Stand. Mag. **6**(4), 14–20 (2022)
17. Sutton, R.S., Barto, A.G.: Reinforcement Learning: An Introduction. MIT Press, Cambridge (2018)
18. Vaswani, A., et al.: Attention is all you need. Adv. Neural Inf. Process. Syst. **30** (2017)

Learning Broadcast Protocols with LeoParDS

Noa Izsak[1(✉)], Dana Fisman[1], and Swen Jacobs[2]

[1] Ben Gurion University, Beer-Sheva, Israel
izsak@post.bgu.ac.il, dana@bgu.ac.il
[2] CISPA Helmholtz Center for Information Security, Saarbrücken, Germany
jacobs@cispa.de

Abstract. **LeoParDS** is a new tool for learning broadcast protocols (BPs) from a set of positive and negative example traces. It is the first tool that enables learning of a distributed computational model in a *parameterized* setting, i.e., with a parametric number of processes running the BP concurrently. We describe the tool along a running example, discuss some implementation details, and present experimental results on randomly generated BPs.

Keywords: learning computational models · broadcast protocols · parameterized verification · concurrent systems

1 Introduction

We present **LeoParDS**[1], an automatic tool for passive learning of broadcast protocols from example traces. Broadcast protocols are one of the most powerful computational models for which some parameterized verification problems are still decidable, and are strictly more expressive than protocols using communication primitives such as pairwise rendezvous [32] or disjunctive guards [22].

A **Broadcast Protocol**, in short **BP**, is a tuple (S, s_0, L, R) consisting of a finite set of states S with an initial state $s_0 \in S$, a set of labels L and a transition relation $R \subseteq S \times L \times S$, where $L = \{a!!, a?? \mid a \in A\}$ for some set of actions A (see Fig. 1). A transition labeled with $a!!$ is a broadcast *sending transition* (for action a), and a transition labeled with $a??$ is a broadcast *receiving transition* (for action a), also called a *response*. For each action $a \in A$, there is a unique state for the outgoing sending transition, and there must be exactly one outgoing response from every state. That is, when a process p is in a certain state s, and action a was broadcast by some other process q, the process p must respond by taking the unique $a??$ transition from s.

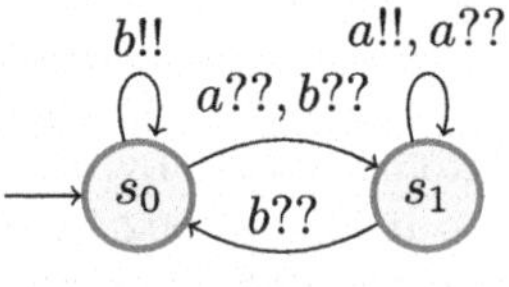

Fig. 1. BP $\mathcal{B}_{toy}$ with 2 states

[1] **LeoParDS** can be accessed by GitHub or Zenodo (DOI 10.5281/zenodo.10968037).

N. Izsak—Supported by ISF grant 2507/21.

S. Akshay et al. (Eds.): ATVA 2024, LNCS 15054, pp. 220–234, 2025.
https://doi.org/10.1007/978-3-031-78709-6_11

Given a BP $\mathcal{B} = (S, s_0, L, R)$ we use $\mathcal{B}^n$ to denote the system composed of n indistinguishable (i.e., identical) processes that execute $\mathcal{B}$ in parallel. Let $[n]$ denote the set $\{0, 1, \ldots, n\}$. A *configuration* of $\mathcal{B}^n$ is a function $\mathbf{q} : S \to [n]$, assigning to each state $s \in S$ the number of processes that are currently in local state s. The *initial configuration* $\mathbf{q}_0$ is the configuration with $\mathbf{q}_0(s_0) = n$ and $\mathbf{q}_0(s) = 0$ for all $s \neq s_0$. In a *global transition*, all processes make a move: One process takes a sending transition (labeled $a!!$), modeling that it broadcasts the value a to all the other processes in the system. Simultaneously, all of the **other** processes take the receiving transition (labeled $a??$) from their current state. Note that in $\mathcal{B}^1$, namely when the system is composed of a single process, this process takes only sending transitions, and there are no responses since there are no other processes. For those less familiar with broadcast protocols, more definitions, examples, and intuitions are given in [28].

One of the important definitions is the *language* of a broadcast protocol. With a particular $n \in \mathbb{N}$ we use $\mathcal{L}(\mathcal{B}^n)$ to denote the set of words that are *feasible* in $\mathcal{B}^n$. For instance, consider the BP $\mathcal{B}_{toy}$ of Fig. 1. Then bbb is feasible in $\mathcal{B}^1_{toy}$, and ba is feasible in $\mathcal{B}^2_{toy}$ but not in $\mathcal{B}^1_{toy}$ (since the single process remains in s_0 after taking b and a cannot be broadcast from s_0). A BP $\mathcal{B}$ defines an infinite family of systems $\{\mathcal{B}^n\}_{n \in \mathbb{N}}$, often referred to as a *parameterized system*. We use $\mathcal{L}(\mathcal{B})$ for the set of words feasible by at least one member $\mathcal{B}^n$ of this family, namely $\mathcal{L}(\mathcal{B}) = \bigcup_{n \in \mathbb{N}} \mathcal{L}(\mathcal{B}^n)$.

LeoParDS deal with *fine BPs* [28]. A BP is *fine* if it does not have hidden states[2] and there exists a cutoff k, such that the language of $\mathcal{B}^k$ is equal to the language of $\mathcal{B}^n$ for any $n > k$.

The learning problem we are interested in is inferring a broadcast protocol $\mathcal{B}'$ from a sample consisting of (execution) traces of members of a family $\{\mathcal{B}^n\}_{n \in \mathbb{N}}$ for some unknown BP $\mathcal{B}$ such that $\mathcal{L}(\mathcal{B}')$ is consistent with the sample. In addition, if the sample subsumes a *characteristic sample* for $\mathcal{B}$ then we require that $\mathcal{L}(\mathcal{B}') = \mathcal{L}(\mathcal{B})$. A *characteristic sample*, in short CS, is an important notion from the literature on passive learning of automata [37]. Loosely speaking, a CS is a set of labeled words from the unknown target language U from which a learner can infer an automaton B whose language is *equivalent* to U.

LeoParDS can also be used to generate a CS for fine BPs, as well as automatically detecting the cutoff of a fine BP. Additional functionalities of **LeoParDS** are listed in the *overview* paragraph. What makes **LeoParDS** unique is that it supports learning for a parametric number of processes, namely without assuming a fixed known number of processes that run in parallel.[3]

LeoParDS relies on the theoretical ideas developed in [28]. There, a learning algorithm is devised that can infer a correct BP from a sample that is consistent with a fine BP, and it is proven that it will derive a minimal equivalent BP if the sample is sufficiently complete (i.e., subsumes a CS). Various other learning problems concerning fine BPs are answered in [28], unfortunately on the negative

[2] A hidden state is a state where there are no outgoing broadcast sending transition.

[3] As far as we know, it is the first tool that enables learning of a distributed computational model in a *parameterized* setting. Hence the name **LeoParDS**, which stands for *Learning of Parameterized Distributed Systems*.

side. In particular, it is shown (i) that the consistency problem for fine BPs is NP-hard, (ii) that characteristic samples may be of size exponential w.r.t. the number of the states of the BP, and (iii) that under standard cryptographic assumptions, fine BPs are not polynomially predictable.

These negative results, and the fact that the inference algorithm also relies on a constraint solver (an SMT solver to be precise), make one wonder whether inferring a BP can be made practical, and may deter one from trying to invest in an implementation. Since availability of such a tool can benefit the scientific community, we took on ourselves the mission of implementing the first such tool. This paper is here to show that the single positive result from [28] actually holds in it many opportunities and deserves to be further studied by both theoreticians and practitioners. We note that many research fields such as studies of multi-agent systems [21,26,57], verifying concurrent systems and protocols [18,23] and distributed decision-making processes and strategies among multiple agents or players [15,43] in game-theory can use the techniques implemented in this tool to uncover novel insights and approaches in distributed computing.

To start bridging the gap between the theoretical results and their application in practice, we have implemented the techniques presented in [28]. Furthermore, for cases where the theory does not give us a complete solution, we implemented approximate methods that enhance the applicability of these techniques (at the cost of strong correctness guarantees). The result is a tool that allows us to demonstrate that even the techniques with a high theoretical complexity scale surprisingly well in practice (on randomly generated BPs), and that can solve a number of tasks that could benefit anyone interested in learning-based techniques for BPs, and potentially other parameterized distributed systems.

Related Work. Learning of computational models is broadly classified into active and passive learning algorithms. The algorithms for active and passive learning of DFAs [2,17,39,41,42,52,56] have been extended to various other computational models including non-deterministic and alternating automata [5,12,20], symbolic and lattice automata [7,27,30], ω-automata [3,4,6,11,25,45,46], register automata [16,38], multiplicity, weighted and probabilistic automata and grammars [8,9,29,54], and more. The concurrent models for which a learning algorithm has been developed include communicating automata [13], workflow Petri nets [24], and negotiation protocols [48]. The main difference between our work and these works is that we assume that an *arbitrary* number of processes can interact while these works assume a *fixed* number of processes.

Our learning algorithm belongs to the class of constraint-based learning algorithms. The first constraint-based algorithm for DFAs is due to Biermann and Feldman [10]. This algorithm was refined and improved [34,36,50]. Constraint-based algorithms are also used for learning temporal logic-formulas [49,53].

In terms of tools, the open source libraries LibAlf [14] and LearnLib [40] implement many of the algorithms for learning DFAs, Mealy and Moore machines, as well as for more powerful computational models such as visibly-pushdown automata. For ω-regular languages there are the tools ROLL [44] and ALMA [31]. We are not aware of tools for learning the concurrent models mentioned above.

Overview. The central task of **LeoParDS** is to infer a BP from a given sample. This is task BPInf (BPInfMin) listed under 3 below. In addition to that, it can solve four related tasks. The five main tasks that the tool can solve are:

1. **CSGen**: Given a fine BP $\mathcal{B}$, return a characteristic sample $\mathcal{S}_{\mathcal{B}}$ for it.
2. **RSGen**: Given a BP $\mathcal{B}$, subject to certain parameters, return a random sample $\mathcal{S}$ of words with labels corresponding to $\mathcal{B}$.
3. **BPInf** (and **BPInfMin**): Given a sample $\mathcal{S}$, return a (minimal) BP that is consistent with $\mathcal{S}$.
4. **BPGen**: Given bounds on the numbers of states and actions, return a random BP $\mathcal{B}$ within these bounds.
5. **AEQ**: Given two BPs $\mathcal{B}_1$ and $\mathcal{B}_2$, return whether they are equivalent (i.e. accept the same language) up to some approximation.

Even though each of these 5 tasks can stand by itself, the experiments that we describe later on use all of them. First we generate a BP (BPGen). Given a BP one can do one of two things, (1) learn an equivalent (and potentially minimal) fine BP. This can be done by generating a CS (CSGen), and inferring a BP from it (BPInf). Or (2) learn a consistent BP that is not necessarily equivalent to the original BP. This can be done by generating a random consistent sample (RSGen) (which is not necessarily a CS) and inferring a BP that is consistent with the sample. For option (1), in order to evaluate the tool (i.e., to show that we indeed learned an equivalent BP) we run AEQ and check that the language of the original and the generated BP are indeed equivalent. We discuss these tasks in detail in Sect. 2–Sect. 6. In Sect. 7 we discuss empirical results gathered on runs of **LeoParDS** on a large collection of randomly generated BPs.

2 Characteristic Sample Generation

Roughly speaking, a characteristic sample (CS) $\mathcal{S}_{\mathcal{B}}$ is a set of labeled words from which a learner can correctly infer the target model $\mathcal{B}$, i.e., given $\mathcal{S}_{\mathcal{B}}$ or any sample subsuming it, a learner can generate a BP $\mathcal{B}'$ such that $\mathcal{L}(\mathcal{B}) = \mathcal{L}(\mathcal{B}')$. The generation of a CS for BPs [28, Sec.5] is more involved than that for DFAs [33]. This section explains how the module CSGen generates a CS for a given fine BP.

In the context of BPs, a *sample* is a set of triples (w, n, b), where $w \in A^*$, i.e., a word over the actions A of the given BP $\mathcal{B}$, $n \in \mathbb{N}$ is a number of processes, and b is a truth value stating whether this word is feasible with n processes that execute $\mathcal{B}$ in parallel. When b is T (resp. F) this example is termed a *positive* (resp. *negative*) example. For the BP $\mathcal{B}_{toy}$ from Fig. 1, the triple $(bb, 1, \text{T})$ states that the sequence of actions bb is feasible in $\mathcal{B}^1_{toy}$ (as a single process can take the

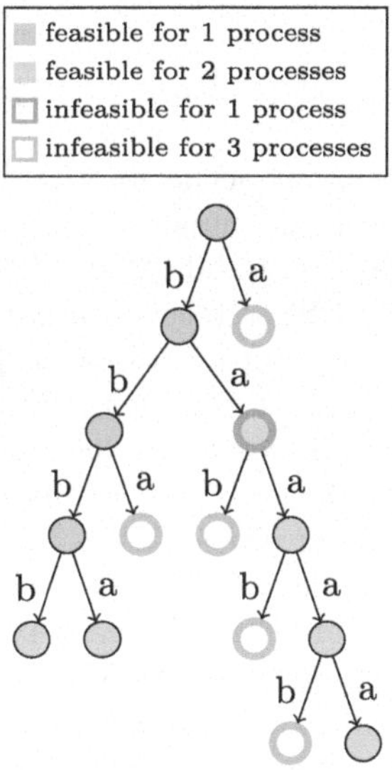

Fig. 2. Tree representing the CS of $\mathcal{B}_{toy}$

sending transition labeled with $b!!$ from the initial state an arbitrary number of times). The triple $(ba, 1, \text{F})$ states that the sequence of actions ba is infeasible in $\mathcal{B}^1_{toy}$ (as a single process can only execute b^*, but is not able to move from s_0 to s_1). The triple $(ba, 2, \text{T})$ states that ba is feasible in $\mathcal{B}^2_{toy}$ (if one process executes $b!!$, the second will move along the receiving transition labeled $b??$ from its current state s_0 to s_1, which will enable the sending transition on $a!!$, thus making ba feasible).

A tree representing the characteristic sample $\mathcal{S}_\mathcal{B}$ for $\mathcal{B}_{toy}$ is sketched in Fig. 2. Note that for any BP, feasibility of word w for n processes, i.e., (w, n, T), implies that (w, m, T) for any $m \geq n$. Similarly, infeasibility of a word w for n processes, i.e., (w, n, F), implies that w is also infeasible for any $m \leq n$. We use these implications to avoid clutter in the figure by only representing feasible (resp., infeasible) examples for the minimal (resp., maximal) number of processes with which they appear in the sample. In Fig. 2, nodes in violet signify that $(w, 1, \text{T}) \in \mathcal{S}_\mathcal{B}$, stating that w, the sequence of actions from the root to the given node, is feasible in $\mathcal{B}^1_{toy}$. Nodes in teal represent a triple $(w, 2, \text{T}) \in \mathcal{S}_\mathcal{B}$, corresponding to words that are feasible in $\mathcal{B}^2_{toy}$, but *not* making any assumption about feasibility of w in $\mathcal{B}^1_{toy}$ (e.g., $bbbb$ is feasible both in $\mathcal{B}^2_{toy}$ and in $\mathcal{B}^1_{toy}$, but $\mathcal{S}_\mathcal{B}$ only contains $(bbbb, 2, \text{T})$). If a node has a violet border, we also have $(w, 1, \text{F}) \in \mathcal{S}_\mathcal{B}$, stating that w is infeasible in $\mathcal{B}^1_{toy}$. Similarly, nodes with a blue border such as $(w, 3, \text{F}) \in \mathcal{S}_\mathcal{B}$, signify that w is infeasible in $\mathcal{B}^3_{toy}$.

In order to ensure termination also in case the given BP has no cutoff, CSGen assumes a given bound, $\overline{\text{M}}_p$, on the number of processes. If the input BP $\mathcal{B}$ has cutoff $c \leq \overline{\text{M}}_p$, procedure CSGen generates a CS $\mathcal{S}_\mathcal{B}$ for $\mathcal{B}$. Otherwise, i.e., if either $c > \overline{\text{M}}_p$ or $\mathcal{B}$ does not have a cutoff, it will generate the trimming of the CS that consists only of triples where the number of processes is bounded by $\overline{\text{M}}_p$.

3 Random Sample Generation

In many scenarios the data set given to the learning algorithm may not necessarily subsumes a characteristic set. **LeoParDS** can also be given a user-defined sample. In addition, RSGen can be used to generate a random sample. The module RSGen receives a parameter F_w that describes the number of words required to be in the sample, a parameter $\overline{\text{M}}_\ell$ that bounds the length of words in the sample, a parameter $\overline{\text{M}}_p$ that bounds the number of processes, and an optional parameter F_r to determine the ratio of positive words in the sample (out of the total number of words in the sample). If the optional parameter is not given, RSGen repeatedly calls procedure RWGen, which draws uniformly at random a number ℓ in 1 to $\overline{\text{M}}_\ell$ and then constructs a word w of length ℓ by randomly drawing an action for each position of the word. It then draws uniformly at random a number p in 1 to $\overline{\text{M}}_p$ and checks whether w is feasible in $\mathcal{B}$ with p processes, and adds the triple with the respective answer (w, p, T) or (w, p, F) to the sample.

Since the probability that a randomly drawn word is in the language of a given BP is very small and decreases with increasing length of words, the optional parameter F_r can be used to obtain a sample with the desired ratio of positive examples. If this parameter is given, an alternative procedure RPWGen is used to generate positive words, which randomly draws a number of processes p in 1 to $\overline{\mathrm{M}}_p$, and a length ℓ in 1 to $\overline{\mathrm{M}}_\ell$, and then simulates a random run of those p processes for ℓ steps as follows. It holds a state vector, a configuration, that records the position of all processes. At first, they are all at the initial state. At step $i \in [1..\ell]$ it checks what are the enabled actions A' according to current positions of the processes. It then randomly chooses an action a from A' and simulates the transition on this action (one process, the sender, takes the sending transition, and the rest of the processes follow the receiving transition). The negative words, i.e., a $(1 - F_r)$ of the words, will be randomly generated and checked to be negative examples, if so then they will be added to the sample.

As a small example, if we call RSGen with the BP $\mathcal{B}_{toy}$ from Fig. 1 and parameters $F_w = 5$, $\overline{\mathrm{M}}_\ell = 5$, $\overline{\mathrm{M}}_p = 3$, $F_r = 0.2$, the output could be the sample $\mathcal{S} = \{(aabab, 2, \mathrm{F}), (abbb, 2, \mathrm{F}), (baa, 3, \mathrm{T}), (bba, 2, \mathrm{F}), (ba, 1, \mathrm{F})\}$.

4 Inference of a BP from a Sample

The modules BPInf and BPInfMin are the central part of the tool **LeoParDS**. The module BPInf infers a BP from a given sample as described in [28]. As usual in passive learning algorithms, it guarantees to return a *minimal* representation *only if* the sample subsumes a CS. The module BPInfMin is a modification of BPInf that is guaranteed to always return the minimal BP consistent with the sample, i.e., even if the sample does not subsumes a CS. The high-level architecture of BPInf and BPInfMin are given in Fig. 3.

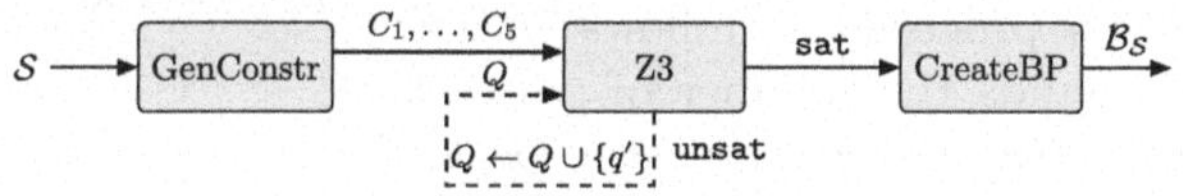

(a) High-level architecture of BPInf

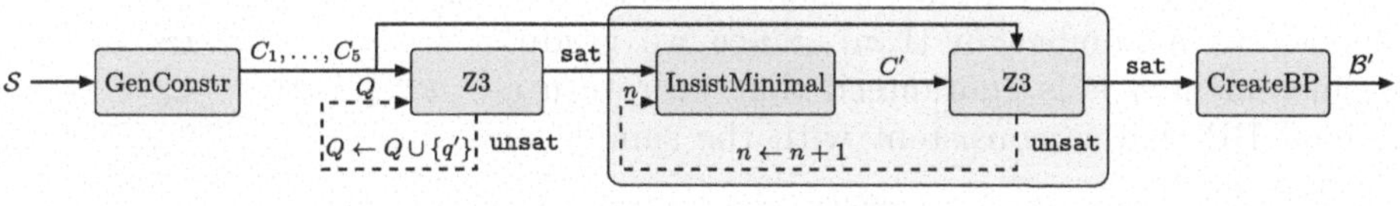

(b) High-level architecture of BPInfMin

Fig. 3. The high-level architectures of BPInf and BPInfMin.

The procedure GenConstr generates from a given sample $\mathcal{S}$ five sets of constraints $C_1, \ldots, C_5$, as described in [28, Sec.4]. These constraints are passed to the SMT solver Z3 [47].[4] If the result is sat, i.e., the constraints are satisfiable,

[4] Note that all variables in our SMT constraints are over finite domains with known size, implying that our constraints are decidable, and Z3 provides a decision procedure for such constraints.

then a satisfying assignment is passed to CreateBP that constructs from it a BP $\mathcal{B}'$ that is consistent with $\mathcal{S}$ as per [28, Thm 4.1]. Moreover, if the sample $\mathcal{S}$ subsumes a CS of some BP $\mathcal{B}$ then $\mathcal{B}'$ will be *correct*, namely equivalent to $\mathcal{B}$ and minimal among all BPs that are equivalent to $\mathcal{B}$ [28, Thm 5.3].

The constraints $C_1, \ldots, C_5$ are defined with respect to a set of states Q, a set of actions A, and partial functions $f^{\mathsf{st}} : A \rightarrow Q$, $f^{!!} : A \rightarrow Q$, and $f_a^{??} : Q \rightarrow Q$ for every $a \in A$. Functions f^{st} and $f^{!!}$ associate with each action the origin and target state, respectively, and each function $f_a^{??}$, for each action $a \in A$, associates with each state q the target state for the receiving $a??$ transition from q. Initially, A consists of all actions in the sample and Q consists of one state per action, namely $Q = \{f^{\mathsf{st}}(a) \mid a \in A\}$. If from some states more than one action is enabled, then fewer states will be required. For example, if $f^{\mathsf{st}}(a) = f^{\mathsf{st}}(b)$, then the set of states will have a single value representing both $f^{\mathsf{st}}(a)$ and $f^{\mathsf{st}}(b)$.

If the sample subsumes a CS then the constraints $C_1, \ldots, C_5$ are satisfiable and the BP $\mathcal{B}'$ constructed by CreateBP is correct and minimal. If the sample does not subsume a CS then there are two options. The first option is that the constraints $C_1, \ldots, C_5$ are immediately satisfiable, although the sample does not subsumes a CS. The second is that the constraints are not satisfiable. In this case, we incrementally add states to Q. (See the loop in Fig. 3a at the middle.) Each new state is associated with an action that does not appear in the sample. We add the states incrementally and try to satisfy the constraints $C_1, \ldots, C_5$ relative to the larger set of states Q until they become satisfiable, at which point CreateBP will return a consistent BP that agrees with the sample.

In both cases it could be that the satisfying assignment used more states in Q than necessary. Hence, if we want to insist that a minimal BP is returned, BPInfMin proceeds as follows. A new parameter n that bounds the number of states to n is introduced. (See the loop on the gray part of Fig. 3b.) BPInfMin tries to satisfy the constraints with the additional requirement that each state corresponds to a number in $[1..n]$. Since we gradually increment n it is guaranteed that we return a minimal BP that is consistent with the sample in this case too.[5]

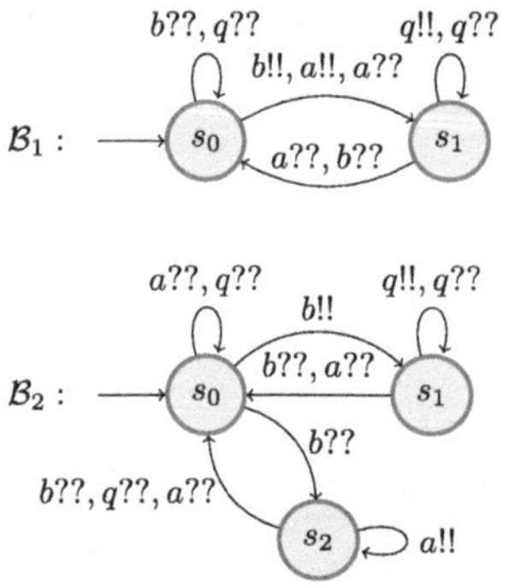

Fig. 4. Two BPs $\mathcal{B}_1$ and $\mathcal{B}_2$ that agree with sample $\mathcal{S} = \{(aa, 1, \text{F}), (ba, 1, \text{F}), (bb, 1, \text{F}), (bab, 2, \text{T}), (baabb, 2, \text{T})\}$.

Note that even in the second case, i.e., when the constraints are not satisfiable immediately and states were added incrementally until the constraints became satisfiable, unless we use BPInfMin, the returned BP might not be minimal. To see how this can happen consider the sample $\mathcal{S} = \{(aa, 1, \text{F}), (ba, 1, \text{F}), (bb, 1, \text{F}), (bab, 2, \text{T}), (baabb, 2, \text{T})\}$, which agrees with the BP $\mathcal{B}_1$ of Fig. 4.

[5] Alternatively we can search for the exact n using a binary search, but we have not yet implemented this option.

In order to have a satisfying assignment for this sample, we must have more states than $f^{\mathsf{st}}(a)$ and $f^{\mathsf{st}}(b)$ (which are the initial value of the set of Q). Note that from the sample, we know that $f^{\mathsf{st}}(b)$ is the initial state (since bab is feasible). However, $f^{!!}(b) \neq f^{\mathsf{st}}(a)$ (since $(ba, 1, \text{F}) \in \mathcal{S}$) and $f^{!!}(b) \neq f^{\mathsf{st}}(b)$ (since $(bb, 1, \text{F}) \in \mathcal{S}$). Therefore, a new state is required so that $f^{!!}(b)$ will be equal to it. Let $f^{\mathsf{st}}(q)$ be the state added in the loop in order to find a satisfying assignment. Now, with $Q = \{f^{\mathsf{st}}(a), f^{\mathsf{st}}(b), f^{\mathsf{st}}(q)\}$ the constraints are satisfiable. However, as we can see in Fig. 4, both of the BPs $\mathcal{B}_1, \mathcal{B}_2$ agree with the sample $\mathcal{S}$. Yet, the SMT solver may return the one with three states rather than the one with two. The language of the two BPs is different (note that $a \in \mathcal{L}(\mathcal{B}_1^1)$ but a is infeasible in $\mathcal{L}(\mathcal{B}_2^1)$) yet both are consistent with the given sample.

5 Generation of Random BPs

LeoParDS can be used to generate a sample for a user-defined BP with no hidden states. To generate a random BP, the module BPGen randomly generates BPs with no hidden states. The module receives parameters $\underline{\text{M}}_s, \overline{\text{M}}_s$ that bound the number of states and $\underline{\text{M}}_a, \overline{\text{M}}_a$ that bound the number of actions. It first chooses at random a number $n_s > 1$ between $\underline{\text{M}}_s$ and $\overline{\text{M}}_s$; this will be the number of states. Each state s is initially associated with a unique action a that is the sending action from s. This assures us that the generated BP will have no hidden states. Then a random number n_a between $\underline{\text{M}}_a$ and $\overline{\text{M}}_a$ of additional actions is chosen; these actions are distributed randomly between the states. After this step there could be more than one sending transition from each state, as is the case in state s_0 in $\mathcal{B}_1$ in Fig. 4.

Finally, for every action a, its broadcast sending and receiving transitions are determined: the sending transition is an edge from the state s associated with a to a randomly chosen target state s', and is labelled by $a!!$. Furthermore, for every state s and every action $a \in A$, a receiving transition is determined by picking a random target state s', and this transition is labelled with $a??$.

As an example, if BPGen is called with $\underline{\text{M}}_s = 2, \overline{\text{M}}_s = 3, \underline{\text{M}}_a = 0, \overline{\text{M}}_a = 2$, the output could be the BP $\mathcal{B}_1$ or $\mathcal{B}_2$ shown in Fig. 4.

6 Checking Approximate Equivalence of Two BPs

Since checking equivalence of BPs is probably infeasible[6], we implemented an approximate equivalence check. The module AEQ receives two BPs $\mathcal{B}_1$ and $\mathcal{B}_2$, a bound $\overline{\text{M}}_c$ for the cutoff, a bound $\overline{\text{M}}_\ell$ on the length of words, a bound $\overline{\text{M}}_w$ on the number of words, and a bound $\overline{\text{M}}_t$ on the running time.

The first approach tries to generate a CS for both $\mathcal{B}_1$ and $\mathcal{B}_2$ incrementally, first for 1 process, then for 2 processes, etc., until reaching the bound $\overline{\text{M}}_c$. For each triple (w, n, b) where $w \in A^*$, $n \in \mathbb{N}$, $b \in \{\text{T}, \text{F}\}$ that is added to the CS

[6] Checking reachability of local states has Ackermannian complexity [55]. To the best of our knowledge no better complexity algorithm for checking equivalence is known.

of $\mathcal{B}_1$ it checks whether w is feasible (resp. infeasible) with n processes in $\mathcal{B}_2$ iff $b = \text{T}$ (resp. $b = \text{F}$), and similarly for each triple added to the CS of $\mathcal{B}_2$. If it is feasible in one but not in the other it returns "no", otherwise it continues until reaching $\overline{\mathrm{M}}_c$ at which point it returns "yes".

The second approach instead of exhaustively generating the CS of both BPs conducts a random walk on the BPs (and again checks for disagreement between the two BPs on some word and some number of processes). For a given number of processes n_c in $[1, \overline{\mathrm{M}}_c]$, starting with $n_c = 1$, it maintains a pair of configurations (state-vectors) $(\mathbf{v}_1, \mathbf{v}_2)$, one for each of the BPs. Initially $\mathbf{v}_i$ is the state-vector where all n_c processes are in the initial state of $\mathcal{B}_i$. It then defines A_i (for $i \in \{1, 2\}$) to be the set of actions enabled from $\mathbf{v}_i$ in $\mathcal{B}_i$. If $A_1 \neq A_2$ it returns "no". Otherwise, it randomly chooses an action $a \in A_i$ and updates the current pair of configurations to be those obtained by the broadcast of action a. It continues this way until either $A_1 \neq A_2$ or the limit on the length of words is reached. If the limit on the length of a word is reached, it restarts the walk. If the limit on the number of words is reached, we increase n_c and repeat the process. If $n_c = \overline{\mathrm{M}}_c$ or the time bound is reached it returns "yes".

7 Experiments

Our experimental results may lack the fireworks associated with groundbreaking discoveries, but they carry immense value:

(1) **Practical Applicability: LeoParDS** consistently solved the generated instances. It navigated the intricacies of the inference problem, demonstrating its practical utility. The gap between theory and reality narrowed significantly.
(2) **Scalability:** As the problem complexity increased, **LeoParDS** maintained predictable performance. This scalability bodes well for future applications.
(3) **Broader Implications:** Our contribution extends beyond the inference problem for BPs. Researchers in diverse fields: verification, multi-agent learning, concurrent systems, strategies among multiple agents or players and others can leverage **LeoParDS**. By releasing it to the scientific community, we lay the foundation for future advancements.

Table 1. Statistical information

(a)

#states	**%BPs**
[2, 5)	36.64%
[5, 10)	37.27%
[10, 15)	16.87%
[15, 20]	9.23%

(b)

#words	**%BPs**
[0, 25)	21.67%
[25, 50)	44.28%
[50, 75)	24.74%
[75, 100]	9.30%

(c)

pos-ratio	**%BPs**
[0.0, 0.10)	40.46%
[0.10, 0.25)	39.22%
[0.25, 0.50)	16.50%
[0.50, 1.0]	3.82%

(d)

SMT(min)	**#BPs**
[0, 5)	2914
[5, 30)	773
[30, 60]	161
timeout	301

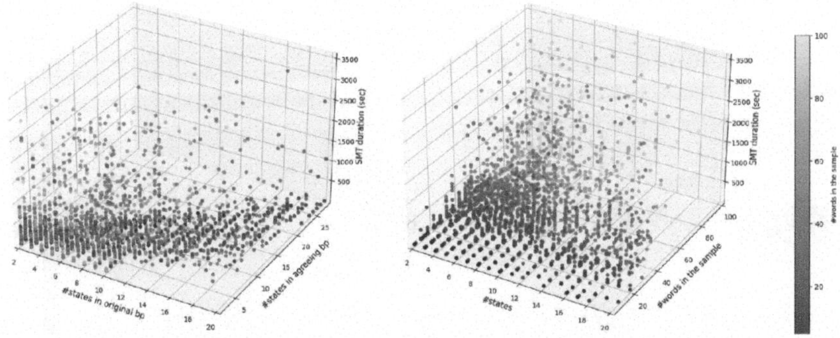

(a) (b)

Fig. 5. SMT duration according to several parameters

We ran all experiments on a cluster with Intel Xeon E5-2620 v4 CPUs. We allocated one CPU core and 30GB of RAM with time limit of 1 h. For our experiments we randomly generated 4149 BPs with a number of states in [2, 20], number of actions in [0, 8]. For each of these BPs we generated a random sample with a random number of words, F_w, in [5, 100]; with a bound of $\overline{\mathrm{M}}_\ell$=20 on the length of the words, and a bound of $\overline{\mathrm{M}}_p$=20 for the number of processes. The ratio of positive examples in the sample ranges between 0 and 1.

Table 1a provides details on the number of states of the generated BPs. Note that the number of states of a minimal equivalent BP might be smaller. Table 1b provides details on the number of words in the generated samples. In the first 850 generated random samples we used RWGen to randomly generate words. As discussed in Sect. 3, words generated by RWGen are more likely to be negative, and the probability increases with the length of words. Therefore, the ratio of positive words is generally low. To address this phenomenon, we implemented RPWGen which generates positive words. Table 1c provides details on the ratio of positive words in all the samples. We run BPInf on each of the generated samples. Table 1d provides details on the time (in minutes) it took the SMT-solver to find a satisfying assignment. The time to generate the BP from the assignment is negligible. We can see that 70.23% of the examples terminated in less than 5 min, and 7.25% timed out. Tables 1a–1c provide information only on the samples that did not time out.

Figure 5 shows the time needed for SMT solving (in seconds) relative to various parameters. In both Figs. 5a and 5b the z-axis is the SMT solving time, and the colors correspond to the number of words in the sample. In Fig. 5a the x-axis (resp. y-axis) shows the number of states in the randomly generated BP (resp. in the BP learned by BPInf). We can see that the number of states in the inferred BP is very close to the number of states in the generated BP. Recall that it could be smaller, since the randomly generated BP might not be minimal.

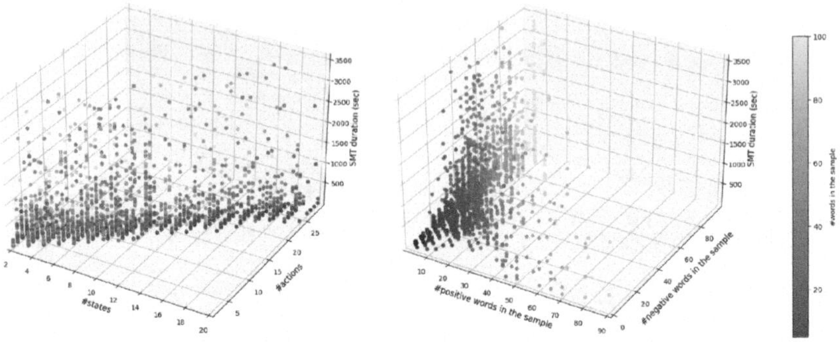

(a) (b)

Fig. 6. More plots for SMT duration according to several parameters

In Fig. 5b the x-axis shows the number of states in the randomly generated BP, and the y-axis shows the number of words in the sample. We can see that while the SMT time is affected mostly by the number of words in the sample, for BPs with a large number of states and actions the SMT time is larger even with fewer words, see Fig. 6a. When comparing the effect of positive vs negative words in the sample, we can see that the SMT time is mostly affected by the number of negative words. Note also that negative words are relatively longer, and may include more actions, both factors may affect the SMT time, see Fig. 6b.

8 Conclusions and Future Work

We have presented **LeoParDS**, the first automatic tool for passive learning of parameterized distributed systems, in particular in the form of broadcast protocols (BPs). In addition to its main task, the inference of a BP from a sample, **LeoParDS** supports the generation of random BPs, the generation of a characteristic or a random sample from a BP, as well as approximate equivalence checks between two BPs. All of these tasks come with a number of parameters that give the user control over the precision and the required resources. Based on the tasks that are already implemented, **LeoParDS** can be used for instance in the field of robotics and autonomous systems to learn control policies from observed sensor data, as well as a toolbox for future developments in the learning of parameterized distributed systems.

In future work, we plan to investigate both practice-oriented extensions of **LeoParDS**, such as the integration of other SMT solvers or heuristical support for non-fine BPs, and fundamental extensions to support other computational models, such as reconfigurable broadcast networks [19], rendezvous systems [1, 32], or Petri nets/VASS [35, 51]. In conclusion, **LeoParDS** is not just a solution; it's an invitation to explore uncharted territories.

References

1. Aminof, B., Kotek, T., Rubin, S., Spegni, F., Veith, H.: Parameterized model checking of rendezvous systems. In: Baldan, P., Gorla, D. (eds.) CONCUR 2014. LNCS, vol. 8704, pp. 109–124. Springer, Heidelberg (2014). https://doi.org/10.1007/978-3-662-44584-6_9
2. Angluin, D.: Learning regular sets from queries and counterexamples. Inf. Comput. **75**(2), 87–106 (1987)
3. Angluin, D., Antonopoulos, T., Fisman, D.: Query learning of derived ω tree languages in polynomial time. Log. Methods Comput. Sci. **15**(3) (2019)
4. Angluin, D., Antonopoulos, T., Fisman, D.: Strongly unambiguous büchi automata are polynomially predictable with membership queries. In: 28th EACSL Annual Conference on Computer Science Logic, CSL 2020, pp. 8:1–8:17 (2020)
5. Angluin, D., Eisenstat, S., Fisman, D.: Learning regular languages via alternating automata. In: Proceedings of the Twenty-Fourth International Joint Conference on Artificial Intelligence, IJCAI 2015, pp. 3308–3314 (2015)
6. Angluin, D., Fisman, D.: Learning regular omega languages. Theor. Comput. Sci. **650**, 57–72 (2016)
7. Argyros, G., D'Antoni, L.: The learnability of symbolic automata. In: Chockler, H., Weissenbacher, G. (eds.) CAV 2018. LNCS, vol. 10981, pp. 427–445. Springer, Cham (2018). https://doi.org/10.1007/978-3-319-96145-3_23
8. Balle, B., Mohri, M.: Learning weighted automata. In: Maletti, A. (ed.) CAI 2015. LNCS, vol. 9270, pp. 1–21. Springer, Cham (2015). https://doi.org/10.1007/978-3-319-23021-4_1
9. Beimel, A., Bergadano, F., Bshouty, N.H., Kushilevitz, E., Varricchio, S.: Learning functions represented as multiplicity automata. J. ACM **47**(3), 506–530 (2000)
10. Biermann, A.W., Feldman, J.A.: On the synthesis of finite-state machines from samples of their behavior. IEEE Trans. Comput. **21**(6), 592–597 (1972)
11. Bohn, L., Löding, C.: Constructing deterministic ω-automata from examples by an extension of the RPNI algorithm. In: 46th International Symposium on Mathematical Foundations of Computer Science, MFCS 2021, pp. 20:1–20:18 (2021)
12. Bollig, B., Habermehl, P., Kern, C., Leucker, M.: Angluin-style learning of NFA. In: IJCAI 2009, Proceedings of the 21st International Joint Conference on Artificial Intelligence, 2009, pp. 1004–1009 (2009)
13. Bollig, B., Katoen, J., Kern, C., Leucker, M.: Learning communicating automata from MSCs. IEEE Trans. Software Eng. **36**(3), 390–408 (2010)
14. Bollig, B., Katoen, J.-P., Kern, C., Leucker, M., Neider, D., Piegdon, D.R.: `libalf`: the Automata Learning Framework. In: Touili, T., Cook, B., Jackson, P. (eds.) CAV 2010. LNCS, vol. 6174, pp. 360–364. Springer, Heidelberg (2010). https://doi.org/10.1007/978-3-642-14295-6_32
15. Boutilier, C.: Planning, learning and coordination in multiagent decision processes. In: TARK, vol. 96, pp. 195–210. Citeseer (1996)
16. Cassel, S., Howar, F., Jonsson, B., Steffen, B.: Active learning for extended finite state machines. Formal Aspects Comput. **28**(2), 233–263 (2016). https://doi.org/10.1007/s00165-016-0355-5
17. Castellanos, A., Vidal, E., Varó, M.A., Oncina, J.: Language understanding and subsequential transducer learning. Comput. Speech Lang. **12**(3), 193–228 (1998)
18. Clarke, E.M., Emerson, E.A., Sistla, A.P.: Automatic verification of finite-state concurrent systems using temporal logic specifications. ACM Trans. Program. Lang. Syst. **8**(2), 244–263 (1986). https://doi.org/10.1145/5397.5399

19. Delzanno, G., Sangnier, A., Traverso, R., Zavattaro, G.: On the complexity of parameterized reachability in reconfigurable broadcast networks. In: FSTTCS. LIPIcs, vol. 18, pp. 289–300. Schloss Dagstuhl - Leibniz-Zentrum für Informatik (2012)
20. Denis, F., Lemay, A., Terlutte, A.: Residual finite state automata. In: Ferreira, A., Reichel, H. (eds.) STACS 2001. LNCS, vol. 2010, pp. 144–157. Springer, Heidelberg (2001). https://doi.org/10.1007/3-540-44693-1_13
21. Dorri, A., Kanhere, S.S., Jurdak, R.: Multi-agent systems: a survey. IEEE Access **6**, 28573–28593 (2018). https://doi.org/10.1109/ACCESS.2018.2831228
22. Emerson, E.A., Kahlon, V.: Reducing model checking of the many to the few. In: McAllester, D. (ed.) CADE 2000. LNCS (LNAI), vol. 1831, pp. 236–254. Springer, Heidelberg (2000). https://doi.org/10.1007/10721959_19
23. Emerson, E.A., Namjoshi, K.S.: Automatic verification of parameterized synchronous systems. In: Alur, R., Henzinger, T.A. (eds.) CAV 1996. LNCS, vol. 1102, pp. 87–98. Springer, Heidelberg (1996). https://doi.org/10.1007/3-540-61474-5_60
24. Esparza, J., Leucker, M., Schlund, M.: Learning workflow petri nets. Fundam. Informaticae **113**(3–4), 205–228 (2011)
25. Farzan, A., Chen, Y.-F., Clarke, E.M., Tsay, Y.-K., Wang, B.-Y.: Extending automated compositional verification to the full class of omega-regular languages. In: Ramakrishnan, C.R., Rehof, J. (eds.) TACAS 2008. LNCS, vol. 4963, pp. 2–17. Springer, Heidelberg (2008). https://doi.org/10.1007/978-3-540-78800-3_2
26. Ferber, J., Weiss, G.: Multi-agent Systems: An introduction to Distributed Artificial Intelligence, vol. 1. Addison-Wesley, Reading (1999)
27. Fisman, D., Frenkel, H., Zilles, S.: Inferring symbolic automata. Log. Methods Comput. Sci. **19**(2) (2023)
28. Fisman, D., Izsak, N., Jacobs, S.: Learning broadcast protocols. Proc. AAAI Conf. Artif. Intell. **38**(11), 12016–12023 (2024). https://doi.org/10.1609/aaai.v38i11.29089, https://ojs.aaai.org/index.php/AAAI/article/view/29089
29. Fisman, D., Nitay, D., Ziv-Ukelson, M.: Learning of structurally unambiguous probabilistic grammars. Log. Methods Comput. Sci. **19**(1) (2023)
30. Fisman, D., Saadon, S.: Learning and characterizing fully-ordered lattice automata. In: Automated Technology for Verification and Analysis - 20th International Symposium, ATVA 2022, Proceedings, pp. 266–282 (2022)
31. George, N.: ALMA: automata learner using modulo 2 multiplicity automata. CoRR **abs/2301.04077** (2023). https://doi.org/10.48550/ARXIV.2301.04077
32. German, S.M., Sistla, A.P.: Reasoning about systems with many processes. J. ACM **39**(3), 675–735 (1992)
33. Gold, E.M.: Complexity of automaton identification from given data. Inf. Control **37**(3), 302–320 (1978)
34. Grinchtein, O., Leucker, M., Piterman, N.: Inferring network invariants automatically. In: Furbach, U., Shankar, N. (eds.) IJCAR 2006. LNCS (LNAI), vol. 4130, pp. 483–497. Springer, Heidelberg (2006). https://doi.org/10.1007/11814771_40
35. Hack, M.: Decidability questions for Petri Nets. Ph.D. thesis, Massachusetts Institute of Technology, Cambridge, MA, USA (1976)
36. Heule, M.J.H., Verwer, S.: Exact DFA identification using SAT solvers. In: Sempere, J.M., García, P. (eds.) ICGI 2010. LNCS (LNAI), vol. 6339, pp. 66–79. Springer, Heidelberg (2010). https://doi.org/10.1007/978-3-642-15488-1_7
37. de la Higuera, C.: Characteristic sets for polynomial grammatical inference. Mach. Learn. **27**(2), 125–138 (1997)

38. Howar, F., Steffen, B., Jonsson, B., Cassel, S.: Inferring canonical register automata. In: Kuncak, V., Rybalchenko, A. (eds.) VMCAI 2012. LNCS, vol. 7148, pp. 251–266. Springer, Heidelberg (2012). https://doi.org/10.1007/978-3-642-27940-9_17
39. Isberner, M., Howar, F., Steffen, B.: The TTT algorithm: a redundancy-free approach to active automata learning. In: Runtime Verification - 5th International Conference, RV 2014. Proceedings, pp. 307–322 (2014)
40. Isberner, M., Howar, F., Steffen, B.: The open-source LearnLib. In: Kroening, D., Păsăreanu, C.S. (eds.) CAV 2015. LNCS, vol. 9206, pp. 487–495. Springer, Cham (2015). https://doi.org/10.1007/978-3-319-21690-4_32
41. José Oncina, P.G.: Identifying regular languages in polynomial time. In: Advances in Structural and Syntactic Pattern Recognition, pp. 99–108 (1992). https://doi.org/10.1142/9789812797919_0007
42. Kearns, M.J., Vazirani, U.V.: An Introduction to Computational Learning Theory. MIT Press, Cambridge (1994)
43. Kraus, S.: Automated negotiation and decision making in multiagent environments. In: Luck, M., Mařík, V., Štěpánková, O., Trappl, R. (eds.) ACAI 2001. LNCS (LNAI), vol. 2086, pp. 150–172. Springer, Heidelberg (2001). https://doi.org/10.1007/3-540-47745-4_7
44. Li, Y., Chen, Y.F., Zhang, L., Liu, D.: A novel learning algorithm for büchi automata based on family of DFAs and classification trees. Inf. Comput. **281**, 104678 (2021). https://doi.org/10.1016/j.ic.2020.104678, https://www.sciencedirect.com/science/article/pii/S0890540120301711
45. Maler, O., Pnueli, A.: On the learnability of infinitary regular sets. Inf. Comput. **118**(2), 316–326 (1995)
46. Michaliszyn, J., Otop, J.: Learning infinite-word automata with loop-index queries. Artif. Intell. **307**, 103710 (2022)
47. de Moura, L., Bjørner, N.: Z3: an efficient SMT solver. In: Ramakrishnan, C.R., Rehof, J. (eds.) TACAS 2008. LNCS, vol. 4963, pp. 337–340. Springer, Heidelberg (2008). https://doi.org/10.1007/978-3-540-78800-3_24
48. Muscholl, A., Walukiewicz, I.: Active learning for sound negotiations. In: LICS '22: 37th Annual ACM/IEEE Symposium on Logic in Computer Science, 2022, pp. 21:1–21:12 (2022)
49. Neider, D., Gavran, I.: Learning linear temporal properties. In: 2018 Formal Methods in Computer Aided Design, FMCAD 2018, pp. 1–10 (2018)
50. Oliveira, A.L., Silva, J.P.M.: Efficient algorithms for the inference of minimum size DFAs. Mach. Learn. **44**(1/2), 93–119 (2001)
51. Rackoff, C.: The covering and boundedness problems for vector addition systems. Theor. Comput. Sci. **6**, 223–231 (1978)
52. Rivest, R.L., Schapire, R.E.: Inference of finite automata using homing sequences. Inf. Comput. **103**(2), 299–347 (1993)
53. Roy, R., Fisman, D., Neider, D.: Learning interpretable models in the property specification language. In: Proceedings of the Twenty-Ninth International Joint Conference on Artificial Intelligence, IJCAI 2020. pp. 2213–2219 (2020). https://doi.org/10.24963/ijcai.2020/306
54. Sakakibara, Y.: Learning context-free grammars using tabular representations. Pattern Recognit. **38**(9), 1372–1383 (2005)
55. Schmitz, S., Schnoebelen, P.: The power of well-structured systems. In: D'Argenio, P.R., Melgratti, H. (eds.) CONCUR 2013. LNCS, vol. 8052, pp. 5–24. Springer, Heidelberg (2013). https://doi.org/10.1007/978-3-642-40184-8_2

56. Vaandrager, F., Garhewal, B., Rot, J., Wißmann, T.: A new approach for active automata learning based on apartness. In: TACAS 2022. LNCS, vol. 13243, pp. 223–243. Springer, Cham (2022). https://doi.org/10.1007/978-3-030-99524-9_12
57. Weiss, G.: Multiagent Systems: A Modern Approach to Distributed Artificial Intelligence. MIT Press, Cambridge (1999)

Greybox Learning of Languages Recognizable by Event-Recording Automata

Anirban Majumdar, Sayan Mukherjee(✉), and Jean-François Raskin

Université Libre de Bruxelles, Brussels, Belgium
sayan.mukherjee@ulb.be

Abstract. In this paper, we revisit the active learning of timed languages recognizable by event-recording automata. Our framework employs a method known as greybox learning, which enables the learning of event-recording automata with a minimal number of control states. This approach avoids learning the region automaton associated with the language, contrasting with existing methods. We have implemented our greybox learning algorithm with various heuristics to maintain low computational complexity. The efficacy of our approach is demonstrated through several examples.

Keywords: Automata learning · Greybox learning · Event-recording automata

1 Introduction

Formal modeling of complex systems is essential in fields such as requirement engineering and computer-aided verification. However, the task of writing formal models is both laborious and susceptible to errors. This process can be facilitated by learning algorithms [22]. For example, if a system can be represented as a finite state automaton, and thus if the system's set of behaviors constitutes a regular language, there exist thoroughly understood passive and active learning algorithms capable of learning the minimal DFA of the underlying language[1]. We call this problem the specification discovery problem in the sequel. In the realm of active learning, the L^* algorithm [5], pioneered by Angluin, is a celebrated approach that employs a protocol involving membership and equivalence queries, and enabling an efficient learning process for regular languages.

In this paper, we introduce an active learning framework designed to acquire timed languages that can be recognized by *event-recording automata* (ERA, for

[1] Minimal DFAs are a canonical representation of regular languages and are closely tied to the Myhill-Nerode equivalence relation.

Professor Jean-François Raskin receives support from the Foundation ULB. Dr. Anirban Majumdar and Dr. Sayan Mukherjee's post-doctoral research are also funded by a grant from the same foundation.

S. Akshay et al. (Eds.): ATVA 2024, LNCS 15054, pp. 235–256, 2025.
https://doi.org/10.1007/978-3-031-78709-6_12

short) [3]. The class of ERA enjoys several nice properties over the more general class of Timed Automata (TA) [2]. First, ERA are determinizable and hence complementable, unlike TA, making it particularly well suited for verification as inclusion checking is decidable for this class. Second, in ERA, clocks are explicitly associated to events and implicitly reset whenever its associated event occurs. This property leads to automata that are usually much easier to interpret than classical TA where clocks are not tied to events. This makes the class of ERA a very interesting candidate for learning, when interpretability is of concern.

Adapting the L^* algorithm for ERA is feasible by employing a canonical form known as the *simple deterministic event-recording automata* (SDERA). These SDERAs, introduced in [11] specifically for this application, are essentially the underlying region automaton of the timed language. Although the region automaton fulfills all the necessary criteria for the L^* algorithm, its size is generally excessive. Typically, the region automaton is significantly larger than a deterministic ERA (DERA, for short) with the minimum number of locations for a given timed language (and it is known that it can be *exponentially* larger). This discrepancy arises because the region automaton explicitly incorporates the semantics of clocks in its states, whereas in a DERA, the semantics of clocks are implicitly utilized. The difficulty to work directly with DERA is related to the fact that there is no natural canonical form for DERA and usually, there are several DERA with minimum number of states that recognize the same timed language. To overcome this difficulty, we propose in this paper an innovative application of the *greybox learning* framework, see for example [1], and demonstrate that it is possible to learn an automaton whose number of states matches that of a minimum DERA for the underlying timed language.

In our approach, rather than learning the region automaton of the timed language, we establish an active learning setup in which the semantics of the regions are already *known* to the learning algorithm, thus eliminating the need for the algorithm to learn the semantics of regions. Our greybox learning algorithm is underpinned by the following concept:

$$\mathsf{RW}_K(L) = L(C) \cap \mathsf{RegL}(\Sigma, K) \tag{1}$$

Here, $\mathsf{RW}_K(L)$ is a set of *consistent region words* that exactly represents the target timed language L. Meanwhile, $\mathsf{RegL}(\Sigma, K)$ denotes the regular language of consistent region words across the alphabet Σ and a maximal constant K. This language is precisely defined once Σ and K are fixed and remains independent of the timed language to be learned; therefore, it does not require learning. Essentially, deciding if a region word belongs to $\mathsf{RegL}(\Sigma, K)$ or not reduces to solving the following "consistency problem": given a region word, are there concrete timed words *consistent* with this (symbolic) region word? The answer to this question does *not* depend on the timed language to be learned but *only* on the semantics of clocks. This reduces the consistency problem to the problem of solving a linear program, which is known to be solvable efficiently.

The target of our greybox learning algorithm is a DERA C recognizing the timed language L. We will demonstrate that if a DERA with n states can accept the timed language to be learned, then the DERA C returned by our algorithm has at most n many states. Here is an informal summary of our learning protocol: within the context of the L^* vocabulary, we assume that the `Teacher` is capable of responding to membership queries of *consistent* region words. Additionally, the `Teacher` handles *inclusion* queries, unlike equivalence queries in L^* by determining whether a timed language is contained in another. If a discrepancy exists, `Teacher` provides a counter-example in the form of a region word.

This learning framework can be applied to specification discovery problem presented in the motivations above: we assume that the requirements engineer has a specific timed language in mind for which he wants to construct a DERA, but we assume that he is not able to formally write this DERA on his own. However, the requirement engineer is capable of answering membership and inclusion queries related to this language. Since the engineer cannot directly draft a DERA that represents the timed language, it is crucial that the queries posed are *semantic*, focusing on the language itself rather than on a specific automaton representing the language. This distinction ensures that the questions are appropriate and manageable given the assumptions about the engineer's capabilities. This is in contrast with [14], where queries are syntactic and answered with a specific DERA known by the `Teacher`. We will give more details about this comparison later in Sect. 3.

Technical Contribution. First, we define a greybox learning algorithm to derive a DERA with the *minimal number* of states that recognizes a target timed language. To achieve the learning of a minimal automaton, we must solve an NP-hard optimization problem: calculating a minimal finite state automaton that separates regular languages of positive and negative examples derived from membership and equivalence queries [10]. For that, we adapt to the timed setting the approach of Chen et al. in [7]. A similar framework has also been studied using SMT-based techniques by Moeller et al. in [16]. Second, we explore methods to circumvent this NP-hard optimization problem when the requirement for minimality is loosened. We introduce a heuristic that computes a candidate automaton in polynomial time using a greedy algorithm. This algorithm strives to maintain a small automaton size but does not guarantee the discovery of the absolute minimal solution, yet guaranteed to terminate with a DERA that accepts the input timed language. We have implemented this heuristic and demonstrate with our prototype that, in practice, it yields compact automata.

Related Works. Grinchtein et al. in [11] also present an active learning framework for ERA-recognizable languages. However, their learning algorithm generates simple DERAs – these are a canonical form of ERA recognizable languages, closely aligned with the underlying region automaton. In a simple DERA, transitions are labeled with region constraints, and notably, every path leading to an accepting state is satisfiable. This means the sequence of regions is consistent (as in the region automaton), and any two path prefixes reaching the same state are region equivalent. Typically, this results in a prohibitively large number of states in the automaton that maintains explicitly the semantics of regions. In contrast, our approach, while also labeling automaton edges with region constraints, permits the merging of prefixes that are not region equivalent. Enabled by Eq. 1, this allows for a more compact representation of the ERA languages (we generate DERA with minimal number of states). While our algorithm has been implemented, there is, to the best of our knowledge, no implementation of Grinchtein's algorithm, certainly due to high complexity of their approach.

Lin et al. in [14] propose another active learning style algorithm for inferring ERA, but with zones (coarser constraints than regions) as guards on the transitions. This allows them to infer smaller automata than [11]. However, it assumes that `Teacher` is familiar with a *specific* DERA for the underlying language and is capable of answering syntactic queries about this DERA. In fact, their learning algorithm is recognizing the regular language of words over the alphabet, composed of events and zones of the specific DERA known to `Teacher`. Unlike this approach, our learning algorithm does not presuppose a known and fixed DERA but only relies on queries that are semantic rather than syntactic. Although the work of [14] may seem superficially similar to ours, we dedicate in Sect. 3 an entire paragraph to the formal and thorough comparison between our two different approaches.

Recently, Masaki Waga developed an algorithm [25] for learning the class of Deterministic Timed Automata (DTA), which includes ERA recognizable languages. Waga's method resets a clock on every transition and utilizes region-based guards, often producing complex automata. Consequently, this algorithm does not guarantee the minimality of the resulting automaton, but merely ensures it accepts the specified timed language. In contrast, our approach guarantees learning of automata with the minimal number of states, featuring implicit clock resets that enhance readability. In the experimental section, we detail a performance comparison of our tool against their tool, LearnTA, across various examples. Further, in [21], the authors extend Waga's approach to reduce the number of clocks in learned automata, though they also do not achieve minimality. Their method also requires a significantly higher number of queries to implement these improvements.

Several other works have proposed learning methods for different models of timed languages, such as, One-clock Timed Automata [26], Real-time Automata [4], Mealy-machines with timers [6,23]. There have also been approaches other than active learning for learning such models, for example, using Genetic programming [20] and passive learning [8,24].

The missing proofs can be found in the longer version of the paper [15].

2 Preliminaries and Notations

DFA and 3DFA. Let $\Sigma = \{\sigma_1, \sigma_2, \ldots, \sigma_k\}$ be a finite *alphabet.* A deterministic finite state automaton (DFA) over Σ is a tuple $A = (Q, q_{\mathsf{init}}, \Sigma, \delta, F)$ where Q is a finite set of states, $q_{\mathsf{init}} \in Q$ is the initial state, $\delta : Q \times \Sigma \to Q$ is a partial transition function, and $F \subseteq Q$ is the set of final (accepting) states. When δ is a total function, we say that A is *total.* A DFA $A = (Q, q_{\mathsf{init}}, \Sigma, \delta, F)$ defines a regular language, noted $L(A)$, which is a subset of Σ^* and which contains the set of words $w = \sigma_1\sigma_2 \dots \sigma_n$ such that there exists an *accepting run* of A over w, *i.e.*, there exists a sequence of states $q_0q_1 \dots q_n$ such that $q_0 = q_{\mathsf{init}}$, and for all i, $1 \leq i \leq n$, $\delta(q_{i-1}, \sigma_i) = q_i$, and $q_n \in F$. We then say that the word w is *accepted* by A. If such an accepting run does not exist, we say that A *rejects* the word w.

A 3DFA D over Σ is a tuple $(Q, q_{\mathsf{init}}, \Sigma, \delta, \mathsf{A}, \mathsf{R}, \mathsf{E})$ where Q is a finite set of states, $q_{\mathsf{init}} \in Q$ is the initial state, $\delta : Q \times \Sigma \to Q$ is a total transition function, and $\mathsf{A} \uplus \mathsf{R} \uplus \mathsf{E}$ forms a partition of Q into a set of accepting states A, a set of rejection states R, and a set of 'don't care' states E. The 3DFA D defines the function $D : \Sigma^* \to \{0, 1, ?\}$ as follows: for $w = \sigma_0\sigma_1 \dots \sigma_n$ let $q_0q_1 \dots q_{n+1}$ be the unique run of D on w. If $q_{n+1} \in \mathsf{A}$ (resp. $q_{n+1} \in \mathsf{R}$), then $D(w) = 1$ (resp. $D(w) = 0$) and we say that w is *strongly accepted* (resp. *strongly rejected*) by D, and if $q_{n+1} \in \mathsf{E}$, then $D(w) = ?$. We interpret "?" as *either way*, *i.e.*, so the word can be either accepted or rejected. We say that a regular language L is consistent with a 3DFA D, noted $L \models D$, if for all $w \in \Sigma^*$, if $D(w) = 0$ then $w \notin L$, and if $D(w) = 1$ then $w \in L$. Accordingly, we define D^- as the DFA obtained from D where the partition $\mathsf{A} \uplus \mathsf{R} \uplus \mathsf{E}$ is replaced by $F = \mathsf{R}$, clearly $L(D^-) = \{w \in \Sigma^* \mid D(w) = 0\}$, it is thus the set of words that are strongly rejected by D. Similarly, we define D^+ as the DFA obtained from D where the partition $\mathsf{A} \uplus \mathsf{R} \uplus \mathsf{E}$ is replaced by $F = \mathsf{A}$, then $L(D^+) = \{w \in \Sigma^* \mid D(w) = 1\}$, it is thus the set of words that are strongly accepted by D. Now, it is easy to see that $L \models D$ iff $L(D^+) \subseteq L$ and $L(D^-) \subseteq \overline{L}$.

Timed Words and Timed Languages. A *timed word* over an alphabet Σ is a finite sequence $(\sigma_1, t_1)(\sigma_2, t_2) \dots (\sigma_n, t_n)$ where each $\sigma_i \in \Sigma$ and $t_i \in \mathbb{R}_{\geq 0}$, for all $1 \leq i \leq n$, and for all $1 \leq i < j \leq n$, $t_i \leq t_j$ (time is monotonically increasing). We use $\mathsf{TW}(\Sigma)$ to denote the set of all timed words over the alphabet Σ.

A *timed language* is a (possibly infinite) set of timed words. In existing literature, a timed language is called *timed regular* when there exists a timed automaton 'recognizing' the language. Timed Automata (TA) [2] extend deterministic finite-state automata with *clocks*. In what follows, we will use a subclass of TA, where clocks have a pre-assigned semantics and are not reset arbitrarily. This class is known as the class of Event-recording Automata (ERA) [3]. We now introduce the necessary vocabulary and notations for their definition.

Constraints. A *clock* is a non-negative real valued variable, that is, a variable ranging over $\mathbb{R}_{\geq 0}$. Let K be a positive integer. An *atomic K-constraint* over a clock x, is an expression of the form $x = c$, $x \in (c, d)$ or $x > K$ where $c, d \in \mathbb{N} \cap [0, K]$. A *$K$-constraint* over a set of clocks X is a conjunction of atomic K-constraints over clocks in X. Note that, K-constraints are closely related to the notion of *zones* [9] as in the literature of TA. However, zones also allow difference between two clocks, that are not allowed in K-constraints.

An *elementary K-constraint* over a clock x, is an atomic K-constraint where the intervals are restricted to unit intervals; more formally, it is an expression of the form $x = c$, $x \in (d, d+1)$ or $x > K$ where $c, d, d+1 \in \mathbb{N} \cap [0, K]$. A *simple K-constraint* over X is a conjunction of elementary K-constraints over clocks in

X, where each variable $x \in X$ appears exactly in one conjunct. The definition of simple constraints also appear in earlier works, for example [11]. One can again note that, simple constraints closely relate to the classical notion of *regions* [2]. However, again, regions consider difference between two clocks as well, which simple constraints do not. Interestingly, we do not need the granularity that regions offer (by comparing clocks) for our purpose, because a sequence of simple constraints induce a unique region in the classical sense (see Lemma 3).

Satisfaction of Constraints. A *valuation* for a set of clocks X is a function $v \colon X \to \mathbb{R}_{\geq 0}$. A valuation v for X satisfies an atomic K-constraint ψ, written as $v \models \psi$, if: $v(x) = c$ when $\psi := x = c$, $v(x) \in (c, d)$ when $\psi := x \in (c, d)$ and $v(x) > K$ when $\psi := x > K$.

A valuation v satisfies a K-constraint over X if v satisfies all its conjuncts. Given a K-constraint ψ, we denote by $[\![\psi]\!]$ the set of all valuations v such that $v \models \psi$. We say that a simple constraint r satisfies an elementary constraint ψ, noted $r \models \psi$, if $[\![r]\!] \subseteq [\![\psi]\!]$. It is easy to verify that for any simple constraint r and any elementary constraint ψ, either $[\![r]\!] \cap [\![\psi]\!] = \emptyset$ or $[\![r]\!] \subseteq [\![\psi]\!]$.

Let $\Sigma = \{\sigma_1, \sigma_2, \ldots, \sigma_k\}$ be a finite *alphabet*. The set of *event-recording clocks* associated to Σ is denoted by $X_\Sigma = \{x_\sigma \mid \sigma \in \Sigma\}$. We denote by $\mathsf{C}(\Sigma, K)$ the set of all K-constraints over the set of clocks X_Σ and we use $\mathsf{Reg}(\Sigma, K)$ to denote the set of all simple K-constraints over the clocks in X_Σ. For simple K-constraints we adopt the notation Reg, since, as remarked earlier, these kinds of constraints relate closely to the well-known notion of regions. Since simple K-constraints are also K-constraints, we have that $\mathsf{Reg}(\Sigma, K) \subset \mathsf{C}(\Sigma, K)$.

Definition 1 (ERA). *A K-Event-Recording Automaton (K-ERA) A is a tuple $(Q, q_{\mathsf{init}}, \Sigma, E, F)$ where Q is a finite set of states, $q_{\mathsf{init}} \in Q$ is the initial state, Σ is a finite alphabet, $E \subseteq Q \times \Sigma \times \mathsf{C}(\Sigma, K) \times Q$ is the set of transitions, and $F \subseteq Q$ is the subset of accepting states. Each transition in A is a tuple (q, σ, g, q'), where $q, q' \in Q$, $\sigma \in \Sigma$ and $g \in \mathsf{C}(\Sigma, K)$, g is called the* guard *of the transition. A is called a K-*deterministic-*ERA (K-DERA) if for every state $q \in Q$ and every letter σ, if there exist two transitions (q, σ, g_1, q_1) and (q, σ, g_2, q_2) then $[\![g_1]\!] \cap [\![g_2]\!] = \emptyset$.*

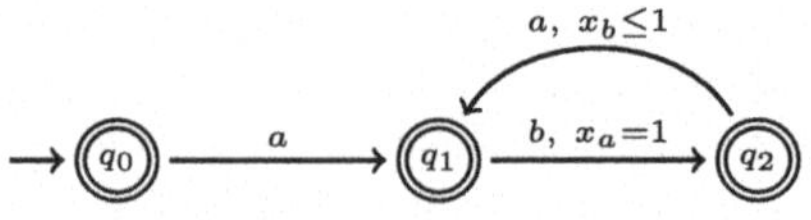

Fig. 1. A DERA that accepts timed words where every a is followed by a b after exactly 1 time unit and every b is followed by an a within 1 time units

For the semantics, initially, all the clocks start with the value 0 and then they all elapse at the same rate. For every transition on a letter σ, once the transition is taken, its corresponding recording clock x_σ gets reset to the value 0.

Clocked Words. Given a timed word $\mathsf{tw} = (\sigma_1, t_1)(\sigma_2, t_2)\dots(\sigma_n, t_n)$, we associate with it a *clocked word* $\mathsf{cw}(\mathsf{tw}) = (\sigma_1, v_1)(\sigma_2, v_2)\dots(\sigma_n, v_n)$ where each $v_i : X_\Sigma \to \mathbb{R}_{\geq 0}$ maps each clock of X_Σ to a real-value as follows: $v_i(x_\sigma) = t_i - t_j$ where $j = \max\{l < i \mid \sigma_l = \sigma\}$, with the convention that $\max(\emptyset) = 0$. In words, the value $v_i(x_\sigma)$ is the amount of time elapsed since the last occurrence of σ in tw; which is why we call the clocks x_σ 'recording' clocks. Although not explicitly, clocks are implicitly reset after every occurrence of their associated events.

Timed Language of a K-ERA. A timed word $\mathsf{tw} = (\sigma_1, t_1)(\sigma_2, t_2)\dots(\sigma_n, t_n)$ with its clocked word $\mathsf{cw}(\mathsf{tw}) = (\sigma_1, v_1)(\sigma_2, v_2)\dots(\sigma_n, v_n)$, is *accepted* by A if there exists a sequence of states $q_0 q_1 \dots q_n$ of A such that $q_0 = q_{\mathsf{init}}$, $q_n \in F$, and for all $1 \leq i \leq n$, there exists $e = (q_{i-1}, \sigma, \psi, q_i) \in E$ such that $\sigma_i = \sigma$, and $v_i \models \psi$. The set of all timed words accepted by A is called the *timed language* of A, and will be denoted by $L^{\mathsf{tw}}(A)$. We now ask a curious reader: is it possible to construct an ERA with two (or less) states that accepts the timed language represented in Fig. 1? We will answer this question in Sect. 5.

Lemma 1 ([3]). *For every K-ERA A, there exists a K-DERA A′ such that* $L^{\mathsf{tw}}(A) = L^{\mathsf{tw}}(A')$ *and there exists a K-DERA* $\overline{A'}$ *such that* $\overline{L^{\mathsf{tw}}(A)} = L^{\mathsf{tw}}(\overline{A'})$.

A timed language L is K-ERA (resp. K-DERA) definable if there exists a K-ERA (resp. K-DERA) A such that $L^{\mathsf{tw}}(A) = L$. Now, due to Lemma 1, a timed language L is K-ERA definable iff it is K-DERA definable.

Symbolic words over (Σ, K) are finite sequences $(\sigma_1, g_1)(\sigma_2, g_2)\dots(\sigma_n, g_n)$ where each $\sigma_i \in \Sigma$ and $g_i \in \mathsf{C}(\Sigma, K)$, for all $1 \leq i \leq n$. Similarly, a *region word* over (Σ, K) is a finite sequence $(\sigma_1, r_1)(\sigma_2, r_2)\dots(\sigma_n, r_n)$ where each $\sigma_i \in \Sigma$ and $r_i \in \mathsf{Reg}(\Sigma, K)$ is a simple K-constraint, for all $1 \leq i \leq n$. Lemma 3 will justify why we refer to symbolic words over simple constraints as 'region' words.

We are now equipped to define when a timed word tw is compatible with a symbolic word sw. Let $\mathsf{tw} = (\sigma_1, t_1)(\sigma_2, t_2)\dots(\sigma_n, t_n)$ be a timed word with its clocked word being $(\sigma_1, v_1)(\sigma_2, v_2)\dots(\sigma_n, t_n)$, and let us consider a symbolic word $\mathsf{sw} = (\sigma'_1, g_1)(\sigma'_2, g_2)\dots(\sigma'_m, g_m)$. We say that tw is compatible with sw, noted $\mathsf{tw} \models \mathsf{sw}$, if we have that: *(i)* $n = m$, *i.e.*, both words have the same length, *(ii)* $\sigma_i = \sigma'_i$ and *(iii)* $v_i \models g_i$, for all i, $1 \leq i \leq n$. We denote by $[\![\mathsf{sw}]\!] = \{\mathsf{tw} \in \mathsf{TW}(\Sigma) \mid \mathsf{tw} \models \mathsf{sw}\}$. We say that a symbolic word sw is *consistent* if $[\![\mathsf{sw}]\!] \neq \emptyset$, and *inconsistent* otherwise. We will use $\mathsf{RegL}(\Sigma, K)$ to denote the set of all *consistent* region words over the set of all K-simple constraints $\mathsf{Reg}(\Sigma, K)$.

Example 1. Let $\Sigma = \{a, b\}$ be an alphabet and let $X_\Sigma = \{x_a, x_b\}$ be its set of recording clocks. The symbolic word $\mathsf{rw}_1 := (a,\ x_a = 0 \land x_b = 0)(b,\ x_a = 1 \land x_b = 1)$ is consistent, since the timed word $(a, 0)(b, 1) \models \mathsf{rw}_1$. On the other hand, consider the symbolic word $\mathsf{rw}_2 := (a,\ x_a = 0 \land x_b = 1)(b,\ x_a = 1 \land x_b = 0)$. Let $\mathsf{tw} = (a, t_1)(b, t_2)$ be a timed word and $\mathsf{cw}(\mathsf{tw}) = (a, v_1)(b, v_2)$ be the clocked word of tw. Then $\mathsf{tw} \models \mathsf{rw}_2$ would imply $t_1 = 0$ and $t_2 - t_1 = 1$, but in that case, $v_2(x_b) = 1$, that is, $v_2 \not\models x_a = 1 \land x_b = 0$. Hence, rw_2 is inconsistent.

Lemma 2. *For every timed word* tw *over an alphabet* Σ*, for every fixed positive integer* K*, there exists a unique region word* $\mathsf{rw} \in \mathsf{RegL}(\Sigma, K)$ *where* $\mathsf{tw} \in [\![\mathsf{rw}]\!]$.

Lemma 3. *For every* K*-ERA* A *over an alphabet* Σ *and for every region word* $\mathsf{rw} \in \mathsf{RegL}(\Sigma, K)$*, either* $[\![\mathsf{rw}]\!] \subseteq L^{\mathsf{tw}}(A)$ *or* $[\![\mathsf{rw}]\!] \cap L^{\mathsf{tw}}(A) = \emptyset$*. Equivalently, for all timed words* $\mathsf{tw}_1, \mathsf{tw}_2 \in [\![\mathsf{rw}]\!]$*,* $\mathsf{tw}_1 \in L^{\mathsf{tw}}(A)$ *iff* $\mathsf{tw}_2 \in L^{\mathsf{tw}}(A)$.

The above lemma states that, two timed words that are both compatible with one region word, cannot be 'distinguished' using a DERA. This can be proved using Lemma 18 of [11].

Symbolic Languages. Note that, every K-DERA A can be transformed into another K-DERA A' where every guard present in A' is a simple K-constraint. This can be constructed as follows: for every transition (q, σ, g, q') in A where g is a K-constraint (and not a simple K-constraint), A' contains the transitions (q, σ, r, q') such that $r \models g$. Since, for every K-constraint g, there are only finitely-many (possibly, exponentially many) simple K-constraints r that satisfy g, this construction indeed yields a finite automaton. As for an example, the transition from q_1 to q_2 in the automaton in Fig. 1 contains a non-simple K-constraint as guard. This transition can be replaced with the following set of transitions without altering its timed language: $(q_1, b, x_a = 1 \wedge x_b = 0, q_2), (q_1, b, x_a = 1 \wedge 0 < x_b < 1, q_2), (q_1, b, x_a = 1 \wedge x_b = 1, q_2), (q_1, b, x_a = 1 \wedge x_b > 1, q_2)$. Note that, A' in the above construction is different from the "simple DERA" for A, as defined in [11]. A key difference is that, in A' there can be paths leading to an accepting state that are not satisfiable by any timed words, which is not the case in the simple DERA of A. This relaxation ensures, A' here has the same number of states as A, in contrast, in a simple DERA of [11], the number of states can be exponentially larger than the original DERA.

With the above construction in mind, given a K-DERA A, we associate two regular languages to it, called the *syntactic region language* of A and the *region language* of A, both over the finite alphabet $\Sigma \times \mathsf{Reg}(\Sigma, K)$, as follows:

- the syntactic region language of A, denoted $L^{\mathsf{s}\cdot\mathsf{rw}}(A)$, is the set of region words $\mathsf{rw} = (\sigma_1, r_1)(\sigma_2, r_2)\ldots(\sigma_m, r_m)$ such that there exists a sequence of states $q_0 q_1 \ldots q_n$ in A and (i) $q_0 = q_{\mathsf{init}}$, $q_n \in F$, and for all $1 \leq i \leq n$, there exists $e = (q_{i-1}, \sigma, \psi, q_i) \in E$ such that $\sigma_i = \sigma$, and $r_i \models \psi$. It is easy to see that A plays the role of a DFA for this language and that this language is thus a regular language over $\Sigma \times \mathsf{Reg}(\Sigma, K)$.
- the (semantic) region language of A, denoted $L^{\mathsf{rw}}(A)$, is the subset of $L^{\mathsf{s}\cdot\mathsf{rw}}(A)$ that is restricted to the set of region words that are consistent. This language is thus the intersection of $L^{\mathsf{s}\cdot\mathsf{rw}}(A)$ with $\mathsf{RegL}(\Sigma, K)$. And so, it is also a regular language over $\Sigma \times \mathsf{Reg}(\Sigma, K)$. (This is precisely the language accepted by a "simple DERA" corresponding to A, as defined in [11]).

Example 2. Let A be the automaton depicted in Fig. 1. Now, consider the region word $\mathsf{rw} := (a, x_a = 1 \wedge x_b = 1)(b, x_a = 1 \wedge x_b = 3)$. Note that, $\mathsf{rw} \in L^{\mathsf{s}\cdot\mathsf{rw}}(A)$, since there is the path $q_0 \xrightarrow{a,\ \top} q_1 \xrightarrow{b,\ x_a=1} q_2$ in A and (i) $(x_a = 1 \wedge x_b = 1) \models \top$, and (ii) $(x_a = 1 \wedge x_b = 3) \models (x_a = 1)$. However, one can show that $\mathsf{rw} \notin L^{\mathsf{rw}}(A)$. Indeed, $[\![\mathsf{rw}]\!] = \emptyset$, since for every clocked word $\mathsf{cw} = (a, v_1)(b, v_2)$, $\mathsf{cw} \models \mathsf{rw}$ only if $v_2(x_a) = 1$ and $v_2(x_b) = 3$, however, this is not possible, since in order for $v_2(x_a)$ to be 1, the time difference between the a and b must be 1-time unit, in which case, $v_2(x_b)$ will always be 2 (because, $v_1(x_b) = 1$) (Table 1).

Remark 1. Given a DFA C over the alphabet $\Sigma \times \mathsf{Reg}(\Sigma, K)$, one can interpret it as a K-DERA and associate the two –syntactic and semantic– languages as defined above. Then, the regular language $L(C)$ is the set of all region words in $L^{\mathsf{s\text{-}rw}}(C)$, when C is interpreted as a DERA. Similarly, abusing the notation, we write $L^{\mathsf{rw}}(C)$ to denote the set of all consistent region words accepted by C, and $L^{\mathsf{tw}}(C)$ to denote the set of all timed words accepted by C. This is a crucial remark to note, as *we will use this notation often* in the rest of the paper.

Table 1. Different symbolic languages for the automaton A in Fig. 1.

symbolic word	$L(A)$	$L^{\mathsf{s\text{-}rw}}(A)$	$L^{\mathsf{rw}}(A)$
$(a, \top)$	✓	✗	✗
$(a,\ x_a = 1 \wedge x_b = 1)(b,\ x_a = 0 \wedge x_b = 1)$	✗	✓	✓
$(a,\ x_a > 1 \wedge x_b > 1)(b,\ x_a > 1 \wedge x_b = 0)$	✗	✓	✗

3 Greybox Learning Framework

In this work, we are given a target timed language L, and we are trying to infer a DERA that recognizes L. To achieve this, we propose a greybox learning algorithm that involves a `Teacher` and a `Student`. Before giving details about this algorithm, we first make clear what are the assumptions that we make on the interaction between the `Teacher` and the `Student`. We then introduce some important notions that will be useful when we present the algorithm in Sect. 4.

3.1 The Learning Protocol

The purpose of the greybox active learning algorithm that we propose is to build a DERA for an ERA-definable timed language L using the following protocol between a so-called `Teacher`, that knows the language, and `Student` who tries to discover it. We assume that the `Student` is aware of the alphabet Σ and the maximum constant K that can appear in a region word, thus, due to Lemma 4, the `Student` can then determine the set of *consistent* region words $\mathsf{RegL}(\Sigma, K)$.

Lemma 4. *Given an alphabet Σ and a positive integer K, the set $\mathsf{RegL}(\Sigma, K)$ consisting of all consistent region words over (Σ, K), forms a regular language over the alphabet $\Sigma \times \mathsf{Reg}(\Sigma, K)$ and it can be recognized by a finite automaton. In the worst case, the size of this automaton is exponential both in $|\Sigma|$ and K.*

Since the Student can compute the automaton for $\mathsf{RegL}(\Sigma, K)$, we assume that the Student only poses membership queries for *consistent* region words, that is, region words from the set $\mathsf{RegL}(\Sigma, K)$. The Student, that is the learning algorithm, is allowed to formulate two types of queries to the Teacher:

Membership queries: given a *consistent* region word rw over the alphabet $\Sigma \times \mathsf{Reg}(\Sigma, K)$, Teacher answers Yes if $[\![\mathsf{rw}]\!] \subseteq L$, and No if $[\![\mathsf{rw}]\!] \not\subseteq L$ which, for region words, is equivalent to $[\![\mathsf{rw}]\!] \cap L = \emptyset$ (cf. Lemma 3).

Equivalence queries: given a DERA A, Student can ask two types of inclusion queries: $L^{\mathsf{tw}}(A) \subseteq L$, or $L \subseteq L^{\mathsf{tw}}(A)$. The Teacher answers Yes to an inclusion query if the inclusion holds, otherwise returns a counterexample.

Comparison with the Work in [14]. The queries that are allowed in our setting are *semantic* queries, so, they can be answered if the Teacher knows the timed language L and the answers to the queries are not bound by the particular ERA that the Teacher has for the language. This is in contrast with the learning algorithm proposed in [14]. Indeed, the learning algorithm proposed there considers queries that are answered for a specific DERA that the Teacher uses as a reference to answer those queries. In particular, a membership query in their setting is formulated according to a symbolic word w_z, i.e. a finite word over the alphabet $\Sigma \times \mathsf{C}(\Sigma, K)$. The membership query about the symbolic word w_z will be answered positively if there is a run that follows edges exactly annotated by this symbolic word in the automaton and that leads to an accepting state. For the equivalence query, the query asks if a candidate DERA is equal to the DERA that is known by the Teacher. Again, the answer is based on the syntax and not on the semantics. For instance, consider the automaton A in Fig. 1. When a membership query is performed in their algorithm for the symbolic word $w_z := (a, \top)(b, x_a = 1)(a, x_a = 1)$, even though $[\![w_z]\!] \subseteq L^{\mathsf{tw}}(A)$, their Teacher will respond negatively – this is because the guard on the transition $q_2 \xrightarrow{a, x_a \leq 1} q_1$ in A, does not syntactically match the expression $x_a = 1$, which is present in the third position of w_z. That is, when treating A as a DFA with the alphabet being $\Sigma \times \mathsf{C}(\Sigma, K)$, $w_z \notin L(A)$. So, the algorithm in [14] essentially learns the regular languages of symbolic words over the alphabet $\Sigma \times \mathsf{C}(\Sigma, K)$ rather than the semantics of the underlying timed language. As a corollary, our result (which we develop in Sect. 4) on returning a DERA with the minimum number of states holds even if the input automaton has more states, contrary to [14].

3.2 The Region Language Associated to a Timed Language

Definition 2 (The region language). *Given a timed language L, we define its K-region language as the set* $\mathsf{RW}_K(L) := \{\mathsf{rw} \in \mathsf{RegL}(\Sigma, K) \mid [\![\mathsf{rw}]\!] \subseteq L\}$.

For every ERA-definable timed language L, its K-region language $\mathsf{RW}_K(L)$ is uniquely determined due to Lemma 3. We now present a set of useful results regarding the set $\mathsf{RW}_K(L)$.

Lemma 5. *Let L be an ERA-definable timed language, and let A be a K-DERA recognizing L. Then: (1)* $\bigcup_{\mathsf{rw} \in \mathsf{RW}_K(L)} [\![\mathsf{rw}]\!] = L$, *and (2)* $\mathsf{RW}_K(\overline{L}) = \overline{\mathsf{RW}_K(L)} \cap \mathsf{RegL}(\Sigma, K)$, *where $\overline{L}$ denotes the complement*[2] *of L.*

In [11], the authors prove that for every ERA-definable timed language L, there exists a K-DERA A, for some positive integer K, such that $L^{\mathsf{tw}}(A) = L$. From the construction of such an A, it in fact follows that $L^{\mathsf{rw}}(A) = \mathsf{RW}_K(L)$. The authors then present an extension of the L^*-algorithm [5] that is able to learn a minimal DFA for the language $L^{\mathsf{rw}}(A)$. Now, the following lemma shows that a minimal DFA for the regular language $L^{\mathsf{rw}}(A)$ can be *exponentially* larger than a minimal DFA for the language $L^{\mathsf{s\cdot rw}}(A)$. In this paper, we show how to cast the problem of learning a minimal DFA for $L^{\mathsf{s\cdot rw}}(A)$ using an adaptation of the greybox active learning framework proposed by Chen et al. in [7].

Lemma 6. *Let L be an ERA-definable timed language and A be a K-DERA recognizing L. Then: (1)* $\mathsf{RW}_K(L) = L^{\mathsf{s\cdot rw}}(A) \cap \mathsf{RegL}(\Sigma, K) = L^{\mathsf{rw}}(A)$, *(2)* $\mathsf{RW}_K(\overline{L}) = L^{\mathsf{s\cdot rw}}(\overline{A}) \cap \mathsf{RegL}(\Sigma, K) = L^{\mathsf{rw}}(\overline{A})$, *(3) The minimal DFA over $\Sigma \times \mathsf{Reg}(\Sigma, K)$ that recognizes $L^{\mathsf{s\cdot rw}}(A)$ can be exponentially smaller than the minimal DFA that recognizes $L^{\mathsf{rw}}(A)$, and (4) There exists a DFA with a number of states equal to the number of states in A that accepts $L^{\mathsf{s\cdot rw}}(A)$.*

Note that, the first equation in Lemma 6 is similar to Eq. 1 that we introduced in Sect. 1. This equation is the cornerstone of our approach, and this is what justifies the advantage of our approach over existing approaches. It is crucial to understand that for a fixed Σ and K, the regular language $\mathsf{RegL}(\Sigma, K)$ present in this equation is already known and does not require learning. Consequently, the learning method we are about to describe focuses on discovering an automaton C that satisfies this equation, and thereby it is a *greybox* learning algorithm (as coined in [1]) since a part of this equation is already known.

In order for an automaton C to satisfy the first equation in Lemma 6, we can deduce that C must (i) accept all the region words in $\mathsf{RW}_K(L)$, *i.e.* all consistent region words rw for which $[\![\mathsf{rw}]\!] \subseteq L$, (ii) reject all the consistent region words rw for which $[\![\mathsf{rw}]\!] \subseteq \overline{L}$, and (iii) it can do either ways with inconsistent region words. This is precisely the flexibility that allows for solutions C that have fewer states than the minimal DFA for the language $\mathsf{RW}_K(L)$. The fourth statement in Lemma 6 implies that there is a DFA over the alphabet $\Sigma \times \mathsf{Reg}(\Sigma, K)$ that has the same number of states as that of a minimal DERA recognizing the timed language L. We give an overview of our greybox learning algorithm in Sect. 4.

In the following, we establish a strong correspondence between the timed languages and the region languages of two DERAs:

Lemma 7. *Given two DERAs A and B, $L^{\mathsf{rw}}(A) \subseteq L^{\mathsf{rw}}(B)$ iff $L^{\mathsf{tw}}(A) \subseteq L^{\mathsf{tw}}(B)$.*

[2] The complement of L is also ERA-definable, since the class of ERA is closed under complementation [3].

3.3 (Strongly-)complete 3DFAs

In this part, we define some concepts regarding 3DFAs that we will use in our greybox learning algorithm. These concepts are adaptations of similar concepts presented in [7] to the timed setting.

Definition 3 (Completeness). *A 3DFA D over $\Sigma \times \mathsf{Reg}(\Sigma, K)$ is* complete *w.r.t. the timed language L if the timed language of D^+, when interpreted as a DERA, is a subset of L,* i.e., *$L^{\mathsf{tw}}(D^+) \subseteq L$; and the timed language of D^-, when interpreted as a DERA, is a subset of $\overline{L}$,* i.e., *$L^{\mathsf{tw}}(D^-) \subseteq \overline{L}$.*

Applying Lemma 6 and 7 to the above definition, we get the following result:

Lemma 8. *Let L be a timed language over Σ recognized by a K-DERA A over Σ, then for any 3DFA D over $\Sigma \times \mathsf{Reg}(\Sigma, K)$, D is complete w.r.t. L iff $L^{\mathsf{rw}}(D^+) \subseteq L^{\mathsf{rw}}(A) = \mathsf{RW}_K(L)$ and $L^{\mathsf{rw}}(D^-) \subseteq L^{\mathsf{rw}}(\overline{A}) = \mathsf{RW}_K(\overline{L})$.*

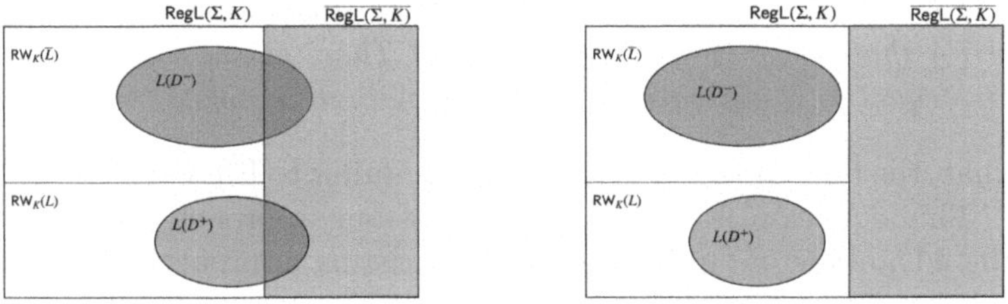

(a) Completeness (b) Strong-completeness

Fig. 2. Illustration of the two completeness criteria

However, to show the minimality in the number of states of the final DERA returned by our greybox learning algorithm, we introduce *strong-completeness*, by strengthening the condition on the language accepted by a 3DFA D as follows: $L(D^+) = L^{\mathsf{rw}}(D^+)$, and $L(D^-) = L^{\mathsf{rw}}(D^-)$. In other words, we require that all the inconsistent words lead to a "don't care" state in D.

Definition 4 (Strong-completeness). *A 3DFA D over $\Sigma \times \mathsf{Reg}(\Sigma, K)$ is* strongly-complete *w.r.t. the timed language L if D is complete w.r.t. L and additionally, every region word that is strongly accepted or strongly rejected by D must be consistent,* i.e., *if $L^{\mathsf{tw}}(D^+) \subseteq L$ and $L(D^+) = L^{\mathsf{rw}}(D^+)$; and $L^{\mathsf{tw}}(D^-) \subseteq \overline{L}$ and $L(D^-) = L^{\mathsf{rw}}(D^-)$.*

Corollary 1. *Let L be a timed language over Σ recognized by a K-DERA A over Σ, then for any 3DFA D over $\Sigma \times \mathsf{Reg}(\Sigma, K)$, D is strongly-complete w.r.t. L iff $L(D^+) \subseteq L^{\mathsf{rw}}(A) = \mathsf{RW}_K(L)$ and $L(D^-) \subseteq L^{\mathsf{rw}}(\overline{A}) = \mathsf{RW}_K(\overline{L})$. D is strongly-complete w.r.t. L iff $L(D^+) \subseteq \mathsf{RW}_K(L)$ and $L(D^-) \subseteq \mathsf{RW}_K(\overline{L})$.*

A pictorial representation of completeness and strong-completeness are given in Fig. 2. A dual notion of completeness, called *soundness* can also be defined in this context, however, since we will only need that notion for showing the termination of tLSep, we will introduce it in the next section.

4 The tLSep Algorithm

To learn a ERA-recognizable language L, we adopt the following greybox learning algorithm, that is an adaptation of the separation algorithm proposed in [7]. The main steps of the algorithm are the following: we first learn a (strongly-) complete 3DFA D_i that maps finite words on the alphabet $\Sigma \times \mathsf{Reg}(\Sigma, K)$ to $\{0, 1, ?\}$, where 1 means "accept", 0 means "reject", and ? means "don't care". The 3DFA D_i is used to represent a family of regular languages L such that $L \models D_i$. We then extract from D_i a minimal automaton C_i that is compatible with the 3DFA D_i, *i.e.*, such that $L(C_i) \models D_i$. Finally, we check, using two inclusion queries, if C_i satisfies the equation $L^{\mathsf{tw}}(A) = L^{\mathsf{tw}}(C_i)$. If this is the case then we return C_i, otherwise, we use the counterexample to this equality check to learn a new 3DFA D_{i+1}. We now give details of the greybox in the following subsections, and we conclude this section with the properties of our algorithm.

4.1 Learning the 3DFA D_i

In this step, we learn the 3DFA D_i, by relying on a modified version of L^*. Similar to L^*, we maintain an observation table (S, E, T), where S (the set of 'prefixes') and E (the set of 'suffixes') are sets of region words. $T : (S.E) \to \{0, 1, ?\}$ is a function that maps the region words $s.e$, where $s \in S, e \in E$, to 1 if $[\![s.e]\!] \subseteq L$, 0 if $[\![s.e]\!] \cap L = \emptyset$ and to ? if $[\![s.e]\!] = \emptyset$. Crucially, we restrict *membership queries* exclusively to consistent region words. The rationale is that queries for inconsistent words are redundant, given our understanding that such words invariably yield a "?" response from the `Teacher`. This approach streamlines the learning phase by reducing the number of necessary membership queries. We can see the 3DFA D_i defining a space of solutions for the automaton C that must be discovered.

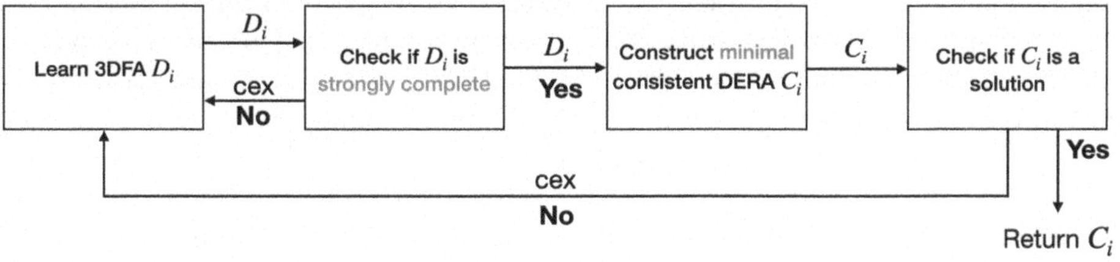

Fig. 3. Overview of the tLSep algorithm

4.2 Checking if the 3DFA D_i Is (Strongly-)complete

We can interpret the 3DFA D_i as the definition for a space of solutions for recognizing the region language $\mathsf{RW}_K(L)$. To ensure that the final DERA of our algorithm has the minimum number of states, we rely on the fact that at every iteration i, D_i is *strongly-complete*. To this end, we show the following result:

Lemma 9. *Let L be a timed language, and $A = (Q, q_{\mathsf{init}}, \Sigma, E, F)$ be a K-DERA with the* minimum *number of states accepting L. Let $C_i = (Q', q'_{\mathsf{init}}, \Sigma \times \mathsf{Reg}(\Sigma, K), \delta, F')$ be the minimal consistent DFA such that $L(C_i) \models D_i$. If D_i is strongly-complete, then $|Q| \geq |Q'|$.*

Proof. We shall show that $L^{\mathsf{s\text{-}rw}}(A)$ is consistent with D_i. First, if $\mathsf{w} \in L(D_i^+)$, then $\mathsf{w} \in L^{\mathsf{rw}}(D_i^+)$ (since strongly-complete), therefore from Corollary 1, $\mathsf{w} \in L^{\mathsf{rw}}(A)$ and hence $\mathsf{w} \in L^{\mathsf{s\text{-}rw}}(A)$. For the other side, if $\mathsf{w} \in L(D_i^-)$, then $\mathsf{w} \in L^{\mathsf{rw}}(D_i^-)$, and again from Corollary 1, $\mathsf{w} \in L^{\mathsf{rw}}(\overline{A})$, which is equivalent to $\mathsf{w} \in L^{\mathsf{s\text{-}rw}}(\overline{A}) \cap \mathsf{RegL}(\Sigma, K)$. Now note that $L^{\mathsf{s\text{-}rw}}(\overline{A}) = \overline{L^{\mathsf{s\text{-}rw}}(A)}$, and hence $\mathsf{w} \in \overline{L^{\mathsf{s\text{-}rw}}(A)} \cap \mathsf{RegL}(\Sigma, K)$, and so, $\mathsf{w} \in \overline{L^{\mathsf{s\text{-}rw}}(A)}$. Therefore, $L^{\mathsf{s\text{-}rw}}(A)$ is consistent with D_i. From hypothesis, C_i is the *minimal* DFA that is consistent with D_i. Therefore, it follows that $|Q| \geq |Q'|$.

The lemma above implies that if we compute a minimal consistent DFA C_i from a strongly-complete 3DFA D_i w.r.t. the timed language L and if this C_i satisfies Eq. 1, then C_i recognizes (when it is interpreted as a DERA) L and it has the minimum number of states among every DERA recognizing L. The two requirements – D_i being *strongly*-complete and C_i being a *minimal* consistent DFA – are necessary to ensure that the resulting DERA for L has the minimum number of states. However, checking both of these requirements are computationally expensive. First, for *strong*-completeness, one needs to check that no inconsistent region word is strongly accepted or strongly rejected by the 3DFA D_i. This can be done by checking if every region word that is either strongly accepted or strongly rejected by D_i is accepted by a DFA recognizing the regular language $\overline{\mathsf{RegL}(\Sigma, K)}$ – this is computationally hard due to the size of the latter. Second, computing a minimal consistent DFA C_i from D_i requires essentially to find a DFA that accepts every region word that is strongly accepted by D_i and rejects every region word that is strongly rejected by D_i. This is a generalization of the problem of finding a DFA with minimum number of states accepting a set of positive words and rejecting a set of negative words, which is known – due to the works of Gold [10] – to be a computationally hard problem. In practice, we generally do not require (as is also remarked in [7]) the automaton with the *minimum* number of states, instead it is sufficient to compute an automaton with a *small* number of states – provided it makes the algorithm computationally easier. To this end, instead of implementing the algorithm depicted in Fig. 3, we instead implement the algorithm depicted in Fig. 4 that employs two relaxations – (i) we only compute a *complete* 3DFA D_i, and (ii) we only compute a *small* (not necessarily minimal) C_i consistent with D_i. Whereas checking whether a 3DFA is complete or not can be done by checking the two inclusions mentioned in Definition 3, we present a heuristic for computing a small consistent DFA in the next section. These two relaxations come at the cost of minimality of the solution, however, we show in Theorem 2 that this version of our algorithm still correctly computes a DERA recognizing L. As we will see in Sect. 5, our implementation returns an automaton with a reasonably small, sometimes minimum, number of states.

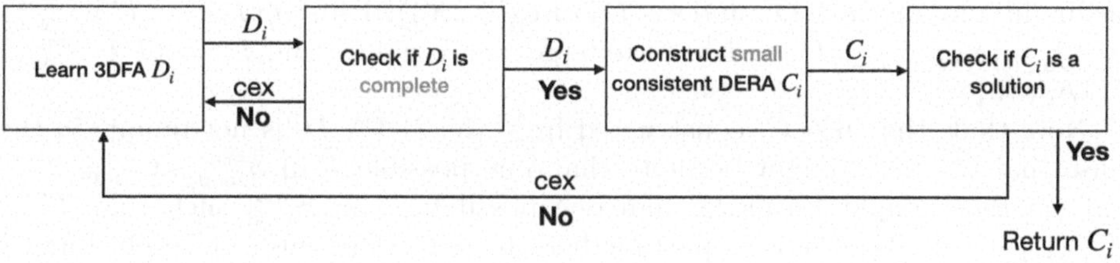

Fig. 4. Overview of the tLSep algorithm with heuristics

4.3 Computing a Small Candidate C_i from D_i

In this section, we detail a heuristic that computes a small candidate DFA C_i from a 3DFA D_i that is complete with respect to L. For the rest of this section, we fix the notation for the 3DFA $D_i = (Q_i, q_{\mathsf{init}}, (\Sigma \times \mathsf{Reg}(\Sigma, K)), \delta_i, \mathsf{A_i}, \mathsf{R_i}, \mathsf{E_i})$.

The first step is to find the set of all pairs of states that are *incompatible* in D_i. Two states are *incompatible* if there exists a region word $\mathsf{w} \in (\Sigma \times \mathsf{Reg}(\Sigma, K))^*$ s.t. w leads one of them to an accepting state in $\mathsf{A_i}$ and another to a rejecting state in $\mathsf{R_i}$. Notice that, in the above definition, one does not take into account the timing constraints of a word, and that is precisely the reason why in the final automaton, the *inconsistent* words may lead to any state, unlike in a "simple DERA" for the corresponding timed language, where the inconsistent words must be rejected syntactically by the automaton, enabling it to be (possibly) smaller than the "minimal simple DERA".

We recursively compute the set S_{bad} of incompatible pairs of states as follows: initially add every pair (q, q') into S_{bad} where $q \in \mathsf{A_i}$, $q' \in \mathsf{R_i}$; then recursively add new pairs as long as possible: add a new pair (q_1, q_2) into S_{bad} s.t. there exists a letter $e \in \Sigma \times \mathsf{Reg}(\Sigma, K)$ s.t. $q_1 \xrightarrow{e} q_1'$ and $q_2 \xrightarrow{e} q_2'$ and $(q_1', q_2') \in S_{\mathsf{bad}}$.

The second step is to find the set of all $\subseteq$-*maximal sets* that are compatible in D_i. A set of states of D_i is *compatible* if it does not contain any incompatible pair. The set of maximal sets of compatible pairs, denoted by $S_{\mathsf{good}}^{\mathsf{max}}$, can be computed recursively as follows: initially, $S_{\mathsf{good}}^{\mathsf{max}} = \{Q_i\}$; at any iteration, if there exists a set $T \in S_{\mathsf{good}}^{\mathsf{max}}$ s.t. there exists a pair $(q, q') \in T \cap S_{\mathsf{bad}}$, we do the following operation: $S_{\mathsf{good}}^{\mathsf{max}} := (S_{\mathsf{good}}^{\mathsf{max}} \setminus T) \cup (T \setminus \{q\}) \cup (T \setminus \{q'\})$, with the condition that $T \setminus \{q\}$ is added to the set $S_{\mathsf{good}}^{\mathsf{max}}$ only if there exists no T' in $S_{\mathsf{good}}^{\mathsf{max}}$ such that

$T' \supseteq T \setminus \{q\}$, and similarly for $T \setminus \{q'\}$. Then we can prove the correctness of the above procedure in the following manner.

Theorem 1. *The above procedure terminates. Moreover, the set* $S_{\mathsf{good}}^{\mathsf{max}}$ *returned by the algorithm is the set of all maximal compatible sets in the 3DFA* D_i.

In the final step, we define a DFA $C_i = (Q'_i, q'_{\mathsf{init}}, (\Sigma \times \mathsf{Reg}(\Sigma, K)), \delta'_i, F_i)$, where: $Q'_i = S_{\mathsf{good}}^{\mathsf{max}}$; $q'_{\mathsf{init}} = T \in S_{\mathsf{good}}^{\mathsf{max}}$ s.t. $q_{\mathsf{init}} \in T$, and T has the highest cardinality; for any $T \in Q'_i$, and $e \in (\Sigma \times \mathsf{Reg}(\Sigma, K))$, define $\delta'_i(T, e) = T' \in S_{\mathsf{good}}^{\mathsf{max}}$ s.t. $\bigcup_{q \in T}\{\delta_i(q, e)\} \subseteq T'$, and has the largest cardinality; and $F_i := \{T \in S_{\mathsf{good}}^{\mathsf{max}} \mid T \cap \mathsf{A_i} \neq \emptyset\}$.

Note that, the DFA C_i constructed from the 3DFA D_i is not unique in the sense that (1) there might be more than one possible T in $S_{\mathsf{good}}^{\mathsf{max}}$ s.t. $q_{\mathsf{init}} \in T$, and (2) there might be more than one possible T' in $S_{\mathsf{good}}^{\mathsf{max}}$ such that $T' \supseteq \bigcup_{q \in T}\{\delta_i(q, e)\}$. Also, it is important here to note that, one can apply further heuristics at this step, in particular, while adding a new transition from T on e, if there is already some maximal set T' that has been discovered previously, set the target of this transition to T', even if it is not of maximum cardinality.

Lemma 10. *For any 3DFA* D_i, *the procedure described above is well-defined. Then for any* C_i *constructed according to the procedure,* C_i *is consistent with* D_i, i.e., $L(D_i^+) \subseteq L(C_i)$ *and* $L(D_i^-) \subseteq \overline{L(C_i)}$.

Taking intersection with $\mathsf{RegL}(\Sigma, K)$ on both sides, together with Lemma 6, we get the following corollary:

Corollary 2. $L^{\mathsf{rw}}(D_i^+) \subseteq L^{\mathsf{rw}}(C_i)$, *and* $L^{\mathsf{rw}}(D_i^-) \subseteq \overline{L^{\mathsf{rw}}(C_i)} \cap \mathsf{RegL}(\Sigma, K)$.

4.4 Checking if C_i Is a Solution

Now that C_i has been extracted from D_i, we can query the `Teacher` with two inclusion queries that check if $L^{\mathsf{tw}}(C_i) = L$. If the answer is yes, then C_i is a solution to our the learning problem, and we return the automaton C_i; otherwise, the `Teacher` returns a counterexample – a consistent region word that is either accepted by C_i but is not in $\mathsf{RW}_K(L)$, or a consistent region word that is rejected by C_i but is in $\mathsf{RW}_K(L)$. Notice that the equality check has been defined above as an equality check between two timed languages, whereas, the counterexamples returned by the `Teacher` are region words. This is not contradictory, indeed, one can show a similar result to Lemma 7 that $L^{\mathsf{tw}}(C_i) = L$ iff $L^{\mathsf{rw}}(C_i) = \mathsf{RW}_K(L)$. More details on how the counter-example is extracted from the answer received from the `Teacher` is described in Sect. 5. We will show in Lemma 11 that a counterexample to the equality check is also a 'discrepancy' in the 3DFA D_i. Therefore, this counterexample is used to update the observation table as in L^* to produce the subsequent hypothesis D_{i+1}.

4.5 Correctness of the tLSep Algorithm

Definition 5 (Soundness). *A 3DFA D over $\Sigma \times \mathsf{Reg}(\Sigma, K)$ is* sound *w.r.t. the timed language L if the timed language of D^+, when interpreted as a DERA, contains L,* i.e., *$L \subseteq L^{\mathsf{tw}}(D^+)$; and the timed language of D^-, when interpreted as a DERA, contains $\overline{L}$,* i.e., *$\overline{L} \subseteq L^{\mathsf{tw}}(D^-)$.*

The following lemma shows that a counter-example of the equality check in Sect. 4.4 is also a counter-example to the soundness of D_i:

Lemma 11. *If a counter-example is generated for the equality check against C_i, then the corresponding 3DFA D_i is not sound w.r.t. $\mathsf{RW}_K(L)$.*

We can prove the following using similar lines of arguments as in [7].

Theorem 2. *Let L be a timed language over Σ recognizable by a ERA given as input to the* tLSep *algorithm. Then: (1) the algorithm* tLSep *terminates, (2) the algorithm* tLSep *is correct,* i.e., *letting C be the automaton returned by the algorithm, $L^{\mathsf{tw}}(C) = L$, and (3) at every iteration of* tLSep*, if strong-completeness is checked for 3DFA D_i, and if a minimization procedure is used to construct C_i, then C has a minimal number of states.*

5 Implementation and Its Performance

We have made a prototype implementation of tLSep in PYTHON. Parts of our implementation are inspired from the implementation of L^* in AALpy [18]. For the experiments, we assume that the `Teacher` has access to a DERA A recognizing the target timed language L. Below, we describe how we implement the sub-procedures. Note that, in our implementation, we check for completeness, and not for strong-completeness, of the 3DFA's.

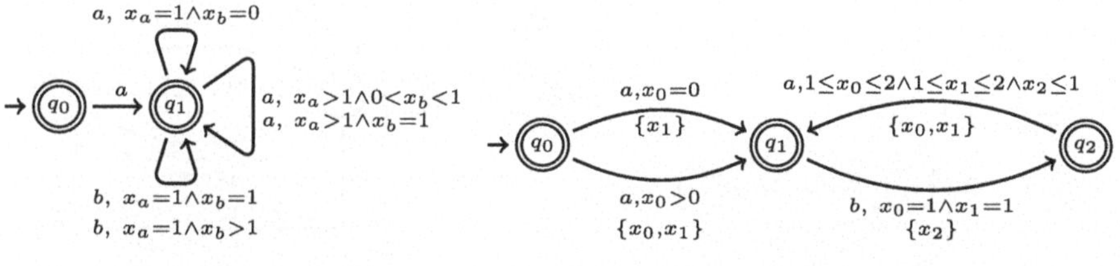

(a) output of tLSep (b) output of LearnTA

Fig. 5. The automata computed by the two algorithms on Fig. 1

Emptiness of Region Words. Since we do not perform a membership query for inconsistent region words, before every membership query, we first check if the region word is consistent or not (in agreement with our greybox learning framework described in Page 9). The consistency check is performed by encoding the region word as an SMT formula in Linear Real Arithmetic and then checking (using the SMT solver Z3 [17]) if the formula is satisfiable or not. Unsatisfiability of the formula implies the region word is inconsistent.

Inclusion of Timed Languages. We check inclusion between timed languages recognizable by ERA in two situations: (i) while making the 3DFA D_i complete (cf. Definition 3), and (ii) during checking if the constructed DERA C_i recognizes L (cf. Definition 5). Both of these checks can be reduced to checking emptiness of appropriate automata. We perform the emptiness checks using the reachability algorithm (covreach) implemented inside the tool TChecker [12].

Counterexample Processing. When one of the language inclusions during completeness checking returns False, we obtain a 'concrete' path from TChecker that acts as a certificate for non-emptiness. The path is of the form:

$$\mathsf{cex} := (q_0, v_0) \xrightarrow[\{x_{\sigma_1}\}]{\sigma_1,\ g_1} (q_1, v_1) \xrightarrow[\{x_{\sigma_2}\}]{\sigma_2,\ g_2} (q_2, v_2) \ldots (q_{n-1}, v_{n-1}) \xrightarrow[\{x_{\sigma_n}\}]{\sigma_n,\ g_n} (q_n, v_n)$$

Since the guards present in the automata D_i^+, D_i^- are region words, every guard present in the product automaton is also a region word. From cex we then construct the region word $(\sigma_1, g_1)(\sigma_2, g_2)\ldots(\sigma_n, g_n)$. We then use the algorithm proposed by Rivest-Schapire [13,19] to compute the 'witnessing suffix' ws from cex and then add ws to the set of suffixes (E) of the observation table. On the other hand, when we receive a counterexample during the soundness check, we add all the prefixes of this counterexample to the set S instead. Note that, the guards on transitions in our output are simple constraints, and not constraints.

We now compare the performance of our prototype implementation of tLSep against the algorithm proposed by Waga in [25] on a set of synthetic timed languages and on a benchmark taken from their tool LearnTA. We witness encouraging results, among those, we stress on the important ones below.

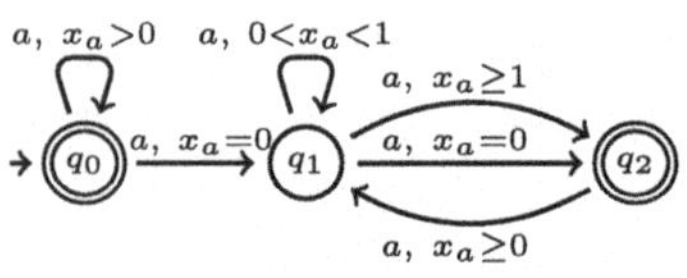

(a) Example-4

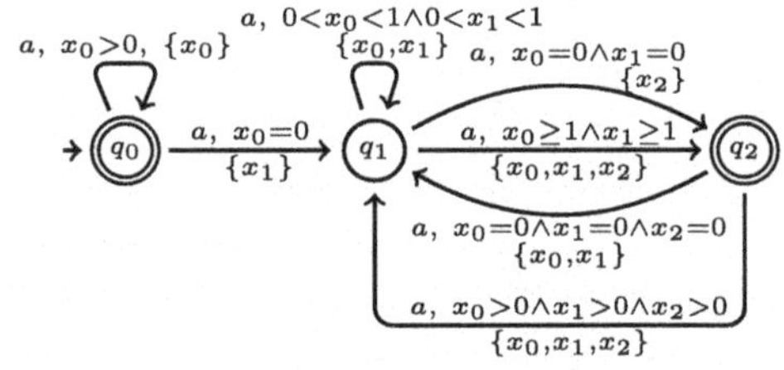

(b) DTA computed by LearnTA on Figure 6a

Fig. 6. Explainability of tLSep

Minimality. We have shown in Sect. 4 that if one ensures strong-completeness of the 3DFAs throughout the procedure, then the minimality in the number of states is assured. However, this is often the case even with only checking completeness. For instance, recall our running example from Fig. 1. For this language, our algorithm was able to find a DERA with only two states (depicted in Fig. 5a) – which is indeed the minimum number of states. On the other hand,

LearnTA does not claim minimality in the computed automaton, and indeed for this language, they end up constructing the automaton in Fig. 5b instead. Note that for the sake of clarity, we draw a single edge from q_0 to q_1 on a in Fig. 5a, however, our implementation constructs several parallel edges (on a) between these two states, one for each constraint in $\mathsf{Reg}(\Sigma, K)$.

Explainability. From a practical point of view, explainability of the output automaton is a very important property of learning algorithms. One would ideally like the learning algorithm to return a 'readable', or easily explainable, model for the target language. We find some of the automata returned by tLSep are relatively easier to understand (due to better readability of ERA over TA) than the model returned by LearnTA. A comparative example can be found in Fig. 6.

Efficiency. We treat completeness checks for a 3DFA and language-equivalence checks for a DERA, as equivalence queries (EQ). Note that, EQ's are not new queries, these are merely (at most) two Inclusion Queries (IQ). We report on the number of queries for tLSep and LearnTA in Table 2 on a set of examples. For both the algorithms, we only report on the number of queries 'with memory' in the sense that we fetch the answer to a query from the memory if it was already computed. Notice that LearnTA uses two types of membership queries, called *symbolic queries* (s-MQ) and *timed-queries* (t-MQ), and in most of the examples, tLSep needs much lesser number of membership queries than LearnTA.

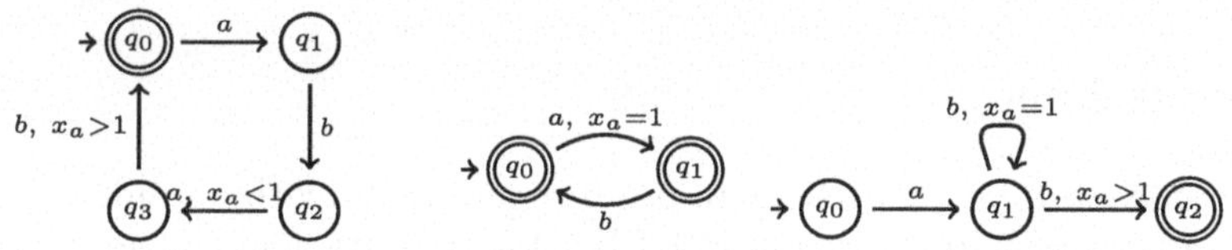

(a) Example-1 (b) Example-2 (c) Example-3

Fig. 7. Automata corresponding to the models ex1, ex2 and ex3 of the table

Below we give brief descriptions of languages mentioned in Table 2. The timed language (ex1) has untimed language $(abab)^*$, where in every such four letter block, the second a must occur before 1 time unit of the first a and the second b must occur after 1 time unit since the first a. The language (ex2) has untimed language $(ab)^*$, where the first a happens at 1 time unit and every subsequent a occurs exactly 1 time unit after the preceding a. The timed language (ex3) consists of timed words whose untimed language is ab^*b, and the first a can occur at any time, then there can be several b's all exactly 1 time unit after a, and then the last b occurs strictly after 1 time unit since the first a (Fig. 7). The language (ex4) is the language represented by the automaton in Fig. 6a.

Although the class of ERA-recognizable languages is a strict subclass of DTA-recognizable languages, we found a set of benchmarks from the LearnTA tool, that are in fact event-recording automata (after renaming the clocks). This example is called *Unbalanced*, Table 2 shows that tLSep uses significantly lesser number of queries than LearnTA for these, illustrating the gains of our greybox approach.

Table 2. Experimental results. Here K denotes the maximum constant appearing in the automaton provided as input to the algorithm, $|Q|$ and $|\Sigma|$ denote the numbers of states and the alphabet. Note that, for some of these automata, $|Q|$ specified in the table is one more than what are depicted in the figures. This is because, in our implementation, we need to provide automata that are total.

Model	K	$\|Q\|$	$\|\Sigma\|$	tLSep			LearnTA		
				MQ	IQ	EQ	s – MQ	t – MQ	EQ
Figure 1	1	4	2	98	8	5	230	219	4
ex1	1	5	2	219	11	6	296	365	4
ex2	1	3	2	220	12	7	247	233	5
ex3	2	4	2	87	7	4	123	173	3
ex4	1	3	1	26	5	3	40	43	2
Unbalanced-1	1	5	3	421	17	12	1717	2394	6
Unbalanced-2	2	5	3	1095	27	20	7347	13227	10
Unbalanced-3	3	5	3	2087	37	28	21200	45400	17

6 Discussions

Our grey box learning algorithm can produce automata with a minimal number of states, equivalent to the minimal DERA for the target language. Currently, the transitions are labeled with region constraints. In the future, we plan to implement a procedure that consolidates edges labeled with the same event and regions, whose unions are convex, into a single edge with a zone constraint. This planned procedure aims to not only maintain an automaton with the fewest possible states, but also to minimize the number of edges and zones. Such optimization could further enhance the readability of the models we produce, thereby improving explainability—an increasingly important aspect of machine learning.

Building on our proposed future work above, we also aim to refine our approach to membership queries. Instead of defaulting to queries on regions where it may not be necessary, we plan to consider queries on zones. If the response from the `Teacher` is not uniform across the zone, only then will we break down the queries into more specific sub-queries, ending in regions if necessary. This strategy will necessitate revising the current learning protocol we use, but exploring these alternatives could enhance the efficiency and effectiveness of our learning process. Similar ideas have been used in [14].

Throughout this paper, we follow the convention used in prior research [11,25] that the parameter K is predetermined (the maximal constant against which the clocks are compared). Similarly, in our experimental section, we assume we know which events need to be tracked by a clock. While these assumptions are typically reasonable in practice, it is possible to consider a more flexible approach. We could start with no predetermined events to track with clocks and only introduce clocks for events and update the maximum constant, as needed. These could be inferred from the counterexamples provided by the `Teacher`.

Overall, we believe the greybox learning framework described in this work may also be well-suited for other classes of languages that enjoy a similar condition like Eq. 1, where the automaton C can be of relatively smaller size, while a canonical model recognizing L might be too large.

References

1. Abel, A., Reineke, J.: Gray-box learning of serial compositions of mealy machines. In: Rayadurgam, S., Tkachuk, O. (eds.) NFM 2016. LNCS, vol. 9690, pp. 272–287. Springer, Cham (2016). https://doi.org/10.1007/978-3-319-40648-0_21
2. Alur, R., Dill, D.L.: A theory of timed automata. Theor. Comput. Sci. **126**(2), 183–235 (1994)
3. Alur, R., Fix, L., Henzinger, T.A.: Event-clock automata: a determinizable class of timed automata. Theor. Comput. Sci. **211**(1–2), 253–273 (1999)
4. An, J., Wang, L., Zhan, B., Zhan, N., Zhang, M.: Learning real-time automata. Sci. China Inf. Sci. **64**(9) (2021)
5. Angluin, D.: Learning regular sets from queries and counterexamples. Inf. Comput. **75**(2), 87–106 (1987)
6. Bruyère, V., Garhewal, B., Pérez, G.A., Staquet, G., Vaandrager, F.W.: Active learning of mealy machines with timers. CoRR **abs/2403.02019** (2024). https://doi.org/10.48550/arXiv.2403.02019
7. Chen, Y.-F., Farzan, A., Clarke, E.M., Tsay, Y.-K., Wang, B.-Y.: Learning minimal separating DFA's for compositional verification. In: Kowalewski, S., Philippou, A. (eds.) TACAS 2009. LNCS, vol. 5505, pp. 31–45. Springer, Heidelberg (2009). https://doi.org/10.1007/978-3-642-00768-2_3
8. Cornanguer, L., Largouët, C., Rozé, L., Termier, A.: TAG: learning timed automata from logs. In: AAAI, pp. 3949–3958. AAAI Press (2022)
9. Dill, D.L.: Timing assumptions and verification of finite-state concurrent systems. In: Sifakis, J. (ed.) CAV 1989. LNCS, vol. 407, pp. 197–212. Springer, Heidelberg (1990). https://doi.org/10.1007/3-540-52148-8_17
10. Gold, E.M.: Complexity of automaton identification from given data. Inf. Control **37**(3), 302–320 (1978). https://doi.org/10.1016/S0019-9958(78)90562-4
11. Grinchtein, O., Jonsson, B., Leucker, M.: Learning of event-recording automata. Theor. Comput. Sci. **411**(47), 4029–4054 (2010)
12. Herbreteau, F., Point, G.: Tchecker. https://github.com/ticktac-project/tchecker
13. Isberner, M., Steffen, B.: An abstract framework for counterexample analysis in active automata learning. In: ICGI. JMLR Workshop and Conference Proceedings, vol. 34, pp. 79–93. JMLR.org (2014)
14. Lin, S.-W., André, É., Dong, J.S., Sun, J., Liu, Y.: An efficient algorithm for learning event-recording automata. In: Bultan, T., Hsiung, P.-A. (eds.) ATVA 2011. LNCS, vol. 6996, pp. 463–472. Springer, Heidelberg (2011). https://doi.org/10.1007/978-3-642-24372-1_35

15. Majumdar, A., Mukherjee, S., Raskin, J.F.: Greybox learning of languages recognizable by event-recording automata (2024). https://arxiv.org/abs/2408.12551
16. Moeller, M., Wiener, T., Solko-Breslin, A., Koch, C., Foster, N., Silva, A.: Automata learning with an incomplete teacher. In: ECOOP. LIPIcs, vol. 263, pp. 21:1–21:30. Schloss Dagstuhl - Leibniz-Zentrum für Informatik (2023)
17. de Moura, L., Bjørner, N.: Z3: an efficient SMT solver. In: Ramakrishnan, C.R., Rehof, J. (eds.) TACAS 2008. LNCS, vol. 4963, pp. 337–340. Springer, Heidelberg (2008). https://doi.org/10.1007/978-3-540-78800-3_24
18. Muškardin, E., Aichernig, B., Pill, I., Pferscher, A., Tappler, M.: AALpy: an active automata learning library. Innovations Syst. Softw. Eng. **18**, 1–10 (2022). https://doi.org/10.1007/s11334-022-00449-3
19. Rivest, R.L., Schapire, R.E.: Inference of finite automata using homing sequences. Inf. Comput. **103**(2), 299–347 (1993)
20. Tappler, M., Aichernig, B.K., Larsen, K.G., Lorber, F.: Time to learn – learning timed automata from tests. In: André, É., Stoelinga, M. (eds.) FORMATS 2019. LNCS, vol. 11750, pp. 216–235. Springer, Cham (2019). https://doi.org/10.1007/978-3-030-29662-9_13
21. Teng, Y., Zhang, M., An, J.: Learning deterministic multi-clock timed automata. In: HSCC, pp. 6:1–6:11. ACM (2024)
22. Vaandrager, F.W.: Model learning. Commun. ACM **60**(2), 86–95 (2017)
23. Vaandrager, F., Bloem, R., Ebrahimi, M.: Learning mealy machines with one timer. In: Leporati, A., Martín-Vide, C., Shapira, D., Zandron, C. (eds.) LATA 2021. LNCS, vol. 12638, pp. 157–170. Springer, Cham (2021). https://doi.org/10.1007/978-3-030-68195-1_13
24. Verwer, S., de Weerdt, M., Witteveen, C.: One-clock deterministic timed automata are efficiently identifiable in the limit. In: Dediu, A.H., Ionescu, A.M., Martín-Vide, C. (eds.) LATA 2009. LNCS, vol. 5457, pp. 740–751. Springer, Heidelberg (2009). https://doi.org/10.1007/978-3-642-00982-2_63
25. Waga, M.: Active learning of deterministic timed automata with Myhill-Nerode style characterization. In: Enea, C., Lal, A. (eds.) CAV 2023. LNCS, vol. 13964, pp. 3–26. Springer, Cham (2023). https://doi.org/10.1007/978-3-031-37706-8_1
26. Xu, R., An, J., Zhan, B.: Active learning of one-clock timed automata using constraint solving. In: Bouajjani, A., Holík, L., Wu, Z. (eds.) ATVA 2022. LNCS, vol. 13505, pp. 249–265. Springer, Cham (2022). https://doi.org/10.1007/978-3-031-19992-9_16

Query Learning Bounds for Advice and Nominal Automata

Kevin Zhou(✉)

University of Illinois Chicago, Chicago, IL 60607, USA
kzhou23@uic.edu

Abstract. Learning automata by queries is a long-studied area initiated by Angluin in 1987 with the introduction of the L^* algorithm to learn regular languages, with a large body of work afterwards on many different variations and generalizations of DFAs. Recently, Chase and Freitag introduced a novel approach to proving query learning bounds by computing combinatorial complexity measures for the classes in question, which they applied to the setting of DFAs to obtain qualitatively different results compared to the L^* algorithm. Using this approach, we prove new query learning bounds for two generalizations of DFAs. The first setting is that of advice DFAs, which are DFAs augmented with an advice string that informs the DFA's transition behavior at each step. For advice DFAs, we give the first known upper bounds for query complexity. The second setting is that of nominal DFAs, which generalize DFAs to infinite alphabets which admit some structure via symmetries. For nominal DFAs, we make qualitative improvements over prior results.

Keywords: Advice automata · Nominal automata · Query learning

1 Introduction

Learning various forms of automata with queries is a well-studied class of problems with many applications, including in AI, automatic verification, and model checking. The field was initiated by Angluin in 1987 with the introduction of the L^* algorithm that learns deterministic finite automata (DFAs) using a polynomially bounded number of equivalence and membership queries [1]. The L^* algorithm has seen many applications and has also inspired generalizations to other types of automata, such as tree automata [21], nondeterministic finite automata [6], ω-automata [2], symbolic automata [9], and fully-ordered lattice automata [11]. The setting of learning with queries is especially well-suited for learning automata—in real-world applications where the task is to identify the behavior of some black-box system that can be modelled by an automaton, queries can be simulated by interacting with the system and observing the output.

Historically, the study of query learning of automata has centered around adapting Angluin's L^* algorithm to different settings. We do not do this, and instead build on a method introduced by Chase & Freitag [8], who give query

S. Akshay et al. (Eds.): ATVA 2024, LNCS 15054, pp. 257–278, 2025.
https://doi.org/10.1007/978-3-031-78709-6_13

learning bounds in terms of *Littlestone dimension* and *consistency dimension*, which are complexity measures for concept classes. One can then prove a query learning bound in a given setting by computing the Littlestone and consistency dimensions. This approach seems to be particularly effective for learning automata, since many types of automata exhibit form of Myhill-Nerode characterization, which can be used to bound the consistency dimension. For example, Chase and Freitag apply this method for regular languages and regular ω-languages and obtain qualitatively different results from prior work. Our work serves as further proof of concept of this method.

Our work studies the learnability of two generalizations of DFAs. The first is advice DFAs, which were studied as early as 1968 by Salomaa [22], though we follow the notation of Kruckman et al. [15]. Advice DFAs generalize classical DFAs by allowing the automata access to an additional advice string that it reads concurrently with the input, and are useful in modeling situations where the transition behavior can vary over time. They are also of interest to the logic community: it is a classical result that DFAs correspond to weak monadic second-order formulas over the structure of natural numbers with the successor operation; advice DFAs correspond to formulas over expansions of this structure by unary predicates, a frequently studied setting; see e.g. [4,7,10,20]. Another motivating factor for advice DFAs comes from the study of *automatic structures*, which are structures whose domain and atomic relations are recognized by DFAs. It turns out some natural structures are not automatic or even isomorphic to an automatic structure, such as $(\mathbb{Q}, +)$, the additive group of the rationals [23]. However, $(\mathbb{Q}, +)$ *is* isomorphic to a structure whose domain and atomic relations are recognized by advice DFAs [15,18].

The second setting we consider is that of nominal DFAs, introduced by Bojańczyk, Klin, and Lasota [5], which generalize DFAs to infinite alphabets. Generalizing formal language theory to infinite alphabets is highly non-trivial, since without any restrictions, the fact that there are uncountably many subsets of any infinite set makes computation intractable. However, in most reasonable applications, there is additional structure that can be leveraged to make computation reasonable, and nominal DFAs utilize the notion of *nominal sets* (first introduced by Gabbay & Pitts [12]) to formalize this idea. Aside from the development of the theory of automata over infinite alphabets, nominal sets have also found much use in the concurrency and semantics communities as a formalism for modeling name binding (see e.g. [17,19]).

Organization of Paper and Summary of Results. In Sect. 2, we present the basic definitions and notation necessary for the remainder of the paper.

In Sect. 3, we study query learning of advice DFAs, and give the first known bound for the query complexity of advice DFAs. Our result for advice DFAs is as follows: let $\mathcal{L}_k^{\mathrm{adv}}(n, m)$ be the set of languages over an alphabet of size k recognized by an advice DFA on at most n states, restricted to strings of length at most m.

Theorem 4. *The (EQ+MQ)-query complexity of* $\mathcal{L}_k^{adv}(n, m)$ *with queries from* $\mathcal{L}_k^{adv}(2n, m)$ *is* $O(n^3 mk \log n)$.

In Sect. 4, we study query learning of nominal DFAs. Query learning of nominal DFAs was previously studied by Moerman et al. [16]. We give a qualitative improvement over this previous result; a detailed comparison is given in the discussion below. Our result for nominal DFAs is as follows: given a G-alphabet A, let $\mathcal{L}_A^{\mathrm{nom}}(n, k)$ denote the set of G-languages recognized by a nominal DFA with at most n orbits and nominal dimension at most k.

Theorem 6. *For a fixed G-alphabet A, the (EQ+MQ)-query complexity of* $\mathcal{L}_A^{nom}(n, k)$ *with queries from* $\mathcal{L}_A^{nom}(n, k)$ *is at most* $\frac{n^{O(k)}}{k^k}$.

Due to space constraints, some proofs are omitted, and given in the appendix of the full version of this paper.

Discussion and Related Work. The approach of Chase & Freitag of deriving query complexity bounds by computing bounds on various combinatorial notions of dimension is a fairly novel one, and in [8] they illustrate its usefulness by easily proving polynomial query learning bounds for regular languages. The approach gives a qualitatively different bound compared to the one given by the L^* algorithm—their results have no dependence on the length of the longest counterexample returned by the oracle (while the L^* algorithm does), but a worse dependence on the number of states. They also do not give any computational complexity guarantees—their algorithm requires computing the Littlestone dimension and finding witnesses to the consistency dimension, which in general may be hard computational problems.

As mentioned, in the setting of advice DFAs, we give the first known bounds on the query complexity. The restriction on the length of the strings in $\mathcal{L}_k^{\mathrm{adv}}(n, m)$ is necessary to make the problem tractable and can be thought of as giving a dependence on the length of the longest counterexample for equivalence queries. It may be of interest to see if there is an analogous version of the L^* algorithm for advice DFAs, and if so, how the bounds with that approach compare to ours.

The prior best known bound for query complexity of nominal DFAs is given by Moerman et al. in [16], using a generalization of Angluin's L^* algorithm to nominal DFAs. The bound that they derive is a complicated quantity (see [16, Corollary 1]), but in particular we observe the following: if the target automaton has n orbits and nominal dimension k, p is the nominal dimension of the (fixed) alphabet, and m is the length of the longest counterexample returned by the oracle, then their bound is lower bounded by both

(a) $\min\left(\left(\frac{nk}{e}\right)^m, \left(\frac{m}{e}\right)^{nk}\right)$ and
(b) $(k^n n!)^p$.

These are not explicitly stated in the original work, but follow with some additional work (see Remark 4).

Our result improves on (a) since our bound does not depend on the length of the longest counterexample, and improves the asymptotic dependence on n compared to (b) (polynomial in n with respect to k, instead of factorial in n). This is especially important in light of Corollary 1, which says that in this setting, k is at most a constant multiple of n. However, as with Chase & Freitag's result on classical DFAs, we give no computational complexity guarantees.

2 Preliminaries

2.1 Query Learning

Let X be a set (the *instance space*). A *concept* is a function $C : X \to \{0, 1\}$, and a *concept class* $\mathcal{C}$ on X is a nonempty set of concepts. We note that a concept is sometimes equivalently defined as a subset of X, but for our purposes it will be easier to work with functions. Fix a concept $C \in \mathcal{C}$, which we call the *target*, and another concept class $\mathcal{H} \supseteq \mathcal{C}$, which we call the *hypothesis class*. An *equivalence query* (EQ) consists of a hypothesis $H \in \mathcal{H}$, to which the oracle answers *yes* if $H = C$, or with a counterexample $x \in X$ for which $H(x) \neq C(x)$. A *membership query* (MQ) consists of an element $x \in X$, to which the oracle responds with the value of $C(x)$. The learning procedure proceeds interactively in rounds: in each round, the learner poses a query to the oracle, and the oracle responds with the corresponding answer. The learner is allowed to choose queries based on the responses to previous queries, and succeeds if they submit the target as an equivalence query. In *EQ-learning*, the learner is only allowed to submit equivalence queries, while in *(EQ+MQ)-learning*, the learner can use both equivalence and membership queries.

Definition 1 (Query Complexity). *Let $\mathcal{C} \subseteq \mathcal{H}$ be two concept classes. The* EQ-query complexity of $\mathcal{C}$ with queries from $\mathcal{H}$ *is defined to be the least n such that there is an algorithm for the learner to submit equivalence queries from $\mathcal{H}$ with the property that for any $C \in \mathcal{C}$, the learner can identify C within at most n queries, or ∞ if no such n exists.*

The (EQ+MQ)-query complexity of $\mathcal{C}$ with queries from $\mathcal{H}$ *is defined in the same way, except that the learner is allowed to also use membership queries.*

A significant stream of prior work studied bounds for the query complexity of $\mathcal{C}$ with hypotheses from $\mathcal{H}$ in terms of combinatorial complexity measures of $\mathcal{C}$ and $\mathcal{H}$ [3,8,13,14]. These bounds are formulated in terms of the *Littlestone dimension*, *consistency dimension*, and *strong consistency dimension* (also known as the *dual Helly number*), which we define now.

A *binary element tree* is a complete binary tree whose internal nodes are labeled by elements of X. A binary element tree T is *shattered* by $\mathcal{C}$ if there is a way to label all the leaves of T with elements of $\mathcal{C}$ such that the following condition holds: given a leaf node labeled by $A \in \mathcal{C}$, for each internal node above A labeled by $x \in X$, $A(x) = 1$ if and only if the (unique) path from the root to A goes through the left child of x.

An example of a (labelled) binary element tree of height 2 is given below, where $x_0, x_1, x_2 \in X$, and $C_0, C_1, C_2, C_3 \in \mathcal{C}$:

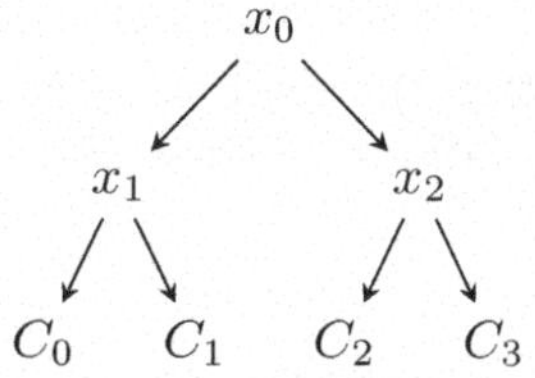

This tree is shattered exactly when $C_0(x_0) = C_0(x_1) = 1$, $C_1(x_0) = 1$ but $C_1(x_1) = 0$, $C_2(x_0) = 0$ but $C_2(x_2) = 1$, and $C_3(x_0) = C_3(x_2) = 0$.

Definition 2 (Littlestone dimension). *The* Littlestone dimension *of a concept class $\mathcal{C}$, denoted* $\mathrm{Ldim}(\mathcal{C})$, *is the maximum n such that there exists a binary element tree T of height n which is shattered by $\mathcal{C}$. If no such n exists, we say that* $\mathrm{Ldim}(\mathcal{C}) = \infty$.

Remark 1. A straightforward bound for the Littlestone dimension of a finite class $\mathcal{C}$ is $\mathrm{Ldim}(\mathcal{C}) \leq \log |\mathcal{C}|$. To see this, note that a binary element tree T of height $> \log |\mathcal{C}|$ has more than $|\mathcal{C}|$ leaves, so there must be two leaves labeled by the same element $C \in \mathcal{C}$. Consider the internal node where the paths leading to these two leaves differ; suppose it is labeled by x. Then there is a root-to-leaf path ending at C that goes through the left child of x, implying that $x \in C$. However, there is also a root-to-leaf path ending at C that goes through the right child of x, implying that $x \notin C$, so T cannot be shattered.

We now define consistency dimension. For the following bulleted definitions, let A, B be partial functions from X to $\{0, 1\}$.

- $\mathrm{dom}(A)$ denotes domain of A.
- The *size* of A refers to the cardinality of $\mathrm{dom}(A)$.
- For a set $Y \subseteq \mathrm{dom}(A)$, the *restriction* of A to Y is the partial function $A|_Y$ defined by $A|_Y(x) = A(x)$ for $x \in Y$ and undefined outside of Y.
- We say that B *extends* A if $\mathrm{dom}(A) \subseteq \mathrm{dom}(B)$ and $B|_{\mathrm{dom}(A)} = A$. On the other hand, we say that A is a *restriction* of B.
- Given a concept class $\mathcal{C}$, A is *n-consistent with* $\mathcal{C}$ if every size n restriction of A has an extension in $\mathcal{C}$. Otherwise, A is *n-inconsistent.*

Definition 3 (Consistency Dimension). *The* consistency dimension *of $\mathcal{C}$ with respect to $\mathcal{H}$, denoted* $\mathrm{Cdim}(\mathcal{C}, \mathcal{H})$, *is the least n such that for every concept $A : X \to \{0, 1\}$ that is n-consistent with $\mathcal{C}$, we have that $A \in \mathcal{H}$. If no such n exists, we say that* $\mathrm{Cdim}(\mathcal{C}, \mathcal{H}) = \infty$. *In the case that $\mathcal{H} = \mathcal{C}$, we will write* $\mathrm{Cdim}(\mathcal{C})$ *to denote* $\mathrm{Cdim}(\mathcal{C}, \mathcal{C})$.

Remark 2. By contrapositive, $\mathrm{Cdim}(\mathcal{C}, \mathcal{H}) \leq n$ if for every concept $A \notin \mathcal{H}$, A is n-inconsistent with $\mathcal{C}$. That is, we can find a subset $Y \subseteq X$ of size n such that $A|_Y$ cannot be extended to anything in $\mathcal{C}$.

It is often easier to work concretely with the contrapositive characterization of consistency dimension. Our proofs of bounds on consistency dimension will go through this direction.

Theorem 1 ([8, **Theorem 2.24**]). *Let $\mathcal{C} \subseteq \mathcal{H}$ be two concept classes on a set X, $c = \mathrm{Cdim}(\mathcal{C}, \mathcal{H})$, and $d = \mathrm{Ldim}(\mathcal{C})$. Then (EQ+MQ)-query complexity of $\mathcal{C}$ with queries from $\mathcal{H}$ is $O(cd)$.*

2.2 Deterministic Finite Automata

In this subsection, we set notation and terminology for deterministic finite automata and regular languages, and briefly review the Myhill-Nerode theorem.

Definition 4 (Deterministic Finite Automata). *Let Σ be a finite set (the* input alphabet*). A* deterministic finite automaton (DFA) *over Σ consists of the following data:*

- *a finite set Q (the set of* states*);*
- *a function $\delta : Q \times \Sigma \to Q$ (the* transition function*);*
- *a state $q_0 \in Q$ (the* initial state*); and*
- *a set of states $F \subseteq Q$ (the set of* accepting states*).*

As is typical, Σ^* will denote the set of finite strings over Σ. Given an input string $x = x_1 x_2 \cdots x_n \in \Sigma^*$, and a DFA M, define the *run* of M on x to be the sequence of states $\alpha_0, \dots, \alpha_n \in Q$ such that $\alpha_0 = q_0$, and for $1 \leq i \leq n$, we have that $\delta(\alpha_{i-1}, x_i) = \alpha_i$. A string $x \in \Sigma^*$ is *accepted* by M if the last state appearing in the run of M on x is in F. A *language* is a function $L : \Sigma^* \to \{0, 1\}$. We note that languages are often defined as subsets of Σ^*, but here we use functions in order to align with our definition of a concept. A language is *recognized* by a DFA M if M accepts a string x if and only if $x \in L$. We say that a language L is *regular* if it is recognized by some DFA.

The Myhill-Nerode theorem provides a useful syntactic characterization of regular languages. Given a language $L : \Sigma^* \to \{0, 1\}$, define an equivalence relation $\equiv_L$ on Σ^* as follows: for strings $x, y \in \Sigma^*$, we say that $x \equiv_L y$ iff $L(xz) = L(yz)$ for all $z \in \Sigma^*$.

Theorem 2 (Myhill-Nerode). *A language L is regular if and only if $\equiv_L$ has finitely many equivalence classes. Moreover, $\equiv_L$ has exactly n classes if and only if the minimal DFA recognizing L has exactly n states.*

3 Learning Advice DFAs

3.1 Overview of Advice DFAs

In this subsection, we give an introduction to automata with advice. For a more comprehensive overview, see [15].

Definition 5 (Advice DFA). *Let Σ and Γ be finite sets (the* input *and* advice alphabets, *respectively). An* advice DFA M over Σ with advice from Γ *consists of the following data:*

- *a finite set Q (the set of* states*);*
- *an infinite length string $A \in \Gamma^\omega$ over the advice alphabet (the* advice string*);*
- *a function $\delta : Q \times \Sigma \times \Gamma \to Q$ (the* transition function*);*
- *a state $q_0 \in Q$ (the* initial state*); and*
- *a set of states $F \subseteq Q$ (the set of* accepting states*).*

Given an input string $x = x_1 x_2 \cdots x_n \in \Sigma^*$ and advice DFA M, define the *run* of M on x to be the sequence of states $\alpha_0, \ldots, \alpha_n \in Q$ such that $\alpha_0 = q_0$, and for $1 \leq i \leq n$, we have that $\delta(\alpha_{i-1}, x_i, A_i) = \alpha_i$. A string $x \in \Sigma^*$ is accepted by M if the last state appearing in the run of M on x is in F. A language L is *recognized* by an advice DFA M if M accepts a string x if and only if $x \in L$. We say that a language L is *regular with advice* if it is recognized by some advice DFA.

Advice DFAs extend classical DFAs with the addition of the (infinite) advice string A (which is fixed beforehand as part of the automaton). The advice string is read in parallel with the input string; i.e., when M reads the nth character of the input, it also has access to the nth character of the advice when deciding which transition to make. One way to think about the advice string is that it allows the transition function to vary at each step of the computation (although at a fixed step i, the transition behavior is the same regardless of the input string).

Advice DFAs satisfy a Myhill-Nerode characterization, under a variant of the $\equiv_L$ relation. Define an equivalence relation $\equiv_{L,m}$ on Σ^m by $x \equiv_{L,m} y$ iff $xz \in L \iff yz \in L$ for all $z \in \Sigma^*$. Notice that $\equiv_{L,m}$ is simply $\equiv_L$ restricted to strings of length m.

Theorem 3 (Myhill-Nerode for advice DFAs, cf. [15, Theorem 4]). *Let L be a language.*

(i) Suppose L is accepted by an advice DFA that has n states. Then $\equiv_{L,m}$ has at most n classes for all $m \in \mathbb{N}$.
(ii) Suppose $\equiv_{L,m}$ has at most n classes for all $m \in \mathbb{N}$. Then there is an advice DFA on $2n$ states that recognizes L.

In general, the bound of $2n$ states in the second item is tight. Also, note that this statement is more precise than the original version in [15]; in particular, the relationship between the number of states and the number of $\equiv_{L,m}$-classes does not appear in the original theorem. However, this relationship is easily derived from its proof.

3.2 Learning Bound for Advice DFAs

For the remainder of the section, fix $k \in \mathbb{N}$ and let Σ be an alphabet of size k. We will not fix the advice alphabet Γ; however, notice that if we are constructing an automaton with at most n states, we may take Γ to have size n^{nk}, since the advice string can be thought of as coding the transition function at a given step, and there are n^{nk} functions from $Q \times \Sigma \to Q$ (possible transition functions).

Note that the language consisting of the finite prefixes of any ω-word A is regular with advice A, and each of these languages is distinct, so there are uncountably many languages that are regular with advice. Thus we cannot have any finitary representation of arbitrary languages that are regular with advice. Hence, we consider the case where we restrict to strings of bounded length. Let $\mathcal{L}_k^{\text{adv}}(n,m)$ denote the set

$$\mathcal{L}_k^{\text{adv}}(n,m) := \{L \subseteq \Sigma^{\leq m} \mid L \text{ is recognized by an advice DFA with at most } n \text{ states}\},$$

and let $\mathcal{E}_k(n,m)$ denote the set

$$\mathcal{E}_k(n,m) := \{L \subseteq \Sigma^{\leq m} \mid \equiv_{L,\ell} \text{ has at most } n \text{ classes for all } \ell \leq m\}.$$

By Theorem 3, $\mathcal{L}_k^{\text{adv}}(n,m) \subseteq \mathcal{E}_k(n,m) \subseteq \mathcal{L}_k^{\text{adv}}(2n,m)$ for any $n,m \in \mathbb{N}$. Because of this, it is more convenient to compute the query complexity of $\mathcal{L}_k^{\text{adv}}(n,m)$ with queries $\mathcal{L}_k^{\text{adv}}(2n,m)$.

Proposition 1. *The consistency dimension of $\mathcal{L}_k^{adv}(n,m)$ with respect to $\mathcal{L}_k^{adv}(2n,m)$ is at most $n(n+1)$.*

Proof. Let $L : \Sigma^{\leq m} \to \{0,1\}$, and suppose that $L \notin \mathcal{L}_k^{\text{adv}}(2n,m)$. Since $\mathcal{E}_k(n,m) \subseteq \mathcal{L}_k^{\text{adv}}(2n,m)$, we have that $L \notin \mathcal{E}_k(n,m)$. This means that there are strings $x_0,\ldots,x_n \in \Sigma^\ell$ which are pairwise $\equiv_{L,\ell}$-inequivalent for some $\ell \leq m$. For each $0 \leq i < j \leq n$, let $z_{ij} \in \Sigma^*$ such that $L(x_i z_{ij}) \neq L(x_j z_{ij})$ (i.e., z_{ij} distinguishes x_i and x_j according to $\equiv_{L,\ell}$). Consider the set

$$B = \{x_k z_{ij} \mid 0 \leq i < j \leq n, k = i,j\},$$

which has size $2\binom{n+1}{2} = n(n+1)$. Let $L' : \Sigma^{\leq m} \to \{0,1\}$ extend $L|_B$. L' must have at least $n+1$ $\equiv_{L',\ell}$-classes, since $x_0,\ldots,x_n$ are forced to be $\equiv_{L',\ell}$-inequivalent. Hence $L' \notin \mathcal{E}_k(n,m)$, so in particular $L' \notin \mathcal{L}_k^{\text{adv}}(n,m)$. Since we found a set of size $n(n+1)$ which witnesses the fact that L is n-inconsistent with $\mathcal{L}_k^{\text{adv}}(n,m)$, the consistency dimension of $\mathcal{L}_k^{\text{adv}}(n,m)$ with respect to $\mathcal{L}_k^{\text{adv}}(2n,m)$ is at most $n(n+1)$. □

Proposition 2. *The Littlestone dimension of $\mathcal{L}_k^{adv}(n,m)$ is $O(nmk \log n)$.*

Proof. We can bound the Littlestone dimension of $\mathcal{L}_k^{\text{adv}}(n,m)$ by bounding the size of $\mathcal{L}_k^{\text{adv}}(n,m)$ and applying Remark 1. As noted at the beginning of the section, we may interpret Γ as coding all possible transition functions, so the advice string A simply tells the automaton which transition function to use at each step.

Consider an advice DFA such that $Q = [n]$ and $q_0 = 1$. Then to fully specify the behavior of the automaton on strings of length m, it is enough to choose one transition function for each step, as well as the set of accepting states. There are $(n^{nk})^m = n^{nmk}$ ways to choose the transition functions, and 2^n ways to choose the set of accepting states. So there are $n^{nmk}2^n$ total possible advice DFAs of this form.

Now notice that every language on strings of length up to m that is accepted by an advice DFA with at most n states is accepted by an advice DFA of this form, simply by appropriately permuting the states and the letters of the advice string. So indeed the size of the class $\mathcal{L}_k^{\text{adv}}(n, m)$ is upper bounded by $n^{nmk}2^n$. Therefore

$$\begin{aligned}\text{Ldim}(\mathcal{L}_k^{\text{adv}}(n, m)) &\leq \log |\mathcal{L}_k^{\text{adv}}(n, m)| \\ &= \log(n^{nmk}2^n) \\ &= nmk \log n + n \\ &= O(nmk \log n).\end{aligned}$$

□

Combining Propositions 1 and 2 with Theorem 1(1), we obtain:

Theorem 4. *The (EQ+MQ)-query complexity of* $\mathcal{L}_k^{\text{adv}}(n, m)$ *with queries from* $\mathcal{L}_k^{\text{adv}}(2n, m)$ is $O(n^3 mk \log n)$.

4 Learning Nominal DFAs

4.1 Overview of Nominal DFAs

In this subsection, we give an introduction to nominal automata. For a more comprehensive treatment, see [5].

As mentioned in the introduction, one must leverage some underlying structure to properly generalize automata theory to infinite alphabets. For example, consider the alphabet $A = \mathbb{N}$, and define $L : A^* \to \{0, 1\}$ by $L(w) = 1$ if and only if $w = aa$ for some $a \in A$. An equivalently defined language over a finite alphabet is easily seen to be regular, and so we expect this example to be "regular" as well. We can draw an infinite automaton that recognizes L in the following way:

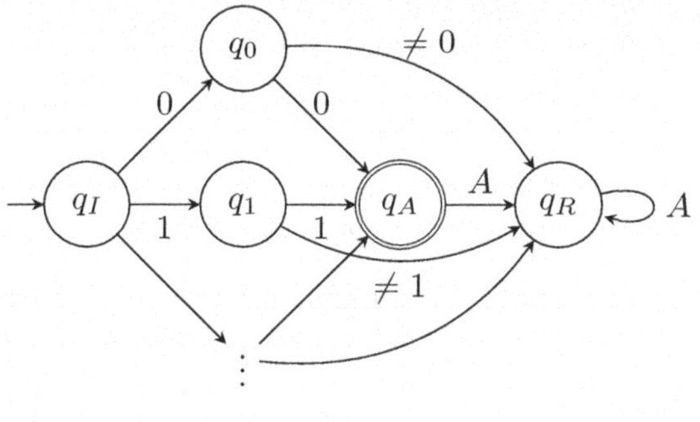

Notice that in some cases, we have combined infinitely many transitions into a single arrow—here, we assume that we are able to compare whether or not two data values are equal, and so are leveraging a form of symmetry. We can further condense this representation into an actually finite diagram:

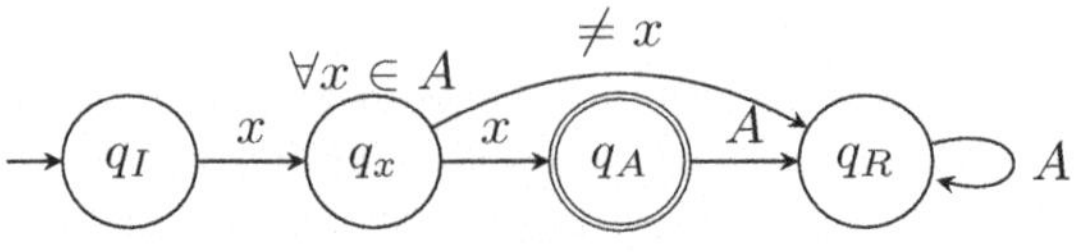

We can compress the distinct states for each character from A into a single "state" because it is enough to be able to compare whether or not the first and second characters read are equal or not. In order to formalize this intuition, we use the notion of *nominal sets.* Note: we do not work in the most general setting of [5], and instead only focus on what they call the *equality symmetry.* However, it is reasonable to expect that our results can generalize to other well-behaved symmetries.

Given a set A, let $\mathrm{Sym}(A)$ denote the group of permutations on A, i.e., the set of bijections from A to A with the operation of function composition. For the rest of the paper, let G denote $\mathrm{Sym}(\mathbb{N})$ Given a set X, a *(left) action* of G on X is an operation $\cdot : G \times X \to X$ such that:

1) for all $x \in X$, $e \cdot x = x$, where e is the identity function on $\mathbb{N}$, and
2) for all $\pi, \pi' \in G$ and $x \in X$, $(\pi \circ \pi') \cdot x = \pi \cdot (\pi' \cdot x)$.

Example 1. Let $X = \mathbb{N}^2$. Define an action of G on X by $\pi \cdot (n, m) = (\pi(n), \pi(m))$. Observe that there is a permutation π for which $\pi \cdot (n_1, m_1) = (n_2, m_2)$ if and only if either (1) $n_1 = m_1$ and $n_2 = m_2$, or (2) $n_1 \neq m_1$ and $n_2 \neq m_2$. This example illustrates the action of $\mathrm{Sym}(\mathbb{N})$ can be used to formalize the idea of being able to compare data values for equality.

Definition 6 (Support; Least Support). *Fix X and an action of G on X. Given a subset $D \subseteq \mathbb{N}$ and an element $x \in X$, we say that D* supports *x if for every $\pi \in G$ such that π fixes every element of D, we have that $\pi \cdot x = x$.*

A finite set $D \subseteq \mathbb{N}$ is called the least support *of x if*

(1) D supports x,
(2) no proper subset of D supports x, and
(3) no other finite subset of $\mathbb{N}$ has properties (1) and (2).

We will use $supp(x)$ to denote the least support of x.

An equivalent characterization of an element having least support is that the intersection of any two finite supports of x also supports x.

Definition 7 (Nominal Set). *A* nominal set *is a set X along with an action of G on X such that every element of X has a least support.*

Lemma 1 ([5, Lemma 4.9]). *Let X be a nominal set and let $x \in X$. If D supports x, then for any $\pi \in G$, $\pi(D)$ supports $\pi \cdot x$.*

As a corollary, $|supp(x)| = |supp(\pi \cdot x)|$ for any $\pi \in G$.

Definition 8 (Nominal Dimension). *Let X be a nominal set. The* nominal dimension *of X is $\sup_{x \in X} |supp(x)|$ (i.e., the largest size of a least support).*

In the literature on nominal sets, this is simply referred to as the dimension of X. However, in order to prevent confusion with other notions of dimension used in this paper, we will use the term nominal dimension.

Definition 9 (Orbit; Orbit-finiteness). *Let X be a nominal set. The* orbit *of an element $x \in X$, denoted $G \cdot x$, is the set*

$$G \cdot x = \{\pi \cdot x \mid \pi \in G\}.$$

Every nominal set is partitioned into the disjoint union of its orbits. We say that X is orbit-finite *if X is the union of only finitely many orbits.*

By Lemma 1, elements in the same orbit have the same size of least support, so orbit-finite nominal sets have finite nominal dimension.

Example 2. Let $X = \mathbb{N}^2$, and define the action of G on X as in Example 1. The orbits of X are $G \cdot (n, n)$ and $G \cdot (n, m)$, where $n, m \in \mathbb{N}$ and $n \neq m$. These are the sets of pairs whose coordinate are either equal or unequal, respectively. Thus X is orbit-finite with two orbits. Additionally, every element (n, m) has least support $\{n, m\}$, and so the nominal dimension of X is 2.

For $i = 1, \ldots, n$, let X_i be a set with an action of G on X_i. The *pointwise action* of G on $\prod_{i=1}^{n} X_i$ is the action given by $\pi \cdot (x_1, \ldots, x_n) = (\pi \cdot x_1, \ldots, \pi \cdot x_n)$.

Definition 10 (Equivariance). *Let X be a nominal set. A subset $Y \subseteq X$ is* equivariant *if for any $y \in Y$ and $\pi \in G$, $\pi \cdot y \in Y$.*

A relation R on $\prod_{i=1}^{n} X_i$, where each X_i is a nominal set, is equivariant *if it is equivariant when considered as a subset of the product equipped with the pointwise action.*

In particular, a function $f : X \to Y$ is equivariant exactly when

$$f(\pi \cdot x) = \pi \cdot f(x).$$

Remark 3. Y is an equivariant subset of X if and only if Y is a union of orbits.

The following lemmas demonstrate how equivariant functions behave nicely with orbits and supports.

Lemma 2. *Let $f : X \to Y$ be an equivariant function, and let $x \in X$. The image of the orbit of x (in X) under f is equal to the orbit of $f(x)$ (in Y).*

As a corollary, if f is surjective, then Y has at most as many orbits as X.

Proof. The orbit of $f(x)$ is the set $\{\pi \cdot f(x) \mid \pi \in G\}$. By equivariance of f, this is equal to $\{f(\pi \cdot x) \mid \pi \in G\} = f(\{\pi \cdot x \mid \pi \in G\})$, which is the image under f of the orbit of x. □

Lemma 3 ([5, Lemma 4.8]). *Let $f : X \to Y$ be an equivariant function, $x \in X$, and $D \subseteq \mathbb{N}$. If D supports x, then D supports $f(x)$.*

As a corollary, supp$(f(x)) \subseteq$ supp(x), and hence if f is surjective, the nominal dimension of Y is at most the nominal dimension of X.

We will work extensively with quotients by equivariant equivalence relations, so we state some important general facts about them. Recall that if R is an equivalence relation on X, X/R denotes the set of equivalence classes of R, and is called the *quotient* of X by R.

Lemma 4 ([5, Lemma 3.5]). *Let X be a nominal set and $R \subseteq X \times X$ be an equivariant equivalence relation. Then the quotient X/R is a nominal set, under the action $\pi \cdot [x]_R = [\pi \cdot x]_R$, and the quotient map $x \mapsto [x]_R$ is a surjective equivariant function.*

Lemma 5. *Let X be a nominal set and $R \subseteq X \times X$ be an equivariant equivalence relation. Then supp$([x]_R) \subseteq$ supp(x) for every $x \in X$, and the nominal dimension of X/R is at most the nominal dimension of X.*

Proof. This follows immediately from Lemma 3 and the fact that the quotient map $x \mapsto [x]_R$ is surjective and equivariant. □

Lemma 6. *Let X, Y be nominal sets. An equivariant function $F : X \to Y$ and equivariant equivalence relation $\equiv_Y$ on Y induce an equivariant equivalence relation $\equiv_X$ on X and an equivariant function $f : X/\equiv_X \to Y/\equiv_Y$.*

Furthermore, f is injective, and if F is surjective, then f is also surjective.

We are now ready to define nominal DFAs and state the nominal Myhill-Nerode theorem. Fix an orbit-finite nominal set A, which we will call the *G-alphabet.* The action of G on A naturally extends to A^*: given a string $w \in A^*$, $\pi \cdot w$ is the string obtained by letting π act on each individual character of w.

Definition 11 (G-language). *A G-*language *is a function $L : A^* \to \{0, 1\}$ such that the set $\{x \in A^* \mid L(x) = 1\}$ is an equivariant subset of A^*.*

Definition 12 (Nominal DFA). *Let A be an orbit-finite nominal set (the* input alphabet*). A* nominal DFA M over *A consists of the following data:*

- *an orbit-finite nominal set Q (the set of* states*);*
- *an equivariant function $\delta : Q \times A \to Q$ (the* transition function*)*
- *a state $q_0 \in Q$ such that the orbit of q_0 is $\{q_0\}$ (the* initial state*)*
- *an equivariant subset $F \subseteq Q$ (the set of* accepting states*)*

As a shorthand, we say that a nominal DFA M has n orbits or nominal dimension k when the state set has n orbits or nominal dimension k.

Given an input string $x = x_1x_2 \cdots x_n \in A^*$, define the *run* of M on x to be the sequence of states $\alpha_0, \ldots, \alpha_n \in Q$ such that $\alpha_0 = q_0$, and for $1 \leq i \leq n$, we have that $\delta(\alpha_{i-1}, x_i) = \alpha_i$. A string $x \in \Sigma^*$ is *accepted* by M if the last state appearing in the run of M on x is in F. We say that a langauge L is *recognized* by a nominal DFA M if M accepts a string x if and only if $x \in L$. As noted in [5, Definition 3.1], the language recognized by a nominal DFA must be a G-language. We say that a G-language L is *nominal regular* if it is recognized by some nominal DFA.

Example 3. Let $A = \mathbb{N}$, and let $L : A \to \{0, 1\}$ be defined by $L(w) = 1$ if and only if $w = aa$ for some $a \in A$ as in the previous example. It is straightfoward to see this language is a G-language. Additionally, in the automaton that recognizes L, we can define an action of G on the set of states by $\sigma \cdot q_i = q_{\sigma(i)}$ for any $\sigma \in G$ and $i \in \mathbb{N}$, while $\sigma \cdot q = q$ for all $\sigma \in G$ for the states q_I, q_A, and q_R. This automaton is a nominal DFA, and hence L is nominal regular.

Let L be a G-language, and define the usual relation $\equiv_L$ on A^* by: $x \equiv_L y$ if and only if for all $z \in A^*$, we have $L(xz) = L(yz)$. This relation is equivariant (see [5, Lemma 3.4]), and hence by Lemma 4, $A^*/\equiv_L$ is a nominal set. We will write $[x]_L$ to denote the $\equiv_L$-equivalence class of a string $x \in A^*$.

Theorem 5 (Myhill-Nerode for nominal DFAs [5, Theorem 5.2]). *Let A be an orbit-finite nominal set, and let L be a G-language. Then the following are equivalent:*

1. *$A^*/\equiv_L$ has at most n orbits and has nominal dimension at most k;*
2. *L is nominal regular, and in particular is recognized by a nominal DFA with at most n orbits and nominal dimension at most k.*

Note that this statement is more precise than the original version in [5]; in particular, the conditions on the number of orbits and the nominal dimension do not appear in the original theorem. However, these conditions are easily derived from its proof.

4.2 Littlestone Dimension of Nominal DFAs

To prove bounds on the Littlestone dimension of nominal automata, we wish to bound the number of possible nominal automata. Since automata involve transition functions, we will need to understand products of nominal sets. Nominality is easily seen to be preserved under Cartesian products:

Proposition 3. *The product of two nominal sets is nominal. In particular, the nominal dimension of the product of two nominal sets $X \times Y$ is at most the sum of the nominal dimensions of X and Y.*

Proof. Suppose X and Y are nominal with nominal dimensions k and ℓ, respectively. Let $(x, y) \in X \times Y$. Notice that $supp(x) \cup supp(y)$, which has size at most $k + \ell$, supports $(x, y) \in X \times Y$. □

On the other hand, in the most general setting, products of orbit-finite nominal sets need not be orbit-finite [5, Example 2.5]. However, in our context of Sym($\mathbb{N}$), products of orbit-finite sets are known to be orbit-finite [5, Section 10]. We will need an explicit bound on the number of orbits of products of orbit-finite sets, which is the purpose of the following discussion.

For a natural number k, define $\mathbb{N}^{(k)} := \{(a_1, \ldots, a_k) \mid a_i \neq a_j \text{ for } i \neq j\}$. $\mathbb{N}^{(k)}$ is a single-orbit nominal set when equipped with the pointwise action of G.

Lemma 7 ([5, Lemma 4.13]). *Given a nominal set X of nominal dimension k that has exactly one orbit, there is an equivariant surjection $f_X : \mathbb{N}^{(k)} \to X$.*

Definition 13 (cf. [16, Section 3]). *Given $k_1, \ldots, k_n \in \mathbb{N}$, let $f_{\mathbb{N}}(k_1, \ldots, k_n)$ denote the number of orbits of $\mathbb{N}^{(k_1)} \times \cdots \times \mathbb{N}^{(k_n)}$.*

Proposition 4 (cf. [16, Section 3]). *Let X_i be a nominal set with ℓ_i orbits and nominal dimension k_i for $i = 1, \ldots, n$. Let $X := X_1 \times \cdots \times X_n$ and $\ell = \ell_1 \cdots \ell_n$. Then X has at most $\ell f_{\mathbb{N}}(k_1, \ldots, k_n)$ many orbits.*

In light of Proposition 4, we can find bounds on the number of orbits of a product of nominal sets by bounding the value of $f_{\mathbb{N}}$. We do so for the case $n = 2$:

Proposition 5. *Suppose (without loss of generality) that $k_1 \geq k_2$. Then*

$$\left(\frac{k_1}{e}\right)^{k_2} \leq \binom{k_1}{k_2} k_2! \leq f_{\mathbb{N}}(k_1, k_2) \leq (2k_1)^{k_2}.$$

In particular, if k_2 is a constant, then $f_{\mathbb{N}}(k_1, k_2) = \Theta(k_1^{k_2})$.

Proposition 5 will help us to calculate an explicit upper bound on the Littlestone dimension of nominal automata later, but we can first use it to substantiate a comment from the introduction about previously known query bounds.

The bound in [16, Corollary 1] involves a $f_{\mathbb{N}}(p(n+m), pn(k + k \log k + 1))$ factor, where n is the number of orbits of the state set of the target automaton, k is the nominal dimension of the target automaton, p is the nominal dimension of the alphabet, and m is the length of the longest counterexample. Notice that $f_{\mathbb{N}}$ is non-decreasing in all coordinates. Therefore, $f_{\mathbb{N}}(p(n+m), pn(k + k \log k + 1))$ is lower bounded by both $f_{\mathbb{N}}(pn, pnk)$ and $f_{\mathbb{N}}(m, nk)$. Applying the lower bounds from Proposition 5 yields the following:

Remark 4. The bound on the (EQ+MQ)-query complexity of nominal automata given in [16, Corollary 1] is at least $(k^n n!)^p$, and at least $\min\left(\left(\frac{nk}{e}\right)^m, \left(\frac{m}{e}\right)^{nk}\right)$.

We are now at a point where we can calculate a bound on the number of possible nominal DFAs and hence bound the Littlestone dimension. First, we state a general result on the number of single-orbit nominal sets:

Proposition 6. *The number of distinct (up to isomorphism) single-orbit nominal sets of nominal dimension at most k is at most $2^{O(k^2)}$.*

We note that it is a completely general result about nominal sets and may be of independent interest. For us, it will allow us to bound the number of possible state sets.

Lemma 8. *The number of possible state sets for a nominal DFA with n orbits and nominal dimension k is $2^{O(nk^2)}$.*

Proof. Since the state set Q is an orbit-finite nominal set with n orbits and nominal dimension k, we count the number of such sets. We can view Q as the disjoint union of n single-orbit nominal sets, each with nominal dimension at most k, just by considering each orbit independently. By Proposition 6, the number of single-orbit nominal sets of nominal dimension $\leq k$ is at most $2^{O(k^2)}$. An upper bound on the number of nominal sets with n orbits and nominal dimension k can be found by raising this number to n, i.e., $\left(2^{O(k^2)}\right)^n = 2^{O(nk^2)}$. □

Now, we count the number of possible transition behaviors. Fix an input alphabet A, where A has ℓ orbits and nominal dimension p.

Lemma 9. *The number of possible transition behaviors for a nominal DFA with n orbits and nominal dimension k is at most*

$$(n(k+p)!)^{O(nk^p)}.$$

The proof of Lemma 9 is given in Appendix ??.

Let $\mathcal{L}_A^{\mathrm{nom}}(n,k)$ denote the set of G-languages over A recognized by a nominal DFA with at most n orbits and nominal dimension at most k.

Proposition 7. *The Littlestone dimension of $\mathcal{L}_A^{nom}(n,k)$ is at most*

$$O\left(nk^p\left(\log n + k\log k\right)\right)$$

Proof. We bound the Littlestone dimension by bounding the size of $\mathcal{L}_A^{\mathrm{nom}}(n,k)$. To choose a nominal DFA with at most n orbits and nominal dimension at most k, we must choose the state set, transition function, initial state, and set of accepting states. By Lemma 8, there are at most $2^{O(nk^2)}$ choices for the state set. By Lemma 9, there are at most $(n(k+p)!)^{O(nk^p)}$ choices for the transition function. There are at most n choices for the initial state (since the initial state must be an orbit of its own) and 2^n choices for the accepting states (since the set of accepting states is a union of orbits). So in total, we can upper bound $|\mathcal{L}_A^{nom}(n,k)|$ by

$$|\mathcal{L}_A^{nom}(n,k)| \leq 2^{O\left(nk^2\right)}\left(n(k+p)!\right)^{O\left(nk^p\right)} n2^n.$$

Applying Remark 1, taking logs, using Stirling's approximation, and remembering that p is constant, we find that

$$\begin{aligned}\mathrm{Ldim}(\mathcal{L}_A^{nom}(n,k)) &\leq \log|\mathcal{L}_A^{nom}(n,k)| \\ &\leq O\left(nk^2\right) + O\left(nk^p\right)\left(\log n + \log((k+p)!)\right) + \log n + n \\ &\leq O\left(nk^p\left(\log n + (k+p)\log(k+p)\right)\right) \\ &= O\left(nk^p\left(\log n + k\log k\right)\right).\end{aligned}$$

□

4.3 Consistency Dimension of Nominal DFAs

It remains to bound the consistency dimension. To do this, we need to show that if L is a language that is not recognized by a nominal DFA with at most n orbits and nominal dimension at most k, then there is a set of strings B of bounded size such that the restriction of L to B cannot be extended to any G-language recognized by such a nominal DFA. By the nominal Myhill-Nerode theorem, L not being recognized by a nominal DFA with at most n orbits and nominal dimension at most k is equivalent to $A^*/\equiv_L$ either having greater than n orbits or having nominal dimension greater than k. We first address the case where $A^*/\equiv_L$ has large nominal dimension.

Lemma 10. *Let X be any nominal set, let $x \in X$, and let $D = supp(x)$. Suppose that $\tau \in G$ fixes every element of D except for one. Then $\tau \cdot x \neq x$.*

Proposition 8. *Let L be a G-language over alphabet A, and suppose that $A^*/\equiv_L$ has nominal dimension at least $k+1$. Then there is a set $B \subseteq A^*$ of size $2(k+1)$ such that for any G-language L', if $L|_B = L'|_B$, then $A^*/\equiv_{L'}$ also has nominal dimension at least $k+1$.*

Proof. Since $A^*/\equiv_L$ has nominal dimension $\geq k+1$, there is some $x_0 \in A^*$ such that $|supp([x_0]_L)| \geq k+1$. Let D denote $supp([x_0]_L)$, and let D_0 be a subset of D of size $k+1$. Let $j = \max(D)+1$, and for each $i \in D_0$, let $\tau_i = (i\ i+j) \in G$ (the permutation that swaps i and $i+j$). Notice that τ_i fixes all but one element of D, and so by Lemma 10, $[\tau_i \cdot x_0]_L = \tau_i \cdot [x_0]_L \neq [x_0]_L$. Thus for each $i \in D_0$, there is some $z_i \in A^*$ such that $L((\tau_i \cdot x_0)z_i) \neq L(x_0 z_i)$. Let

$$B = \{(\tau_i \cdot x_0)z_i \mid i \in D_0\} \cup \{x_0 z_i \mid i \in D_0\},$$

which has size $2(k+1)$.

Now, let L' be a G-language extending $L|_B$, and suppose for contradiction that $A^*/\equiv_{L'}$ has nominal dimension at most k. That is, for every $w \in A^*$, $|supp([w]_{L'})| \leq k$. In particular, $|supp([x_0]_{L'})| \leq k$. For each $i \in D_0$, L' agrees with L on $(\tau_i \cdot x_0)z_i$ and $x_0 z_i$, so $L'((\tau_i \cdot x_0)z_i) \neq L'(x_0 z_i)$. This shows that $\tau_i \cdot [x_0]_{L'} = [\tau_i \cdot x_0]_{L'} \neq [x_0]_{L'}$. Since the only elements not fixed by τ_i are i and $i+j$, it must be that at least one of i and $i+j$ are in the least support of $[x_0]_{L'}$. Thus for each $i \in D_0$, $supp([x_0]_{L'})$ contains at least one of i and $i+j$. Since $j > \max(D)$, all values $i, i+j$ for $i \in D_0$ are distinct, and so $|supp([x_0]_{L'})| \geq |D_0| = k+1$, which contradicts the fact that $|supp([x_0]_{L'})| \leq k$. □

Next, we address the case where $A^*/\equiv_L$ has a large number of orbits.

Lemma 11. *Let L be a G-language such that $A^*/\equiv_L$ has n orbits. Then for every orbit $G \cdot [x]_L$ of $A^*/\equiv_L$, there is a string $x' \in A^*$ such that $|x'| < n$ such that $[x']_L \in G \cdot [x]_L$.*

Proposition 9. *Let L be a G-language over alphabet A, where A has nominal dimension p, and suppose that $A^*/\equiv_L$ has at least $n+1$ orbits. Then there is a set $B \subseteq A^*$ of size $2\binom{n+1}{2}\binom{pn}{k}(3pn)^k$ such that for any G-language L', if $L|_B = L'|_B$, then $A^*/\equiv_{L'}$ also has at least $n+1$ orbits.*

Proof. Since $A^*/\equiv_L$ has at least $n+1$ orbits, there are strings $x_0, \ldots, x_n$ such that $[x_i]_L$ all belong to distinct orbits. That is, for every $\tau \in G$ and $0 \le i < j \le n$, $[\tau \cdot x_i]_L = \tau[x_i]_L \neq [x_j]_L$, and thus there is $z_{ij}^\tau \in A^*$ such that

$$L((\tau \cdot x_i)z_{ij}^\tau) \neq L(x_j z_{ij}^\tau).$$

Moreover, by Lemma 11, we may assume that $|x_i| \le n$ for each $0 \le i \le n$.

For each $0 \le i \le n$, let $D_i = supp(x_i)$. Since the nominal dimension of A is p, we have that $|D_i| \le p \cdot |x_i| \le pn$. Also, let D be some subset of $\mathbb{N}$ such that D is disjoint from $D_0, \ldots, D_n$, and $|D| = \max_{0 \le i \le n} |D_i| \le pn$.

Now, for each $0 \le i < j \le n$, let

$$\Sigma'_{ij} := \{\sigma' : D'' \to D_i \cup D_j \cup D \mid D'' \subseteq D_i \text{ of size } k \text{ and } \sigma' \textit{ is an injection}\}.$$

Notice that Σ'_{ij} has size at most $\binom{pn}{k}(3pn)^k$: to choose a σ', we choose a subset of D_i of size k and a value from $D_i \cup D_j \cup D$ for each of the k inputs. For each $\sigma' \in \Sigma'_{ij}$, let $\sigma \in G$ be an arbitrary but fixed extension of σ' to a permutation of $\mathbb{N}$, and let Σ_{ij} consist of all such σ (so $|\Sigma_{ij}| = |\Sigma'_{ij}| \le \binom{pn}{k}(3pn)^k$).

Now, let

$$B = \{(\sigma \cdot x_i)z_{ij}^\sigma \mid 0 \le i < j \le n,\ \sigma \in \Sigma_{ij}\} \cup \{x_j z_{ij}^\sigma \mid 0 \le i < j \le n,\ \sigma \in \Sigma_{ij}\}.$$

B has size at most $2\binom{n+1}{2}\binom{pn}{k}(3pn)^k$. Let L' be a G-language extending $L|_B$, and assume for contradiction that $A^*/\equiv_{L'}$ has at most n orbits. Thus there must be $0 \le i < j \le n$ such that $[x_i]_{L'}$ is in the same orbit as $[x_j]_{L'}$. Let $\pi \in G$ such that $\pi \cdot [x_i]_{L'} = [x_j]_{L'}$. π does not have to be in Σ_{ij}, and so we cannot directly derive a contradiction. Instead, we will alter π in order to obtain a $\sigma \in \Sigma_{ij}$ such that $\sigma \cdot [x_i]_{L'} = [x_j]_{L'}$.

Define $\pi' \in G$ in the following way: first, let $\pi(D_i)$ denote the image of D_i under π. For each element $a \in \pi(D_i) \setminus (D_i \cup D_j \cup D)$, select a unique element $b_a \in D \setminus \pi(D_i)$. This is possible because $|D| \ge |D_i| = |\pi(D_i)|$, and so $|D \setminus \pi(D_i)| \ge |\pi(D_i) \setminus D| \ge |\pi(D_i) \setminus (D_i \cup D_j \cup D)|$. Let π' be the permutation that transposes each $a \in \pi(D_i) \setminus (D_i \cup D_j \cup D)$ with its corresponding $b_a \in D \setminus \pi(D_i)$, and fixes every other element of $\mathbb{N}$.

Notice that $\pi'|_{D_j} = \mathrm{id}_{D_j}$, and so $\pi' \cdot x_j = x_j$. Also, if $a \in D_i$, then $\pi' \circ \pi(a) \in D_i \cup D_j \cup D$: if $\pi(a) \in D_i \cup D_j \cup D$, then by definition π' does not affect $\pi(a)$ and so $\pi'(\pi(a)) = \pi(a) \in D_i \cup D_j \cup D$, whereas if $\pi(a) \in \pi(D_i) \setminus (D_i \cup D_j \cup D)$, π' will transpose $\pi(a)$ with an element in D. Let D_i' denote $supp([x_i]_{L'})$. Since $A^*/\equiv_{L'}$ has nominal dimension at most k, $|D_i'| \leq k$. Also, by Lemma 5, $D_i' \subseteq supp(x_i) = D_i$. Therefore, $(\pi' \circ \pi)|_{D_i'}$ is an injection from a subset of D_i of size at most k into $D_i \cup D_j \cup D$. Therefore, there is some $\sigma \in \Sigma_{ij}$ such that

$$\sigma|_{D_i'} = (\pi' \circ \pi)|_{D_i'}.$$

We may then deduce that

$$\begin{aligned}
[\sigma \cdot x_i]_{L'} &= \sigma \cdot [x_i]_{L'} \\
&= (\pi' \circ \pi) \cdot [x_i]_{L'} \\
&= \pi' \cdot (\pi \cdot [x_i]_{L'}) \\
&= \pi' \cdot [x_j]_{L'} \\
&= [\pi' \cdot x_j]_{L'} \\
&= [x_j]_{L'}.
\end{aligned}$$

This means that for all $z \in A^*$, $L'((\sigma \cdot x_i)z) = L'(x_j z)$. In particular, we may choose $z = z_{ij}^{\sigma}$. However, since $(\sigma \cdot x_i)z_{ij}^{\sigma}$ and $x_j z_{ij}^{\sigma}$ are in B, it must be that

$$\begin{aligned}
L((\sigma \cdot x_i)z_{ij}^{\sigma}) &= L'((\sigma \cdot x_i)z_{ij}^{\sigma}) \\
&= L'(x_j z_{ij}^{\sigma}) \\
&= L(x_j z_{ij}^{\sigma}),
\end{aligned}$$

a contradiction! So we may finally conclude that $A^*/\equiv_{L'}$ has at least $n+1$ orbits. □

Lemma 11 yields an interesting consequence, which we do not use in any of our proofs but may be of independent interest:

Corollary 1. *If L is a G-language over an alphabet A which has nominal dimension p such that $A^*/\equiv_L$ has n orbits, then $A^*/\equiv_L$ has nominal dimension at most $(n-1)p$.*

This result suggests that ultimately it is the number of orbits, and not the nominal dimension, of $A^*/\equiv_L$ which characterizes the complexity of L.

We now have all the ingredients we need to bound the consistency dimension.

Proposition 10. *The consistency dimension of $\mathcal{L}_A^{nom}(n,k)$ with respect to itself is at most $2\binom{n+1}{2}\binom{pn}{k}(3pn)^k$.*

Proof. Let $L : A^* \to \{0,1\}$, and suppose that $L \notin \mathcal{L}_A^{nom}(n,k)$, i.e., L is not recognized by any nominal DFA with at most n orbits and nominal dimension at most k. We must find a set B of at most $2\binom{n+1}{2}\binom{pn}{k}(3pn)^k$ strings such that any function extending $L|_B$ is not in $\mathcal{L}_A^{nom}(n,k)$.

Case 1: L is not equivariant. Then there is $x_0 \in A^*$ and $\pi \in G$ such that $L(x_0) \neq L(\pi \cdot x_0)$. Set $B = \{x_0, \pi \cdot x_0\}$. Any function L' extending $L|_B$ cannot be equivariant, and therefore cannot be nominal regular, so $L' \notin \mathcal{L}_A^{nom}(n,k)$.

Case 2: L is equivariant, and is recognized by some nominal DFA with at most n orbits. By Theorem 5, $A^*/\equiv_L$ has at most n orbits. Thus the nominal dimension of $A^*/\equiv_L$ must be at least $k+1$, or else another application of Theorem 5 would imply that L is recognized by a nominal DFA with at most n orbits and nominal dimension at most k, contradicting the assumption that $L \notin \mathcal{L}_A^{nom}(n,k)$. Let $B \subseteq A^*$ of size $2(k+1)$ be as given by Proposition 8.

Now, let $L' : A^* \to \{0,1\}$ extend $L|_B$, and suppose for contradiction that $L' \in \mathcal{L}_A^{nom}(n,k)$. Since L' is recognized by a nominal DFA, it must be a G-language, so by the definition of B, $A^*/\equiv_{L'}$ has nominal dimension at least $k+1$. However, by Theorem 5 and the fact that L' is recognized by a nominal DFA with at most n orbits and nominal dimension at most k, $A^*/\equiv_{L'}$ has nominal dimension at most k, a contradiction! So $L' \notin \mathcal{L}_A^{nom}(n,k)$.

Case 3: L is equivariant, and L is not recognized by any nominal DFAs with at most n orbits. By Theorem 5, $A^*/\equiv_L$ has at least $n+1$ orbits. Let $B \subseteq A^*$ of size $2\binom{n+1}{2}\binom{pn}{k}(3pn)^k$ be as given by Proposition 9.

Now, let $L' : A^* \to \{0,1\}$ extend $L|_B$, and suppose for contradiction that $L' \in \mathcal{L}_A^{nom}(n,k)$. Since L' is recognized by a nominal DFA, it must be a G-language, so by the definition of B, $A^*/\equiv_{L'}$ has at least $n+1$ orbits. However, by Theorem 5 and the fact that L' is recognized by a nominal DFA with at most n orbits and nominal dimension at most k, $A^*/\equiv_{L'}$ has at most n orbits, a contradiction! So $L' \notin \mathcal{L}_A^{nom}(n,k)$.

In all three cases, we found a set B of size at most $2\binom{n+1}{2}\binom{pn}{k}(3pn)^k$ such that any language extending $L|_B$ cannot be in $\mathcal{L}_A^{nom}(n,k)$. We can then conclude that the consistency dimension of $\mathcal{L}_A^{nom}(n,k)$ with respect to itself is at most $2\binom{n+1}{2}\binom{pn}{k}(3pn)^k$. □

4.4 Learning Bound for Nominal DFAs

We can now use the bounds we proved for Littlestone dimension and consistency dimension to prove our main result on nominal DFAs:

Theorem 6. *For a fixed G-alphabet A, the (EQ+MQ)-query complexity of* $\mathcal{L}_A^{\mathrm{nom}}(n,k)$ *with queries from* $\mathcal{L}_A^{\mathrm{nom}}(n,k)$ *is at most* $\frac{n^{O(k)}}{k^k}$.

Proof. By Proposition 7, the Littlestone dimension of $\mathcal{L}_A^{nom}(n,k)$ is at most $O\left(nk^p\left(\log n + k\log k\right)\right)$. By Proposition 10, the consistency dimension of $\mathcal{L}_A^{nom}(n,k)$ with respect to itself is at most $2\binom{n+1}{2}\binom{pn}{k}(3pn)^k$. This is upper bounded by $n(n+1)\frac{(e \cdot pn)^k}{k^k}(3pn)^k$, which is in turn at most $\frac{n^{O(k)}}{k^k}$ (since p is a constant). Applying Theorem 1, the query complexity of $\mathcal{L}_A^{nom}(n,k)$ with queries from $\mathcal{L}_A^{nom}(n,k)$ is at most $O\left(nk^p\left(\log n + k\log k\right)\frac{n^{O(k)}}{k^k}\right) = \frac{n^{O(k)}}{k^k}$. □

5 Conclusion

In this paper, we derive query learning bounds for advice DFAs and nominal DFAs; the bounds for advice DFAs are the first known bounds for the setting, while the bounds for nominal DFAs improve upon prior results, at the cost of not making any computational guarantees about the learning algorithm.

The bounds for advice DFAs are derived in almost the exact same manner as the bounds for DFAs given by Chase and Freitag [8]. However, to the complexity of the setting of nominal DFAs requires a much deeper analysis of the structure of nominal sets and nominal DFAs. This leads to several auxillary results which may be of independent interest; namely, Proposition 5, which analyzes the asymptotics of the number of orbits of products of nominal sets; Proposition 6, which counts the number of single-orbit nominal sets of a given dimension; and Corollary 1, which bounds the nominal dimension of $A^*/\equiv_L$ in terms of the number of orbits of $A^*/\equiv_L$ and the nominal dimension of A.

One natural extension of our work is to adapt the results for nominal automata to other well-behaved symmetries beside the equality symmetry, such as the total order symmetry, as described in [5]. Our approach is general enough that it should apply to these symmetries; however, there are many details that would need to be verified. It would also be natural to explore what the approach of Chase and Freitag yields for other previously-studied forms of automata that admit versions of the Myhill-Nerode theorem. For example, Bollig et al. [6] study query learning of NFAs via *residual finite-state automata*, which crucially utilize the Myhill-Nerode correspondence to find canonical NFA representations of regular languages. A final potential direction for future work would be to consider the generalization of nominal automata to ω-languages; i.e., nominal DFAs with a Büchi-style acceptance criteria. Angluin and Fisman have adapted the L^* algorithm to the classical setting of ω-regular languages [2], and Chase and Freitag apply their method in the same setting [8]. To our knowledge, no work has been done studying the learnability of ω-nominal regular languages, so it would be of interest to find results using both Angluin's method and Chase and Freitag's method.

References

1. Angluin, D.: Learning regular sets from queries and counterexamples. Inf. Comput. **75**, 87–106 (1987)
2. Angluin, D., Fisman, D.: Learning regular omega languages. Theoret. Comput. Sci. **650**, 57–72 (2016). https://doi.org/10.1016/j.tcs.2016.07.031, https://www.sciencedirect.com/science/article/pii/S0304397516303760, algorithmic Learning Theory
3. Balcázar, J.L., Castro, J., Guijarro, D., Simon, H.U.: The consistency dimension and distribution-dependent learning from queries. Theoretical Computer Science **288**(2), 197–215 (2002). https://doi.org/10.1016/S0304-3975(01)00400-5, https://www.sciencedirect.com/science/article/pii/S0304397501004005, algorithmic Learning Theory

4. Bárány, V.: A hierarchy of automatic ω-words having a decidable MSO theory. RAIRO - Theoret. Inform. Appl. - Informatique Théorique et Applications **42**(3), 417–450 (2008). https://doi.org/10.1051/ita:2008008, http://www.numdam.org/articles/10.1051/ita:2008008/
5. Bojańczyk, M., Klin, B., Lasota, S.: Automata theory in nominal sets. Log. Meth. Comput. Sci. **10**(3) (2014). https://doi.org/10.2168/LMCS-10(3:4)2014, https://lmcs.episciences.org/1157
6. Bollig, B., Habermehl, P., Kern, C., Leucker, M.: Angluin-style learning of NFA. In: IJCAI, pp. 1004–1009 (2009)
7. Carton, O., Thomas, W.: The monadic theory of morphic infinite words and generalizations. In: Nielsen, M., Rovan, B. (eds.) MFCS 2000. LNCS, vol. 1893, pp. 275–284. Springer, Heidelberg (2000). https://doi.org/10.1007/3-540-44612-5_23
8. Chase, H., Freitag, J.: Bounds in query learning. In: Abernethy, J., Agarwal, S. (eds.) Proceedings of Thirty Third Conference on Learning Theory. Proceedings of Machine Learning Research, vol. 125, pp. 1142–1160. PMLR (2020). http://proceedings.mlr.press/v125/chase20a.html
9. Drews, S., D'Antoni, L.: Learning symbolic automata. In: Legay, A., Margaria, T. (eds.) TACAS 2017. LNCS, vol. 10205, pp. 173–189. Springer, Heidelberg (2017). https://doi.org/10.1007/978-3-662-54577-5_10
10. Elgot, C.C., Rabin, M.: Decidability and undecidability of extensions of second (first) order theory of (generalized) successor. J. Symb. Log. **31**, 169–181 (1966)
11. Fisman, D., Saadon, S.: Learning and characterizing fully-ordered lattice automata. In: Bouajjani, A., Holík, L., Wu, Z. (eds.) Automated Technology for Verification and Analysis. LNCS, vol. 13505, pp. 266–282. Springer, Cham (2022). https://doi.org/10.1007/978-3-031-19992-9_17
12. Gabbay, M.J., Pitts, A.M.: A new approach to abstract syntax with variable binding. Formal Aspects Comput. **13**(3), 341–363 (2002). https://doi.org/10.1007/s001650200016
13. Hanneke, S., Livni, R., Moran, S.: Online learning with simple predictors and a combinatorial characterization of minimax in 0/1 games. In: COLT (2021)
14. Hellerstein, L., Pillaipakkamnatt, K., Raghavan, V., Wilkins, D.: How many queries are needed to learn? J. ACM **43**(5), 840–862 (1996). https://doi.org/10.1145/234752.234755
15. Kruckman, A., Rubin, S., Sheridan, J., Zax, B.: A myhill-nerode theorem for automata with advice. Electron. Proc. Theoret. Comput. Sci. **96** (2012). https://doi.org/10.4204/EPTCS.96.18
16. Moerman, J., Sammartino, M., Silva, A., Klin, B., Szynwelski, M.: Learning nominal automata. In: Proceedings of the 44th ACM SIGPLAN Symposium on Principles of Programming Languages, New York, NY, USA, pp. 613–625. POPL 2017, Association for Computing Machinery (2017). https://doi.org/10.1145/3009837.3009879
17. Montanari, U., Pistore, M.: An introduction to history dependent automata. Electr. Notes Theor. Comput. Sci. **10**, 170–188 (1997). https://doi.org/10.1016/S1571-0661(05)80696-6
18. Nies, A.: Describing groups. Bull. Symbol. Logic **13**(3), 305–339 (2007). http://www.jstor.org/stable/4493323
19. Pitts, A.M.: Nominal Sets: Names and Symmetry in Computer Science. Cambridge Tracts in Theoretical Computer Science, Cambridge University Press (2013). https://doi.org/10.1017/CBO9781139084673

20. Rabinovich, A., Thomas, W.: Decidable theories of the ordering of natural numbers with unary predicates. In: Ésik, Z. (ed.) CSL 2006. LNCS, vol. 4207, pp. 562–574. Springer, Heidelberg (2006). https://doi.org/10.1007/11874683_37
21. Sakakibara, Y.: Learning context-free grammars from structural data in polynomial time. In: Proceedings of the First Annual Workshop on Computational Learning Theory. COLT '88, San Francisco, CA, USA, pp. 330–344. Morgan Kaufmann Publishers Inc. (1988)
22. Salomaa, A.: On finite automata with a time-variant structure. Inf. Control **13**(2), 85–98 (1968). https://doi.org/10.1016/S0019-9958(68)90706-7, https://www.sciencedirect.com/science/article/pii/S0019995868907067
23. Tsankov, T.: The additive group of the rationals does not have an automatic presentation. J. Symbol. Logic **76**(4), 1341–1351 (2011). http://www.jstor.org/stable/23208221

Guiding Word Equation Solving Using Graph Neural Networks

Parosh Aziz Abdulla[1], Mohamed Faouzi Atig[1], Julie Cailler[2], Chencheng Liang[1(✉)], and Philipp Rümmer[1,2(✉)]

[1] Uppsala University, Uppsala, Sweden
{parosh.abdulla,mohamed_faouzi.atig,chencheng.liang}@it.uu.se
[2] University of Regensburg, Regensburg, Germany
{philipp.ruemmer,julie.cailler}@ur.de

Abstract. This paper proposes a Graph Neural Network-guided algorithm for solving word equations, based on the well-known Nielsen transformation for splitting equations. The algorithm iteratively rewrites the first terms of each side of an equation, giving rise to a tree-like search space. The choice of path at each split point of the tree significantly impacts solving time, motivating the use of Graph Neural Networks (GNNs) for efficient split decision-making. Split decisions are encoded as multi-classification tasks, and five graph representations of word equations are introduced to encode their structural information for GNNs. The algorithm is implemented as a solver named DragonLi. Experiments are conducted on artificial and real-world benchmarks. The algorithm performs particularly well on satisfiable problems. For single word equations, DragonLi can solve significantly more problems than well-established string solvers. For the conjunction of multiple word equations, DragonLi is competitive with state-of-the-art string solvers.

Keywords: Word equation · Graph neural network · String theory

1 Introduction

Over the past few years, reasoning within specific theories, including arithmetic, arrays, or algebraic data structures, has become one the main challenges in automated reasoning. To address the needs of modern applications, new techniques have been developed, giving rise to *SMT* (Satisfiability Modulo Theories) solvers. SMT solvers implement efficient decision procedures and reasoning methods for a wide range of theories, and are used in applications such as verification.

Among the theories supported by SMT solvers, the theory of *strings* has in particular received attention in the last years. Strings represent one of the most important data-types in programming, and string constraints are therefore relevant in various domains, from text processing to database management systems and web applications. One of the simplest kind of constraints supported by the SMT-LIB theory of strings [12] are *word equations,* i.e., equations in a free semigroup [30]. Makanin's work [36] demonstrated the decidability of the word equation problem, which was later confirmed to be in PSPACE [44]. However, even

S. Akshay et al. (Eds.): ATVA 2024, LNCS 15054, pp. 279–301, 2025.
https://doi.org/10.1007/978-3-031-78709-6_14

the leading SMT solvers with support for string constraints (including cvc5 [10], Z3 [39], Norn [5], TRAU [6], Ostrich [16], Woorpje [19], and Z3-Noodler [17]) tend to be incomplete for proving the unsatisfiability of word equations, illustrating the hardness of the theory.

Solving a word equation is to check for the existence of string values for variables that make equal both sides of the equation. For example, consider the equation $Xab = YaZ$, where X, Y, and Z are variables ranging over strings, and a and b are letters. This equation is satisfiable and has multiple solutions. For example, assigning a to both X and Y and b to Z results in $aab = aab$.

This paper presents an algorithm that makes use of *Graph Neural Networks* (GNN) [13] in order to solve word equations. It is an extension of the method proposed in [4] and implemented in Norn [5], referred to as the *split algorithm*. The split algorithm is, in turn, based on the well-known Nielsen transformation [40]. It builds a proof tree by iteratively applying a set of inference (split) rules on a word equation.

One critical aspect of the algorithm lies in selecting the next branch to be explored while constructing the proof tree, which significantly influences the solving time. To address this, we present a heuristic that leverages deep learning to determine the exploration order of branches. GNNs [13] represent one of the paradigms in neural network research, tailored for non-Euclidean, graph-structured data. This makes them suited for scenarios where data points are interconnected, such as social networks [22], molecular structures [23], programs [9,38], and logical formulae [18,29,41,50]. Our work represents, to the best of our knowledge, the first use of deep learning in the context of word equations.

Figure 1 illustrates the workflow of our approach. During the training stage, we initially employ the split algorithm (without GNN guidance) to solve word equation problems drawn from a training dataset. For each satisfiable (SAT) problem, we generate a corresponding proof tree. Within this tree, each branch (pair of a node and a direct child) is evaluated to determine whether it leads to a solution, as well as its distance to the corresponding leaf. Based on this information, we assign labels to each branch to indicate whether it is a favorable choice for reaching a solution. Subsequently, we model each branching point comprising the node and its child nodes as a graph. These graph representations, along with their associated labels, are then used to train the GNN.

In the prediction stage, word equations from an evaluation dataset are processed using the split algorithm, now guided by GNN. At each branching point, the current branch is first transformed into a graph representation, which is in turn fed to the trained GNN model. The GNN, using its learned insights, advises on which branch should be prioritized and explored first.

We implemented this algorithm in the DragonLi tool. Experiments were conducted using four word equation benchmarks: three of them are artificially generated and inspired by Woorpje [19]; a fourth one is extracted from SMT-LIB benchmarks [1] and encodes real-world problems. Results show that for SAT problems, the pure split algorithm without GNNs is already competitive with some leading string solvers (Z3 [39], cvc5 [10], Ostrich [16], Woorpje [19], Z3-

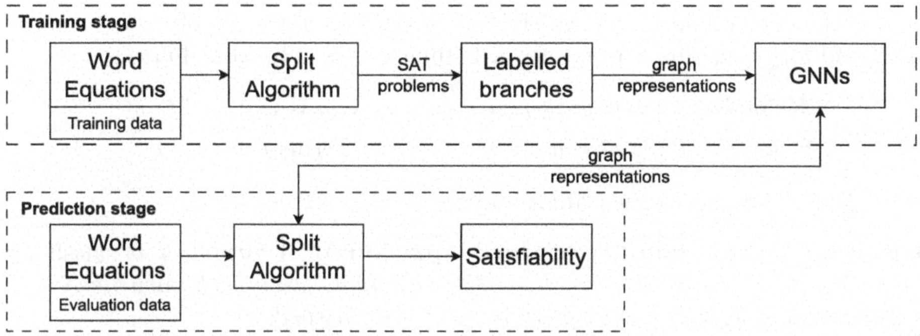

Fig. 1. The workflow diagram for the training and prediction stage

Noodler [17]), while it performs less well on UNSAT problems. We conjecture that this is due to the (relatively straightforward) depth-first search performed by our implementation of the split algorithm, which is a good strategy for finding solutions, whereas other solvers devote more time (e.g., using length reasoning) to show that formulas are unsatisfiable. Enabling GNN guidance in DragonLi uniformly improves performance on SAT problems, allowing it to outperform all other solvers in one specific benchmark. Specifically, in Benchmark 2, the GNN-guided version of DragonLi solves 115% more SAT problems than its non-GNN-guided counterpart and 43.0% more than the next best string solver, Woorpje.

In summary, the contributions of this paper are as follows:

- We define a proof system based on the split algorithm for solving word equations, tailored to combining symbolic reasoning with GNN-based guidance.
- Based on the proof system, we introduce an algorithm for integrating GNN-based guidance with the proof system.
- To train a GNN on the data obtained from solving word equations, we present five possible graph representations of word equations.
- We present an extensive experimental evaluation on four word equation benchmarks, comparing, in particular, the different graph encodings and different backtracking strategies of the algorithm.

2 Preliminaries

We start by defining the syntax of word equations, as well as the notion of satisfiability. Then, we explain the fundamental mechanism of Graph Neural Networks (GNNs), along with a description of the specific GNN model we have employed in our experiments.

Word Equations. We assume a finite non-empty alphabet Σ and write Σ^* for the set of all strings (or words) over Σ. We work with a set Γ of string variables, ranging over words in Σ^*, and denote the empty string by ϵ. The symbol $\cdot$

denotes the concatenation of two strings; in our examples, we often write uv as shorthand for $u \cdot v$. The syntax of word equations is defined as follows:

$$\text{Formulae } \phi ::= \mathit{true} \mid e \wedge \phi \qquad \text{Words } w ::= \epsilon \mid t \cdot w$$
$$\text{Equations } e ::= w = w \qquad \text{Terms } t ::= X \mid c$$

where $X \in \Gamma$ ranges over variables and $c \in \Sigma$ over letters.

Definition 1 (Satisfiability of word equations). *A formula ϕ is* satisfiable *if there exists a substitution $\pi : \Gamma \to \Sigma^*$ such that, when each variable $X \in \Gamma$ in ϕ is replaced by $\pi(X)$, all equations in ϕ are satisfied.*

Graph Neural Networks. A *Graph Neural Network* (GNN) [13] uses *Multi-Layer Perceptrons* (MLPs) to extract features from a given graph. MLPs, also known as multi-layer neural networks [25], transform an input space to make different classes of data linearly separable, and this way learn representations of data with multiple levels of abstraction. Each layer of an MLP consists of neurons that apply a nonlinear transformation to the inputs received from the previous layer. This allows MLPs to learn increasingly complex patterns as data moves from the input layer to the output layer.

Message passing-based GNNs (MP-GNNs) [24] are designed to learn features of graph nodes (and potentially the entire graph) by iteratively aggregating and transforming feature information from the neighborhood of a node. For instance, if we represent variables in a word equation by nodes in a graph, then node features could represent symbol type (i.e., being a variable), possible assignments, or the position in the word equation.

Consider a graph $G = (V, E)$, with V as the set of nodes and $E \subseteq V \times V$ as the set of edges. Each node $v \in V$ has an initial representation $x_v \in \mathbb{R}^n$ and a set of neighbors $N_v \subseteq V$. In an MP-GNN comprising T message-passing steps, node representations are iteratively updated. At each step t, the representation of node v, denoted as h_v^t, is updated using the equation:

$$h_v^t = \eta_t(\rho_t(\{h_u^{t-1} \mid u \in N_v\}), h_v^{t-1}), \tag{1}$$

where $h_v^t \in \mathbb{R}^n$ is the updated representation of node v after t iterations, starting from the initial representation $h_v^0 = x_v$. The node representation of u in the previous iteration $t-1$ is h_u^{t-1}, and node u is a neighbor of node v. In this context, $\rho_t : (\mathbb{R}^n)^{|N_v|} \to \mathbb{R}^n$ is an aggregation function with trainable parameters (e.g., an MLP followed by sum, mean, min, or max) that aggregates the node representations of v's neighboring nodes at the t-th iteration. Along with this, $\eta_t : (\mathbb{R}^n)^2 \to \mathbb{R}^n$ is an update function with trainable parameters (e.g., an MLP) that takes the aggregated node representation from ρ_t and the node representation of v in the previous iteration as input, and outputs the updated node representation of v at the t-th iteration.

MP-GNNs operate under the assumption that node features can capture structural information from long-distance neighbors by aggregating and updating features of neighboring nodes. After T message-passing steps, an MP-GNN yields an updated node representation (feature) that includes information from neighbors within a distance of T, applicable to various downstream tasks like node or graph classification.

In this study, we choose *Graph Convolutional Networks* (GCNs) [31] to guide our algorithm. In GCNs, the node representation h_v^t of v at step $t \in \{1, ..., T\}$ where $T \in \mathbb{N}$ is computed by

$$h_v^t = \text{ReLU}(\text{MLP}^t(\text{mean}\{h_u^{t-1} \mid u \in N_v \cup \{v\}\})), \tag{2}$$

where each MLP^t is a fully connected neural network, ReLU (Rectified Linear Unit) [8] is the non-linear function $f(x) = max(0, x)$, and $h_v^0 = x_v$.

3 Search Procedure and Split Algorithm

In this section, we define our proof system for word equations, the notion of a proof tree, and show soundness and completeness. We then introduce an algorithm to solve a conjunction of word equations.

3.1 Split Rules

We introduce four types of proof rules in Fig. 2, each corresponding to a specific situation. The proof rules are inspired by [4], but streamlined and formulated differently. Each proof rule is of the form:

$$\mathit{Name}\ \frac{P}{\begin{array}{c|c|c} [\mathit{cond}_1] & & [\mathit{cond}_n] \\ C_1 & \cdots & C_n \end{array}}$$

Here, *Name* is the name of the rule, P is the premise, and C_is are the conclusions. Each $cond_i$ is a substitution that is applied implicitly to the corresponding conclusion C_i, describing the case handled by that particular branch. In our case, P is a conjunction of word equations and each C_i is either a conjunction of word equations or a final state, SAT or UNSAT.

To introduce our proof rules, we use distinct letters $a, b \in \Sigma$ and variables $X, Y \in \Gamma$, while u and v denote sequences of letters and variables.

Rules R_1, R_2, R_3, and R_4 (Fig. 2a) define how to simplify word equations, and how to handle equations in which one side is empty. In R_3, note that the substitution $X \mapsto \epsilon$ is applied to the conclusion ϕ. Rules R_5 and R_6 (Fig. 2b) refer to cases in which each word starts with a letter. The rules simplify the current equation, either by removing the first letter, if it is identical on both sides (R_5), or by concluding that the equation is UNSAT (R_6). Rule R_7 (Fig. 2c) manages cases where one side begins with a letter and the other one with a variable. The rule introduces two branches, since the variable must either denote the empty string ϵ, or its value must start with the same letter as the right-hand side. Rule R_8 (Fig. 2d) handles the case in which both sides of an equation start with a variable, implying that either both variables have the same value or the value of one is included in the value of the other.

We implicitly assume symmetric versions of the rules R_3, R_4, and R_7, swapping left-hand side and right-hand side of the equation that is rewritten. For instance, the symmetric rule for R_3 would have premise $\epsilon = X \wedge \phi$.

$$R_1 \ \frac{true}{\mathrm{SAT}} \qquad R_2 \ \frac{\epsilon = \epsilon \wedge \phi}{\phi} \qquad R_3 \ \frac{X = \epsilon \wedge \phi}{\begin{matrix}[X \mapsto \epsilon] \\ \phi\end{matrix}} \qquad R_4 \ \frac{a \cdot u = \epsilon \wedge \phi}{\mathrm{UNSAT}}$$

with $X \in \Gamma$ and $a \in \Sigma$.

(a) Simplification rules

$$R_5 \ \frac{a \cdot u = a \cdot v \wedge \phi}{u = v \wedge \phi} \qquad R_6 \ \frac{a \cdot u = b \cdot v \wedge \phi}{\mathrm{UNSAT}}$$

with a, b two different letters from Σ.

(b) Letter-letter rules

$$R_7 \ \frac{X \cdot u = a \cdot v \wedge \phi}{\begin{matrix}[X \mapsto \epsilon] \\ u = a \cdot v \wedge \phi\end{matrix} \ \Bigg| \ \begin{matrix}[X \mapsto a \cdot X'] \\ X' \cdot u = v \wedge \phi\end{matrix}}$$

with X' a *fresh* element of Γ.

(c) Variable-letter rules

$$R_8 \ \frac{X \cdot u = Y \cdot v \wedge \phi}{\begin{matrix}[X \mapsto Y] \\ u = v \wedge \phi\end{matrix} \ \Bigg| \ \begin{matrix}[X \mapsto Y \cdot Y'] \\ Y' \cdot u = v \wedge \phi\end{matrix} \ \Bigg| \ \begin{matrix}[Y \mapsto X \cdot X'] \\ u = X' \cdot v \wedge \phi\end{matrix}}$$

with X', Y' *fresh* elements of Γ.

(d) Variable-variable rule

Fig. 2. Rules of the proof system for word equations

Although our proof system is not complete for proving the unsatisfiability of word equations, we can observe that the proof rules are sound and locally complete. A proof rule is said to be *sound* if the satisfiability of the premise implies the satisfiability of one of the conclusions. It is said to be *locally complete* if the satisfiability of one of the conclusions implies the satisfiability of the premise.

Lemma 1. *The proof rules in Fig. 2 are sound and locally complete.*

3.2 Proof Trees

Iteratively applying the proof rules to a conjunction of word equations gives rise to a *proof tree* growing downwards. Given the proof rules $R_1, \ldots, R_8$ in Fig. 2, we represent a proof tree as a tuple $\tau = (N, \alpha, E, \lambda)$ where:

- N is a finite set of nodes;
- $E \subseteq N \times N$ is a set of edges, such that (N, E) is a directed tree. An edge $(n_i, n_j) \in E$ implies that n_j is derived from n_i by applying a proof rule;
- $\alpha : N \to For \cup \{\text{SAT}, \text{UNSAT}\}$ is a function mapping each node $n \in N$ to a formula or to a label SAT, UNSAT;
- $\lambda : E \to R$ is a function that assigns to each edge a proof rule.

A *path* in the proof tree is a sequence of edges starting from the root and ending with a leaf node. Due to local completeness, if there is a leaf node that is SAT, then the word equation at the root node is satisfiable. Due to soundness, if all the leaf nodes are UNSAT, then the formula at the root node is unsatisfiable.

Figure 3 illustrates the proof tree generated by applying the proof rules in Fig. 2 on the word equation $\phi = (XbY = bXXZ)$. In this example, $b \in \Sigma$ and $X, Y, Z \in \Gamma$. The application of R_7 on the root generates two branches. While exploring the left branch first yields a solution (SAT) at a depth of 3, iteratively navigating through the right branch of R_7 leads to non-termination since the length of the word equation keeps increasing.

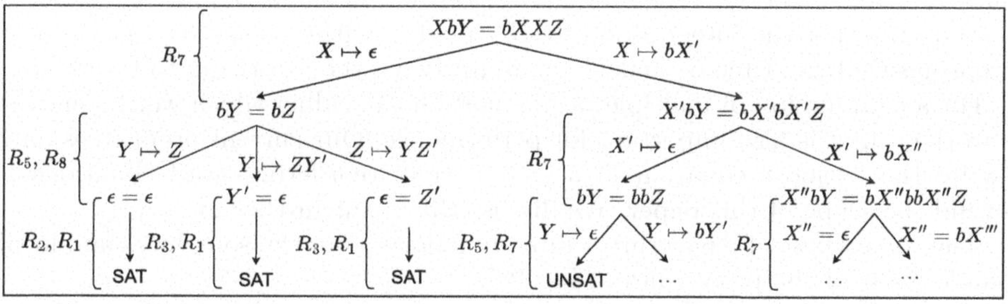

Fig. 3. Proof tree resulting from the word equation $XbY = bXXZ$

3.3 GNN-Guided Split Algorithm

We use the proof rules in Fig. 2 and the idea of iterative deepening from [32] (combination of depth- and breadth-first search in a tree) to solve word equations, as shown in Algorithm 1. This algorithm aims to check the satisfiability of word equations $\phi = (\bigwedge_{i=1}^{n} w_i^l = w_i^r)$.

Algorithm 1 receives as parameter a backtrack strategy $BT \in \{BT_1, BT_2, BT_3\}$, which determines when to stop exploring a path of the proof tree and return to a previous branching point. The algorithm calls the function *solveEqsRec* (Algorithm 2), which returns the satisfiability status by exploring a proof tree recursively. At each branching point in this tree, if at least one child node is SAT, the algorithm concludes that ϕ is SAT and terminates (Line 13 of *solveEqsRec*). Conversely, if every child node is UNSAT, the current node is marked as UNSAT (Line 19 of *solveEqsRec*), and the algorithm backtracks to the last branching point. A formula ϕ is considered UNSAT only after all branches have been checked and found to be UNSAT.

We explore three different backtrack strategies, BT_1, BT_2, and BT_3:

- BT_1: This strategy performs depth-first search until it finds a SAT node or exhausts all branches to conclude UNSAT. It may lead to non-termination of the algorithm in proof trees with infinite branches, and can miss solutions; an example for this is the rightmost branch of Fig. 3.
- BT_2: This hybrid strategy imposes a limit, l_{BT_2}, on the depth to which a proof branch is explored. When the maximum depth l_{BT_2} is reached, the proof search backtracks to the last branching point, and l_{BT_2} is globally increased by $l_{BT_2}^{step}$ (line 3 of *solveEqsRec*). Similarly as BT_1, this strategy can miss solutions of word equations.
- BT_3: This strategy performs the classical depth-first search with iterative deepening, by setting an initial limit l_{BT_3} on the exploration depth. This limit is increased (line 8 of *solveEqs*) when no node with label SAT is found but the tree was not fully explored yet. This strategy is complete in the sense that it will eventually find a solution for every satisfiable formula.

The performance and termination of the algorithm are highly influenced by the order in which we explore the proof tree. This order is determined by the *orderBranches* function (Line 8 of *solveEqsRec*). Our main goal in this paper is to study whether the integration of GNN models within *orderBranches* is able to optimise solving time or make it more likely for the algorithm to terminate.

For a conjunction of multiple word equations, deciding which word equation to work on first is also important for performance. Our current proof rules only rewrite the leftmost equation in a conjunction; reordering word equations is beyond the scope of this paper. We discuss this point further in Sect. 7.

The correctness of Algorithm 1 directly follows from the soundness and local completeness of the proof rules in Fig. 2:

Lemma 2 (Soundness of Algorithm 1). *For a conjunction of word equations ϕ, if Algorithm 1 terminates with the result* SAT *or* UNSAT, *then ϕ is* SAT *or* UNSAT, *respectively.*

```
Input: Alphabet Σ and variables Γ;
       Word equations φ = (⋀_{i=1}^n w_i^l = w_i^r);
       Backtrack strategy BT ∈ {BT1, BT2, BT3};
       Global backtrack limits l_BT2, l_BT2^step, l_BT3.
Output: The status of φ: SAT, UNSAT, or UNKNOWN
1  begin
2      res ← UNKNOWN
3      if BT ∈ {BT1, BT2} then
4          res ← solveEqsRec(φ, 0, BT, Σ, Γ)
5      if BT = BT3 then
6          do
7              res ← solveEqsRec(φ, 0, BT3, Σ, Γ)
8              l_BT3 ← l_BT3 + 1
9          while res ≠ UNKNOWN
10     return res
```

Algorithm 1: The top-level algorithm *solveEqs* for word equations

4 Guiding the Split Algorithm

This section describes how to train and apply the GNNs in the *orderBranches* function in Algorithm 2. We start by describing five graph representations for a conjunction of word equations, which encode word equations in form of text to graph representations to be readable by GNNs. Then, we explain how to train our classification tasks on GNNs and collect the training data. Finally, we describe different ways to apply the predicted results back to algorithm.

Input: Alphabet Σ and variables Γ;
Word equations $\phi = (\bigwedge_{i=1}^{n} w_i^l = w_i^r)$;
Backtrack strategy $BT \in \{BT_1, BT_2, BT_3\}$;
Current exploration depth *currentDepth*;
Global backtrack limits $l_{BT_2}, l_{BT_2}^{step}, l_{BT_3}$.
Output: The state of ϕ: SAT, UNSAT, or UNKNOWN

begin
  if $BT = BT_2 \land currentDepth \geq l_{BT_2}$ **then**
    $l_{BT_2} \leftarrow l_{BT_2} + l_{BT_2}^{step}$
    return UNKNOWN
  if $BT = BT_3 \land currentDepth \geq l_{BT_3}$ **then**
    return UNKNOWN
  $branches \leftarrow applyRules(\phi, \Sigma, \Gamma)$
  $branches \leftarrow orderBranches(branches)$
  $unknownFlag \leftarrow false$
  foreach *child in branches* **do**
    $res \leftarrow solveEqsRec(child, currentDepth + 1, BT, \Sigma, \Gamma)$
    if res = SAT **then**
      return SAT
    if res = UNKNOWN **then**
      $unknownFlag \leftarrow true$
  if $unknownFlag$ **then**
    return UNKNOWN
  else
    return UNSAT

Algorithm 2: Recursive exploration *solveEqsRec* of word equations

4.1 Representing Word Equations by Graphs

Graph representations can capture the structural information in word equations and are the standard input format for GNNs. To understand the impact of the graph structure on our framework, we have designed five graph representations for word equations.

In order to extract a single graph from the equations, we first translate a conjunction $\bigwedge_{i=1}^{n} w_i^l = w_i^r$ of word equations to a single word equation, by inserting a distinguished letter $\# \notin \Sigma$ as follows:

$$w_1^l \# w_2^l \# ... \# w_n^l = w_1^r \# w_2^r \# ... \# w_n^r, \tag{3}$$

Then, we construct the graph representations for the word equation in (3). A graph representation $G = (V, E, V_{\mathrm{T}}, V_{\mathrm{Var}})$ of a word equation consists of a set of nodes V, a set of edges $E \subseteq V \times V$, a set of terminal nodes $V_{\mathrm{T}} \subseteq V$, and a set of variable nodes $V_{\mathrm{Var}} \subseteq V$. We start constructing the graph by drawing the "=" symbol as the root node. Its left and right children are the leftmost terms of both sides of the equation, respectively. The rest of the graph is built following the choice of the graph type:

- **Graph 1:** Inspired by Abstract Syntax Trees (ASTs). Each letter and variable is represented by its own node, and words are represented by singly-linked lists of nodes.
- **Graph 2:** An extension of Graph 1, introducing additional edges from each term node back to the root node.
- **Graph 3:** An extension of Graph 1 which incorporates unique variable nodes. In this design, nodes representing variables are added, which are connected to their respective occurrences in the linked lists. This representation aims at facilitating the learning of long-distance variable relationships by GNNs.
- **Graph 4:** Similar in approach to Graph 3, but introducing unique nodes for letters instead of variables.
- **Graph 5:** A composite structure that merges the concepts of Graphs 3 and 4. It includes unique nodes for both variables and letters..

Figure 4 illustrates the five graph representations of the conjunction of word equation $aXY\#bc = XY\#Zc$, where $\{X, Y, Z\} \subseteq \Gamma$ and $\{a, b, c\} \subseteq \Sigma$.

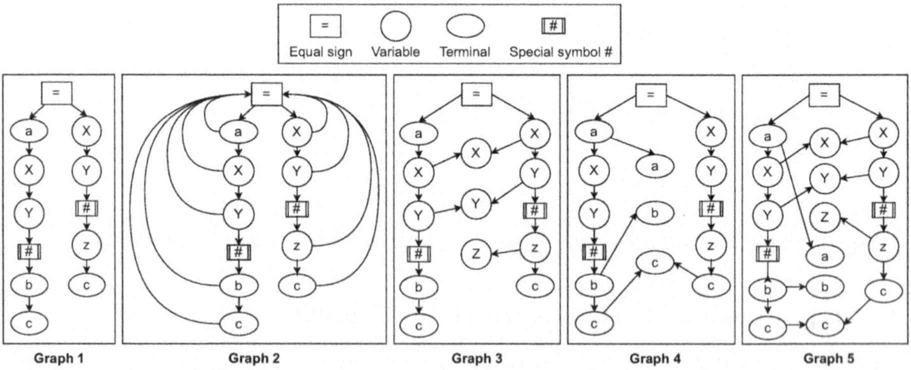

Fig. 4. The five graph representations for the word equation $aXY\#bc = XY\#Zc$ where X, Y, Z are variables and a, b, c are terminals

4.2 Training of Graph Neural Networks

Forward Propagation. In the *orderBranches* function of Algorithm 1, we sort the branches by using the predictions from a trained GNN model. This GNN model performs a multi-classification task. Given a list of branches $(b_1, \ldots, b_n)$ resulting from a rule application, we expect the trained GNN model to output a list of floating-point numbers $\hat{Y}_n = (\hat{y}_1, \ldots, \hat{y}_n)$, representing priorities of the branches. A higher value for $\hat{y}_i$ indicates a higher priority of the branch. For instance, given a node with two children b_1 and b_2, the output from the model could be $\hat{Y}_2 = (0.3, 0.7)$, expressing the prediction that b_2 will lead to a solution more quickly than b_1 and should be explored first. We detail the process of deriving $\hat{Y}_n$ at each split point using GNNs, exemplified by using $n = 2$.

Propagation on Graphs. To explain forward propagation, suppose a node labelled with formula ϕ_0 in the proof is rewritten by applying rule R_7, resulting in direct children labelled with ϕ_1, ϕ_2. The situation is similar for applications of R_8.

Formulas ϕ_0, ϕ_1, and ϕ_2 are transformed to graphs $G_0 = (V^0, E^0, V^0_{\mathrm{T}}, V^0_{\mathrm{Var}})$, $G_1 = (V^1, E^1, V^1_{\mathrm{T}}, V^1_{\mathrm{Var}})$, and $G_2 = (V^2, E^2, V^2_{\mathrm{T}}, V^2_{\mathrm{Var}})$, respectively, according to one of the encodings in Sect. 4.1. Each node in those graphs is then assigned an initial node representation in $\mathbb{R}^m$, which is determined by the node type: variable, letter, $=$, or $\#$. This gives rise to three initial node representation functions $H^0_i : V^i \to \mathbb{R}^m$ for $i \in \{1, 2, 3\}$, mapping the nodes of the graphs to vectors of real numbers.

Equation (2) defines how node representations are updated. Iterating the update rule, we obtain node representations $H^t_i = \mathrm{GCN}(H^{t-1}_i, E^i)$ for $i \in \{1, 2, 3\}$ and $t \in \{1, \ldots, T\}$, where the relation E^i is used to identify neighbours. Subsequently, representation of the graphs as a whole are derived by summing up the node representations at point T, resulting in $H_{G_i} = \sum_{v \in V^i} H^T_i(v)$.

Finally, these graph representations are concatenated and fed to a classifier $\mathrm{MLP} : (\mathbb{R}^m)^3 \to \mathbb{R}^2$ to calculate scores $\hat{Y}_2 = \mathrm{MLP}(H_{G_0} || H_{G_1} || H_{G_2})$, where $||$ denotes concatenation of vectors. The whole process generalizes in a straightforward way to branching points in the proof tree with n children.

Backward Propagation. The trainable parameters of the model, as described above, are the initial node representations for the four types of graph nodes and the parameters of the GCNs. Those trainable parameters are optimized together by minimizing the categorical cross-entropy loss between the predicted label $\hat{y}_i \in \hat{Y}_n$ and the true label $y_i \in Y_n$, using the following equation:

$$loss = -\frac{1}{N} \sum_{1}^{N} y_i \log(\hat{y}_i) \tag{4}$$

where N is the number of split points in a training batch. We explain how to collect the training data Y_n in the next section.

4.3 Training Data Collection

With our current algorithm, UNSAT problems always require an exhaustive exploration of a proof tree; branch ordering therefore does not affect the solving time. We have thus focused on optimizing the process of finding solutions and only extract training data from SAT problems.

To collect our training labels, we construct the complete proof tree for given conjunctions of word equations, up to a certain depth. The tree enables us to identify cases of multiple SAT pathways within the tree, and to identify situations where one branch leads to a solution more quickly than other branches.

Each node v of the proof tree with multiple children is labelled based on two criteria: the satisfiability status (SAT, UNSAT, or UNKNOWN) of the formula, and the size of the proof sub-tree underneath each of the direct children. Assume that node v has n children, each of which has status SAT, UNSAT, or UNKNOWN, respectively. If there is exactly one child of v, say the i'th child, that is SAT, then the label of v is a list of integers $(x_1, \ldots, x_n)$ with $x_i = 1$ and $x_j = 0$ for $j \neq i$. If multiple children are SAT, we examine the size of the sub-tree underneath each of those children, and label all children with minimal sub-trees with 1 in the list $(x_1, \ldots, x_n)$.

More formally, suppose a proof tree $\tau = (N, \alpha, E, \lambda)$. The satisfiability status $\sigma(v)$ of a node $v \in N$ is determined by:

$$\sigma(v) = \begin{cases} \alpha(v) & \text{if } \alpha(v) \in \{\text{SAT}, \text{UNSAT}, \text{UNKNOWN}\} \\ \text{SAT} & \text{if there is } u \in V \text{ with } \sigma(u) = \text{SAT and } (v,u) \in E \\ \text{UNKNOWN} & \text{otherwise, if there is } u \in V \text{ with } \sigma(u) = \text{UNKNOWN} \\ & \quad \text{and } (v,u) \in E \\ \text{UNSAT} & \text{otherwise} \end{cases} \tag{5}$$

The size $\Delta(v)$ of the sub-tree underneath a node v is defined by:

$$\Delta(v) = 1 + \sum_{u \in N, (v,u) \in E} \Delta(u)$$

Finally, the label $Y_n^v = (y_1, ..., y_n)$ of a node v with $\sigma(v) = \text{SAT}$ and n children $v_1, \ldots, v_n$, where $y_i \in \{0, 1\}$, is defined by:

$$y_i = \begin{cases} 1 & \text{if } \sigma(v_i) = \text{SAT and } \Delta(v_i) = \min S \\ 0 & \text{otherwise} \end{cases}$$

$$S = \{\Delta(v_i) \mid \sigma(v_i) = \text{SAT}\}$$

When $\sum_{i=1}^{n} y_i > 1$, we discard some children with label 1 until $\sum_{i=1}^{n} y_i = 1$ to make sure that the label for each split point is consistent.

4.4 Guidance for the Split Algorithm Using the GNN Model

In Algorithm 1, we introduce five strategies for the *orderBranches* function implementation, designed to evaluate the efficiency of deterministic versus stochastic methods in branch ordering and to investigate the interplay between fixed and variable branch ordering approaches:

- **Fixed Order:** Use a predetermined branch order, defined before execution. In our experiments, we simply use the order in which the branches are displayed in Fig. 2.
- **Random Order:** Reorder branches randomly.
- **GNN (S1):** Exclusively use the GNN model for branch ordering.
- **GNN-fixed (S2):** A balanced approach with a 50% chance of using the GNN model and a 50% chance of using the fixed order.
- **GNN-random (S3):** Similar to S2, but with the alternative 50% chance dedicated to random ordering.

5 Experimental Results

This section presents the benchmarks used for our experiments and details the results with the different versions of our algorithm. It also provides a comprehensive comparison with other state-of-the-art solvers.

5.1 Implementation of DragonLi

DragonLi [2] is developed from scratch using `Python 3.8` [49]. We train the models with `PyTorch` [42] and construct the GNNs using the `Deep Graph Library (DGL)` [51]. For tracking and visualizing training experiments, `mlflow` [15] is employed. Proof trees and graph representations of word equations are stored in `JSON` [43] format, while `graphviz` [21] is utilized for their tracking and visualization.

5.2 Benchmarks Selection

We consider two kinds of benchmarks: benchmarks that are artificially generated based on the benchmarks used to evaluate the solver Woorpje [19], as well as benchmarks extracted from the non-incremental QF_S, QF_SLIA, and QF_SNLIA track of the SMT-LIB benchmarks [1]. We summarize the benchmarks as following:

- **Benchmark 1** is generated by the mechanism used in Woorpje track I. Given finite sets of letters C and variables V, we construct a string s with maximum length of k by randomly concatenating selected letters from C. We then form a word equation $s = s$ and repeatedly replace substrings in s with the concatenation of between 1 and 5 fresh variables. This procedure guarantees that the constructed word equation is SAT.

- **Benchmark 2** is generated by the mechanism used in Woorpje track III. It first generates a word equation using the following definition:

$$X_n a X_n b X_{n-1} b X_{n-2} \cdots b X_1 = \\ a X_n X_{n-1} X_{n-1} b X_{n-2} X_{n-2} b \cdots b X_1 X_1 baa \quad (6)$$

  where $X_1, ..., X_n$ are variables and a and b are letters. We then generate a word equation using the mechanism for Benchmark 1, and replace letters b in (6) randomly with the left-hand side or the right-hand side of that equation.
- **Benchmark 3** is generated by conjoining multiple word equations that were randomly generated using the mechanism described in Benchmark 1. This procedure mainly produces benchmarks that are UNSAT.
- **Benchmark 4** is extracted from benchmarks from the non-incremental QF_S, QF_SLIA, and QF_SNLIA tracks of SMT-LIB. We obtain word equations by removing length constraints, regular expressions, and unsupported Boolean operators, which are not considered in this paper. As a result, benchmarks after transformation can be SAT even if the original SMT-LIB benchmarks were UNSAT.

Table 1. Number of SAT (✓), UNSAT (×), UNKNOWN (∞), and evaluation (Eval) problems in the four benchmarks

Benchmark 1 Total: 3000				Benchmark 2 Total: 21000				Benchmark 3 Total: 41000				Benchmark 4 Total: 2310			
2000			Eval	20000			Eval	40000			Eval	1855			Eval
✓	×	∞		✓	×	∞		✓	×	∞		✓	×	∞	
1997	0	3	1000	1293	0	18707	1000	1449	1137	37414	1000	1673	16	166	455

Table 1 presents the number of problems in each benchmark. Benchmark 4 originates from a collection of 100805 SMT-LIB problems; after transformation, we obtain 2310 problems. For evaluation, we selected hold-out sets of 1000 (Benchmarks 1–3) and 455 (Benchmark 4) problems were selected uniformly at random; those sets were exclusively used for evaluation, not for training or for tuning hyper-parameters. All benchmarks, as well as our implementation and chosen hyper-parameters are available on Zenodo [3].

We then applied the split algorithm (Algorithm 1) to all benchmarks with the *fixed* reordering strategy, to determine the number of SAT, UNSAT and UNKNOWN problems. After the dispatch phase, we only retained SAT problems for the construction of the training dataset.

5.3 Experimental Settings

DragonLi was parametrized with values $l_{BT2} = 500$, $l_{BT2}^{step} = 250, l_{BT3} = 20$ for Algorithm 1. In addition, we chose a hidden layer of size 128 for all neural

Table 2. Evaluation on three metrics for different solvers. The labels SAT, UNS, UNI, CS, and CU are abbreviation of SAT, UNSAT, unique solved, commonly solved SAT, and commonly solved UNSAT, respectively. The labels Fixed, Random, and GNN are the three variations of DragonLi in Sect. 4.4. Entries marked "-" do not apply. Values less than 0.1 are rounded to 0.1. GNN rows for benchmarks 1–4 share the configuration $(BT_2, S1, G5)$.

Bench	Solver	Number of solved problems					Average solving time (split numbet)			
		SAT	UNS	UNI	CS	CU	SAT	UNS	CS	CU
1 (1000 SAT)	Fixed	999	-	0	777	0	4.1 (182.0)	- (-)	4.0 (169.0)	- (-)
	Random	996	-	0			4.2 (349.6)	- (-)	4.1 (269.8)	- (-)
	GNN	995	-	0			7.6 (215.7)	- (-)	7.0 (162.3)	- (-)
	cvc5	**1000**	-	0			0.1 (-)	- (-)	0.1 (-)	- (-)
	Ostrich	918	-	0			20.4 (-)	- (-)	19.6 (-)	- (-)
	Woorpje	967	-	0			1.6 (-)	- (-)	0.5 (-)	- (-)
	Z3	902	-	0			3.4 (-)	- (-)	2.4 (-)	- (-)
	Z3-Noodler	935	-	0			1.9 (-)	- (-)	1.1 (-)	- (-)
2 (1000 in total)	Fixed	33	0	10	1	0	13.2 (1115.2)	- (-)	4.8 (7)	- (-)
	Random	41	0	6			11.7 (3879.5)	- (-)	4.2 (60)	- (-)
	GNN	**71**	0	27			46.0 (1813.5)	- (-)	5.1 (5)	- (-)
	cvc5	4	2	4			2.0 (-)	0.1 (-)	0.1 (-)	- (-)
	Ostrich	14	**43**	44			40.7 (-)	31.8 (-)	2.5 (-)	- (-)
	Woorpje	23	0	2			38.3 (-)	- (-)	0.1 (-)	- (-)
	Z3	6	0	2			0.1 (-)	- (-)	4.2 (-)	- (-)
	Z3-Noodler	19	0	0			45.8 (-)	- (-)	4.2 (-)	- (-)
3 (1000 in total)	Fixed	32	79	0	23	50	5.2 (1946.2)	65.8 (4227.0)	3.6 (57.0)	38.3 (796.6)
	Random	32	79	0			9.5 (3861.8)	65.0 (4227.0)	3.8 (61.7)	38.5 (796.6)
	GNN	32	65	0			214.3 (1471.2)	1471.2 (1471.2)	4.6 (63.7)	84.0 (796.6)
	cvc5	32	943	2			0.1 (-)	0.3 (-)	0.1 (-)	0.3 (-)
	Ostrich	27	926	0			5.8 (-)	4.7 (-)	4.6 (-)	4.5 (-)
	Woorpje	**34**	723	1			12.4 (-)	12.3 (-)	0.1 (-)	23.2 (-)
	Z3	26	**953**	10			5.6 (-)	0.5 (-)	4.7 (-)	0.1 (-)
	Z3-Noodler	28	926	0			22.7 (-)	0.3 (-)	8.9 (-)	0.1 (-)
4 (455 in total)	Fixed	416	6	0	403	2	5.1 (105.5)	17.7 (17119.5)	5.1 (51.0)	5.0 (246)
	Random	415	6	0			4.9 (61.3)	17.9 (17119.5)	4.9 (38.1)	4.4 (246)
	GNN	418	5	0			5.5 (118.3)	31.8 (5019.6)	5.3 (49.0)	8.8 (246)
	cvc5	406	34	0			0.1 (-)	0.1 (-)	0.1 (-)	0.1 (-)
	Ostrich	406	6	0			1.4 (-)	1.2 (-)	1.4 (-)	1.2 (-)
	Woorpje	**420**	2	0			0.2 (-)	3.6 (-)	0.2 (-)	3.6 (-)
	Z3	**420**	10	0			0.1 (-)	0.1 (-)	0.1 (-)	0.1 (-)
	Z3-Noodler	**420**	**35**	1			0.1 (-)	0.1 (-)	0.1 (-)	0.1 (-)

Table 3. Detailed results for number of solved problems of DragonLi in terms of five graph representations (G1 to G5 represent Graph 1 to 5 in Sect. 4.1), three strategies to apply GNN back to the algorithm (S1, S2, S3 in Sect. 4.4), and three backtracking strategies (BT_1, BT_2, BT_3 in Sect. 3.3). The column GT denotes graph type.

GT	Benchmark 1									Benchmark 2								
	BT_1			BT_2			BT_3			BT_1			BT_2			BT_3		
	S1	S2	S3	S1	S2	S3	S1	S2	S3	S1	S2	S3	S1	S2	S3	S1	S2	S3
G1	991	**1000**	996	997	999	999	584	627	624	57	48	44	53	45	40	3	3	3
G2	998	1000	1000	998	1000	998	584	627	624	49	46	41	53	40	50	3	3	3
G3	997	1000	998	998	1000	999	584	627	624	53	43	49	65	46	55	3	3	3
G4	985	999	997	984	999	995	584	627	624	65	52	38	59	54	44	3	3	3
G5	995	1000	999	995	1000	995	584	627	624	64	46	44	**71**	54	50	3	3	3
GT	Benchmark 3									Benchmark 4								
	BT_1			BT_2			BT_3			BT_1			BT_2			BT_3		
	S1	S2	S3	S1	S2	S3	S1	S2	S3	S1	S2	S3	S1	S2	S3	S1	S2	S3
G1	32	32	31	32	32	32	14	16	16	413	415	413	417	417	416	400	404	402
G2	34	32	32	34	32	34	13	16	16	416	416	416	418	418	417	400	402	403
G3	32	32	32	31	32	33	13	16	16	416	416	417	418	417	415	400	402	404
G4	**35**	32	32	34	32	32	14	16	16	414	413	415	417	417	416	400	403	403
G5	31	31	31	32	31	32	14	16	16	415	416	414	**418**	417	416	400	402	402

networks, and used a two message-passing layer (i.e. $t = 2$ in Eq. 1) for the GNN. Each problem in the benchmarks is evaluated on a computer equipped with two Intel Xeon E5 2630 v4 at 2.20 GHz/core and 128GB memory. The GNNs are trained on A100 GPUs. We measured the number of solved problems and the average solving time (in seconds), with timeout of 300 s for each proof attempt.

5.4 Comparison with Other Solvers

In Table 2, we evaluate three versions of our algorithm based on their implementation of the *orderRules* function: the fixed, random, and GNN-guided order versions (listed in Sect. 4.4). The performance of the GNN-guided DragonLi (row GNN in Table 2) for each benchmark is selected from the best results out of 45 experiments (see Table 3). These experiments use different combinations of five graph representations, three backtrack strategies, and three GNN guidance strategies, as shown in bold text in Table 3. We compare the results with those of five other solvers: Z3 (v4.12.2) [39], Z3-Noodler (v1.1.0) [17], cvc5 (v1.0.8) [10], Ostrich (v1.3) [16], and Woopje (v0.2) [19].

The primary metric is the number of solved problems. DragonLi outperforms all other solvers on SAT problems in benchmark 2. Notably, the GNN-based DragonLi solves the highest number of SAT problems. For the conjunction of multiple word equations (benchmark 3 and 4), DragonLi's performance is comparable to the other solvers. The order of processing word equations is crucial for those problems; currently, our solver uses only a predefined sequence, indicating significant potential for improvement. A limitation of DragonLi is determining UNSAT cases, as it requires an exhaustive check of all nodes in the proof tree.

In terms of average solving time for solved problems, GNN-based DragonLi does not hold an advantage. This is mainly due to the overhead associated with encoding equations into a graph at each split point and invoking GNNs. Furthermore, DragonLi is written in Python and not particularly optimized at this point, so that there is ample room for improvement in future efforts.

The measurement of the average number of splits in solved problems is used to gain insight into the efficiency of the different versions of our algorithm. For benchmark 1 and 2, the GNN-guided version outperforms the others on the commonly solved problems. However, for benchmarks 3 and 4, the GNN-guided version does not show advantages. This is for the same reason mentioned in the metric of the number of solved problems; namely, the performance is also influenced by the order of processing equations when dealing with the conjunction of multiple word equations.

We summarize the experimental results compared with some of the leading string solvers as follows:

1. DragonLi shows better or comparable performance on SAT problems but is limited on UNSAT problems. This occurs because the split algorithm concludes SAT upon finding one SAT node, but can conclude UNSAT only after exhaustively exploring the proof tree. In contrast, other solvers may invest more time in proving UNSAT cases, for instance by reasoning about string length or Parikh vectors.
2. DragonLi performs better than other solvers on single word equations (e.g., benchmark 2) and comparably on conjunctions of multiple word equations. This performance difference is because the initial choice of word equation for splitting is crucial for the split algorithm, and this aspect is not optimized currently.
3. Incorporating GNN guidance into the proof tree search enhances the performance of the pure split algorithm for SAT problems, but currently does not lead to an improvement for UNSAT problems.

5.5 Ablation Study

Table 3 displays the number of problems solved in 45 experiments across all benchmarks using the GNN-guided version.

In terms of backtrack strategies, BT_1 performs a pure depth-first search, but it already has good performance. BT_2 performs a depth-first search controlled by parameters l_{BT_2} and $l_{BT_2}^{step}$, and in many cases, it delivers the best performance. BT_3 conducts a systematic search on the proof tree, which is complete for proving problems SAT, but turns out to be relatively inefficient in the experiments and solves the fewest problems given a fixed timeout. This indicates that more sophisticated search strategies may lead to even better performance.

In terms of the guiding strategies (S1, S2, S3), using the GNN alone (S1) to guide the branch order is better than combining it with predefined and random orders (S2 and S3) in most cases. This indicates that the GNN model successfully learns useful patterns at each split point and can be used as a stand-alone heuristic for branching.

In terms of the five graph representations, Graph 1 has the simplest structure, which represents the syntactic information of the word equations and thus incurs the least overhead when we call the model at each split point. This yields average performance compared to other graph representations. The performances of Graph 2 are weaker than others; this is probably due to the extra edges not providing any benefits for prediction, but leading to additional computational overhead. Graphs 3 and 4 emphasize the relationships between terminals and variables, respectively, thus the performance is biased by individual problems. Graph 5 considers the relationships for both terminals and variables, thus it has bigger overhead than Graphs 1, 3, and 4, but it offers relatively good performance. This shows that representing semantic information of the word equations well in graphs helps the model to learn important patterns. In summary, the setting $(BT_2, S1, Graph5)$ performs the best.

6 Related Work

There are many techniques within solvers supporting word equations, as well as in stand-alone word equation solvers. For instance, the SMT solvers Norn [5] and TRAU [6] introduce several improvements on the inference rules [4], including length-guided splitting of equalities and a more efficient way to handle disequalities. The stand-alone word equation solver Woorpje [19] reformulates the word equation problem as a reachability problem for nondeterministic finite automata, then encodes it as a propositional satisfiability problem which can be handled by SAT solvers. In [20], the authors propose a transformation system that extends the Nielsen transformation [34] to work with linear length constraints. This transformation system can be integrated into existing string solvers such as Z3STR3 [14], Z3SEQ [39], and CVC4 [11], thereby advancing the efficiency of word equation resolution.

GNNs excel at analyzing the graph-like structures of logic formulae, offering a complementary approach to formal verification. FormulaNet [50] is an early study guiding the premise selection for Automated Theorem Provers (ATPs). It uses MP-GNNs [24] to process the graph representation of the formulae in the proof trace extracted from HOL Light [26]. With more studies [18,29,41] exploring this path, this trend quickly expands to related fields. For instance, for SAT solvers [33,52], NeuroSAT [45,46] predicts the probability of variables appearing in unsat cores to guide the variable branching decisions for Conflict-Driven Clause Learning (CDCL) [37]. Moreover, GNNs have been combined with various formal verification techniques, such as scheduling SMT solvers [28], loop invariant reasoning [47,48], or guiding Constraint Horn Clause (CHC) solvers [7, 27,35]. They provide the empirical foundations for designing the learning task in Sect. 4, such as the graph representation of word equations and forming the learning task in split points.

7 Conclusion and Future Work

This study introduces a GNN-guided split algorithm for solving word equations, along with five graph representations to enhance branch ordering through a multi-classification task at each split point of the proof tree. We developed our solver from scratch instead of modifying a state-of-the-art SMT solver. This decision prevents the confounding influences of pre-existing optimizations in state-of-the-art SMT solvers, allowing us to isolate and evaluate the specific impact of GNN guidance more effectively.

We investigate various configurations, including graph representations, backtrack strategies, and the conditions for employing GNN-guided branches, aiming to analyze the behaviors of the algorithm across different settings.

The evaluation tables reveal that while the split algorithm effectively solves single word equations, it does not demonstrate marked improvements for multiple conjunctive word equations relative to other solvers. This discrepancy is attributed to the significance of the processing order for conjunctive word equations, where our current solver employs a predefined order. It is possible to make use of a GNN to compute the best equation to start with. However, this involves ranking a list of elements with variable lengths, rather than performing a fixed-category classification task, and requires completely different training for this specific task. Consequently, as future work, we aim to investigate both deterministic and stochastic strategies to optimize the ordering of conjunctive word equations for the split algorithm. Our algorithm is also limited in handling UNSAT problems because it can only conclude UNSAT by exhausting the proof tree. This can be improved in future work.

Acknowledgement. The computations were enabled by resources provided by the National Academic Infrastructure for Supercomputing in Sweden (NAISS) at Chalmers Centre for Computational Science and Engineering (C3SE) and Uppsala Multidisciplinary Center for Advanced Computational Science (UPPMAX) partially funded by the Swedish Research Council through grant agreement no. 2022-06725. The research was also partially supported by the Swedish Research Council through grant agreement no. 2021-06327, by a Microsoft Research PhD grant, the Swedish Foundation for Strategic Research (SSF) under the project WebSec (Ref. RIT17-0011), and the Wallenberg project UPDATE.

References

1. The satisfiability modulo theories library (SMT-LIB). Accessed 25 April 2024. https://smtlib.cs.uiowa.edu/benchmarks.shtml
2. DragonLi github repository (2024). Accessed 28 June 2024. https://github.com/ChenchengLiang/boosting-string-equation-solving-by-GNNs
3. Zenodo record of DragonLi (2024). Accessed 21 Aug 2024. https://zenodo.org/records/13354774
4. Abdulla, P.A., et al.: String constraints for verification. In: Biere, A., Bloem, R. (eds.) Computer Aided Verification, pp. 150–166. Springer International Publishing, Cham (2014)
5. Kroening, D., Păsăreanu, C.S. (eds.): Norn: an SMT solver for string constraints. In: Computer Aided Verification, pp. 462–469. Springer International Publishing, Cham (2015)
6. Abdulla, P.A., et al.: TRAU: SMT solver for string constraints. In: 2018 Formal Methods in Computer Aided Design (FMCAD), pp. 1–5 (2018). https://doi.org/10.23919/FMCAD.2018.8602997
7. Abdulla, P.A., Liang, C., Rümmer, P.: Boosting constrained Horn solving by unsat core learning. In: Dimitrova, R., Lahav, O., Wolff, S. (eds.) Verification, Model Checking, and Abstract Interpretation, pp. 280–302. Springer Nature Switzerland, Cham (2024)
8. Agarap, A.F.: Deep Learning using Rectified Linear Units (ReLU). arXiv:1803.08375 (Mar 2018). https://doi.org/10.48550/arXiv.1803.08375
9. Allamanis, M., Brockschmidt, M., Khademi, M.: Learning to represent programs with graphs. CoRR arxvi preprint arxiv: abs/1711.00740 (2017). http://arxiv.org/abs/1711.00740
10. Barbosa, H., et al.: cvc5: a versatile and industrial-strength SMT solver. In: Fisman, D., Rosu, G. (eds.) Tools and Algorithms for the Construction and Analysis of Systems, pp. 415–442. Springer International Publishing, Cham (2022)
11. Barrett, C., et al.: CVC4. In: Gopalakrishnan, G., Qadeer, S. (eds.) CAV 2011. LNCS, vol. 6806, pp. 171–177. Springer, Heidelberg (2011). https://doi.org/10.1007/978-3-642-22110-1_14
12. Barrett, C., Fontaine, P., Tinelli, C.: The SMT-LIB Standard: Version 2.6. Tech. rep., Department of Computer Science, The University of Iowa (2017). Available at www.SMT-LIB.org
13. Battaglia, P.W., et al.: Relational inductive biases, deep learning, and graph networks. CoRR **abs/1806.01261** (2018). http://arxiv.org/abs/1806.01261
14. Berzish, M., Ganesh, V., Zheng, Y.: Z3str3: a string solver with theory-aware heuristics. In: 2017 Formal Methods in Computer Aided Design (FMCAD), pp. 55–59 (2017). https://doi.org/10.23919/FMCAD.2017.8102241
15. Chen, A., et al.: Developments in MLflow: a system to accelerate the machine learning lifecycle. In: Proceedings of the Fourth International Workshop on Data Management for End-to-End Machine Learning. DEEM '20, Association for Computing Machinery, New York, NY, USA (2020). https://doi.org/10.1145/3399579.3399867
16. Chen, T., Hague, M., Lin, A.W., Rümmer, P., Wu, Z.: Decision procedures for path feasibility of string-manipulating programs with complex operations. Proc. ACM Program. Lang. **3**(POPL), 49:1–49:30 (2019). https://doi.org/10.1145/3290362

17. Chen, Y.F., Chocholatý, D., Havlena, V., Holík, L., Lengál, O., Síč, J.: Z3-Noodler: an automata-based string solver. In: Finkbeiner, B., Kovács, L. (eds.) Tools and Algorithms for the Construction and Analysis of Systems, pp. 24–33. Springer Nature Switzerland, Cham (2024)
18. Chvalovsky, K., Korovin, K., Piepenbrock, J., Urban, J.: Guiding an instantiation prover with graph neural networks. In: Piskac, R., Voronkov, A. (eds.) Proceedings of 24th International Conference on Logic for Programming, Artificial Intelligence and Reasoning. EPiC Series in Computing, vol. 94, pp. 112–123. EasyChair (2023). https://doi.org/10.29007/tp23, https://easychair.org/publications/paper/5z94
19. Day, J.D., Ehlers, T., Kulczynski, M., Manea, F., Nowotka, D., Poulsen, D.B.: On solving word equations using SAT. In: Filiot, E., Jungers, R., Potapov, I. (eds.) Reachability Problems, pp. 93–106. Springer International Publishing, Cham (2019)
20. Day, J.D., Kulczynski, M., Manea, F., Nowotka, D., Poulsen, D.B.: Rule-based word equation solving. In: Proceedings of the 8th International Conference on Formal Methods in Software Engineering, pp. 87–97. FormaliSE '20, Association for Computing Machinery, New York, NY, USA (2020). https://doi.org/10.1145/3372020.3391556
21. Ellson, J., Gansner, E.R., Koutsofios, E., North, S.C., Woodhull, G.: Graphviz and Dynagraph — Static and Dynamic Graph Drawing Tools, pp. 127–148. Springer Berlin Heidelberg, Berlin, Heidelberg (2004). https://doi.org/10.1007/978-3-642-18638-7_6
22. Fan, W., et al.: Graph neural networks for social recommendation. In: The World Wide Web Conference, pp. 417–426. WWW '19, Association for Computing Machinery, New York, NY, USA (2019). https://doi.org/10.1145/3308558.3313488
23. Gilmer, J., Schoenholz, S.S., Riley, P.F., Vinyals, O., Dahl, G.E.: Neural message passing for Quantum chemistry. In: Proceedings of the 34th International Conference on Machine Learning - Volume 70, pp. 1263–1272. ICML'17, JMLR.org (2017)
24. Gilmer, J., Schoenholz, S.S., Riley, P.F., Vinyals, O., Dahl, G.E.: Neural message passing for quantum chemistry. CoRR **abs/1704.01212** (2017), http://arxiv.org/abs/1704.01212
25. Goodfellow, I.J., Bengio, Y., Courville, A.: Deep Learning. MIT Press, Cambridge, MA, USA (2016). http://www.deeplearningbook.org
26. Harrison, J.: HOL light: an overview. In: Proceedings of the 22nd International Conference on Theorem Proving in Higher Order Logics, pp. 60–66. TPHOLs '09, Springer-Verlag, Berlin, Heidelberg (2009)
27. Hojjat, H., Rümmer, P.: The ELDARICA horn solver. In: 2018 Formal Methods in Computer Aided Design (FMCAD), pp. 1–7 (2018). https://doi.org/10.23919/FMCAD.2018.8603013
28. Hůla, J., Mojžíšek, D., Janota, M.: Graph neural networks for scheduling of SMT solvers. In: 2021 IEEE 33rd International Conference on Tools with Artificial Intelligence (ICTAI), pp. 447–451 (2021). https://doi.org/10.1109/ICTAI52525.2021.00072
29. Jakubův, J., Chvalovský, K., Olšák, M., Piotrowski, B., Suda, M., Urban, J.: Enigma anonymous: symbol-independent inference guiding machine (system description). In: Peltier, N., Sofronie-Stokkermans, V. (eds.) Automated Reasoning, pp. 448–463. Springer International Publishing, Cham (2020)
30. Khmelevskii, Y.I.: Equations in a free semigroup. Proc. Steklov Inst. Math. **107**, 1–270 (1971)

31. Kipf, T.N., Welling, M.: Semi-supervised classification with graph convolutional networks. In: 5th International Conference on Learning Representations, ICLR 2017, Toulon, France, April 24-26, 2017, Conference Track Proceedings. OpenReview.net (2017). https://openreview.net/forum?id=SJU4ayYgl
32. Korf, R.E.: Depth-first iterative-deepening: an optimal admissible tree search. Artif. Intell. **27**(1), 97–109 (1985)
33. Kurin, V., Godil, S., Whiteson, S., Catanzaro, B.: Improving SAT solver heuristics with graph networks and reinforcement learning (2020). https://openreview.net/forum?id=B1lCn64tvS
34. Levi, F.W.: On semigroups. Bull. Calcutta Math. Soc. **36**(141–146), 82 (1944)
35. Liang, C., Rümmer, P., Brockschmidt, M.: Exploring representation of horn clauses using GNNs. In: Konev, B., Schon, C., Steen, A. (eds.) Proceedings of the Workshop on Practical Aspects of Automated Reasoning Co-located with the 11th International Joint Conference on Automated Reasoning (FLoC/IJCAR 2022), Haifa, Israel, August, 11 - 12, 2022. CEUR Workshop Proceedings, vol. 3201. CEUR-WS.org (2022). https://ceur-ws.org/Vol-3201/paper7.pdf
36. Makanin, G.S.: The problem of solvability of equations in a free semigroup. Math. Sb. (N.S.) **103(145)**(2(6)), 147–236 (1977)
37. Marques-Silva, J., Sakallah, K.A.: GRASP: a search algorithm for propositional satisfiability. IEEE Trans. Computers **48**, 506–521 (1999). https://api.semanticscholar.org/CorpusID:13039801
38. Mou, L., Li, G., Zhang, L., Wang, T., Jin, Z.: Convolutional neural networks over tree structures for programming language processing. In: Proceedings of the Thirtieth AAAI Conference on Artificial Intelligence, pp. 1287–1293. AAAI'16, AAAI Press (2016)
39. de Moura, L., Bjørner, N.: Z3: an efficient SMT solver. In: 2008 Tools and Algorithms for Construction and Analysis of Systems, pp. 337–340. Springer, Berlin, Heidelberg (March 2008)
40. Nielsen, J.: Die Isomorphismen der allgemeinen, unendlichen Gruppe mit zwei Erzeugenden. Mathematische Annalen **78**, 385–397 (1917). https://api.semanticscholar.org/CorpusID:119726936
41. Paliwal, A., Loos, S.M., Rabe, M.N., Bansal, K., Szegedy, C.: Graph representations for higher-order logic and theorem proving. CoRR arxiv preprint arxiv: abs/1905.10006 (2019)
42. Paszke, A., et al.: Pytorch: an imperative style, high-performance deep learning library. In: Advances in Neural Information Processing Systems 32, pp. 8024–8035. Curran Associates, Inc. (2019). http://papers.neurips.cc/paper/9015-pytorch-an-imperative-style-high-performance-deep-learning-library.pdf
43. Pezoa, F., Reutter, J.L., Suarez, F., Ugarte, M., Vrgoč, D.: Foundations of JSON schema. In: Proceedings of the 25th International Conference on World Wide Web, pp. 263–273. International World Wide Web Conferences Steering Committee (2016)
44. Plandowski, W.: An efficient algorithm for solving word equations. In: Proceedings of the Thirty-Eighth Annual ACM Symposium on Theory of Computing, pp. 467—-476. STOC '06, Association for Computing Machinery, New York, NY, USA (2006). https://doi.org/10.1145/1132516.1132584
45. Selsam, D., Bjørner, N.: Neurocore: Guiding high-performance SAT solvers with unsat-core predictions. CoRR arxiv preprint arxiv: abs/1903.04671. (2019)

46. Selsam, D., Lamm, M., Bünz, B., Liang, P., de Moura, L., Dill, D.L.: Learning a SAT solver from single-bit supervision. In: 7th International Conference on Learning Representations, ICLR 2019, New Orleans, LA, USA, May 6-9, 2019. OpenReview.net (2019). https://openreview.net/forum?id=HJMC_iA5tm
47. Si, X., Dai, H., Raghothaman, M., Naik, M., Song, L.: Learning loop invariants for program verification. In: Bengio, S., Wallach, H., Larochelle, H., Grauman, K., Cesa-Bianchi, N., Garnett, R. (eds.) Advances in Neural Information Processing Systems, vol. 31. Curran Associates, Inc. (2018)
48. Si, X., Naik, A., Dai, H., Naik, M., Song, L.: Code2Inv: a deep learning framework for program verification. In: Lahiri, S.K., Wang, C. (eds.) CAV 2020. LNCS, vol. 12225, pp. 151–164. Springer, Cham (2020). https://doi.org/10.1007/978-3-030-53291-8_9
49. Van Rossum, G., Drake, F.L.: Python 3 Reference Manual. CreateSpace, Scotts Valley, CA (2009)
50. Wang, M., Tang, Y., Wang, J., Deng, J.: Premise selection for theorem proving by deep graph embedding. In: Proceedings of the 31st International Conference on Neural Information Processing Systems, pp. 2783—-2793. NIPS'17, Curran Associates Inc., Red Hook, NY, USA (2017)
51. Wang, M., et al.: Deep graph library: a graph-centric, highly-performant package for graph neural networks. arXiv preprint arXiv:1909.01315 (2019)
52. Wang, W., Hu, Y., Tiwari, M., Khurshid, S., McMillan, K.L., Miikkulainen, R.: Neurocomb: improving SAT solving with graph neural networks. CoRR **abs/2110.14053** (2021). https://arxiv.org/abs/2110.14053

Author Index

S. Akshay et al. (Eds.): ATVA 2024, LNCS 15054, pp. 303–304, 2025.
https://doi.org/10.1007/978-3-031-78709-6

The manufacturer's authorised representative in the EU is Springer
Nature Customer Service Centre GmbH, Europaplatz 3, 69115 Heidelberg,
Germany. If you have any concerns regarding our products, please
contact ProductSafety@springernature.com

Printed and bound by CPI Group (UK) Ltd, Croydon, CR0 4YY
01/10/2026
02225908-0010